Handbook of Design in Educational Technology

The *Handbook of Design in Educational Technology* provides up-to-date, comprehensive summaries and syntheses of recent research pertinent to the design of information and communication technologies to support learning. Readers can turn to this handbook for expert advice about each stage in the process of designing systems for use in educational settings, from theoretical foundations to the challenges of implementation, the process of evaluating the impact of the design, and the manner in which it might be further developed and disseminated.

The volume is organized into the following four sections: Theory, Design, Implementation, and Evaluation.

The more than forty chapters reflect the international and interdisciplinary nature of the educational technology design research field.

Rosemary Luckin is Professor of Learner Centered Design at the London Knowledge Lab, Institute of Education, University of London, UK.

Sadhana Puntambekar is Professor of Learning Sciences in the Educational Psychology department at the University of Wisconsin-Madison, USA.

Peter Goodyear is an Australian Laureate Fellow and Professor of Education at the University of Sydney, Australia.

Barbara Grabowski is Professor Emerita of Education at The Pennsylvania State University, USA.

Joshua Underwood is an independent Learner Centered Design consultant and PhD candidate at the London Knowledge Lab, Institute of Education, University of London, UK.

Niall Winters is a Senior Lecturer in Learning Technologies for Development at the London Knowledge Lab, Institute of Education, University of London, UK.

Handbook of Design in Educational Technology

Edited by

Rosemary Luckin, Sadhana Puntambekar, Peter Goodyear, Barbara Grabowski, Joshua Underwood, and Niall Winters

NEW YORK AND LONDON

First published 2013
by Routledge
711 Third Avenue, New York, NY 10017

Simultaneously published in the UK
by Routledge
2 Park Square, Milton Park, Abingdon, Oxon OX14 4RN

Routledge is an imprint of the Taylor & Francis Group, an informa business

Library of Congress Cataloging in Publication Data
Handbook of design in educational technology / Edited by Rosemary Luckin, Peter Goodyear, Barbara Grabowski, Niall Winters, Joshua Underwood, and Sadhana Puntambekar.
pages cm
Includes bibliographical references and index.
1. Educational technology—Handbooks, manuals, etc.
I. Luckin, Rosemary, editor of compilation.
LB1028.3.H354 2013
371.33—dc23
2012037152

ISBN: 978–0–415–80734–0 (hbk)
ISBN: 978–0–415–80735–7 (pbk)
ISBN: 978–0–203–07522–7 (ebk)

Typeset in Minion
by Swales & Willis Ltd, Exeter, Devon
Printed and bound by TJ International Ltd, Padstow, Cornwall

CONTENTS

FOREWORD

The complex act of design is an enterprise engaged in by multiple disciplines across the Arts and Sciences from the formality of Engineers to the creative individualism of the Arts. There is much active debate about what constitutes design, how design should be done and who can participate in the process of designing. The purpose of the *Handbook of Design in Educational Technology* is to provide a practical guide for students and professionals that mines this complexity to extract and explain key approaches and tools. The design of educational technology is a young discipline that is evolving quickly. It is concerned with both designing the learning situation and designing the technology. It is also concerned with the people who will eventually use what results from the design process and with finding a way to engage them in the design process.

When the editors of this volume first started to discuss the type of book that we wanted to produce it was clear that we were embarking on a process that needed to mirror the subject matter of the product. The handbook would need to be carefully designed so that it would draw together a collection of chapters that were:

- interdisciplinary and that spanned social and technical expertise;
- reflective of advances in innovative technologies and methodologies;
- theoretically grounded to substantiate pedagogical integrity;
- carefully evaluated and reviewed to ensure quality; and
- contemporary so that the needs of modern designers, learners and teachers would be met.

We wanted to design a book that we would want to read and recommend.

There were few models on which to base our design, with little currently available to offer the reader a complete account from theory through to evaluation with descriptions of each step in-between. There were books that discussed research approaches to the use of technology to support learning, books that covered Instructional Design, manuals about the technical aspects of designing educational computing, from particular programming languages to methods and interface design. However, there was nothing that harnessed the social and the technical to offer readers a comprehensive account of the process of designing educational technology, a synthesis of recent research and expert advice about each stage in the process of designing from theoretical foundations to the challenges of implementation and impact evaluation.

The *Handbook of Design in Educational Technology* offers a compendium of 43 chapters written by an international community of authors that discuss the design of educational technology to support learners of all ages from within formal and informal education, and the work place. The technologies encompassed include mobile, ubiquitous and tangible as well as more traditional desktop and on-line computing resources. The volume is organized into four sections: Foundations, Design Methods, Implementation, and Evaluation. Each of these sections has been carefully commissioned, reviewed and organized by expert editors to provide a comprehensive tool for researchers and practitioners wishing to develop and use technologies for learning.

Rosemary Luckin
The London Knowledge Lab, London

Part I
Foundations

INTRODUCTION

Peter Goodyear

THE CHAPTERS

The chapters in this section of the handbook combine to provide some foundational ideas that can be used for thinking about design for technology-enhanced learning.

Ertmer, Parisio and Wardak provide a timely review of empirical research into how design gets done—who is involved, and how their goals, methods and contexts affect the processes of design for learning. It provides a useful overview of design, as well as a launchpad into an active, widely dispersed literature.

Keppell and Riddle open up a neglected dimension of design: work on innovative learning spaces. They use two case studies to explain how design principles can be used to align pedagogy and place. They also introduce the complicating but unavoidable challenges that arise when design needs to help with the integration of the material world, digital technologies and modern pedagogy.

Luckin, Clark and Underwood build on ideas of space, environment and situated activity in outlining the Ecology of Resources framework for design. The 'materialist turn' in educational research is broadening appreciation of the significance of networks of tools and artefacts in shaping human activity, including study activities. Luckin's model shows how complex learning environments can be subjected to analysis—to distinguish the many entities that affect learning—and how such analysis can inform and improve subsequent design work.

Reimann presents the theoretical roots of Design-Based Research and discusses how and when to apply the method in an aim to 'shed light on the processes through which technology gets interpreted and appropriated by teachers and learners'. This work highlights the importance of authentic educational settings and identifying the 'real needs' that technology should serve. A particularly interesting aspect of this work is the emphasis upon developing learning trajectories as an essential step in the design process.

Griffin, Bui and Care draw on major, contemporary efforts to define and assess '21st-century' capabilities to sketch some links between assessment of learning and design for learning. Combining criterion-referenced assessment of learning with Rasch modelling, the authors are able to show how actionable information about what students can do can be elicited and employed to (re)direct teaching. Design for learning needs to be able to design in opportunities for assessment.

Knowing what students are ready to learn can make a huge difference to pedagogical decisions—whether they are made by a human being, an adaptive machine, or a combination of the two. Knowing how students interpret the spaces in which they work, and how their activities are influenced by their surroundings, is vital if one needs to design supportive learning environments. Finally, being able to integrate thinking about design, environment, learning activity and outcomes is key to progress in this field.

1

THE PRACTICE OF EDUCATIONAL/INSTRUCTIONAL DESIGN

Peggy A. Ertmer, Martin L. Parisio, and Dewa Wardak

WHAT IS DESIGN?

Design has been defined in a number of ways, with designers from various fields (e.g., architecture, fashion, and education) conceptualizing and defining their work in slightly different ways. Although design can be used to describe both a process and a product (Smith & Boling, 2009), in this chapter, we focus primarily on the process, or 'work', of design. Thus, design is defined here as a *goal directed, problem-solving activity* (Archer, 1965; Rowland, 1993), *which results in the creation of something useful that did not exist previously* (Reswick, 1965). Furthermore, we include the idea, proposed by Cross (2007), which describes design as occurring within a complex conceptual space, comprising both opportunities and constraints, which must be resolved in order to achieve desired and effective results. This definition, then, encapsulates the complex space within which designers work, while also suggesting that design often involves the resolution of competing tensions or priorities. In educational/instructional design, these tensions arise from competition between such things as learning outcomes, policy guidelines, graduate attributes, and students' needs and expectations (Bird, Morgan, & O'Reilly, 2007).

For many years, Cross has emphasized the importance of 'understanding the design process through an understanding of design cognition, or the 'designerly' ways of knowing and thinking' (2007, p. 41). According to Cross (2006, p. 22), 'design . . . encompasses unique things to know, ways of knowing, and ways of finding out about them'. By considering the work of educational/instructional designers as a 'kind of design', we are better positioned to see parallels between the processes, expertise, and languages of instructional design and those of other fields. This is supported by the results of Rowland's (1993) work, which highlighted many similarities between instructional design-focused studies and those in other design fields. Indeed, this similarity was initially noted by Simon (1969) over 40 years ago when he boldly proclaimed, 'design is the core of all professional training' (pp. 55–56). Moreover, recent research has demonstrated that much of what a designer does is common across design domains (Blackwell, Eckert, Bucciarelli, & Earl, 2009; Eckert, Blackwell, Bucciarelli, & Earl, 2010). For example,

Eckert and colleagues (2010) found designers of different domains shared common stories about getting the right brief from the client and embraced descriptions of design as a 'conversation' with materials and tools. Interestingly, designers from different fields were able to comprehend each other even when unfamiliar terminology was used.

According to Rowland (1993), designing instruction is a subset of designing, in general, and as such, the general characteristics of design hold true for the more narrow instances of educational/instructional design. More specifically he defines instructional design as being '*directed toward the practical purpose of learning, i.e., the designer seeks to create new instructional materials or systems in which students learn*' (p. 87). This includes, then, the entire process of '*the analysis of learning and performance problems, and the design, development, implementation, evaluation, and management of instructional and non-instructional processes and resources intended to improve learning and performance in a variety of settings, particularly educational institutions and the workplace*' (Reiser, 2007, p. 7).

WHO PARTICIPATES IN DESIGN WORK?

In educational contexts, design work is undertaken by both multi-professional teams and solo designers. While some designers hold design-focused titles such as instructional designer, educational or curriculum designer, others engage in design work primarily as teachers, students, or library media specialists. In general, larger organizations often employ designers as part of their workforce, while smaller organizations tend to hire designers, as consultants, on an as-needed basis. However, regardless of whether designers are internal or external to the organization, their designs are influenced by the various contexts in which they occur.

DIFFERENT APPROACHES TO DESIGN WORK

Depending on work contexts, designers may function as members of a team or individually, and as external or internal to the organization they are serving. In large design teams, the division of labour often maps to individuals' skills; for example, an instructional design team might include a multimedia designer, graphic artist, pedagogy specialist, and so on. In a study of design-intensive industries, Dell'Era & Verganti (2010) found that innovators in design often collaborated with external designers to draw on knowledge diversity (p. 135).

Another common approach, participatory- or user-design, involves the end-user in significant design decisions (Carr, 1997). In general, end-users comprise those for whom the instruction is intended; in instructional/educational design, then, end-users can include teachers *or* students, depending on the specific design. Carr-Chellman, Cuyar, & Breman (1998) noted that this approach enabled all stakeholders to have a voice in the decision-making process, creating a greater sense of unity and project momentum. A good example of a participatory design approach is rapid prototyping (Jones & Richey, 2000) in which the end-users are involved throughout the design and development stages, resulting in a higher likelihood of successful implementation. However, increased time is required to educate participants about basic terminology and project-design techniques. Similarly, there is an interesting line of inquiry into the roles of *learners* as designers (e.g., Cameron & Gotlieb, 2009; Kolodner et al., 2003; Lim, 2008) and co-designers

(Könings, Brand-Gruwel, & van Merriënboer, 2010, 2011). Jonassen (1994) took this line of inquiry even further by arguing, 'We should take the tools away from the instructional designers and give them to the learners, as tools for knowledge construction, rather than media of conveyance and knowledge acquisition' (online, para. 5).

TEACHERS AS DESIGNERS

Recently, Goodyear (2010) emphasized the importance of broadening our conception of educational praxis to incorporate the concept of teaching-as-design. Hoogveld, Paas, Jochems, and van Merriënboer (2001, 2002) present a useful line of research in this area. For example, Hoogveld, Paas, and Jochems (2005) found that teachers who were trained in an instructional systems design methodology, the four-component instructional design model (4C-ID; van Merriënboer, 1997), performed better as designers than those who were not trained. In a more recent study, Bennett and colleagues (2011) interviewed 30 teachers across 16 Australian universities to examine various aspects of teachers' design activities including their teaching approaches, the contexts in which they worked, their approaches to designing, the key influences on their design activities, and the support mechanisms they accessed. Results indicated teachers frequently engaged in design and redesign of units, in both teams and individually, and were often given extensive flexibility in their design activities. In a similar vein, Lovitt and Clarke (2011) analysed several quality lesson plans to distil a set of generalizable and transferable design features that teachers tended to incorporate into their lessons. Components observed across lessons included a focus on group work and multiple ability levels, establishing challenges for students to grapple with, facilitating problem-solving, and instilling ownership in multiple interconnected content areas.

INSTRUCTIONAL DESIGNERS AS PROJECT MANAGERS

Design work often occurs alongside project management. Although the literature describes various models for instructional design project management (e.g., Gentry, 1994; Greer, 1992; Layng, 1997; Yang, Moore, & Burton, 1995), Van Rooij (2010) indicated a mismatch between the project management skills required of instructional designers in the workplace and the skills and knowledge taught in formal education courses. Indeed, Merrill and Wilson (2007) stated that ID graduates tend to spend the majority of their time on the job managing projects and training others to design instruction. As reported by Cox and Osguthorpe (2003), instructional designers in corporate and educational settings can spend up to 35% of their time in meetings and project management activities. Although the results might not generalize to other settings, this finding emphasizes the fact that project management can be a significant aspect of an instructional designer's work.

LEVELS AND CONTEXTS OF DESIGN

When conceptualizing phenomena, it is useful to consider the macro, micro, and meso contexts in which they occur (Goodyear & Ellis, 2008; Jones, Dirckinck-Homfeld, & Lindstrom, 2006). For example, before students enter a programme of study, curriculum designers work at the macro level to delineate a configuration of courses through which the students must progress. At the meso level, designers and teachers work to create individual learning tasks for students, and at the micro level learners design individual study practices. In theory, at least, design is practised at each of these levels when there is a need to achieve a desired goal, with the expectation being that design outcomes will be communicated across each level.

Undoubtedly, context shapes both the design process and design outcomes; what is often not considered, however, is how the design subsequently reshapes the context. Designers must frequently reflect on the design situation and respond appropriately. In education, such reflection involves gathering qualitative feedback from learners and quantitative feedback from formal course evaluations. In this way it can be said that the designer is in constant 'conversation' with the design situation (Schön, 1995). In the next section we describe, in more detail, the various factors that influence the design process.

WHAT FACTORS INFLUENCE THE DESIGN PROCESS AND HOW?

During the instructional design process, there are a number of factors that influence the process as well as the final product, including: (1) *people* (e.g., the client and/or audience for whom the design is being developed, the prior knowledge and previous experiences of the designer him/herself, and the knowledge and experience of production staff), (2) *contexts* (e.g., environments in which the design is developed and implemented, and (3) *expected learning outcomes* (e.g., impact of assessment and evaluation practices).

People-based Factors

CLIENTS: Impact of Designing for Diverse Clients

Designing for clients who are different from oneself requires a certain level of awareness and sensitivity (Ertmer, York, & Gedik, 2009; York & Ertmer, 2011). Clients can become quickly discouraged, or even upset, if designers downplay or ignore their needs or preferences (Ertmer & Cennamo, 2007). According to Summers, Lohr, and O'Neil (2002), although it is important for designers to communicate credibility, data, and feelings, in that order, clients will remember the information in the reverse order: feelings, data, and credibility. This is supported by the work of Dicks and Ives (2008), who reported that instructional designers consider 'building client relationships' as an important and significant aspect of their work. Designers can increase their credibility with clients by applying effective communication, interpersonal, and leadership skills (Summers et al., 2002). According to the participants in the Ertmer et al. (2009) study, designers should listen more than they talk and utilize responsive communication strategies that demonstrate sensitivity to clients' unique cultural, political, and interpersonal traits. Finally, it is important for instructional designers to avoid using technical language or instructional design jargon (Keppell & Gale, 2007), which typically serves to separate, rather than unite, clients and designers.

LEARNERS: Impact of Designing for Diverse Learners

Cultural differences between the designer and audience can greatly influence the design process. According to Rogers, Graham, and Mayes (2007), factors influencing the design processes include awareness of general cultural and social expectations, teaching and learning expectations, and differences in the use of language and symbols. For example, designers need to know how roles and responsibilities, such as student–teacher relationships, are defined by the cultural group for whom they are designing. Because symbols are interpreted differently in different cultures, designers need to avoid using languages and symbols that have the potential to be offensive to others. Even different conceptions of time and humour need to be considered. Based on the results of their work, Rogers and colleagues (2007) found that designers tended to be aware that cultural differences existed between themselves and the audience for whom they were designing but did not know what those differences were.

Johari, Bentley, Tinney, and Chia (2005), through a review of literature, identified at least eight factors that influenced how learners perceive the quality of instruction received, and as such, designers need to be aware of these. These factors include: (1) language, (2) educational culture, (3) technical infrastructure, (4) primary audience, (5) learning styles, (6) reasoning patterns, (7) cultural context, and (8) social context. According to Johari et al. (2005), language and culture are intertwined and impossible to understand independently. Furthermore, students from different cultures are likely to have strong ideas about how they learn best. For example, students from some cultures are not as familiar with group discussion and, thus, might not participate in these activities. For this reason, designers might need to provide familiar frameworks for the specific learners who will participate in their instruction (Gunawardena, Wilson, & Nolla, 2003). Still, there could be times when unfamiliar approaches are beneficial for introducing learners to new ways of learning and knowing.

In general, educational designers develop instruction in isolation (i.e., removed from the intended learners) with merely a list of learning aims to guide them. This often ignores the gap between the intentions of the designer when creating learning tasks and students' interpretation of them. One solution to filling this gap is participatory design, as described earlier, where students' perspectives are integrated into the instructional design process. Participatory instructional design can contribute considerable improvements to students' perceptions of learning and thus their learning outcomes (Könings et al., 2010, 2011).

DESIGNERS: Impact of designers' knowledge and experiences

Experienced designers bring a wealth of knowledge, gained from both formal education and personal experiences, to each design project in which they are involved (Ertmer et al., 2008). Designer-specific factors that influence how an instructional need is translated into instructional materials and/or activities include the designer's knowledge and use of instructional design theories and models and his/her previous experiences with the design process.

DESIGNERS' KNOWLEDGE: USE OF THEORIES AND MODELS

Based on the results of a number of recent studies (Ertmer et al., 2009; York & Ertmer, 2011), instructional designers appear to apply ID models, learned at university, to guide their practice (Martin, 2011), although they use them in a more fluid manner than advocated by formal ID textbooks (Ertmer et al., 2009). According to Ertmer and colleagues (2008), experienced designers create a mental model of the ID process, for example the ADDIE model, and use it to structure their design processes. Additionally, designers tend to use these mental models heuristically, as opposed to procedurally. Similar results have been reported by Romiszowski (1981) and Kirschner, Carr, van Merriënboer, and Sloep (2002): experienced designers use heuristics, or general guidelines, when making decisions under uncertain conditions (Dudczak, 1995). These heuristics are influenced by both prior conceptual knowledge and practical knowledge based on past experience. For example, the participants in the Ertmer et al. (2009) study reported that communicating successfully in design projects is critical; as such, most experienced designers have developed their own heuristics for communicating with clients.

In contrast to how instructional designers use ID *models*, results of a study by Yanchar, South, Williams, Allen, and Wilson (2010) demonstrated that designers, although generally favourable toward using *theory* in their designs, reported using only a limited number (e.g., Bloom's Taxonomy, Merrill's Component Display Theory, Reigeluth's Elaboration Theory). In general, the designers in the Yanchar et al. study described theories as being too abstract, rigid, or complex to apply readily in practice. Rather, similar to how ID models were applied, theories were used, more heuristically, to make sense of a situation and to guide decision-making.

DESIGNERS' EXPERIENCE: USE OF PRIOR EXPERIENCE

When solving design problems, instructional designers often use tacit or intuitive knowledge, derived from past experience (Winn, 1990). For instance, Rowland (1992) reported that expert instructional designers rely on their experiences as designers, whereas novice designers rely more on their experiences as learners. Furthermore, expert designers retrieve relevant information in the form of what Rowland calls 'templates' or 'mental models' that are triggered by a match to specific experiences. This is supported by the results of the Ertmer et al. (2008) study in which experienced designers narrowed the problem space of an unfamiliar problem situation using their personal experiences and unique 'frames of reference'. According to the authors, these frames of reference were built from an 'amalgam of knowledge and experience' (p. 28).

Hardré, Ge, and Thomas (2006) discovered a clear connection between an individual's background knowledge and his/her development from a student to an instructional designer. Thus, a background in teaching, instruction, or a related field supported the development of sophisticated design thinking, enabling students to create more complex designs than students with backgrounds in less-related fields. More specifically, students with backgrounds in teacher training or the military performed well in acquiring ID knowledge in comparison to a student with a background in philosophy who initially found it hard to integrate ID knowledge with his prior experience.

PRODUCTION STAFF: Impact of Knowledge and Experience

Another factor that can have an impact on how instructional design is translated into practice is the level of experience the instructional *developers* bring to the project. More experienced developers can produce instructional environments higher in both pedagogical and technical quality compared to developers with less experience (Boot, van Merriënboer, & Veerman, 2007). Furthermore, instructional design documents can be misinterpreted by novice developers (Boot, Nelson, Van Merriënboer, & Gibbons, 2007). This problem is exacerbated by the fact that most of those responsible for production are not professional developers and the job can be given to domain specialists or software experts who are not necessarily experienced in the production of instructional programs. In these situations it is recommended that the instructional designer divide the design document into interrelated layers and describe each layer in enough detail to guide both the developers and production personnel.

Context-based Factors

Designing for Diverse Implementation Contexts

Context is another important factor that shapes design work; instructional designers must be able to adapt their design processes and products based on where their designs will be implemented. Larson and Lockee (2004), categorized the different environments in which instructional designers work as: (a) business and industry, (b) higher education, (c) K–12 education, (d) government/military, (e) non-profit, and (f) health care. Significantly different values prevail in these various environments, which can make it particularly difficult for instructional designers to adapt to them, especially if they have gained little experience outside the higher education arena in which they received their formal training (Tasker & Packham, 1993).

Impact of Infrastructure and Technology

In addition to the type of organization being designed for, designers also need to consider issues such as the availability of technological infrastructure, speed of access, and even access to electricity for contexts occurring in underdeveloped countries or even in rural areas in some developed countries. With more educational institutions pushing to incorporate technologies into educational programmes, it is important for designers to determine how technologies will be used to facilitate learning. Each technology tool should have a stated purpose in the learning environment and should be linked to pedagogy (Mereba, 2003). A learning technology is a powerful tool, 'but one that may not be appropriate in all situations' (Cook, 2007, p. 39). Used inappropriately, technologies may actually hinder learning. For example, a study by Smith, Torres-Ayala, and Heindel (2008) found that some disciplines may not benefit from the use of technologies as a designer might imagine. For example, mathematics instructors reported that the use of Common Course Management Systems (CMSs) did not work well for incorporating mathematical diagrams and notation systems into instruction and, as a result, placed extraneous cognitive load on the learners.

Impact of Content

The type of content being designed, as well as how it will be delivered, also play important roles in the design of educational environments. For example, Jin and Boling (2010) discovered that instructional designers often included images in their content in order to attract attention, reduce cognitive load, facilitate understanding, assist in learning transfer, build mental models, and increase memory. However, learners perceived the meaning and purposes of these images differently. The study found that learners' perceptions were in congruence with the designers' intentions for only half of the images analysed.

Another challenge exists when designers try to design instruction for a highly interactive and/or constructivist environment using a very linear, structured model. According to Der-Thanq, Hung, and Wang (2007), learning activities often do not match the desired learning outcomes because there is a lack of design tools and methods to support new learning approaches. For example, designers may often use traditional design methods, such as task analysis, to design non-traditional activities such as collaborative projects. To solve this challenge, designers may need new design tools and methods to support progressive pedagogies and learning theories.

Outcomes-related Influences

Designing with the End in Mind: The Impact of Assessment and Evaluation

According to Reeves (2006), eight factors need to be aligned to ensure the success of any learning environment. These factors are: (1) goals, (2) content, (3) instructional design, (4) learner tasks, (5) instructor roles, (6) student roles, (7) technological affordances, and (8) assessment. According to Reeves, among these eight factors, assessment is the most commonly misaligned factor.

Assessment is often confused with evaluation. Whereas *evaluation* comprises judging the effectiveness of educational programmes and products, *assessment* involves measuring student learning (Reeves, 2000). However, often the same data are used for both tasks. For example, the results of final examinations are used to assess students' learning but can also be used to measure the success of the programme (Reeves, 2000).

The Impact of Assessment on Design Practices

When designing instruction, it is important to ask at the outset how the resulting design will have an impact on the learners. In other words 'how will you know they are learning?' (Reeves, 2006, p. 307). The design of assessments is an important factor in the design process because it influences the actions and approaches learners take towards studying (Struyven et al., 2005). For example, formal examinations, mostly consisting of multiple-choice questions, are common in student assessment because they are easy to implement. However, these methods encourage a surface approach to learning, with a focus on memorizing facts and demonstrating static knowledge, rather than the application of critical thinking skills (Tian, 2007). Herrington and Oliver (2000) recommended integrating assessment with authentic learning tasks so that assessment comprises the results of investigations, not formal tests. Technological affordances present new opportunities for rapid and radical changes in assessment, however, it is essential that assessment measures what is important, not what is easy to assess (Reeves, 2006; Griffin et al., this volume).

Sluijsmans, Prins, and Martens (2006) recommended that assessment, particularly summative assessment, be integrated into the learning design by engaging students throughout the learning process in authentic tasks, which gradually become more complex. By successfully completing increasingly complex tasks, learners master the required knowledge and skills. This idea is based on the whole-task approach (Sluijsmans et al., 2006) in which the first task is the simplest version of the tasks that professionals encounter in real working environments. Subsequent tasks represent more complex versions until the final task comprises the most complex task that professionals encounter. In an example given by van Merriënboer, Kirschner, and Kester (2003), students are given an assignment to search for literature. The first task involves searching for clearly defined concepts, which will lead to a smaller number of articles. Subsequent tasks involve searching for complex undefined concepts where a larger number of articles are available and students are required to search larger databases.

The traditional individualistic types of assessment practices have been challenged by various forms of student-centered, collaborative or cooperative activities that facilitate student mastery of a variety of 21st-century learning outcomes (e.g., collaboration, problem-solving—*see* Griffin et al., this volume). One example of this type of assessment is peer assessment, which has demonstrated great learning benefits for both small and large groups of students (Ballantyne, Hughes, & Mylonas, 2002). The implementation of peer assessment in groups is a challenge to designers but if done right has numerous learning benefits for students. In particular, designers need to be aware of factors such as the need to judge students on collective rather than individual efforts, a shift away from defined learning outcomes to dynamic learning processes, and the need to understand how results should be used—that is, to support or modify another grade, rather than as a graded assessment itself (Boud, Cohen, & Sampson, 1999).

Recently, the function of assessment has evolved from being an event at the end of learning programmes that measure 'what' has been learned, to a series of events aimed at monitoring learning and focusing on 'how' students transform information into usable knowledge (Hagstrom, 2006). In real-world situations, once students graduate, they must be able to judge the adequacy of their own learning. To become life-long learners, students need to become adept at self-assessment and to be able to make judgements about their own work and that of others (Boud & Falchikov, 2006).

Peer assessment and self-assessment give greater autonomy to the learner. According to Taras (2002), 'we need to implicate students as active participants and protagonists in the assessment process' (p. 508). This type of design changes the relationship between designers and users including students, teachers, and trainers.

The Impact of Evaluation on Design Practices

According to Williams, South, Yanchar, Wilson, and Allen (2011), the instructional design literature rarely, if ever, focuses on the actual evaluation activities carried out by designers. Furthermore, conducting formal evaluations is generally not encouraged by the designers' own organizations or disbursed by the clients. Project constraints such as budget and deadlines often push evaluation to the bottom of the priority list. As a result, instructional designers report spending less than 2% of their time engaging in evaluation activities (Cox & Osguthorpe, 2003). Similarly, Hoogveld and colleagues (2001, 2002) found that teachers spent little time on the evaluation stage of design.

Some instructional designers feel that it is important to deliver their work on time rather than spend extra time evaluating their designs. For example, one of the participants in the Rogers et al. (2007) study explained, 'there might be a desperate need for HIV training or training for refugees where people don't want to wait until it is perfected' (p. 208). The same participant elaborated,

> The ideal situation is that you create a pilot testing phase that is planned into the development process when you are preparing the materials for the first time. Now, often this kind of pre-test gets squeezed out because you never have enough time to do what you want to do even if you want to do it' (p. 208).

Williams and colleagues (2011) reported that instructional designers do conduct evaluation activities but in less formal ways. For example, instructional designers used the principles of evaluation in their work to integrate assessment into learning experiences to encourage students to apply what they had learned. This supports the idea, alluded to earlier, that the results of student assessments can be used to evaluate the success of instructional design programmes or products (Reeves, 2000).

Communicating the Design

Communication plays an important role in the design and development of instructional systems. According to Liang (2000), communication is one of the top four competencies of successful corporate professionals. The 31 participants in the York and Ertmer (2011) Delphi study identified effective communication, in visual, oral, and written form, as a key component in the instructional design process. In complex projects, instructional designers need to communicate different types of information to different stakeholders including managers, producers, instructors, subject matter experts, and software programmers (Boot & Kremer, 2006). According to Derntl, Figl, Botturi, and Boot (2006), misinterpretation can be reduced by representing ID products and processes using formal design languages: 'A design language is a set of concepts that support structuring a design task and conceiving solutions' (p. 1216).

An example of a formal design language, not bound to the instructional design field, is the Unified Modeling Language (UML) used to analyse, specify, and design software systems. The language has been in existence since the late 1980s and has been refined through practice (Booch et al., 2007). Using formal design languages entails practical and theoretical benefits for instructional design, such as improving communication within design teams; improving communication between designers, producers, and clients; promoting innovation in design; easing the integration of theory within designs; improving design sharing and comparison; improving designer education; and, automating design and production tasks (Gibbons, Botturi, Boot, & Nelson, 2008).

In instructional design, however, there is a lack of formal standardized languages that are understood and interpreted similarly by both designers and producers (Boot, van Merriënboer, & Theunissen, 2008). Still, lessons can be learned from other areas that have utilized design languages and notations systems successfully. For example, dance choreography has a clear standardized notation system that must be agreed upon and understood by the choreographer, the dancer, the stage manager, and other production staff members in order to synchronize participants' actions and produce a dance performance (Waters & Gibbons, 2004).

Design languages are mostly expressed through notation systems, which usually appear in visual form, using text and diagrams. Conole (2010) identified seven types of representations in instructional design: (1) textual summary, (2) content map, (3) task swimlane, (4) pedagogy profile, (5) principles matrix, (6) component map, and, (7) course map. The type of visual representation used is dependent on its purpose. For example, mind maps and models can be used for conceptual representation. Some formal instructional design languages utilize visualization in order to enhance team communication, improve design, and contribute to the development of high-quality instruction. Regardless of form, visualization allows designers to externalize their thinking, thus making their ideas available for reflection and better understanding (Botturi, 2008). Visual form is mostly preferred because it is instantly recognizable, thus encouraging interpretation, abstraction, and the simplification of complex ideas (Hokanson, 2008). Furthermore, visualization enables further development of design ideas by making them available for reflection, criticism, and reaction.

E^2ML (Educational Environment Modeling Language) is an example of a visual language used in the design of educational environments (Botturi, 2006). E^2ML is a tool used to develop a visual representation of instruction that all stakeholders in a design process can similarly comprehend. It has a limited number of basic concepts supported by a visual notation system and can be used at any stage of the design process. The use and potential effectiveness of the language was tested in an experimental setting with 12 designers from different disciplinary backgrounds (Botturi, 2005). The 12 designers agreed that E²ML was potentially powerful, flexible, and adaptable to different design situations. Interestingly, the designers stated that they usually developed a mental, but unexpressed, image of the course, and that using a visual language such as E²ML would help them organize their thinking, speed-up collaboration, compare different design solutions, and help maintain overall consistency in their designs (Botturi, 2005). Figure 1.1 presents an example of how E²ML can be used to illustrate dependencies in an instructional programme. The aim of the dependencies diagram is to show that learning activities are connected in deep and meaningful ways, which can, then, enable designers to control the effects that local changes can have on whole environments.

SUMMARY

The foundational design literature portrays design in educational technology 'as a highly systematic, problem-solving process, executed by individuals who specialize in portions of the larger process, and informed by empirical evidence gathered throughout the design process' (Smith & Boling, 2009, p. 13). Yet, in practice, design work is rarely as systematic as portrayed, as designer judgements and contextual variables influence both the processes and resulting products in unexpected ways (Stolterman, 2009). It is important that design teams understand and plan for these variations so as to both capitalize on positive influences as well as control for negative ones, thus ultimately assuring that the best possible designs will emerge.

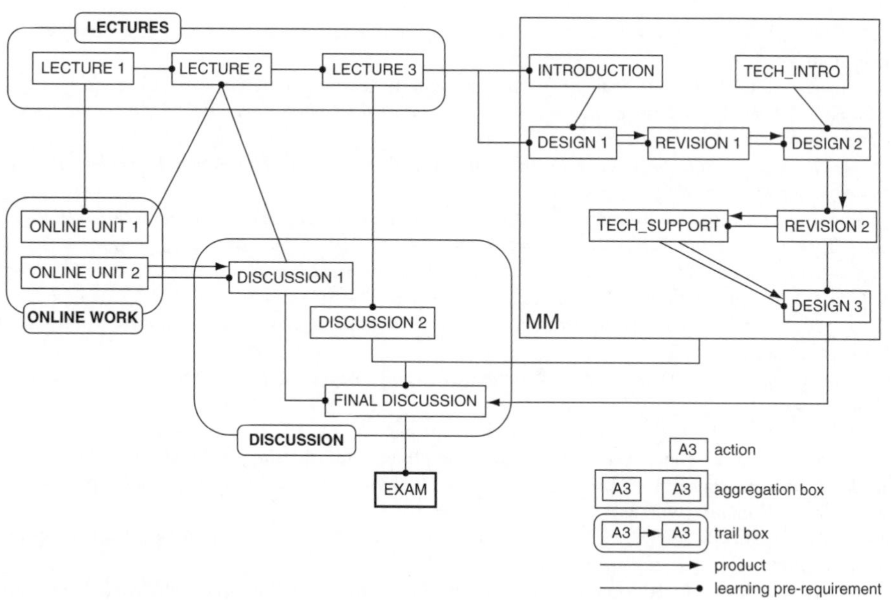

Figure 1.1 Example of dependencies diagram (Botturi, 2006).

REFERENCES

Archer, L. B. (1965). *Systematic Method for Designers*. London: Council for Industrial Design.

Ballantyne, R., Hughes, K., & Mylonas, A. (2002). Developing procedures for implementing peer assessment in large classes using an action research process. *Assessment & Evaluation in Higher Education, 27*, 427–441.

Bennett, S., Thomas, L., Agostinho, S., Lockyer, L., Jones, J., & Harper, B. (2011). Understanding the design context for Australian university teachers: Implications for the future of learning design. *Learning, Media and Technology, 36*(2), 151–167.

Bird, J., Morgan, C., & O'Reilly, M. (2007). Exploring the tensions in educational and instructional design in Australian universities. In M. Keppell (Ed.), *Instructional Design: Case Studies in Communities of Practice* (pp. 19–35). Hershey, PA: Information Science.

Blackwell, A. F., Eckert, C. M., Bucciarelli, L. L., & Earl, C. F. (2009). Witnesses to design: A phenomenology of comparative design. *Design Issues, 25*(1), 36–47.

Booch, G., Maksimchuk, R. A., Engle, M. W., Young, B. J., Conallen, J., & Houston, K. A. (2007). *Object-oriented Analysis and Design with Applications* (3rd ed.). Boston, MA: Addison-Wesley.

Boot, E., & Kremer, J. (2006). Communicating complex instructional designs to different stakeholders. Paper presented at the The Interservice/Industry Training, Simulation & Education Conference (I/ITSEC). Retrieved November 30, 2011, from http://ntsa.metapress.com/link.asp?id=0xhtb2jpq75ftq69.

Boot, E., Nelson, J., Van Merriënboer, J. J., & Gibbons, A. S. (2007). Stratification, elaboration and formalisation of design documents: Effects on the production of instructional materials. *British Journal of Educational Technology, 38*, 917–933.

Boot, E., van Merriënboer, J. J., & Theunissen, N. C. M. (2008). Improving the development of instructional software: Three building-block solutions to interrelate design and production. *Computers in Human Behavior, 24*, 1275–1292.

Boot, E., van Merriënboer, J., & Veerman, A. (2007). Novice and experienced instructional software developers: Effects on materials created with instructional software templates. *Educational Technology Research and Development, 55*, 647–666.

Botturi, L. (2005). A framework for the evaluation of visual languages for instructional design: The case of E^{2}ML. *Journal of Interactive Learning Research, 16*(4), 329–351.

Botturi, L. (2006). E^{2}ML: A visual language for the design of instruction. *Educational Technology Research and Development, 54*, 265–293.

Botturi, L. (2008). E^{2}ML: A tool for sketching instructional designs. In L. Botturi & T. Stubbs (Eds.), *Handbook of Visual Languages for Instructional Design: Theories and Practices*. New York: Information Science Reference.

Boud, D., & Falchikov, N. (2006). Aligning assessment with long-term learning. *Assessment & Evaluation in Higher Education, 31*, 399–413.

Boud, D., Cohen, R., & Sampson, J. (1999). Peer learning and assessment. *Assessment & Evaluation in Higher Education, 24*, 413–426.

Cameron, L., & Gotlieb, C. (2009). Students participating in the learning design process using LAMS. In L. Cameron & J. Dalziel (Eds.), *Proceedings of the 4th International LAMS Conference 2009: Opening Up Learning Design*. Sydney: LAMS Foundation.

Carr, A. (1997). User-design in the creation of human learning systems. *Educational Technology Research and Development, 45*(3), 5–22.

Carr-Chellman, A., Cuyar, C., & Breman, J. (1998). User-design: A case application in health care training. *Educational Technology Research and Development, 46*(4), 97–114.

Conole, G. (2010). *An overview of design representations*. Paper presented at the 7th International Conference on Networked Learning. Aalborg, Denmark.

Cook, D. A. (2007). Web-based learning: Pros, cons and controversies. *Clinical Medicine: Journal of the Royal College of Physicians, 7*(1), 37–42.

Cox, S., & Osguthorpe, R. (2003). How do instructional design professionals spend their time? *TechTrends, 47*(3), 45–47.

Cross, N. (2006). *Designerly Ways of Knowing*. London: Springer.

Cross, N. (2007). From a design science to a design discipline: Understanding designerly ways of knowing and thinking. In R. Michel (Ed.), *Design Research Now: Essays and Selected Projects* (Part 2; pp. 41–54). Basel, Switzerland: Birkhauser Verlag.

Dell'Era, C., & Verganti, R. (2010). Collaborative strategies in design-intensive industries: Knowledge diversity and innovation. *Long Range Planning, 43*(1), 123–141.

Derntl, M., Figl, K., Botturi, L., & Boot, E. (2006). *A classification framework for educational modeling languages in instructional design*. Paper presented at the IEEE International Conference on Advanced Learning Technologies (ICALT 2006). Retrieved December 10, 2011, from http://eprints.cs.univie.ac.at/539/.

Der-Thanq, C., Hung, D., & Wang, Y. M. (2007). Educational design as a quest for congruence: The need for alternative learning design tools. *British Journal of Educational Technology, 38*, 876–884.

Dicks, D., & Ives, C. (2008). Instructional designers at work: A study of how designers design. *Canadian Journal of Learning and Technology, 32*(2), 91–108.

Dudczak, C. A. (1995, November). *Heuristic elements of plausible reasoning.* Paper presented at the Annual Meeting of the Speech Communication Association. San Antonio, Texas.

Eckert, C. M., Blackwell, A. F., Bucciarelli, L. L., & Earl, C. F. (2010). Shared conversations across Design. *Design Issues, 26*(3), 27–39.

Ertmer, P. A., & Cennamo, K. C. (2007). The Denny Clifford case. In P. A. Ertmer & J. Quinn (Eds.), *The ID Case-Book: Case Studies in Instructional Design* (pp. 27–31). Upper Saddle River, NJ: Pearson.

Ertmer, P. A., Stepich, D. A., York, C. S., Stickman, A., Wu, X., Zurek, S., et al. (2008). How instructional design experts use knowledge and experience to solve ill-structured problems. *Performance Improvement Quarterly, 21*(1), 17–42.

Ertmer, P. A., York, C. S., & Gedik, N. (2009). Learning from the pros: How experienced designers translate ID models into practice. *Educational Technology, 49*(1), 19–26.

Gentry, C. (1994). *Introduction to Instructional Development: Process and Technique.* Belmont, CA: Wadsworth.

Gibbons, A., Botturi, L., Boot, E., & Nelson, J. (2008). Design languages. In M. J. Spector et al. (Eds.), *Handbook of Research on Educational Communications and Technology* (3rd ed.) (pp. 633–645). New York: Erlbaum.

Goodyear, P. (2010). Emerging methodological challenges for educational research. In L. Markauskaite, P. Freebody, & J. Irwin (Eds.), *Methodological Choice and Design: Scholarship, Policy and Practice in Social and Educational Research* (pp. 253–266). London: Springer.

Goodyear, P., & Ellis, R. (2008). University students' approaches to learning: Rethinking the place of technology. *Distance Education, 29*(2), 141–152.

Greer, M. (1992). *ID Project Management: Tools and Techniques for Instructional Designers and Developers.* Englewood Cliffs, NJ: Educational Technology Publications.

Gunawardena, C., Wilson, P., & Nolla, A. (2003). Culture and online education. In M. Moore & W. Anderson (Eds.), *Handbook of Distance Education* (pp. 753–775). Mahwah, NJ: Erlbaum.

Hagstrom, F. (2006). Formative learning and assessment. *Communication Disorders Quarterly, 28*(1), 24–36.

Hardré, P. L., Ge, X., & Thomas, M. K. (2006). An investigation of development toward instructional design expertise. *Performance Improvement Quarterly, 19*(4), 63–90.

Herrington, J., & Oliver, R. (2000). An instructional design framework for authentic learning environments. *Educational Technology Research and Development, 48*(3), 23–48.

Hokanson, B. (2008). The virtue of paper: Drawing as a means to innovation in instructional design. In L. Botturi & T. Stubbs (Eds.), *Handbook of Visual Languages for Instructional Design: Theories and Practices.* New York: Information Science Reference.

Hoogveld, A. W., Paas, F., Jochems, W. M., & van Merriënboer, J. J. (2001). The effects of a Web-based training in an instructional systems design approach on teachers' instructional design behavior. *Computers in Human Behavior, 17*, 363–371.

Hoogveld, A. W., Paas, F., Jochems, W. M., & van Merriënboer, J. J. (2002). Exploring teachers' instructional design practices from a systems design perspective. *Instructional Science, 30*, 291–305.

Hoogveld, A. W., Paas, F., & Jochems, W. M. G. (2005). Training higher education teachers for instructional design of competency-based education: Product-oriented versus process-oriented worked examples. *Teaching and Teacher Education, 21*(3), 287–297.

Jin, S. H., & Boling, E. (2010). Instructional designer's intentions and learners' perceptions of the instructional functions of visuals in an e-Learning context. *Journal of Visual Literacy, 29*(2), 143–166.

Johari, A., Bentley, J., Tinney, M., & Chia, B. (2005). Intercultural Internet-based learning: Know your audience and what it values. *Educational Technology Research and Development, 53*(2), 117–127.

Jonassen, D. H. (1994). Technology as cognitive tools: Learners as designers. *ITForum Paper, 1*, 1–7. Retrieved December 10, 2011 from http://it.coe.uga.edu/itforum/paper1/paper1.html.

Jones, C., Dirckinck-Homfeld, L., & Lindstrom, B. (2006). A relational, indirect, meso-level approach to CSCL design in the next decade. *International Journal of Computer-Supported Collaborative Learning, 1*(1), 35–56.

Jones, T., & Richey, R. (2000). Rapid prototyping methodology in action: A developmental study. *Educational Technology Research and Development, 48*(2), 63–80.

Keppell, M. J., & Gale, T. (2007). *Instructional Design: Case Studies in Communities of Practice.* Hershey, PA: Information Science.

Kirschner, P., Carr, C., van Merriënboer, J., & Sloep, P. (2002). How expert designers design. *Performance Improvement Quarterly, 15*(4), 86–104.

Kolodner, J. L., Camp, P. J., Crismond, D., Fasse, B., Gray, J., Holbrook, J., et al. (2003). Problem-based learning meets case-based reasoning in the middle-school science classroom: Putting learning by design into practice. *Journal of the Learning Sciences, 12*(4), 495–547.

Könings, K., Brand-Gruwel, S., & van Merriënboer, J. (2011). Participatory instructional redesign by students and teachers in secondary education: Effects on perceptions of instruction. *Instructional Science, 39*, 737–762.

Könings, K., Brand-Gruwel, S., & van Merriënboer, J. J. G. (2010). An approach to participatory instructional design in secondary education: An exploratory study. *Educational Research, 52*(1), 45–59.

Larson, M., & Lockee, B. (2004). Instructional design practice: Career environments, job roles, and a climate of change. *Performance Improvement Quarterly, 17*(1), 22–40.

Layng, J. (1997). Parallels between project management and instructional design. *Performance Management, 36*(6), 16–20.

Liang, C. C. (2000). Patterns of expert ID practitioners in the corporate world: A literature review. *TechTrends, 44*(1), 16–18.

Lim, C. P. (2008). Spirit of the game: Empowering students as designers in schools? *British Journal of Educational Technology, 39*, 996–1003.

Lovitt, C., & Clarke, D. (2011). A designer speaks. *Educational Designer, 1*(4), 1–25.

Martin, F. (2011). Instructional design and the importance of instructional alignment. *Community College Journal of Research and Practice, 35*(12), 955–972.

Mereba, T. (2003). Managing transformation: Aligning technology initiatives with institutional priorities. *TechTrends, 47*(3), 42–44.

Merrill, M., & Wilson, B. (2007). The future of instructional design (Point/Counterpoint). In R. Reiser & J. Dempsey (Eds.), *Trends and Issues in Instructional Design and Technology* (2nd ed., pp. 335–351). Upper Saddle River, NJ: Pearson.

Reeves, T. C. (2000). Alternative assessment approaches for online learning environments in higher education. *Journal of Educational Computing Research, 23*(1), 101–111.

Reeves, T. C. (2006). How do you know they are learning? The importance of alignment in higher education. *International Journal of Learning Technology, 2*(4), 294–309.

Reiser, R. A. (2007). What field did you say you were in? Defining and naming our field. In R. A. Resier & J. V. Dempsey (Eds.), *Trends and Issues in Instructional Design and Technology* (2nd ed., pp. 2–9). Upper Saddle River, NJ: Pearson.

Reswick, J. B. (1965). *Prospectus for an Engineering Design Center.* Cleveland, OH: Case Institute of Technology.

Rogers, P. C., Graham, C. R., & Mayes, C. T. (2007). Cultural competence and instructional design: Exploration research into the delivery of online instruction cross-culturally. *Educational Technology Research and Development, 55*(2), 197–217.

Romiszowski, A. J. (1981). *Designing Instructional Systems: Decision Making in Course Planning and Curriculum Design.* New York: Kogan Page.

Rowland, G. (1992). What do instructional designers actually do? An initial investigation of expert practice. *Performance Improvement Quarterly, 5*(2), 65–86.

Rowland, G. (1993). Designing and instructional design. *Educational Technology Research and Development, 41*(1), 79–91.

Schön, D. A. (1995). *The Reflective Practitioner: How Professionals Think in Action.* Aldershot: Ashgate.

Simon, H. (1969). *The Sciences of the Artificial.* Boston, MA: Massachusetts Institute of Technology.

Sluijsmans, D., Prins, F., & Martens, R. (2006). The design of competency-based performance assessment in E-learning. *Learning Environments Research, 9*(1), 45–66.

Smith, G., Torres-Ayala, A., & Heindel, A. (2008). Disciplinary differences in E-learning instructional design: The case of mathematics. *The Journal of Distance Education, 22*(3), 63–88.

Smith, K. M., & Boling, E. (2009). What do we make of design? Design as a concept in educational technology. *Educational Technology, 49*(4), 3–17.

Stolterman, E. (2009). The nature of design practice and implications for interaction design research. *International Journal of Design, 2*(1), 55–65.

Struyven, K., Dochy, F., & Janssens, S. (2005). Students' perceptions about evaluation and assessment in higher education: A review. *Assessment & Evaluation in Higher Education, 30*, 325–341.

Summers, L., Lohr, L., & O'Neil, C. (2002). Building instructional design credibility through communication competency. *TechTrends, 46*(1), 26–32.

Taras, M. (2002). Using assessment for learning and learning from assessment. *Assessment & Evaluation in Higher Education, 27*, 501–510.

Tasker, M., & Packham, D. (1993). Industry and higher education: A question of values. *Studies in Higher Education, 18*(2), 127–136.

Tian, X. (2007). Do assessment methods matter? A sensitivity test. *Assessment & Evaluation in Higher Education, 32*, 387–401.

van Merriënboer, J. J. (1997). *Training Complex Cognitive Skills: A Four Component Instructional Design Model for Technical Training*. Englewood Cliffs, NJ: Educational Technology Publications.

van Merriënboer, J. J., Kirschner, P. A., & Kester, L. (2003). Taking the load off a learner's mind: Instructional design for complex learning. *Educational Psychologist, 38*(1), 5–13.

Van Rooij, S. W. (2010). Project management in instructional design: ADDIE is not enough. *British Journal of Educational Technology, 41*, 852–864.

Waters, S., & Gibbons, A. (2004). Design languages, notation systems, and instructional technology: A case study. *Educational Technology Research and Development, 52*(2), 57–68.

Williams, D., South, J., Yanchar, S., Wilson, B., & Allen, S. (2011). How do instructional designers evaluate? A qualitative study of evaluation in practice. *Educational Technology Research and Development, 59*(6), 885–907.

Winn, W. (1990). Some implications of cognitive theory for instructional design. *Instructional Science, 19*(1), 53–69.

Yanchar, S., South, J., Williams, D., Allen, S., & Wilson, B. (2010). Struggling with theory? A qualitative investigation of conceptual tool use in instructional design. *Educational Technology Research and Development, 58*(1), 39–60.

Yang, C., Moore, D., & Burton, J. (1995). Managing courseware production: An instructional design model with a software engineering approach. *Educational Technology Research and Development, 43*(4), 60–70.

York, C., & Ertmer, P. (2011). Towards an understanding of instructional design heuristics: An exploratory Delphi study. *Educational Technology Research and Development, 59*(6), 1–23.

2

PRINCIPLES FOR DESIGN AND EVALUATION OF LEARNING SPACES

Mike Keppell and Matthew Riddle

INTRODUCTION

Interest in the influence of learning spaces on learning and teaching has been growing in recent times (e.g. Boys, 2011; Ellsworth, 2005; Goodyear, 2008; Luckin, 2010). Projects such as the Spaces for Knowledge Generation Project (Souter, Riddle, Sellers, & Keppell, 2011) explicitly focused on the influence of technology, economic and social developments in relation to learning spaces and how space influences both the role of the teacher and the learner and the range of learning approaches that can be undertaken within the space.

> The SKG project found that students move in nomadic but purposeful ways across a learning landscape of which the university is only part. Students are already enmeshed in a work/home/study continuum, and the problem for the university is to indeed advance these open and flexible communities on campus.
>
> (Souter et al. 2011, p. 1)

We define learning spaces as:

- physical, blended or virtual learning environments that enhance as opposed to constrain learning;
- physical, blended or virtual 'areas' that motivate a user to participate for learning benefits;
- spaces where both teachers and students optimize the perceived and actual affordances of the space; and
- spaces that promote authentic learning interactions.

(Keppell & Riddle, 2011, p. 5)

Formal physical learning spaces within higher education often have a preconceived function determined by traditional conceptions of teaching and learning that position the teacher as authority and the student as a relatively passive participant in the learning process. In order to provide a motivating and rich learning environment, formal physical learning spaces need to be adaptable and flexible for learning and teaching as opposed to being designed for one purpose. These spaces also need to emphasize authentic learning interactions. Informal physical learning spaces include learning commons that encourage both independent and peer learning. They allow students to repurpose the informal space to suit their own learning needs. Chairs, tables, access to Wi-Fi and power points need to be carefully considered to allow this individual customization (Keppell & Riddle, 2011).

Within this chapter we argue that design and evaluation are iterative and integral aspects of the design process, and that designers of learning spaces need to be involved in both aspects of the process to fully contribute to the design of learning spaces for contemporary learning and teaching. This chapter examines two cases that utilize seven principles of learning space design that support a constructivist approach to learning and support a learning environment that is student-centered, collaborative, active and experiential. These principles comprise: comfort, aesthetics, flow, equity, blending, affordances and repurposing (Souter et al., 2011). The first case utilizes the principles to inform the design of a space and the second case uses the principles to informally evaluate an existing learning space.

DESIGN PRINCIPLES FOR LEARNING SPACE DESIGN

The use of design principles to guide learning space design is quite common in the literature and such principles have been successfully utilized to design 21st-century learning spaces (Boys, 2011; Jamieson, Fisher, Gilding, & Taylor, 2000; JISC, 2006; Mitchell, White, & Pospisil, 2010). Previous research considering appropriate learning space designs for contemporary higher learning has identified the need for more attention to this area in suggesting that

> we need a better understanding of the role of space in the dynamics of creating more productive higher education communities (potentially involving considerations of institutional academic and managerial organisation and their part in social capital formation, as well as space design and maintenance issues), and its connections with learning and research. This should be the subject of further research.
>
> (Temple, 2007, p. 6; see also Temple, 2008)

Jamieson et al. (2000) suggested seven learning space design principles:

1. Design space for multiple uses concurrently and consecutively
2. Design to maximize the inherent flexibility within each space
3. Design to make use of the vertical dimension of facilities
4. Design to integrate previously discrete campus functions
5. Design features and functions to maximize teacher and student control
6. Design to maximize alignment of different curricular activities
7. Design to maximize student access to and use/ownership of the learning environment.

By considering the alignment of curricular activities with spaces there is an intention to integrate discipline pedagogies into the discussion. This is an inherent strength of these design principles.

JISC (2006, p. 3) suggested six principles for learning space design:

1. Flexible—to accommodate both current and evolving pedagogies
2. Future-proofed—to enable space to be re-allocated and reconfigured
3. Bold—to look beyond tried and tested technologies and pedagogies
4. Creative—to energize and inspire learners and tutors
5. Supportive—to develop the potential of all learners
6. Enterprising—to make each space capable of supporting different purposes.

A major strength of the JISC principles is the notion of 'being bold' and designing space that incorporates new technologies and new pedagogies. While physical spaces may endure for many years, technology needs to be updated on a more regular timescale than the actual physical space.

Mitchell et al. (2010) focused on the development of principles to guide the *redevelopment* of existing spaces in a project titled 'Retrofitting University Learning Spaces'. They developed eight principles and further categorized these principles under the headings of engagement, empowerment, ease-of-use and confidence. The eight principles are outlined below.

Engagement Principles

1. Spaces should support a range of learners and learning activities.
2. Spaces should provide a quality experience for users.

Empowerment Principles

3. Spaces should help foster a sense of emotional and cultural safety.
4. Spaces should enable easy access by everyone.

Ease-of-Use Principles

5. Spaces should emphasize simplicity of design.
6. Spaces should integrate seamlessly with other physical and virtual spaces.

Confidence Principles

7. Space should be fit-for-purpose, now and into the future.
8. Spaces should embed a range of appropriate, reliable and effective technologies.

A distinctive strength of these design principles is the emphasis on 'fostering emotional and cultural safety'. Mitchell et al. (2010) suggest an inclusive approach that focuses on multi-cultural awareness in the design of spaces. This is also a distinguishing characteristic in their learning space design principles.

The SKG project (Souter et al., 2011) posed questions about the design of learning spaces to suit the needs of learners as they generate knowledge. Acknowledging Barnett's (2000, p. 43) proposition that the pace at which knowledge is expanding makes the world 'radically unknowable', SKG focused on informal spaces and collaborative spaces. This shifts attention away from the design of traditional university learning spaces such as lecture theatres, and towards what Savin-Baden (2008) terms *dialogic spaces*, emphasizing a transformation through the contestability of knowledge and the exchange of ideas involved in academic work (p. 51), and *troublesome spaces*, where disjunction occurs (p. 95).

Souter et al. (2011) suggested seven principles of learning space design which support a constructivist approach to learning and support a learning environment that is student-centered, collaborative and experiential. The development of these principles explicitly embraced the student voice and we believe that this is a neglected area. Next generation learning spaces need to co-partner with students who are major stakeholders in the design and evaluation of learning spaces which they will occupy for a major part of their education. In fact, if occupation of a space determined the influence of the stakeholder then students would be the predominant stakeholders in the design process. The SKG design principles include:

1. *Comfort*: a space which creates a physical and mental sense of ease and well-being.
2. *Aesthetics*: pleasure which includes the recognition of symmetry, harmony, simplicity and fitness for purpose.
3. *Flow*: the state of mind felt by the learner when totally involved in the learning experience.
4. *Equity*: consideration of the needs arising from cultural and physical differences.
5. *Blending*: a mixture of technological and face-to-face pedagogical resources.
6. *Affordances*: the 'action possibilities' the learning environment provides the users, including such things as kitchens, natural light, Wi-Fi, private spaces, writing surfaces, sofas, and so on.
7. *Repurposing*: the potential for multiple usage of a space.

The SKG project was based on the philosophy that constructivist approaches to learning, as well as to research and study, should make use of technologies and approaches that students favour, and that learning spaces should therefore be organized to accommodate learner-generated aspects of learning. SKG provides a model for designing student learning environments that is future-focused and sustainable for the medium term (Souter et al., 2011). A legacy of this sustainable project has been the ability of the design team to apply these principles to the design of new spaces or to redesign existing spaces using the seven principles outlined above. The following case at La Trobe University provides an example of how the principles were utilized to repurpose an existing learning space. The second case at Charles Sturt University will outline how the principles were utilized for informally evaluating an existing learning space.

CASE STUDY 1: THE DESIGN OF A TECHNOLOGY-ENRICHED LEARNING SPACE

The Exemplar Learning Facilities Project

In July 2011 at La Trobe University, a project steering committee was formed to undertake a programme of upgrades to existing teaching spaces. The project, named 'Exemplar Learning Facilities' (ELF), was established after a comprehensive audit of the utilization rates and configuration of the university's teaching and learning spaces, which found, among other things that: 'there is currently an inadequate spatial provision per seat/student which inhibits the adoption of alternative teaching and learning modes particularly at the Melbourne campus' and 'the existing furniture style (typically tablet chairs, long narrow tables or small 500 × 500 tables) is inappropriate for a tertiary institution which seeks to promote team and peer to peer learning' (La Trobe University, 2011, p. 1).

The audit report refers to La Trobe's curriculum renewal process under the banner of *Design for Learning* (La Trobe University, 2009) in stating that the guidelines were established in order to: 'complement other University initiatives to improve learning outcomes and a *Design for Learning* aim that graduates acquire a capability to work in teams and understand the dynamics of teamwork' and 'inform and direct design decision-making in both new and adaptive reuse learning space projects' (La Trobe University, 2011, p. 2).

These design guidelines were produced by a working party of La Trobe's Learning Spaces and Technologies Committee. Considering a suite of teaching spaces, the guidelines outline principles including the design of adaptable and flexible flat-floored teaching spaces with adequate special standards to support collaborative, peer-to-peer learning.

The ELF project scope included six rooms across campus, with priority placed on the development of two new, experimental learning spaces in the Social Sciences Building in order to prototype these ideas. It proposed the establishment of 'highly adaptive and interactive (technology-enriched) collaborative cross-discipline spaces fitted out with loose tables' (ELF Project Steering Committee, Terms of Reference). The establishment of state of the art facilities would require reducing the capacity of two existing seminar rooms from 108 to approximately 60 students in each, according to the spatial standards proposed in the new guidelines.

Project Approach

The project steering committee decided that the best way to go about the project was using two different prototypes. One of the prototypes would trial a more conservative design response, while the other would push the current technological boundaries to develop a collaborative learning space design with a sharper future focus.

ELF Learning Space Design Principles

Development of these experimental spaces, known in the project as Prototype A and Prototype B, involved a careful consideration of the primary point of focus of the room. In the traditional configuration used prior to the project and shown in Figure 2.1, fixed rows of chairs faced towards a fixed lectern, lengthways in the room. A single projector focused on the wall behind the lectern. Under the ELF project, these rooms were designed to have less of a focus on a single delivery point, allowing for team teaching and group work to be supported and suggested. This aspect of the design was seen as particularly important to the ability of the room to be flexible in supporting didactic teaching as well as enquiry-based and problem-based learning. This follows from the SKG principle of *repurposing*, and is important to the overall success of the design.

Comfort and *aesthetics* are two principles that were absolutely central to the ELF project. The existing configuration of the space was uncomfortable for students in a number of important ways. Due to the use of fixed tablet chairs in rows without any

Figure 2.1 This photo, taken prior to the ELF project, shows the orientation of fixed furnishings towards a lectern used in both the spaces redesigned with Prototype A and B.

room for a central aisle, students were not able to move freely in the room, and those at the back were forced to look at the projector display with an uncomfortably small viewing angle. Hearing clearly in these rooms could also be challenging, and lecturers complained about strained voices at the end of long days. Visual comfort was addressed in the redesigned spaces through the provision of dual projection on the long wall (Figures 2.2 and 2.3) and acoustic comfort was improved with the use of acoustic dampening on ceiling beams. Aesthetically, the rooms were quite plain, and their design suggested a pedagogy that no longer matched with the desire for redesigned pedagogies under *Design for Learning* (La Trobe University, 2009) that involve active learning and team work. As Figures 2.1, 2.2 and 2.3 show, the redesigned spaces are considerably more attractive and make use of engaging colours and shapes.

Figure 2.2 Prototype A after completion. Floor markings in the carpet tiles indicate the home position of tables. The lectern has been moved to the long wall and dual projection is in place.

Figure 2.3 Prototype B after completion. This room employs a subtle lectern design, tables in pairs and six team pods with wireless video capability.

The principle of *flow* was also at work in the development of the design. Csikszentmihalyi (1990, p. 4) describes *flow* as 'the state in which people are so involved in an activity that nothing else seems to matter'. The SKG design principles adapt this concept to inform the design of learning spaces, suggesting that spaces should be configured to enhance rather than interrupt the process of finding *flow* in the generation of knowledge. In particular, teaching staff involved in the ELF design team were concerned that the reconfiguration of furniture in the rooms should not distract or divert the flow of learning during class time. These academics also advocated for adequate provision for breakout discussion spaces to promote creative thinking, with discussion groups ranging from three to eight students.

The ELF spaces are designed to support students in subjects making use of collaborative learning approaches such as Enquiry-Based Learning (EBL) and Problem-Based Learning (PBL). EBL is 'a broad umbrella term to describe approaches to learning that are driven by a process of enquiry' (Kahn & O'Rourke, 2005, p. 1). The purpose of using EBL and PBL approaches is to promote active learning and to constructively align the outcomes, teaching and learning and assessment of courses (Biggs, 2012). In this way, the ELF spaces have been designed with *pedagogically informed* principles as recommended by Jamieson et al. (2000). To achieve this, two lecturers coordinating courses that involve EBL and collaborative project work were co-opted to the project steering committee. These academics made it clear that the need for students to work in groups of three or four was particularly important to the learning design of their courses. This was a crucial turning point for the design of the furniture layout in the ELF rooms. Two different default layouts are offered by the prototypes chosen by the project shown in Figures 2.2 and 2.3, with each allowing alternative layouts with separate tables to support small groups.

The ELF spaces have been designed to support active learning, creating what Savin-Baden (2008, p. 104) calls *troublesome* learning spaces, because learners are placed in a mode of enquiry that causes a disjunction—a key catalyst to engage learners prior to transformation of knowledge. Those involved in the ELF project were keenly aware that the pedagogical design and the learning design go together to create these circumstances for learning.

Both prototype designs make use of hardwearing flip-top tables on casters that can be quickly and easily repositioned, or folded away altogether. Each room includes both chairs with casters and on sleds in order to fully test both approaches. In each case the chairs were chosen to be durable, light and easy to move.

Floor markings in the carpet design show the 'home position' of moveable furniture. In the case of Prototype A (Figure 2.2) this arranges ten tables of six students each individually in two gentle arcs, with three additional breakout spaces created by banquette seating. In Prototype B (Figure 2.3) 14 tables are arranged in pairs, accommodating eight students at each of seven large tables in the 'home position'. These can be drawn apart towards the wall for smaller group discussions, and the room includes two breakout spaces with banquette seating.

The ELF project has a particular focus on the SKG principles of the *affordances* of learning space technologies, as well as the *blending* of face-to-face learning with students' own digital devices. The most striking addition in Prototype B is the inclusion of six extra digital monitors fitted with wireless video presentation capabilities as well as input panels supporting physical input of video from laptops and other devices. The wireless video capability is an affordance of this space that represents a new approach for La Trobe, and allows videos and presentations to be sent directly to any of the monitors without plugging in any cables.

Each room also includes a state of the art document camera, as well as the tried and tested low-tech group work technologies of huddle-boards, fixed whiteboards and pin-boards. Huddle-boards are small, lightweight whiteboards that can be used by groups at a table and then hung on a rail or placed underneath a document camera for presentation to a larger group. These technologies are particularly useful in supporting learning designs that require students to make presentations, work in groups and demonstrate active listening skills.

CASE STUDY 2: EVALUATING THE THURGOONA LEARNING COMMONS

The Thurgoona Learning Commons (TLC) is located on the Albury-Wodonga Campus at Charles Sturt University. The TLC houses the library collections, learning skills advisors and Indigenous Student Services. More recently, other campus services have migrated to the Learning Commons as it has become a hub for student engagement and has become the *agora* or community centre of the campus. (The agora was a gathering place or assembly point in ancient Greek city-states and represented a lively market place of the city.)

The TLC has been designed and built to conform to the environmentally friendly ethos of the campus, which has a strong emphasis on sustainability.

> The Albury-Wodonga campus was designed to function autonomously, drawing minimally on external services, using material resources sparingly and generating significantly less waste. The comprehensive, environmentally sensitive design process

> that encompassed all stages from site planning to the selection of materials, succeeded in creating a campus based on far more rigorous principles of sustainability than any project of comparable size in Australia.
>
> (Rafferty, 2012, p. 53)

The TLC has natural ventilation and natural lighting to align with the principles of this environmentally friendly campus. The TLC has a diverse range of spaces that were designed to enhance independent and peer learning (Oakley, 2008).

The seven principles of learning space design were utilized to informally evaluate this 21st-century space in order to test the framework in relation to evaluation of learning spaces. In terms of *comfort* the TLC space creates a physical and mental sense of ease and well-being through the use of natural lighting including high ceilings and visual connection to the outside quadrangle through large glass windows at the front of the building. This area in the front of the building is also the 24-hour access area where students can congregate and socialize with other students. It is a place for students to meet and discuss their work on an informal basis. It also introduces students to the milieu of studying at the Thurgoona campus.

As can be seen from the photo in Figure 2.4, the *aesthetics* of the learning space demonstrate principles of symmetry, harmony, simplicity and fitness for purpose. The space is designed to be welcoming and allow students to undertake peer-related discussions. It is also the area where students enjoy congregating. As staff or students enter the learning space there is an appreciation of thoughtful and considered design.

Figure 2.4 The Thurgoona Learning Commons 24-hour access area.

> The aesthetic appeal of a learning space, then, will not just be the utilitarian fact that it has a particular level of technology or affordances, but the way the technology or affordances fit into the whole. It may also include the non-utilitarian enjoyment of the design of the space, the outlook, the furnishings, colours, light, view.
>
> (SKG Website, 2011)

In addition it is hoped that the space would facilitate students to engage with their learning and experience *flow* (Csikszentmihalyi, 1990).

The TLC also aligns with the principle of *equity* as it considers cultural and physical differences. It has an inclusive approach to students and teachers who utilize the space. The entrance and entire learning space have been designed so that they are accessible to students and staff with disabilities. The inclusion of the Indigenous Student Services sends a positive message to all staff and students working in the area. In addition the range of spaces—from noisy, social learning spaces, group study areas, to quiet

Figure 2.5 Range of group and independent spaces throughout the Thurgoona Learning Commons.

individual areas—allow the students to decide how they wish to study within the space. A student can transition through each of the spaces depending on the task on which they wish to focus.

In addition, the *timescape* of the semester will influence the mix of peer and independent study that is required. Timescape refers to the different use of the same learning space over a semester. For example, early in the semester a student might wish to discuss an assignment topic with a group of students in the learning space. When students are getting closer to exams they might wish to gravitate to a quiet, individual space toward the back of the TLC to prepare for the impending exam. The lower ceilings toward the back of the TLC also assist in minimizing noise and creating a sense of privacy.

The TLC has explicitly accounted for a mixture of technological and face-to-face pedagogical resources through a *blended* approach. 'Blended and flexible learning' is a design approach that examines the relationships between flexible learning *opportunities*, in order to optimize student engagement (Keppell, 2010). The blended learning environment is a necessity for teaching and learning. The design of learning spaces needs to embrace the nomadic student who needs wireless and other technology, seamless connection and uninterrupted usage irrespective of the type of technology being used (Taylor, 2012). Within the TLC, there is an explicit need to blend face-to-face pedagogical experiences with access to CSU Interact, the university's virtual learning space. There are both PC and Mac computers for students to access resources and applications that require the greater bandwidth provided by a fixed network. In addition, since students are coming to regard the use of laptops and mobile devices as the norm, wireless access is pervasive within the TLC. Residential students also appreciate the ability to easily access the wireless network within the 24-hour access area and the TLC is a major space for interactions on the campus.

There are multiple 'action possibilities' for this learning space. As suggested previously, there are noisy social spaces, group study rooms and individual study areas *affording* informal peer learning, structured peer learning and independent learning, respectively. An important aspect of affordances is that the student needs to appreciate both the perceived and actual affordances of the learning space. By recognizing the perceived possibilities of the space for learning the student will be more likely to utilize the space when needed. The variety of spaces promotes student learning and is enhanced by Wi-Fi, vending machines for snacks, and comfortable sofas that can be reconfigured by the students. Students can repurpose the spaces by moving chairs and tables into group settings or *repurposing* the space to suit their needs for group discussion, group projects or independent study.

CONCLUSION

The two cases discussed suggest that the SKG seven principles of learning space design have potential in assisting the design of learning space and in the evaluation of learning space. In undertaking both the design and evaluation of the spaces at two universities the authors have elaborated the design principles to include questions that may further guide design and evaluation for multiple stakeholders. These are summarized in Table 2.1.

The SKG design principles focus on questions to ask both staff and students working in an informal learning space.

Table 2.1 SKG Design Principles and Focus Questions

Principle	Questions
Comfort: a space that creates a physical and mental sense of ease and well-being.	How comfortable do you feel in this learning space?
	Do aspects of the learning space distract you from learning?
	What area in the learning space do you spend most of your time in and why?
	Is there an area where you don't feel comfortable in the learning space?
Aesthetics: pleasure, which includes the recognition of symmetry, harmony, simplicity and fitness for purpose.	What features of the learning space do you appreciate?
	Is the space fit for purpose in relation to learning?
Flow: the state of mind felt by the learner when totally involved in the learning experience.	Do you feel you can engage with your work in the learning space?
	Are there areas in the learning space where you can focus on your individual work?
Equity: consideration of the needs of cultural and physical differences.	Do you think the learning space is inclusive of all people?
	What features of the space promote an inclusive approach?
Blending: a mixture of technological and face-to-face pedagogical resources.	Do you utilize your own mobile device in the learning space?
	How easy is it for you to connect to the network?
	How often do you rely on the technology within the space?
Affordances: the 'action possibilities' the learning environment provides the users, including such things as kitchens, natural light, Wi-Fi, private spaces, writing surfaces, sofas, and so on.	What does this learning space allow you to do that you cannot complete in another space?
	Do you learn from other users about how to use the space?
	Are there parts of the learning space that you avoid because you don't know how to use them?
Repurposing: the potential for multiple usage of a space.	Do you move tables and chairs to create your own learning area?
	What parts of the learning space do you reconfigure to suit your learning style?
	Are there areas in the learning space that you constantly reuse for this reason?

Future design and evaluation of our spaces will utilize these questions to enable further insight into the use of learning spaces by both staff and students. By focusing on the key stakeholder perspectives we should be able to provide insightful feedback on the usefulness of the SKG principles for both design and evaluation of learning spaces in higher education.

REFERENCES

Barnett, R. (2000). University knowledge in an age of supercomplexity. *Higher Education, 40,* 409–422.

Biggs, J. (2012). What the student does: teaching for enhanced learning. *Higher Education Research and Development, 31*(1), 39–55.

Boys, J. (2011). *Towards Creative Learning Spaces: re-thinking the architecture of post-compulsory education.* New York: Routledge.

Csikszentmihalyi, M. (1990). *Flow: the psychology of optimal experience,* 1st ed. New York: Harper & Row.

Ellsworth, E. (2005). *Places of Learning: media, architecture, pedagogy.* New York: Routledge.

Goodyear, P. (2008). Flexible learning and the architecture of learning places. In M. Spector, D. Merrill, J. van Merrienboer & M. Driscoll (Eds) *Handbook of Research on Educational Communications and Technology,* pp. 251–257. New York: Routledge.

Jamieson, P., Fisher, K., Gilding, T., & Taylor, P. (2000). Place and space in the design of new learning environments. *Higher Education Research and Development, 19*(2), 221–237.

JISC. (2006). Designing learning spaces for effective learning: A guide to 21st century learning space design. Retrieved 10 March, 2012, from http://www.jisc.ac.uk/uploaded_documents/JISClearningspaces.pdf

Kahn, P. & O'Rourke, K. (2005). Understanding Enquiry-Based Learning. In T. Barrett, I. Mac Labhrainn, & H. Fallon (Eds) *Handbook of Enquiry & Problem Based Learning.* Galway: CELT. Available at: http://www.nuigalway.ie/celt/pblbook/

Keppell, M. (2010). *Blended and Flexible Learning Standards.* Charles Sturt University.

Keppell, M. & Riddle, M. (2011). Distributed learning places: physical, blended and virtual learning spaces in higher education. In Mike Keppell, Kay Souter, & Matthew Riddle (Eds.) *Physical and Virtual Learning Spaces in Higher Education: concepts for the modern learning environment* (pp. 1–20). New York: IGI Global.

La Trobe University (2009). *Design for Learning: Curriculum Review and Renewal at La Trobe University.* Retrieved 15 February, 2012, from http://www.latrobe.edu.au/ctlc/assets/downloads/dfl/DFL-booklet.pdf

La Trobe University (2011). *Teaching & Learning Spaces—Design Guidelines.* Retrieved 15 February, 2012, from http://www.latrobe.edu.au/policy/documents/teaching-learning-spaces-guidelines.pdf

Luckin, R. (2010). *Re-designing Learning Contexts: technology-rich, learner-centred ecologies.* New York: Routledge.

Mitchell, G., White, B., & Pospisil, R. (2010). Retrofitting university learning spaces: report for Australian Learning and Teaching Council. Retrieved 10 March, 2012, from http://learnline.cdu.edu.au/retrofittingunispaces/resources/content/ALTC final report - Retrofitting Part A.pdf

Oakley, S. (2008). The Thurgoona learning commons. In D. Radcliffe, H. Wilson, D. Powell, & B. Tibbetts *Proceedings of the Next Generation Learning Spaces 2008 Colloquium* (pp. 93–98). University of Queensland.

Rafferty, J. (2012). Design of outdoor and environmentally integrated learning spaces. In M. J. Keppell, M. Riddle, & K. Souter (Eds.) *Physical and Virtual Learning Spaces in Higher Education: concepts for the modern learning environment.* New York: IGI Global.

Savin-Baden, M. (2008). *Learning Spaces: creating opportunities for knowledge creation in academic life.* Buckingham: Open University Press.

SKG Website. (2011). Spaces for knowledge generation. http://www.skgproject.com/

Souter, K., Riddle, M., Sellers, W., & Keppell, M. (2011). Spaces for Knowledge Generation, final report. Australian Learning and Teaching Council. Retrieved 10 March, 2012, from http://documents.skgproject.com/skg-final-report.pdf

Taylor, G. (2012). Personal communication. Charles Sturt University.

Temple, P. (2007). Learning spaces for the 21st century: A review of the literature. York, UK: Higher Education Academy. Retrieved from http://www.heacademy.ac.uk/assets/documents/research/Learning_spaces_v3.pdf.

Temple, P. (2008). Learning spaces in higher education: An under-researched topic. *London Review of Education, 24*(4), 402–412.

3

THE ECOLOGY OF RESOURCES

A Theoretically Grounded Framework for Designing Next Generation Technology-Rich Learning

Rosemary Luckin, Wilma Clark and Joshua Underwood

INTRODUCTION

William Gibson (1999) eloquently noted that our progress towards the future is 'not evenly distributed'. It happens in 'fits and starts' and in different places to different extents and at different times. The theories and frameworks upon which design activity is based must therefore be capable of engaging with the potential of the cutting edge, yet at the same time be capable of graceful degradation to meet the needs of those who are less technologically sophisticated. Participatory design methods can help designers to understand and address the reality of their beneficiaries, and a greater understanding of learners' contexts can inform this participatory enterprise. However, these methods need to be grounded on a sound theoretical foundation if they are to enhance learning and enable us to reap the full benefits of what modern technologies have to offer. For example, Web 2.0 and crowd sourcing can enable massive, global-scale collaboration, as employed by Galaxy Zoo (http://www.galaxyzoo.org/). Such developments in information-sharing and collaboration have the potential to provide the cognitive tools we need to enable us to act as 'epistemic engineers' and to build 'better tools to think with' (Clark, 2008) so that we can develop more effective educational practices:

> [We] self-engineer ourselves to think and perform better in the world we find ourselves in. We self-engineer worlds in which to build better worlds to think in. We build better tools to think with and use these very tools to discover still better tools to think with. We tune the way we use these tools by building educational practices to train ourselves to use our best cognitive tools better. We even tune the way we tune the way we use our best cognitive tools by devising environments that help build better environments for educating ourselves in the use of our own cognitive tools.
>
> (Clark, 2008, pp. 59–60)

In this chapter we therefore offer a theoretical framework for designing learning activities and technologies that takes advantage of the sophisticated knowledge and equipment that are increasingly available on a large scale. We present and discuss the Ecology of Resources model and associated design framework, which offer a way in which a learner's context can be integrated into the manner in which technology supports their learning.

THE THEORETICAL BACKGROUND FOR THE ECOLOGY OF RESOURCES

Context is a concept that is discussed across many disciplines and from a variety of perspectives. However, previous research into the manner in which context impacts upon learning has been largely limited to specific environmental locations, such as school classrooms. School classrooms are only one kind of context. Much of the literature about context and space is not specifically about education and learning, and yet it deals with issues, such as institutions and social interaction, that are also fundamental to learning. The proliferation of ubiquitous technologies has added to the complexity of the discussions about context. These technologies also provide an increasing impetus for the integration of research into the built environment and research into digital technology, or the blended physical and digital environment (see Keppell & Riddle, this volume).

> The proliferation of the microchip renders the everyday spaces of our existence alive, capable of interacting and reacting to our passage.
>
> (Kerckhove & Tursi, 2009)

Context can be viewed as a multiplicity, with individual people experiencing 'exposure to multiple "contexts" in time and space' (Cummins, Curtis, Diez-Roux & Macintyre, 2007). Context is 'perhaps the most prevalent term used to index the circumstances of behaviour' (Cole, 1996, p. 132). It requires that we interpret mind 'as distributed in the artifacts which are woven together and which weave together individual human actions in concert with and as part of the permeable, changing, events of life' (Cole, 1996, p. 136). This is a perspective that has roots in the work of Vygotsky (1978; 1986) and echoes through the literature on the situated approaches to cognition and learning (for example, Brown, Collins & Duguid, 1989; Brown, 1990; Lave, 1988; Lave & Wenger, 1991).

The Ecology of Resources model of context draws upon this research and provides a model and design framework based upon a learner-centered definition of context:

> Context is dynamic and associated with connections between people, things, locations and events in a narrative that is driven by people's intentionality and motivations. Technology can help to make these connections in an operational sense. People can help to make these connections have meaning for a learner. A learner is not exposed to multiple contexts, but rather has a single context that is their lived experience of the world; a 'phenomenological gestalt' (Manovich, 2006) that reflects their interactions with multiple people, artefacts and environments. The partial descriptions of the world that are offered to a learner through these resources act as the hooks for interactions in which action and meaning are built. In this sense, meaning is distributed amongst these resources. However, it is the manner in which the learner at the centre of their context internalizes their interactions that is the core activity of importance.

> These interactions are not predictable but are created by the people who interact, each of whom will have intentions about how these interactions should be.
>
> (Luckin, 2010, p. 18)

This definition of context is integrated with an interpretation of Vygotsky's Zone of Proximal Development (ZPD), which is conceptualized as a context for productive interactivity. This conceptualization emphasizes the important role played by the society within which the learner interacts and, in particular, by the more knowledgeable, or more able, members of that society: lecturers, teachers, trainers and parents, for example. The need for further clarification and specification of the ZPD concept (Wertsch, 1984; Wood, Bruner & Ross, 1976) is addressed through its re-interpretation in the Zone of Collaboration. The Zone of Collaboration involves two constructs, namely: the Zone of Available Assistance (ZAA) and the Zone of Proximal Adjustment (ZPA). The ZAA describes the variety of resources within a learner's world that could provide different qualities and quantities of assistance that may be available to the learner at a particular point in time. The ZPA represents a subset of the ZAA that is deemed appropriate for a learner's needs.

The concept of the Zone of Collaboration is integrated with the description of context outlined above to form the Ecology of Resources model of context.

THE ECOLOGY OF RESOURCES MODEL OF CONTEXT

The Ecology of Resources model is illustrated in Figure 3.1. It develops the ZAA and ZPA concepts into a characterization of a learner along with the interactions that form that learner's context. Its full detail can be found in Luckin (2010). Here we describe it briefly to situate the presentation of the design framework and to ground the empirical examples that follow.

The resources that comprise a learner's ZAA embrace a wide range of categories, including: the knowledge and skills that are the subject of their learning ('Knowledge

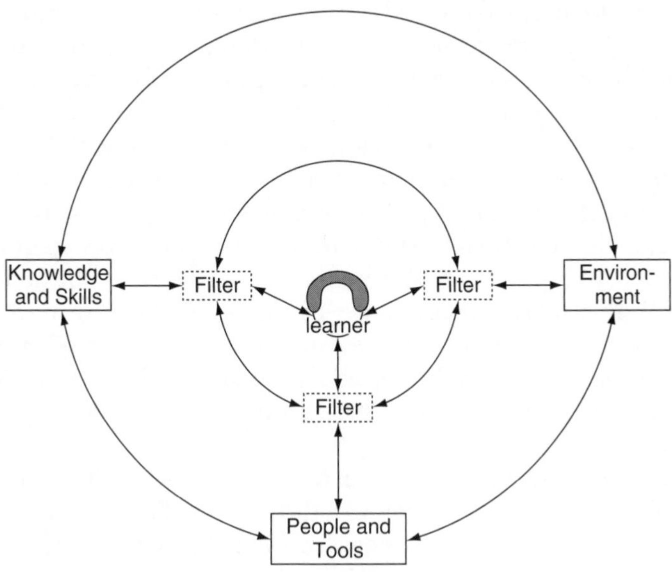

Figure 3.1 The Ecology of Resources Model (Luckin, 2010).

and Skills' in Figure 3.1); the books, pens and paper, technology and other people who know more about the knowledge or skill to be learnt than the learner does ('Tools and People' in Figure 3.1); and the location and surrounding environment with which the learner interacts, for example, a school classroom, a park, a virtual world, or a place of work ('Environment' in Figure 3.1). To support learning, it is necessary to identify and understand the relationships between the different types of resource with which the learner interacts. In addition, it is necessary to explore the manner in which a learner's interactions with these resources is, or might be, constrained. These constraints are identified by the 'Filter' labels in Figure 3.1. For example, a teacher might filter learners' interactions with the world to focus upon and illustrate a particular concept. The teacher is probably only available during a class, or perhaps at some other times via email, and a learner's access to their environment is mediated by that environment's organization and any rules and conventions that apply to it. Filters can be positive or negative and may also be inter-related. The coherence of the learner's experience can be enhanced through careful consideration of existing relationships between filter elements and between individual resource elements and their associated filters.

In addition, it is also important to understand that all of the elements in any Ecology of Resources bring with them a history that defines them, as well as the part they play in the wider cultural and political system. Likewise, the individual at the centre of the Ecology of Resources has their own history of experience that impacts upon their interactions with each of the elements in the Ecology.

THE ECOLOGY OF RESOURCES DESIGN FRAMEWORK

The Ecology of Resources model helps to identify the forms of assistance available to a learner that make up the resource elements with which that learner interacts. The Ecology of Resources model could be viewed statically as merely a snapshot of the set of elements that describe a learner's ZAA and that can be 'optimized' by design and/or by practice. The model can also be viewed as a dynamic process of instigating and maintaining learning interactions in technology-rich environments. The objective of the framework presented here is to support the dynamic process of developing technology-rich learning activities. The aim of the Ecology of Resources framework is to map out the complexity of this design process so that it can be conducted with an enhanced awareness of the subtleties of a learner's context. This does not mean that the entire complexity of a learner's context can be taken into account within the process, merely that a greater understanding of the complexity enables the process, and the resultant technology-rich learning activities, to be more effectively situated. In particular, the design process supported by the Ecology of Resources framework identifies the ways in which technology, people and the learners themselves can best support learning. If the Ecology of Resources model and its associated design framework are to be useful to a design team, the overarching aim of their design process must be to engage with the learner's context as part of that process.

The Ecology of Resources Design Framework offers a structured process based upon the Ecology of Resources model of context, through which educators and technologists can develop technologies and technology-rich learning activities that take a learner's wider context into account. The process is iterative and has three phases, each of which has several steps.

Phase 1: Create an Ecology of Resources Model to identify and organize the potential forms of assistance that can act as resources for learning. This comprises the following steps:

1. Brainstorm Potential Resources to identify learners' ZAA
2. Specify the Focus of Attention
3. Categorize Resource Elements
4. Identify potential Resource Filters
5. Identify the Learners' Resources
6. Identify potential More Able Partners (MAPs)
7. Iterate through Steps 1–6

Phase 2: Identify the relationships within and between the resources produced in Phase 1. Identify the extent to which these relationships meet a learner's needs and how they might be optimized with respect to that learner.

Phase 3: Develop the Scaffolds and Adjustments to support learning and enable the negotiation of a ZPA for a learner. Phase 3 of the framework is about identifying the possible ways in which the relationships identified in Phase 2 might best be supported or scaffolded. This support might, for example, be offered through the manner in which technology is introduced, used or designed.

Each phase and step should be completed through collaboration between beneficiaries and designers in a participatory design process. A full account of the framework can be found in Luckin (2010).

THE ECOLOGY OF RESOURCES DESIGN FRAMEWORK IN USE

The Ecology of Resources approach has been used in a variety of projects including: science learning in school, informal and formal learning in the developing world, home education in the UK, and adult foreign-language learning. In the following section of this chapter we present an example of the Ecology of Resources design framework in use. (Further detail about the Ecology of Resources design method can be found in the design section of this handbook and a fuller explanation of this and other examples can be found at http://eorframework.pbworks.com/)

Empirical Example

This example is drawn from a study completed with students and staff at a learning centre in the South East of England; this centre operates a self-managed learning (SML) process for 11–16-year-old learners in an 'out-of-school' environment. SML involves learning to learn within the context of the individual and the wider community. Consequently, learning within the centre is not formalized to the same extent as it is in more traditional educational settings. Nonetheless, many of the learners at the centre are seeking to gain formal educational qualifications. A key aim of the design process described in this case study was to *explore and model learners' contexts to identify ways in which available resources might best be used to support their learning needs.* These issues were addressed through the Ecology of Resources iterative, participatory design approach, in collaboration with learners and staff at the learning centre, as described in Phases 1 to 3 below.

Phase 1 Mapping Learners' Ecology of Resources

STEP 1—BRAINSTORMING POTENTIAL RESOURCES TO IDENTIFY THE LEARNERS' ZAA

Initial explorations with learners and staff at the centre revealed that, although learners had access to a wide range of technologies for both formal and informal learning, they did not find it easy to make connections between these technologies, their learning activities and the available spaces for learning. A preliminary generic ZAA was generated, based on a loosely framed design motivation, which focused on learners' selection and use of technologies on trips. This was later refined to supporting a trip to the Royal Observatory, Greenwich to learn about astronomy, as described in Step 2 below. The preliminary, widely framed, ZAA is consistent with the aims of the initial step of Phase 1 of the design framework; that is: to provide the widest possible ZAA, such that it may be revisited across several iterations to address multiple foci of attention. During subsequent iterations of the design process, Step 1 was used to produce a gradually refined ZAA, an extract from which is illustrated in Table 3.1.

STEP 2—SPECIFYING THE FOCUS OF ATTENTION

At the end of the first iteration of Step 1, the goal of the design process had been specified as: *Linking learners and technologies to specific trips.* A further set of iterations that moved between Steps 1 and 2 of the design framework was required to produce a sufficiently narrow and fine-grained focus of attention to enable progress to Step 3. The refinements that occurred through this process required further dialogue and interaction with participants and involved researcher participation in two trips organized by learners: one to a local farm, which focused on formal study and learning about biology and becoming a vet; and one to the BBC, which focused on leisure and learn-

Table 3.1 Refined ZAA after specification of the Royal Observatory trip Focus of Attention

Refined ZAA (Trip to Royal Observatory to learn about Astronomy)
Learners, staff from learning centre, siblings, peers, group/community rules, staff at trip site (museum guides, show narrators specialists, ticket attendants, shop assistants), other learners/visitors, trip site rules, interactive exhibits, simulations, models, trip site activities, trip site environment and facilities, weather, environment (indoors, outdoors, secure, unsecured, private), time, security, mobility, size, weight, money (mobile phone credit), posters, leaflets, flyers, books, digital information screens (adverts, exhibit information), mobile phones, batteries, memory cards, iPods or mp4 players, mp3 players (audio only), voice recorder, digital still image camera, digital video camera, combined still image/video camera, headphones (quality, size, comfort, ability to share—dual jacks), energy, co-ordination, information, filming (with video), reviewing photos of past trips/events (using iPod, mobile phone), discussing use of Internet to locate interesting facts, understanding technologies, newsletter (taking photos, writing notes, planning trip reports, sketching, drawing, recording information), activity ideas, watching downloaded or previously captured video clips, generating questions to ask *in situ* trip experts, communication (email, talk, text messaging, GPS networks sensors 'pushing' information, Flickr, Google Docs, blog, paper, pen, pencils, notepad, YouTube, Wikipedia, Google, digital video archives, films, DVDs, videos, Internet, computer literacy, media literacy, information literacy, maths, science, engineering, geography, history, culture, astronomy, learning models, process curriculum, Greenwich, Royal Observatory, Planetarium, Planetarium exhibits (information on universe, galaxies, stars, black holes, Milky Way, Meridian line, shows, video clips).

ing through film studies and becoming a film producer. In each of these instances, the design team (comprising researcher, learners and learning advisors) was able to observe and discuss available resources, with a particular focus on the category elements and filters of the Ecology of Resources framework. With the increased understandings of the learner's learning context across multiple locations gained through this participatory design process, it was then possible to generate an appropriate focus of attention: *How can we support the learner to make appropriate selection and use of available technologies to learn about the Milky Way whilst on a trip to the Peter Harrison Planetarium at the Royal Observatory?*

STEP 3—CATEGORIZING RESOURCE ELEMENTS

The identification of a preliminary set of resources (the ZAA) enabled the generation of a preliminary Ecology of Resources model (Figure 3.2) that was subsequently further refined and reshaped through application of Steps 4–6.

Steps 3–6 are enumerated sequentially, but it can be useful to develop these steps in parallel, because identifying relevant filters and constraints requires a negotiation back and forth between resource elements and learner resources as well as consideration of the role of potential MAPs. It is not a matter, here, of trying to incorporate Steps 4–6 into the Ecology of Resources model generated at Step 3. It is, rather, a matter of identifying relevant resources and asking these follow-on questions at each step.

4—identify resource filters
5—identify learner's resources
6—identify More Able Partners

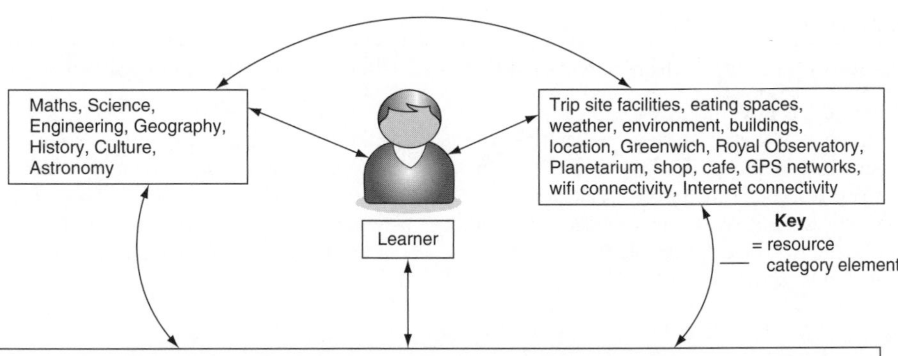

Figure 3.2 An Ecology of Resources model after an initial design iteration.

STEP 4—IDENTIFY POTENTIAL RESOURCE FILTERS

Filters can act as constraints or as opportunities, each of which can have positive/negative qualities. In this example, for instance, learners who want to learn more about the Milky Way might attend the Planetarium where they will learn about the Milky Way as part of a particular scheduled show. The show as a resource is filtered by time (show times, length of narrative/visuals about the Milky Way), and by rules (no audio recording or photography allowed, meaning that learners must remember or record what they see in a different way). The ability to make notes about the show is filtered by ambiance. Lack of light in the darkened room acts as a constraining filter for writing. However, if, for example, learners have a mobile phone, backlighting enables note-taking. Listening to the narrator, the presence of the audience and respect for the rules of quiet listening when in company also act as a constraining filter on the learner's ability to use available MAPs as *in situ* resources. Some of these issues could be addressed in the design process, for example, by considering the use of GPS sensors, which 'push' information to learners' mobile phones at various locations, or, for example, the learner could opt to receive additional digital information about specific knowledge concepts via Bluetooth to their mobile phone. All of these things act as potential filters in the learner's interactions with her context. Table 3.2 illustrates resources and filters identified for the Planetarium trip example.

STEP 5—IDENTIFY THE LEARNER'S RESOURCES

Here, we must consider what resources and filters the learner brings to the situation. For example, some possible resources in this example were the learner's: coordination, curiosity, motivation/interest, existing knowledge, problem-solving skills, decision-making skills, planning skills, technical skills, learning models, learning styles, relationships, social skills, collaborative skills, communication skills, self-esteem.

Table 3.2 Resources and Filters

Resources (some of which are potential MAPs)	Filters (can be positive or negative)
Knowledge & Environment	
Astronomy, Planetarium show, interactive exhibits, simulations, models, digital information screens, information about the universe, galaxies, stars, black holes, Milky Way, film or video clips, audio commentaries, Planetarium learning workshops, Planetarium shop	Milky Way, design and layout of exhibit space, content/relevance/organization of exhibits, access (to show, exhibits, workshops, shop), Internet connectivity, network connectivity, language, location, Planetarium rules, time
People	
Learners, staff from learning centre, peers, researcher-designer, Planetarium show narrator, museum guides, Planetarium ticket collectors, shop assistants, other museum staff, other learners/visitors	Relationship, accessibility, time, location, existing knowledge, environment, confidence, opportunity, group/community rules
Tools	
Mobile phones, batteries, memory cards, voice recorder, digital still image camera, digital video camera, combined still image/video camera, headphones, mp3 player/iPod, DVDs	Connectivity, Planetarium rules, copyright, power, storage capacity, technology skills, availability, quality, ambiance (e.g. light levels, sound levels)

STEP 6—IDENTIFY POTENTIAL MORE ABLE PARTNERS

We also need to consider who or what the MAPs are and what role they might play. For example, a range of potential MAPs can be identified in the scenario of the learner at the Planetarium who wishes to learn more about the Milky Way. Here, the MAPs could include: the narrator at the Planetarium show; the learning mentor from the learning centre who travelled on the trip; and/or peer learners and even technology capable of providing adaptive help.

Phase 2 Identifying Relationships and Filters

The aim of Phase 2 of the Ecology of Resources design framework is the identification of relationships and interactions that might influence the ways in which the resources, filters and MAPs may or may not be appropriated to act as forms of assistance for learners. The resources identified in this example are organized into groups according to the category elements and the relationships between the elements. Figure 3.3 illustrates a sample Ecology of Resources model of a learner's trip to the Planetarium incorporating resources and filters based on the preliminary output generated at Phase 2.

The model also incorporates arrows that highlight the relationships between these resources and filters. This Ecology of Resources model is still quite broadly framed, but can nevertheless be used and reused to consider scenarios and options and to explore the learner's potential interactions with resource elements. The relationships and filters framing available resources and potential MAPs can be made more explicit. Opportunities for cross-location activities can also be generated and made visible. Mapping a learner's interactions in this way can provide a preliminary model for considering ways

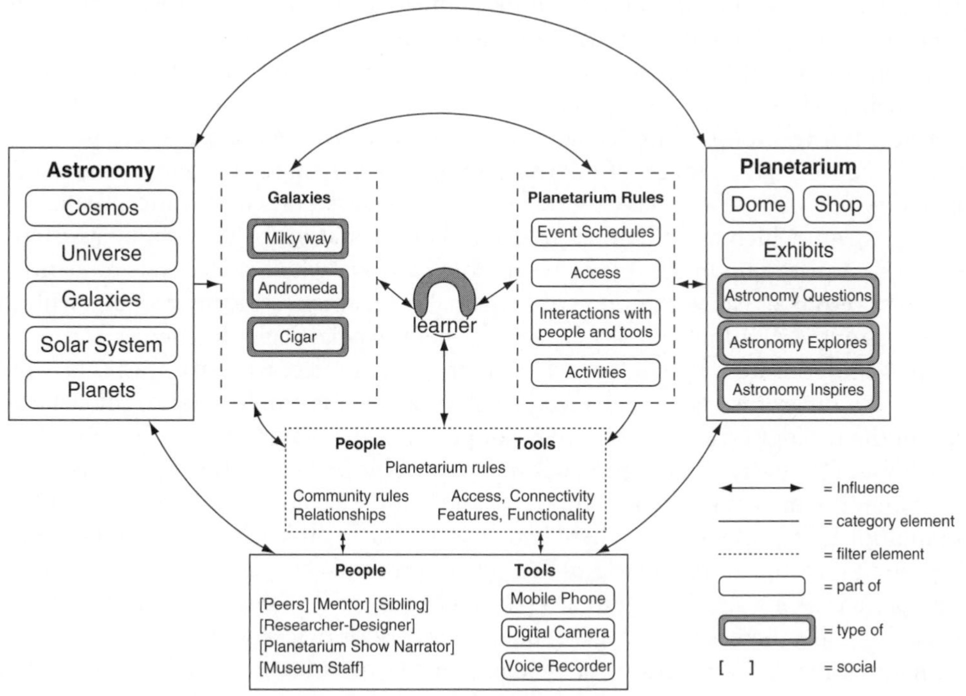

Figure 3.3 Ecology of Resources illustration for the Planetarium visit example.

of developing effective scaffolds in both the learning process and the design process. Each of these resources and filters can influence any of the others, and it is perhaps only with this understanding that the value of the Ecology of Resource framework really starts to become apparent and the interdependency of the component parts of the learner's context begins to emerge.

Phase 3 Identifying Scaffolds and Adjustments

The research for this example was largely exploratory and focused on supporting learners' decision-making processes about appropriate and effective technology use to support their learning on educational visits and field trips. Phase 3 in this instance, therefore, focused more on identifying, for future iterations, potential scaffolding opportunities. For example, an adjustment to the rules framed by copyright has been made in relation to the Planetarium Exhibits hall, thus permitting learners to utilize their technology to capture data about their interests in astronomy, which they are later able to share with others, via Flickr, for example. A further example adjustment to this scenario could be made by making *in situ* provision within the Planetarium for visitors to share digital data captured in this way online, such as via a shared visitor website.

DISCUSSION

The Ecology of Resources model and its associated design framework offer a way to talk about learners and learning holistically—to sensitize designers to the range of interactions that constitute their contexts. The Ecology of Resources is based upon a definition of context that recognizes both the subjective and the objective nature of learners' experiences with the world, and the interconnectedness of all the elements with which they interact and that shape their understanding of the world. A learner's context is made up of the billions of interactions that they have with other people, with artefacts, and with their environment. These interactions provide 'partial descriptions of the world' that help learners to build understandings that are distributed and that are personally crystallized through a process of internalization. The Ecology of Resources is grounded in an interpretation of Vygotsky's Zone of Proximal Development. It conceptualizes the resources with which an individual interacts as potential forms of learning assistance. Emphasis is placed upon the role of More Able Partners, who help learners to identify a subset of resources called the Zone of Proximal Adjustment. It is interactions with the resources of the ZPA that will be of specific benefit to a particular learner.

The Ecology of Resources approach is an on-going project with many aspects, which are more complex than have been recognized to date. For example, the current instantiation of the Ecology of Resources model adopts an individual learner as the central unit of analysis. However, collaboration between more able and less able people is also a vital component of the approach, and this leads to multiple Ecologies of Resources centered on multiple different learners. These Ecologies interact with each other in complex and important ways to form networks of Ecologies. A second complexity is that of time. For example, a learning activity begins at a particular time and, whilst learning can continue throughout life, there is a time when a particular episode of learning, of which there may be many, comes to completion. These complexities need further development and are the subject of current attention that will further develop the theory, design, method and evaluation of the Ecology of Resources.

ACKNOWLEDGEMENTS

We thank the participants who have made our empirical work possible and the Engineering and Physical Sciences Research Council for funding our research.

REFERENCES

Brown, J. S. (1990) Toward a new Epistemology for Learning. In: Frasson, C. & Gauthier, G. (eds.) *Intelligent Tutoring Systems: At the Crossroads of Artificial Intelligence and Education.* Norwood: Ablex, pp. 262–286.

Brown, J. S., Collins, A. & Duguid, P. (1989) Situated Cognition and the Culture of Learning. *Educational Researcher*, 18, 32–42.

Clark, A. (2008) *Supersizing the Mind: Embodiment, Action and Cognitive Extension.* New York: Oxford University Press.

Cole, M. (1996) *Cultural Psychology: A Once and Future Discipline.* Cambridge, MA: Harvard University Press.

Cummins, S., Curtis, S., Diez-Roux, A. & Macintyre, S. (2007) Understanding and Representing 'Place' in Health Research: A Relational Approach. *Social Science and Medicine*, 65, 1825–38.

Gibson, W. (1999) The Science in Science Fiction, *Talk of the Nation*, National Public Radio, November 1999.

Kerckhove, D. D. & Tursi, A. (2009) The Life of Space. *Architectural Design*, 79(1), 48–53.

Lave, J. (1988) *Cognition in Practice.* Cambridge: Cambridge University Press.

Lave, J. & Wenger, E. (1991) *Situated Learning: Legitimate Peripheral Participation.* Cambridge: Cambridge University Press.

Luckin, R. (2010) *Re-designing Learning Contexts: Technology Rich, Learner-Centered Ecologies.* London: Routledge.

Manovich, L. (2006) The Poetics of Augmented Space. *Visual Communication*, 5(2), 219–240.

Vygotsky, L. S. (1978) *Mind in Society: The Development of Higher Psychological Processes.* Trans. M. Cole, V. John-Steiner, S. Scribner, & E. Souberman. Cambridge, MA: Harvard University Press.

Vygotsky, L. S. (1986) *Thought and Language.* Cambridge, MA: MIT Press.

Wertsch, J. V. (1984) The Zone of Proximal Development: Some Conceptual Issues. In: Rogoff, B. & Wertsch, J. V. (eds.) *Children's Learning in the 'Zone of Proximal Development'.* San Francisco, CA: Jossey-Bass, pp. 7–18.

Wood, D. J., Bruner, J. S. & Ross, G. (1976) The Role of Tutoring in Problem Solving. *Journal of Child Psychology and Psychiatry*, 17(2), 89–100.

4

DESIGN-BASED RESEARCH—DESIGNING AS RESEARCH

Peter Reimann

1. INTRODUCTION

Design-based research (DBR) is usually introduced as a *research* methodology, not a *design* methodology; this chapter looks at DBR primarily from a design perspective. As such, DBR can be seen in the tradition of participatory design, as a design method that incorporates strong involvement of the end user.

DBR is increasingly applied in educational software projects. This is because it is seen as helpful in understanding some of the "deep" problems of learning, such as bringing about conceptual change, and in shedding light on the processes through which technology gets interpreted and appropriated by teachers and students. Studies show that adoption of technology-supported innovations depends largely on how well teachers perceive them to fit within their goals for students, teaching strategies, and expectations for student learning (Penuel, Roschelle, & Shechtman, 2007). Perceived fit of technology is a function of current teaching practices, social and technical capacities of schools to support implementation, and alignment with standards of learning and assessment regimens (Blumenfeld, Fishman, Krajcik, Marx, & Soloway, 2000). Since DBR is focused on the analysis of learning processes in authentic educational settings, and is sensitive to the role of context in the analysis of processes and effects, it can be put to use for informing designers about the "real needs" a software tool should serve, and about the "fate" that this tool undergoes as it is introduced into educational settings.

What can DBR concretely bring to technology design? I think the most interesting contribution is a more direct relation to learning research, in particular research that aims at theory development. While the general design process is comparable with other as well as older models of instructional design (Reigeluth, 1999), an important contribution from DBR lies in the element of developing learning trajectories as an essential step in the design process, and as an extension to formulating learning/teaching goals. The learning trajectory needs to be theory-based, and as such makes for a "boundary object" between the designer/developer community and the research community. Following Cobb and Gravemeijer (2008), a learning trajectory (also known as a *learning progression*) is a conjecture how learning in a specific context and for a specific concept will develop over time under the influence of instruction, and theory in this context means more general knowledge about, yet specific enough to anchor the conjectured trajectory in that knowledge.

DBR brings a qualitative change in the relation between design and research. Educational technology designers have of course always taken research findings into account, minimally by finding out what is known about "what works." However, reading articles with evaluation studies, if possible in the form of meta-analysis and review articles in order to get a sense of cumulated research findings, is quite different from having research fully integrated as a key component of an ongoing design process and from engaging in long-term collaborations with researchers and practitioners.

Hence, DBR and other variants of design research (Plomp & Nieveen, 2009), may be just what is needed for educational technology, and educational technology research to address the concern that it is not achieving its potential (Cuban, 2001; Reeves, 2006), and that simple control-group studies, stand on shaky ground (House, 1991).

2. THEORETICAL INFLUENCES

DBR's intellectual pedigree can be traced back to three roots: Experimental educational psychology, design research, and participatory software development methods.

DBR has its roots in educational research. Conceived by Anne Brown to overcome challenges with doing experimental research in classrooms (Brown, 1992), and by Alan Collins to better capture pedagogical innovations suggested by teachers (Collins, 1992), it has been further developed in the Learning Sciences (Bransford, Brown, & Cocking, 2000; Sawyer, 2006; The Design-Based Research Collective, 2003). Technology development has not been the driving force behind DBR. DBR was and is mainly concerned with innovations in teaching and learning that pertain to pedagogy rather than technology. However, due to the rise of personal technologies and then of the Internet many DBR studies have had an additional focus on technological innovation.

While Anne Brown started the turn towards experimentation in real classrooms from the methodological perspective of Experimental Psychology, Allan Collins' (1992) perspective is more representative for the second pedigree line: design research. This methodology has been developed mainly in Europe, in the context of math education (van den Akker, Gravemeijer, McKenney, & Nieveen, 2006). In a recent definition, design research is

> the systematic study of designing, developing and evaluating educational interventions (such as programs, teaching-learning strategies and materials, products and systems) as solutions for complex problems in educational practice, which also aims at advancing our knowledge about the characteristics of these interventions and the processes of designing and developing them.
>
> (Plomp, 2009, p. 13)

Design research can be seen as broader in scope than DBR as it addresses also challenges from a system and product orientation, whereas DBR has more of a classroom orientation (following the taxonomy suggested by Gustafson & Branch (2002), and used here to include other educational settings, e.g., seminar room, workplace learning, as well), but these levels are increasingly addressed in DBR type studies as well (e.g., Fishman, Marx, Blumenfeld, Krajcik, & Soloway, 2004; Roschelle, Knudsen, & Hegedus, 2010).

The third pedigree line can be found in traditions of design methods in industry, in particular methods of participatory design. As Penuel et al. (2007, p. 52) note, DBR is specifically related to the so-called "semantic turn" in design (Krippendorf, 2006), i.e., the insight that design artifacts have meaning, and are interpreted by users in their context in reference to specific practices that are meaningful in that context. Design theories (now in the sense of theories of design) that are aligned with this view are, for instance, value-sensitive design (Friedman, 1996), participatory design (Muller & Kuhn, 1993), team-based fast prototyping (Snyder, 2003), and co-design (Penuel et al., 2007).

It is also a potential source of confusion in terminology that Design Research and Design-Based Research do not make a systematic distinction between the "design" as a kind of artifact distinct from the "product." In architecture, for example, the design of a building is different from the building itself, whereas in most cases in Design (Based) Research the design of a learning environment is essentially the learning environment. This conflation is unfortunate not only because it can raise terminological confusion, but also because there are many advantages in distinguishing design from product.

3. HOW DBR IS DONE

The "practice" of DBR—and I am putting this into "scare marks" because this is as much aspirational as it is descriptive—corresponds to its theoretical lineage by putting two trajectories, or process models, or narratives, into the center: a *learning* trajectory, and a *design* trajectory. The first trajectory focuses on how learning (in students, learners, etc.) takes place and how the pedagogical-technical intervention will affect learning. The design trajectory focuses on the design process itself, how it unfolds over time, and what can be learned from it for design methodology. The yield of DBR, correspondingly, is threefold: (a) information about the way an innovation is used, plays out in a specific context, and what impact it has in that context; (b) contributions to learning theories; and (c) contributions to design methodologies.

A prototypical study would go through three main stages: (1) developing the learning trajectory and the learning environment; (2) conducting a design experiment; and (3) generalizing the findings. Steps 1 and 2 are performed iteratively, should the experiment show that the research and development goals have not been achieved yet, or result in new questions that need answering.

3.1. Developing the Learning Trajectory and the Learning Environment

Using the terminology provided by Cobb and Gravemeijer (2008), this stage can be split into four steps: (1) Clarifying the instructional goals; (2) documenting the instructional learning goals; (3) delineating an envisioned learning trajectory; and (4) placing the design study in an theoretical context.

(1) *Clarifying the instructional goals* to be addressed is pivotal. Relying on curricular documents and goals can only sometimes do this, but usually this step requires an in-depth analysis of the curricular document along with an identification of central domain concepts around powerful ideas.

(2) *Documenting the instructional starting points* involves identifying students' current level and learning in terms of their prior instructional histories. Usually, this step involves going into the learning setting and working with learners. Cobb and Gravemeijer (2008) recommend such methods as interviews with individual students and whole-class performance assessment using video rather than written forms of assessment for evaluating students' reasoning.

(3) *Delineating an envisioned learning trajectory*: The designer/researcher here will "formulate testable conjectures about both significant shifts in students' reasoning and the means of supporting and organizing these shifts" (Cobb & Gravemeijer, 2008, p. 70). This requires formulating a process model of learning—how learning unfolds over time—which in turn necessitates mobilizing theory. This process model needs also to spell out the materials, tasks, and technologies that support students' learning trajectory—the learning design. The trajectory model will need to take into account factors that affect the enactment of the design, i.e., contextual factors such as classroom norms and the nature of classroom discourse. The model further needs to be explicit about the teacher's role, should the technology be used in classroom settings.

More often than not, this step of the analysis will result in additional demands on designers: Not only do they have to conceive of a technological tool, in addition they will need to give due attention to the design of curriculum materials, learning tasks, assessments, and materials specifically designed for teachers. Furthermore, at this stage it often also becomes clearer what kind of capacities need to be in place, such as requirements on teachers' subject matter knowledge and technical knowledge, and correspondingly which elements of capacity building the overall design will need to include. Roschelle et al. (2010) speak of a "curricular activity system" that needs to be designed, and stress that "activity" is not simply the identification of what students and teachers will be doing ("presentation," "web search"), but instead an activity comprises "its objective (for the participants), available materials, the intended use of tools, the roles of the different participants, and the key thing we would like the participants to do and notice" (p. 239). Given the central mediating role of teachers in classrooms, this often means designing tasks and materials (including software) as a resource in the hand of the teacher, and to involve teachers as co-designers early on in the research planning.

(4) *Placing the experiment in a theoretical context* helps to produce knowledge that will be useful in providing guidance to others as they attempt to support similar learning processes. "Theory" in this regard is quite a practical concept: A (micro) theory of learning should spell out *how and why* learning evolves over time, and how it is affected by the pedagogical-technical intervention. The theory is, hence, part and parcel of the *design rationale* (Buckingham Shum, 1996), and provides both the designers as well as the users of the design with knowledge that is needed to make modification decisions. Without an explicit design rationale, it is just too easy to confuse essential elements of the design with incidental ones.

3.2. Experimenting to Support Learning

The focus of experimenting in DBR is on supporting learning; the purpose is not to show that the intervention "works," but to improve the envisioned design by testing and revising conjectures about both the prospective learning process and the specific means of supporting it (Cobb & Gravemeijer, 2008). Hence, data collection will need to be carefully planned so that the data acquired speak to the conjectures and do so in a manner such that later retrospective analyses with a potentially wider theoretical framework can be performed rigorously.

Design experiments can involve a "control group," but since they are conducted in real educational settings over longer durations, this can raise ethical as well as practical concerns. The prototypical design experiment is, hence, not of the control-group type, but employs "within-subject" comparisons in a kind of repeated measurements design (Creswell, 2009).

Because of the different kinds of data collected in design studies—most of them taking an open format, e.g. classroom discourse, answers to semi-structured interviews, non-standard classroom assessments—and because of the tentativeness of applicable theoretical models, making sense of the data is typically a highly inferential, interpretative, and cyclical process. Furthermore, these interpretations and the decisions based on them will profoundly shape the development of the design. This necessitates articulating carefully the key constructs that were used making interpretations and decisions, so that other designers (either working concurrently, or as potential re-users of the design at later stage in time) can interpret the design modifications. The *interpretive framework* will hardly stay static over the course of a design experiment, hence articulating, critiquing, and refining the framework need not only to be practiced, but also to be documented.

Design-based researchers use either purely qualitative or mixed-method approaches to data gathering and data analysis. Examples for important methods are content analysis (Strijbos, Martens, Prins, & Jochems, 2006), discourse analysis (Gee, 2005), interaction analysis (Jordan & Henderson, 1995), and methods specifically developed for video analysis (Pea & Lindgren, 2008). Computational methods for data and text mining (Yacef & Baker, 2009), for process mining (Reimann & Yacef, this volume) and for educational analytics in general are being rapidly developed and find increasingly entry into DBR research as well. However, it remains the case that all of the methods frequently deployed in DBR studies require high effort and deep familiarity with the methodology, the subject matter, and the context. This contributes substantially to the fact that a typical DBR study is closer in duration to a PhD project than to a typical experimental study.

3.3. Generalizing Beyond the Local Solution

While the design as such may be seen as "finished" once some criterion for success in the iteration of (re-)design and experimentation is reached, the designer-as-researcher would move on identifying points that can be generalized beyond the local solution, from both the learning trajectory as well as from the design trajectory.

The manner in which findings in DBR studies are generalized is different from experimental studies that follow a control-group logic. There, the generalization is statistical; here, it is analytic (Yin, 2003). That is to say, the generalization is performed by relating the specific design, and specific observations on how the design works out, to theories that relate to these. The specific observations are not taken as applying in an identical manner to a "population," but are related to similar processes, and/or more abstract types of processes. It is not the specific participants in the study who are seen as instances of a (in a statistical sense meaningful) "population"; instead, the specific observation is treated as "an instance of" something more abstract (and in that sense, more general). The theory, then, provides warrants for the interpretation of local observations. The theory itself, however, needs to be warranted by other local findings.

Because the generalization is not performed as a statistical inference, but in an interpretive manner, this step needs to be as carefully documented as the substantial observations and their transformations and interpretations. Barab, Baek, Schatz, Scheckler, & Moore (2008, p. 322) recommend therefore that every DBR study includes the following information:

- The designed product.
- The context within which the design was implemented.
- Warrants for evidence of the local impact.
- The theoretical assertions and their relations to the design work.
- The conditions through which the theoretical assertions are generated.
- Warrants for evidence of the theoretical assertions.

Barab et al. (2008) argue for the *design narrative* as the form for documenting the design process, building on a suggestion by Hoadley (2002). The design narrative serves the purpose to "characterize the complexity, fragility, messiness, and eventual solidity of the design so that others may benefit from it" (Barab et al., 2008, p. 322). In DBR studies one needs to be explicit about the design and how it came about in order to allow other designers to modify the design based on an understanding of it and the context within which and for which it was developed. From a research perspective, being explicit about the design and its development is important for establishing the validity of the design seen as an intervention that changes learning; this is because the validity (and reliability) of DBR studies can usually not be established by replication.

4. WHEN AND FOR WHOM IS THE METHOD APPROPRIATE?

DBR does not establish new methods for designing and developing educational technology. Due to its focus on design changes driven by research on end-users, it does go well along with agile software development methods (Beck, 1999), but a large range of other software development methods can be applied. Given the close relationship with the development of learning theory, DBR is perhaps best applied when one has to design for learning that is, as yet, not well understood, that is, when there is a research need in addition to a design need. Also, given the substantial effort that goes into DBR type of work, the learning problem should be a significant one (for theoretical and practical reasons). DBR has rarely been used for fully online learning settings, but is more typically used for developing classroom-integrated technologies (such as graphics calculators (Roschelle et al., 2010)), or for technologies that can be blended into face-to-face learning settings.

DBR is mostly done in multi-disciplinary teams because the design/development and the research aspect are of equal importance. The cooperation with researchers means that the problem must also be worth their attention, hence has relations to theories of learning, including teachers' learning.

5. DBR IN USE

Space does not allow to provide a detailed example, in particular as the iterative nature of the DBR process as well as the rich data that are analyzed in the course of it are not easily summarized. Instead, I will introduce in a summative fashion three prototypical

DBR studies, all of which are accessible in the literature and which are described in sufficient detail to provide the interested reader with a fuller picture of how DBR is done in practice.

The first example (Cobb & Gravemeijer, 2008) focuses on middle school statistics and describes a number of design cycles for creating computational representations that help teachers to introduce notions such as center, skewness, spread, and relative frequency coherently from the concept of a mathematical distribution. Based on statistics education literature and classroom observations, the authors formulate as an important step in the learning trajectory that students will initially need to learn to appreciate the difference between numbers and data. Therefore tasks and computer-generated graphical representations that are intended to make students aware of the fact that they are analyzing data need to be developed. As a theoretical framing, the specific learning trajectory becomes contextualized in the wider context of mathematical reasoning, in particular learning about data generation and about developing and critiquing data-based arguments. The chapter describes in some depth three different computational tools, with different, but synergistic representational notations, that in concert with capable teachers began to move students' conceptions of distributions into a mathematically fruitful direction.

The second example (Roschelle et al., 2010) also situated in math education, goes beyond the development of single representational tools, analyzing a whole research program that stretched over multiple years, with the goal to develop a technical classroom infrastructure and to create the kind of learning activities that make sufficient use of this infrastructure so that difficult mathematical concepts become accessible for the majority of students. This infrastructure goes by the name of MathWorlds software, available for PCs, Macs, and Texas Instruments Graphics Calculators. The MathWorlds studies as summarized by Roschelle et al. (2010) are of particular interest, as this line of work illustrates not only multiple design cycles to get the infrastructure right (in particular the representational part, which Roschelle and colleagues developed themselves), but also how much (re-)design work needs to go into building the "curricular activity systems" and into the development of capacity in teachers to work with the infrastructure and the activities.

The third DBR study recommended here for instructional purposes is Barab et al. (2008). This study is important, in our context, for two reasons: First, it shows how DBR can be employed when the audience is not students but (in-service) teachers, and when the learning is not about disciplinary subject matter but about teachers' professional learning. Second, this study is important because it illustrates how to document the design process—by unfolding a design narrative, as introduced above—for the purpose of informing the work of future designers of the same artifact (re-design) and more generally as a contribution to design methodology. The design artifact described in this publication is ILF, the Inquiry Learning Forum. It is meant to be an online platform for a community that "seeks to improve student learning by supporting teachers in better understanding inquiry-based teaching and learning" (p. 326). ILF underwent some major re-designs, largely triggered by data on users' ways of engaging with the resources on the site, including tools for facilitating end-user communication and interaction. For instance, while ILF initially was designed with a view to attract members from the general population of mathematics and science teachers, it was later re-designed for being useful for pre-existing groups—for community support rather than community building.

These are just three out of a large range of design-based research studies. They are different in user groups, learning goals, scale, methods used, and many other aspects. What they share, however, is a commitment to end-user orientation, rigorous methodology, and to scaling-up, some in numbers, all in conceptual scope (theory building). Many others could be mentioned, such as Penuel et al. (2007), which provides valuable insights into the challenges of including teachers as co-designers. Books such as the *Handbook of Design Research Methods in Education* (Kelly, Lesh, & Baek, 2008) and journals such as the *Journal of the Learning Sciences* provide many more instances.

6. CONCLUSION

DBR as a design methodology necessitates a deep integration of research into the design process. This is very important at this stage, I believe, because it is an opportunity to move beyond an overly simplistic view of both learning and technology in conceptual terms, and beyond the simple control-group design that characterizes so many educational technology studies in methodological terms. It is good that the price is high, because the challenges are considerable; not only does the research and design community need to create capacity (in particular amongst PhD students) to perform and innovate this kind of research and development process, it also needs to convince policy makers that this kind of research can create the knowledge needed to improve upon educational systems at scale.

7. REFERENCES

Barab, S. A., Baek, E.-O., Schatz, S., Scheckler, R., & Moore, J. (2008). Illuminating the braids of change in a web-supported community. In A. E. Kelly, R. A. Lesh, & J. Y. Baek (Eds.), *Handbook of Design Research Methods in Education* (pp. 320–352). New York: Routledge.

Beck, K. (1999). *Extreme Programming Explained: Embrace Change.* New York: Addison-Wesley.

Blumenfeld, P., Fishman, B. J., Krajcik, J., Marx, R. W., & Soloway, E. (2000). Creating usable innovations in systemic reform: scaling-up technology-embedded project-based science in urban schools. *Educational Psychologist, 35*(3), 149–164.

Bransford, J. D., Brown, A. L., & Cocking, R. C. (Eds.). (2000). *How People Learn: Brain, Mind, Experience and School.* Washington, DC: National Academy Press.

Brown, A. L. (1992). Design experiments: Theoretical and methodological challenges in creating complex interventions. *The Journal of the Learning Sciences, 2,* 141–178.

Buckingham Shum, S. (1996). Design Argumentation as Design Rationale. *The Encyclopedia of Computer Science and Technology* (Vol. 35 Supp. 20, pp. 95–128).

Cobb, P., & Gravemeijer, K. (2008). Experimenting to support and understand learning processes. In A. E. Kelly, R. A. Lesh, & J. Y. Baek (Eds.), *Handbook of Design Research Methods in Education* (pp. 68–95). New York: Routledge.

Collins, A. (1992). Toward a design science of education. In E. Scanlon & T. O'Shea (Eds.), *New Directions in Educational Technology.* Berlin: Springer.

Creswell, J. W. (2009). *Research Design: Qualitative, Quantitative, and Mixed Methods Approaches.* Los Angeles: Sage.

Cuban, L. (2001). *Oversold and Underused. Computers in the Classroom.* Cambridge, MA: Harvard University Press.

Fishman, B., Marx, R. W., Blumenfeld, P., Krajcik, J., & Soloway, E. (2004). Creating a framework for research on systemic technology innovations. *The Journal of the Learning Sciences, 13*(1), 43–76.

Friedman, B. (Ed.). (1996). *Human Values and the Design of Computer Technology.* New York: Cambridge University Press.

Gee, J. P. (2005). *An Introduction to Discourse Analysis* (2nd ed.). New York: Routledge.

Gustafson, K. L., & Branch, R. M. (2002). *Survey of Instructional Development Models* (4th edition). Syracuse, NY: ERIC Clearinghouse on Information & Technology.

Hoadley, C. P. (2002). Creating context: Design-based research in creating and understanding CSCL. In G. Stahl (Ed.), *Proceedings of the Computer Supported Collaborative Learning Conference* (pp. 453–462). Boulder, CO: Erlbaum.

House, E. R. (1991). Realism in research. *Educational Researcher, 20*(6), 2–9.

Jordan, B., & Henderson, A. (1995). Interaction analysis: Foundations and practice. *The Journal of the Learning Sciences, 4*(1), 39–103.

Kelly, A. E., Lesh, R. A., & Baek, J. Y. (Eds.). (2008). *Handbook of Design Research Methods in Education.* New York: Routledge.

Krippendorf, K. (2006). *The Semantic Turn: A New Foundation for Design.* New York: Taylor & Francis.

Muller, M. J., & Kuhn, S. (1993). Participatory design. *Communications of the ACM, 36*(3), 24–28.

Pea, R., & Lindgren, R. (2008). Video collaboratories for research and education: An analysis of collaboration design patterns. *IEEE Transactions on Learning Technologies, 1*(4), 235–247.

Penuel, W. R., Roschelle, J., & Shechtman, N. (2007). Designing formative assessment software with teachers: An analysis of the co-design framework. *Research and Practice in Technology Enhanced Learning, 2*(1), 51–74.

Plomp, T. (2009). Educational design research: An introduction. In T. Plomp & N. Nieveen (Eds.), *An Introduction to Educational Design Research* (pp. 9–35). SLO—Netherlands Institute for Curriculum Development.

Plomp, T., & Nieveen, N. (Eds.). (2009). *An Introduction to Educational Design Research.* SLO—Netherlands Institute for Curriculum Development.

Reeves, T. (2006). Design research from a technology perspective. In J. van den Akker, K. Gravemeijer, S. McKenney, & N. Nieveen (Eds.), *Educational Design Research* (pp. 52–66). London: Routledge.

Reigeluth, C. M. (Ed.). (1999). *Instructional-design Theories and Models. A New Paradigm of Instructional Theory* (Vol. 2). Mahwah, NJ: Erlbaum.

Roschelle, J., Knudsen, J., & Hegedus, S. (2010). From new technological infrastructures to curricular activity systems: Advanced designs for teaching and learning. In M. J. Jacobson & P. Reimann (Eds.), *Designs for Learning Environments of the Future* (pp. 233–262). New York: Springer.

Sawyer, R. K. (Ed.). (2006). *The Cambridge Handbook of the Learning Sciences.* New York: Cambridge University Press.

Snyder, C. (2003). *Paper Prototyping: The Fast and Easy Way to Design and Refine User Interfaces.* San Francisco, CA: Morgan Kaufmann.

Strijbos, J. W., Martens, R. L., Prins, F. J., & Jochems, W. M. G. (2006). Content analysis: What are they talking about? *Computers & Education, 46*, 29–48.

The Design-Based Research Collective. (2003). Design-based research: An emerging paradigm for educational inquiry. *Educational Researcher, 32*(1), 5–8.

van den Akker, J., Gravemeijer, K., McKenney, S., & Nieveen, N. (Eds.). (2006). *Educational Design Research.* London: Routledge.

Yacef, K., & Baker, S. J. D. (2009). The state of educational data mining in 2009: A review and future vision. *JEDM—Journal of Educational Data Mining, 1*(1), 3–17.

Yin, R. K. (2003). *Case Study Research: Design and Methods* (3rd ed.). Thousand Oaks, CA: Sage.

5

UNDERSTANDING AND ANALYSING 21ST-CENTURY SKILLS LEARNING OUTCOMES USING ASSESSMENTS

Patrick Griffin, Myvan Bui, and Esther Care

INTRODUCTION

This chapter is intended as an introduction to how assessments can be created and used to understand learning outcomes (including those for 21st-century skills), to assist with the development of appropriate teaching strategies. Thus, it is written for those wishing to learn about developing assessments, but also outlines how assessments should be used to understand and improve learning outcomes. It outlines key principles and considerations needed for designing, developing and validating assessment instruments; as well as methodology for linking assessment data with appropriate teaching strategies. Assessment design is an important, and relatively neglected, aspect of the design of technology-based systems for learning. Implications for technology design are discussed in the final sections of the chapter.

IDENTIFYING READINESS TO LEARN THROUGH ASSESSMENTS

Students achieve the best learning outcomes when what is taught is what they are ready to learn. Assessments can be used to identify what students are ready to learn. *Assessment* involves the process of gathering data and making inferences about what the learner has learnt or how well they have learnt it (Griffin & Nix, 1990). The process of gathering data can take many forms, from tests to performances or work samples. The interpretation usually involves some form of measurement—a process of assigning number codes (such as scores) to the gathered data and a way to interpret what the numbers mean. The scores from assessments are often thought of as representing summative achievement at the time of testing and used to identify problems—the difference between what the learner should know and what they do know. Unfortunately, this approach often results in teachers teaching one group of students what they are not yet ready to learn in an attempt to make up for the deficit, another group coasting ahead of the pack and the rest of the class being taught as a homogeneous group (Griffin, 2009b). A more effective approach is to focus on student development (Griffin, 2007), such that scores are viewed as an indication of the student's Zone of Proximal Development (Vygotsky, 1986). The Zone of Proximal Development is the level at which the student is most ready to learn and where intervention for the student will have the greatest impact. It is a state of readiness where a student will be able to make certain conceptual connections but not others—anything too simple for the student will be considered boring and anything too difficult will be demoralising (Burbles, 1993).

This developmental approach requires knowledge of the skill driving performance on the score, and its developmental progression (Griffin, 2009b). Good assessments have a psychometric basis in that they attempt to measure a specific skill and take into account its developmental progression. It is the skill and progression that is of primary importance, not the specific choice of test items. Individual items are replaceable, merely representing one of many ways to operationalise the skill of interest. Once the skill and its developmental progression are defined based on theoretical and empirical evidence, teachers can use the assessment data to gain an understanding of what students are ready to learn by their position or level on the developmental progression. This focus on the student's position on the progression moves the emphasis away from specific test scores (and 'teaching to the test') to a more general interpretation of what the student can do. This idea (referred to as *criterion referencing*) was originally proposed by Glaser (1963) and elucidated in Glaser (1981), where criterion referencing is described as, 'the development of procedures whereby assessments of proficiency could be referred to stages along progressions of increasing competence' (p. 935). Criterion referencing involves description of performance in terms of the tasks performed and the quality of the behaviours displayed. Descriptions of the levels of quality can be used to form the descriptions of the stages along progressions of increasing competence, and a criterion can be considered a threshold separating levels on the developmental progression.[1] Once stage descriptions are established, a person's development can be interpreted by referring to the relative positions of stages in the progression (Griffin, 2007). This will be elucidated with an example involving a complex 21st-century skill—*collaborative problem solving*.

The process requires the development of rubrics from which the latent trait (i.e. collaborative problem-solving ability) can be inferred. Rubrics for collaborative problem solving were developed by a group of subject matter experts (SME) drawn from a cross-section of academic backgrounds, representing a variety of perspectives. Rubrics are sets of scoring guidelines that characterise levels of performance. These levels are the ordered categories of performance that comprise a description of the cognitive, affective and psychomotor skills embedded in competent performance (Griffin, 2007). Underpinning the concept of rubrics is the criterion-referenced interpretation in which an individual's achievement or competence is described in terms of the behaviour they demonstrate or the tasks they can perform (Glaser, 1981).

Questionnaire items were presented in a structured and consistent format. Each item consisted of a Performance Indicator as the stem and Ordered Criteria as alternative choices. The order of increasing quality performance in the criteria was important so that a partial credit item response model (Masters, 1988) could be employed to integrate the responses from the multiple observers over multiple items. The structure of the items is illustrated in Figure 5.1.

This approach to analysing and understanding learning outcomes is generally the same for 'traditional' skills as well as more complex 21st-century skills. However, understanding and analysing complex 21st-century skills poses some unique challenges. The

Item Structure	Example Item
Capability	Participation
Indicator	Interaction: Interacting with, prompting and responding to the contributions of others.
Criteria	1 Acknowledges communication
	2 Responds to cues in communication
	3 Initiates and promotes interaction or activity

Figure 5.1 Item Structure and Sample Item illustrating Indicator and Ordered Criteria.

following section outlines the nature of some of these complex 21st-century skills and briefly describes some of the barriers to their assessment and development.

COMPLEX 21ST-CENTURY SKILLS

A number of organisations, educators and researchers around the world are currently concerned with 21st-century skills education and assessment (Binkley et al., 2012; Griffin, McGaw, & Care, 2012; Trilling & Fadel, 2009). Although frameworks for 21st-century skills differ considerably in terms of their content (Binkley et al., 2012), there is general agreement that 21st-century skills are any that are necessary for operating in the 21st century, including traditional skills currently in most curricula. However, the 21st-century skills movement has concerns about currently required skills that are neglected and not properly addressed by curricula (Kozma & Roth, 2012). Often, these skills are high-order, complex, multi-faceted skills that are not well understood, hard to define and operationalise, and therefore difficult to assess and teach. Examples of these skills include (Binkley et al., 2012):

- creativity and innovation
- critical thinking, problem solving, decision making
- learning to learn, metacognition
- communication
- collaboration
- information literacy
- ICT literacy
- citizenship
- life and career
- personal and social responsibility.

Traditionally, assessments have been by pencil and paper, designed to be fast to administer, easy to score and completed by individuals. Some therefore take the view that education measures what is easy to measure, rather than what is important to measure, and phenomena such as team processes are neglected (Kozma & Roth, 2012). However, demands of the 21st century, such as the shift in the context of work from the industrial age to the information age, the proliferation of information, and the diversification of modes of communication in society, have made urgent the need for the teaching and assessment of these complicated, high-level 21st-century skills.

Fortunately, the increased availability of computers in schools and various developments in computerised assessments are making it potentially easier for a wider range of skills and knowledge to be assessed, understood and developed. Computerised assessments can include elements such as dynamic environments, tools and resources that can be manipulated by the student. Computerised assessments can also capture process data and interactions, including group dynamics. This permits the collection of cognitive evidence to produce and report instructionally useful information not available through traditional paper and pencil assessment approaches, thus making 'students' thinking more visible' (Binkley et al., 2012; Csapo, Ainley, Bennett, Latour, & Law, 2012; Noss, 2012; Zoanetti, 2010). For example, Zoanetti (2010) demonstrated how strengths and weaknesses at different stages of problem solving can be diagnosed by a computer-based problem-solving assessment to support targeted instruction for students.

However, such work in education is far from ubiquitous and there are currently still many technological, practical and conceptual barriers to the assessment and teaching of complex 21st-century skills. The technological and practical barriers are beyond the scope of this chapter and more detail can be found in Griffin et al. (2012), and McKay (2013). Conceptual challenges largely revolve around the issue of grappling with skills that are new, difficult to characterise and currently ill-defined. Although the principles for understanding and analysing learning outcomes are the same as those for traditional skills, more groundwork is needed for the complex 21st-century skills. First, close attention needs to be paid to the latest research findings about the nature of the skill. This might not be a straightforward matter, as there may not exist consensus on how these new skills should be defined. Hence, validation of the assessment materials might also involve elucidation of the nature of the skill itself and lead to revisions of how the skill and its developmental progression are defined. Second, creativity might be required to operationalise the construct for assessment, especially if it is a construct that in the real world requires a lot of time and resources to demonstrate. Third, intensive work may be required in developing scoring methods that can distinguish between different levels of complex behaviours and yet still be practical—such as being conducive to automated scoring and feedback for providing timely and instructionally relevant information. Fourth, how to improve students' skills—to move them from one developmental level to the next—might not yet be fully known or documented. Thus, there exist many obstacles to understanding and analysing 21st-century learning outcomes and many opportunities for those interested in this area to make contributions to the field.

APPLICATION OF ASSESSMENT DESIGN PRINCIPLES TO A 21ST-CENTURY SKILL: COLLABORATIVE PROBLEM SOLVING

This section provides an example of how principles of assessment design and analysis of learning outcomes (outlined above) are being applied to the assessment of a complex 21st-century skill: collaborative problem solving. Collaborative problem solving has been identified by the Assessment and Teaching of 21st Century Skills (ATC21S) project (Griffin et al., 2012) as a skill of interest due to the role it is thought to play in negotiating the 21st century. The ATC21S project is a large-scale international research collaboration between industry, academics, governments and schools aimed at developing ways of assessing and teaching 21st-century skills and encourages the teaching and adoption of those skills in the classroom. Collaborative problem solving is a skill brought to bear in face-to-face situations, is well entrenched in some workplaces and is increasingly required as groups of people solve problems in virtual space. It has been seen in the workplace as a set of skills that is desirable, yet has lacked clear definition. Collaborative problem solving rests on the existence and development of sets of sub-skills, both cognitively and socially based. Resting on theoretical and empirical research, collaborative problem solving is conceptualised within ATC21S as consisting of five broad strands (or sub-domains) (Griffin et al., 2012). It is conceptualised as the capacity of an individual to:

- recognise the perspective of other persons in a group ('perspective taking')
- participate as a member of the group by contributing their knowledge, experience and expertise in a constructive way ('participation')
- recognise the need for contributions and how to manage them ('social regulation')
- identify structure and procedure involved in resolving a problem as a member of the collaborative group ('task regulation')
- build and develop knowledge and understanding ('knowledge building').

For the purposes of developing assessments and understanding learning outcomes, the multiple strands that constitute collaborative problem solving can be described in the context of underlying developmental progressions. The framework for this can be found in Griffin, Gillis and Calvitto (2004) and Griffin (2009a). Within these works, a skill or abstract domain of learning can be broken into strands and then into statements of capabilities that can be used to define each strand. Next, each capability is expressed in concrete terms as a set of performance indicators, which are written in the form of observable behaviours, and each of these behavioural indicators is then defined in terms of criteria that describe the relative quality of performance that might be expected. The latter are specific, ordered categories that describe how well each of the indicative behaviours can be demonstrated. These details for the 'participation' strand are presented in Table 5.1 to exemplify indicative criteria for assessing students' capacity. This is based on the research work of Lave and Wenger (1991) and information from workshops with SMEs on the nature of participation. It is also based on considerations of what types of evidence are required to make inferences about at what level a person is operating on the construct. This forms the basis of the *hypothesised* developmental progression for the construct, which must subsequently be empirically validated.

Once the hypothesised learning progression is documented for each of the strands, consideration can be given to the nature of assessment tasks that would be suitable for eliciting the required student evidence. Figure 5.2 shows an example of a computerised collaborative problem-solving assessment task trialled in the ATC21S project, the 'Olive Oil Task'. Based on a well-known single-person problem-solving task, it has been

Table 5.1 Example of performance indicators and quality criteria to describe the Participation strand

Indicators	Description	Quality criteria		
		Low	Medium	High
1. Action	Activity within environment	No or very little activity	Activity in familiar contexts	Activity in familiar and unfamiliar contexts
2. Interaction	Interacting with, prompting and responding to the contributions of others	Acknowledges communication	Responds to cues in communication	Initiates and promotes interaction or activity
3. Task completion	Undertaking and completing a task or part of a task individually	Maintains presence only	Identifies and attempts the task	Perseveres in task as indicated by repeated attempts or multiple strategies

Figure 5.2 Student A and Student B view of the 'Olive Oil' task.

modified and designed for two students (Student A and Student B) to work together to solve the problem. The aim is for the students to work out how Student A can transfer oil to Student B using only a three-litre jar so that Student B can fill a five-litre jar with four litres of oil. Players have different views of the task and must communicate to coordinate resource use. Thus, students must engage with the process via a number of dependencies. They have a common goal but each possesses different information and resources, which are also of use to the other student. Good collaborative problem solvers will tend to explore and learn about their respective resources, use a chat facility to share salient information, and frequently report back to each other. They will also tend to solve the problem correctly and more efficiently, that is, in fewer moves. Poor collaborative problem solving will involve fewer interactions, more random moves and a reduced chance of correct solution. Logged data such as activity timing and counts and chat message timing and counts can be automatically computer-scored to describe performance differences. That is, complex process data can be scored and treated as item response data in a similar way to data from traditional tests; naturally scoring such complex process data requires high-level programming and modelling expertise, of the kind being developed in the related fields of educational data mining and learning analytics.

Due to the complex nature of collaborative problem solving, with its multiple strands, the development of the Olive Oil Task was designed to indicate only some of the capabilities within the strands of 'participation', 'perspective taking', 'knowledge building', 'social regulation' and 'task regulation'. However, the task can be administered with other tasks to include other capabilities. Within the ATC21S project, each task is 'bundled' with other tasks for administration to students to ensure coverage of the full capabilities.

Task evaluation is necessary throughout the task development cycle (Parshall & Harmes, 2009). This is particularly critical for tasks designed to assess new constructs. Collaborative problem-solving tasks developed by the ATC21S project were put through several evaluation processes including reviews by teachers and cognitive laboratories. These laboratories involved recording observations of students' behaviours as they undertook the tasks. Students were asked about what they were thinking and doing as they worked through the tasks and this was recorded with audio and screen capture software for later analysis. This not only provided evidence about the validity and usability of tasks, it also provided information about the nature of collaborative problem solving itself. Tasks were then modified based on information gathered from the laboratories. Tasks were then trialled with large groups of students in multiple classes and schools. Data from trials were used to refine scoring procedures, calibrate item response data, validate the tasks, and validate the hypothesised development learning progressions.[2]

One methodology for linking student performance data on an assessment with a hypothesised developmental progression is using Item Response analysis, such as the Rasch model (Rasch, 1960) applied within the criterion-referenced assessment design framework (Griffin, 2007) introduced above. This method involves using the Rasch model to scale item response data and to construct a hierarchy of competencies. The hypothesised developmental progression and empirically derived hierarchy of competencies are then compared for agreement. Item Response Theory describes the relationship between a person's ability on some latent trait (skill), measured by a task and the person's observed response to items on that test (Lord, 1980). It enables the construction of scales where both items and persons are assigned values representing their respective difficulty and ability. These values are mapped onto a common metric and can be presented visually on a 'variable map' (for a more detailed account of Item Response Theory, see Hambleton, Swaminathan and Rogers (1991)). An example of a variable map is presented in Figure 5.3.

The variable map has several sections to it. Working from left to right, the first feature of the map is the scale that ranges from approximately −7.0 to +5.0. This is a logit scale and is the main metric of the Rasch model that enables person ability and item difficulty to be mapped concurrently. Higher values represent more difficulty or higher ability. The distribution of student ability is represented by the 'X's. The next feature on the map is the distribution of items and their relative difficulty. Students represented by the Xs adjacent to a cluster of items have about a 50/50 chance of being able to solve those items, less than 50/50 chance of solving items above their cluster and higher than 50/50 chance of solving items below their cluster.

Items tend to cluster together at different points along the scale. It is necessary to determine whether these clusters can be interpreted as having something in common conceptually. It is also necessary to consider whether increases in difficulty for clusters of items coincide with a change in the nature of the underpinning cognitive skill and whether items are sufficiently spread out to cover the full domain of interest. This

```
 5           |           |7.2
             |           |
             |           |
             |           |
 4           |           |5.2                     12.2 19.2
             |           |
             |           |6.2
             |           |
 3           |           |1.2 3.2 4.2             10.2
             |           |9.2                     14.2 18.2
             |           |                        13.2
             |           |                        15.2
 2           |           |
            X|           |
            X|           |
           XX|           |
 1       XXXX|           |
         XXXX|          X|                        16.2
          XXX|           |8
         XXXX|          X|
 0        XXX|         XX|7.1
       XXXXXX|        XXX|
       XXXXXX|        XXX|                        13.1 17
-1      XXXXX|        XXX|                        20
          XXX|         XX|9.1                     10.1 19.1
   XXXXXXXXXX|         XX|4.1 5.1                 18.1
         XXXX|        XXX|2.2 6.1                 14.1
-2       XXXX|       XXXX|12.1
        XXXXX|      XXXXX|
          XXX|         XX|
       XXXXXX|       XXXX|                        11
-3        XXX|      XXXXX|                        15.1 16.1
          XXX|       XXXX|
             |   XXXXXXXX|
             |        XXX|
-4          X|      XXXXX|
             |      XXXXX|2.1
             |        XXX|
             |        XXX|
-5           |         XX|
             |       XXXX|
             |         XX|
             |           |
-6           |          X|3.1
             |           |
             |           |
-7           |           |
             |           |1.1
             |           |
             |           |
```

Figure 5.3 An example of a variable map displaying logit scale, student distribution, item distribution and empirically derived competency levels and social and cognitive dimensions of collaborative problem solving.

requires an understanding of the underpinning cognitive skill involved in obtaining the correct answer and how the student thinks when they are responding to the items. If items within the clusters do not suggest an interpretable, cognitive skill level, some of the items might need to be removed from the assessment. If items do not sufficiently cover the domain of interest, more items will need to be written and added. From the interpretation of the underlying skill level which is required for successful performance on items in each of the clusters, empirically derived competency level descriptions can be written for each of the clusters. These descriptions should be of a general nature, not just a list of narrow skills needed for each of the items in the cluster, but a general description of the construct level. The last feature in the variable map in Figure 5.3 presents examples of empirically derived competency level descriptions. Students represented by the Xs at the same level as a particular competency are developing the skills located at the level and are able to fully demonstrate the skills located below that competency level. That is, a student's Zone of Proximal Development is indicated by their position on the scale.

If the empirically derived competency levels match or closely approximate the original hypothesised developmental progression used to design the assessment task, it can be used as evidence of construct validity. A poor match would require an examination of the discrepancy, which might lead to a revision of the items or revision of the hypothesised developmental progression. Consideration of various statistical indices is an important part of this refinement process. For example, examination of model fit can provide information about how justified it is to measure the underlying construct with the particular set of items chosen (Wright & Stone, 1979). Good fit to the model suggests that the items are measuring the same uni-dimensional construct—another evidence of construct validity. Other indices that should be considered include test reliability, item measurement error, item discrimination and differential item functioning (for detailed accounts of establishing validity using Rasch modelling refer to Zoanetti et al. (2009), or Woods (2010). Information from these indices can assist with refinement of the assessment task, refinement of the competency level descriptions, as well as with establishing a better understanding of the construct.

LINKING LEARNING OUTCOMES TO TEACHING STRATEGIES

Once the assessment tasks and competency levels have been validated and finalised and student data have been gathered using the refined assessment instrument, information about student skill can be communicated to teachers. This information provides teachers with an organising framework within which teaching decisions can be made (Griffin, 2007). The more student skills are observed, the more accurately generalised learning can be inferred. Assessments should help teachers interpret observations and infer learning, through documenting observable skills (Griffin, 2009b). Student results should be reported in the form of developmental progressions interpreted in criterion-referenced manner (Griffin, Murray, Care, Thomas, & Perri, 2010). Teachers can then review a student's generalised level of skill by reading the level description that corresponds to the student's position on the progression, derived from their score on the instrument. Teachers can use this information to establish appropriate goals, targets and teaching strategies, as students at different levels on the progression benefit from different teaching strategies.

Teachers can improve student learning outcomes by means of teachers' critical and collaborative analysis and discussion of student assessment data in professional learning teams (Griffin et al., 2010; Hawley & Valli, 1999; Phillips, McNaughton, & MacDonald, 2004; Woods, 2010). Professional learning teams provide teachers with the opportunity to test their understanding of the data, have their colleagues examine their interpretation and teaching strategies from a critical perspective, as well as provide support. Collaboration enables teachers to have access to a greater number and diversity of theories against which to test their theories and draw on different expertise.

An example of a protocol for this is outlined in Woods (2010). Teachers review student reports within the context of collegial meetings which, over time, leads teachers through a cycle of examination of student assessment results, objective setting, planning and review. Thus, it is recommended teachers:

- set learning objectives for students by referring to their level on the developmental progression

- establish teaching strategies for working with all of their students at a particular level of proficiency
- identify the resources they needed to support their teaching programme
- document the evidence of student learning they expected to observe
- set time to review student results and their decisions.

Woods (2010) recommends that teachers set between one and four learning goals for students at each level, review their decisions in light of evidence of student progress at subsequent meetings based on their observations of their students in everyday classroom interactions, and adjust plans to suit strengths or interests of students. These protocols are aimed at setting well-targeted and appropriate learning objectives; to assist teachers to know where to take students next, and prevent teachers from feeling under pressure to set goals for student learning that are unrealistic or too general to inform programmes of teaching. Thus, developmental progressions are a means of making and sharing decisions about specific and appropriate targets and objectives for student learning.

IMPLICATIONS FOR DESIGN OF LEARNING TECHNOLOGIES

We will focus on two sets of implications for the improvement of design methods. First, we would argue that the design of technologies for learning ought also to take into account opportunities for gathering actionable assessment data. That is, design should not merely be concerned with the more obvious elements of the learning and teaching process. It should also aim to create subsystems concerned with what the student is doing, saying, creating or writing and what might be inferred about what they are ready to do next (see Luckin et al., this volume). Such assessment capabilities can be quite visible to the student, or they may operate in the background so as not to interrupt the learning process (see, for example, Shute (2011) on 'stealth assessment'). Second, such design work ought to be informed by the best of what is known about complex 21st-century skills and about techniques for their assessment. There is little point in making sophisticated use of technologies if the underpinning conceptions of target skills are flawed.

CONCLUSION

To optimise learning outcomes, assessment data can be used as indicators of what students are ready to learn, rather than merely to identify what they can and cannot do. However, this requires a certain developmental approach. The one we have outlined is based on the work of Griffin (2007) which combines the work of Glaser (1981) on criterion referencing, Rasch's (1960) work on item response modelling and Vygotsky's (1986) work on Zones of Proximal Development. The approach requires an understanding of the skill being assessed and its developmental progression. Assessment performance can then be reported in terms of criterion and levels, such that the score is simply a code for a level of development and helps to indicate Vygotsky's Zone of Proximal Development—where the student is ready to learn and where teaching intervention will have the best learning outcomes. This information can then be used to assist teachers develop appropriate teaching strategies, targeted specifically at what students are ready to learn. Likewise, it can be used within adaptive learning systems to provide timely and appropriate support for the student's next task. It should be noted that this approach is not the only developmental approach available to designers and users of assessments. However, regardless of the developmental approach used, the importance of using evidence to establish an understanding of what students are ready to learn will always be an essential element of optimising learning outcomes.

NOTES

1. Criterion referencing can be combined with item response modelling (Griffin, 2007) such as the Rasch model (Rasch, 1960; Wright & Stone, 1979) for statistical validation and for linking students' scores to their Zone of Proximal Development. The Rasch model maps student performance on assessment items and clusters items in terms of their modelled relative difficulty. These different clusters can be directly linked to levels of increasing competence, providing empirical evidence for the order and nature of the levels. This, in turn, helps give meaning to test scores and helps with the interpretation of the nature of the skill, as once the levels are ordered the skill can be better described (Griffin, 2007). Rasch showed that when the amount of the skill possessed by the student is greater than the task demand for that skill, the likelihood is of success. When the ability is less than the difficulty, failure is likely. However, when student ability and item difficulty are equal, the probability that the person can demonstrate the behaviour is 0.5. Good tests should contain items spread out in terms of their difficulty so that at least some items are equal in difficulty to the ability of each pupil. There should be items that the student can complete easily, items that challenge the student or with which they struggle, and items where the chance of success for the student is low. If the test is designed well, this experience will be had by every student. The 'struggle items' will differ for every student, depending on the student's ability. This region of 'struggle items' is, in theory, where the student ability is at the same level as the item difficulty—the chance of success for the student on these items is approximately 50 per cent. This zone where success has odds of 50:50 points to the location on the progression where teaching intervention has the best chance of success; that is, it is the Zone of Proximal Development. Teaching concepts located at levels above this will be too difficult for the student to grasp and teaching concepts located at levels below this will be too easy and uninteresting for the student.
2. At the time this chapter was being written, this process was under way.

REFERENCES

ATC21S. (2012). Assessment and Teaching of 21st Century Skills Project Website. Retrieved 28/03/2012.

Binkley, M., Erstad, O., Herman, J., Raizen, S., Ripley, M., Miller-Ricci, M. et al. (2012). Defining twenty-first century skills. In P. Griffin, B. McGaw & E. Care (Eds.), *Assessment and teaching of 21st century skills*. Dordrecht: Springer.

Burbles, N. C. (1993). Savage inequalities: An interview with Jonathan Kozol. *Education Theory, 43*(1), 55–70.

Csapo, B., Ainley, J., Bennett, R. E., Latour, T., & Law, N. (2012). Technological issues for computer-based assessment. In P. Griffin, B. McGaw & E. Care (Eds.), *Assessment and teaching of 21st century skills*. Dordrecht: Springer.

Glaser, R. (1963). Instructional technology and the measurement of learning outcomes: Some questions. *American Psychologist, 18*, 519–521.

Glaser, R. (1981). The future of testing: A research agenda for cognitive psychology and psychometrics. *American Psychologist, 36*, 923–936.

Griffin, P. (2007). The comfort of competence and the uncertainty of assessment. *Studies in Educational Evaluation, 33*, 87–99.

Griffin, P. (2009a). Developmental frameworks for writing quality criteria in rubrics. Melbourne: Assessment Research Centre, University of Melbourne.

Griffin, P. (2009b). Teachers' use of assessment data. In C. Wyatt-Smith & J. J. Cumming (Eds.), *Educational Assessment in the 21st Century*. Dordrecht: Springer Science + Business Media B. V.

Griffin, P., Gillis, S., & Calvitto, L. (2004). Connecting competence and quality: Scored assessment in Year 12 VET. A report to the New South Wales Department of Education. Melbourne: Assessment Research Centre, University of Melbourne.

Griffin, P., McGaw, B., & Care, E. (Eds.). (2012). *Assessment and teaching of 21st century skills*. Dordrecht: Springer.

Griffin, P., Murray, L., Care, E., Thomas, A., & Perri, P. (2010). Developmental assessment: Lifting literacy through Professional Learning Teams. *Assessment in Education: Principles, Policy and Practice, 17*(4), 383–397.

Griffin, P., & Nix, P. (1990). *Educational assessment and reporting: A new approach.* Sydney: Harcourt, Brace, Jovanovic.

Hambleton, R. K., Swaminathan, H., & Rogers, H. J. (1991). *Fundamentals of Item Response Theory.* Newbury Park, CA: Sage Publications.

Hawley, W. D., & Valli, L. (1999). The essentials of effective professional development: A new consensus. In L. Darling-Hammond & G. Sykes (Eds.), *Teaching as a learning profession.* San Francisco, CA: Jossey-Bass.

Kozma, R. B., & Roth, M. (2012). Foreword. In P. Griffin, B. McGaw & E. Care (Eds.), *Assessment and teaching of 21st century skills.* Dordrecht: Springer.

Lave, J., & Wenger, E. (1991). *Situated learning: Legitimate peripheral participation.* New York: Cambridge University Press.

Lord, F. M. (1980). *Application of Item Response Theory to practical testing problems.* Hillsdale, NJ: Erlbaum.

Masters, G. (1988). The analysis of partial credit scoring. *Applied Measurement in Education, 1*(4), 279–297.

McKay, E. (Ed.). (2013). *ePedagogy in online learning: New developments in web mediated human computer interaction.* Hershey, New York: IGI Global.

Noss, R. (2012). Learning the unlearnable: Teaching the unteachable. *Dean's Lecture Series 2012 Melbourne Graduate School of Education, University of Melbourne.* Retrieved 26/03/2012, from http://www.edfac.unimelb.edu.au/news/lectures/2012series.html.

Parshall, C. G., & Harmes, J. C. (2009). Improving the quality of innovative item types: Four tasks for design and development. *Journal of Applied Testing Technology, 10*(1), 1–20.

Phillips, G., McNaughton, S., & MacDonald, S. (2004). Managing the mismatch: Enhancing early literacy progress for children with diverse language and cultural identities in mainstream urban schools in New Zealand. *Journal of Educational Psychology, 96*(2), 309–323.

Rasch, G. (1960). *Probabilistic models for some intelligence and attainment tests.* Copenhagen: Paedaogiske Institut.

Shute, V. J. (2011). Stealth assessment in computer-based games to support learning. In S. Tobias & J. D. Fletcher (Eds.), *Computer games and instruction* (pp. 503–524). Charlotte, NC: Information Age Publishers.

Trilling, B., & Fadel, C. (2009). *21st century skills: Learning for life in our times.* San Francisco, CA: Jossey-Bass.

Vygotsky, L. S. (1986). *Thought and language.* Boston, MA: MIT Press.

Woods, K. (2010). *The design and validation of measures of communication and literacy to support the instruction of students with learning disabilities.* (PhD Thesis), University of Melbourne.

Wright, B. D., & Stone, M. (1979). *Best test design.* Chicago, IL: MESA Press.

Zoanetti, N. (2010). Interactive computer based assessment tasks: How problem-solving process data can inform instruction. *Australasian Journal of Educational Technology, 26*(5), 585–606.

Zoanetti, N., Griffin, P., Beaves, M., & Wallace, E. M. (2009). Rasch scaling procedure for informing development of a valid Fetal Surveillance Education Program multiple-choice assessment. *BMC Medical Education, 9*(20).

Part II

Design Methods

INTRODUCTION

Joshua Underwood and Rosemary Luckin

The process of design is the point at which theory meets practice and the partnership must be operationalized in order to enable implementation. In the early days of educational technology development, such as exemplified in Skinner's teaching machine for example (1968) it is hard to recognize design from an aesthetic standpoint, but easy to see the pedagogical drivers. Now learners and teachers rightly expect sound design: aesthetically, pedagogically, technically and interactionally. The chapters in this section are a contemporary mix of high-quality contributions that could be described according to a range of categorizations. For example, one could collect the chapters by Balaam, Duncan, Craft and Robertson under the heading Design: Practical Tools and Methods; Fischer, Mwanza, Looi & Wong, Luckin et al., under the heading Design: Frameworks; Mavrikis et al., Kay et al. and du Boulay under the heading Design: Adaptive Systems, and Prieto et al. and Mor under the heading Design: Narratives and Patterns. However, there is a critical, crosscutting theme within the chapters in this section, a theme around which we prefer to view the work presented. This central theme is *Design: Enabling end-user and stakeholder involvement.* The chapters in this section of the book derive and demonstrate methods that go beyond simply inviting users to comment on and contribute to designs post-hoc. Contributors offer frameworks, approaches and practical methods that have been tried and tested with a wide range of participants.

Getting users to genuinely engage with design is particularly difficult when the intention is to transform learning and create new opportunities, which may be quite different from learners' current experience.

Balaam and Mavrikis et al. address the issue of how to enable users (both teachers and learners) to contribute to design even when design involves unfamiliar scenarios such as those afforded by new technologies. Mavrikis et al. provide a worked example of an approach they call Iterative Context Engineering that enables them to collaboratively explore and design new learning and teaching scenarios afforded by intelligent systems with teachers and learners in authentic settings. This approach will have evident appeal to those concerned that exciting new opportunities for learning opened up by new technology should converge with real-world needs and constraints. Balaam also provides a worked example of how to enable users to explore, think about and communicate their needs and feelings about unfamiliar new learning scenarios. She introduces technology probes and describes her use of a probe as a tool for understanding learners' and teachers' feelings about opportunities for emotional feedback in classroom learning scenarios.

Craft, too, addresses the issue of how to facilitate collaboration and participation in design. He provides advice and a highly practical account of how collaborative sketch-ins can be used to help all kinds of participants think about design issues and contribute to design. This approach brings designers and other participants together and uses sketching to support communication of design issues and opportunities, and creative collaboration around these, in ways that conversation alone may not.

The approaches described so far are not mutually exclusive and are applicable to participants of all ages. There are, however, certain user groups who need particular attention. Robertson et al. discuss specific issues relating to young people and offer a framework and methods for engaging young people in design. They argue that involving young users in design is not only ideological in terms of democracy and empowerment but can also lead to better design, provided that participation is appropriately managed and learners' developmental stages are taken into account. Issues of levels of participation are discussed elsewhere in the handbook (see Winters, Chapter 26) but empowerment ultimately leading to end-user design is taken up by Kay et al., Prieto et al. and Fischer in this section though in each case in somewhat different ways.

Prieto et al. look specifically at teachers and the issue of how to enable them to re-use and share, apply and adapt learning designs, particularly at enactment time—that is to say on the fly in the classroom (virtual or face-to-face). They use observation and workshops to identify and describe highly contextualized learning design patterns, which they refer to as 'atomic patterns', which can then be used to orchestrate and enact Computer-Supported Collaborative Learning scenarios.

Kay et al. also wish to empower teachers to design but in this case they are concerned with support for learner self-regulation. They point out that teachers now regularly use learning management systems to design and deliver at least part of their course but that these systems do not as yet incorporate widgets that support learners' meta-cognition and self-regulation despite strong evidence that metacognitive interface elements could make such materials more effective. Kay et al. draw on their own extensive work to provide examples of the form such widgets might take and propose a research agenda for creating a toolkit of metacognitive interface elements. Again, Kay et al. emphasize the importance of involving users (particularly teachers) in the design of this toolkit. Prieto et al. empower teachers by providing highly practical and contextualized but nevertheless re-usable learning design patterns. Kay et al. aim to provide widgets that make it easy for teachers to design and implement materials and an environment that promotes and supports learners' self-regulation.

Fischer goes a step further in presenting Meta-Design, a tried and tested theoretical framework that supports design that aims to empower all stakeholders in co-design. Fischer argues that such a framework can transform learning by empowering all stakeholders to participate, contribute, share content, provide feedback and criticality because it empowers learners to act as co-designers in personally meaningful problems and supports cultures of participation in which all voices are heard. That is to say, the framework supports the design of environments for lifelong learning, informal learning and self-directed learning. Interestingly, Kay et al. also point to the utility of their metacognitive widgets for lifelong and self-directed learning. In fact, as Winne (Chapter 42) points out even in formal situations where learning goals are typically assigned, learners 'always set their own goals; sometimes, these match assigned goals'. Empowering learners to set and assess their own goals and manage their learning and the resources they access to help them achieve these goals then becomes a central objective across all learning.

The empowerment of learners through multiple resources and settings is also a characteristic in Looi & Wong's chapter on Seamless Learning. They draw on their own extensive empirical work and a review of others' work to characterize dimensions of Seamless Learning. They then describe how various affordances of new technologies (particularly mobile devices) can be exploited to support learning across these dimensions. However, they recognize that learners need scaffolding towards effective exploitation of these affordances. They describe a collaborative design process they employed with teachers in order to foster self-directed seamless planned and emergent learning inside and outside the classroom. The nine strategies for facilitated seamless learning will be of particular interest to teachers and other educators interested in exploiting technology to empower learners both in and beyond classrooms.

Luckin et al. also provide a chapter at the framework level expanding upon their introduction of the Ecology of Resources conceptualization of context in the Foundations section of this handbook. Here, though, they present methods for understanding learner perspectives on resource ecologies and the relationships within these and demonstrate the use of these methods in two language learning design activities. As with Fischer, Luckin et al. are concerned to empower learners through participation in design and they look here at some ways this can be done along with ethical complexities. Luckin et al. are also concerned, like Looi & Wong, to help learners connect across experiences. Here they describe a visualization approach that can help focus design attention on transitions in learning experiences and the connections we may need to help learners make.

The remaining chapters all also recognize the importance of engaging with users in design. Their central focuses are all different, but they all link in interesting ways to the other chapters in this section. Du Boulay addresses affective issues. We have already seen that it must ultimately be the learner that interprets learning goals and manages learning and we have looked at ways in which learners and teachers can be involved in designing systems to help learners realize their own goals and manage their own learning. However, goal setting and management of learning is clearly not only a cognitive issue, motivation and feelings interact very significantly. There has been substantial research in adaptive systems in this area and Du Boulay provides a useful overview of such systems and dimensions along which they may be classified. Du Boulay also helpfully highlights the various choices designers, interested in addressing affective issues, face.

Mwanza-Simwami focuses on understanding, and designing for (and in) authentic settings. She uses Activity Theory to focus more on socio-cultural settings and understand the motivations and contradictions that will influence the success of designs. She presents a worked example of the use of her Activity Oriented Design Method in the design of a mobile learning system.

Mor also provides a chapter at the framework level, though with many highly practical examples drawn from his own design work. He is particularly concerned to facilitate the communication and re-use of design knowledge. He demonstrates how design narrative, design patterns and design scenarios can be used together to support learning from past experiences and projecting design claims into the future. Again this approach can be used to facilitate multi-perspective collaborative design and hence genuine engagement with users and other stakeholders.

Finally, from a refreshingly different angle, Duncan looks at how we can better understand ourselves, both as designers and learners. She argues that our primary pieces of educational technology are our own minds and that what we have been missing most are ways of looking into these. She provides an accessible introduction to auto-ethnography and highly practical advice on how we as designers can employ auto-ethnography to look at, learn from and share our own experience. Importantly, this approach recognizes that we too set our own goals, have our own motivations and feelings and that these influence our designs. Just as learners interpret our designs we interpret their needs and we need to understand how this influences our designs.

REFERENCE

Skinner, B. F. (1968) *The Technology of Teaching*. New York: Appleton-Century-Crofts.

6

USING TECHNOLOGY PROBES TO UNDERSTAND EDUCATIONAL DESIGN SPACES

Madeline Balaam

INTRODUCTION

Learner-centred design (LCD) is an orientation to design that focuses on the needs, motivations, requirements and practices of the learner and, ideally, also the context within which the learning interaction is taking place. In doing so, the designer hopes to create an intervention that works to provide a rich, effective learning experience for the learner in question (Good & Robertson, 2006). There are many possible ways of involving a learner in the process of LCD. LCD can be interpreted as the designer deeply engaging with theory to infer a learner's needs. Taking this approach, the end product is informed by an understanding of learners' needs and practices as derived from theory. LCD can also be concerned with involving a learner in the testing of high-fidelity prototypes to ensure that the product is easy to use and aesthetically appealing. The term LCD might also be used to evoke a situation where the learner acts alongside the designer to aid the design process, from identifying the types of places and situations in their life where technology might support them, through to exploring the types of interactions that might be beneficial, to developing the packaging and aesthetics of the end product.

One of the issues raised through discussions around LCD is how you might involve learners in designing educational interventions for learning objectives which they have not already been taught (Good & Robertson, 2006). In effect, learners might not have the vocabulary and experience required to play such a central role in the design process. In this chapter I will describe one design method used within Human Computer Interaction (HCI) that might help overcome this problem. This HCI practice, the Technology Probe, aims to provide participants (or learners) with a concrete experience of technology in order to scaffold participation in the design process. This chapter will provide a background to the Technology Probe as well as describing a case study which explores the use of a Technology Probe within the design of an educational technology.

FROM CULTURAL PROBES TO TECHNOLOGY PROBES

As a design method the term 'probe' has been used in HCI since the work of Gaver (Gaver, Dunne, & Pacenti, 1999). Gaver's probes are *designed* objects produced to aid the process of coming to know the person for whom one is designing. The probes are intended to act almost as a conversation between the participant and the designer, allowing the participant to get to know the designer better through the process of using and responding to the probes. In this sense cultural probes are also about recognising the desires and needs of the designer and establishing these subjectivities as an important part of the process of design. Cultural probes, which stem from the situationalist and surrealist movements, are designed to provoke, and in some cases disrupt, the common narratives of experience and understanding that participants might ordinarily bring to the design process. Through the application of probes, the designer seeks to gather a set of stimuli (rather than data) that might be taken, hand-in-hand with theoretical understandings and practical considerations, to inspire design.

Cultural probes have had a prolific impact upon HCI practice (Boehner, Vertesi, & Sengers, 2007). The popularity of the method has led the community to produce a number of different types of design probes. One example is the Technology Probe (Hutchinson et al., 2003). Hutchinson et al. sought to devise a method that would allow participants to more directly inspire and shape technologies, enabling participants to become more actively involved in the design, rather than being the inspiration for, or the evaluators of the design. Similarly to the original writing around cultural probes, Hutchinson et al. (2003) sought to create a set of Technology Probes that would provide their participants with some experience of the kind of technology they would like to design, or the kind of concept/phenomenon they would like to design for. In this sense, the conversation between designer and participant begins, and is put into context by the initial Technology Probe. Hutchinson et al. (2003) describe the goal of a Technology Probe as combining: 'the social science goal of collecting data about use of the technology in a real-world setting, the engineering goal of field testing the technology and the design goal of inspiring users (and designers) to think of new kinds of technology' (p. 18). A Technology Probe is not a mocked up demonstration of a technological interaction. It is a working design, robust enough to be deployed 'in the wild' for an extended period so that participants can interact with the new technology and integrate it into their practices.

According to Hutchinson et al. (2003) Technology Probes should:

- be simple;
- collect data about its usage;
- not be iterated on or developed further during its deployment;
- be flexible and open-ended in terms of how it is and can be used;
- be used to test novel ideas and provoke new narratives and practices.

Technology Probes have the advantage of being able to make salient to the designer the dynamics of a particular context. As a result, a well-designed probe can be a useful tool for uncovering practices that might not be easily observable by a researcher or a designer. Technology Probes can also help to uncover users' values, particularly if these values might be difficult, or perhaps socially unacceptable for a user to articulate (Maitland & Chalmers, 2009). Such design goals can often result in probes that are provocative as a means of promoting reflection amongst users, feeding into a designer's comprehension of the design space. In addition, Technology Probes have been posited as a means of overcoming the perceived distance between designers and those being designed for/with. For example, probes have been used to bridge the age-gap between the designer and the community being designed for (Gaver et al., 1999). This suggests a clear advantage to using such a method when designing for a younger, perhaps school-based community. Perhaps most commonly though, Technology Probes have been used to provide users' with a concrete experience of technology that otherwise might not be easily imaginable.

At the crux of the Technology Probe method is the deployment of a prototype that is stable enough to operate 'in the wild'. It can be a costly route for design, with significant development effort needed at the start of an iterative design cycle, especially as Technology Probes are not a design that will be iterated on and improved, but rather a technology whose single function is to understand the design space better (Hutchinson et al., 2003). It is also worth bearing in mind that the Technology Probe is not an unbiased means of understanding the design space. A Technology Probe embodies the designer's values (whether these be conceptual, aesthetic, or otherwise), and since these values will likely be communicated to users through their use and appropriation of the probe, the designer inevitably shapes the way in which they understand the design space.

What follows is a case study where a Technology Probe was used within an educational design context and discussion of how this design method can be used to support LCD.

A CASE STUDY OF A TECHNOLOGY PROBE AS A TOOL TO INSPIRE DESIGN

The LCD process at the heart of this case study began with the theoretically derived principle that emotion is crucial to the success of learning and teaching interactions (Meyer & Turner, 2002), as well as mounting evidence that teachers find it hard to understand the emotional experiences of their learners, both in the classroom (Alsmeyer, Luckin, Good, & Harris, 2009), and in lab-based experiments (D'Mello, Taylor, Davidson, & Graesser, 2008). In part, data suggest that learners (at least in the classroom) do not strongly use facial features or body language to express their emotional experiences (Alsmeyer et al., 2009). Additionally, given the social context of the classroom, learners may deliberately suppress the expression of particular emotions (Boekaerts, 1994). Given these foundations, the question became whether a carefully designed technology could support emotion in the classroom, both in terms of helping learners to better understand their own emotional experiences and also supporting teachers in attending to the emotional impact of their teaching strategies and the emotional experiences of their learners.

Initial empirical work in the area (Alsmeyer et al., 2009) indicated that young learners found it difficult to talk about their emotional experiences. This was in part because these young learners were unsure what an emotion was and because they were unsure what emotions had to do with their learning experiences, outcomes and schoolings. Such lack of understanding, experience and vocabulary around emotion and its impact on learning processes limited the extent to which it was considered useful to encourage participation from learners through typical LCD methods (workshops, interviews, low-fidelity prototyping sessions) in the design of an affective technology for the classroom. Nevertheless, it was considered integral that the learners (and teachers) had a central role in the design process, in particular due to the relatively sensitive and personal nature of the proposed role for the technology—a technology that seeks to support emotional understanding and communication within learning interactions. A Technology Probe was designed and deployed in order to provide learners and teachers with a direct experience of an affective technology. The experiences of the probe can potentially not only prompt a greater understanding of emotion and its role in learning, but also stimulate reflection on the role for affective technologies in the classroom.

Design sensitivities garnered through initial empirical work in the classroom led to a set of simple design requirements for a Technology Probe (Alsmeyer et al., 2009; Alsmeyer, Luckin, & Good, 2008), which should:

- support real-time communication between the learner and their teacher;
- support private communication between the learner and their teacher;
- promote reflection on emotion;
- be both easy to use and easy to interpret.

These requirements led to the design of the Subtle Stone (see Figure 6.1). The Subtle Stone is a handheld, squeezable orb that allows for the communication (or self-report) of emotion from learner to teacher in real time through the use of a colour-based language. The Subtle Stone is covered in ribbed rubber containing 6 LED lights and a switch that is operated through a squeeze. It displays seven separate colours: blue, green, red, purple, light blue, yellow and white. To engender privacy each learner creates their own colour:emotion language, by deciding for themselves which colour communicates which emotion to their teacher. When a learner decides to communicate an emotion to their teacher, they select the colour associated with that emotion in their own colour:emotion language by squeezing their Subtle Stone until it displays the colour they require. The colour continues to be emitted until the learner decides to change the colour (and hence the emotion communicated) by squeezing the Subtle Stone or by switching it off.

Figure 6.1 The Subtle Stone.

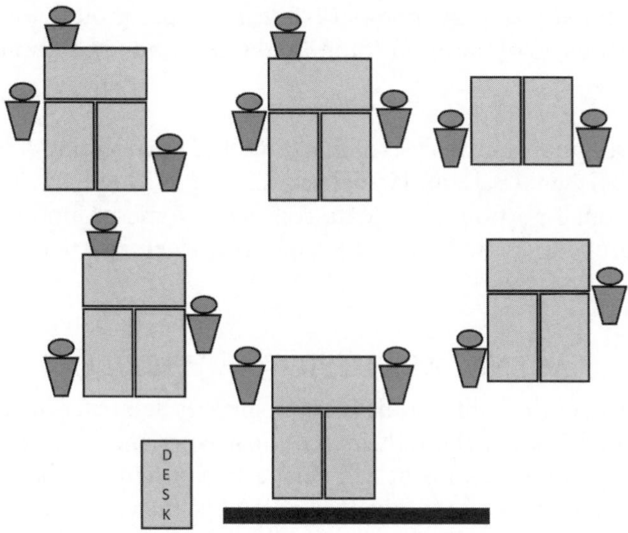

Figure 6.2 The teacher interface.

Each Subtle Stone wirelessly transmits the displayed colour to a tablet PC that translates and presents the learners' communications to the class teacher. Effectively the tablet PC displays a map of the classroom (see Figure 6.2.). Each person-shaped icon represents a learner in the classroom with a Subtle Stone. The teacher interface gives the teacher a general overview of the emotions experienced by the learners in the classroom by indicating to the teacher through colour which learners are reporting a 'positive' emotion (represented by a green learner icon) and which learners are reporting a 'negative' emotion (represented by a red learner icon), and which learners are not reporting any emotions (represented by a grey learner icon). Rollover text is provided should the teacher wish to know the specific emotion communicated by a learner.

DEPLOYING A TECHNOLOGY PROBE TO INSPIRE DESIGN

Fifteen Subtle Stones were deployed in a year eight German language class (aged 12–13 years) at a high school in the UK. The study involved 15 learners (10 female and 5 male) who each had access to a Subtle Stone during their lessons. The Subtle Stones were available for the learners to use throughout four weeks of classes. Some learners kept their Subtle Stones on their laps, other learners kept the Subtle Stone on their desks, while others kept their Subtle Stone inside its box.

A range of data was collected to help understand the learners' experiences and usage of the Subtle Stone including:

- a log file which described each learner's use of the Subtle Stone;
- a questionnaire completed by learners at the beginning and end of each class, describing the learner's general mood and current experience of seven emotions;
- a diary where each learner was asked to make entries reflecting on their emotional experiences in their German classes;

- semi-structured group interviews (2–5 learners per group) which explored students' experiences of the Subtle Stone and were conducted towards the end of the study.

A detailed description and analysis of this study and the resulting design requirements can be found elsewhere (Balaam, Fitzpatrick, Luckin, & Good, 2010). In what follows I will present a small portion of the data collected by and around the deployment of a Technology Probe to show how it can support learners' participation in the design process.

AGENCY AS A DESIGN REQUIREMENT

One of the features of the Subtle Stone is that it gives each learner full control over what they disclose to their teacher about their emotional experience, and when they choose to disclose this information. From a design perspective, insight can be gained about what learners would want from an affective technology in the classroom by exploring how they exercised choice around this feature as well as how they talked about their use of this feature. What follows is a description of how one learner in the classroom (John) used his Subtle Stone. This description is based not only on the Subtle Stone log data, but also on questionnaires completed by John before and after each lesson, John's entries into his diary and interviews with John and other students.

Table 6.1 outlines the emotional experiences that John reports to his teacher via the Subtle Stone throughout the course of the deployment. It illustrates that John reports mostly positive and activating emotions (i.e. happy, pride) to his teacher when using his Subtle Stone. But John's diary entries tell a slightly different story. Over the course of the study John writes nine entries in his diary, each of which briefly reflects upon a German lesson and his emotional experiences within that lesson. John's diary entries also indicate that John's recollections of the emotions experienced in his German lessons are markedly positive, yet the percentage of emotions, such as angry, frustrated and nervous, recorded in his diary is double to that reported using the Subtle Stone. Further, John's reporting of boredom in his diary entries is three times that reported using his Subtle Stone. A closer look at John's use of the Subtle Stone, questionnaire and diary from one particular lesson during the deployment is useful to illustrate more specifically how John chooses to use the Subtle Stone to communicate his emotional experiences to his teacher.

At the start of this lesson John reports (using the pre-class emotion questionnaire) that he feels moderately happy and tired, as well as a little bit proud and bored. He also reports that the class teacher, a learner in the class, and the resources he suspects will

Table 6.1 An overview of the emotions reported by John throughout the study

Emotional Term	Time spent reporting emotion (%)	Number of reports of emotion
Happy	62.4	23
Tired	15.2	11
Proud	6.8	3
Bored	5.8	8
Nervous	5.1	9
Angry	3.0	8
Frustrated	1.7	6

be used throughout the day's lesson are having a moderately strong positive influence over his emotional experiences. The class focuses on the construction of sentences in the perfect tense, and is divided up into six main tasks, some of which are completed in small groups, others of which are completed independently. Throughout the lesson John predominantly reports that he is feeling happy to his teacher, reporting happiness throughout just under 80% of his Subtle Stone use, and frustrated for 10% of his Subtle Stone use. However, at the end of the class John uses the post-class questionnaire to report that by the end of the class he is feeling most strongly bored, and a bit happy. John also reports that the class teacher has had a strong positive influence over his emotional experiences, and another learner in the class and the resources that were used in the session continue to have a moderately strong positive influence over his emotional experiences. John's diary entry for this session reads: 'Came into the lesson very happy. The first activity made me bored. I remained fairly happy for the remainder of the lesson.'

In just under half of the lessons observed as part of this study John reports boredom as the emotion most strongly felt at the end of his German lessons. Yet, only 6% of John's overall use of the Subtle Stone is reporting boredom to his teacher. In tandem with this, John reports throughout the study in both the pre- and post-class emotion questionnaires that the class teacher has a strong positive influence on his emotional experiences. These data hint that John may be making conscious decisions as to what to communicate to his teacher with regard to his emotional experience. John rarely reports to his teacher that he feels bored, even though questionnaires completed at the end of each lesson suggest that boredom is the strongest change in his emotional experiences while in the classroom. By triangulating the data sources collected by and around the Technology Probe it is possible to ascertain that John values the opportunity of being in control of what his teacher knows and, importantly, does not know, about his emotional experiences. This notion of the importance of control is also reflected in the interviews conducted with learners after the deployment of the Subtle Stone. For instance, in the following interview excerpt, a group of female students are discussing whether they always told their class teacher everything about their emotional experiences with the Subtle Stone. While the majority of her group believed they did, Josie says: 'When I'm like not really interested in what we're learning I don't like putting it onto bored, because even if I was bored I wouldn't say that I was bored.'

Two learners also report making decisions about what is important to tell their teacher, and what they consider not important or necessary. In the following interview the group of girls are discussing whether the Subtle Stones were distracting for their learning. During this discussion Ciara says:

> No, I think [the Subtle Stones] are fun. I don't really take notice of mine. I normally put it on an emotion at the beginning of the lesson and put it in the box. If my emotion changes completely then I'll change it, but if it changes for like one minute while I like, I need a wee or something, then I don't change it. I don't change it like that if something little happens.

CONCLUSION

The glimpse of data provided in this chapter describes one aspect of how learners used the Technology Probe as well as how they talked about their use of the probe, illustrating the role this design method can play in enabling learners to articulate their values for technologies that support emotion in the classroom. The case study has shown that learners can effectively contribute to the design process even though the concept of emotion and its relation to learning is one that is both abstract and foreign to young learners (Alsmeyer et al., 2009). In addition, these young learners were able to contribute to the design process regardless of the fact that the design team were exploring a role for technology that would be out of the range of experience for most everyday users of technology. It is in these types of design situations where the real strength of a Technology Probe lies. The Technology Probe appears to be a helpful design method to utilise in exactly those situations when a designer wants to involve learners in the design of something where they might not yet have a great deal of experience.

The data described here show, through the learners' use and experience of the Subtle Stone, the learners' desire to control what their teacher knows about their emotional experiences. We see John actively making decisions about what he feels is appropriate to express to his class teacher. Such a need was also reflected in how students talked about their use of the Subtle Stone. The learners shaped the emotions they expressed to their teacher based in part upon their conceptions about how a given emotional expression would be received by their teacher. This suggests classroom affective technologies should offer students control about what is conveyed about their emotional experiences, when, and to whom. As such, a carefully designed Technology Probe can scaffold learners' contributions to the design process by both giving learners a greater vocabulary of experience around which to base their contributions to the design process as well as allowing a design team to understand more about a group's particular needs, values and desires through exploring how a probe is used and incorporated in the learners' practice. The Technology Probe provided the learners with a concrete example and experience of an affective technology and it was through the learners' use of this probe that they were able to think through and talk about the implications of such technologies.

As mentioned previously, the Technology Probe is not a valueless approach to design. Both Hutchinson et al. (2003) and Gaver et al (1999) emphasise that probes at their heart speak something of the desires and beliefs of the designer. The instantiation of a design into a concrete interaction with a technology will likely shape the way in which users can participate in the design process. The Subtle Stone is no exception. One explicit choice made by the design team in creating the Subtle Stone was to support privacy around the communication of emotion in the classroom. Data collected throughout the deployment of the probe suggest that learners responded to this value. As already discussed, the learners controlled what they communicated to the teacher. The learners were able to exert this control exactly because the Subtle Stone, in supporting privacy, gave them choice about what they told their teacher and when. In addition to this, the learners generally kept their colour:emotion languages secret from their peers, and sometimes even hid their Subtle Stones on their laps, or under the desk during classes. Furthermore, the learners also talked about the importance of knowing that not everyone in the classroom knew how they were feeling. It is plausible, however, that these observable and articulated values around privacy were shaped by the original design intention of the Subtle Stone to explicitly give learners a private means of communicating emotion. Such idiosyncrasies of the method need to be both acknowledged and carefully navigated by a designer to ensure the design requirements, sensitivities or inspiration derived from the use of a Technology Probe are reflective of the participants' values, rather than simply those of the designer. One prime means of navigating these issues is to ensure the Technology Probe is flexible enough to enable those using it to usurp any particular designer-led values for a piece of technology to instead reflect their own. In the case of the Subtle Stone, the learners could have chosen to leave their colour:emotion language crib sheets open on their desk for others to use. Or, they could have decided to make their colour:emotion languages match their friends, or the other learners who sat near to them.

To conclude, a key challenge often identified in LCD is concerned with how to include learners actively in the design process of educational technologies when those learners might not have the experience or understanding of the concepts or learning that the designed technology is seeking to address. In other words, how can a learner meaningfully contribute to the design of educational technologies when they do not know about, or have not experienced the concepts or ideas that the designed technology should respond to? This chapter has introduced the Technology Probe as one design method that scaffolds learners' contributions to the design process by giving learners a concrete experience upon which to start basing their articulation of needs, values and requirements.

REFERENCES

Alsmeyer, M., Luckin, R., Good, J., & Harris, E. (2009). Supporting Affective Communication in the Classroom with the Subtle Stone. *International Journal of Learning Technologies, 4*, pp. 188–215.

Alsmeyer, M., Luckin, R., & Good, J. (2008). Developing a Novel Interface for Capturing Self Reports of Affect. *CHI'08 Extended Abstracts on Human Factors in Computing Systems*, pp. 2883–2888. ACM.

Balaam, M., Fitzpatrick, G., & Good, J. (2010). Exploring Affective Technologies for the Classroom with the Subtle Stone. *Proceedings of the 28th International Conference on Human Factors in Computing Systems*, pp. 1623–1632. ACM.

Boehner, K., Vertesi, J., & Sengers, P. (2007). How HCI Interprets the Probes. *Proceedings of the 25th International Conference on Human Factors in Computing Systems*, pp. 1077–1086. ACM.

Boekaerts, M. (1994). Anger in Relation to School Learning. *Learning and Instruction, 3*(4), pp. 269–280. Elsevier.

D'Mello, S., Taylor, R., Davidson, K., & Graesser, A. (2008). Self Versus Teacher Judgments of Learner Emotions during a Tutoring Session with AutoTutor. *Intelligent Tutoring Systems*, pp. 9–18. Springer.

Gaver, B., Dunne, T., & Pacenti, E. (1999). Cultural Probes. *Interactions, 6*(1), pp. 21–29. ACM.

Good, Judith, & Robertson, J. (2006). CARSS: A Framework for Learner-Centred Design with Children. *International Journal of Artificial Intelligence in Education, 16*, pp. 381–413.

Hutchinson, H., Mackay, W., Westerlund, B., Bederson, B. B., Druin, A., Plaisant, C., et al. (2003). Technology Probes: Inspiring Design For and With Families. *Proceedings of the SIGCHI Conference on Human Factors in Computing Systems*, pp. 17–24.

Maitland, J., & Chalmers, M. (2009). Probelems: Reflecting on a Technology Probe into Peer Involvement in Cardiac Rehabilitation. *Pervasive Health*, pp. 1–4.

Meyer, D. K., & Turner, J. C. (2002). Discovering Emotion in Classroom Motivation Research. *Educational Psychologist, 37*(2), pp. 107–114.

7

ITERATIVE CONTEXT ENGINEERING TO INFORM THE DESIGN OF INTELLIGENT EXPLORATORY LEARNING ENVIRONMENTS FOR THE CLASSROOM

Manolis Mavrikis, Sergio Gutierrez-Santos, Eirini Geraniou, Celia Hoyles, George Magoulas, Richard Noss, and Alex Poulovassilis

1 INTRODUCTION

This chapter presents the design approach that emerged from the efforts of the MiGen team to develop an intelligent exploratory learning environment (ELE) for the classroom. The MiGen system supports students directly when possible, and also provides information to teachers aiming to assist them in their role in the classroom. Designing such a learning environment entails a set of challenges that differ somewhat from those faced in the design of 'traditional' Intelligent Tutoring Systems or other learning environments, which typically have a clear delimitation of the domain and well-defined sequences of possible steps to be performed. In this chapter we focus on two challenges rooted in the different style of interaction and epistemology underlying exploratory environments, coupled with the need for iterative design and development that considers carefully the context within which such environments would be used.

The first challenge emerges mostly when designing a novel exploratory environment which aims to provide students the opportunity to develop certain ways of thinking. As the system is being iteratively developed and evaluated, its design, the tasks it affords, and the relationship between the system itself and the knowledge domain (also known as 'epistemological validity' of an environment (Balacheff and Sutherland, 1994)) co-evolve (Disessa and Cobb, 2004). Appreciating this resonates with the emphasis on recognising context and its dynamic dimension in engineering (Dourish, 2004) or design-based research (Luckin, 2011). The challenge is to reconcile the paradox introduced by the fact that a typical knowledge elicitation process requires expertise which, in our case, is not available until after the system is implemented, evaluated and used.

The second challenge arises from our belief that one of the reasons that many technology-enhanced learning (TEL) systems, and particularly intelligent ones, have not reached their full potential is the lack of attention to the teacher's role in the classroom. Although the need to co-design systems with teachers has been recognised in TEL research and development (e.g. Disessa, Azevedo, and Parnafes, 2004, Luckin, 2011), collecting requirements for tools whose functionalities are novel and which are not similar to existing tools with which users may be familiar is not straightforward and requires an agile, iterative methodology in which successive prototypes are co-designed, trialled and evolved.

The chapter describes an approach that we refer to as 'Iterative Context Engineering' that responds to these challenges by engineering particular didactical situations and conducting in-situ studies that allow us to inform the design of the intelligent support components as well as to appreciate the complexities of the classroom context and the information that can be provided to teachers in order to support them during and after the lesson.

2 ITERATIVE CONTEXT ENGINEERING (ICE)

The design of intelligent systems can be based on relevant theories of learning or observation of human tutors (du Boulay and Luckin, 2001; Self, 1999). In relation to theories of learning or frameworks, Disessa and Cobb (2004) argue that although these may provide general principles, perspectives for conceptualising instructional design or prescriptions of pedagogical strategies, they usually lack the descriptive power required to develop specific designs in practice. Self (1999) also observes that such theories are not adequate for facilitating the implementation of computational support and advocates 'a mixture of theory and empiricism'.

On the other hand, relying for this necessary empiricism on observation of human tutors' strategies presents several difficulties. The first difficulty arises from the lack of users' experience with a novel learning environment. The problem is compounded by the fact that the communication means available to a human (e.g. teacher) are very different to those achievable with a system implemented on a computer. The computer is limited in the amount of information it can obtain from the student, and in the amount and types of feedback it can provide. These limitations are both technical—for example, limitations of the state of the art in natural language processing and generation—and pragmatic—humans simply behave differently from computers, for example, they listen, read and interact with interest and attention. In some cases, especially in well-structured and well-researched and understood domains, the mapping of human tutors' strategies to computer-based ones is relatively straightforward; that is, knowledge can be elicited from experts, and can be directly implemented as intelligent support within the system. In other cases, however, apart from a lack of deep understanding of the processes involved in learning, the difference in language and behaviour between humans and computers makes a straightforward implementation difficult—an issue already noted in Rizzo et al. (2005), Dahlback et al. (1993) and Maulsby et al. (1993).

In early research in the human–computer interaction (HCI) field (Gould and Lewis, 1985; Wilson and Rosenberg, 1988; Chignell, 1990) similar realisations led to the recognition of the fact that in-depth understanding of user behaviour requires observing and analysing situations in their actual context. This is the main thrust behind *contextual design* approaches (Beyer and Holtzblatt, 1997). In the field of intelligent systems, this led to the development of methods that rely on computer-mediated sessions where unimplemented components of an intelligent system are emulated by a human who is interacting with a user remotely, a method often referred to as *wizard-of-Oz* (inspired by the famous children's story); this is especially appropriate when the user is not privy to the existence of the other human (Wilson and Rosenberg, 1988; Maulsby et al., 1993; Bernsen et al., 1998; Fiedler et al., 2004).

Section 2.1 presents how we approach contextual design with iterative wizard-of-Oz cycles that also take into account the need for feeding from and into theory in order to explain the phenomena of interest (Disessa and Cobb, 2004). This falls within the design-based research paradigm which, despite its challenges, offers an approach for dealing with the complexity of naturalistic contexts by 'iteratively changing the learning environment over time, collecting evidence of the effect of these variations and feeding it recursively into future designs' (Barab, 2006).

However, such studies are not sufficient for deriving requirements for the actual context of usage, i.e. intelligent support for *classroom-deployed* ELE. To achieve this, there is a need for direct observation and active participation in the context. While these are typical approaches in the HCI field (e.g. Wilson and Rosenberg, 1988; Gould and Lewis, 1985), where they are used to determine how users interact with systems under realistic situations, the need to conduct such empirical observations is only recently starting to be understood in the educational field (c.f. Conati and Maclaren, 2004; Porayska-Pomsta and Pain, 2004; Luckin et al., 2006). We present in Section 2.2 our approach of incrementally eliciting requirements while increasingly approximating authentic classroom situations.

2.1 *Iterative Communication Capacity Tapering*

Inspired by the wizard-of-Oz methodology, but also recognising the need to iteratively design and evaluate the design of the intelligent system, we purposefully engineer a series of didactical situations where we manipulate the available modalities and speed of communication—also known as *interaction bandwidth*. Based on previous studies, we script the support that can be provided in order to limit (to the extent possible) the *feedback improvisation* by the human tutor and, therefore, simulate specific aspects of the intelligent system. We refer to the combination of interaction bandwidth and feedback improvisation as *communication capacity*. By explicitly modifying and manipulating the communication capacity, we enable the investigation of effective pedagogic strategies and the design of intelligent components of the overall system. We refer to this approach as 'Iterative Communication Capacity Tapering' to emphasise its iterative nature and the fact that, in each iteration, we are tapering down the available communication bandwidth (Mavrikis and Gutierrez-Santos, 2010).

In the early stages of the design, a facilitator interacts face-to-face with students in order to establish useful pedagogical strategies. Useful as this may be, it does not lead directly to the development of the intelligent support components that will support the student. To this end, we gradually match the 'interaction bandwidth' of the didactical situation with the envisaged context. In other words, we engineer the context in which the facilitator has to progressively use communication channels that can provide the same sort of interaction as the one that will be possible with the intelligent system. In this way, we achieve a gradual transition from a system supported by a human facilitator to a system in which most of the support is computer-based (see Figure 7.1). The process is presented in more detail in Mavrikis and Gutierrez-Santos (2010).

2.2 *Iterative Classroom Authenticity*

To appreciate the range and complexity of classrooms, we conduct in-situ studies where the ELE and associated activities are integrated into normal classroom lessons, including among other things the fact that there are several students undertaking the same task

Figure 7.1 Interaction bandwidth tapering. Initial face-to-face interactions with students establish useful pedagogical strategies. Subsequently, we engineer the context using computer-mediated sessions, gradually moving from a system supported by a human to a system in which the support is computer-based (with permission, from Mavrikis and Gutierrez-Santos, 2010).

(with implications such as distractions, peer-pressure, and opportunities for help), the possibility of obtaining help from the teacher and teaching assistants, and a strict time-frame for performing the task. Recognising the difficulty of immediately evaluating a new system in the classroom, we follow an iterative process similar to the one in Section 2.1, but this time we gradually increase the number of students and the ecological validity of the situation. To approximate, therefore, the envisaged context of usage, we first involve a small group of students—we found six to eight students to be a manageable number—and their teacher in a session that resembles as much as possible the classroom set-up. That is, instead of inviting them to a session in our lab, we ensure that the session is conducted in an appropriate classroom at their school.

By incrementally approximating an authentic classroom set-up we are able to observe the impact of the system's actual use and the issues under consideration in an—as much as possible—ecologically valid context. One researcher observes the sessions while at least one other acts as a teaching assistant in order to provide the support that students require in this exploratory learning context. The sources of data collected include: (a) field notes with observations; (b) video of the whole classroom and screen recordings of the individual students when possible; (c) audio-recording of the teacher and the teaching assistants (and particularly their interventions); and (d) post-session interviews with teachers. The data in (b) are synchronised and are later analysed and annotated with the help of the observations and the audio recordings. Such a rich pool of data enables in-depth analyses from multiple perspectives. In our case, they have helped us identify which intelligent support strategies within the system need amendment in order to better support the classroom context. After a series of such evaluations, and resultant evolutions of the system, we are in a position to trial the system in an actual classroom. The next section provides examples.

3 ICE FOR INFORMING THE DESIGN OF MIGEN

3.1 The MiGen Project

The MiGen project set out to develop a system that contributes to the teaching and learning of algebra in secondary education (Noss et al., 2012). The system revolves around a mathematical microworld, called eXpresser, designed to help students develop algebraic ways of thinking (see Mavrikis et al., 2013). In brief, in eXpresser students undertake activities that require them to construct algebraic rules that underpin figural patterns composed of square tiles (see Figure 7.2). Similar activities are often found in the UK National Curriculum and have the potential to help students understand that their algebraic rules can derive from the structure they observe in the pattern and thus provide a rationale for using algebra to express generalisations. For more details the reader is referred to Noss et al. (2012) where key difficulties that students face in this domain are presented along with references to related work. Figure 7.2 describes the main features of eXpresser.

In order to support students (and, indirectly, the teacher) in the classroom, MiGen's intelligent components analyse students' interactions and, in combination with information stored in the MiGen database about students and tasks, generate real-time feedback for students. In order to determine the most appropriate form of feedback, a set of rules are used to combine information about the student's current construction and recent history of actions (Gutierrez-Santos et al., 2012a). The possible types of feedback were identified by following the Iterative Communication Capacity Tapering methodology (Mavrikis and Gutierrez-Santos, 2010), core findings of which are presented in Section 3.2.

The system's intelligent components also detect or infer a series of interaction indicators which are notified to the teacher via the Teacher Assistance (TA) tools (Pearce-Lazard et al., 2010; Gutierrez-Santos et al., 2012b). This is a suite of tools aimed at assisting the teacher in monitoring students' activities, informing her own interventions in

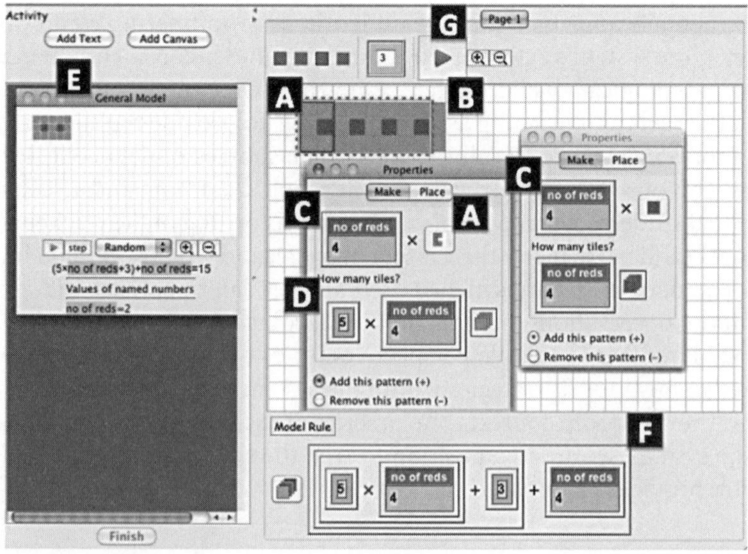

Figure 7.2 The eXpresser microworld. Letters highlight its main features: (A) a C-shaped building block made of five tiles is repeated to make a pattern; (B) a pattern made out of one tile repeated three times in the vertical direction completes the model; (C) the number of repetitions of the building block (A) is 'no of reds'; (D) the number of green (light grey) tiles in this pattern; (E) in the Computer's Model, the system chooses different values for the unlocked number, 'no of reds', and in this case it has chosen the value 2; (F) the student's Model Rule that specifies the total number of tiles in their model; (G) students can click this button to animate their model.

the class, and reviewing students' achievements so as to plan the next lesson. These tools run on the teacher's computer (or device such as a tablet) and provide graphical representations of the occurrence of significant events during students' constructions, students' accomplishment of task goals, students' possible disengagement from the task, and students in need of help. The identification of appropriate interaction indicators to notify to the teacher via the TA tools was also accomplished through application of our contextualised iterative methodology (see Gutierrez-Santos et al., 2012).

3.2 Iterative Communication Capacity Tapering

In order to help the reader appreciate the Iterative Context Engineering methodology, we present here three key findings related to design of the MiGen system.

First, following the Iterative Communication Capacity Tapering described in Section 2.1 facilitated the fine-tuning of the intrusiveness of the intelligent support provided by the system to the student. General pedagogic principles and early face-to-face sessions suggested that a microworld environment provides interesting learning opportunities, particularly when students reach an impasse and the system's support is likely to be perceived by the student as being welcome rather than intrusive. The iterative methodology we followed allowed us to identify such moments and to design the intelligent support to detect and deal with such cases (see examples in Mavrikis et al., in press).

Second, the wizard-of-Oz sessions established that even the pedagogical experts observing students' interactions had difficulties identifying the type of help the students required. Despite the fact that the experts had access to a larger bandwidth of information than the system (including being able to see the whole of the student's screen, mouse movements, etc.), we had restricted on purpose the possibility of natural language interaction, since implementing natural language processing and understanding was out of the scope of our system development. The difficulties that the experts faced and the mismatch between what students required and the type of help that the experts offered, led us to develop a list of possible types of help that would be available from the system at any given time for the student. These alternatives appear in a drop-down menu from which the student selects the option that is most appropriate for them at that moment.

Last, early design sessions demonstrated a clear need for drawing students' attention to parts of their constructions on screen through language and gestures (see Figure 7.3).

In these sessions the context of the interaction was not only the computer, but included a human facilitator. Moving the design on to the next stage, suppressing the communication capacity of the human facilitator, introduced difficulties as objects on the screen could only be referred to through the use of ambiguous anaphoric and deictic language. To test whether these difficulties could be overcome, we first used screen-sharing software that includes annotation facilities.[1] After evaluating the potential of this type of interaction, we subsequently undertook studies close to the conventional wizard-of-Oz paradigm, where the only means of communication is an interface to display messages as well as the interactive support features of the system. This led to the development of computer-based support messages designed to be co-located with the student's construction on the student's screen and to be able to point to parts of their model. In other words, we had to adapt a perceived need for support in the learning process from one context to another; in this case, the computer alone without a human expert on hand to point to the student's screen. An example of the final implementation of the computer-based support messages appears in Figure 7.3b (and more details in Gutierrez-Santos et al., 2012a).

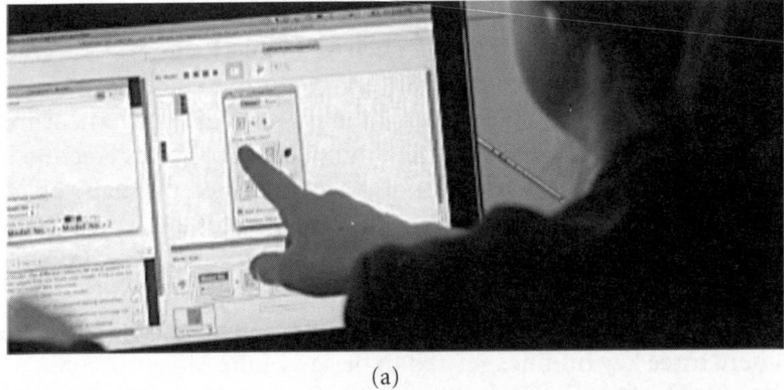

(a)

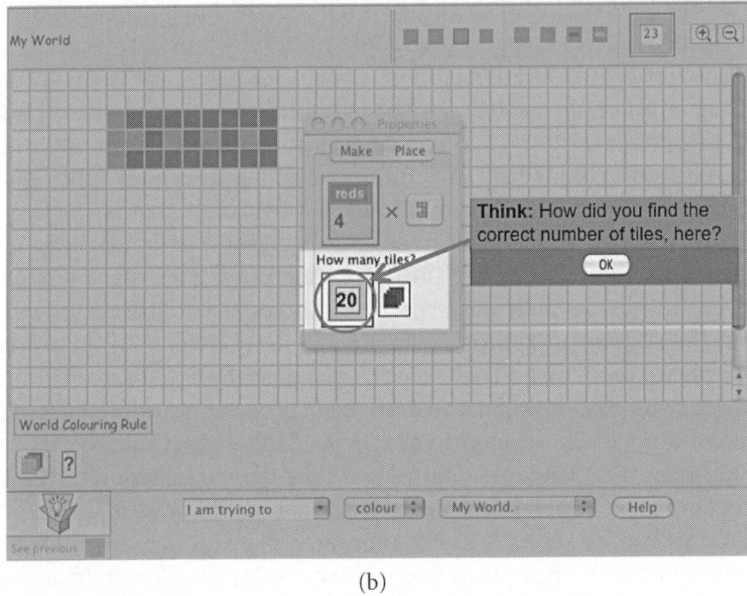

(b)

Figure 7.3 From deictic language and gestures (a) in face-to-face sessions to co-located automated feedback messages (b) With permission from Mavrikis et al. (in press).

3.3 Iterative Classroom Authenticity

In the context of the MiGen project, approximating a classroom set-up (even with small groups of students, as discussed earlier) allowed us to identify the difference between one-to-one feedback provided by a teacher in a single-student context and that of a classroom situation, and to prioritise the types of feedback that were more appropriate for the envisaged context of use. For example, we quickly identified that support for some pragmatic and technical aspects in relation to eXpresser (e.g. how to create tiles for the first time) was less important as these could be resolved by peer interaction and discussion.

In addition, early sessions with the system helped to overcome the difficulties arising from teachers' lack of familiarity with using such tools in their lessons. In early design workshops, it proved extremely difficult for us to derive a coherent set of requirements from our teacher collaborators. By adopting an agile, iterative methodology that comprised successive phases of prototyping and by actively engaging the teachers who were collaborating with us in actual experiences using the system in the classroom, we were able to give them the opportunity to provide more informed feedback for future development of the system based on their practical observations and reflections from the real context of the classroom, with students working with the eXpresser in real time, rather than commenting on a hypothetical scenario. This is crucially important since, in our experience, teachers are able to reflect more deeply and to provide better insights into the effectiveness of a system when they are able to use it in practice for themselves. Also, being able to observe different teachers who might have different teaching styles can suggest a variety of requirements and inform the design of a more complete system that can be used effectively by most teachers.

As an example, when we began running sessions with a larger number of students, the need to detect students who are off-task became evident. The design team (including the teachers) had overlooked the fact that in some schools students have access to the Internet and can use it to perform off-task activities (e.g. playing web games) when the teacher cannot see their computer screens. In some cases we realised that this behaviour was a common occurrence due to the placement of computers in the classroom—the teacher could only see a few computer screens at a time. An example of such a situation is shown in Figure 7.4.

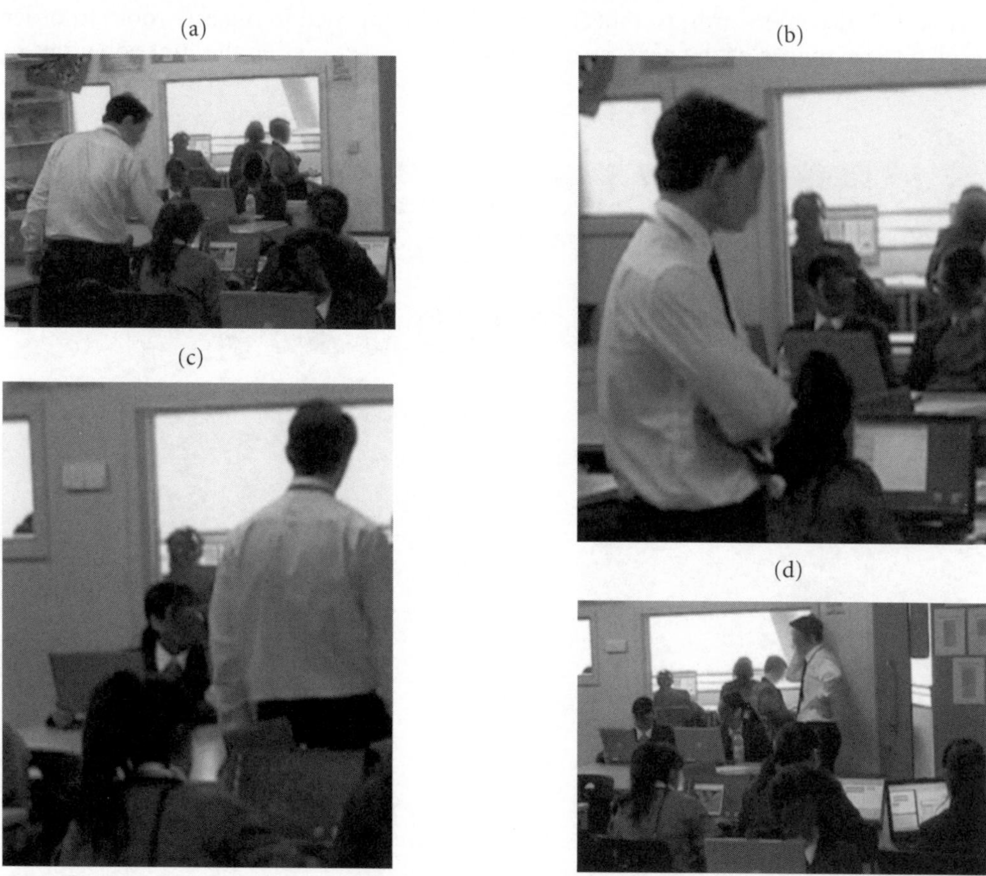

Figure 7.4 (a) The teacher brings a student (who is playing a web game) back onto the eXpresser task. (b) The student is working in the eXpresser while the teacher is nearby. (c) The minute the teacher moves away the student closes eXpresser again. (d) The student reverts to playing the web game while the teacher is interacting with other students..

These realisations led to the design of a Classroom Dynamics (CD) tool for the teacher (Pearce-Lazard et al., 2010; Gutierrez-Santos et al., 2012). This tool is designed to increase the teacher's awareness of the classroom state at all times, so as to decide which students to prioritise in helping and which students might be inactive or not achieving the task goals. Figure 7.5 illustrates the visual display of the CD tool. Each student in the classroom is represented by a circle containing their initials. The circles are arranged in a display that matches the students' positions in the classroom (the teacher can do this quickly at the start of the lesson). A green circle indicates that the student is currently working on the task set, while an amber circle indicates that the student is likely to be off-task. Also contained in each circle is an indication of how many of the task goals the student has achieved so far in the lesson (e.g. 2/4 indicates that 2 out of the total of 4 goals have been achieved).

As we gradually developed early prototypes of this tool, we observed teachers using it in the classroom and even publicly displaying it to the class as a means of regulating students' interaction: as one of the teachers put it, 'I can see everything that you are doing, so you'd better focus on the task'. Similarly, by conducting a series of classroom sessions, we identified that teachers wanted to use the TA tools not only during the classroom session but also afterwards, to reflect on what had happened in the classroom in order to plan the activities of the next lesson. This allowed us to refine the functionalities of

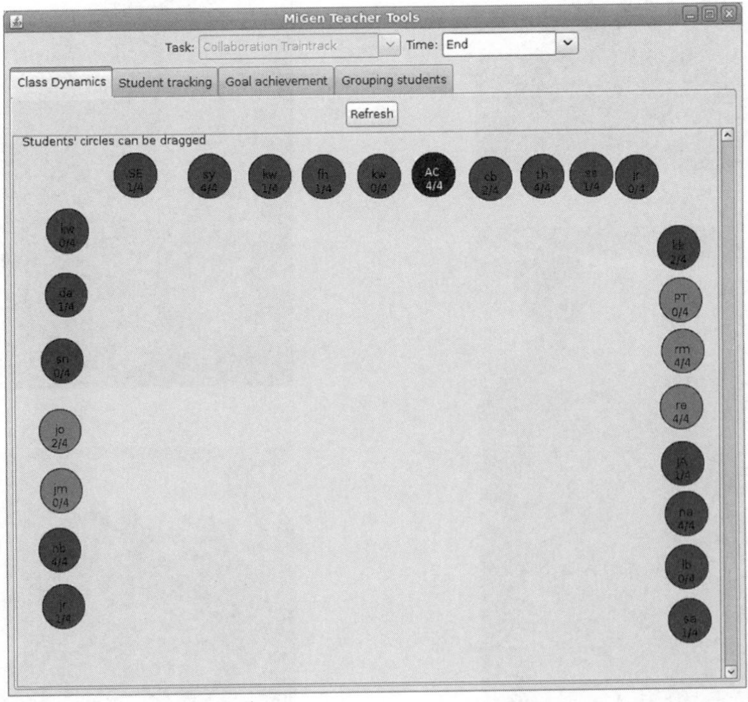

Figure 7.5 A screenshot of the Class Dynamics tool. The tool shows students as working (green shown as dark grey in print), inactive (amber, light grey), or waiting for the teacher to help (red, black), showing teachers at a glance where to focus their attention. In this example, the students are shown in the arrangement they had in the classroom, (a U-configuration) but the teacher can choose any arrangement by moving the circles accordingly.

the Student Tracking (ST) tool (see Pearce-Lazard et al., 2010; Gutierrez-Santos et al., 2012) so that teachers were presented with a small set of the most significant interaction indicators to track using this tool during the lesson but were able to have access to the full range of indicators to reflect on after the lesson.

Another example from the suite of TA tools is the Grouping Tool, which helps the teacher to create groups for collaborative activities that follow students' individual constructions using the eXpresser. The Grouping Tool suggests groupings of students based on how students have undertaken the task in order to maximise their opportunities of discussion, and therefore their opportunities for reflection and learning (Noss et al., 2012). This grouping of students is a complicated process that would require a significant amount of time to undertake manually (in our early observations, before the Grouping Tool was developed, it took an experienced teacher around one hour to perform). In practice that meant that either teachers created groups based on their own observations of how students were approaching the task while walking around the classroom, or they were postponing the collaborative activities to the next lesson, after they had had a chance to view each student's construction and to perform the grouping manually. In contrast, our Grouping Tool is able to provide grouping suggestions to the teacher within a few seconds, helping them to quickly initiate productive discussion-intensive collaborative activities between students, using the discussion tool that the MiGen system also provides.

4 CONCLUSION

This chapter has outlined key aspects of the methodology underlying our design-based research, with the aim of informing the design of intelligent components that can provide support to students and teachers in ELEs. Our research methodology follows iterative cycles of research and development that recognise the potentially transformative nature of intelligent support and the particular requirements arising in response to the need to design systems that support not only the students but also their teacher.

Our approach has enabled us to derive theoretically motivated and empirically validated pedagogical strategies for support and has provided a framework for modelling the teacher's role while establishing useful strategies to help students in approaching the ideal (but impossible to achieve) one-to-one setting. We highlighted the need for empirical fine-tuning of the relevant educational theories and the gradual tapering of the interaction bandwidth in wizard-of-Oz studies that help the knowledge elicitation process. We also described the methodology and rationale behind in-situ studies that help us refine the design of the system and provide the teachers collaborating with us the experience of contributing actively and significantly to the design of the system. This approach helps us to take into account, as the MiGen system is developed and refined, the range and complexity of the classroom context in which the system will be deployed.

NOTE

1. We used Vision, a classroom sharing tool equipped with Netop's Pointer plugin (see http://www.codework.com/vision/pointer.php).

REFERENCES

Balacheff, N. and Sutherland, R. (1994). Epistemological domain of validity of microworlds: the case of logo and cabri-géomètre. In *Proceedings of the IFIP TC3/WG3.3 Working Conference on Lessons from Learning*, pages 137–150, Amsterdam, the Netherlands. North-Holland Publishing Co.

Barab, S. (2006). Design-based research: a methodological toolkit for the learning sciences. In Sawyer, K., editor, *Handbook of the Learning Sciences* (pp. 153–169). Cambridge, MA: Cambridge University Press.

Bernsen, N. O., Dybkjaer, H., and Dybkjaer, L. (1998). *Designing Interactive Speech Systems. From First Ideas to User Testing*. Berlin: Springer.

Beyer, H. and Holtzblatt, K. (1997). *Contextual Design: Defining Customer-Centered Systems (Interactive Technologies)*. San Francisco: Morgan Kaufmann.

Chignell, M. H. (1990). A taxonomy of user interface terminology. *SIGCHI Bull.*, 21(4): 27.

Conati, C. and Maclaren, H. (2004). Evaluating a Probabilistic Model of Student Affect. In *Proceedings of Intelligent Tutoring Systems 2004*, LNCS 3220, pages 55–66. Berlin: Springer.

Dahlback, N., Jonsson, A., and Ahrenberg, L. (1993). Wizard of Oz studies: why and how. In *IUI '93: Proceedings of the 1st International Conference on Intelligent User Interfaces*, pages 193–200, New York: ACM Press.

Disessa, A. A., Azevedo, F. S., and Parnafes, O. (2004). Issues in component computing: a synthetic review. *Interactive Learning Environments*, 12(1): 109–159.

Disessa, A. A. and Cobb, P. (2004). Ontological innovation and the role of theory in design experiments. *Journal of the Learning Sciences*, 13(1): 77–103.

Dourish, P. (2004). What we talk about when we talk about context. *Personal Ubiquitous Computing*, 8: 19–30.

du Boulay, B. and Luckin, R. (2001). Modelling human teaching tactics and strategies for tutoring systems. *International Journal of Artificial Intelligence in Education*, 12: 235–256.

Fiedler, A., Gabsdil, M., and Horacek, H. (2004). A tool for supporting progressive refinement of wizard-of-oz experiments in natural language. In *International Conference on Intelligent Tutoring Systems*, pages 325–335, New York.

Gould, J. D. and Lewis, C. (1985). Designing for usability: key principles and what designers think. *Communications of the ACM*, 28(3): 300–311.

Gutierrez-Santos, S., Mavrikis, M., and Magoulas, G. D. (2012). A Separation of Concerns for Engineering Intelligent Support for Exploratory Learning Environments. Journal of Research and Practice in Information Technology, 44(3), August 2012, ISSN 1443–458X.

Gutierrez-Santos, S., Geraniou, E., Pearce-Lazard, D., and Poulovassilis, A. (2012). The design of teacher assistance tools in an exploratory learning environment for algebraic generalisation. *IEEE Transactions in Learning Technologies*, 5(4): 366–376.

Luckin, R. (2011). *Re-designing learning contexts: technology-rich, learner-centred ecologies*. London: Routledge.

Luckin, R., Underwood, J., du Boulay, B., Holmberg, J., Kerawalla, L., O'Connor, J., et al. (2006). Designing educational systems fit for use: A case study in the application of human centred design for AIED. *International Journal of Artificial Intelligence in Education*, 16(4): 353–380.

Maulsby, D., Greenberg, S., and Mander, R. (1993). Prototyping an intelligent agent through Wizard of Oz. In *CHI '93: Proceedings of the INTERACT '93 and CHI '93 conference on Human factors in computing systems*, pages 277–284. New York: ACM.

Mavrikis, M. and Gutierrez-Santos, S. (2010). Not all wizards are from Oz: Iterative design of intelligent learning environments by communication capacity tapering. *Computers & Education*, 54(3): 641–651.

Mavrikis, M., Noss, R., Hoyles, C., and Geraniou, E. (2013). Sowing the seeds of algebraic generalisation: designing epistemic affordances for an intelligent microworld. *Special Issue on Knowledge Transformation, Design and Technology, Journal of Computer Assisted Learning*, 29(1): 68–85.

Mavrikis, M., Gutierrez-Santos, S., Geraniou, E., Noss, R. (in press). Design requirements, student perception indicators and validation metrics for intelligent exploratory learning environments. *Personal and Ubiquitous Computing*.

Noss, R., Poulovassilis, A., Geraniou, E., Gutierrez-Santos, S., Hoyles, C., Kahn, K., et al. (2012). The design of a system to support exploratory learning of algebraic generalisation. *Computers and Education*, 59(1): 68–81.

Pearce-Lazard, D., Poulovassilis, A. and Geraniou, E. (2010). The design of teacher assistance tools in an exploratory learning environment for mathematics generalisation. In Cress, U., Dimitrova, V., and Specht, M., editors, *Sustaining TEL: From Innovation to Learning and Practice*, volume 6383, pages 260–275. Berlin/Heidelberg: Springer.

Porayska-Pomsta, K. and Pain, H. (2004). Exploring methodologies for building socially and emotionally intelligent learning environments. In *Workshop on Social and Emotional Intelligence in Learning Environments*, Maceio, Brazil.

Rizzo, P., Lee, H., Shaw, E., Johnson, L. W., Wang, N., and Mayer, R. E. (2005). A semi-automated Wizard of Oz interface for modeling tutorial strategies. In *User Modeling 2005*, pages 174–178. Springer.

Self, J. (1999). The defining characteristics of intelligent tutoring systems research: ITSs care, precisely. *International Journal of Artificial Intelligence in Education*, 10: 350–364.

Wilson, J. and Rosenberg, D. (1988). Rapid prototyping for user interface design. In Helander, M., editor, *Handbook of Human-Computer Interaction*, pages 859–875. Elsevier Science Publishers.

8

SKETCH-INS: A METHOD FOR PARTICIPATORY DESIGN IN TECHNOLOGY-ENHANCED LEARNING

Brock Craft

INTRODUCTION

One of the most useful and inexpensive tools for designing technology-enhanced learning (TEL) systems is probably on your desk right now. I am not referring to lightweight programming environments, developer tools, mock-ups and wireframes, or even paper prototypes. No, I mean the humble bit of graphite enrobed within a couple of pieces of wood—the pencil. In this chapter, I will describe 'Sketch-ins', a participatory design approach that leverages the value of freehand sketching for creativity, collaboration, and problem solving in TEL design teams with two or more participants. A Sketch-in is a group design activity in which participants use freehand sketching to collaboratively identify, process, and resolve design problems. The approach is simple, rapid, requires only a few inexpensive tools, and is suitable for a wide variety of TEL design problems, including creating new software or re-engineering existing systems. I will explain the kind of problems you might expect to solve, how to set up and run a Sketch-in, and what you can expect to get out of it. Along the way, I will also highlight some of the research on why and how sketching works.

Designers of TEL systems[1] are continuing to leverage experiences and knowledge drawn from other software engineering communities of practice and it is generally accepted that iterative, user-centred approaches are essential in building TEL tools. Participatory design techniques, learner context-focused approaches (Luckin, 2010), and the use of design patterns (Mor & Winters, 2007; Laurillard & Ljubojevic, 2011) have seen significant research and adoption in recent years. While these have proved fruitful, substantial interest remains in new approaches to solving design problems in TEL.

Sketching is such a successful method that it is central to the design-oriented disciplines, including architecture, engineering, and visual communication. It is also a significant part of the pedagogy of these disciplines (Laseau, 2000). Freehand sketching is a way of playing with ideas, visually rendering the concepts that are in the mind of the person doing the sketching. It facilitates externalising the internal and involves creating and eliminating, modifying and compromising, and weighing possibilities (Fallman, 2003).

Sketching also encourages creative exploration of ideas that might not be fully formed, but where there is a specific goal in mind. It is one part of the larger design process that consists of 'a spectrum of design activities dealing with both precise and vague ideas, . . . systematic and chaotic thinking, . . . imaginative thought and mechanical calculation' (Lawson, 1997, p. 4).

Bill Buxton, a respected designer of interactive systems within the human–computer interaction (HCI) community, emphasises the importance of sketching and further contends that it is essential for designing software and interfaces (Buxton, 2007). Drawing from Goel's (1995) research into how sketching supports cognition, he contends that sketching is a fundamental part of any design process and that designers use sketching in specific ways to help them with their creative activities. Yet, although experienced designers use sketching in quite different ways (see Goel (1995) and Schön (1983)), it can also be employed by those who might not normally consider themselves designers.

Current research has provided concrete evidence of the value and cognitive mechanisms of sketching in the design process, in three ways: controlled experiments (see Balasubramanian, Turoff, & Ullman, 1998; van der Lugt, 2002; Heiser, Tversky, & Silverman, 2004), linking sketching with creativity (see Suwa & Tversky, 1997; Suwa, Tversky, Gero, & Purcell, 2001; Goldschmidt, 1991), and identifying cognitive supports of sketching (see Boden, 2004; Goel, 1992; Plimmer & Apperley, 2002; Tversky et al., 2003). Notably, Van der Lugt's research employed a technique referred to as 'brainsketching', in which participants generated individual sketches and presented them for group evaluation. These were used as a source of inspiration for additional iterations of sketching and evaluation activity. Sketching supported individual re-interpretive cycles of idea generation, and enhanced individual and group access to earlier ideas. Sketch-ins can be seen as an extension of this technique for TEL.

Recognising the benefits in other design disciplines, the HCI community has long acknowledged the role of sketching along with other techniques, such as low-fidelity prototyping and modelling (Fallman, 2003). Since freehand sketching can facilitate ideation, creativity, and problem solving in design processes for a variety of human–machine systems, it then follows that the design of TEL systems can also benefit. Although the value of sketching for the design of learning has begun to be identified and discussed (see, notably, Botturi & Stubbs, 2008; Hokanson, 2008), few authors have described the role of sketching in facilitating the design of software for learning (Stubbs & Gibbons, 2008), or how to use sketching for this purpose. Sketch-ins, as one of a variety methods for participatory design of TEL systems, aim to address this.

RUNNING A SKETCH-IN

Overview

Sketch-in sessions yield concrete outcomes: problems identified, ideas generated, internal representations elicited, and often, problems solved. Moreover, sketches cost almost nothing to produce, whereas a prototype requires more time, effort, and money to build. Supplementary data collected during the sessions, such as audio or video recordings, can also be useful. Sketch-ins can be employed with mixed teams of experienced and novice designers, as well as stakeholders not writing the software, most importantly teachers and students. Consider the following characteristics in determining whether Sketch-ins will work for you.

Sketch-ins are learner-centred, exploratory, and generative. They are ideal for grappling with design ideas that might not yet be in focus, or for situations in which you need to elicit a variety of perspectives from within the design team, and should be seen as a way to supplement design knowledge around the problems at hand. You can use Sketch-ins to:

- invite a wide range of design ideas;
- raise questions about the design;
- identify and explore design problems;
- elicit representations of/views on these problems;
- spark creativity;
- suggest alternatives and solutions.

Sketch-ins will be fruitful if the above are among your goals, and if you can marshal a small team who are familiar enough with your project to have an opinion about how it should look, operate, the tasks it might support, and how learners might interact with it. You can run a Sketch-in session in about two hours. If you have more time or participants at your disposal, consider running a series of sessions to iteratively explore design issues. Sketch-ins can be used at any stage of the design process, but are particularly useful for early work, when ideas are most nascent and unformed. They can also be used for re-design activities, when specific problems must be addressed, such as deciding on the elements of a user interface, identifying sequences of steps needed to complete a task, or even uncovering major conceptual differences among participants about the purpose of the software. Sketching can crystallise issues users might have with existing software and help them to elaborate solutions. These kinds of problems and needs can serve to frame the sketching activities that the team will explore.

The Sketch-in process comprises the following stages:

- framing the area of enquiry for the Sketch-in session(s);
- organising the session and selecting participants;
- running the session and collecting data;
- reflecting upon the generated results.

From a high-level perspective, Sketch-ins follow several phases of expansion and idea generation, followed by contraction, refinement, and idea crystallisation. Buxton (2007), drawing upon Laseau (2000), asserts that the design process is one in which there are overlapping objectives of exploring and elaborating ideas whilst gradually narrowing the possibilities through decision-making. These can be represented as overlapping funnels in the Sketch-in process. In this model, Elaboration is a process of embellishment that emphasises increasing alternatives; Reduction through decision-making refers to paring down options with the objective of arriving at possible design(s).

This is similar to Laseau's model of the early phases of design, which emphasises generating a widening set of possibilities, represented by diverging lines in Figure 8.1. The following sections describe each of the Sketch-in stages in more detail, with examples of what you might expect from your work.

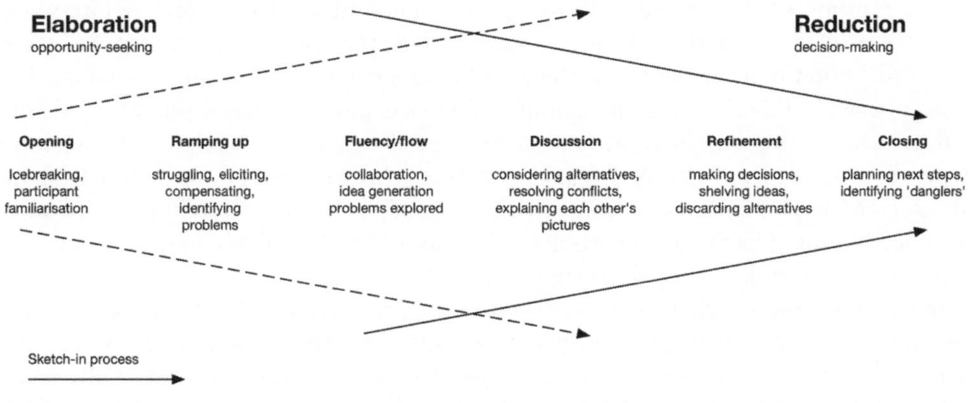

Figure 8.1 Overview of Sketch-ins within the design process, adapted from Buxton (2007).

Framing the Work

Prior to starting, you will need to frame the Sketch-in around a particular question or topic. Otherwise, participants could be confused and the work will lack focus. Try to formulate a general area for the work to be centred on. In one project from my work involving a learning tool for the human liver (Craft, 2006), the participants felt that they needed a common representation of the same problem. Each stakeholder had a different understanding of what the problem 'looked like'. We framed the Sketch-ins around eliciting everyone's views on how to visually represent the topic to learners. This gave the participants a focus for the session and elicited the many different ways participants represented the problem to themselves. It also exposed the differences in how they thought the key learning goals should be addressed. One of the broad questions related to how to ensure learners would understand a sequence of calculations about liver metabolism. This was used as one of the framing topics for the Sketch-in. The participants used sketching to engage with and share their own conceptions about this topic and arrived at the rough idea of using a 'jigsaw puzzle' metaphor for widgets in the user interface, where each piece would represent an algorithm. This would limit learners to only connecting together valid sequences of calculations, and support their understanding of how metabolism algorithms are constructed.

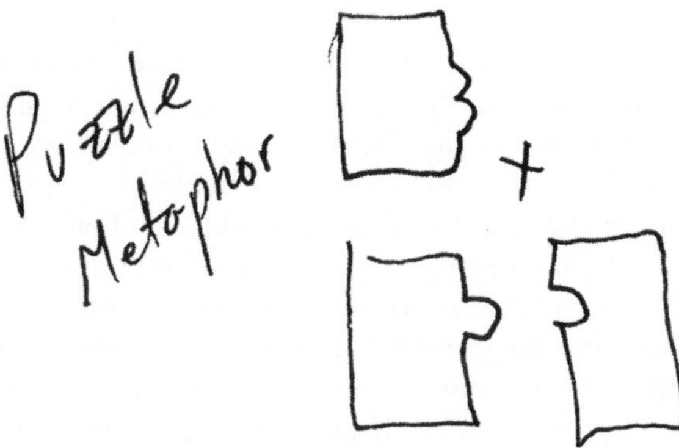

Figure 8.2 Creating a visual metaphor for software behaviour.

The framing of the problem can be quite vague and need not even be phrased in terms of a specific question. As the work proceeds, the way that a problem is framed and understood typically shifts, as the stakeholders begin to share and crystallise their conceptions. In this situation, sketching facilitates exploring what is relevant and what is not. How the problem is framed and the degree to which this shifts over the session is dependent on the state of the system under development. Are you in the initial phases of research, do you have some simple working prototypes already? Will participants be completely unfamiliar with the problem domain, or are they likely to have some ideas about how to start designing the system?

In framing your Sketch-in, consider these questions and try to identify the most pressing questions about the project. With a few starter questions in mind, it can be useful to write down an idea or two about the topics you will want to address. You can also solicit help from your participants in framing/reframing the work in an icebreaker activity (see below).

Assembling the Team

If possible, select a group of three to five participants for the work. In small groups each person can reflect and act, but there is not usually enough social space for one of the participants to remain completely idle. Groups of two work less well, because the activity tends to become dialogic. More than five is unworkable, because large groups tend to be dominated by one or two people and to get into 'design by committee' discussions; worse, few people actually end up sketching. Break large groups into smaller teams of three or four. Small groups also ensure that everyone has easy access to the paper where sketching is happening.

Sketch-ins should involve various stakeholders and their situations on the project. Participants might include: project leaders, software engineers, non-technical end users, and ideally teachers and learners. Consider anyone with a general idea of the project subject domain as a potential candidate and, of course, try to include people who might actually use such a system to learn from. In fact, it can be quite beneficial to intentionally enlist team members who are from very different parts of the TEL project you are investigating. They will have very different perspectives on the problem and these wide differences can have the effect of reframing boundaries, exposing more clearly what is relevant and what is not.

Facilitating

In leading the Sketch-in, you will likely take on the role of facilitator. The challenge for the facilitator is to provide motivation to keep your participants working without overly influencing the direction of the discussion. In participatory design, it is reasonable to provide input into the work of the session, particularly in cases where your knowledge and expertise are important for solving the problems that informants are working through. It is sufficient to provide support to spark alternative ideas and keep the discussion going, but without taking too much time away from others. Your aim is to help the participants to feel comfortable working together and to guide them in the process.

If you have another person who can also facilitate, this can be helpful. Having an extra colleague to help provides not only extra eyes, but also extra hands for recording observations. If you are working with more than one group, it is handy to be able to switch among teams with another facilitator to monitor progress and to provide input and assistance. Managing the tools and resources you will use is also easier with a second set of eyes.

Materials

There are only a few tools you will need to facilitate the work and to capture the activity. The most obvious are the sketching tools, but the environment itself also acts as a tool to structure the work. You may also want to use some additional methods of data collection.

Sketching tools: you will want to have a wide variety of writing tools for people to be able to make their own aesthetic choices. This will engage participants with the kind of mark they are going to produce and make it personal to them. It can also be useful for tracking who sketched what, during analysis. Make sure to have at least three implements per participant, ideally many more.

Pencils: the unsung heroes on your desk. Use good quality HB or No. 2 pencils that make a clean, dark mark. I prefer pencils without erasers so that the false starts, errors, and changes in approach are preserved on the paper.

Pens: make sure to provide them in a range of colours and thicknesses. Very fine line pens are not ideal because they are often hard to see from afar and if the drawings will be used for group reflection or presentation later, the fine lines will not be readable. A good variety of liquid ball pens or marker pens are best. Multipack marker pen selections are a good solution.

Paper: Use uncoloured, A3 size at a minimum. Flip charts are a good source of large paper sheets, made with just good enough quality to do the work, and at a reasonable price. Choose a durable paper if you intend to keep the results. It is also good to have masking and clear adhesive tape to hold down the paper, and some sticky notes.

Setting: a small conference room is sufficient. It should be well lit and comfortable. It is very important that your groups can sit in-the-round at a table. This is why small groups are essential. Place the sketching tools at the centre of the table and make sure everyone can access the materials. You are creating a collaborative sketch space, and even though people will often make individual sketches, others might want to add, embellish, or sketch upon the work of their teammates. If you have multiple groups, each should be working in an area where they will not be disturbed by the discussions of the other work groups.

Data collection: the primary source of data will be the sketched artefacts that your participants produce—the sheets of paper. You might also want to keep track of what goes on in a session by recording audio. Portable MP3 audio recorders provide enough detail to reconstruct what was being considered as sketches were being made. Video is only really useful if you can see both the sketches and the participants who are speaking, and this is rarely practical. The additional burden of setting up cameras and tripods, their intrusiveness, and the labour-intensiveness of video analysis are all major drawbacks compared to audio. Unless you need video evidence for some reason or can use unobtrusive cameras such as on smart phones, it is usually not worth the effort.

You will also need a clock or timer to track your progress and keep to deadlines for the various activities. Bear in mind that some of the best work occurs in the middle and end of the session, after people have generated some ideas and considered alternatives, so do not short-change yourself by running out of time. You need not adhere to a strict schedule, but it is useful to note the following stages of a session (as illustrated in Figure 8.1), and pace the work accordingly.

Opening: a few minutes of introducing your participants to each other and the problems at hand. The facilitator begins by describing what the group will do, how long it will take, and what the results might be. You should then organise people into groups and familiarise them with the sketching materials. You can use an icebreaker activity to get everyone comfortable with working together, particularly if members of the team have not met before. One such activity might be to have participants write ideas on slips of paper as a spark. These are collected and ranked together. Then the facilitator asks participants to draw out what the highly ranked ideas might look like.

Ramping up: about 15–20 minutes of uncertainty, as people overcome their fears about sketching and try to begin to express themselves. Here is where the sketching begins. The facilitator should ask people to begin sketching out some of the ideas they might have and relate these to the framing topic. Participants begin to create diagrams and sketches of their thinking. People will often need a good nudge to sketch something out, so give them encouragement by asking them to draw anything at all—not to worry about the details of whether something is right or wrong.

Fluency/flow: the bulk of the work during which ideas are generated, representations made, and problems uncovered. Participants discuss ideas about how to solve interaction problems with the system and when they are working well, are able to identify learning problems that are addressed. At this point, if a really valuable sketch is generated, it can be useful to add a timestamp to the sketch right away, to be used for later reference if you are recording audio.

Regrouping (if in multiple groups)/discussion: At some point, the idea will start to be 'played out' and the conversations will begin to mature, or you might be running out of time. Participants may also begin to go over the same ground in finer detail. It can be helpful to kick this off with a question such as, 'What picture from this group is most intriguing/important?'

Refinement: This is where the sketches start to take on less importance generatively, and instead become talking points for discussion and refinement. You can pick out the best suggestions later for discussion.

Denouement/closure: Discuss what you have accomplished and what problems have been raised. Decide upon future steps and whether further sessions would be beneficial.

WHAT TO EXPECT

The use of generic kinds of user-interface widgets is fairly firmly established within the collective experience of computer users and will likely be very familiar to the members of your design team. As the work progresses, participants will often suggest using familiar user-interface widgets and as part of a solution to a design problem the team has uncovered. It is common for someone to suggest, 'We'll need a drop-down menu here' or 'Let's add a button here for that', or other GUI-based solutions. It is important to let these ideas play out, whether they seem like good ideas or not. The objective is to get information on paper. It is not the time to test whether or not a particular solution will actually do the job.

For example, in another project I worked on involving teachers-in-training, one participant was confident that a specific sequence of learning activities and the ratios of their learning types would improve students' learning. She represented the ratios with pie and bar charts. This particular representation did not end up being developed for the final

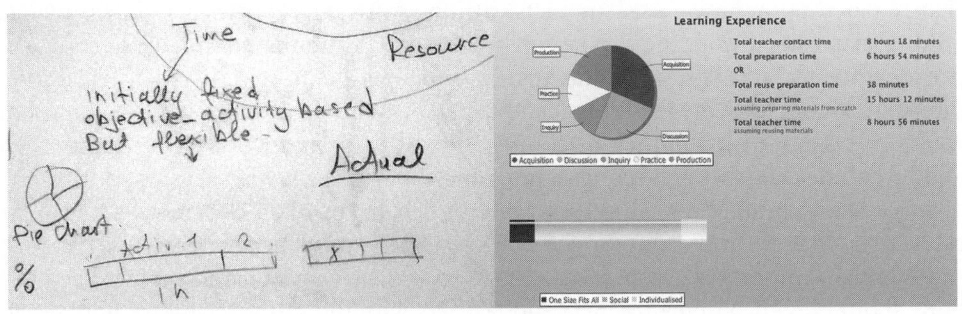

Figure 8.3 Identification of user-interface elements as sketched (left) and as implemented (right).

interface design, but it highlighted the importance of representing the ratios of learning types, when creating learning sequences. Later design work refined this representation and interaction for the final user interface.

Getting Stuck

Sometimes, participants will get hung up on a particular problem or will seem to have run out of steam. In these situations, it can be a bit awkward if there is nothing to fall back on and no guidance that you can provide. Thus, it is a good idea to have a selection of questions ready to prompt further work.

Sometimes you might notice that a group seems to be having a good and lively discussion but there is nothing on the paper. Although the point of the session is to get people to collaborate, keep in mind the goal of elucidating what is inside people's heads. It can be helpful to explicitly remind participants to sketch. One way of doing this is by prompting people at key junctures in the discussion. You might gently intervene at such points and ask simple prompting questions:

'Can you show me what that might look like?'

'Could you draw that out for me?'

'What does that look like for you?

'Can you sketch it out?'

It is also important to provide positive feedback on progress. Some of your participants will not have drawn a sketch since kindergarten. Just as with children, a little encouragement goes a long way.

As the session draws to a close, allow a few minutes to review the design activity. This can be some of the most valuable work that the team will do, because it allows them to reflect upon their work together and verbalise their experience of each other's sketches, thinking, and conceptualisations of the problem. Underscore the key ideas for later use and jot down notes about what particularly important sketches mean and the problems they solve. Write descriptive notes on the sketches themselves. The sketches can be used as evidence for later decisions and can serve as foci for subsequent Sketch-in sessions.

Following the Sketch-in approach will generate many ideas and will help to identify key design problems and potential solutions in your TEL system. However, there are a few limitations. One is that sketches often cannot tackle highly interactive visualisations where the dynamic representation is a key part of the interaction. People tend to work around this by drawing storyboards. But in situations where the data or representation change based upon how a user interacts with the software, sketches can only provide a limited snapshot of what the system might look like. You might also have to cope with participants who are resistant to drawing. Some people are more verbal than visual and it can be uncomfortable for them to pick up a pen. 'I'm no good at drawing' is a common apology. It is best to accept their discomfort, provide reassurances, and encourage them to do what they can. More often than not, others on the team will make up for this.

Successfully conducting a Sketch-in session will help you to quickly and effectively elucidate ideas that are important for your TEL system. You will be able to inspire creativity and highlight important design ideas. The team will also develop and explore key questions about how to support teachers and learners with the software, and explore design problems more deeply. The sketches could also lay the groundwork for future Sketch-ins and frame additional problems you will want to address. The results are captured by the work itself—the sketches and audio become the evidence to support your decisions and can lead to refinement of more effective TEL systems as your project matures.

NOTE

1. By 'TEL systems', I mean not only TEL software itself, but also the physical and social context within which such software exists. Sketch-ins are likely to uncover not just questions around the software, but the learner's context, too.

REFERENCES

Balasubramanian, V., Turoff, M., & Ullman, D. (1998). A Systematic Approach to Support the Idea Generation Phase of the User Interface Design Process, *Proceedings of the Thirty-First Hawaii International Conference on System Sciences*, January 1998, Maui, Hawaii, (Vol. 6, pp. 425–434).

Boden, M. A. (2004). *The Creative Mind: Myths and mechanisms* (p. 344). London: Routledge.

Botturi, L., & Stubbs, S. T. (2008). *Handbook of Visual Languages for Instructional Design: Theories and practices* (p. 480). Hershey, PA: Information Science Reference.

Buxton, B. (2007). *Sketching User Experiences: Getting the design right and the right design* (p. 443). San Francisco: Morgan Kaufmann.

Craft, B. (2006). Using Sketching to Support Visualisation Design. *British HCI 2006 Conference Workshop on Combining Visualisation and Interaction to Facilitate Scientific Exploration and Discovery*, London, UK, 11 September, 2006.

Fallman, D. (2003). Design-oriented Human-Computer Interaction, *Proceedings of CHI2003, Conference on Human Factors in Computing Systems*, CHI Letters, Vol. 5, Issue No. 1 (Fort Lauderdale, Florida, April 5–10), New York: ACM Press, pp. 225–232.

Goel, V. (1992). 'Ill-structured representations' for ill-structured problems. *Fourteenth Annual Conference of the Cognitive Science Society*, Bloomington, IN, Hillsdale, NJ: Erlbaum.

Goel, V. (1995). *Sketches of Thought* (p. 279). Cambridge: The MIT Press.

Goldschmidt, G. (1991). The dialectics of sketching. *Creativity Research Journal*, *4*(2), 122–143.

Heiser, J., Tversky, B., & Silverman, M. (2004). Sketches for and from collaboration. *Visual and Spatial Reasoning in Design*, *3*, 69–78.

Hokanson, B. (2008). The virtue of paper: Drawing as a means to innovation in instructional design. In L. Botturi & T. Stubbs (Eds.), *Handbook of Visual Languages for Instructional Design: Theories and practices*. Hershey, PA: Information Science Reference, 76–89.

Laseau, P. (2000). *Graphic Thinking for Architects & Designers* (p. 246). New York: Wiley.

Laurillard, D., & Ljubojevic, D. (2011). Evaluating learning designs through the formal representation of pedagogical patterns. In C. Kohls & J. W. Wedekind (Eds.), *Investigations of e-learning Patterns: Context factors, problems and solutions* (pp. 86–105). Hershey, PA: IGI Global.

Lawson, B. (1997). *How Designers Think: The design process demystified*. London: Architectural Press, 3rd Edition.

Luckin, R. (2010). *Re-designing Learning Contexts: Technology-rich, learner-centred ecologies*. New York: Routledge.

Mor, Y., & Winters, N. (2007). Design approaches in technology enhanced learning. *Interactive Learning Environments*, *15*(1), 61–75.

Plimmer, B., & Apperley, M. (2002). Computer-aided sketching to capture preliminary design. *Australian Computer Science Communications, 24*(4), 9–12.

Schön, D. A. (1983). *The Reflective Practitioner: How practitioners think in action.* New York: Basic Books.

Stubbs, S. T., & Gibbons, A. S. (2008). The pervasiveness of design drawing in ID. In *Handbook of Visual Languages for Instructional Design: Theories and practices* (pp. 345–365). Hershey, PA: Information Science Reference.

Suwa, M., & Tversky, B. (1997). How do designers shift their focus of attention in their own sketches? *Reasoning with Diagrammatic Representations: Papers from the 1997 AAAI Spring*, pp. 102–108.

Suwa, M., Tversky, B., Gero, J., & Purcell, T. (2001). Seeing into sketches: Regrouping parts encourages new interpretations. In J. S. Gero, B. Tversky, & T. Purcell (Eds.), *Visual and Spatial Reasoning in Design* (pp. 207–219). Sydney: Key Centre of Design Computing and Cognition, University of Sydney.

Tversky, B., Suwa, M., Agrawala, M., Heiser, J., Stolte, C., Hanrahan, P., et al. (2003). Sketches for design and design of sketches. In U. Lindemann (Ed.), *Human Behavior in Design: Individuals, teams, tools* (pp. 79–86). Berlin: Springer.

Van der Lugt, R. (2002). Functions of sketching in design idea generation meetings. In E. Edmonds, L. Candy, T. Kavanagh, & T. Hewett (Eds.), *C&C'02. Proceedings of the 4th Conference on Creativity & Cognition*, pp. 72–79.

9

ISSUES AND METHODS FOR INVOLVING YOUNG PEOPLE IN DESIGN

Judy Robertson, Judith Good, Katy Howland, and Andrew Macvean

1 INTRODUCTION

The concept of involving users in the design of the technology which affects them has been an area of interest since the politically inspired research on participatory design in the Scandinavian workplace during the early 1980s (Spinuzzi, 2002). Ehn identifies two important features of the participatory design strategy: the political aspect of democracy in which users are empowered through contributing to design, and the technical aspect in which the participation of users results in more successful design and higher quality products (Ehn, 1993). This chapter considers the ways in which children and young people can contribute to the design of educational software that they use. In doing so it considers the trade-off between Ehn's two features: while it might be ideologically important to empower young people in the design of such learning technology, does their participation also result in more effective tools for learning? We argue that young people's participation in the design of learning technology can indeed provide important design insights, which would not otherwise be possible, but that the design process needs to be carefully managed to facilitate this. We revisit our CARSS framework for learner-centred design (Good & Robertson, 2006) that aims to provide design teams with strategies to appropriately involve younger users as part of a design process while taking account of their developmental stage, domain knowledge and skills. In light of our experiences on educational technology design projects since CARSS was published in 2006, we further consider: what can be done to resolve the potentially conflicting requirements that emerge from young designers and other stakeholders? And we ask if there are methods that can be used to invite input from young people at key points in the project which do not require costly investment in a full participatory design process?

2 LITERATURE REVIEW

The CARSS framework was developed to guide other researchers through the often complex process of designing educational technology with young people, and is based on our experiences of technology design projects with learners and teachers in school settings. We aimed to provide a practical and realistic charting of the requirements and challenges of involving learners and other stakeholders in the process. However, we believe that young people's voices are important and their views should be heard. Druin's (1999, 2002) influential work on the cooperative inquiry process, with roots in cooperative and participatory design, contextual inquiry, activity theory and situated action, argued passionately for the benefits that intergenerational design teams could bring to the design of children's technology.

Druin's work offered young people a place during the *process* of technology design, something that had previously not been considered in educational software design models such as Soloway's TILT model (Soloway, Guzdial, & Hay, 1994), which was product focused, or Conlon and Pain's PCM model, which focused on the involvement of teachers (Conlon & Pain, 1996). However, learner-centred design (LCD) raised a number of assumptions that cooperative inquiry did not address. The focus in cooperative inquiry was on children as technology *users*, whereas in LCD, the focus must necessarily be more constrained, and focus on children as technology *learners*, i.e. children who use the technology as a vehicle for learning. We intended the CARSS framework to address the gap between ignoring children as valuable participants in the design process and the somewhat naive view of children as equal design partners. In the framework, we examined the context, activities, roles, stakeholders and skills involved in the design of educational technology projects. In the next section of this chapter the framework is summarised, followed by a discussion of the practical questions researchers may consider when using the framework.

From a theoretical perspective, the CARSS framework has its roots in distributed cognition (Hutchins, 1995; Hollan, Hutchins, & Kirsh, 2000). The LCD context can be seen as a cognitive system, with cognitive processes distributed across that system. Hollan et al. (2000) note that human activity which occurs 'in the wild' involves the distribution of cognitive processes across group members, 'coordination between internal and external (material or environmental) structure' (p. 176), and the distribution of processes across time such that 'the products of earlier events can transform the nature of later events' (p. 176). These processes are evident in the work of our LCD teams: novel ideas arise through the interactions between team members, involve the coordination of internal and external structure (in the form of cognitive off-loading, and the use of numerous external artefacts, tools and representations), and the design, and indeed the design activities, evolve over time as a partial function of the team's earlier activities. From a practical perspective, our use of the term 'framework' is consistent with Rogers and Muller (2006) who suggest that 'within HCI, it is commonly used to describe a form of guidance that is explicated in a particular way to inform design and analysis' (p. 3). They further suggest that frameworks fulfil various functions, ranging from explanatory to predictive. The position of a framework along this continuum will determine whether it consists of 'a series of steps or principles to be followed' (p. 3), in the case of a predictive framework, or 'a set of concepts or dimensions to be considered' (p. 3), in the case of an explanatory framework. We feel that CARSS sits in the middle of the predictive–explanatory continuum: on the one hand, it aims to allow researchers and/or project managers to plan and lead a learner-centred project with an awareness of the numerous parameters that constitute a design context (predictive). At the same time, it can be useful in determining the extent to which the design process was successful (explanatory). Nonetheless, it would be unwise to view the framework as a sort of recipe that somehow guarantees a successful design project. When using CARSS, simply including every possible stakeholder into the mix will not guarantee a successful design outcome. Instead, the list of potential stakeholders should be weighed up within the context of the project and its overall aims, in order to determine the most relevant stakeholders.

CARSS has been applied in a number of contexts with children and young people of different age ranges (Coyle, McGlade, & Doherty, 2011; Robertson & Howells, 2008; Good, Howland, & Nicholson, 2010; Romero, du Boulay, Robertson, Good, & Howland, 2009) including teenagers and with both typically developing children and children with developmental disorders such as autism (Frauenberger, Good, & Keay-Bright, 2011).

3 CARSS

CARSS is a framework for the participatory, learner-centred design of educational software, comprising five components:

- *Context* focuses on the environments in which the design activities take place, and the constraints inherent in these environments.
- *Activities* describes the sequence of steps comprising the standard educational software design cycle, noting those specifically relevant to work with children.
- *Roles* describes the functions that a design team member can fulfil within the team.
- *Stakeholders* covers all of the individuals with a vested interest in the design process.
- *Skills* describes the personal attributes and abilities needed by both adult and child design partners to conduct successful design sessions.

The CARSS framework is shown in Figure 9.1, and its subcomponents are described below.

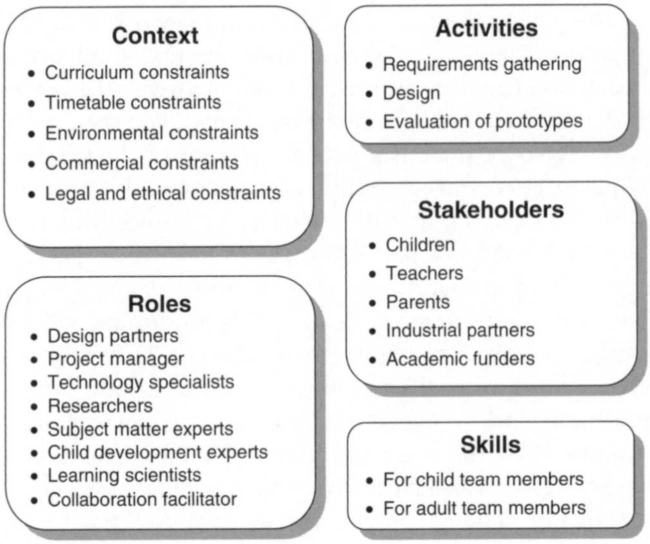

Figure 9.1 A summary of the CARSS framework.

4 CONTEXT

Learner-centred design with children is subject to a number of constraints. An awareness of such constraints will allow researchers to plan for them and ensure that the research progresses as smoothly as possible. We have identified five main constraints, although there are undoubtedly others.

- *Curriculum constraints*—curricula differ widely from country to country or even across regions. Researchers designing educational software for use in schools must ensure that they align with the curriculum, or are sufficiently open-ended to be adapted by teachers.
- *Timetable constraints*—design sessions taking place during the school day might be quite brief, school holidays can fall at inopportune points in the design cycle and sessions might be cancelled due to changes to the timetable. It is therefore crucial to plan and prepare for the sessions in order to extract the maximum benefit.
- *Environmental constraints*—it is important to find a regular venue for the session which has space for the children to write and draw, and where they will not be interrupted by other pupils. If computer access is required, it should be in a similarly quiet environment.
- *Commercial constraints*—projects with commercial partners might involve working to short time scales, and ensuring that the product is both feasible to develop and profitable. Care must be taken to manage these constraints in the best way possible so that the project accomplishes its goals, and children do not feel frustrated, rushed, or devalued.
- *Legal and ethical constraints*—formal approvals are likely to be required when working with children, for example, ethical approval from the researcher's institution, and approval from the school. Consent will be needed from parents and children. Child team members should be informed of their role in the project before agreeing to take part, and have the option of dropping out of the team if desired. Adults working with children need to be aware of relevant child protection laws and to have undergone the required background checks.

5 ROLES

Roles refers to the different functions that design team members may fulfil. In the case of small projects, a single person might fulfil several of the following roles:

- *Design partners*—within CARSS, children take on this role, contributing to design tasks from requirements gathering to evaluation. They also represent child learners more broadly, so that adult designers do not have to second guess children's capabilities and preferences.
- *Project manager*—ensures that the project keeps to schedule, and external deadlines are met.
- *Technology specialists*—provide expertise in current and emerging technologies, determine the technical feasibility of team members' ideas, and implement high-fidelity prototypes.
- *Researchers*—play a vital role in projects with a research component, serving to theoretically ground the project and choose appropriate empirical methodologies.

- *Subject matter experts*—might be needed to assist in developing domain materials (if teachers cannot fill this role).
- *Child development experts*—might be needed in projects for younger children to ensure the learning environment is developed in an age-appropriate manner.
- *Learning scientists*—needed to ensure that the software is grounded in, and consistent with, current theories of learning.
- *Collaboration facilitator*—might be needed to manage the collaboration (face to face or virtual) between industrial partners and children. Similarly, during requirements gathering, can act to integrate child and teacher perspectives.

6 STAKEHOLDERS

The CARSS framework considers the broadest possible range of stakeholders, thus increasing the chances that the project will be successful. Potential stakeholders include:

- *Children*—the primary stakeholders in the CARSS framework, children play a role throughout the design process, from co-designer to expert evaluator.
- *Teachers*—are also considered to be primary stakeholders. They provide pedagogical expertise and curriculum knowledge.
- *Parents*—should be included when, for example, the software is targeted at the home environment and/or a younger age group.
- *Industrial partners*—are relevant in commercially funded projects.
- *Academic funders*—are a key stakeholder in research council funded projects. With the increasing focus on impact, both the academic community and the community at large could be considered as stakeholders.

7 ACTIVITIES

The CARSS framework assumes a rapid prototyping approach. Design starts with requirements gathering, consulting stakeholders about the features the software should contain. This is followed by collaborative design and low-tech prototyping. After a period of high-fidelity prototyping, the team evaluates a working prototype. Prototypes can be iteratively refined until an alpha release is ready, at which point it is beneficial to introduce the software to another group of target users who can identify problems that were missed by stakeholders in previous iterations. Although stakeholders cannot always be involved at each phase, they should at least be represented at the requirements gathering and prototype evaluation phases.

7.1 Requirements Gathering

Requirements gathering should start with a wide range of stakeholder perspectives. Learners can provide input on difficulties they typically encounter, and software support features they would appreciate. Teachers can supplement this information, and also describe their usual approach to teaching. Data can be gathered via questionnaires, with particular issues followed up through focus groups or interviews. Other methods for gathering requirements include:

- Observing current practice, e.g., existing classroom teaching, software, textbooks or current curricula. This also sheds light on the broader context of use.

- Evaluating similar software packages.
- Consulting the academic literature for theoretical insights and empirical studies.
- Analysing learners' work for common misconceptions, and teachers' assessments, to understand their assessment criteria, and ways of giving feedback.

7.2 Design

Brainstorming is a key part of the design phase, and children can take part in the process by sketching out designs on paper or using software tools to create low-fidelity prototypes, working with adults as appropriate.

Having established a design, specific aspects can be refined using pen and paper walk-throughs, or implementing high-fidelity prototypes.

7.3 Evaluation of Prototypes

At the prototype stage, evaluation can begin, either through watching a developer demonstrate the software (in the early stages) or having the children try it out themselves. The Wizard of Oz (WOZ) technique, where a learner interacts with the software prototype but a human simulates some of the software's responses, can also be useful.

8 SKILLS

In order to successfully function as a member of the design team, team members require a set of core skills and attitudes. Sternberg (2003) discusses three of these, namely: (1) the synthetic skill to see problems in a new way and propose new solutions; (2) the analytic skill to recognise potentially successful ideas; and (3) the practical contextual skill to convince others of their merit. Knowledge of the domain is also required in order to generate new ideas within the design space. Personality traits and attitudes are also important: Sternberg identifies perseverance in the face of obstacles, the conviction to oppose convention by introducing new ideas, willingness to take sensible risks, and strong intrinsic motivation to focus on the creative task.

The specific skills required by children and adult facilitators in educational software design projects are discussed in turn below. It is important to note that these skills are not prerequisites to taking part, but can be fostered. Indeed, particularly in the case of children, acquiring new skills as part of a design team is a rich educational experience in and of itself.

8.1 Skills for Child Team Members

Working in a design team can be very challenging for children. It places them in an unfamiliar social situation in which they are collaborating with unfamiliar adults, over a long period of time, on a project that is of significance in the real world. Given these challenges, the adult team members need to ensure that children have the opportunity to develop any skills they lack and, furthermore, to ensure that tasks are adequately matched to children's developmental, social and cognitive skill levels so that children feel valued as members of the team. We have identified a number of skills that are necessary for the child team members:

- ability to contribute one's perspective to a group discussion, and listen without interruption to other group members;

- ability to take part in sustained work, both in working on the same task over a period of time, and on the same project over a longer period;
- proficiency in the target domain in order to understand the design problem;
- ability to develop project-specific skills, e.g. learn new software packages;
- a degree of literacy (unless it is appropriate to include team members who cannot read/write, in which case one-on-one support should be budgeted for);
- ability to present design ideas to the other team members, either orally or in writing (with appropriate facilitation from the adult team members);
- ability to give and receive critical feedback. If carefully moderated by the adult facilitator, this is also a very good opportunity for children to learn important skills around critiquing.

8.2 Skills for Adult Team Members

The adult team member essentially plays two roles with respect to the design. The first is to act as a liaison between the child design team and those adult members of the team who cannot work directly with the children because of time and/or budgetary constraints. Second, they act as facilitators for the child design team.

With respect to the liaison role, the following abilities are necessary:

- Communicate the adult team's designs to children in an understandable and engaging format, and relay adult feedback to the children in a constructive and positive way.
- Explain and interpret the children's design ideas to the adult designers, convey the children's suggestions for improving the software and provide observations of children using early prototypes of the software.
- Balance the perspectives of both parties, so as to meet the project's objectives, while ensuring the children feel heard and respected, and the project does not simply pay lip service to the notion of participatory design.

With respect to the facilitation role, the adult team member must have the skills to:

- Model such qualities as enthusiasm, patience, flexibility and confidence. Sessions must be enjoyable, and children should feel that their contributions are valued, even in trying situations such as software malfunctions or timetable changes.
- Help the team determine boundaries for acceptable behaviour, either implicitly by modelling positive attitudes and behaviours, or explicitly, by agreeing on a set of group rules.
- Model the behaviour of designers, including teaching children the vocabulary of this new world, whilst ensuring that they are not overwhelmed by it.
- Oversee all aspects of practical organisation, e.g. planning sessions such that children do not become tired or bored.
- Make a personal commitment to the children, who are themselves making an investment in the design process. The facilitator must ensure that children feel valued, and that they have achieved something worthwhile by taking part. This could be manifested tangibly, for example through an end of project party.

9 MAKING CARSS WORK IN PRACTICE

We discuss some practical issues which researchers might consider when deciding whether to adopt CARSS using three example projects: (1) the design of Flip, a visual language for games programming (Good, Howland, & Nicholson, 2010), (2) the design of Narrative Threads, a tool to support game-based storytelling (Howland, 2011) and (3) the iFitQuest project where teenagers and a Physical Education (PE) teacher contributed to the design of a location-based fitness game for use within PE classes (Macvean & Robertson, 2012).

9.1 What if the Target Audience Does Not Know Enough About the Domain to Contribute Useful Input?

Children can make a range of important contributions that do not rely on specialist knowledge and skills, such as giving feedback on motivational elements or information about their own current knowledge of a domain. In the Flip project, target users were asked to write down, in their own words, rules which explained the events happening in a computer game. This allowed the designers to better understand how young people without programming experience express computational concepts and, in turn, begin to design a programming language that would be easy to use. In this case, their lack of domain knowledge was exactly what made their input relevant to the requirements-gathering activity.

Children can also make useful contributions on tasks which do require domain knowledge with the right training. In the Narrative Threads project, young people who received training in game creation were able to take on the role of designer to develop their own low-fidelity prototypes of a character creation tool. In the case of well-funded projects, particularly those which have active research questions around the role of child designers, the skills of the design team members can be developed over a number of years.

9.2 What if There Are Tensions between the Aim of the System and the Goals of the Target User?

As developers, we are used to balancing the needs of various, often conflicting, stakeholders. This issue is particularly prevalent when designing with young people, as the 'bigger picture' aim of the system is often of little relevance to the direct interests of the young people themselves.

One emerging area where child designers are often used is exercise games or exergames, where the goal is to motivate and facilitate physical exercise while also providing an enjoyable game experience. Here we see potential tension where the entertainment elements specified by the young person and the exercise elements specified by a domain expert are often in natural conflict, and thus the developer is faced with the challenge of balancing these tensions.

An effective way of achieving this is to highlight the overall aims of the system, so that the younger members of the design team are fully aware of the context in which their goals must be constrained. In the case of the iFitQuest exergame project, focus groups involving 12–15 year olds were used to help shape the style and themes of the game. However, prior to this, two exergaming play sessions were used to familiarise each young person with the type of game being developed, and examples of feasible game content.

By framing the design task with tangible examples, the young people are less likely to stray from the goals of the system.

An iterative development approach is another effective way of minimising the potential for design tensions. During the iFitQuest exergame project, the young person design team helped to develop the game elements, these ideas were then shown to a PE teacher who helped turn game elements into more appropriate fitness tasks. The development team then developed the prototype and took this back to the design team so that they could see their ideas in tangible form, for further consideration and alteration.

9.3 What if I Cannot Get Users Involved Throughout the Design Process and Only Have Limited Opportunities for Input?

To achieve the most effective and suitable designs it is preferable to involve young target users throughout all stages of the design process. However, this can be challenging due to issues such as limitations on time and staff availability, and difficultly getting prolonged contact with stakeholders, particularly children. For learner-centred design techniques to be useful in real-world projects, a certain amount of pragmatism is necessary. Very limited levels of engagement risks the production of a design which fails its target users, but some input on some aspects of the design is preferable to no involvement, and the more focused this input is on the crucial issues the more helpful it will be.

In the design process of any system or tool, there will be hundreds of decisions to make and it is not necessary, possible or even appropriate to get input from children on every aspect. Therefore, in order to maximise the time and resources available for participatory design the activities should be focused on those questions where a genuine gap in knowledge exists, and where the constraints are relaxed enough to mean that design ideas and change suggestions can actually be incorporated. Formulating the most appropriate questions for participatory design input should be based on requirements gathering and reviewing related work, as well as findings from previous design activities.

On some projects, children may only be able to take part in evaluation activities, but using low-fidelity prototypes can make these more powerful and design focused than traditional evaluation activities. For example, on the Flip project, when target users evaluated an early paper-based version of the interface they were also able to create any new visual and textual blocks that they felt were necessary to express their ideas.

10 CONCLUSIONS

The CARSS framework is appropriate for use by researchers or developers of educational software who believe it is important to include the views of stakeholders—particularly learners and teachers—in their designs. The advantages of using this approach are that it increases the likelihood of the software being regarded as motivating and enjoyable by learners, and as educationally useful in real classroom settings by teachers. The main limitations of the approach are that it is time-consuming and resource intensive to regularly consult with learners. However, these factors can be mitigated by carefully considering the design activities during which the learners or teachers can provide most useful input.

REFERENCES

Conlon, T., & Pain, H. (1996). Persistent collaboration: A methodology for applied AIED. *Journal of Artificial Intelligence in Education, 7*(3/4), 219–252.

Coyle, D., McGlade, N., & Doherty, G. (2011). Exploratory evaluations of a computer game supporting cognitive behavioural therapy for adolescents. *Proceedings of the 2011 Annual Conference on Human Factors in Computing Systems* (pp. 2937–2946). ACM Press.

Druin, A. (1999). Cooperative inquiry: Developing new technologies for children with children. *Proceedings of CHI 99* (pp. 592–599). Pittsburgh, PA: ACM Press.

Druin, A. (2002). The role of children in the design of new technology. *Behaviour and Information Technology, 21*(1), 1–25.

Ehn, P. (1993). Scandinavian design: on participation and skill. In D. Schuler & A. Namioka (Eds.), *Participatory Design: Principles and Practices* (pp. 41–77). Hillsdale, NJ: Lawrence Erlbaum.

Frauenberger, C., Good, J., & Keay-Bright, W. E. (2011). Designing technology for children with special needs—bridging perspectives through participatory design. CoDesign: *International Journal of CoCreation in Design and the Arts, 7*, 1–28.

Good, J., & Robertson, J. (2006). CARSS: A framework for learner-centred design with children. *International Journal of Artificial Intelligence in Education, 16*(4), 381–413.

Good, J., Howland, K., & Nicholson, K. (2010). Young people's descriptions of computational rules in role-playing games: An empirical study. *Proceedings of the 2010 IEEE Symposium on Visual Languages and Human-Centric Computing* (pp. 67–74).

Hollan, J., Hutchins, E., & Kirsh, D. (2000). Distributed cognition: Toward a new foundation for human computer interaction research. *ACM Transactions on Computer-Human Interaction, 7*, 174–196. ACM Press.

Howland, K. (2011). Designing an interface for multimodal narrative creation. *Proceedings of the 2011 Annual Conference Extended Abstracts on Human Factors in Computing Systems* (pp. 1077–1080). ACM Press.

Hutchins, E. (1995). *Cognition in the Wild.* Cambridge, MA: MIT Press.

Macvean, A., & Robertson, J. (2012). iFitQuest: A school based study of a mobile location-aware exergame for adolescents. *Proceedings of the 14th International Conference on Human–Computer Interaction with Mobile Devices and Services (Mobile HCI '12)* (pp. 359–368). New York: ACM. Available at: http://doi.acm.org/10.1145/2371574.2371630.

Robertson, J., & Howells, C. (2008). Computer game design: Opportunities for successful learning. *Journal of Computers & Education, 50*(2), 559–578.

Rogers, Y., & Muller, H. (2006). A framework for designing sensor-based interactions to promote exploration and reflection in play. *International Journal of Human-Computer Studies, 64*(1), 1–14.

Romero, P., du Boulay, B., Robertson, J., Good, J., & Howland, K. (2009). Is embodied interaction beneficial when learning programming? *Proceedings of Virtual and Mixed Reality, Third International Conference* (pp. 97–105).

Soloway, E., Guzdial, M., & Hay, K. E. (1994). Learner-centered design: The challenge for HCI in the 21st century. *Interactions, 1*(2), 36–48.

Spinuzzi, C. (2002). A Scandinavian challenge, a US response: Methodological assumptions in Scandinavian and US prototyping approaches. *Proceedings of the 20th annual International Conference on Computer Documentation* (pp. 208–215). ACM Press.

Sternberg, R. (2003). The development of creativity as a decision making process. In K. Sawyer, V. John-Steiner, S. Moran, R. Sternberg, D. Feldman, J. Nakamura, & M. Csikszentmihalyi (Eds.), *Creativity and Development* (pp. 139–185). Oxford: Oxford University Press.

10

ORCHESTRATING CLASSROOM CSCL

A Multi-Level Pattern Approach for Design and Enactment

Luis P. Prieto, Sara Villagrá-Sobrino, Yannis Dimitriadis, and Iván Jorrín-Abellán

1 INTRODUCTION

Mark Weiser stated in 1991 that the most profound technologies are those that disappear, the ones that 'weave themselves into the fabric of everyday life until they are indistinguishable from it' (Weiser, 1991). However, although ICT is slowly permeating all aspects of our lives, technology has certainly not 'weaved itself into the fabric of everyday' learning.

Today, classrooms are complex technological ecosystems (Luckin, 2008), where practitioners are asked to design and enact non-trivial pedagogical learning activities, integrating a wide variety of tools (from pen and paper to digital whiteboards, laptops, web-based tools, etc.). Designing learning activities in this complex landscape, and managing them in real time within the multiple constraints of authentic educational contexts (lack of time, curriculum restrictions, student scaffolding, discipline, etc.) has been termed, 'orchestration' by TEL researchers (Prieto, Holenko Dlab, Gutiérrez, Abdulwahed & Balid, 2011a). Fischer and Dillenbourg (2006) define orchestration as 'the process of productively coordinating supportive interventions across multiple learning activities occurring at multiple social levels'. Integrating all these technological and pedagogical aspects in everyday teacher practice (and, hence, integrating orchestration in learning design thinking) is a challenge for researchers and practitioners in TEL.

Learning design for orchestration requires making sense of this complexity, in order to come up with designs that optimize learning within the multiple restrictions and opportunities of authentic settings. This chapter presents a multi-level pattern approach to learning design for orchestration. The aim of this approach is *to produce pedagogically sound learning activities that comply with the complex constraints and opportunities of authentic educational settings*, such as available resources, or making deviations from the original plans (e.g. contingent teaching, improvisation).

This chapter first describes the overall phases of our multi-level approach, its objectives and its main target audience. Then, we present in depth an example of how the approach has been used to implement professional development actions in authentic settings, to foster learning design and enactment of Computer Supported Collaborative Learning (CSCL). Later on, we discuss the advantages, disadvantages and challenges of the approach. Finally, we draw out implications for the orchestration of TEL activities.

2 MULTI-LEVEL PATTERN APPROACH

2.1 Overview

In this section we provide a general overview of the multi-level pattern approach. This work is mostly inspired by Alexander's notion of design patterns: abstractions based on empirical observation of recurring phenomena and their representation as successful solutions to recurrent problems in a field of practice, so that they can be reused across different contexts (Alexander, Ishikawa, & Silverstein, 1977). Generally, patterns are expressed stating the *problem* they are trying to tackle, the *forces* at work, and the general *solution* that the pattern proposes. Pattern approaches have already been applied to different fields ranging from software development (Gamma, Helm, Johnson, & Vlissides, 1995) to the design of learning activities (Conole, McAndrew, & Dimitriadis, 2011; Hernández-Leo, Villasclaras-Fernández, Dimitriadis, & Asensio-Pérez, 2010).

In this chapter we propose a variant of the design patterns approach, based on the combination of patterns of different kinds, *at different levels of contextualization*. We use existing pedagogical design patterns coming from different sources (Retalis, Georgiakakis, & Dimitriadis, 2006), such as the Pyramid technique (in which participants try to solve a problem through several phases in groups of increasing size, to finally achieve an overall consensus solution, see section 3.4). However, our proposal relies on combining this kind of pattern with a less-formal kind of pattern that makes explicit reference to contextual elements in the classroom (e.g. 'Disallow ICT tool usage', 'Use interactive whiteboard to exemplify a task'), as opposed to the more formal, de-contextualized advice provided by typical design patterns. We have called these 'atomic patterns'. These atomic patterns have been extracted from CSCL and TEL orchestration practice (i.e. from the design and enactment of learning activities) in authentic settings.

2.2 Bridging the Gap: Using Atomic Patterns to Help Contextual Teaching

By combining these two kinds of patterns, learning designs take explicitly into account the particular contextual restrictions and opportunities of each classroom (e.g. specific tool affordances). The resulting designs provide a more complete view of the plans to be enacted in the concrete setting, thus helping practitioners to 'bridge the gap' between the de-contextualized advice of Alexandrian patterns and the contextualized performance that practitioners must deliver in the classroom (Prieto et al., 2011b). Research evidence supports the hypothesis that these atomic patterns are easily understandable and recognizable for practitioners, who can use them to enrich their learning designs and reflect about how to enact them (Prieto, Villagrá-Sobrino, Jorrín-Abellán, Martínez-Monés, & Dimitriadis, 2011c). Thus, using this approach, the elegant simplicity of the more de-contextualized design patterns is lost, but part of the richness and complexity of the authentic contextual classroom is regained.

This approach has been used by the authors in the role of researchers trying to understand orchestration in authentic TEL settings, as well as to foster CSCL practice through teacher professional development actions. However, the approach is motivated mainly by the needs of teachers and learning design practitioners. Thus, the process described here is aimed at researchers, learning design experts or teacher trainers trying to foster learning design practice within a particular focus of interest, in authentic settings. That said, nothing precludes teachers themselves from using the process to produce more contextualized learning designs.

2.3 Multi-Level Pattern Approach Phases

As we can see in Figure 10.1, the approach follows four main phases. The first step is the *elicitation* of atomic patterns from authentic teacher practice (including the design of activities and their implementation and enactment in the classroom). Atomic patterns are recurrent elements in authentic teacher practices that practitioners use to solve problems taking into account a pedagogical objective and the contextual restrictions.

Then, so that they can be used more easily later, this corpus of elicited atomic patterns is *refined* (e.g. are two atomic patterns slight variants of the same practice?) and *categorized* (e.g. in which moment is the atomic pattern used? Is it associated with a concrete ICT tool or task?). This classification can be guided by theoretical and pedagogical viewpoints, by the aims of the research effort, as well as by practical limitations (e.g. the number of them that can be used in a specific professional development action such as a workshop).

Afterwards, the atomic patterns can be *combined with existing design patterns* and pattern languages available for the target pedagogical approach (e.g. CSCL, inquiry-based learning, formative assessment and contingent teaching). This step aims to connect the overarching, pedagogically sound structures that design patterns provide with the contextual elements of the authentic setting that atomic patterns represent. For example, we can take the aforementioned Pyramid design pattern as a base, and provide more richness and detail to our design by stating that in some phase students are to do a 'conceptual mapping', or that we are going to 'distribute participants physically to facilitate interaction' (both of which are atomic patterns). Finally, this extended pattern set can be *applied in the field* (e.g. in teacher workshops, to design and enact learning experiences) to promote orchestration in teacher practice. Eventually, data can be gathered to further refine the combined set of patterns, or to guide further iterations of the research or professional development intervention.

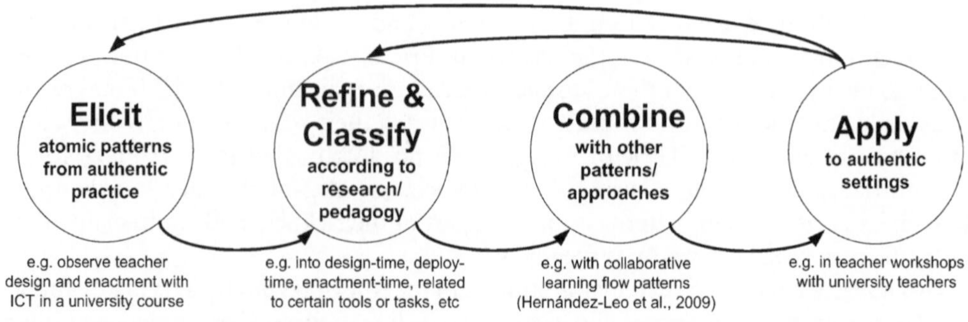

Figure 10.1 Graphical representation of the multi-level pattern approach.

2.4 Audience

The multi-level pattern approach is mainly aimed at researchers and teacher educators. However, the products of the approach (e.g. a catalogue of atomic patterns, a teacher workshop using these patterns) are aimed at teachers and other learning design practitioners. These products can be especially useful for novice pre-service and in-service teachers with little experience in designing TEL scenarios and enacting them in authentic settings.[1]

2.5 Requirements

The use of this multi-level approach has certain base requirements:

1. To have a concrete pedagogical approach or any other focus of practice in mind (e.g. what kind of activities will be designed and enacted).
2. To have access to real educational contexts where information about authentic design and enactment practice within that focus can be gathered.
3. The focus of practice should be formalized as design patterns, such as Collaborative Learning Flow Patterns for CSCL (Hernández-Leo et al., 2010); Interactive Formative Assessments to promote contingent teaching (DeBarger, Penuel, Harris, & Schank, 2011), etc.

3 THE APPROACH IN USE

This multi-level pattern approach has been successfully used to design and enact a number of CSCL activities, both by the authors as learning designers of professional development actions (so far, in primary and higher education), as well as by practitioners themselves (e.g. as participants in professional development actions).

In this section, we demonstrate how to use the multi-level pattern approach. We illustrate each phase with examples from our own use of the approach in the design of a teacher professional development workshop on the design and enactment of CSCL activities in higher education.

3.1 Phase 1: Eliciting Atomic Patterns from Authentic Practice

The first step in this approach is to elicit recurrent orchestration elements from real teacher practice within our focus of interest. This includes gathering data through interviews about how teachers design their learning activities and also how they implement those activities with the available ICT and non-ICT resources, and how those designed activities are finally enacted in authentic settings (e.g. through observations). This kind of data is normally gathered from teachers who have previously applied the pedagogical approach of interest in their everyday practice (especially experienced/successful teachers).

In this example, we were trying to foster the design and enactment of CSCL activities in higher education in the context of the University of Valladolid (UVa), where blended learning and the use of Moodle and Web 2.0 tools are common. In order to elicit orchestration patterns, we observed 10 CSCL experiences within UVa courses, taking audio recordings and/or observation notes. We complemented this first-hand data with more indirect methods, such as discussions in a teacher workshop (Ferracutti, 2010), as well as three interviews with university teachers who included CSCL practice in their courses.[2]

3.1.1 Design Analysis

First, practitioners' learning *designs* in the authentic setting have to be analysed, considering all data sources and formats at our disposal: teachers' notebooks, wikis, the design's implementation in a Learning Management System (LMS) such as Moodle, and even non-written depictions of the designs (e.g. formal or informal interviews). This analysis aims at eliciting recurrent elements in teachers' learning designs, identifying typical activities and tasks, their flow in the overall plan, and how available ICT and non-ICT resources in the classroom are used.

In our concrete case, we analysed the designs of the aforementioned CSCL experiences. Figure 10.2 depicts the analysis of one of the studied teacher's designs of CSCL experiences, which was in the form of a wiki page. In Prieto et al. (2011c) we give an example from a primary school teacher's notebook.

3.1.2 Deployment analysis

After this first design analysis, similar steps are taken to analyse the *deployment* (i.e. how the design ideas, are implemented concretely with the available ICT and non-ICT infrastructures of the classroom, and within other setting constraints): how does an activity get reflected into the LMS, how the group formation will be done, how learning materials will be delivered to students, how students will deliver their constructed artefacts to the teacher, and a long etcetera.

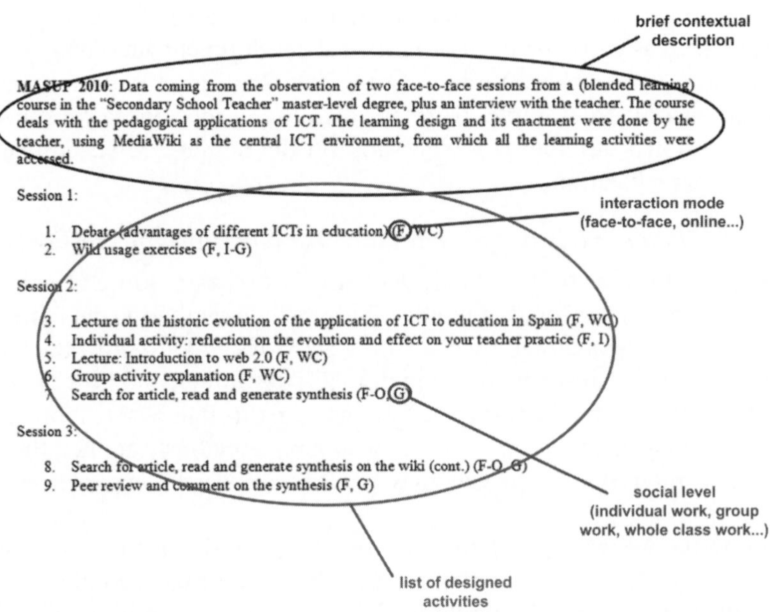

Figure 10.2 Example of our analysis of a learning design implemented by a teacher (translated from Spanish). Sessions, tasks, social levels (whole class—WC, small group—G, individual work—I) and interaction modes (face-to-face—F, online work—O) are indicated.

3.1.3 *Enactment analysis*

Finally, we analyse how each learning design considered was *enacted* in the classroom, paying special attention to deviations, improvisations and other emergent occurrences, and how the teacher orchestrated them. Here again, it is very important to count on different data sources and techniques for triangulation (observation notes, computer system log files, access to the actual activities in the learning platform, audio and video recordings of the lesson, interviews, etc.). Moreover, if at all possible, multiple researchers should perform this analysis in parallel, for analysis triangulation purposes.

In our case, we analysed the observation notes, audio recordings and post-experience. Our deployment and enactment analysis produced a synthesized description of the activity enactment, both in narrative/outline form (see Figure 10.3), as well as through graphical representations depicting the different activity phases, and the social levels and tools that were used at each moment, by teachers and students (Prieto, Dimitriadis, & Villagrá-Sobrino, 2011). Examples from primary education are available in Prieto, et al. (2011c).

3.2 *Phase 2: Refine and Classify*

From the design, deployment and enactment analyses we extract recurrent elements of teacher practice that have a certain pedagogical aim, or serve to help teachers to comply with the many restrictions of authentic settings (time restrictions, class management, discipline, etc.). These recurrent elements are collected from the analyses and refined

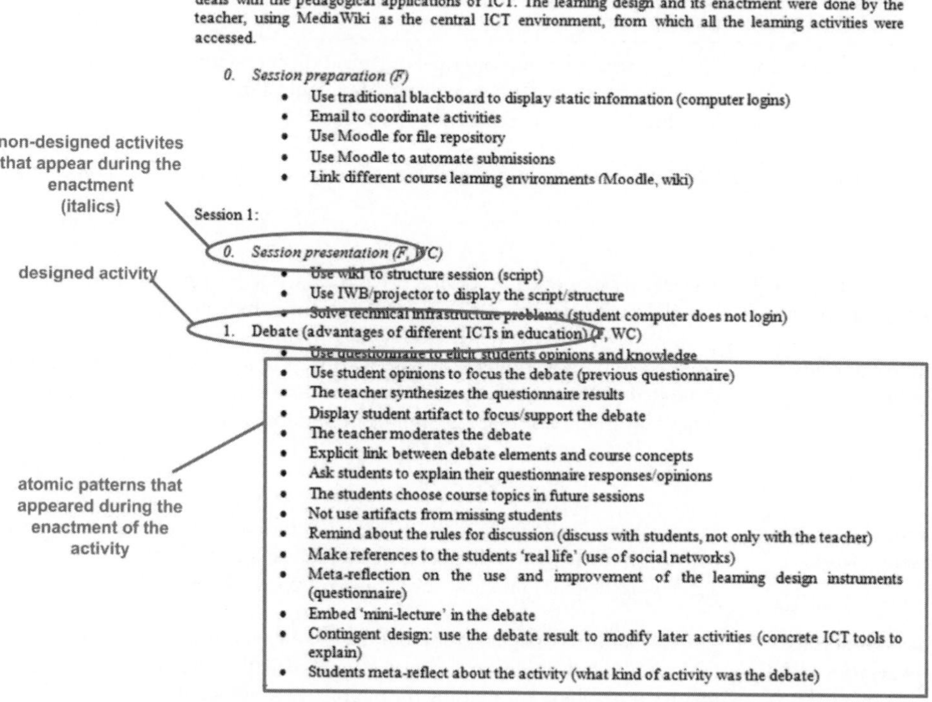

MASUP 2010: Data coming from the observation of two face-to-face sessions from a (blended learning) course in the "Secondary School Teacher" master-level degree, plus an interview with the teacher. The course deals with the pedagogical applications of ICT. The learning design and its enactment were done by the teacher, using MediaWiki as the central ICT environment, from which all the learning activities were accessed.

0. *Session preparation (F)*
   - Use traditional blackboard to display static information (computer logins)
   - Email to coordinate activities
   - Use Moodle for file repository
   - Use Moodle to automate submissions
   - Link different course learning environments (Moodle, wiki)

Session 1:

0. *Session presentation (F, WC)*
   - Use wiki to structure session (script)
   - Use IWB/projector to display the script/structure
   - Solve technical infrastructure problems (student computer does not login)
1. Debate (advantages of different ICTs in education) (F, WC)
   - Use questionnaire to elicit students opinions and knowledge
   - Use student opinions to focus the debate (previous questionnaire)
   - The teacher synthesizes the questionnaire results
   - Display student artifact to focus/support the debate
   - The teacher moderates the debate
   - Explicit link between debate elements and course concepts
   - Ask students to explain their questionnaire responses/opinions
   - The students choose course topics in future sessions
   - Not use artifacts from missing students
   - Remind about the rules for discussion (discuss with students, not only with the teacher)
   - Make references to the students 'real life' (use of social networks)
   - Meta-reflection on the use and improvement of the learning design instruments (questionnaire)
   - Embed 'mini-lecture' in the debate
   - Contingent design: use the debate result to modify later activities (concrete ICT tools to explain)
   - Students meta-reflect about the activity (what kind of activity was the debate)

Figure 10.3 Example of our analysis of the deployment and enactment of the same teacher's learning design as in Figure 10.2 (excerpt, translated from Spanish).

into 'atomic patterns' (being 'atomic' in the sense that they are not normally subdivided into smaller steps). These atomic patterns do not follow the typical Alexandrian formalism of design patterns (problem, forces, solution), being at this stage formalized only through a *title*, a short *description*, and a number of *examples* of use in real practice.

Moreover, since these catalogues may have a large number of atomic patterns, it is very important to *classify* them. Multiple classifications can emerge in this stage: according to the *implementation* phase in which they appeared (design time, deployment time or enactment time), specific *tasks* to which they are related (e.g. assessment, debates, teacher explanations, online work), specific *technological elements* that appear in them (e.g. related to the use of *Moodle*, *Google Docs*, the physical blackboard in the classroom), or other categorizations specific to the researchers' or designers' pedagogical focus. These classifications can ease the retrieval of patterns and the drawing of relationships with one another, and with contextual elements in the classroom situation.

In our example, we were able to extract 169 atomic patterns. Table 10.1 depicts a short selection of this atomic pattern catalogue, categorized by the implementation phase in which they appeared. Also, each atomic pattern was related to multiple contextual elements, in the form of tags (see, for example, Figure 10.4 below).[3]

3.3 Phase 3: Combine Patterns to Foster Learning Design Orchestration

Once a catalogue of categorized atomic patterns is in place, we can combine them with other available pedagogical patterns that have proved useful for learning design within

Table 10.1 Atomic patterns catalogue (excerpt). See Figure 5 for more complete examples

Routine	Description	Type/phase
Conceptual mapping	Students create a model or visual organization of concepts related to the course (often in groups, but could also be individually)	Design-time
Peer review	Students revise one or more artifacts generated by their peers	Design-time
. . .	. . .	. . .
Use open-access ICT to do peer review	The teacher uses open-access ICTs (e.g. a wiki, open-access GoogleDocs) to facilitate the peer review among students	Deployment-time
Publish partial products	Students publish incomplete or partial artifacts to be generated by them, so that partial assessments are possible (especially in the case of long-running or iterative activities)	Deployment-time
. . .	. . .	. . .
Random evaluation of group work	The teacher will choose randomly the part or the component of a group work to be evaluated, to ensure that all members of a group participate and know the whole group's work	Enactment-time
Use IWB to trace conversation/debate	The teacher (or a designated student) takes notes about the topics and interventions in a conversation or debate, either in textual or graphical form, using the interactive whiteboard	Enactment-time
. . .	. . .	. . .

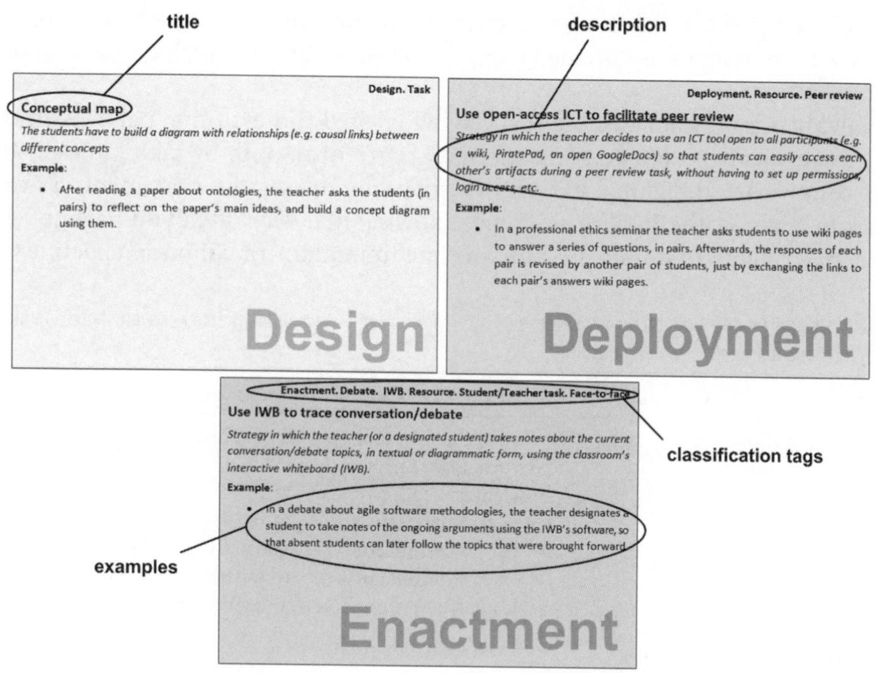

Figure 10.4 Atomic pattern card examples, as used in a teacher professional development workshop. Design (top left), deployment (top right), and enactment (bottom) atomic patterns are depicted.

our focus of interest (e.g. the pedagogical approach we wish to promote). The pedagogical patterns may come from different origins: educational practice, pedagogical theories, or combinations of both (Retalis et al., 2006). Aiming to foster the design and enactment of CSCL experiences, we combined the atomic patterns uncovered so far with the notion of collaborative learning flow patterns (CLFPs), a set of general strategies that proved to be useful for the design of collaborative learning (Hernández-Leo et al., 2010). In the following section we show how these two kinds of patterns were combined into a concrete learning design for professional development.

3.4 Phase 4: Applying the Patterns in the Field: the Design of a Teacher Workshop

Once we have a clear idea of how to combine the elicited atomic patterns with other pedagogical patterns in our field of interest, it is finally time to apply this pattern set in authentic educational settings, to design activities, implement them and enact them (and, eventually, to evaluate and refine the pattern set itself, which can always be improved).

For example, we used the aforementioned approach combining CLFPs and atomic patterns in designing a professional development workshop for university teachers, to help them in designing and enacting non-trivial CSCL activities in their everyday practice. We designed the first part of the workshop using this very same approach that we were presenting to the teachers, so that they could experience a CSCL activity of the kind they were learning about.

Thus, the first three-hour face-to-face session of the workshop was designed following the Pyramid CLFP[4] as the basic structure. In this case, the Pyramid's activities tried to tackle the problem of designing a small CSCL activity (also using the Pyramid CLFP and a subset of the elicited atomic patterns in the form of cards—see Figure 10.4). This general session design was enriched using our atomic patterns catalogue, as can be seen in Table 10.2.

Finally, it is important to note that having elicited those atomic patterns from real practice can also help in facing unexpected occurrences, both by taking these patterns into account when designing, as well as a reminder during the enactment of available options to react on-the-fly. For example, knowing that very often you have to 'change face-to-face activity to online' because of time limitations (a common enactment rou-

Table 10.2 Design for the first face-to-face session in a professional development teacher workshop, combining the Pyramid CLFP and a number of atomic patterns.

Activity	Grouping	(partial) List of atomic patterns used
Session presentation	Whole class	• Introduction to the subject/experience • Anticipate script • Centralized file repository • Distribute participants physically to facilitate interaction • Explicit connection between activity and learning objectives • Use traditional blackboard to show static information • Use wireless mouse as a computer remote
First design phase (Pyramid Level 1)	8 groups, 2–3 people each	• Conceptual mapping • Form groups • Teacher determines group formation • Students choose their work topic • Wander and solve doubts
Peer review (Pyramid Level 1)	8 groups, 2–3 people each	• Peer review • Freeze intermediate artefact • Reuse generated artefacts • Use ICT for persistence of intermediate artefacts
Second design phase (Pyramid Level 2)	4 groups, 5 people each	• Conceptual mapping • Group computer use • Teacher determines group formation • Make monitoring explicit • Monitoring web browser • Pen and paper plan B • Teacher chooses tools • Use ICT for persistence of intermediate artefacts • Use ICTs for real-time monitoring • Use open-access ICT to do peer review • Use shared whiteboard to make student concepts explicit
Break	Whole class	• Take a break during the session
Medium-group design presentations (Pyramid Level 3)	Whole class	• Oral presentation
Debate (Pyramid Level 3)	Whole class	• Debate/discussion • Synthesis/comparison among presentations • Use IWB to trace conversation/debate
Tool demo & closure	Whole class	• Meta-reflection • Demonstration • Discussion synthesis

tine), the teacher might decide that it is better that the peer review is done using a wiki instead of pen and paper (which makes the change seamless). Also, for instance, knowing that you might want to do 'on-the-fly assessment' (another enactment atomic pattern) may prompt you to open all groups' online documents in a browser during the activity, for easier monitoring of the groups' advances.

4 DISCUSSION: ADVANTAGES, DISADVANTAGES AND CHALLENGES

This multi-level approach to learning design has the following *advantages*, which mainly stem from the notion and usage of atomic patterns:

- The atomic patterns are *easy for practitioners to identify and to use*, because they are simpler and only slightly formalized (as opposed to the typical Alexandrian pattern, which is much more complex and formalized). Also, the fact that these atomic patterns have been extracted from real practice and contain explicitly classroom contextual elements, make them *easily identifiable* for a practitioner.
- The atomic patterns allow practitioners to *reflect* not only about the design but also *about the enactment* of activities in the classroom, and its many aspects and restrictions. This is an emerging issue in the Learning Design field, where the enactment phase traditionally has been neglected. In this sense, atomic patterns could be a useful tool to guide practitioners in the orchestration of complex activities in TEL scenarios.
- Although this approach could also be useful for expert teachers, it is especially indicated in the case of *novice* (even pre-service) teachers and learning designers, and for those who have very limited experience with the use of ICT for education. Atomic patterns, rather than being normative rules about classroom practice, can provide nice starting points to bootstrap their practice with ICT in the classroom.

However, this method is not without its *disadvantages*:

- The first, most obvious disadvantage of this approach is that it is quite *costly* in terms of time and effort for the researchers and/or teacher trainers who apply the method, since it requires the observation and analysis of teacher practice in authentic settings, to extract atomic patterns.
- Related to the previous one, it is important to note that the application of these atomic patterns is strongly *contextual*, and thus atomic pattern catalogues might not be completely reusable across very different contexts. However, even if the complete catalogue of patterns is not entirely reusable, given their number, and following the principles of 'naturalistic generalization' (Stake, 2005), a part of the catalogue might probably be applicable to different contexts.
- Given that the atomic patterns are extracted from existing teacher practice, this approach has limited power in developing *revolutionary* designs, from a pedagogical point of view.

Among the main *challenges* that the application of this approach poses, the difficulties of abstracting, refining and classifying the atomic patterns are probably the most prominent (e.g. obtaining feedback from real contexts about the atomic patterns' effectiveness, triangulating the design and enactment data and analyses, etc.). The proliferation of atomic patterns could also be problematic (tens or even hundreds of them might emerge from a single application of the approach); the sheer number of available patterns might make it difficult for practitioners to manage and use them in practice. This chapter has outlined some possible criteria for classification and usage (see section 3), although more formal databases, classification schemes and refining instruments can be very helpful in making atomic patterns and this overall approach more sustainable and easy to use. In fact, supporting the reusability of practices with value among practitioners is not a trivial issue, and it remains an open challenge in learning design in general. The design principles database (Kali, 2008), as a pedagogical model that aims to assist graduate students in the educative design of technology-enhanced curriculum modules, provides a good example of this kind of system. Also, in the field of CSCL, Chacón, Hernández-Leo and Blat (2011), propose a pattern ontology for the design of CSCL scripts, in order to assist practitioners in selecting a set of patterns for the design of meaningful CSCL scripts.

5 CONCLUSIONS

The process described in this chapter tries to acknowledge and address the complexity of designing and enacting CSCL activities in a 'messy classroom'. To that end, we have considered the combination of 'atomic patterns' (which are finer-grained, less-formal, and contextual) with existing pedagogical patterns (more abstract, formal and de-contextualized) to build learning designs. Furthermore, we also try to help practitioners in reflecting about the implementation and enactment of activities, the deviations that often take place, the inevitability (and the necessity) of improvisation and the non-linearity of the whole learning activity lifecycle. This multi-level pattern approach can be seen as a first attempt in better understanding teacher orchestration practice and promoting design strategies for professional development that help teachers in orchestrating TEL scenarios.

6 ACKNOWLEDGEMENTS

This research has been partially funded by the Spanish Ministry of Science and Innovation Projects. TIN2008-03023, TIN2011-28308-C03-02 and IPT-430000-2010-054, and the Autonomous Government of Castilla and León, Spain, project VA293A11-2.

7 NOTES

1. Alternatively, the practitioners could assume the role of action researchers, as a strategy for encouraging more reflective teaching practice (Schön, 1983).
2. For these semi-structured interviews we followed an interview guide developed specifically to elicit recurrent orchestration patterns, guided by the conceptual framework for orchestration depicted in Prieto et al. (2011a).
3. A more researcher-oriented classification of the atomic patterns follows the orchestration conceptual framework in Prieto et al. (2011a). This classification, accessible at http://www.gsic.uva.es/%7Elprisan/Prieto2012_HDET_AtomicPatternsClassification.zip (last visit: 24 November 2011), is being used, for example, as requirements input for the implementation of technological systems to support orchestration in higher education blended learning contexts.
4. See http://pandora.tel.uva.es/wic2/patterns/en/pyramid/ (last visit: 1 December 2011) for a more detailed description of the Pyramid pattern.

8 REFERENCES

Alexander, C., Ishikawa, S., & Silverstein, M. (1977). *A pattern language: Towns, buildings, construction.* New York: Oxford University Press.

Chacón, J., Hernández-Leo, D., & Blat, J. (2011). From a pattern language to a pattern ontology approach for CSCL script design. *In proceedings of the international conference on computational science and its applications.* Santander (Spain).

Conole, G., McAndrew, P., & Dimitriadis, Y. (2011). The role of CSCL pedagogical patterns as mediating artefacts for repurposing open educational resources. In F. Pozzi & D. Persico (Eds.), *Techniques for fostering collaboration in online learning communities: Theoretical and practical perspectives.* (pp. 206–223). IGI Global Publishing.

DeBarger, A. H., Penuel, W., Harris, C. J., & Schank, P. (2011). Teaching routines to enhance collaboration using classroom network technology. In F. Pozzi & D. Persico (Eds.), *Techniques for fostering collaboration in online learning communities: Theoretical and practical perspectives* (pp. 224–244). IGI Global Publishing.

Ferracutti, V. M. (2010). *Integration of telematics services to support teaching and learning in the research University Master on Information Technologies and Telecommunications.* School of Telecommunications Engineering, University of Valladolid (in Spanish).

Fischer, F., & Dillenbourg, P. (2006). Challenges of orchestrating computer-supported collaborative learning. *Paper Presented at the 8th Annual Meeting of the American Educational Research Association (AERA).*

Gamma, E., Helm, R., Johnson, R., & Vlissides, J. (1995). *Design patterns: Elements of reusable object-oriented software.* Addison-Wesley.

Hernández-Leo, D., Villasclaras-Fernández, E. D., Dimitriadis, Y., & Asensio-Pérez, J. I. (2010). Pattern languages for generating CSCL scripts: From a conceptual model to the design of a real situation. In P. Goodyear, & S. Retalis (Eds.), *E-learning, design patterns and pattern languages* (pp. 49–64). Rotterdam: Sense Publishers.

Kali, Y. (2008). The design principles database as means for promoting design based research. In A. E. Kelly, R. A. Lesh, & J. Y. Baek (Eds.), *Handbook of design research methods in education: Innovations in science, technology, engineering and mathematics learning and teaching* (pp. 423–438). Mahwah, NJ: Lawrence Erlbaum Associates.

Luckin, R. (2008). The learner centric ecology of resources: A framework for using technology to scaffold learning. *Computers & Education, 50*(2), 449–462.

Prieto, L. P., Dimitriadis, Y., & Villagrá-Sobrino, S. (2011). Representing learning design and classroom orchestration through atomic patterns. *Paper Presented at the 'Art & Science of Learning Design' Workshop (ASLD 2011)*, London, UK.

Prieto, L. P., Holenko Dlab, M., Gutiérrez, I., Abdulwahed, M., & Balid, W. (2011a). Orchestrating technology enhanced learning: A literature review and a conceptual framework. *International Journal of Technology Enhanced Learning, 3*(6), 583–598. doi:10.1504/IJTEL.2011.045449.

Prieto, L. P., Villagrá-Sobrino, S., Dimitriadis, Y., Schank, P., Penuel, W., & DeBarger, A. H. (2011b). Mind the gaps: Using patterns to change everyday classroom practice towards contingent CSCL teaching. *CSCL2011 Proceedings.* Hong Kong, China. Volume I, 518–525.

Prieto, L. P., Villagrá-Sobrino, S., Jorrín-Abellán, I. M., Martínez-Monés, A., & Dimitriadis, Y. (2011c). Recurrent routines: Analyzing and supporting orchestration in technology enhanced primary classrooms. *Computers & Education,* 57(1), 1214–1227.

Retalis, S., Georgiakakis, P., & Dimitriadis, Y. (2006). Eliciting design patterns for e-learning systems. *Computer Science Education, 16*(2), 105–118.

Schön, D. A. (1983). *The reflective practitioner: How professionals think in action.* New York: Basic Books.

Stake, R. (2005). Qualitative case studies. In N. Denzin & Y. Lincoln (Eds.), *The SAGE handbook of qualitative research* (pp. 443–466). Thousand Oaks, CA: Sage.

Weiser, M. (1991). The computer for the 21st century. *Scientific American, 265*(3), 94–104.

11

EMPOWERING TEACHERS TO DESIGN LEARNING RESOURCES WITH METACOGNITIVE INTERFACE ELEMENTS

Judy Kay, Sabina Kleitman, and Roger Azevedo

1 INTRODUCTION

Metacognition refers to the executive processes of reflecting on and regulating one's own thinking, that is, 'thinking about thinking' (Flavell, 1979). These processes, central to learning, are one of the three fundamentals of self-regulated learning (Schraw et al., 2006). This makes it important for most learning contexts and especially for the many uses of digital learning resources for independent and lifelong learning (Azevedo et al., 2012; Kay, 2008). Given its importance, it is unsurprising that there is a large body of research about metacognition; for example, see reviews (Dunlosky & Bjork, 2008; Dunlosky & Lipko, 2007). These provide powerful insights into how real-world learning can be improved. This metacognition research also has the potential to serve as a foundation for the design of interface elements that can improve learning and be useful in many different learning resources.

It is particularly timely to make it easier for teachers to build upon the existing body of knowledge about metacognition. This is because it is becoming increasingly common for teachers to create their own digital learning resources or to modify or adapt existing ones. This chapter argues for the creation of a new class of interface element that is part of the authoring toolkit for digital learning resources. This would pave the way for teachers to readily incorporate these metacognitive interface elements into a learning resource.

For example, within schools, learner management systems have become mainstream and these provide authoring environments for teachers. It has also become increasingly common for teachers to use general tools to create web sites, wikis and blogs. These have important roles outside formal, school and university, settings. They are relevant for a broad range of learning needs, including lifelong concerns, such as those associated with learning about health and wellness.

In this chapter, we illustrate how research in metacognition has the potential to provide valuable guidance about interface elements that can support metacognitive processes. This chapter is intended for teachers who create learning resources in authoring environments. We also write for designers of environments supporting authoring of learning resources since it would be valuable if they created these elements for authors to include into their learning materials.

In the next section, we introduce one metacognitive interface element, chosen because it is simple to implement within real-life learning environments, easy for the user to understand, and has broad applicability. Then we present an overview of MetaTutor, a sophisticated example with multiple, integrated metacognitive interface elements. We conclude with our vision for broad adoption of metacognitive interface elements in learning resources.

2 METACOGNITIVE ELEMENTS

One of the challenges in adopting the results of research on metacognition is due to the complexity of the concept (Azevedo and Aleven, 2012). For example, Azevedo (Azevedo and colleagues, in press) identified 33 self-regulatory processes:

> (a) planning variables including planning, goal setting, activating prior knowledge, and recycling goal in working memory; (b) monitoring activities including feeling of knowing (FOK), judgement of learning (JOL), monitoring progress towards goals, content evaluation, identifying the adequacy of information, evaluating the content as the answer to a goal, and self-questioning; (c) learning strategies including hypothesizing, coordinating informational sources, inferences, mnemonics, drawing, summarizing, goal-directed search, selecting new informational sources, free search, rereading, taking notes, knowledge elaboration, finding location in environment, memorizing, reading notes, and reading a new paragraph; (d) handling task difficulties and demands including help-seeking behavior, expect adequacy of information, control of context, time and effort planning, and task difficulty; and (e) interest in the task or the content domain of the task.

Most of these involve metacognitive processes. This chapter gives several examples of one class of interface element, then shows a combination of metacognitive processes used by students when using an intelligent tutoring system to develop a conceptual understanding of human biology.

2.1 Feeling of Confidence

Confidence levels are an important component of FOK as they reflect the degree of certainty about the accuracy of one's own performance while doing a task. They index key metacognitive experiences that are closely tied to self-monitoring, learning, self-regulation, and decision making (Allwood and Granhag, 1999; Efklides, 2008; Flavell, 1979; Koriat, 2012; Stankov and Kleitman, 2008). This section introduces interface elements that enable learners to consider and report their confidence levels in their answers to tasks in a learning environment.

With the premise that 'confidence controls action' (Gilovich et al., 2002, p. 248), measures of confidence in one's own knowledge, opinions and answers have been used in a wide range of scientific and real-life domains including self-regulated learning, memory, metacognition, decision making, intelligence, eyewitness testimonies, neuroscience, and perception (see Dunlosky and Metcalfe (2008) and Koriat (2012) for reviews). Typically, a person is asked to express their confidence about their answers, opinions, decisions, and perceptions during on-task cognitive activity, thus prompting immediate reflection on current performance (see Allwood and Granhag (1999), Kleitman (2008) and Koriat (2012) for reviews).

These confidence levels, captured on a variety of seemingly unrelated cognitive tasks (opinions, mathematics, verbal, reasoning testing stimuli), are demonstrated to converge into the construct of Confidence (see Kleitman (2008) and Stankov and Kleitman (2008) for reviews)—a broad psychological trait spanning a variety of cognitive domains, and reflects the habitual way in which people assess the accuracy of their decisions, memories, and opinions.

Kleitman (2008) also showed that both over- and under-confidence, tend to be stable characteristics of a person. Both can be damaging. 'No problem in judgment and decision making is more prevalent and more potentially catastrophic than overconfidence' (Plous, 1993, p. 217). On the other hand, under-confidence can also pose problems (Want and Kleitman, 2006), including anxiety and detrimental tendencies such as procrastination and negative thinking. Within formal settings, this makes it valuable for a teacher to learn whether a student tends to be over- or under-confident. For a learner, there is potential benefit in becoming self-aware, based on formative assessment of their confidence, for example in terms of the FOK. We now introduce examples of simple interface elements that enable a learner to think about their certainty about their response to questions in a learning interface.

For instance, in a recent study, Kleitman and Costa (2012) included a metacognitive interface element in the quizzes for a statistics subject. This was part of a tool for formative assessment, the Statistical Metacognitive Instrumentation Quizzes (Stats-mIQ). It was designed for a typical learning environment, as part of a senior compulsory for psychology students' undergraduate statistics subject. The students see this as a series of quizzes, each comprised of multiple choice questions. The metacognitive element can be seen in the middle of Figure 11.1. It asks students to rate how confident they are that their answer was correct. Afterwards, they see feedback on their answers as can be seen at the bottom of the figure. After completing the whole quiz, the students were provided with more feedback on their overall accuracy, confidence (overall, and separately for correct and incorrect answers) and bias levels for this and the other quizzes (and attempts).

Demonstrating the effectiveness of the quizzes, the final exam mark was positively predicted by the total number of quiz attempts, a composite accuracy and confidence score, and students' prediction of their exam mark. The metacognitive feedback was shown to be of real benefit, subjective and objective, for the students struggling with the content of the course. That is, poorly performing students reported that they found the confidence procedure was very useful for their learning. Importantly, even a small degree of engagement with quizzes improves the accuracy of the exam mark prediction (minimizing mark-prediction bias). Although replication and extension are required, these findings highlight the important role metacognitive feedback plays in an authentic tertiary education setting.

In another study (Gluga et al., 2012a, b), confidence ratings were used for two purposes. They served to evaluate a learner's perception of their progress, based on confidence judgements at each stage of learning. They were also valuable input to the *authors* of the materials since they gave clear evidence about the appropriateness and difficulty levels of their learning stimuli. The interface element is illustrated in Figure 11.2. This

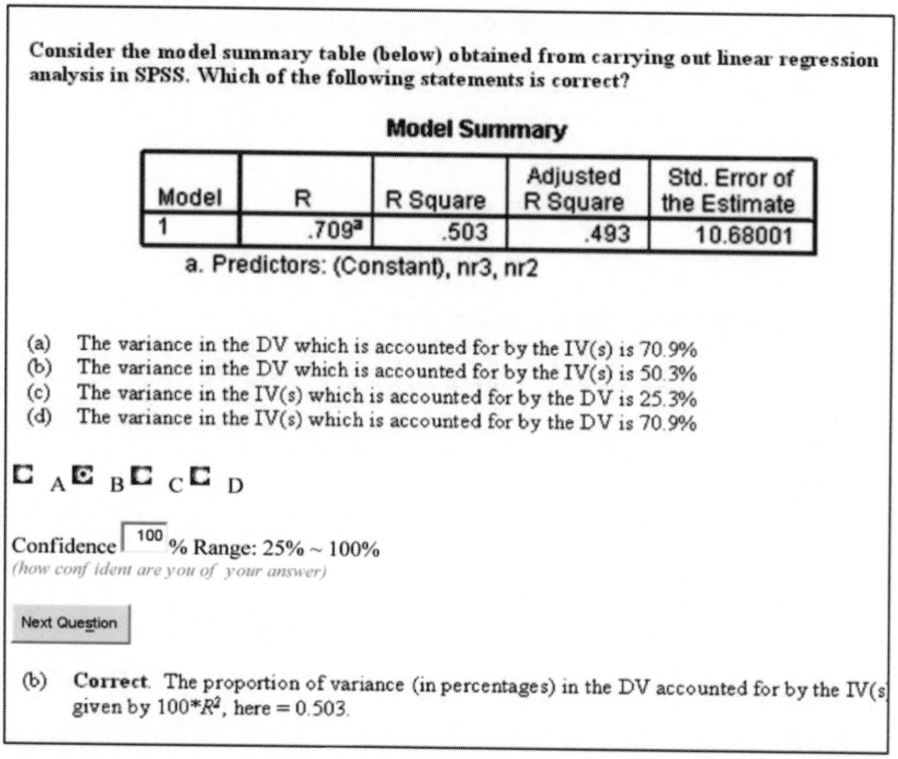

Consider the model summary table (below) obtained from carrying out linear regression analysis in SPSS. Which of the following statements is correct?

Model Summary

Model	R	R Square	Adjusted R Square	Std. Error of the Estimate
1	.709[a]	.503	.493	10.68001

a. Predictors: (Constant), nr3, nr2

(a) The variance in the DV which is accounted for by the IV(s) is 70.9%
(b) The variance in the DV which is accounted for by the IV(s) is 50.3%
(c) The variance in the IV(s) which is accounted for by the DV is 25.3%
(d) The variance in the IV(s) which is accounted for by the DV is 70.9%

A B C D

Confidence 100 % Range: 25% ~ 100%
(how confident are you of your answer)

Next Question

(b) **Correct**. The proportion of variance (in percentages) in the DV accounted for by the IV(s given by 100*R^2, here = 0.503.

Figure 11.1 Example of a quiz question format, with confidence rating and showing the feedback for the correct response.

is an online tutorial system designed to help teachers learn how to use the Bloom taxonomy to classify examination tasks in terms of the level of learning that they can assess. In the example shown, the system makes use of examples from computer programming fundamentals. The system has the following stages.

- It asks learners to assess their initial knowledge of Bloom—*original feeling of knowing*.
- Then, for each of the six Bloom levels, it presents a brief description and an example of a task. Learners self-assess their ability to correctly classify tasks at each Bloom level—their *prediction of performance*.
- The third stage involves working through a series of examples (see Figure 11.2) where the learner reads the example and selects the classification they consider most appropriate. In the figure, this is Synthesis. They also indicate their confidence, in this case 95% (*on-task confidence*). As shown in the figure, this interface asks learners to also indicate the reason for their classification and any reasons for uncertainty. Afterwards, the interface presents the remaining information visible in the figure: the expert classification and its explanation. If this differs from the learner's classification, they are invited to explain that.

This interface element provided a valuable means to evaluate the effectiveness of the material in each part of the tutorial. Results indicate that for each learning category

▾ Example 5

Example Exam Question: Write a function that will return a boolean indicating if the given integer array is sorted in ascending order. Use the following header as a starting point.

```
public boolean isSorted(int[] data) {
    ...
}
```

Which category would you classify this example as?

Synthesis

How confident are you in your above answer?

95%

Please explain why you consider this is the correct classification.

Creating a solution requires putting lots of ideas together.

Please explain any uncertainties in your rating, or why you think it is not any of the other categories.

I am fairly confident of this.

Ideal Classification:

Application

Here the student is required to identify the neccessary abstractions for completing this task, namely a loop to go over the array elements, an if statement to compare the values, and a local variable or return statement to terminate the loop and return the correct result.

If you disagree with the above explanation, please state why.

I think the rating as application would only apply if the student had been taught some recipes for problems like this, and had a good reason to think that the question would fit a recipe.

Please proceed to the next example below when ready.

▸ Example 6

▸ Example 7

Figure 11.2 Tutorial system for learning how to classify examination questions in terms of the Bloom taxonomy, with learners assessing their self-confidence in the classification.

(i.e., the six Bloom levels), on-task judgements were higher than prediction judgements, indicating that participants felt more competent to apply the material learned after completing the tutorial.

To evaluate appropriateness of the learning stimuli, the on-task confidence levels were matched with the on-task accuracy scores (their difference being the bias scores). It is well established that misleading items result in high degrees of overconfidence for most learners, irrespective of their levels of knowledge (Gigerenzer et al., 1991; Juslin, 1994). A high degree of overconfidence for a task strongly indicates it might be 'tricky' or misleading (see Harvey (1997) for a review), suggesting a need to reconsider this choice of example in the future. Indeed, reviewing the material involved and the free comments provided by study participants, it became apparent that there was indeed a tricky and contentious case. This indicates the way that confidence interface elements, easily incorporated in such learning resources, can serve as a valuable diagnostic tool.

In another recent study, Jackson and Kleitman (2012) used confidence levels to investigate the role of confidence in decision-making tendencies. Their Medical Decision-making Test (MDMT) required participants to diagnose patients with fictitious illnesses and to indicate their confidence in the accuracy of their diagnoses. Participants were then asked to make a decision: either to administer treatment matching the diagnosis (direct), or request a blood test to accurately identify the patients' illness state (see Figure 11.3). Four novel *reliable* individual decision-making tendencies were established: ideal decision-making (patients cured without delays 100% of the time); adequate decision-making (patients cured at least 50% of the time); hesitant decision-making (50% of patients die due to *unnecessary* testing); and fatal decision-making (patients die due to incorrect diagnosis and treatment). Confidence predicted these tendencies incrementally after taking account of diagnostic accuracy, cognitive ability, personality, cognitive styles, gender, and age. These results demonstrate that confidence judgements play an important role in decision making, and are valuable where individual differences in decision making are of interest.

Confidence ratings could easily be incorporated within the many computerized learning contexts which require learners to provide answers/decisions/opinions. The judgements could be in terms of percentages (see Figure 11.1), using sliding scales (see Figure 11.2), or using verbal expressions, for example, Not sure, Just Guessing, to Very Sure (see Allwood, Granhag, and Jonsson (2006) for a review). The starting point of the scale must reflect the number of choices available to the learner. For example, a multiple choice question with five, four or two response options would have a minimum confidence level of 20%, 25%, or 50%, respectively (i.e., 100/5; 100/4; 100/2); even if the participant was guessing, there is a 1 in 5/4/2 chance that the answer is correct. With open-ended questions, the scale should start at zero, as the learner is not provided with the answers and has to generate them. The objectivity of these confidence ratings can be verified by comparing them with actual performance ('confidence' minus 'accuracy'), giving immediate and reliable 'bias' scores (Stankov, 1999). Several other scores, or calibration indices, can also be collected (e.g., discrimination—an ability to discriminate between correct and incorrect answers; see Yates (1990) for a review) for each individual, for each performance and across many learning tasks. These would be collected with the aim of fostering learners' self-awareness of the state of their knowledge. When assessed over several occasions, over- and under-estimations reflect individual differences in habitual over- and under-confidence (Stankov, 1999) or habitual difficulties with discrimination (Jackson and Kleitman, 2012). Importantly, the bias scores can also be used for the test's diagnostic purposes, evaluating items to exclude 'misleading' or 'tricky' ones (see Gluga et al. (2012a), Harvey (1997), and Kleitman and Stankov (2001) for reviews).

Symptom	Present?
Coughing	
Headache	√
Rash	
Nausea	√
Swollen Glands	
Sneezing	
Diarrhea	√
Congestion	

Most likely diagnosis?
o*Puneria* o*Zymosis* o*Paralymphnal Free*

How confident are you that your diagnosis is correct?
o*30%* o*40%* o*50%* o*60%* o*70%* o*80%* o*90%* o*100%*

Your final decision?
o*Direct from Diagnosis* o*Request Blood Test*

Figure 11.3 Example of a quiz question format, with confidence rating and showing the feedback for the correct response.

3 INTERFACE ELEMENTS TO FACILITATE METACOGNITION DURING COMPLEX UNDERSTANDING

This section of the chapter deals with the design of interface elements to assess and foster several metacognitive processes used by students during learning with MetaTutor. MetaTutor is a multi-agent, adaptive hypermedia learning environment, designed to train, model, and foster students' self-regulated learning (SRL) while learning about the human circulatory system. The primary goal underlying the design of MetaTutor is to investigate how advanced learning technologies (ALTs) can adaptively scaffold learners' SRL while they learn about complex biological topics. MetaTutor is grounded in a theory of SRL that views learning as an active, constructive process whereby learners set goals for their learning and then attempt to monitor, regulate, and control their cognitive and metacognitive processes in the service of those goals. More specifically, MetaTutor is based on several theoretical assumptions of SRL that emphasize the role of cognitive, affective, metacognitive, and motivational (CAMM) processes. Moreover, there is a fundamental assumption that learners have the potential to monitor and regulate their CAMM processes while developing a conceptual understanding of the science topic (e.g., the human circulatory system). Although all students have the potential to regulate, few students do so effectively, possibly due to inefficient, or a lack of, cognitive, emotional or metacognitive strategies, and knowledge.

As a learning tool, MetaTutor has a host of features that embody and foster SRL (see Figure 11.4). These include four pedagogical agents (PAs) who guide students through the two-hour learning session and prompt them to engage in planning, monitoring, and strategic learning behaviours. In addition, the agents can provide feedback and engage in a tutorial dialogue in order to scaffold students' selection of appropriate sub-goals, accuracy of metacognitive judgements, and use of particular learning strategies. The system also uses natural language processing (NLP) to allow learners to express metacognitive judgements such as JOLs (e.g., 'I do not understand this paragraph on systemic circulation'), FOK (e.g., 'I do not recall reading about the valves in the heart'), content evaluation (e.g., 'this section is not related to my current learning sub-goal'), and monitoring of progress towards goals (by using a colour overlay on the current sub-goal list to indicate to students how much content they have covered that is directly related to their current sub-goal). In addition, the interface elements allow learners to click on the SRL palette and then choose their level of understanding on a 6-item Likert-scale before receiving a quiz. They can also use the interface to summarize a static illustration related to the circulatory system. Additionally, MetaTutor collects information from user interactions using it to provide adaptive feedback on the deployment of students' SRL behaviours. For example, students can be prompted to self-assess their understanding (i.e., system-initiated JOL) and are then administered a brief quiz. Results from the self-assessment and quiz allow pedagogic agents to provide adaptive feedback according to the calibration between students' confidence of comprehension and their actual quiz performance.

As illustrated in Figure 11.4, the system's interface layout also supports SRL processes. For example, an embedded SRL palette provides the opportunity for students to initiate an interaction with the system according to the SRL process selected (e.g., summarize their understanding of the topic). Overall, in line with its theoretical foundations, MetaTutor supports and fosters a variety of SRL behaviours including prior knowledge activation, goal setting, evaluation of learning strategies, integrating information across representations, content evaluation, summarization, note-taking, and drawing. Importantly, it also scaffolds specific metacognitive processes such as judgements of learning, feelings of knowing, content evaluation, and monitoring progress towards goals. Overall, these interface elements have been shown to enhance students metacognitive awareness and monitoring of their learning processes and enhanced their ability to use various learning strategies to enhance their conceptual understanding (Azevedo et al., 2010, 2011, in press).

4 SUMMARY AND CONCLUSIONS

There has been considerable research exploring how best to incorporate metacognitive interface elements into learning environments so that they enhance learning. Some of that work has explored how to explicitly teach metacognitive skills (e.g., Aleven and Koedinger, 2000; Azevedo and Cromley, 2004; Gama, 2004; Hacker et al., 1998; Roll et al., 2011). Indeed, that work has emphasized the need for explicit teaching, arguing that many students do not use metacognitive skills effectively and independently (Aleven and Koedinger, 2000; Aleven et al., 2006; Azevedo and Witherspoon, 2009; Gama, 2004; Roll et al., 2011).

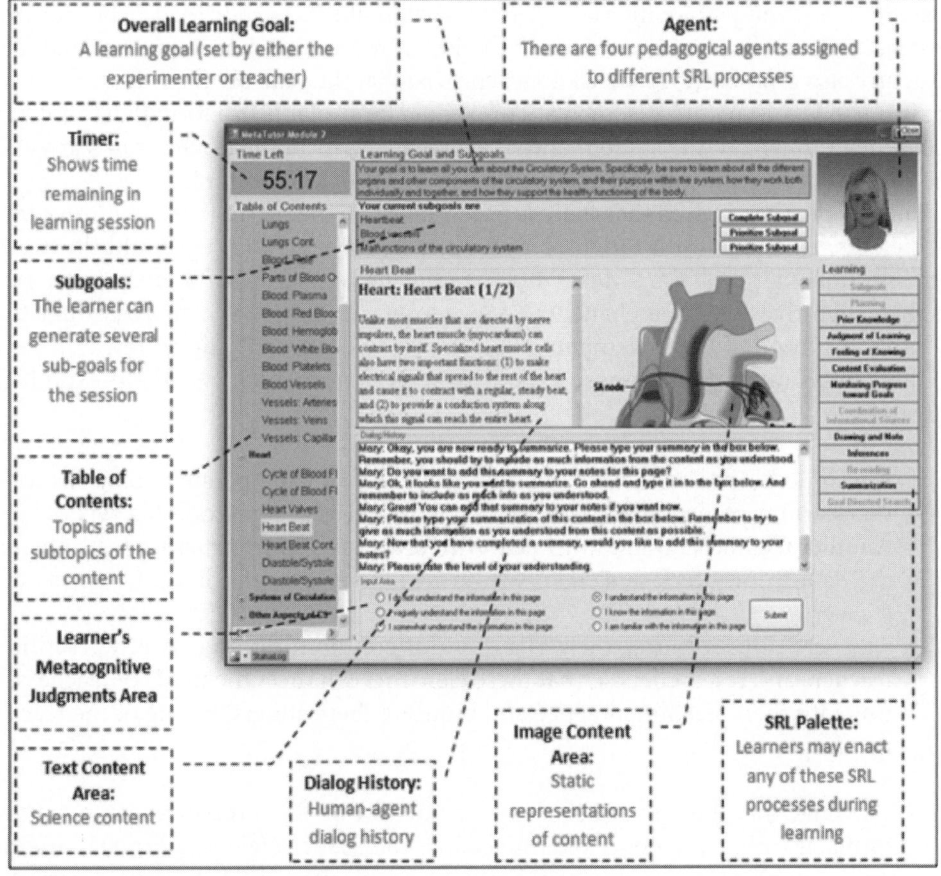

Figure 11.4 Annotated screenshot of MetaTutor (Azevedo et al., in press).

How does this relate to the simple confidence rating interface element? It is easy to create an interface that requires learners to answer questions about their confidence before they can progress. This partially avoids some of the problems identified in previous work where students simply did not use metacognitive interface elements that were available (Aleven and Koedinger, 2000; Azevedo and Cromley, 2004). However, it does not guarantee that learners will take this seriously. In addition, calibration is important here. Just because we provide interface elements for them to assess their confidence, does not mean they will make accurate metacognitive judgements.

One valuable approach is to explicitly teach metacognitive skills and knowledge. This can be done simply, as in Stat-mIQ, which showed summary information about the student's accuracy in self-assessment of their knowledge. Equally, teachers can explain the value of improving this metacognitive skill. These low-tech approaches can help learners calibrate their confidence scores and potentially help them to see greater value in doing the extra work of rating confidence.

There are many benefits that follow from standardization of interface elements, and these apply to those we propose for metacognitive interface elements. When visually consistent interface elements appear in many learning resources, learners will recognize them. This is helpful in terms of usability and learnability of the interface. Learners may also appreciate that it could offer similar benefits to those they came to value in the past. Standard widget-like interface elements will make it easy for the teacher (or other designers of learning resources) to include them. In this case, it is important that infrastructure also gives useful feedback to teachers so that they can see the ways that learners are using the metacognitive elements. This should be available in a form that is useful for individual tutoring of the student and in aggregate form so the teacher can learn about the effectiveness of the learning material (as in our ProGoSs example).

This chapter has argued that there is potential value in creating metacognitive interface elements. We chose to focus on just one of these so that we could illustrate it with several examples. Our MetaTutor overview gave a taste of a far broader range of metacognitive interface elements (Azevedo et al., 2011). We envisage that there is a role for more of these elements, too. The body of metacognition research points to their importance. We propose several strands of a research agenda to exploit this research.

- A technical stand will create *interface elements* that can operate as plug-ins to formal learning environments such as LMSs as well as general tools like wikis.
- Another technical strand must deal with creation of infrastructure that integrates the data from interface elements to provide long-term feedback to learners and teachers.
- At a very different level, there is a need for communication between practitioner teachers and researchers so that these elements can meet the needs of teachers, fitting into their teaching practice and building their understanding of the teaching metacognitive skills.

We envisage that these interface elements have a role that crosses learning contexts, from formal learning in schools and universities to broader lifelong learning. For example, personal informatics involves self-tracking and self-rating (Wolf, 2010). Across these contexts, many people, including teachers in formal settings, create learning resources in many forms. These have not yet begun to include metacognitive interface elements. This chapter has presented examples illustrating potential metacognitive interface elements that could become part of authoring toolkits, so that many teachers can use them to create more effective learning resources.

BIBLIOGRAPHY

Aleven, V., and K. Koedinger (2000). Limitations of student control: Do students know when they need help? In G. Gauthier, C. Frasson, and K. VanLehn (Eds.), *Intelligent Tutoring Systems*, pages 292–303. Berlin: Springer.

Aleven, V., B. Mclaren, I. Roll, and K. Koedinger (2006). Toward meta-cognitive tutoring: A model of help seeking with a cognitive tutor. *International Journal of Artificial Intelligence in Education, 16*(2): 101–128.

Allwood, C. M., and P. A. Granhag (1999). Feelings of confidence and the realism of confidence judgments in everyday life. In P. Juslin and H. Montgomery (Eds.), *Judgment and decision making: Neo-Brunswikian and process-tracing approaches*, pages 123–146. Hillsdale, NJ: Erlbaum.

Allwood, C. M., P. A. Granhag, and A. C. Jonsson (2006). Child witnessess' metamemory realism. *Scandinavian Journal of Psychology, 47*(6): 461–470.

Azevedo, R., and V. Aleven (Eds.) (2012). *International handbook of metacognition and learning technologies.* Amsterdam, the Netherlands: Springer.

Azevedo, R., R. Behnagh, M. Duffy, J. Harley, and G. Trevors (2012). Metacognition and self-regulated learning in student-centered learning environments. In D. Jonassen and S. Land (Eds.), *Theoretical foundations of student-centered learning environments* (2nd ed.), pages 171–197. New York: Routledge.

Azevedo, R., and J. G. Cromley (2004). Does training on self-regulated learning facilitate students' learning with hypermedia? *Journal of Educational Psychology, 96*(3): 523–535.

Azevedo, R., and A. F. Hadwin (2005). Scaffolding self-regulated learning and metacognition: Implications for the design of computer-based scaffolds. *Instructional Science, 33*(5): 367–379.

Azevedo, R., J. Harley, G. Trevors, M. Duffy, R. Feyzi-Behnagh, F. Bouchet, and R. S. Landis (in press). Using trace data to examine the complex roles of cognitive, metacognitive, and emotional self-regulatory processes during learning with multi-agents systems. In R. Azevedo and V. Aleven (Eds.), *International handbook of metacognition and learning technologies.* Amsterdam, the Netherlands: Springer.

Azevedo, R., A. Johnson, A. Chauncey, A. Graesser, B. Zimmerman, and D. Schunk (2011). Use of hypermedia to convey and assess self-regulated learning. In B. Zimmerman and D. Schunk (Eds.), *Handbook of self-regulation of learning and performance*, pages 102–121.

Azevedo, R., D. Moos, A. Johnson, and A. Chauncey (2010). Measuring cognitive and metacognitive regulatory processes used during hypermedia learning: Issues and challenges. *Educational Psychologist, 45*(4): 210–223.

Azevedo, R., and A. M. Witherspoon (2009). Self-regulated learning with hypermedia. In D. J. Hacker, J. Dunlosky, and A. C. Graesser (Eds.), *Handbook of metacognition in education*, pages 319–339. Mahwah, NJ: Routledge.

Dunlosky, J., and R. Bjork (2008). *Handbook of metamemory and memory.* New York: Taylor & Francis.

Dunlosky, J., and A. R. Lipko (2007). Etacomprehension: A brief history and how to improve its accuracy. *Current Directions in Psychological Science, 16*, 228–232.

Dunlosky, J., and J. Metcalfe (2008). *Metacognition.* Thousand Oaks, CA: Sage Publications, Inc.

Efklides, A. (2008) Metacognition: Defining its facets and levels of functioning in relation to self-regulation and co-regulation. *European Psychologist, 13*(4): 277.

Flavell, J. H. (1979). Metacognition and cognitive monitoring. *American Psychologist, 34*(10): 906–911.

Gama, C. (2004). Metacognition in interactive learning environments: The reflection assistant model. In G. Gauthier, C. Frasson, and K. VanLehn (Eds.), *Intelligent Tutoring Systems*, pages 668–677. Berlin: Springer.

Georghiades, P. (2004). From the general to the situated: Three decades of metacognition. *International Journal of Science Education, 26*(3): 365–383.

Gigerenzer, G., U. Hoffrage, and H. Kleinbolting (1991). Probabilistic mental models: A Brunswikian theory of confidence. *Psychological Review, 98*(4): 506–528.

Gilovich, T., D. W. Griffin, and D. Kahneman (2002). *Heuristics and biases: The psychology of intuitive judgement.* New York: Cambridge University Press.

Gluga, R., J. Kay, R. Lister, S. Kleitman, and T. Lever (2012a). Coming to terms with Bloom: An online tutorial for teachers of programming fundamentals. In M. de Raadt and A. Carbone (Eds.), *Australasian Computing Education Conference* (ACE2012), volume 123 of CRPIT, pages 147–156, Melbourne, Australia.

Gluga,R., J. Kay, R. Lister, S. Kleitman, and T. Lever (2012b). Over-confidence and confusion in using Bloom for programming fundamentals assessment. In *Proceedings of the 43rd ACM technical symposium on Computer Science Education, SIGCSE '12*, pages 147–152.

Hacker, D. J., J. Dunlosky, and A. C. Graesser (1998). *Metacognition in educational theory and practice.* Mahwah, NJ: Lawrence Erlbaum.

Harvey, N. (1997). Confidence in judgment. *Trends in Cognitive Sciences, 1*(2): 78–82.

Jackson, A. S., and S. Kleitman (2012). To cure, to kill, or to test? Decision-making tendencies in a medical paradigm: the role of individual differences in feelings of confidence. submitted, 2012.

Juslin, P. (1994). The overconfidence phenomenon as a consequence of informal experimenter-guided selection of almanac items. *Organizational Behavior and Human Decision Processes, 57*(2): 226–246.

Kay, J. (2008). Lifelong learner modeling for lifelong personalized pervasive learning. *IEEE Trans on Learning Technologies, 1*(4): 215–228.

Kleitman, S. (2008). *Metacognition in the rationality debate: Self-confidence and its calibration.* VDM Verlag.

Kleitman, S., and D. S. J. Costa (2012). The role of a novel formative assessment tool (Stats-mIQ) and individual differences in real-life academic performance. *Learning and Individual Differences.* Available online, 3 January 2013, http://dx.doi.org/10.1016/j.lindif.2012.12.001.

Kleitman, S., and L. Stankov (2001). Ecological and person-oriented aspects of metacognitive processes in test-taking. *Applied Cognitive Psychology, 15*(3): 321–341.

Kleitman, S., and L. Stankov (2007). Self-confidence and metacognitive processes. *Learning and Individual Differences, 17*(2): 161–173.

Koriat, A. (2012). The self-consistency model of subjective confidence. *Psychological Review, 119*(1): 80–113.

Plous, S. (1993). *The psychology of judgment and decision making.* New York: McGraw-Hill.

Roll, I., V. Aleven, B. McLaren, and K. Koedinger (2011). Metacognitive practice makes perfect: Improving students' self-assessment skills with an intelligent tutoring system. In G. Biswas (Ed.), *Artificial Intelligence in Education,* pages 288–295. Berlin: Springer.

Schraw, G., K. J. Crippen, and K. Hartley (2006). Promoting self-regulation in science education: Metacognition as part of a broader perspective on learning. *Research in Science Education, 36*(1): 111–139.

Stankov, L. (1999). Mining on the 'no man's land' between intelligence and personality. In P. L. Ackerman, P. C. Kyllonen, and R. D. Roberts (Eds.), *Learning and individual differences: Process, trait, and content determinants,* pages 315–337. Washington, DC: American Psychological Association.

Stankov, L., and S. Kleitman (2008). Processes on the borderline between cognitive abilities and personality: Confidence and its realism, pages 541–555. Thousand Oaks, CA: Sage Publications.

Want, J., and S. Kleitman (2006). Imposter phenomenon and self-handicapping: Links with parenting styles and self-confidence. *Personality and Individual Differences, 40*(5): 961–971.

Wolf, G. (2010). The data-driven life. *The New York Times.*

Yates, J. F. (1990). *Judgment and decision making.* Englewood Cliffs, NJ: Prentice-Hall Inc.

12

META-DESIGN

Empowering all Stakeholders as Co-designers

Gerhard Fischer

1 INTRODUCTION

Learning and education are experiencing a period of profound transformation. Phenomena such as globalization, increasing trends to outsource high-level cognitive tasks, and the need to participate effectively in addressing complex world problems are changing how we think, learn, work, and collaborate. New knowledge and skills for students entering work environments require collaborations with experts from multiple fields, the pursuit of several career paths, and interaction with people from diverse backgrounds. These changes create new educational demands: learners need to be educated for a diverse, technical, problem-oriented world that does not yet exist. Meta-design represents a theoretical framework, supported by innovative information and communication technologies, in which learners of all ages can pursue topics of interest and take responsibility for their own education by empowering them to thrive and participate as co-designers in collaborative environments with ever-changing disciplinary boundaries.

2 FUNDAMENTAL TRANSFORMATIONS

New information and communication technologies (specifically the Internet and the cyberinfrastructure) have been heralded as the major driving forces behind innovation in learning and education. But many approaches have had only a minor impact based on the following limitations:

- *Technology-centered developments*: Technology alone does not determine social structure: it creates feasibility spaces for new social and cultural practice (Benkler, 2006). Changes in complex learning environments are not only dictated by technology; rather, they are the result of an incremental shift in human behavior and social organization and, as such, require the *co-design of social and technical systems.*

- *Gift-wrapping:* Many uses of new media can be characterized as "gift-wrapping": they are used as add-ons to existing practices rather than a catalyst for fundamentally rethinking what education should and can be in the next century (Fischer, 1998). They change the medium, but leave the content unchanged and contribute little to introducing new epistemologies. *Old* frameworks, such as instructionism, fixed curricula, memorization, decontextualized learning, and so forth, are not changed by technology itself. This is true whether we use computer-based training, intelligent tutoring systems, multimedia presentations, or the World Wide Web.

Computational environments are needed to support *new* frameworks for education such as lifelong learning, integration of working and learning, learning on demand, self-directed learning, collaborative learning, and organizational learning (Fischer & Sugimoto, 2006). To overcome these limitations, fundamental transformations need to be grounded in the *co-evolution* of (1) a new science of learning, (2) technological innovations embedded in socio-technical environments, and (3) new learning organizations supporting formal and informal learning.

How Things Are. The current emphasis on learning is focused on formal learning taking place in schools. It is based on instructionist models in which "omniscient teachers tell or show presumably unknowing learners something they presumably know nothing about" (Bruner, 1996). Learning follows prescribed paths defined by curricula. It is conceptualized as "learning when the answer is known" grounded in a transmission model in which the learners should learn what the teachers know.

How Things Could Be. A science of learning for the 21st century needs to explore many types of learning other than traditional curriculum-based classroom learning. It must conceptualize learning as an inclusive, social, informal, participatory, and creative lifelong activity. The learning goals and the content of the learning activity should not only be determined by curricula but by interest-based, self-directed learning objectives. Many problems (specifically design problems) are unique and ill-defined and the knowledge to address them is not "out there," requiring contributions and ideas from all involved stakeholders. Learners in such settings must be *active contributors* rather than passive consumers and the learning environments and learning organizations must foster and support mindsets, tools and skills that help learners become empowered and willing to actively contribute (Fischer, 2002).

Providing learners of all ages with the means to become co-creators of new ideas, knowledge, and products in personally meaningful activities presents one of the most exciting innovations and transformations of digital media, with profound implications in the years to come. Beyond supporting contributions from individuals, learning organizations need to build a culture and mindset of sharing, supported by effective technologies and sustained by personal motivation to work for the benefit of groups and communities. *Learning Webs* (as articulated by Illich 25 years before the Internet came into existence (Illich, 1971)) represent an early vision of such an environment based on two objectives: (1) provide all who want to learn with access to available resources at any time in their lives; and (2) empower all who want to share what they know to find those who want to learn it from them.

The following sections of this chapter explore meta-design as a design methodology to create new learning ecologies and environments to support these objectives. Meta-design supports fluency with IT and it is instrumental for "the ability to reformulate knowledge, to express oneself creatively and appropriately, and to produce and generate information rather than simply to comprehend it" (National Research Council, 1999). It appeals to a diverse audience to engage in interest-driven, self-directed learning by supporting them in designing and building their own socio-technical environments by situating computation in new contexts and by developing tools that democratize design, innovation, and knowledge creation.

3 META-DESIGN

3.1 A Characterization of Meta-Design

Meta-design is a theoretical framework to conceptualize and to cope in unique ways with design problems. *Design* is a ubiquitous activity that is practiced in everyday life as well as in the workplace by professionals (Schön, 1983; Simon, 1996). It is not restricted to any specific discipline, such as art or architecture, but instead is a broad human activity that pursues the question of "how things ought to be," as compared to the natural sciences which study "how things are" (Simon, 1996). It is a fundamental activity within all professions: (1) architects and urban planners design buildings and towns (Rittel, 1984); (2) people in the creative practices design new artifacts with new media (National Research Council, 2003); (3) citizens from around the world engage in cultures of participation (Fischer, 2011; Jenkins, 2009); and (4) learning scientists in collaboration with media developers design innovative environments to support new learning activities and ecologies (Bruner, 1996; Collins & Halverson, 2009).

In a world that is not predictable, improvisation, evolution, and innovation are more than luxuries—they are *necessities.* The challenge of design is not a matter of getting rid of the emergent, but rather of including it and making it an opportunity for more creative and more adequate solutions to problems. Many design approaches force all the design intelligence to the earliest part of the design process, when everyone knows the least about what is really needed. Meta-design provides the enabling conditions for putting owners of problems in charge who act until they experience a breakdown that may lead them to reflection and learning new relevant topics on demand (Schön, 1983). These breakdowns are experienced by end users and not by system builders. End users need the ability to evolve and refine their problem framing and solving attempts without relying on "high-tech scribes." End-user modifiable systems extend the traditional notion of system design beyond the original development of a system to include an ongoing process in which the users of the system become *co-designers.* Meta-designers use their own creativity to produce socio-technical environments in which other people can be creative. They define the *technical* and *social* conditions for broad participation in design activities.

Meta-design is more than a technical problem: it addresses the challenges of fostering new mindsets, new sources of creativity, cultural changes, and innovative societies. It has the potential to create a culture in which all participants in collaborative design processes can express themselves and engage in personally meaningful activities (Engeström & Sannino, 2010).

3.2 Complementing Existing Design Methodologies

To explore the unique aspects of meta-design, it can be contrasted with a number of existing design methodologies:

- *Professional-dominated design* (Rittel, 1984) (serving as the foundation of teacher- and curriculum-driven education (Rogoff et al., 1998)) represents a design methodology founded on the belief that professional experts understand the users' needs. At design time, they create artifacts which users "have to live with" at use time. While professional-dominated design has its place, it often creates systems that are at odds with users' interests, needs, and background knowledge.
- *User-centered design* (Norman & Draper, 1986) has been a major step forward to transcend the limitations of professional-dominated design by analysing the interests, needs, and background knowledge of users and envisioning how users are likely to use an artifact.
- *Learner-centered design* (Luckin, 2010) draws attention to the changing needs of users and it combines interaction principles with educational support for scaffolding and tailoring information and tools to the evolving background knowledge of the learner.
- *Participatory design* (Schuler & Namioka, 1993) seeks to involve users more deeply in the process as co-designers by empowering them to propose and generate design alternatives themselves. It requires the social inclusion and active participation of the users at *design time* by bringing developers and users together to envision the contexts of use.

Different from these approaches, meta-design creates *open systems* that can be modified by their users and evolved at *use time.* Open systems allow significant modifications when the need arises because, despite the best efforts at design time, systems need to be evolvable to fit new needs and account for changing tasks.

3.3 Supporting Meta-Design with the Seeding, Evolutionary Growth, and Reseeding (SER) Model

The *SER model* (Fischer & Ostwald, 2002) is a descriptive and prescriptive model for creating systems that best fit an emerging and evolving context. Instead of attempting to build complete systems, the SER model advocates building *seeds* that can evolve over time. It postulates that systems that evolve over a sustained time span must continually alternate between (1) periods of planned activity and unplanned evolution, and (2) periods of deliberate (re)structuring and enhancement. A seed is something that has the potential to change and grow. In socio-technical environments, seeds need to be designed and created for the technical as well as the social component of the environment.

As illustrated in Figure 12.1, a *seed* is built based on an initial understanding and framing of a problem. It is created by meta-designers, acting as environment developers for future users, to be as complete as possible. However, the understanding of a problem cannot be complete due to the situated and tacit nature of knowledge work (Winograd & Flores, 1986). Furthermore, the constant changes occurring in the environment in which systems are embedded will breed new needs, and the introduction of computational systems themselves generates changes in professional practices and socio-technical environments. Therefore, the initial seed needs to be continuously adapted to the new understanding and new environments.

The *evolutionary growth* phase is one of decentralized evolution as the seed is used and extended by users to do their work or explore new problems. In this phase, the original developers are not directly involved because the focus has shifted to the problem

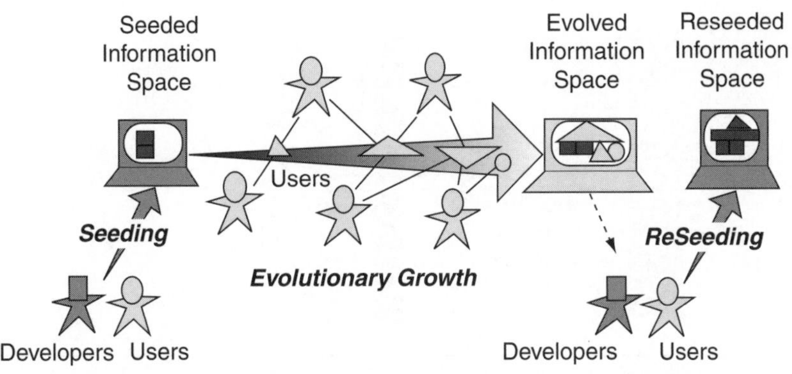

Figure 12.1 The seeding, evolutionary growth, reseeding (SER) model.

framing and problem solving activities of the users. Instead, the development is performed by participants who have a direct stake in the problem at hand (von Hippel, 2005). During the evolutionary growth phase, users focus on solving a specific problem and creating problem-specific solutions rather than on creating general solutions. As a result, the solutions added during this phase may not be well integrated with the rest of the solution in the seed.

Reseeding is a deliberate and centralized effort to organize, formalize, and generalize solutions and artifacts created during the evolutionary growth phase. The goal of reseeding is to create an information space in which useful solutions can be easily found, reused, and extended. As in the seeding phase, developers are needed to perform substantial system and solution space modifications and users must participate because only they can judge what solutions are useful and what structures will serve their work practices.

3.4 Different Models for Knowledge Creation, Accumulation, and Sharing

The process of knowledge creation, accumulation, and sharing in society has undergone major changes. Initially, knowledge was accumulated in the minds of people and communicated by tales, stories, and myths. The oral tradition has been replaced by a written tradition that allows people to permanently record thoughts and widely distribute them (Ong, 1982). Information and communication technologies have created fundamentally new opportunities including the latest shift from consumer cultures to *cultures of participation* (Fischer, 2011). Two models will be briefly described indicating which approaches are preferable in different settings. Rather than being mutually exclusive, these models can complement each other.

Model-Authoritative (see Figure 12.2) underlies *professional-dominated cultures* that are characterized by (1) a small number of experts (such as teachers) acting as contributors, and (2) a large number of passive consumers (such as learners). In such cultures, strong input filters exist based on these requirements:

- substantial knowledge is necessary for contributions (e.g., the in-depth understanding of established fields of inquiry or the need to learn specialized high-functionality tools); and

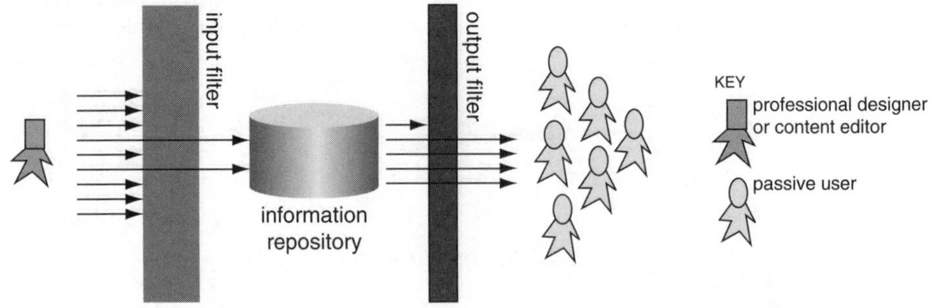

Figure 12.2 Model-Authoritative underlying professional-dominated cultures

- extensive quality control mechanisms exist (e.g., the certification of professionals or low acceptance rates for conference and journal articles); and
- large organizations and high investments for production (e.g., film studios such as Hollywood or newspaper production facilities).

A consequence of the fact that the strong input filters prevent and reject contributions is that relatively small information repositories are created. The advantage of this model (this is at least the basic underlying assumption) is the likelihood that the quality and trustworthiness of the accumulated information is high because the strong input filters will reject unreliable and untrustworthy information. Based on the smaller size of the resulting information repositories, relatively weak output filters are required.

Model-Democratic (see Figure 12.3) underlies *democratized cultures* (Fischer, 2002; von Hippel, 2005); it is characterized by weak input filters allowing users not only to access information but to become active contributors by engaging in *informed participation.* The weak input filters result in much larger information repositories (with information repositories such as the World Wide Web being the prime example).

The meta-design framework supports Model-democratic on the *technical* side with powerful tools for (1) creating content (such as wiki substrates and end-user development environments); (2) organizing content (such as supporting collections); and

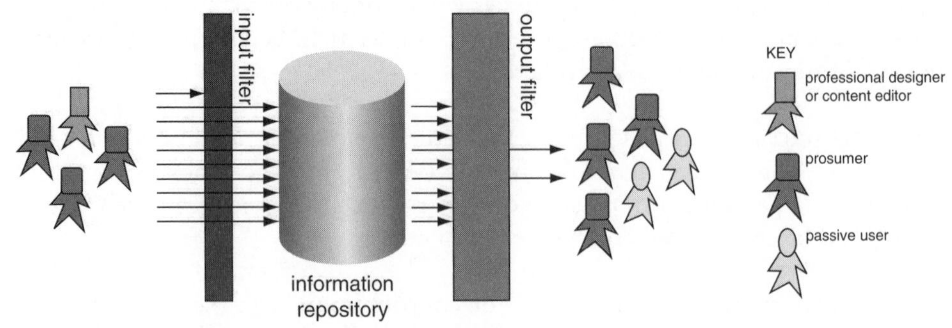

Figure 12.3 Model-Democratic underlying democratized cultures

(3) distributing content (such as powerful search capabilities and recommender systems). And on the *social* side, meta-design supports (1) active contributors (who master design tools and who are motivated to contribute); (2) curators (who organize large information repositories); and (3) coaches (who assist in helping learners to identify and locate relevant information).

The advantages and disadvantages of the two models are complementary. Model-authoritative greatly limits the possibility that "all voices can be heard" thereby excluding relevant information and divergent opinions. Most people in this model are limited to accessing existing information, denying them a voice even in the context of personally meaningful problems and in situations in which specialized idiosyncratic knowledge would represent a unique contribution.

Major limitations of Model-democratic are the potentially reduced trust and reliability of the content of the information repositories based on the weak input filters. The amount of available information is exploding, and since too much information consumes the scarce resource of *human attention*, the large information repositories will be a mixed blessing unless we are able to develop strong new output filters (e.g., powerful search mechanisms to find relevant information, collaborative filtering, recommender and tagging systems, and user and task models to personalize information).

4 EXAMPLES OF CO-DESIGNED ENVIRONMENTS

By empowering designers and teachers to act as meta-designers, users and learners can become co-designers and active contributors rather than being passive consumers of the artifacts and information provided to them. This section briefly describes three different examples instantiating the ideas and models discussed in the previous section.

4.1 SketchUp, 3D Warehouse, and Google Earth: Sharing 3D Models

Google is interested in modeling the whole world in 3D and the use of Google Earth for exploring this world (see Figure 12.4 for an example). A development team at Google alone cannot achieve this objective. The most feasible approach is to engage the whole world in this major undertaking with Model-democratic. To do so poses a number of challenging problems for participants acting as active contributors. They need to learn: (1) SketchUp, a high-functionality environment for 3D modeling (http://sketchup.google.com/); (2) the mechanisms of sharing 3D models by uploading them from SketchUp to the 3D Warehouse; and (3) how to download models from the 3D Warehouse and view them in Google Earth. In order to motivate and empower enough people, we have worked in close collaboration with researchers from Google to explore new learning mechanisms for SketchUp to allow everyone who wants to contribute to do so by reducing the "thickness" of the input filters.

The 3D Warehouse (http://sketchup.google.com/3dwarehouse/) is an information repository for the collection of models created by all users who are willing to share their models. It contains millions of models from different domains and it supports collections to organize models and supports ratings and reviews by the participating community. It lets viewers connect with the owners of models. It has weak input filters (such as content policies), mechanisms to ensure the quality of user contributions (such as tagging and ratings), and an emerging set of output filters (such as search support and

Figure 12.4 Downtown Denver in 3D

different sorting algorithms). It is integrated with SketchUp as the design environment, and Google Earth as the viewing environment, which has the capability of showing 3D objects that consist of users' submissions and were developed using SketchUp. Figure 12.4 shows the downtown area of the city of Denver in 3D. An interesting research challenge is to explore the effectiveness of different reward structures to motivate users to participate in the collaborative effort to model the whole world.

4.2 Distributed Scientific Communities

We have designed and seeded a wiki-based socio-technical environment (http://swiki.cs.colorado.edu/CreativeIT) to foster and support the emerging *CreativeIT Community*, consisting of participants (researchers, artists, graduate students) in the NSF research program on "Creativity and IT" (http://www.nsf.gov/funding/pgm_summ.jsp?pims_id=501096). The unique challenges of supporting this specific community with Model-democratic are that people working in interdisciplinary projects or in niches of their disciplines are often isolated in their local environments and are unaware of relevant work in other disciplines. Based on this research, we have developed a deeper understanding of how technical and social environments can be changed through design interventions.

4.3 Courses-as-Seeds

Courses-as-seeds (dePaula et al., 2001) is an educational model that explores meta-design in the context of fundamentally changing the nature of courses taught in universities. Its goal is to create *cultures of participation* (Fischer, 2011) that are situated in the context of university courses by supporting a *community of learners* model (Rogoff et al., 1998). Traditionally, the resources provided by an instructor such as lectures, readings, and assignments define the content of a course. By involving students as active contributors, courses do not have to rely only on the intellectual capital provided by an instructor. Our courses (a large number of them being available at: http://l3d.cs.colorado.edu/~gerhard/courses/) are conceptualized based on the seeding, evolutionary growth, reseeding model (see Figure 12.1), in which the instructor provides the initial seed rather than a finished product and the content of a course evolves over time through contributions of the students.

5 IMPLICATIONS

Our research to empower learners as co-designers with meta-design is creating new opportunities and challenges for rethinking the co-evolution between a new understanding of learning, innovative technologies and new learning organizations, and exploring new design concepts with important and broad implications (Collins & Halverson, 2009). A few of those are now briefly discussed.

5.1 Harness Social Creativity

Meta-design and cultures of participation challenge the assumption that information must move from teachers and other credentialed professionals to passive learners and consumers. As long as only experts (including: teachers, professionals in different disciplines, commercial producers of software and movies) can determine what is right and worthwhile to be published, we will never be in a position to harness people's creativity and local knowledge (von Hippel, 2005). By arguing that meta-design opens the opportunity to harness social creativity, we do not imply that it is the preferred model for *all* human activities. A deeper understanding is needed under which conditions and for which kinds of activities Model-authoritative is the preferred model rather than Model-democratic.

5.2 Quality of Information Repositories

An analysis (Giles, 2005) of the quality of articles in the Encyclopedia Britannica (based on Model-authoritative) with Wikipedia (based on Model-democratic) has come to the conclusion that "Wikipedia comes close to Britannica in terms of the accuracy of its science entries." This study and the interpretation of its findings have generated a controversy and (Tapscott & Williams, 2006) has challenged the basic assumption that a direct comparison between the two encyclopedias is a relevant issue: "Wikipedia isn't great because it's like the Britannica. The Britannica is great at being authoritative, edited, expensive, and monolithic. Wikipedia is great at being free, brawling, universal, and instantaneous."

There are many more open issues to be investigated including: (1) errors will always exist so the question will be which model is better suited to deal with errors over time?; (2) how do knowledge workers acquire the important skill of being critical of information rather than blindly believing in what others (specifically "experts") are saying?; and (3) ownership may be a crucial dimension because voluntary active contributors have a greater sense of ownership and are thereby more willing to make sure that errors will be fixed.

5.3 Motivation for Participation

Being an active contributor requires more effort and more time than being a passive consumer. In order for Model-democratic to be a viable alternative, we have to explore the fundamental question: *what motivates people to participate?* (Fischer, 2011). Active contributors are often lifelong learners, domain professionals, competent practitioners, and discretionary users and should not be considered simply as naive users. They worry about tasks, they are motivated to contribute and create good products, they care about personal growth, and they want to have convivial tools. The experience of having participated in the framing and solving of a problem or in the creation of an artifact makes a difference to those who are affected by the solution and therefore consider it personally meaningful and important: "people are more likely to like a solution if they have been involved in its generation; even though it might not make sense otherwise" (Rittel, 1984). Active contributors require and value different systems than passive consumers: control, ownership, engagement, expressiveness, usefulness, and sharing are more relevant to them than "ease of use" (Fischer, 2002).

5.4 Supporting the "Long Tail"

In systems supported by Model-democratic there is something for everybody. Not all active contributors are equally creative but *most people have some unique expertise* residing in the "Long Tail" (Anderson, 2006; Collins et al., 2009) which is more likely to become externalized and documented with weak input filters. Providing platforms for user-generated content and motivation for participation, Long Tail environments can achieve coverage that a small team of professionals is unable to generate (as argued and demonstrated with the examples described earlier).

6 CONCLUSIONS

The design of innovative information and communication technologies to support learning and education has the potential to change *what we learn, how we learn, where we learn, and who we learn with.* Meta-design provides a framework for making learning a part of life and thereby characterizing learning as: (1) being more a social than an individual process; (2) not having a beginning or an end; (3) being integrated into human lives; and (4) not being completely dependent on teachers. The fundamental transformation supported by meta-design is to empower learners to be co-designers and active contributors engaged in self-directed learning activities complementing their role as consumers of ideas and knowledge provided to them by teachers and restricted by curricula.

ACKNOWLEDGMENTS

The ideas, concepts, arguments, and system developments described in this chapter have been jointly developed over the last two decades with former and current members of the Center for Lifelong Learning & Design (L3D) at CU Boulder (http://l3d.cs.colorado.edu/wordpress/). Financial support for our research was provided by a large number of research grants from the National Science Foundation.

REFERENCES

Anderson, C. (2006) *The Long Tail: Why the Future of Business Is Selling Less of More*, Hyperion, New York.

Benkler, Y. (2006) *The Wealth of Networks: How Social Production Transforms Markets and Freedom*, Yale University Press, New Haven, CT.

Bruner, J. (1996) *The Culture of Education*, Harvard University Press, Cambridge, MA.

Collins, A., Fischer, G., Barron, B., Liu, C., & Spada, H. (2009) "Long-Tail Learning: A Unique Opportunity for CSCL?" In *Proceedings (Vol 2) of CSCL 2009: 8th International Conference on Computer Supported Collaborative Learning, University of the Aegean, Rhodes, Greece*, pp. 22–24.

Collins, A., & Halverson, R. (2009) *Rethinking Education in the Age of Technology: The Digital Revolution and the School*, Teachers College Press, New York.

dePaula, R., Fischer, G., & Ostwald, J. (2001) "Courses as Seeds: Expectations and Realities." In P. Dillenbourg, A. Eurelings, & K. Hakkarainen (Eds.), *Proceedings of the European Conference on Computer-Supported Collaborative Learning*, Maastricht, Netherlands, pp. 494–501.

Engeström, Y., & Sannino, A. (2010) "Studies of Expansive Learning: Foundations, Findings and Future Challenges," *Educational Research Review*, 5(1), pp. 1–24.

Fischer, G. (1998) "Making Learning a Part of Life—Beyond the 'Gift-Wrapping' Approach of Technology." In P. Alheit, & E. Kammler (Eds.), *Lifelong Learning and Its Impact on Social and Regional Development*, Donat Verlag, Bremen, pp. 435–462.

Fischer, G. (2002) *Beyond "Couch Potatoes": From Consumers to Designers and Active Contributors, in Firstmonday (Peer-Reviewed Journal on the Internet)*, available at http://firstmonday.org/issues/issue7_12/fischer/.

Fischer, G. (2011) "Understanding, Fostering, and Supporting Cultures of Participation," *ACM Interactions* XVIII.3 (May + June 2011), pp. 42–53.

Fischer, G., & Ostwald, J. (2002) "Seeding, Evolutionary Growth, and Reseeding: Enriching Participatory Design with Informed Participation," Malmö University, Sweden, pp. 135–143.

Fischer, G., & Sugimoto, M. (2006) "Supporting Self-Directed Learners and Learning Communities with Sociotechnical Environments," *International Journal Research and Practice in Technology Enhanced Learning (RPTEL)*, 1(1), pp. 31–64.

Giles, J. (2005) "Internet Encyclopedias Go Head to Head," *Nature*, 438, pp. 900–901.

Illich, I. (1971) *Deschooling Society*, Harper and Row, New York.

Jenkins, H. (2009) *Confronting the Challenges of Participatory Cultures: Media Education for the 21st Century*, MIT Press, Cambridge, MA.

Luckin, R. (2010) *Re-Designing Learning Contexts*, Routledge, London.

National Research Council (1999) *Being Fluent with Information Technology*, National Academy Press, Washington, DC.

National Research Council (2003) *Beyond Productivity: Information Technology, Innovation, and Creativity*, National Academy Press, Washington, DC.

Norman, D. A., & Draper, S. W. (Eds.) (1986) *User-Centered System Design, New Perspectives on Human-Computer Interaction*, Lawrence Erlbaum Associates, Inc., Hillsdale, NJ.

Ong, W. J. (1982) *Orality and Literacy*, Routledge, London.

Rittel, H. (1984) "Second-Generation Design Methods." In N. Cross (Ed.), *Developments in Design Methodology*, John Wiley & Sons, New York, pp. 317–327.

Rogoff, B., Matsuov, E., & White, C. (1998) "Models of Teaching and Learning: Participation in a Community of Learners." In D. R. Olsen, & N. Torrance (Eds.), *The Handbook of Education and Human Development—New Models of Learning, Teaching and Schooling*, Blackwell, Oxford, pp. 388–414.

Schön, D. A. (1983) *The Reflective Practitioner: How Professionals Think in Action*, Basic Books, New York.

Schuler, D., & Namioka, A. (Eds.) (1993) *Participatory Design: Principles and Practices*, Lawrence Erlbaum Associates, Hillsdale, NJ.

Simon, H. A. (1996) *The Sciences of the Artificial*, third ed., The MIT Press, Cambridge, MA.

Tapscott, D., & Williams, A. D. (2006) *Wikinomics: How Mass Collaboration Changes Everything*, Portfolio, Penguin Group, New York.

von Hippel, E. (2005) *Democratizing Innovation*, MIT Press, Cambridge, MA.

Winograd, T., & Flores, F. (1986) *Understanding Computers and Cognition: A New Foundation for Design*, Ablex Publishing Corporation, Norwood, NJ.

13

DESIGNING FOR SEAMLESS LEARNING

Chee-Kit Looi & Lung-Hsiang Wong

INTRODUCTION

Seamless learning refers to the synergistic integration of the learning experiences across various dimensions such as across formal and informal learning contexts, individual and social learning, and physical world and cyberspace. The initial exposition by Chan et al. (2006) presents and characterizes a seamless learning notion as a conceptual ideal supported by the setting of one or more mobile device per learner. The basic premise of seamless learning is that it is neither feasible nor productive to equip learners with all the knowledge and skills they need to have based on specific snapshots of episodic time frame, location or scenario (Chen, Seow, So, Toh, & Looi, 2010), which is what happens in much of formal education.

A more productive view of learning sees learning as happening continuously over time and learning experiences as being enriched when similar or related phenomena are studied or seen from multiple perspectives. In more formal settings, learners may learn canonical knowledge about a subject or topic, while in more informal settings, learners experience the subject or topic in its natural settings or in different contexts, thus achieving more holistic notions of learning and literacy. Learners will almost naturally and continually enhance their knowledge and skills to address problems and participate in a process of continuous learning. Their learning moves beyond the developing or acquisition of knowledge and skills to developing the capacity and the attitudes to learn seamlessly.

Traditionally, formal learning is defined as learning that happens at a fixed time following a pre-defined curriculum or plan. Informal learning means a mode of learning driven by self-interest outside of school environment, and is emergent in nature. The design challenge of seamless learning is to enable and support learners to learn whenever they are curious and to seamlessly switch between the different contexts. What does seamless integration mean and what does it mean to design for seamless learning? While learning can be facilitated or scaffolded by teachers or peers; at other times it could be student-initiated, impromptu, and emergent. The relevant issues are:

- What is the role of technology in the design of seamless learning?
- To what extent can we design for or facilitate seamless learning?
- What are the theoretical framework and methodologies for observing and analyzing seamless learning?

This chapter seeks to elucidate these design issues for seamless learning based on our three-year longitudinal research study of primary school students in Singapore doing seamless learning (Looi et al., 2010; Zhang et al., 2010; Toh, So, Seow, Chen, & Looi, in-press). In our ethnographic research of six such students over a period of two years, we observe their learning episodes in different learning spaces (school, home and the local science center), and the continuity and linkages to learning episodes or experiences in the other spaces. By incorporating the temporal and spatial aspects, the research provides new perspectives that not only look at the episodic learning events that happened in our participants' life but their learning trajectory over time through multi-site ethnographies as well. We establish instances where a student's learning experiences are deepened when a virtuous cycle is created, where the students can establish continuity of experiences connecting both the formal and informal learning spaces. Conversely, there are also cases where there are disjunctures in the cycle, learning tends to be more surface and perceived as irrelevant to the lives of participants. These findings make a case for designing seamless learning as establishing virtuous and synergistic linkages to learning across different dimensions.

MOBILE SEAMLESS LEARNING

Personal, portable and wirelessly networked technologies have become ubiquitous in the lives of learners. Quick and ready access to these technologies provides the enabling conditions for seamless learning unconstrained by scheduled class hours or specific locations, and emerging from the availability of one device or more per student ("one-to-one"). Research in one-to-one technology-enabled learning has pushed the frontier of technology use in formal and informal learning. The ingenious, emergent or pervasive uses of one-to-one devices in some usage contexts have suggested the potential for fundamental shifts in the ways students learn in schools and outside of schools. Early mobile learning research, however, has typically focused on either formal or informal settings while neglecting the integrated and synergetic effects of linking these two contexts or environments of learning (Sharples, 2006).

Mobile technology has the potential to mediate seamless learning (Looi et al., 2010). While research on cognition and learning during the past decades has emphasized the importance of linking learning in the classroom and learning in the field, the dominant characteristic of school learning still has a strong focus on individual cognition, pure mental activity without tool use, and decontextualized learning. Moreover, there are tensions between formal learning, which is based on fixed curricula enacted in classroom environments, and informal learning where learners are participating in intentional or unintentional experiences outside school settings. The two forms of learning should not be seen as dichotomous and conflicting situations (Sharples, 2006). Instead, by utilizing the affordances of mobile technology, seamless learning can bridge the gap between formal and informal learning, and encourage students to learn in naturalistic settings for developing context-specific competencies.

DIMENSIONS OF SEAMLESS LEARNING

Our seamless learning framework views learning spaces based on two dimensions or factors: physical setting and learning process as shown in the quadrant of Figure 13.1 (So, Kim, & Looi, 2008; Toh et al., in-press). Type I refers to planned learning in classrooms or formal settings while Type II means planned learning outside of school environments, such as field trips. Type III refers to emergent learning happening outside of school, mostly driven by learners' interests and initiatives. Finally, Type IV means emergent learning in class, such as unplanned teachable moments and serendipitous learning. Mobile devices can be used as a mediating tool facilitating a seamless integration of these different types of learning spaces.

In broadening the dichotomy of dimensions beyond this 2 × 2 model, Wong & Looi (2011) identified ten salient features/dimensions that characterize what "seamlessness" in a mobile seamless environment entails:

(MSL1) Encompassing formal and informal learning;
(MSL2) Encompassing individual and social learning;
(MSL3) Learning across time;
(MSL4) Learning across locations;
(MSL5) Ubiquitous access to learning resources (online information, teacher-supplied materials, student artifacts, student online interactions, etc.) (as revised by Wong (2012));
(MSL6) Encompassing physical and digital worlds;
(MSL7) Combined usage of multiple device types;
(MSL8) Seamless and rapid switching between multiple learning tasks (such as data collection + analysis + communication);

	Planned	Emergent
Out Class	***Type II*** **Planned learning out of class** E.g. Field trip to a heritage site which is part of the school curriculum	***Type III*** **Emergent learning out of class** E.g. Using mobile phones to capture pictures and video clips of animals and directed by self-interest
In Class	***Type I*** **Planned learning in class** E.g. Searching for answers in the classroom or using tools on the phone to create mind maps	***Type IV*** **Emergent learning in class** E.g. Teachable moments not planned by the teacher

Figure 13.1 Matrix of learning spaces (adapted from So, Kim, & Looi, 2008).

(MSL9) Knowledge synthesis (prior and new knowledge as well as multiple levels of thinking skills, and/or multi-disciplinary learning);
(MSL10) Encompassing multiple pedagogical or learning activity models (facilitated by the teachers).

The framing of the design problem becomes either one of blurring the boundaries of the continuum along each of these dimensions, or bridging the learning experiences across these dimensions. One can frame the challenge faced by learning design practitioners as designing to bridge the gaps between two points on the continuum of each dimension.

AFFORDANCES OF TECHNOLOGY IN THE SEAMLESS LEARNING FRAMEWORK

In the context of designing for seamless learning, we envision learning to occur when a learner interacts with others and the environment across time and locations seamlessly through the use of the technology as a mediating tool. Mobile technology serves as a "horizontal technology" which is used to meet students' personal needs across multiple physical contexts (Stroup & Petrosino, 2003). Table 13.1 shows the affordances and the characteristics of mobile technologies which are well suited to support seamless learning.

Building on our research findings, we put forward the notion of mobile device as a "learning hub" for individual seamless learners. The underlying concept is that the mobile device carried by a learner 24 hours a day, seven days a week, integrates all the personal learning tools, resources and self-created artifacts at one place. Learners can foster their routine use of the learning hub to manage their own seamless learning (Zhang et al., 2010). This allows a learner to seamlessly synthesize suitable learning resources that were picked up along the ongoing learning journey to mediate the latest learning task. Thus a "learning hub" should be the nucleus of (1) a suite of affordances to support learning activities, and (2) the learner's learning history (including stored resources and self-created artifacts).

The conventional notion of 1:1, which is in fact "one-device-or-more-per-learner" (Norris & Soloway, 2002), can be expanded and interpreted as a "division of labor" strategy where a learner may employ mobile devices of different form factors for different learning tasks or in different learning contexts. For example, smartphones are perfect tools for rapid learning tasks on the move, such as photo taking, note taking, quick communication, web search and map navigation. Whenever learners have the pockets of free time, they can turn to notebooks or even desktop computers as plausible tools for carrying out more "complex" learning tasks such as data analysis, report writing and learning in 3D virtual worlds.

The proliferation of cloud computing technology offers a broader view of the "learning hub." A personal "learning hub" need not be associated with a hardware device. Instead, it may exist as a learner account (that stores the learner history) on a cloud-based, device-independent seamless learning platform (that provides a suite of learning affordances) (e.g., Wong, Chai, Chin, Hsieh, & Liu, 2012). In this regard, we advocate the combination of a cloud-based "learning hub" account, a smartphone (24/7 access), and additional notebook/desktop computers as an ideal technical setting for a personalized seamless learning environment (Wong, 2012).

Table 13.1 The match of affordances of mobile technology to seamless learning (adapted from Chen et al., 2010)

Characteristics of seamless learning	Ways mobile technology can support seamless learning
Learner-centered/User-centered	Learners can actively use their mobile devices to engage in learning activities by interacting with people, resources and the environment. For instance, learners with mobile devices can go out to the field, explore the world, and share their experiences with others (Roschelle, 2003; Squire & Klopfer, 2007). Gaining ownership of what and how they want to learn, they become co-producers of knowledge.
Everyday life experiences	The ready-at-hand use of the device becomes a routine practice and is assimilated into daily needs for communication, reference, and learning.
Across time	The technology is available anytime 24/7.
Across location	The small size and light weight of mobile devices mean that they can be taken to different sites or moved around within a site, so that they can be available wherever the student needs to learn.
Across social groups	The networked device enable learners' data exchange, communication and collaboration with teachers, experts, friends and family members etc.
Natural flow across different situations	The learners can capture and retrieve *in-situ* information without encroaching into spaces obtrusively.
Situated	Learners can use their mobile devices whenever they need to, enabling them to make rapid connections between ideas and observations. The mobile device can both gather and respond to information specific to the current location, environment and time.
Cumulative	The student's personal accumulation of resources and knowledge is persistent and can be immediately accessible.
Personalized	The device can store, organize and retrieve personal information, cases, events, knowledge structures and processes. It can empower the learner to chart their learning paths with more autonomy. The device use is adapted to the learner's evolving abilities, skills, knowledge and learning styles and is designed to support individualized learning.
Accommodate versatile learning activities	The students can use a variety of learning applications that support different types of learning activities. Students can type, draw, take photos, do audio or video recording, supporting their multi-modal expressions.

TOWARDS A FACILITATED SEAMLESS LEARNING PROCESS FRAMEWORK

Taking a learner-centric view in the practice of seamless learning, we put forward the notions of self-directed seamless learning (SDSL) and facilitated seamless learning (FSL) to highlight the distinction between self- and externally-initiated activities (Wong, in-press; see also: Kukulska-Hulme, Sharples, Milrad, Arnedillo-Sánchez, & Vavoula, 2009). We argue that SDSL is the ultimate aim of the seamless learning practice—to transform learners into life-long autonomous "self-inquirers" who are able to acquire any domain knowledge as well as develop learning skills on their own. Nevertheless, SDSL is indeed a tall order for learners who are more accustomed to the present instructivist-dominated education system. In this regard, we envisage the enactment of long-term FSL where teachers engage learners in an ongoing enculturation process to progressively transform their existing epistemological beliefs and methods of learning. Congruent with Leung and Chan's (2003) argument that m-learning should become part of the learning culture rather than an adjunct to it, Zhang et al. (2010) advocate teachers' modeling of the seamless learning process by systematically incorporating m-learning activities into the formal curriculum, and encouraging learners to extend their learning into the informal context by picking up incidentally learned knowledge, applying their knowledge in daily life, and relating back or questioning the knowledge gained in the formal curriculum. Thus we consider SDSL as the desired outcome and FSL as a means to achieve the stated goal.

The literature on contemporary educational research favors the *blurring* of the boundaries between formal and informal learning (Kuh, 1996; Kukulska-Hulme, Traxler, & Pettit, 2007 in order to develop more holistic views of literacy. In a similar vein, we advocate the facilitation of seamless learning with the aim of *bridging* the two learning settings which are usually seen as disjointed (Mezler et al., 2007). The distinction between the two settings may still hold but it is crucial for learning activities taking place in both settings to be interlinked (MSL1 of the above-stated ten mobile seamless learning dimensions). The same goes for bridging individual and social learning (MSL2), and encompassing physical and digital learning spaces (MSL6).

Thus we propose a design framework for FSL processes, as shown in Figure 13.2. Encompassing MSL1, MSL2 and MSL6, the cyclical four-activity-type process consists of "learning Engagement" (E), "Personalized learning" (P), "online Social learning" (S), and "in-class Consolidation" (C). Though we recommend the basic sequence of E→ P→S→C for each FSL cycle, the actual combination and sequence of the activities are customizable from cycle to cycle, as indicated by the bidirectional arrows. Apart from denoting the possible activity sequences, these arrows may also signify the spill-over effect of knowledge, skills and learning resources as they flow from one activity to another, i.e., knowledge or skills learned with learning resources adopted or student artifacts

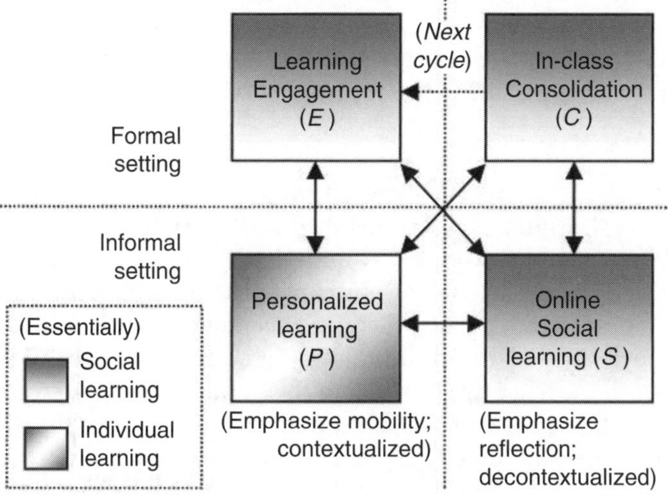

Figure 13.2 The FSL process framework.

generated during one activity may come into use in another activity (which might lead to MSL9—knowledge synthesis). The four activity types are elaborated below.

(E) learning Engagement. Such activities are facilitated by teachers and involve learners from the same class (or other formal learning community) in a face-to-face setting, usually taking place within designated time slots and venues. They may serve as the initialization of a fresh FSL cycle in order to get the learners ready for the subsequent "P" and "S" (which could be relatively personalized and self-paced). They may also serve as "learning checkpoints" in the midst of the learners' seamless learning processes that brings the entire class together to share their learning gains, clarify doubts and get ready for subsequent learning activities. The activities could be in the form of classroom instructions, group activities, outdoor learning or fieldtrips, etc., or any combination of these.

(P) Personalized learning. Individual learners proactively observe, record, make sense of and reflect upon their daily encounters, and associate or contrast those with their prior knowledge, or apply their knowledge into their daily life. By personalized learning, we mean learners exercise greater autonomy than in teacher-facilitated "E" by deciding their learning approaches and pace, and perhaps carrying out incidental learning immersed in authentic contexts. Such activities are not necessarily carried out individually, as learners may involve family members or other people to support their learning.

(S) online Social learning. Learners carry out online peer review and/or discussions mediated by their pooled knowledge, given resources, learning encounters and experiences, thoughts and reflections as well as created artifacts during "E" and "P." The interplay of "P" and "S" constitutes an effective informal learning space where individual contributions shape and reshape the social meaning making; at the same time, individuals' involvement in the social discourses help them in advancing their "P."

(C) in-class Consolidation. Teachers facilitate learners by scaffolding the consolidation process. All forms of knowledge artifacts accessed or created during the entire FSL cycle—from teacher-supplied learning resources to learner online discussions and learner-generated artifacts are consolidated through group or class-wide discussions. Such activities could also come in the form of individual/group report writing or concept mapping, etc.

The four-activity FSL process cuts across time (MSL3), location (MSL4) and multiple pedagogical or learning activities (MSL10). MSL5 (ubiquitous access to learning resources), MSL7 (combined usage of multiple device types) and MSL8 (switching between multiple learning tasks) are not explicitly represented in Figure 13.2—they belong to lower-level design details where teachers might consider incorporating these in their specific activity designs. In addition, the recursive execution of the four-activity process does not mean repetitive learning of the same content or activities that require the application of the same set of skills. Inspired by the concept of the spiral curriculum (Bruner, 1960), we envisage that when the FSL process advances from previous cycles to future ones, new knowledge or skills introduced are inter-related as learners revisit and build on their prior learning acquired in previous cycles, thereby accomplishing knowledge synthesis (MSL9) as well as enculturation towards SDSL.

To date, we have employed this framework mainly in designing seamless language learning activities, namely, "Move, Idioms!" (Wong, Chin, Tan, & Liu, 2010) and MyCLOUD (My Chinese Language ubiquitOUs learning Days) (Wong et al., 2012). However, this framework can also be applied to retrospectively analyze the existing seamless learning process designs, as we have successfully mapped some of the learning processes reported in the literature to the framework to assess their seamless-ness, including the *mobilized* science curriculum designed by our team during 2009–2010 (Wong, in press).

STRATEGIES TO FOSTERING SEAMLESS LEARNING

On top of the FSL Process Framework, we now distill strategies from our design research on fostering seamless learning mediated by mobile technology and our experiences in co-designing lessons with teachers, implementing the lessons, and studying the outcomes of the lessons in the classroom (Chen et al., 2010). The research was conducted across various grade levels and subjects (science, mathematics, Chinese language), over longitudinal time scales of between one to three years in a primary school in Singapore. The intervention comprised transforming the science curriculum to harness the affordances of 1:1 mobile technology for inquiry learning (Zhang et al., 2010). In the spirit of seamless learning, the researchers worked with the teachers, the students and the students' parents to foster the continuous, pervasive, and longitudinal use of mobile technologies for learning anytime and anywhere beyond the confines of classroom.

We identified the following approaches to foster mobile seamless learning (Chen et al., 2010), many of which are indeed reinforced by the FSL process framework.

Extension of Classroom Learning Activities to Other Dimensions

Learning activities can be designed where the students engage in learning beyond the boundaries of the classroom. For example, in primary science learning of plant systems, we encouraged the students to be more observant of their surroundings during the course of everyday activities and learning outside the classroom. They took pictures of the different plants they observed and uploaded them to a class blog. At home, the students conducted experiments and video recorded the experiment with the smartphone.

Design for Holistic and Authentic Learning

We designed activities that are authentic and related to their everyday activities. For example, in "Move, Idioms!" study (Wong et al., 2010), a class of primary school students carried out photo-blogging-like activities on an ongoing basis by using their smartphones to identify or create contexts in their daily lives which could be associated with the Chinese idioms that they learned. They then took photos, made sentences with the idioms to describe the photos, and posted them onto the web for peer review.

Provide a Learning Hub to Integrate Multiple Learning Activities

The affordances of the mobile technologies serve to make it a hub for the learners to integrate their learning activities. The teacher designs learning activities and uploads them to some server. Learners can download the learning activities to their devices. During the course of the activities, learners uploaded their artifacts or work-in-progress to a website for the teacher to review. The activities were centered on the use of the device which allowed them to search the Internet, download resources, collect digital artifacts such as pictures, record their observations, communicate with their friends, view the lessons and work on their assignments, etc. The collection of the learner's work can reside in the cloud from which she can access it anytime, anyplace from any device.

Incorporate Different Learning Modalities (to Personalize Learning)

We made use of multi-modality affordances of the mobile device to engage different learners. In our study (Looi et al., 2010) of primary students learning about plants, the students were required to make a comparison table to understand the characteristics of plants, create an animation of a plant transport system, create a concept of the parts of plants and record pictures of different types of plants they observed outside school. We observed that some students do better when they are engaged in certain forms of modality and representation as compared to other forms.

Design Student-Centered Learning Activities (to Promote Engagement and Self-Directed Learning)

In most lessons, we used a KWL table ("what I Know," "what I Want to know," and "what I Learned") on the mobile devices to engage the students in self-directed learning. The students share their prior knowledge and generate questions on what they would want to know about the topic. They are encouraged to use the device anytime anywhere to embark on their own research as well as to find the answers to any hanging questions they might have. They can use a search engine to find the answers, view videos or take pictures to answer their questions. Subsequently, they review their own learning and synthesize what they have learned.

Make Students' Thinking Process Visible and thus Shareable

We used tools such as animation and concept mapping software on the mobile devices to help students visualize their thinking process. For example, the students drew an animation of the plant transport system showing how water flows through the plant from the roots to the leaves and how food is transported from the leaves to the roots. The visualization tools are useful for teachers as they are able to see the conceptual understanding of the students. They are also a good platform for learning as the whole class can be engaged in meaningful science discussion on what they see.

Facilitate Social Knowledge Building and Collaborative Learning

Rather than relying on teacher and textbooks as sources of knowledge, students conducted their own research and shared what they learned with other classmates. We encouraged the students to share interesting videos or pictures they found with the class. Students brought in sources of knowledge they had found from the Internet and other resources into the classroom. In addition, students shared knowledge on the use of the smartphone. They learned during the process of using the tool and they shared what they learned with others in the classroom.

Assess Formatively from Peers or from the Teacher

We created opportunities for the students to receive feedback from their peers or teacher. In some activities, students exchanged their smartphones and gave feedback on their partner's work. The teacher reviewed the students' work formatively and assessed the student's understanding when they uploaded their work to an online site.

Facilitate Participatory Learning Involving the Family

Family plays an important role in students' learning. We designed activities where parents were involved in participatory learning activities with the students at home. In the "Move, Idioms!" study, some parents took the initiative to brainstorm and co-construct photo/sentence artifacts with their children at home or during their family outings, thus enriching both the students' learning experience as well as the artifacts generated.

THEORETICAL FRAMEWORKS AND METHODOLOGIES FOR STUDYING INFORMAL AND SEAMLESS LEARNING

An important consideration in designing seamless learning with mobile devices is to understand the enactment of learning activities which unfold in various situations. Previous research that examined the use of mobile devices in informal settings has shown both promises and challenges (e.g., Sharples, 2006; Squire & Klopfer, 2007). From the design and research perspectives, however, studying mobile learning in informal settings is challenging because students are "on the move" across different modes of space (both physical and virtual) and time, posing challenges for the collection of data.

Mobile learning researchers also face methodological challenges in terms of the scales of space and time (Lemke, 2000): how to record learning across different physical spaces and different technological media, and how to examine learning in the longer timescale including informal learning outside school contexts. Possible data sources include, but are not limited to, observations, field notes, audio and video recordings, interviews, student artifacts, self-documentation by participants and log files on computers. There are also methodological issues involved in observations such as distorted behaviors and artificial tasks (Gardner, 2000), and also ethics and privacy issues involved with observing students outside school settings. Researchers should aim to minimize potential problems by employing unobtrusive methods such as log files which provide an authentic, time-efficient means of recording student learning behaviors. In-situ sampling of the students' daily experiences with mobile devices can be captured using the Experience Sampling Method (ESM) (Csikszentmihalyi & Larson, 1987).

Ethnographic approaches (Anderson-Levitt, 2006) have been suggested for observing how students are engaged in informal and formal learning settings in their interaction with their handheld devices, peers, teachers, and other people in their learning community. By employing ethnographic methods, cooperative inquiry, in-situ self-report procedures, constant comparisons, and sustained observations as well as analyzing quantifiable measures, researchers can critically examine how learners use mobile technology across subject areas and how different user experiences and motivation levels affect learning over time.

In short, research into seamless learning needs a strong focus on pedagogy, professional development of teachers, co-design of lessons with teachers, a design research perspective, and low-cost affordable mobile learning devices. International collaboration and innovation can contribute towards the broader research agenda. By organizing and sharing information across design experiments in diverse settings, a collaboration of researchers can more rapidly and systematically explore the design space (Hawkins, 1997). For instance, the same-grade classrooms across different countries can implement mobile learning devices for all subject areas, allowing a broad examination of solutions and challenges. By collaborating across the globe, researchers could take advantage of different student device preferences, exchange curriculum ideas, understand cultural differences, and better address issues of scale.

CONCLUSION

This chapter discusses frameworks and dimensions of seamless learning. In emphasizing the role of mobile technologies in fostering seamless learning, we identify practical approaches of matching the affordances of mobile technology to the premises of seamless learning. Drawing on our own research, we discuss the use of the affordances of mobile technology to connect students' learning spaces for the continuity of learning experiences across different scenarios. Learning spaces can be enhanced or extended by mobile technologies that support learning across multiple contexts and time scales.

Our position is that seamless learning can be fostered and scaffolded by appropriate design of learning across the various dimensions of learning. The ideal is for learners to internalize seamless learning as a learning disposition and attitude, so that they become seamless learners in their own right. When they learn, they can find ways to integrate their own learning experiences across space, time, location and the other dimensions, and to be able to self-regulate their own learning. Understanding technology-supported seamless learning is important for researchers and practitioners who are interested in connecting formal learning and informal learning spaces in order to create rich and holistic learning experiences for the students.

REFERENCES

Anderson-Levitt, K. M. (2006). Ethnography. In P. B. Elmore, G. Camilli & J. Green (Eds.), *Handbook of Complementary Methods in Education Research.* Washington, DC & Mahwah, NJ: AERA & Lawrence Erlbaum Associates.

Bruner, J. S. (1960). *The Process of Education.* Cambridge, MA: Harvard University Press.

Chan, T.-W., Roschelle, J., Hsi, S., Kinshuk, Sharples, M., Brown, T., et al. (2006). One-to-one technology-enhanced learning: An opportunity for global research collaboration. *Research and Practice in Technology-Enhanced Learning, 1*(1), 3–29.

Chen, W. L., Seow, P., So, H.-J. Toh, Y., & Looi, C. K. (2010). Connecting learning spaces using mobile technology. *Educational Technology, 50*(5), 45–50.

Csikszentmihalyi, M., & Larson, R. (1987). Validity and reliability of the experience sampling method. *Journal of Nervous and Mental Disease, 175*(9), 526–536.

Gardner, F. (2000). Methodological issues in the direct observation of parent-child interaction: Do observational findings reflect the natural behavior of participants? *Journal of Clinical Child and Family Psychology Review, 3*(3), 185–198.

Hawkins, J. (1997). The national design experiments consortium: Final report. New York: Center for Children and Technology, Educational Development Center.

Kuh, G. D. (1996). Guiding principles for creating seamless learning environments for undergraduates. *College Student Development, 37*(2), 135–148.

Kukulska-Hulme, A., Sharples, M., Milrad, M., Arnedillo-Sánchez, I., & Vavoula, G. (2009). Innovation in mobile learning: A European perspective. *Mobile and Blended Learning, 1*(1), 13–35.

Kukulska-Hulme, A., Traxler, J., & Pettit, J. (2007). Designed and user-generated activity in the mobile age. *Learning Design, 2*(1), 52–65.

Lemke, J. L. (2000). Across the scales of time: Artifacts, activities, and meanings in ecosocial systems. *Mind, Culture, and Activity, 7*(4), 273–290.

Leung, C.-H., & Chan, Y.-Y. (2003). Mobile learning: A new paradigm in electronic learning. *Proceedings of the IEEE International Conference on Advanced Learning Technologies 2003* (pp. 76–80), Athens, Greece.

Looi, C.-K., Seow, P., Zhang, B. H., So, H.-J., Chen, W., & Wong, L.-H. (2010). Leveraging mobile technology for sustainable seamless learning: A research agenda. *British Journal of Educational Technology, 42*(1), 154–169.

Mezler, A., Hadley, L., Glasemann, M., Werner, S., Winkler, T., & Herczeg, M. (2007). Using interactive design and development for mobile learning systems in school projects. *Proceedings of the IADIS International Conference on Cognition and Exploratory Learning in Digital Age 2007* (pp. 65–72), Algarve, Portugal.

Norris, C., & Soloway, E. (2002). Keynote speech. *IEEE International Workshop on Wireless and Mobile Technologies in Education 2002*, Växjö, Sweden.

Roschelle, J. (2003). Keynote paper: Unlocking the learning value of wireless mobile devices. *Journal of Computer Assisted Learning, 19*(3), 260–272.

Sharples, M. (2006). How can we address the conflicts between personal informal learning and traditional classroom education? In M. Sharples (Ed.), *Big Issues in Mobile Learning* (pp. 21–24). Nottingham: LSRI, University of Nottingham.

So, H.-J., Kim, I., & Looi, C.-K. (2008). Seamless mobile learning: Possibilities and challenges arising from the Singapore experience. *Educational Technology International, 9*(2), 97–121.

Squire, K., & Klopfer, E. (2007). Augmented reality simulations on handheld computers. *Journal of the Learning Sciences, 16*(3), 371–413.

Stroup, W. M., & Petrosino, A. J. (2003). An analysis of horizontal and vertical device design for school-related teaching and learning. *Education, Communication & Information, 3*(3), 327–345.

Toh, Y., So, H.-J., Seow, P., Chen, W., & Looi, C.-K. (in-press). Seamless learning in the mobile age: A theoretical and methodological discussion on using cooperative inquiry to study digital kids on-the-move. *Learning, Media and Technology.*

Wong, L.-H. (2012). A learner-centric view of mobile seamless learning. *British Journal of Educational Technology, 43*(1), E19–E23.

Wong, L.-H. (in-press). Enculturating self-directed learners through a facilitated seamless learning process framework. *Technology, Pedagogy and Education.*

Wong, L.-H., Chai, C.-S., Chin, C.-K., Hsieh, Y.-F., & Liu, M. (2012). Towards a seamless language learning framework mediated by the ubiquitous technology. *International Journal on Mobile Learning and Organisation, 6*(2), 156–171.

Wong, L.-H., Chin, C.-K., Tan, C.-L., & Liu, M. (2010). Students' personal and social meaning making in a Chinese idiom mobile learning environment. *Educational Technology & Society, 13*(4), 15–26.

Wong, L.-H., & Looi, C.-K. (2011). What seams do we remove in mobile assisted seamless learning? A critical review of the literature. *Computers & Education, 57*(4), 2364–2381.

Zhang, B. H., Looi, C.-K., Seow, P., Chia, G., Wong, L.-H., Chen, W., et al. (2010). Deconstructing and reconstructing: Transforming primary science learning via a mobilized curriculum. *Computers & Education, 55*(4), 1504–1523.

14

PUTTING THE ECOLOGY OF RESOURCES DESIGN FRAMEWORK TO USE WITH LANGUAGE LEARNERS' CONTEXTS

Rosemary Luckin, Wilma Clark, and Joshua Underwood

1 INTRODUCTION

Modern technology developments present educational practitioners and designers with an exciting array of potential learning benefits and a diverse collection of challenges that need to be addressed if these benefits are to become reality. One of these challenges concerns how best to take into account a learner's context, so that the technologies that enable physical locations, temporal boundaries and personal constraints to be linked, crossed and surmounted can be brought to bear on pedagogy and attainment. Luckin (2010) addresses this challenge and provides a model and design framework based upon a learner-centered definition of context, which also draws (beneficially) on and from research in geography and architecture, anthropology and psychology, and education and computer science. The theoretical basis for this work is discussed in the Foundations section of this handbook together with an example illustrating its use to generate a rich description of a particular learning context.

The structured process of the Ecology of Resources Design Framework is iterative, participatory and has three phases, each of which has several steps (a full account of the framework can be found in Luckin (2010)).

1. Phase 1: Create an Ecology of Resources model to identify and organize the potential forms of assistance that can act as resources for learning.
2. Phase 2: Identify the relationships within and between the resources produced in Phase 1. Identify the extent to which these relationships meet a learner's needs and how they might be optimized with respect to that learner.
3. Phase 3: Develop the scaffolds and adjustments to support learning and enable the negotiation of a Zone of Proximal Adjustment (ZPA) for a learner.

The Ecology of Resources approach is not prescriptive about the exact manner in which these iterations are completed, how many iterations are needed, or exactly how the users and beneficiaries should be engaged. Phase 1 is largely about developing better and shared understandings of learner context, particularly the resources that may be available, and filters that constrain interactions with these (Chapter 3 in the Foundations section of this handbook provides an example application of Phase 1). The emphasis in this current chapter is on using this understanding in design. Consequently we focus on Phases 2 and 3 as these are the phases in which we start to formulate and design the changes we believe will improve learning. Of course, in practice, design thinking tends to extend rather more messily across all three phases, particularly in later iterations through phases.

Phase 1 Creating an Ecology of Resources model

Phase 1 identifies the potential elements of the learners' Ecology of Resources and restricts these elements to those that are relevant for the current design focus of attention. Chapter 3 in the Foundation section of this handbook provides a detailed example of this phase.

Phase 2 Identify the Relationships Within and Between the Resources and Filters of the Ecology of Resources

The relationships and interactions between resource elements and between learner and resource elements are the key to the design process. The design process must support the optimization of these interactions. These relationships are complex, with each category of resource element, and therefore each element in that category, potentially related to every other element, as well as to the learner. In addition resource ecologies and relationships change as learners move through settings and time. Consequently tools that help designers think about these changes over time (at both macro and micro levels) become particularly useful. In the first example provided in this chapter we discuss one such tool.

Finding out about relationships from the learner's perspective is also challenging but essential. Learners' own narrative accounts can provide this perspective (see example 1) as can autoethnography (see Chapter 18 in this handbook). Autoethnography also provides insights into some of the ethical complexities of highly contextual and participatory design methods such as the Ecology of Resource framework. We illustrate this in the second example provided in this chapter.

Phase 3 Developing the Scaffolds and Adjustments

Phases 1 and 2 of the framework enable the design team to map out the elements and interactions of a learner's ZPA. To support learners and MAPs in their negotiation and shaping of a ZPA, the relationships identified in Phase 2 need to be explored to identify opportunities for adjustments and scaffolding to support the interactions of the learner's ZPA. The process continues the iterative approach of Phases 1 and 2 and will involve the design team in both the fine-grained analysis and consideration of how a particular element and interaction fit into the totality of the learner's Ecology of Resources. Both the term 'adjustment' and the term 'scaffold' refer to the identification of ways of supporting a learner's interactions and both are intended to engender learning. Scaffolding involves the evaluation of learner need, the provision of assistance and the withdrawal (or fading) of that assistance in order to engender learner development. The term 'adjustment' refers to less dynamic changes that can be made to resource ecologies in support of the learner, improved connectivity for example.

2 THE ECOLOGY OF RESOURCES DESIGN FRAMEWORK IN USE

This chapter presents two examples of the Ecology of Resources framework in use and is a complement to the example included in our chapter in the Foundations section. The objective of this chapter is a practical one: to illustrate to the reader how the design framework can be used in practice and to demonstrate some of the tools and techniques that we have developed as part of our use of the framework.

3 EMPIRICAL EXAMPLE 1

This first example demonstrates a visualization that is useful for looking at temporal relationships in resource ecologies (Phase 2) and supports design thinking about scaffolding and adjustments (Phase 3). In this example we use narrative data drawn from a study of 15 language learners. More detail on the study can be found in Underwood, Luckin & Winters (2011). In this study participants described memorable language learning experiences. These accounts were summarized from interview transcripts as written narratives. Here we illustrate how a chronological visualization of a single narrative can inform design. We use a narrative provided by Ines (not the real name of the contributor), whose mother tongue is Spanish. The story she told is provided below. Figure 14.1 provides a chronologically ordered representation of interactions with resources in the story.

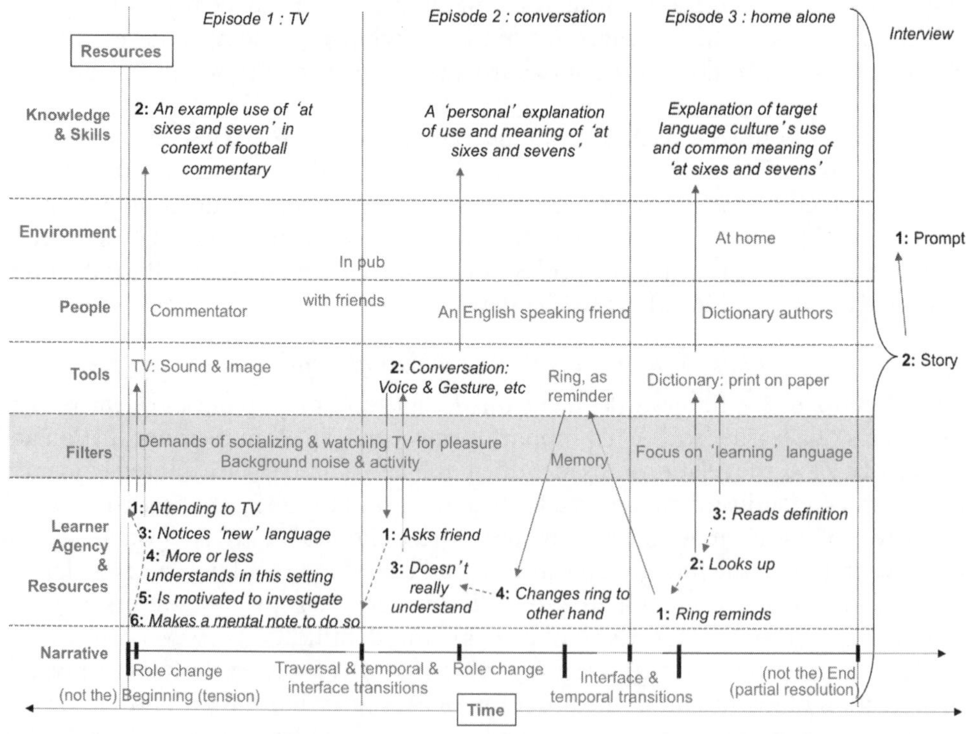

Figure 14.1 Chronologically Ordered Interactions with Resource Ecologies in Narratives (COIREN) chart (Underwood et al., 2011).

> Ines is in the pub with friends. The football is on the TV. She hears the commentator say something like 'he's at sixes and sevens'. She's been living in Ireland for years now and her English is very good but she's never heard that expression before. Her interest is piqued. She more or less gets the meaning in this context but she wants to check and improve her understanding, so she makes a mental note to do so. A little later she asks a friend about the expression. He says it's not an expression he would use. Ines is not very confident with the explanation he gives. She moves her ring from her right hand to her left hand, a habit she has developed to help remind her to look things up. Later at home, she notices her ring and looks up the expression. At first she can't remember exactly what is was, something to do with six and seven. Eventually, she finds it in her dictionary: 'at sixes and sevens—in a state of total confusion or disarray'. She is now more confident she understands. However, Ines's story doesn't end there. She isn't sure whether she has used 'at sixes and sevens' in conversation. She feels doing so might require conscious effort or perhaps she just hasn't had the opportunity.

COIREN: A tool for phase 2 relationship analysis

This chart is described as a Chronologically Ordered Interactions with Resource Ecologies in Narratives (COIREN) chart. It is a further progression of the CORDFU visualization developed previously to try to capture the way that multiple streams of activity interact with each other during learning interactions (Luckin, 2003) and borrows from Suthers, Dwyer, Medina, & Vatrapu (2010) visualization of contingency graphs. (CORDFU is also further developed in Chapter 40 in this handbook).

Figure 14.1 is divided into different horizontal layers. The learner's actions and the goals, feelings and other resources they bring to an interaction are included in the layer labelled Learner Agency & Resources. Other resources are likewise organized in layers labelled Knowledge & Skills, Environment, People, and Tools. A layer labelled Filters is positioned between the learner and these resources. Vertical lines break the narrative into discrete episodes. Key events or actions within episodes are numbered sequentially. *The objective behind representing interactions in this way is to focus designers' attention on dependencies between events (indicated by arrows) and connections across episodes (separated by vertical lines) and other transitions.* Such transitions are often accompanied by changes in filters and resource availability.

Other kinds of transitions in the story are identified and labelled at the bottom of the chart along the time axis in a manner informed by Benford, Giannachi, Koleva, & Rodden (2009). Benford et al. identify six kinds of transition from mixed reality experiences (Beginnings, Endings, Role transitions, Interface transitions, Traversals between physical and virtual worlds, Temporal transitions). Transitions are points where there might be a risk of loss of coherence and continuity and therefore indicate times where scaffolding or other support for learners could be required. The provision of such scaffolding and support is the objective of Phase 3 of the Ecology of Resources design framework. The visualization of Ines's story of successful learning highlights dependencies between events and resources that support her as she moves through such transitions.

From COIREN to Design Scenarios

As designers we can look at dependencies and resources in narratives of learning and consider how to make similar resources available to other learners and optimize their chances of realizing similar opportunities for learning. Developing scenarios can help flesh out and test these design ideas.

One way to redesign Ines' narrative is to adjust access to resources so that an 'authoritative' dictionary is available to Ines and her friend at the time of their conversation. We might even make the friend more aware of his transition into the teaching role and the learner's need for reassurance and perhaps prompt him to refer to a dictionary. Alternatively we might feel that her assessment of his reliability as a resource and her decision to seek further help are key elements of this narrative. Perhaps, then, in designing from this story we should look to prompt learners to solicit help from collaborators and also to assess and check the reliability of help received. Perhaps, also the delay between this episode and the reading of the dictionary and the effort Ines expends in order to connect her experiences across all three episodes are important to her learning. In this case we might want to scaffold learners in engaging in very similar processes as illustrated in the following scenario.

> Lola (not her real name) is in the pub with friends. The football is on the TV. Her ring pulses, this is a prompt to reflect on language she has just heard. She realizes the commentator just said something she more or less understood but she couldn't quite catch it. She taps her ring, this is a signal to her audio-visual recording device, worn as a hairclip, to save the last two minutes of her 'life' and index this to a new vocabulary record. A little later she asks a friend whether he caught what the commentator said. He's not sure what she is referring to and she can't reproduce it so she shows him the clip recorded on her phone and together they identify the phrase as 'at sixes and sevens'. He explains what he thinks it means but it's not an expression he uses much so they look it up in a dictionary also using the phone. Lola then taps her ring twice; this sets a reminder. A couple of days later at home, during the time she usually studies she hears a notification on her phone. She taps the notification and is reminded she heard a new expression and when and where, she thinks back and remembers at sixes and sevens but can't quite remember what it means. She looks it up again and adds a definition of the word to her vocabulary book on the phone. The vocab record includes a section for self-rating her understanding and ability to use the expression, this prompts her to assess her understanding. Still later her English teacher notices she has added the expression to her vocab list (he has access online) but with low confidence. At their next conversation session he shows Lola a picture of a very messy room and asks her to describe it, she says it is very disorganized. He prompts her, saying 'you could describe it as being at s . . .' and she completes the expression for him. She asks him where the expression comes from but he doesn't know, she taps her ring twice and resolves to investigate later.

Clearly, many such scenarios are possible and we are not suggesting that this scenario represents an ideal design for enhancing this kind of learning. Indeed 'any story one may tell about anything is better understood by considering other possible ways in which it can be told' (Bruner, 2004, p. 709). The value of this story is the stories it provokes others to tell: how would you tell it? The aim here is to stimulate rather than constrain design; many alternative scenarios should be generated and discussed. Ultimately different design teams will come up with their own preferred scenarios and these will depend on context, the resources available and the constraining filters.

4 EMPIRICAL EXAMPLE 2

The second empirical example draws upon an auto-ethnographic study, the focus of which was the methodology and practical and ethical implications of the Ecology of Resources design framework itself. The study explored and modelled an adult learner and her context for learning the French language while in France and then on her return to the UK. The learner had access to a range of technologies that she used for a variety of activities including: to communicate; to record in multiple media formats; to search and explore; and for entertainment and leisure. Whilst the underlying desire of the Ecology of Resources design framework is to develop contextualized technology-rich learning activities and the researcher was keen to make explicit the potentials of technology to support learning, the main focus of attention was on the methodology for resource identification and context mapping and its practical and ethical implications.

The main source of data collection and generation was a blog created by the learner to record her experiences of learning the French language as they happened. This blog developed into an aggregation of some of the language-learning resources that were used; it can be found at http://rosequotidienne.wordpress.com/. Other data sources include: the identity and date of visit for websites visited by the learner and other online resources; the learner's web browser bookmarks; the learner's iCal diary of activities; exercises and activities completed by the learner as part of her language classes (these are almost exclusively paper based); learner's phone activity history; sundry paper-based jottings by the learner (examples of all these data sources can be found at http://eorframework.pbworks.com/).

The instance we expand upon for this empirical example is selected from Phase 2 of the Ecology of Resources process, the aim of which is to identify the relationships between resources, filters and the learner. Table 14.1 summarizes the resources and filters that were identified through Phase 1 of the design process. The text in italics offers some more detail about a subset of these resources and their filters (full detail can be found at http://eorframework.pbworks.com/).

Table 14.1 illustrates that *French language TV* is identified as a resource with different types of French TV programme found in the data: *news; Tele matin; advertisements; game shows*. All resources are potentially inter-connected, and the blog entry for 28 April offers some data about the relationships between the French language TV resources. We have identified resources for learning from the *People* and *Tools* categories underscored in *italic*, from the *Knowledge & Skills* category in UPPER CASE and those from the *Environment* category in **bold**:

> As I sat in front of the *TV* doing *my homework* ready for class I was amused to note that I find the gentle flow of *French conversation* in the background useful. This is a very different situation to that in force when I last learnt French many years ago when TV and homework certainly did not mix. I feel I am benefitting from my decision to spend a section of the day in FRENCH IMMERSION as far as possible. This was helped with a good start from *William*, who was on good form this morning and aided by my understanding a little more of the *one o'clock news*. I was very amused to see the tractors in Paris as farmers protested about falling prices and stricter regulation: they would prefer to return to the EU rules. The farmers had taken their tractors to Paris and had travelled from Place de Nation to Place de la Bastille and from Place de la Bastille to Place du Republique. If I understood the *bulletin* correctly the Paris-

Table 14.1 Summary of French Language Learner's Resources and Filters

Resource Element	**Resource Filter**
KNOWLEDGE/SKILLS Fr. Syntax Fr. Semantics Fr. Living Language Fr. Language Skills	The English Language Opinion Learning/philosophy Culture
PEOPLE AND TOOLS Fr. Paper (text & images) ***French TV****: news; Tele matin; advertisements; game shows;* ***Video/Film:*** *Films with subtitles (Fr: Eng; Eng: Fr)—DVDs; YouTube; Cinema; French language adverts;* ***Audio****, French language not language learning specific: Radio; Audio Books; Music & Song: overheard conversations in my proximity; Phone messages; French language—language learning specific (Audio CD course; Listening exercise)* ***Digital Technology*** ***People,*** *for example Language class teacher/staff; Landlady and her husband; Peers; Shop/Restaurant/café proprietors/staff/cashier; Fellow passengers and customers; Colleagues; Family.*	Ownership/access Political/Economic Physical Locale Time Finances/Exchange Distribution ***Power****, e.g. battery or mains electricity; storage e.g. digital storage capacity and ability of devices used* ***Licensing and copyright*** ***Ethos/ownership/political stance of media*** *that filters/edits what is reported about what happens in the world and how it is reported;* ***Distribution*** *of film; TV schedule and production;* NSP land/mobile The lives of others
ENVIRONMENT Fr. Lang school UK. Work Fr. Commercial premises e.g. shops UK. Commercial premises e.g. shops Fr. Travel/ transport UK. Travel/ transport Fr. Living Accommodation UK. Living Accommodation Fr. Landmarks/scenery	Management Weather/Tide/Season Administration Commercial structure Maps/plans/signs/

> ians who were interviewed seemed, as ever, patient and understanding of the protest despite the fact that it seemed to be blocking much of the traffic. Mind you I don't think any motorists were amongst those interviewed. Now that I am back in **France**, after coming from **England**, I continue to notice the difference in *people's* attitudes to industrial action here.

We can also explore the filters (as indicated in Table 14.1) and their potential relationships. We can see in the data example above that there is *homework*, which indicates the existence of the *Learning philosophy* filter and since the homework emanated from the language school then the filters of *Management*, *Administration*, and *Commercial structure* all come into play. These filters are also relevant to the rented accommodation where the learner is watching the TV. The learner is an English speaker and therefore her experience of the French Language TV resource is filtered by *The English Language.* The TV bulletin is about a strike by French farmers and therefore the *Political/Economic* filter is relevant too. The influence of the *Time* filter is also clear in the text, for example: 'spend a section of the day in French immersion' and the 'one o'clock news'. The

Media ethos/editorial filter influences the TV reports and the *Distribution, Power*, and *Network Service Provision* filters will have influenced the availability of the TV and its programmes to the learner.

Other data sources can also be used to clarify the relationships within this TV learning experience. For example, if we look at the diary entry for the day that the blog entry refers to, i.e. 27 April, we can see the record of watching breakfast TV between 7 and 8 am, hence the reference to William: the Breakfast TV host, in the blog text. There is no direct reference to the one o'clock news in the diary, but there is a reference to completing the homework mentioned in the blog post. There is also reference to some resources viewed on the website 'about.com' that deal with prepositions; to listening to the audio course; to working on making some verb conjugation sheets (which were subsequently uploaded to the blog); and to watching the news later in the day at 8 pm.

The blog entry read:

> My particular issue today has been prepositions, particularly when used to describe going to and from places. I have noted previously how I find these little words difficult to handle, so I have decided to focus on these for the Franglais today. I have also added the following resources:
>
> *Regular Verb Examples*—Present, Past Participle and Future
> *Key Irregular Verbs*—Present, Past Participle and Future.

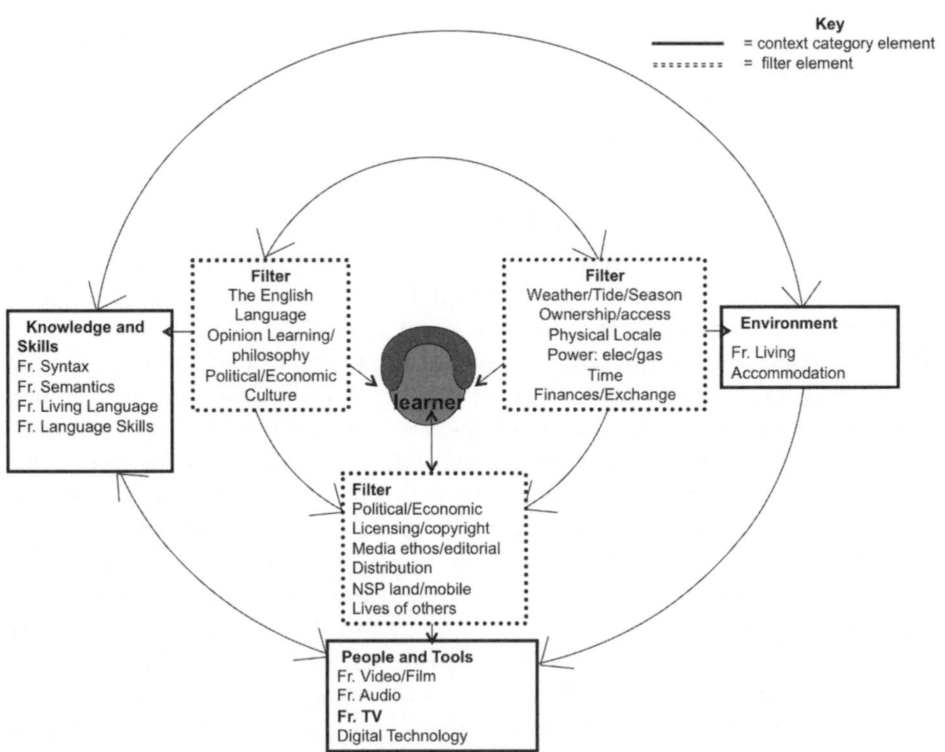

Figure 14.2 Ecology of Resources illustration for language learning example 2.

This indicates the relationship between the blog and the paper resources and between these and the on-line resources at 'about-com' that deals with prepositions.

We could also look at other instances of TV watching within the data to explore what other resources, filters and relationships can be identified, so that we can build up a clearer understanding of the *French language TV* resource and its relationships. For example, the regular references to watching the 8 pm news. These relationships can be seen in the Ecology of Resources model illustrated in Figure 14.2.

5 EXAMPLE 3: AUTOETHNOGRAPHY, COMPLEXITY AND DESIGN REQUIREMENTS

This example illustrates the use of the visualization of the Ecology of Resources model through Figure 14.2. The main purpose of this example is to illustrate the *complex interconnectedness* of the learner's resources and their filters, the potentially intrusive nature of the Ecology of Resources methodology and the possible beneficial use of autoethnography. The detail about a learner's life that can be gained through tracking their web browsing, accessing their diary and their phone logs can yield details about their learning context that could help designers to gain insights into the interventions that might scaffold learning. However, participants must be fully aware of the nature of the data that are to be collected, be able to veto the collection of data about which they are uncomfortable and restrict access to certain sorts of data as they see fit.

These insights can be interpreted as requirements and challenges to inspire design. How can technology-enhanced learning designs help learners collect data about their learning, the resources available to them, filters acting on them and the relationships between these? How can we help learners make sense of these data in ways that help them learn? How can we help them find and solicit appropriate help (including TEL designers) and share the right data with the right helpers?

6 DISCUSSION

The Ecology of Resources model frames a participatory design process that enables us to identify the assistance that could be available to learners, the ways that learners' interactions might be filtered, and the situations where scaffolding might be used. Feedback from participants with whom we have worked has been positive and both the design of activities that use technology to support learning, and the design of the technologies themselves have been developed through the use of the framework. The main purpose of this chapter, however, is to explain the design framework through examples of its use and to present some of the tools and techniques that have been developed to accompany the framework and some of the practical and ethical implications inherent in its use.

Through two empirical examples we have demonstrated some of the phases and steps in the iterative, participatory design process and the use of the following tools: the tabulated representation of the categorized resources and their associated filters in Table 14.1; the Ecology of Resources model in Figure 14.2, and the visualization of learner stories as connected Ecologies of Resources in chronologically ordered visualizations, such as the COIREN chart in Figure 14.1 that can support the identification of scaffolding opportunities. All of these tools are designed to be shared with and used by *all* participants in the design process.

We have also illustrated the complex interconnectedness of the learner's resources and their filters, and highlighted the potentially intrusive nature of the Ecology of Resources methodology. We have stressed the need for participants to be fully aware of the nature of the data that are being collected, and for them to be able to make decisions about how they are used. This latter point is extremely important because it has both a negative and a positive reading. The negative interpretation arises from the potential detriment caused by inappropriate invasive data collection if participants are not fully engaged in the design process. The positive interpretation arises from the realization of the importance of ensuring that participants are full members of the design team with a voice that must be heard and an involvement that results in their being more aware of their own resources for learning.

ACKNOWLEDGEMENT

In particular, we thank the participants who have made our empirical work possible and the Engineering and Physical Sciences Research Council for funding our research.

REFERENCES

Benford, S., Giannachi, G., Koleva, B., & Rodden, T. (2009). From Interaction to Trajectories: designing coherent journeys through user experiences. *Proceedings of the 27th International Conference on Human Factors in Computing Systems*, Boston, MA, ACM.

Bruner, J. (2004). Life as Narrative. *Social Research: An International Quarterly, 71*(3), 691–710.

Luckin, R. (2003). Between the Lines: documenting the multiple dimensions of computer supported collaborations. *Computers and Education (Special issue on Documenting Collaborative Interactions), 41*(4), 379–396.

Luckin, R. (2010). Re-designing Learning Contexts: technology rich, learner-centred ecologies. London: Routledge.

Suthers, D., Dwyer, N., Medina, R., & Vatrapu, R. (2010). A framework for conceptualizing, representing, and analyzing distributed interaction. *International Journal of Computer-Supported Collaborative Learning, 5*(1), 5–42.

Underwood, J., Luckin, R., & Winters, N. (2011). Retelling Stories: setting learner narratives in resource ecologies. *Proceedings of the Conference on Computer Supported Collaborative Learning*, Hong Kong, July 3–8.

15

DESIGNING AFFECTIVE AND COGNITIVE EDUCATIONAL INTERACTION

Benedict du Boulay

INTRODUCTION

When we observe how expert teachers behave, we find that they devote considerable time and effort to affective issues. For example, as Lepper and his colleagues report, expert human teachers include among their goals 'first, to sustain and enhance their students' motivation and interest in learning, . . . and second, to maintain their pupils' feelings of self-esteem and self-efficacy, even in the face of difficult or impossible problems' (Lepper, Aspinwall, Mumme, & Chabay, 1990, p. 219).

This chapter is about the design of educational systems, in other words the design of interactive computer-based educational systems that teach, guide and assess the learner. Knowing that the learner's feelings are an important aspect of how (and how much) they learn, the software designer needs to decide whether to take account of the potential feelings of the users as part of the design of the system, or whether to leave that kind of issue to the human teacher who runs the class within which the system is used.

One advantage of taking such factors as 'motivation', 'interest', 'self-esteem and self-efficacy' into account as part of the design of adaptive and intelligent systems is that such systems are likely to produce greater learning gains either for learners working remotely on their own or for a class of learners, without the need for the human teacher who is managing the class to provide all the individual, minute by minute, affective support needed by each learner (see, for example, Baker et al., 2008; Beal & Lee, 2005; D'Mello et al., 2011; Jaques, Lehmann, & Pesty, 2009; Paas, Tuovinen, van Merriënboer, & Darabi, 2005).

The disadvantage of taking these kinds of factor into account is a considerable increase in design complexity, as the system will need to detect, model and react to the learner's affective state in addition to dealing with cognitive aspects of the learner's state.

So the first question facing the educational interaction designer with 'affect in mind' is what role should affect play in the system being developed. It is a commonplace that the cognitive and affective are intricately intertwined in both learning and teaching (see, for example, Boekaerts, 2007; Forgas, 2008; Kort & Reilly, 2002b; Picard, 2000), but deciding exactly how a human teacher or a system might take account of this is open to a wide range of possibilities (see, for example, Ames, 1992; Balaam, Fitzpatrick, Good, & Luckin, 2010; Porayska-Pomsta, Mavrikis, & Pain, 2008).

The learner's relatively conscious appraisal of events *external* to him or her has both cognitive and affective consequences (Pekrun, 2006). For example, praise from a teacher may make the learner feel pleased, judge himself or herself to be making progress, and so decide to work harder, but in some circumstances it may have other effects (Dweck, 2002). Another is that the learner's relatively conscious appraisal of *internal* cognitive and affective events has both cognitive and affective consequences. For example, detecting that sense of increasing frustration when failing to solve a problem can trigger further affective responses (e.g. shame), as well as further cognitive reactions, such as deciding to give up (Diener & Dweck, 1980). In a similar vein, certain affective processes have relatively unconscious consequences for cognitive processes themselves (Forgas, 2007).

In taking account of this interplay, we distinguish design issues around (i) static aspects of the system that are the same for all learners (*non-adaptive*: see, for example, Malone & Lepper, 1987), from (ii) dynamic aspects that adapt as a one-off to classes of users (*macro-adaptive*: see, for example, Arroyo, Beck, Woolf, Beal, & Schultz, 2000; Shute, 1993), and from (iii) dynamic aspects that adapt to individual learners at run time (*micro-adaptive*). This chapter concentrates on the micro-adaptive aspects of affective design and, to a lesser extent, on the macro-adaptive.

In thinking about how adaptive decisions might be designed it is necessary to choose where the main design focus should lie.

Table 15.1 distinguishes six different kinds of primary design focus. For a more detailed discussion, see du Boulay et al. (2010). In the first row are systems that are designed to try to achieve cognitive gains (either in knowledge or skill). Apart from designing the interaction to be agreeable, but affectively the same for all users, they make only

Table 15.1 Possible design foci for affective and cognitive educational interactions

	Main Goal	
Main Design Focus	**Cognitive**	**Affective**
1. Cognitive	Increasing the learner's knowledge and skill	
2. Metacognitive	Increasing the learner's metacognitive capability, e.g. insight into what she understands and can do, and her ability to regulate her learning process effectively.	
3. Affective		Increasing the learner's overall sense of well-being
4. Meta-affective		Increasing the learner's meta-affective capability, e.g. her insight and regulation of her feelings as a learner.
5. Motivational	Increasing the learner's desire to learn, e.g. her willingness to expend effort on the learning process.	
6. Meta-motivational	Increasing the learner's meta-motivational capability e.g. her insight and regulation of her motivation.	

cognitive micro-level adaptations (see, for example, Koedinger, Anderson, Hadley, & Mark, 1997; Mitrovic, Martin, & Suraweera, 2007). Most adaptive educational software has been designed in this way.

In the second row there are systems that are designed to increase the learner's meta-cognitive skills and adapt at the micro- or macro-level to that purpose. Typically they will also be concerned to achieve cognitive gains, but take the same design stance towards affect as in the first row. There is a growing number of such systems: see, for example, Aleven, McLaren, Roll & Koedinger (2006) and Luckin & Hammerton (2002).

In the third row there are systems that aim primarily to increase the learner's sense of fun, excitement or well-being as a result of the educational interaction, and make either an initial macro-level, or dynamic adjustments at a micro-level to achieve this (see, for example, Yussof & du Boulay, 2010).

The fourth row contains systems that aim to increase the learners' meta-affective capability, so that they are better able to identify and manage their own feelings in educational settings, e.g. working through confusion and disappointment (see, for example, Burleson, 2006), or establishing an affective vocabulary for communication with the teacher (Balaam, Luckin, & Good, 2009).

The fifth row starts to open up a more balanced educational design agenda between the cognitive and the affective. This focuses on the crucial educational issue of motivation. Yes, we want students to achieve cognitive gains but we also want them to be able to deal with the vicissitudes of learning, as well as develop some meta-level skills of both a cognitive and an affective nature, so they are better equipped as learners in future educational interactions. Such systems are rare, but some educational games are beginning to develop capabilities in this design territory (see, for example, Johnson, 2007).

Finally, in the sixth row there are systems designed to achieve all the goals of the systems already mentioned, but also to help learners gain insight into their own motivational processes and capability, for example learning how to manage themselves so as to be able to study despite distractions and temptations, in other words to become self-regulated learners (Zimmerman, 2008).

WHICH AFFECTIVE PEDAGOGICAL THEORY OR STRATEGY?

A number of different theories and strategies have been used by educators to manage learners' affect and motivation. Table 15.2 gives a number of examples, differentiating between macro- and micro-level adaptations. Following Pintrich (2003) we differentiate these examples in terms of whether they focus primarily on the learner's feelings, expectancies or values. Table 15.2 aims to provide a representative sample of theories, strategies and systems rather than an exhaustive list. For more detailed discussions see du Boulay et al. (2010) and Arroyo et al. (2011).

Most of the rows in Table 15.2 are self-explanatory. However, we offer the following gloss on the 'Detect and react' row. Many systems have been built to detect the learner's affective state and, if that state is regarded as unconducive to learning, (e.g. boredom) try to make it more conducive. Care has to be taken as some apparently negative states (e.g. frustration) may be an essential component of some kinds of learning episode (Forgas, 2007), and do not need always to be reacted to (Baker, D'Mello, Rodrigo, & Graesser, 2010). Kort and Reilly (2002b) go further in their theory of affect in learning, which embodies a sequence of affective states that cycles between the negative and the positive.

Table 15.2 Affective theories and strategies

Adapt. Level	Primary focus	Theory or Strategy	Examples
Macro	Values and feelings	Relevance and saving face	Rosiek (2003) gives a number of examples of where human teachers find ways to make the learning material relevant to particular groups or ways to explore controversial topics. For an example of a system that macro-adapts based on gender, see Arroyo et al. (2000).
	Expectancies	Goal orientation	Various researchers have built systems based on Dweck et al.'s (1995) distinction between mastery and performance goals in learning, see for example Martinez-Miron et al. (2005).
Micro	Feelings	Empathy	Various researchers have built systems that attempt to detect the affective state of the learner and acknowledge that perception by adapting the demeanour or feedback from the tutor to demonstrate empathy (see, for example, Arroyo et al., 2009b; Burleson, 2006; Zakharov et al., 2008).
	Feelings and expectancies	Detect and react	Various researchers have built systems that (i) *detect* either affective states, or cycles of states, either through observation of the learner's demeanour or his or her actions, such as gaming the system, and (ii) *react* appropriately. This may be to try to fix things if there is a problem or consolidate the situation if not (see, for example, Baker et al., 2006; Graesser et al., 2007; Kapoor et al., 2007; Kort & Reilly, 2002a; Muldner et al., 2010).
	Feelings, values and expectancies	Model-based	Some researchers have modelled and predicted the affective states of learners. They have often adopted OCC theory (Adam et al., 2009; Ortony, et al., 1988) in the design of their systems, see for example (Conati & Zhou, 2002; Jaques & Vicari, 2007).

In the final row of Table 15.2 we refer to OCC Theory (Ortony, Clore, & Collins, 1988) as it enables systems to reason about learner emotions rather than simply react to them. This has been an important influence in the development of micro-adaptive systems, and so deserves individual mention. It is based on an emotional theory that describes emotions in terms of an individual's cognitive appraisal of events, objects and agents. So, for example, a learner may have feelings of respect for a teacher (an agent) who operates in a very professional manner towards that student, and indeed, to other students whom the learner knows.

WHICH PEDAGOGICAL INTERVENTIONS SHOULD BE AVAILABLE?

The designer will need to consider the design of individual lessons and their components. So a designer may wish to ensure that the introduction to a lesson has both an explicit cognitive and an explicit affective dimension. For this to be automated, the system would need to know something about what was studied last time, how it was received, what the goals and methods of the current session are to be and how they are likely to be received. Considerations of how best to conclude a lesson may well mirror those around how best to start one, as indicated above. This requires both careful logging by the system of what happens as well as modelling derived from those logs.

In terms of ordering concepts and finding the right balance of activities (examples v. problems, say) there are various theories that can be applied; for example there are some based around learner motivational characteristics (mastery v. performance: see, for example, Dweck et al., 1995) or learning style (active v. reflective: see, for example, Graf, Liu, Kinshuk, Chen, & Yang, 2009), or around learner cognitive capacity limitations (see, for example, De Jong, 2010).

WHICH AFFECTIVE STATES ARE TO BE DISTINGUISHED AND HOW ARE THEY TO BE IDENTIFIED/

The 'basic' emotional states, developed for example by Ekman et al. (1972) are not a useful set with which to design educational interactions (Pekrun, 2011). For example, they include anger and disgust, and neither of these tends to occur in educational settings, though other more nuanced negative feelings are important in education such as disappointment, frustration, shame and anxiety. In the search for a more useful set, some research has observed students in educational settings via a mixture of observation, self-report, interviews and questionnaires and has identified a space of affective states: 'enjoyment, hope, pride, relief, anger, anxiety, shame, hopelessness, and boredom' (Pekrun, Goetz, Titz, & Perry, 2002). This space is often portrayed in a two-dimensional form with the degree of arousal (how strong the feeling is) along one dimension, and the valence (negative or positive) along another. Some systems operate simply on valence and distinguish and react to whether the learner is in a broadly positive or broadly negative frame of mind (Zakharov et al., 2008). A set of affective distinctions, commonly used by micro-adaptive system designers, is between 'boredom, flow (engagement), frustration, confusion, delight, surprise, and neutral' (see, for example, Graesser et al., 2007). The main design issue is whether the system is able to differentiate its reactions between all the affective states that can be identified (see, for example, du Boulay, 2011).

The methods and technology for identifying the affective states of learners fall into four categories. First there are various forms of self-report where learners are prompted to indicate their affective state (see, for example, Balaam et al., 2010; Beal & Lee, 2005). Second, there are methods using cameras to identify facial expression and from thence affective state (Craig, D'Mello, Witherspoon, & Graesser, 2008). Third, there are various kinds of sensor to identify body posture, skin conductance, heart rate, brain waves, and grip on the mouse. As yet the jury is still out as to which kind of technology works best (for a comparative analysis, see for example, Arroyo et al., 2009a). Fourth are methods based on observing learner behaviour, either from what they say (D'Mello, Craig, Witherspoon, McDaniel, & Graesser, 2008) or from the balance of off-task and on-task behaviour (Walonoski & Heffernan, 2006).

CONCLUSIONS

This chapter has delineated some of the issues that must be considered by a designer of educational systems, which are to react to affect. The order of description has been top-down from considerations of which affective pedagogical theory to embody in the system, which educational interactions are to be catered for, which affective states are to be identified and distinguished, and what methods are to be used to identify those states in the learner.

ACKNOWLEDGEMENTS

I thank Katerina Avramides, Katy Howland and the editors of this handbook for very helpful comments on earlier drafts of this chapter.

REFERENCES

Adam, C., Herzig, A., & Longin, D. (2009). A logical formalization of the OCC theory of emotions. *Synthese, 168*, 201–248.

Aleven, V., McLaren, B., Roll, I., & Koedinger, K. (2006). Toward meta-cognitive tutoring: A model of help seeking with a Cognitive Tutor. *International Journal of Artificial Intelligence in Education, 16*(2), 101–128.

Ames, C. (1992). Classrooms: Goals, structures, and student motivation. *Journal of Educational Psychology, 84*(3), 261–271.

Arroyo, I., Beck, J. E., Woolf, B. P., Beal, C. R., & Schultz, K. (2000). Macroadapting animalwatch to gender and cognitive differences with respect to hint interactivity and symbolism. In G. Gauthier, C. Frasson, & K. Van-Lehn (Eds.), *5th International Conference on Intelligent Tutoring Systems, ITS 2000* (Vol. Lecture Notes in Computer Science 1839, pp. 574–583). Montreal, Canada: Springer.

Arroyo, I., Cooper, D. G., Burleson, W., Woolf, B. P., Muldner, K., & Christopherson, R. (2009a). Emotion sensors go to school. In V. Dimitrova, R. Mizoguchi, B. du Boulay, & A. Grasser (Eds.), *Artificial Intelligence in Education. Building Learning Systems that Care: from Knowledge Representation to Affective Modelling* (Vol. Frontiers in Artificial Intelligence and Applications 200, pp. 17–24). Amsterdam: IOS Press.

Arroyo, I., du Boulay, B., Eligio, U. X., Luckin, R., & Porayska-Pomsta, K. (2011). In the Mood for Learning: methodology (D. O. Informatics, Trans.) *Cognitive Science Research Papers*: University of Sussex.

Arroyo, I., Woolf, B. P., Royer, J. M., & Tai, M. (2009b). Affective Gendered Learning Companions. In V. Dimitrova, R. Mizoguchi, B. du Boulay & A. Grasser (Eds.), *Artificial Intelligence in Education. Building Learning Systems that Care: from Knowledge Representation to Affective Modelling* (Vol. Frontiers in Artificial Intelligence and Applications 200, pp. 41–48): IOS Press.

Baker, R., Walonoski, J., Heffernan, N., Roll, I., Corbett, A., & Koedinger, K. (2008). Why students engage in 'gaming the system' behaviours in interactive learning environments. *Journal of Interactive Learning Research, 19*(2), 185–224.

Baker, R. S. J. d., Corbett, A. T., Koedinger, K. R., Evenson, S., Roll, I., Wagner, A. Z., et al. (2006). Adapting to when students game an intelligent tutoring system. In M. Ikeda, K. D. Ashley, & T.-W. Chan (Eds.), *Intelligent Tutoring Systems: 8th International Conference, ITS 2006, Jhongli, Taiwan, Proceedings* (Vol. Lecture Notes in Computer Science 4053, pp. 392–401): Springer.

Baker, R. S. J. d., D'Mello, S. K., Rodrigo, M. M. T., & Graesser, A. C. (2010). Better to be frustrated than bored: The incidence, persistence, and impact of learners' cognitive–affective states during interactions with three different computer-based learning environments *International Journal of Human-Computer Studies, 68*(4), 223–241.

Balaam, M., Fitzpatrick, G., Good, J., & Luckin, R. (2010). *Exploring Affective Technologies for the Classroom with the Subtle Stone.* Paper presented at the Proceedings of the 28th international conference on Human Factors in Computing Systems (CHI 2010), Atlanta, Georgia.

Balaam, M., Luckin, R., & Good, J. (2009). Supporting affective communication in the classroom with the Subtle Stone. *International Journal of Learning Technology, 4*(3–4), 188–215.

Beal, C. R., & Lee, H. (2005). Creating a pedagogical model that uses student self reports of motivation and mood to adapt ITS instruction. *Workshop on Motivation and Affect in Educational Software, at AIED2005, 12th International Conference on Artificial Intelligence in Education* (pp. 39–46). Amsterdam.

Boekaerts, M. (2007). Understanding students' affective processes in the classroom. In P. A. Schutz & R. Pekrun (Eds.), *Emotion in Education* (pp. 37–56). Burlington, MA: Acadmic Press.

Burleson, W. (2006). *Affective Learning Companions: strategies for empathetic agents with real-time multimodal affective sensing to foster meta-cognitive and meta-affective approaches to learning, motivation, and perseverance.* PhD, Massachusetts Institute of Technology, Cambridge, MA.

Conati, C., & Zhou, X. (2002). Modeling students' emotions from cognitive appraisal in educational games. In S. A. Cerri, G. Guy, & F. Paraguacu (Eds.), *Intelligent Tutoring Systems. 6th International Conference, ITS2002, Biarritz, France and San Sebastian, Spain, Proceedings* (Vol. Lecture Notes in Computer Science 2363, pp. 944–954). Berlin: Springer.

Craig, S. D., D'Mello, S., Witherspoon, A., & Graesser, A. (2008). Emote aloud during learning with AutoTutor: Applying the Facial Action Coding System to cognitive-affective states during learning. *Cognition & Emotion, 22*(5), 777–788.

D'Mello, S. K., Craig, S. D., Witherspoon, A., McDaniel, B., & Graesser, A. (2008). Automatic detection of learner's affect from conversational cues. *User Modeling and User-Adapted Interaction, 18*(1–2), 45–80.

D'Mello, S., Lehman, B., Sullins, J., Daigle, R., Combs, R., Vogt, K., et al. (2011). A time for emoting: When affect-sensitivity is and isn't effective at promoting deep learning. In R. A. Calvo & S. K. D'Mello (Eds.), *Affective Prospecting.* New York: Springer.

De Jong, T. (2010). Cognitive load theory, educational research, and instructional design: some food for thought. *Instructional Science, 38*(2), 105–134.

Diener, C. I., & Dweck, C. S. (1980). An analysis of learned helplessness: II. The processing of success. *Journal of Personality and Social Psychology, 39*(5), 940–952.

du Boulay, B. (2011). Towards a motivationally-intelligent pedagogy: How should an intelligent tutor respond to the unmotivated or the demotivated? In R. A. Calvo & S. K. D'Mello (Eds.), *New Perspectives on Affect and Learning Technologies* (pp. 41–54). New York: Springer.

du Boulay, B., Avramides, K., Luckin, R., Martinez-Miron, E., Rebolledo-Mendez, G., & Carr, A. (2010). Towards systems that care: A conceptual framework based on motivation, metacognition and affect. *International Journal of Artificial Intelligence in Education, 20*(3), 197–229.

Dweck, C. S. (2002). Messages that motivate: How praise molds students' beliefs, motivation, and performance (in surprising ways). In J. M. Aronson (Ed.), *Improving Academic Achievement: Impact of psychological factors on education* (pp. 37–60). New York: Academic Press.

Dweck, C. S., Chiu, C.-y., & Hong, Y.-y. (1995). Implicit theories and their role in judgments and reactions: A word from two perspectives. *Psychological Inquiry, 6*(4), 267–285.

Ekman, P., Friesen, W. V., & Ellsworth, P. C. (1972). *Emotion in the Human Face.* New York: Pergamon Press.

Forgas, J. P. (2007). When sad is better than happy: Negative affect can improve the quality and effectiveness of persuasive messages and social influence strategies. *Journal of Experimental Social Psychology, 43*(4), 513–528.

Forgas, J. P. (2008). Affect and cognition. *Perspectives on Psychological Science, 3*(2), 94–101.

Graesser, A., Chipman, P., King, B., McDaniel, B., & D'Mello, S. (2007). Emotions and learning with AutoTutor. In R. Luckin, K. R. Koedinger, & J. Greer (Eds.), *Proceeding of the 2007 Conference on Artificial Intelligence in Education: Building Technology Rich Learning Contexts that Work* (Vol. Frontiers in Artificial Intelligence and Applications 158, pp. 569–571). Amsterdam: IOS Press.

Graf, S., Liu, T.-C., Kinshuk, Chen, N.-S., & Yang, S. J. H. (2009). Learning styles and cognitive traits: Their relationship and its benefits in web-based educational systems. *Computers in Human Behaviour, 25*(6), 1280–1289.

Jaques, P. A., Lehmann, M., & Pesty, S. (2009). *Evaluating the Affective Tactics of an Emotional Pedagogical Agent.* Paper presented at the Proceedings of the 2009 ACM symposium on Applied Computing, Honolulu, Hawaii.

Jaques, P. A., & Vicari, R. M. (2007). A BDI approach to infer student's emotions in an intelligent learning environment. *Computers & Education, 49*(2), 360–384.

Johnson, L. W. (2007). Serious use of a serious game for language learning. In R. Luckin, K. R. Koedinger, & J. Greer (Eds.), *Proceeding of the 2007 Conference on Artificial Intelligence in Education: Building Technology Rich Learning Contexts that Work* (Vol. Frontiers in Artificial Intelligence and Applications 158, pp. 67–74). Amsterdam: IOS Press.

Kapoor, A., Burleson, W., & Picard, R. W. (2007). Automatic prediction of frustration. *International Journal of Human-Computer Studies, 65*(8), 724–736.

Koedinger, K. R., Anderson, J. R., Hadley, W. H., & Mark, M. A. (1997). Intelligent tutoring goes to school in the big city. *International Journal of Artificial Intelligence in Education, 8*(1), 30–43.

Kort, B., & Reilly, R. (2002a). an affective module for an intelligent tutoring system. In S. A. Cerri, G. Guy, & F. Paraguacu (Eds.), *Intelligent Tutoring Systems. 6th International Conference, ITS2002, Biarritz, France and San Sebastian, Spain, Proceedings* (Vol. Lecture Notes in Computer Science 2363, pp. 955–962): Springer.

Kort, B., & Reilly, R. (2002b). Theories for deep change in affect-sensitive cognitive machines: A constructivist model. *Educational Technology & Society, 5*(4), 56–63.

Lepper, M. R., Aspinwall, L. G., Mumme, D. L., & Chabay, R. W. (1990). Self perception and social-perception processes in tutoring: Subtle social control strategies of expert tutors. In J. M. Olson & M. P. Zanna (Eds.),

Self-Inference Processes: The Ontario Symposium (Vol. 6, pp. 217–237). Hillsdale, NJ: Lawrence Erlbaum Associates.

Luckin, R., & Hammerton, L. (2002). Getting to know me: helping learners understand their own learning needs through metacognitive scaffolding. *Intelligent Tutoring Systems. 6th International Conference, ITS2002, Biarritz, France and San Sebastian, Spain, Proceedings* (Vol. Lecture Notes in Computer Science 2363, pp. 759–771): Springer.

Malone, T. W., & Lepper, M. R. (1987). Making learning fun: A taxonomy of intrinsic motivations for learning. Aptitude, learning and instruction. In R. E. Snow & M. J. Farr (Eds.), *Aptitude Learning and Instruction* (Volume 3: Conative and Affective Process Analyses, pp. 223–253). Hillsdale, NJ: Lawrence Erlbaum Associates, Inc.

Martinez-Miron, E., Harris, A., du Boulay, B., Luckin, R., & Yuill, N. (2005). The role of learning goals in the design of ILEs: Some issues to consider. In C.-K. Looi, G. McCalla, B. Bredeweg, & J. Breuker (Eds.), *Artificial Intelligence in Education: Supporting Learning through Intelligent and Socially Informed Technology* (Vol. Frontiers in Artificial Intelligence and Applications 125, pp. 427–434). Amsterdam: IOS Press.

Mitrovic, A., Martin, B., & Suraweera, P. (2007). Intelligent tutors for all: The constraint-based approach. *IEEE Intelligent Systems, 22*(4), 38–45.

Muldner, K., Burleson, W., & VanLehn, K. (2010). 'Yes!': Using tutor and sensor data to predict moments of delight during instructional activities. In P. De Bra, A. Kobsa, & D. Chin (Eds.), *User Modeling, Adaptation, and Personalization: Proceedings of 18th International Conference, UMAP 2010.* Berlin: Springer.

Ortony, A., Clore, G. L., & Collins, A. (1988). *The Cognitive Structure of Emotions.* Cambridge University Press.

Paas, F., Tuovinen, J. E., van Merriënboer, J. J. G., & Darabi, A. A. (2005). A motivational perspective on the relation between mental effort and performance: Optimizing learner involvement in instruction. *Educational Technology Research and Development, 53*(3), 25–34.

Pekrun, R. (2006). The control-value theory of achievement emotions: Assumptions, corollaries, and implications for educational research and practice. *Educational Psychology Review, 18*(4), 315–341.

Pekrun, R. (2011) Emotions as Drivers of Learning and Cognitive Development. In R. A. Carlo & S. K. D'Mello (Eds.), New Perspectives on Affect and Learning Technologies (Vol. 3, Explorations in the Learning Sciences, Instructional Systems and Performance Technologies). New York: Springer.

Pekrun, R., Goetz, T., Titz, W., & Perry, R. P. (2002). Academic emotions in students' self-regulated learning and achievement: A program of qualitative and quantitative research. *Educational Psychologist, 37*(2), 91–105.

Picard, R. W. (2000). *Affective Computing.* Cambridge, MA: MIT Press.

Pintrich, P. (2003). Motivation and classroom learning. *Handbook of Psychology: Educational Psychology, 7*, 103–122.

Porayska-Pomsta, K., Mavrikis, M., & Pain, H. (2008). Diagnosing and acting on student affect: The tutor's perspective. *User Modeling and User-Adapted Interaction, 18*(1–2), 125–173.

Rosiek, J. (2003). Emotional scaffolding: An exploration of the teacher knowledge at the intersection of student emotion and the subject matter. *Journal of Teacher Education, 54*(4), 399–412.

Shute, V. J. (1993). A macroadaptive approach to tutoring. *Journal of Artificial Intelligence in Education, 4*(1), 61–93.

Walonoski, J. A., & Heffernan, N. T. (2006). Detection and analysis of off-task gaming behavior in intelligent tutoring systems. In M. Ikeda, K. D. Ashley, & T.-W. Chan (Eds.), *Intelligent Tutoring Systems: 8th International Conference, ITS 2006, Jhongli, Taiwan, Proceedings* (Vol. Lecture Notes in Computer Science 4053, pp. 382–391): Springer.

Yussof, M. Z., & du Boulay, B. (2010). *A tutoring system using an emotion-focused strategy to support learners.* Paper presented at the Proceedings of the 18th International Conference on Computers in Education (ICCE 2010), Putrajaya, Malaysia.

Zakharov, K., Mitrovic, A., & Johnston, L. (2008). Towards emotionally-intelligent pedagogical agents. In B. P. Woolf, E. Aïmeur, R. Nkambou, & S. L. Lajoie (Eds.), *Intelligent Tutoring Systems, 9th International Conference, ITS 2008, Montreal, Canada, Proceedings* (Vol. Lecture Notes in Computer Science 5091, pp. 19–28): Springer.

Zimmerman, B. J. (2008). Investigating self-regulation and motivation: Historical background, methodological developments, and future prospects. *American Educational Research Journal, 45*(1), 166–183.

16

ACTIVITY THEORY AND EDUCATIONAL TECHNOLOGY DESIGN

Daisy Mwanza-Simwami

1 INTRODUCTION—WHAT IS DESIGN?

The term design has different meanings in various fields, such that to understand the type of design being talked about, one needs to understand the philosophy behind the design, its function and timing within the design process. Bruce Archer, a famous 20th-century designer and engineer defines design as follows.

> Design is the field of human experience, skill, understanding and imagination that is concerned with the conception, and realisation of new things and events and particularly with man's appreciation and adaptation of his surroundings in the light of his material and spiritual needs.
>
> (Archer, Baynes & Roberts, 2005, p. 15)

1.1 The Design Process

In this regard, the concept of design incorporates conceptual and practical processes intended to solve problems through analysing human experiences of interacting with each other and with objects of the environment. Also by producing tools and artefacts that humans can use to explore their environment. Meanwhile, within the design process, activities involving analysing experiences and producing artefacts are informed by models and frameworks that enable designers and participants to understand the design rationale (Fischer & Hermann, 2011; Fischer, 2010; Carroll & Rosson, 2003; Dix, Finlay, Abowd & Beale, 1998; Lee & Lai, 1991) and share mental models (Gentner & Stevens, 1983; Jones, Ross, Lynam, Perez & Leitch, 2011; Johnson-Laird, 1983; Moray, 2004; Norman, 1983; Craik, 1943) of what is being designed and the timing for executing design processes and activities. Towards this end, several design methodologies have emerged mainly presenting techniques for product design and usability evaluation (Nielsen, 1994; Norman, 2002). In most cases, design methodologies present models and frameworks that help to understand how a complete system of users, designers, and technology developers interact. Examples include the 'waterfall model' (Royce, 1970) and the 'User-Centred Design' (Norman & Draper, 1986) approach discussed as follows.

1.2 Waterfall Model

The waterfall model is successfully and widely used in the design of software systems for engineering and the construction industry. However, the waterfall model has been criticised for its lack of flexibility in the execution and progression of design activities, e.g. this approach requires that design stages are executed systematically by fulfilling one stage before proceeding to the next stage (Dix et al., 1998; Rogers, Sharp & Preece, 2011; Sharp, Rogers & Preece, 2007). In addition to this, the waterfall model does not adequately consider external influences such as customers changing their minds in the middle of a development project. More importantly, testing or evaluation is done towards the end of the systems development procedure and is focused on correcting systems errors and functionality to ensure smooth operation of the system, therefore neglecting to evaluate usability and the system's fitness for purpose (Nielsen, 1994; Norman, 2002). These criticisms triggered a reaction in systems development which resulted in the establishment of design methods that are more focused on understanding the technology user and the context in which they operate (Norman, 2002; Norman & Draper, 1986; Nardi, 1996; Kaptelinin & Nardi, 2006). An example of a user-focused design method widely used in systems development is the user-centred design philosophy (Norman & Draper, 1986).

1.3 User-Centred Design

User-Centred Design (UCD) (Norman & Draper, 1986), is a broad approach to technology design in which user needs take centre-stage in all processes of systems development. UCD puts emphasis on the inclusion of end-users throughout the systems development processes. Iterative design enables the designer to obtain continuous feedback from users throughout the systems development process (Sharp et al., 2007). In order to obtain user feedback, early prototypes, mock-ups and technology immersion techniques such as software simulations are used to give the user a feel for the interface and functional aspects of the system. The feedback is used to reshape technology in order to improve the 'user experience' or usability of the user interface (Rogers et al., 2011; Shneiderman & Plaisant, 2010). The UCD approach, therefore, aims to understand users and their tasks quite early into the system's development process instead of leaving it to the end during the evaluation stage.

In the meanwhile, rapid increase in the use of technological systems to support teaching and learning have resulted in the establishment of new design fields that are dedicated to empirically understanding how humans learn, how they manage and interact with resources that facilitate learning within their social-cultural environment (Garrison & Anderson, 2003; Bransford, Brown & Cocking, 2001; Kumar, 1997; Rogoff, Matsuov & White, 1998; Mumford, 1987). An example of such a field is educational technology design.

1.4 Educational Technology Design

According to Garrison and Anderson (2003), the term educational technology refers to practices of facilitating learning and improving performance by creating, using and managing appropriate technological processes and resources. Currently, there are several methodologies and philosophies outlining techniques for designing and evaluating educational technology (Jenkins, Browne, Walker & Hewitt, 2010; Fischer and Hermann, 2011;

Luckin, 2010; Shurville, Browne & Whitaker, 2008, 2009). Whilst most design methodologies present models of how people learn and interact with each other and with educational resources, emphasis is increasingly put on offering guidelines and frameworks that help to illuminate context-specific practices and processes that facilitate effective learning. Therefore, emerging educational technology design methods put emphasis on understanding social-cultural practices and motives of those using technology for teaching and learning in addition to enhancing communication between technology users, designers, and technology developers in order to get feedback on user experiences (Luckin, 2008; Mwanza-Simwami, 2009, 2011; Rogers et al., 2011). Furthermore, these methods aim to understand how technology usage practices and settings develop and redevelop over a period of time. This is where theoretical frameworks such as Activity Theory become useful to help understand practices and contexts of technology use (Kaptelinin and Nardi, 2006).

2 A BRIEF INTRODUCTION TO ACTIVITY THEORY

Activity Theory is a descriptive framework for understanding human activities as processes that continuously develop and redevelop over a period of time, and as a result of influences from the context in which human activities are carried out (Leont'ev, 1978, 1981). The basic unit of analysis in Activity Theory is human activity, or 'what people do' (Leont'ev, 1978; Kaptelinin and Nardi, 2006; Mwanza-Simwami, 2009). Central to theorising in Activity Theory is the concept of tool mediation, which presents the view that human beings develop and use tools to help them achieve targeted objectives (Leont'ev, 1978). The concept of 'tools' is used here to refer to both physical tools (e.g. PDAs, mobile phones, etc.) and conceptual tools such as human language and software applications. Activity theory is focused on establishing the means by which human beings master and use tools in everyday activities from a social, cultural and psychological perspective. This line of thinking is based on the understanding that the tools that human beings use to mediate their activities facilitate the performance of actions at hand whilst at the same time they reveal and transform the individual's mind (Leont'ev, 1978). For example, through the development and use of conceptual tools, human beings internally transform their own and other people's perceptions of the activity that they are engaged in. At the same time, by developing and using physical tools, human beings externally transform the activity that they are engaged in. Therefore, the idea of studying human activities as developmental processes is crucial for identifying changes and contradictions that exist in an activity. The term 'contradictions', refer to problems, miss-match or breakdowns that emerge in activity (Engeström, 1987). According to Engeström (1987), contradictions are the means by which new knowledge within an activity emerges. Therefore, Activity Theory seeks to explain the social and cultural embeddedness of human activities by linking them to issues relating to motives of those involved in carrying out activities, and, the nature of the relationships that exist between and among those participating in activity (Leont'ev, 1978). Therefore, Activity Theory is a philosophical framework from which several methods, techniques and guidelines for designing and evaluating the design and use of technology-based tools including educational technology can be based.

2.1 Activity Theory Based Methods for Educational Technology Design

What is disappointing is the fact that there is still no universally acceptable method or guideline for applying Activity Theory based concepts to design and evaluation tasks

(Mwanza, 2011) even though it is well over a decade since Nardi (1996) highlighted the potential benefits of applying activity theoretical concepts to technology design and evaluation. However, in recent years, several methods for applying Activity Theory to practical design and evaluation tasks have been introduced in various fields including educational technology or technology-enhanced learning. One such method is the Activity-Oriented Design Method (Mwanza, 2011) which was originally designed to support the application of Activity Theory based concepts to Human–Computer Interaction (HCI) research and practice.

2.2 Activity-Oriented Design Method

The Activity-Oriented Design Method (AODM) (Mwanza, 2011) is an Activity Theory (Leont'ev, 1978) based iterative approach to analysing and characterising learner practices with tools whilst paying attention to learner motives and social-cultural issues that exist in the context in which activities are carried out. AODM was originally designed to support HCI research and design processes but was initially used to analyse work practices in an engineering organisation (Mwanza, 2002). Recently, AODM has been used to inform the design of a Learning Activity Analysis Tool (LAAT) as part of an e-learning training module (Joyes, 2006). AODM is currently widely used to investigate technology-enhanced learning and design (Greenhow and Belbas, 2007; Dolonen, 2009, Hauge and Dolonen, 2012; Mwanza-Simwami, 2009, 2011).

The conception and operational structure of AODM is based on the acceptance of Engeström's (1987) expanded model of human activity (Figure 16.1) as a representation that captures and unifies key fundamental principles of Activity Theory (Kaptelinin and Nardi, 2006) into a unified whole. Engeström (1987) added the 'rules and regulations', 'community' and 'division of labour' components to Vygotsky's (1978) original model of human activity. The added components together with the 'tools' component that was originally introduced by Vygotsky (1978) serve as mediators of a collective activity system. The various components of an activity system also known as an activity triangle model are shown in Figure 16.1.

Components of an activity system include: *subjects* representing those involved in activity, e.g. learners and teachers; *tools* to represent artefacts, such as technology used to carry out activities; *object* to represent objectives, motives and purposes for engaging in activity (objectives are transformed into *outcomes*); *rules* are mediating elements that represent regulations, cultural norms and practices of those involved in activity; *community* components represent both the physical and conceptual environment in which

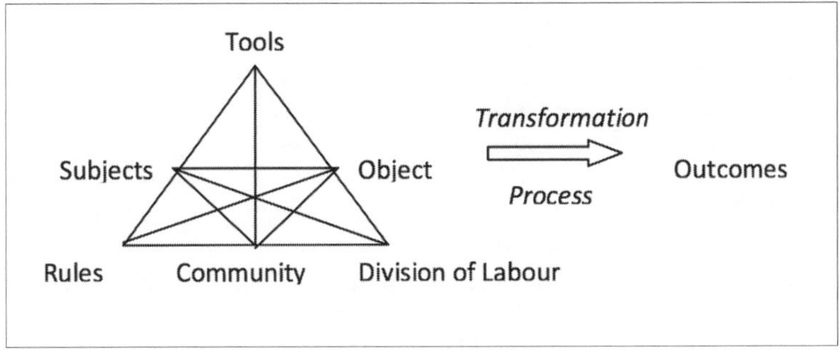

Figure 16.1 Activity triangle model, also known as activity system (Engeström, 1987).

activity is carried out. Finally, the *division of labour* component reflects variations in roles and responsibilities when carrying out human activities. The activity system is suitable for analysing both individual and collaborative practices. At the individual level, the activity system can be used to study a single person's interactions with his or her tools and the environment; whilst an analysis of collaborative practices can be focused on examining shared objectives, also the nature and interrelatedness of several people's interactions with each other, tools and the environment in which activity is carried out. An important feature of this approach to modelling human activities is that it prompts the investigator to understand the:

- structure of an activity or activities being examined;
- relationships that exist between and amongst various components of an activity system;
- objectives or motives of those involved in activity;
- history of the development and use of technologies in the activity being investigated;
- role of tools, rules and regulations, also division of labour as mediators of human activity.

2.2.1 The AODM Toolkit

Activity theory offers a powerful theoretical framework for investigating human activities, however, it is very difficult for new users to apply Activity Theory without a thorough understanding of the underlying basic principles. In order to address this issue, AODM presents: (a) a method for applying fundamental principles of Activity Theory to the phenomenon being investigated, (b) four methodological tools are presented as an analytic scheme for identifying the essential elements of human activity and for examining relationships between and amongst activity elements, (c) guidelines to help identify contradictions that exist in the activity being investigated, all of which are essential for improving the overall activity. A comprehensive description of the various methodological tools incorporated in AODM is given in Mwanza (2011). A brief introduction to AODM tools is presented as follows:

1. *Eight-Step-Model* (Table 16.1)—helps to apply fundamental principles of Activity Theory by translating components of the activity system (Engeström, 1987) in terms of the activity being investigated.

Table 16.1 AODM's Eight-Step-Model (Mwanza, 2011)

The Eight-Step-Model		
Identify the:		*Question to Ask*
Step 1	Activity of interest	What sort of activity am I interested in?
Step 2	Objective	Why is the activity taking place?
Step 3	Subjects	Who is involved in carrying out this activity?
Step 4	Tools	By what means are the subjects performing this activity?
Step 5	Rules & Regulations	Are there any cultural norms, rules or regulations governing the performance of this activity?
Step 6	Division of labour	Who is responsible for what, when carrying out this activity and how are the roles organised?
Step 7	Community	What is the environment in which activity is carried out?
Step 8	Outcome	What is the desired Outcome from carrying out this activity?

2. *Activity Notation* (Table 16.2)—used to reduce complexity in activity analysis by facilitating modelling and decomposition of activity systems in order to produce sub-activity systems.

Table 16.2 AODM's Activity Notation (Mwanza, 2002)

The Activity Notation				
Actors (Doers)	~	*Mediator*	~	*Object-ive (Purpose)*
Subjects	~	Tools	~	Object
Subjects	~	Rules	~	Object
Subjects	~	Division of Labour	~	Object
Community	~	Tools	~	Object
Community	~	Rules	~	Object
Community	~	Division of Labour	~	Object

3. *Technique of Generating Research Questions* (Table 16.3)—provides general and more focused research questions used to further examine learner interactions in sub-activity systems or learning episodes in order to conduct a detailed investigation and identify contradictions.

Table 16.3 AODM's Technique of Generating General Research Questions (Mwanza, 2011)

The Technique of Generating General Research Questions
1) What Tools do the Subjects use to achieve their Objective and how?
2) What Rules affect the way the Subjects achieve the Objective and how?
3) How does the Division of Labour influence the way the Subjects satisfy their Objective?
4) How do the Tools in use affect the way the Community achieves the Objective?
5) What Rules affect the way the Community satisfies their Objective and how?
6) How does the Division of Labour affect the way the Community achieves the Objective?

4. *Technique of Mapping Operational Processes* (Figure 16.2), used to interpret and communicate research findings by presenting visual representations of the transition of activities, sub-activities, activity components and relations, also contradictions or problems identified in focused sub-activities.

The key point to note is that the four methodological tools presented in AODM can be applied independently of each other. There is no need to systematically work through all four tools. A researcher or designer can choose to work with only one tool out of the four tools that are given. AODM tools can also be easily integrated with other methodologies and techniques that are currently available such as the Volere shell (Sharp et al., 2007) when abstracting systems requirements. We will now present a case study to show how AODM was used to support early phases of requirement specifications in the MOBIlearn project.

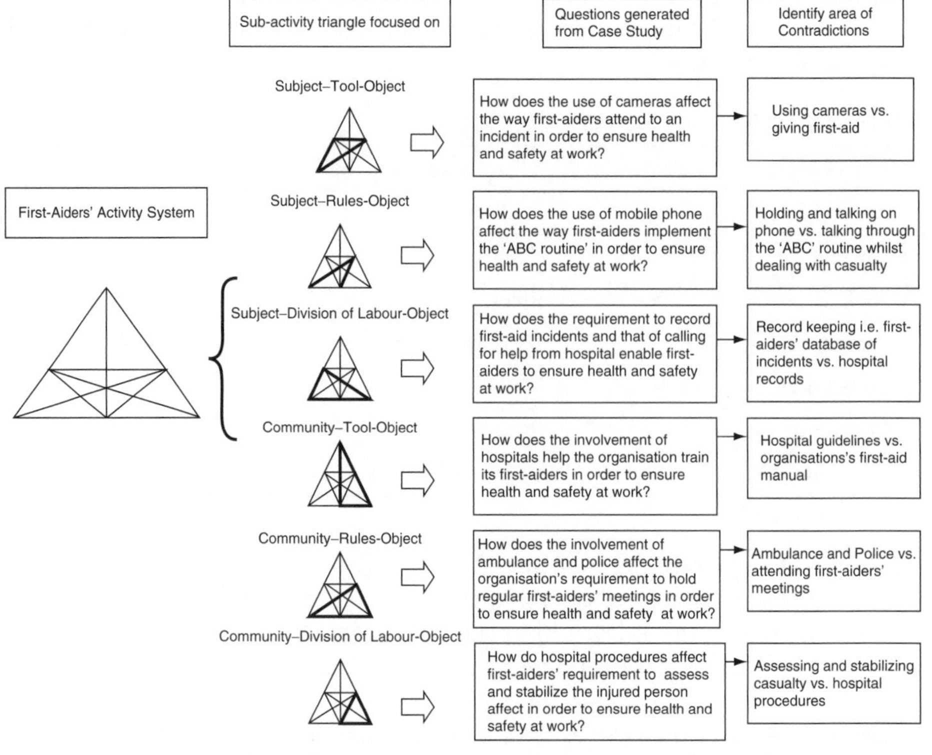

Figure 16.2 AODM's Technique of Mapping Operational Processes.

2.2.2 Using AODM to Support Systems Requirements Capture

AODM has been successfully applied to several systems design projects including eliciting requirements specifications for the design of a prototype mobile learning system for supporting learning using mobile technology, namely, the MOBIlearn project (Sharp et al., 2003). MOBIlearn was a large collaborative multinational research project funded by the European Commission to establish a framework for improved learning using mobile technology (Haley, Nuseibeh, Sharp & Taylor, 2004; Taylor, 2004). This involved conducting pedagogical and contextual research about the effectiveness and usefulness of mobile learning in order to inform the design of a prototype mobile learning environment (Taylor, 2004). Research was organised around three learning domains or strands, namely: museum strand, MBA (business) strand and health strand (Haley et al., 2004). AODM was applied to early phases of requirements capture activities within the health strand of the MOBIlearn project. The health strand was concerned with establishing design requirements for supporting training needs and updating skills of first-aiders in a higher education institution. First-aiders were members of staff who had volunteered to be trained in first-aid at work, and recruited to deal with emergency situations that emerge at the work place. Therefore, first-aiders had to juggle their normal work responsibilities with giving first-aid whenever there was an emergency health incident. This situation meant that first-aiders needed to update and consolidate their practical skills from time to time through re-training, workshops, and knowledge sharing by consulting health-related information resources such as the Internet and medical databases and healthcare organisations. In order to gather suitable requirements for designing a system to support first-aiders' work, the project needed to understand the nature of activities carried out by first-aiders, tools used when carrying out activities, and the context in which activities were carried out. For example, there was a need to understand how first-aiders interacted with each other and other health care provider institutions such as hospitals and ambulance staff. Therefore, in order to address these design issues within the health strand, several research methods and techniques were employed to support requirements specification including: future technology workshops (Vavoula, Sharples & Rudman, 2002); questionnaires, interviews, observations; and Volere shell (Sharp et al., 2003; Taylor, 2004). Given the project's concern for understanding pedagogical issues, relationships between activities, tools and personal interactions in context, AODM and other Activity Theory based methods and techniques such as the task-centred approach to evaluating mobile learning (Taylor, 2004), were used to support early processes of gathering data for systems design requirements specification and evaluation.

AODM's Eight-Step-Model (ESM) was used to support data gathering and guide the analysis of work practices and relationships in context. This involved working through the research questions presented inside the ESM (see Table 16.4). The researcher is free to identify the most appropriate methods for implementing ESM-based questions, although possible techniques for applying ESM-based questions can include interviews and observational studies. Thereafter, researchers identify the various components of the first-aiders' activity system and mediating relationships that exist between and within components or sub-activities. See Table 16.4.

Working through ESM enabled us to gather enough qualitative data to model the first-aiders' activity system as shown in Figure 16.3.

Figure 16.3 shows the various components of the first-aiders' activity system highlighting key sub-activities and relationships that mediate the work of first-aiders. By modelling the first-aiders' activity system, it is possible to identify the various components of an activity system and their interrelatedness. Data gathered enabled the design team to acquire basic understanding of social-cultural practices and contextual issues that are vital for analysing contradictions in tool usage (see Figure 16.2). Finally, context-specific research questions were abstracted around sub-activities and mediating relationships in order to identify areas of research interests from which to gather further information and also meaningful data for requirements abstraction. In order to achieve this, AODM's technique was used to generate research questions based on sub-activity systems and mediators as shown in Table 16.5.

Table 16.5 shows a translation of general research questions into case study related meaningful information that provided the design team with basic understanding of key issues to consider when abstracting a system's requirement. The resulting data were presented in the form of qualitative descriptive statements outlining design requirements. These statements of requirements were then fed into the Volere shell (Sharp et al., 2003) in order to organise and present information to the design team.

3 REFLECTIONS

AODM based investigations enable a descriptive analysis of activities highlighting activity elements and their interrelatedness whilst relating them to the social-cultural context

Table 16.4 AODM's Eight-Step-Model: translation of the MOBIlearn Health Strand

Eight-Step-Model—translation of the MOBIlearn Health Strand		
Identify the:		*Question to Ask*
Step 1	Activity of interest	*What sort of activity am I interested in?* – Learning and training and knowledge sharing activity amongst OU first-aiders
Step 2	Object-ive	*Why is the activity taking place?* – To ensure health and safety at work
Step 3	Subjects	*Who is involved in carrying out this activity?* – OU members of staff volunteering to be trained and recruited to serve as first-aiders at work
Step 4	Tools	*By what means are the subjects performing this activity?* – Defibrillators, bandages, scissors, first-aiders website on the internet, first-aid training, first-aid training manual, telephone, mobile phones, cameras
Step 5	Rules & Regulations	*Are there any cultural norms, rules or regulations governing the performance of this activity?* – Regular first-aiders meetings, first-aiders' refresher course, training in first-aid at work for new volunteers, requirement to follow the 'ABC' routine (Airway, Breathing, Circulation) for assessing a first-aid casualty or incident
Step 6	Division of labour	*Who is responsible for what, when carrying out this activity and how are the roles organised?* – First-aiders are required to assess and stabilise the injured person, then contact the relevant emergency organisation for further assessment and care. This may entail calling an ambulance to take the injured person to a nearby hospital, or telephoning the fire brigade and police if there was fire involved during the incident
Step 7	Community	*What is the environment in which activity is carried out?* – Anywhere at the university's campus or whilst on a university-related business away from campus. Local emergency care providers such as hospitals, ambulances, fire brigade, and police also form part of the operational environment for first-aiders at work
Step 8	Outcome	*What is the desired Outcome from carrying out this activity?* – Safe work environment

in which activities are carried out. The outcome is context-specific qualitative data about activities, sub-activities, relationships between and within an activity, also brief episodes of the focused sub-activities examined in great detail to reveal the developmental patterns of practices. Such detailed and context-specific information is needed to support early stages of systems' requirements gathering so as to enable designers to abstract requirements that are relevant to the context of use. Within MOBIlearn, this information provided a useful starting point for exploring design requirements for a mobile learning system to support first-aiders' practices and evaluation by making elements of first-aiders' activity more explicit and by identifying possible areas of contradictions. In this case study, working through solutions and refining requirements in order to address identified contradictions within the first-aiders' activity system served as a useful basis for generating initial design insights for the system.

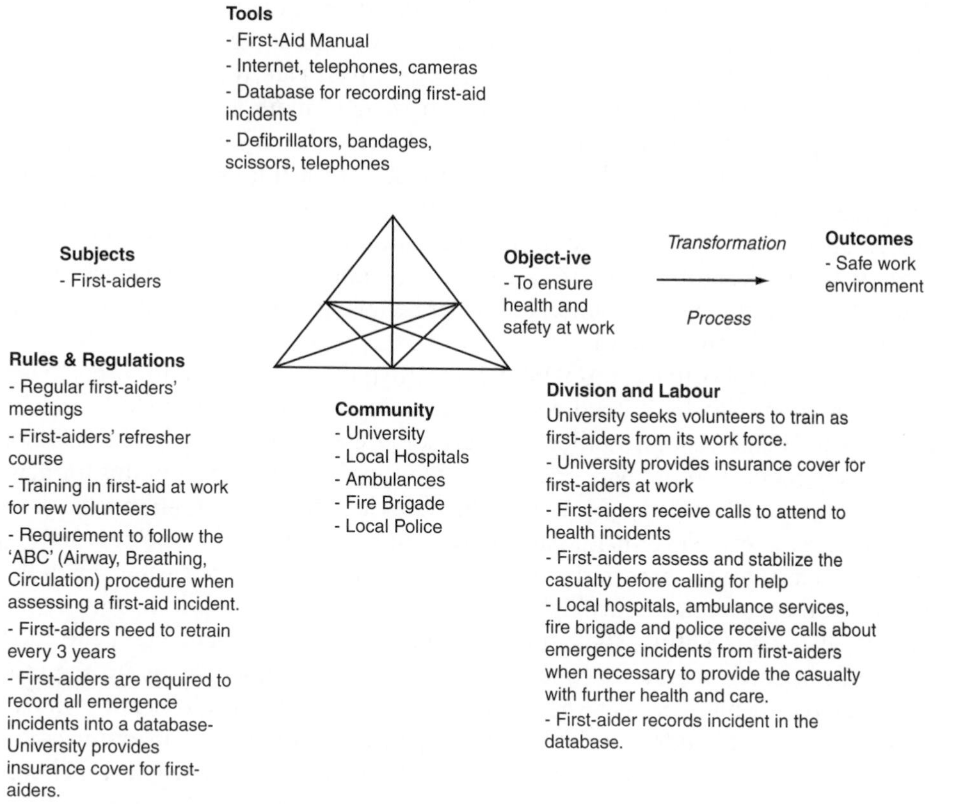

Figure 16.3 First-aiders' activity system.

Table 16.5 Example instantiation of AODM's Technique of Generating General Research Questions in the Health Strand

Example instantiation of AODM's Technique of Generating General Research Questions in the Health strand
1) How does use of the Internet enable first-aiders to ensure health and safety at work?
2) How does the 'ABC' assessment procedure enable/help first-aiders meet the objective of ensuring health and safety at work?
3) How does the practice of receiving calls about first-aid incidents affect the way the first-aiders satisfy the objective of ensuring health and safety at work?
4) How does the use of training manuals influence/affect the way the university ensures health and safety at work?
5) How does the requirement to record first-aid incidents help the university and local hospital ensure health and safety at work?
6) How does the practice of calling the local hospital or/and police affect the way the university ensures health and safety at work?

Notably, key benefits of using AODM to support the design task of gathering systems' requirements for the MOBIlearn project include: First, its capability to allow the researcher to model activity components and to investigate the *relationship* between learner *motives* and technology usage behaviour. AODM methodological tools facilitate a holistic approach to investigating *mediators* of human activities by studying tools in use, rules and regulations, and division of labour, whilst linking observations to targeted goals and desired outcomes. Second, AODM can be used to investigate the interconnectedness of learning episodes in mobile learning through its support for levelled abstractions and decomposition of learner activity models. This approach also helps to capture the developmental transition of learner behaviour and the analysis of contradictions that exist in learner activities.

Weaknesses and shortfalls of AODM include, first, the requirement for users to familiarise themselves with basic theoretical concepts of Activity Theory (Mwanza, 2011; Greenhow and Belbas, 2007). Methodological tools presented in AODM attempt to closely interpret key concepts of Activity Theory so as to capture the richness of this framework in their operational structure. However, this Activity Theory orientation can discourage some researchers. Nevertheless, as pointed out by Greenhow and Belbas (2007), the benefits of being able to characterise the messiness of real-world practices in a way that is valuable to others in context outweigh any possible challenges. Second, studying activities of mobile learners in naturalistic settings or contexts can be challenging due to the fact that mobile learners operate in constantly changing environments (e.g. on the move), therefore, it is difficult to predict when a learning episode or event will occur or what tools will be in use. AODM addresses these issues by providing support for analysing complex social behaviours through decomposition whilst providing a mechanism for making the interrelatedness of interaction processes more explicit. Finally, AODM can easily be integrated with other methods that the researcher chooses to use.

REFERENCES

Archer, L. B., Baynes, K., & Roberts, P. H. (2005). *A Framework for Design and Design Education: A reader containing papers from the 1970s and 80s.* Wellesbourne, UK: DATA, Design and Technology Association, (p. 15). Available at http://www.data.org.uk/generaldocs/dater/Framework%20for%20Design.pdf (accessed 16 May 2012).

Bransford, J. D., Brown, A. L., & Cocking, R. R. (Eds.). (2001). *How People Learn: Brain, Mind, Experience, and School.* Washington, DC: National Academy Press.

Carroll, J. M., & Rosson, M. B. (2003). Design rationale as theory. In J. M. Carroll (Ed.), *HCI Models, Theories, and Frameworks: Toward a Multidisciplinary Science* (pp. 431–461). San Francisco, CA: Morgan Kaufmann Publishers.

Craik, K. (1943). *The Nature of Explanation.* Cambridge: Cambridge University Press.

Dix, A., Finlay, J., Abowd, G., & Beale, R. (1998). *Human-Computer Interaction* (2nd Edn). London: Prentice Hall Europe.

Dolonen, J. A. (2009). Inclusion of teachers and students in the design of educational technology. In J. Molka-Danielsen (Ed.), *Proceedings of the 32nd Information Systems Research Seminar in Scandinavia,* IRIS 32, Norway. Available at http://uio.academia.edu/JanDolonen/Papers/344411/Inclusion_of_Teachers_and_Students_In_the_Design_of_Educational_Technology (accessed 9 June 2011).

Engeström, Y. (1987). *Learning by Expanding: An Activity-Theoretical Approach to Developmental Research.* Helsinki: Orienta-Konsultit Oy, Finland.

Fischer, G. (2010): End-user development and meta-design: foundations for cultures of participation. *Journal of Organizational and End User Computing,* 22(1), pp. 52–82.

Fischer, G., & Hermann, T. (2011): Socio-technical systems—a meta-design perspective. *International Journal for Sociotechnology and Knowledge Development,* January–March, 3(1), pp. 1–33.

Garrison, D. R., & Anderson, T. (2003). *E-Learning in the 21st Century: A Framework for Research and Practice.* New York: Routledge.

Gentner, D. A., & Stevens, A. L. (Eds.) (1983). *Mental Models.* Hillsdale, NJ: Lawrence Erlbaum.

Greenhow, C., & Belbas, B. (2007). Using activity-oriented design methods to study collaborative knowledge-building in e-learning courses within higher education. *International Journal of Computer-Supported Collaborative Learning,* 2(4), pp. 363–391.

Haley, D., Nuseibeh, B., Sharp, H., & Taylor, J. (2004). The conundrum of categorising requirements: managing requirements for learning on the move. In: *12th International Requirements Engineering Conference (RE'04),* 6–10 Sept. 2004, Kyoto, Japan.

Hauge, T. E., & Dolonen, J. A. (2012). Towards an activity-driven design method for online learning resources. In A. D. Olofsson & J. O. Lindberg (Eds.), *Informed Designs of Educational Technologies in Higher Education: Enhanced learning and teaching* (pp. 101–117). Hershey, PA: IGI Global

Jenkins, M., Browne, T., Walker, T., & Hewitt, R. (2010). The development of technology enhanced learning: findings from a 2008 Survey of UK higher education institutions. *Interactive Learning Environments,* 18(1), pp. 1–19.

Johnson-Laird, P. N. (1983). *Mental Models.* Cambridge: Cambridge University Press.

Jones, N. A., Ross, H., Lynam, T., Perez, P., & Leitch, A. (2011). Mental models: an interdisciplinary synthesis of theory and methods. *Ecology and Society,* 16(1), p. 46.

Joyes, G. (2006). An activity theory approach to the exploration of tutors' perceptions of effective online pedagogy. In L. Markauskaite, P. Goodyear, & P. Reimann (Eds.), Who's learning? Whose technology? *Proceedings of the 23rd Annual Conference of the Australasian Society for Computers in Learning in Tertiary Education* (pp. 401–408). Sydney: Sydney University Press.

Kaptelinin, V., & Nardi, B. (2006). *Acting with Technology: Activity Theory and Interaction Design.* Cambridge, MA: MIT Press.

Kumar, K. L. (1997). *Educational Technology: A Practical Textbook for Students, Teachers, Professionals and Trainers.* New Delhi: New Age International.

Lee, J., & Lai, K.-Y. (1991). What's in design rationale? *Human-Computer Interaction special issue on design rationale,* 6(3–4), pp. 251–280.

Leont'ev, A. N. (1978). *Activity, Consciousness, and Personality.* Englewood Cliffs, NJ: Prentice Hall.

Leont'ev, A. N. (1981). The problem of activity in psychology. In J. V. Wertsch (Ed.), *The Concept of Activity in Soviet Psychology: An Introduction.* New York: M. E. Sharpe, Inc.

Luckin, R. (2008). The learner centric Ecology of Resources: A framework for using technology to scaffold learning. *Computers & Education,* 50(2), pp. 449–462.

Luckin, R. (2010). *Re-designing Learning Contexts.* London: Routledge.

Moray, N. (2004). Models of models of . . . mental models. In N. Moray (Ed.), *Ergonomics: Major Writings* (pp. 506–526). London: Taylor & Francis.

Mumford, E. (1987). Sociotechnical systems design: evolving theory and practice. In G. Bjerknes, P. Ehn, & M. Kyng (Eds.), *Computers and Democracy* (pp. 59–77). Brookfield, VT: Avebury.

Mwanza, D. (2002). Conceptualising work activity for CAL systems design. *Journal of Computer Assisted Learning,* 18(1), pp. 84–92.

Mwanza, D. (2011). *Activity-Orientated Design Method (AODM): Towards an Activity-Oriented Design Method for HCI Research and Practice.* Germany: LAP LAMBERT Academic Publishing GmbH & Co. KG.

Mwanza-Simwami, D. (2011). AODM as a framework and model for characterising learner experiences with technology. *Journal of e-Learning and Knowledge Society (Je-LKS)* special issue on Centrality of the experience in TEE: models and frameworks. Guest editors: Carlo Giovannella, Marcus Specht; Guest authors: Kinshuk & Sabine Graf, Rosemary Luckin.

Mwanza-Simwami, D. (2009). Using activity-oriented design methods (AODM) to investigate mobile learning. In G. Vavoula, N. Pachler, & A. Kukulska-Hulme (Eds.), *Researching Mobile Learning: Frameworks, Tools and Research Design* (pp. 97–122). Oxford: Peter Lang Verlag.

Nardi, B. (1996). *Context and Consciousness: Activity Theory and Human-Computer Interaction.* Cambridge, MA: MIT Press.

Nielsen, J. (1994). *Usability Engineering.* San Francisco, CA: Morgan Kaufmann Publishers.

Norman, D. A. (1983). Some observations on mental models. In D. A. Gentner & A. L. Stevens (Eds.), *Mental Models.* Hillsdale, NJ: Lawrence Erlbaum.

Norman, D. A. (2002). *The Design of Everyday Things.* New York: Basic Books.

Norman, D. A., & Draper, S. W. (Editors) (1986). *User-Centered System Design: New Perspectives on Human-Computer Interaction.* Hillsdale, NJ: Lawrence Erlbaum Associates.

Rogers, Y., Sharp, H., & Preece, J. (2011). *Interaction Design: Beyond Human-Computer Interaction (3rd Edn).* Chichester: Wiley.

Rogoff, B., Matsuov, E., & White, C. (1998). Models of teaching and learning: participation in a community of learners. In D. R. Olsen & N. Torrance (Eds.), *The Handbook of Education and Human Development: New Models of Learning, Teaching and Schooling* (pp. 388–414). Oxford: Blackwell.

Royce, W. (1970). Managing the development of large software systems. In: *Proceedings of IEEE WESCON* 26 (August): 1–9.

Sharp, H., Taylor, J., Löber, A., Frohberg, D., Mwanza, D., & Murelli, E. (2003). Establishing user requirements for a mobile learning environment. In: *Conference Proceedings of Eurescom 2003*, 29 Sept.–1 Oct. 2003, Heidelberg, Germany.

Sharp, H., Rogers, Y., & Preece, J. (2007). *Interaction Design: Beyond Human–Computer Interaction* (2nd Edn). New York: John Wiley & Sons Ltd. Shneiderman, B., & Plaisant, C. (2010). *Designing the User Interface: Strategies for Effective Human–Computer Interaction* (5th Edn). Reading, MA: Addison-Wesley.

Shurville, S., Browne, T., & Whitaker, M. (2008). Employing the new educational technologists: A call for evidenced change. In *Hello! Where are you in the landscape of educational technology? Proceedings ascilite Melbourne 2008.*

Shurville, S., Browne, T., & Whitaker, M. (2009). Accommodating the newfound strategic importance of educational technologists within higher education: a critical literature review. *Campus-Wide Information Systems*, 26(3), pp. 201–231.

Taylor, J. (2004). A task-centred approach to evaluating a mobile learning environment for pedagogical soundness. In J. Attewell & C. Savill-Smith (Eds.), *Learning with Mobile Devices: Research and Development* (pp. 167–171). London, UK: Learning and Skills Development Agency.

Vavoula, G. N., Sharples, M., & Rudman, P. D. (2002). Developing the 'Future Technology Workshop' method. In M. M. Bekker, P. Markopoulos, & M. Kersten-Tsikalkina (Eds.), *Proceedings of the International Workshop on Interaction Design and Children* (pp. 65–72), Aug. 28–29, Eindhoven, the Netherlands.

Vygotsky, L. S. (1978). *Mind in Society: The Development of Higher Psychological Processes.* Edited by M. Cole, V. John-Steiner, S. Scribner, & E. Souberman. Cambridge, MA: Harvard University Press.

17

SNaP!

Re-using, Sharing and Communicating Designs and Design Knowledge Using Scenarios, Narratives and Patterns

Yishay Mor

INTRODUCTION

In order to enable a culture of critical, informed and reflective design practice we need a linguistic framework for communicating *design knowledge*: the knowledge of the characteristic features of a domain of practice, the challenges which inhabit it, and the established methods of resolving them. Such an infrastructure must 'serve two masters'; on one hand, it should adhere to the requirements of scientific rigour, ensuring that the proposed conditions and challenges are genuine and the solutions effective. On the other hand, it should maintain pragmatic adequacy, ensuring that the insights it encapsulates are readily available for practitioners to implement in real-world situations. Several representations have been proposed to this effect: design narratives (Barab, Baek, Schatz, Scheckler & Moore, 2008; Bell, Hoadley & Linn, 2004; Hoadley, 2002; Linn & Hsi, 2000; Mor, 2011), design principles (Kali, 2006, 2008; Linn, Bell, & Davis, 2004; Merrill, 2002; Quintana et al., 2004; van den Akker, 1999), and design patterns (Derntl & Motschnig-Pitrik, 2005; Goodyear, 2005; Mor & Winters, 2007; Retalis, Georgiakakis & Dimitriadis, 2006), to name a few. The aim of this chapter is to characterise two of these forms—design narratives and design patterns—and propose a third form, design scenarios, and suggest how these could be embedded in a cycle of reflective learning design.

The combination of design narratives, design patterns and design scenarios is best suited for the social construction of design knowledge in and around the cycle of a design experiment. While the notion of design experiment is derived from the tradition of design-based research in education, it is well suited as a framework for any innovation process, so long as this process is rigorous and reflexive. The cycle of a design experiment (Figure 17.1) iterates through theory, design, implementation, enactment, interpretation and evaluation. Design scenarios offer a viable and reliable form for deriving design postulates from theory, design narratives provide a rich form for interpreting the evidence emerging from the implementation and enactment of such postulates, and design patterns allow the robust and flexible organisation of transferable design knowledge derived

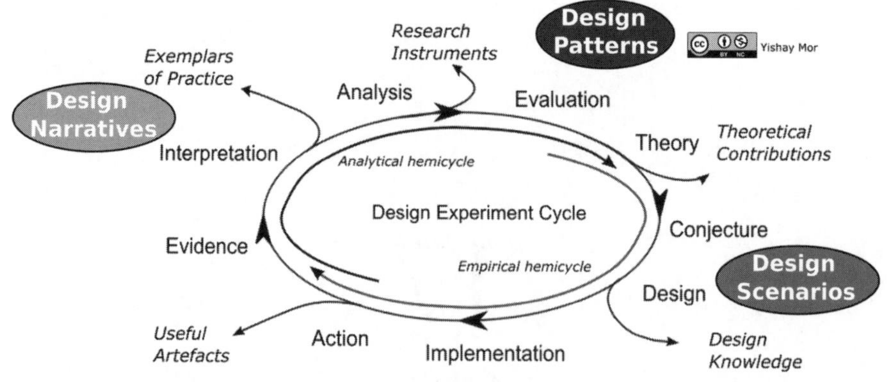

Figure 17.1 The design experiment cycle, with embedded representations.

by analysis and evaluation of design narratives. Together, these representations bridge the gap between theory and practice, mutually informing and directing one another.

DESIGN NARRATIVES: A BASE FORM FOR CAPTURING DESIGN KNOWLEDGE

Design narratives are accounts of critical events from a personal, phenomenological perspective. They focus on design in the sense of problem solving, describing a problem in the chosen domain, the actions taken to resolve it and their unfolding effects. They provide an account of the history and evolution of a design over time, including the research context, the tools and activities designed, and the results of users' interactions with these. They portray the complete path leading to an educational innovation, not just its final form—including failed attempts and the modifications they espoused.

In order for design narratives to provide an effective form of design discourse in education, they need to be shaped in a way that adheres to scientific standards, acknowledges the pragmatic agenda of education, and retains the essential qualities of narrative. A scientific standard demands a transparent audit trail from reliable data to conclusions, and a clear articulation of refutable claims. Where subjectivity is inevitable, it should be reported honestly. A pragmatic stance dictates a functional focus linked to a value dimension, attention to context and representation, and an awareness of the complexity of human situations. Narrative form entails a clear context description, a protagonist, a plot—a temporally and semantically linked sequence of events—and an implied moral. A design narrative presents a single perspective on a single problem to be solved or task to be accomplished. Thus, there can be multiple narratives of the same experiment. All are just as valid, as long as they meet the criteria.

A design narrative should:

- provide an account of an aspect of a design experiment, from the perspective of the designer or that of a participant, and, as much as possible, capturing their voice;
- clearly delineate the context of the design experiment and its educational goals, noting the material, social and intentional factors that define the problem space;
- identify a design challenge within this context; a declaration of the change which the designer wishes to effect;

- specify a theoretical framework that defines the process by which the designer approaches the challenge and the methods by which she evaluates the outcomes;
- present a documented record of the designers'/participants' actions and their effect;
- incorporate data collected and processed in appropriate scientific methods;
- decouple reporting events from their evaluation and reflection;
- be followed by a statement of the derived conclusions, linking them clearly and explicitly back to the narrative.

Beginners often find it hard to distinguish between context and challenge. The rule of thumb is that the challenge is what you are trying to change, the context is what you accept as a given.

It is often helpful to draft a *force map* of the context (Figure 17.2): the various elements at play are given iconic representation, and lines are stretched between them, annotated and marked '+' for supporting relations and '–' for conflicting ones.

The conclusion derived from a design narrative is a design claim, i.e. a statement about how to achieve a particular educational effect in a particular context. This claim is external to the design narrative, but it guides the narrator's choice of which events to include in the narrative.

A template may be provided in order to guide the construction of design narratives, to ensure their adherence to standards, and to facilitate the aggregation and synthesis of knowledge across narratives. An example template is available at: goo.gl/HELaC.

I distinguish between two types of design narratives: designer narratives (DNs) and participant narratives (PNs).

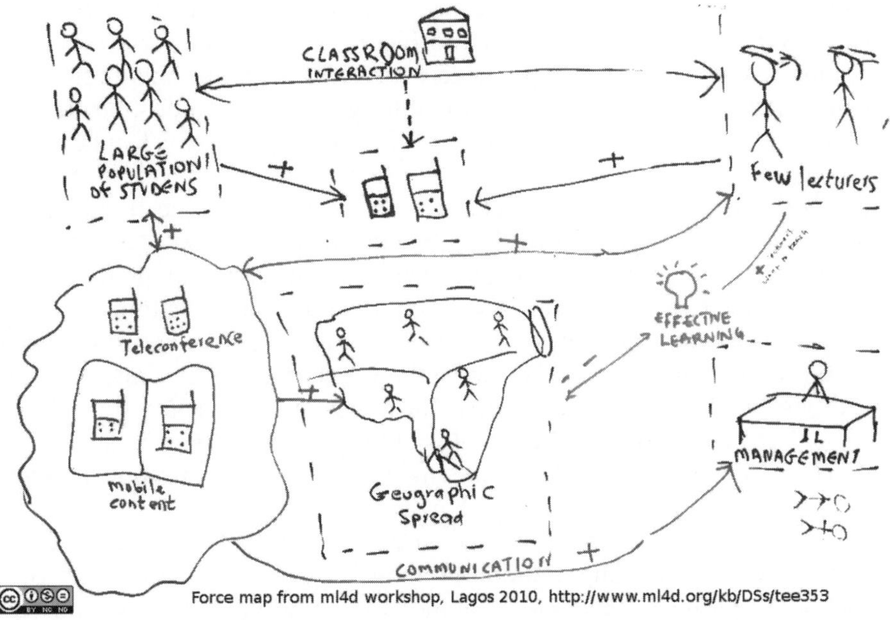

Figure 17.2 Example force map, from the ML4D project (http://www.ml4d.org/kb/DSs/tee353), describing a course at the University of Lagos with over 430 regular students and over 700 distance learning students.

DNs recount a pedagogical problem and its resolution from the designer's point of view. The designer in this case could be an educational practitioner or researcher, devising a learning experience, or the developer of educational tools or content. DNs are first-person accounts of the designer's experience and observations, in the course of a design experiment. In most cases, the focus is on the design and development of activities, social practices and supporting technology. These elements are seen as an integral unit, under the socio-technical stance that these are inseparable and any partial description would lead to unsubstantiated conclusions.

PNs follow the participants in a design experiment—teachers and learners—as designers, contending with problems they encountered in the context of an activity, their use of the resources provided in confronting this problem, and the indications of their learning gains in the process. These are third-person accounts based on the participants' written and verbal articulations and the designer's observations.

These two types of narratives are interdependent; the problems encountered by learners and their resolution are the drivers of their learning trajectory. The designer's problem, from a bird's eye view, is to provide learners with an effective set of problems and the means for resolving them, so as to direct their learning trajectory. Thus, the PNs illuminate and substantiate the DNs.

The following example design narrative is drawn from the FEASST project (http://feasst.wordpress.com/).

COMO: MOBILES + FLICKR = CO-REFLECTIVE PRACTICE

At the Royal Veterinary College, a group of students were engaged in practical work in a vet training hospital. As part of their training, the students were required to capture instances of practice on a mobile phone and the photos collected were automatically uploaded to flickr. The students worked in groups of four or five and each was provided with a mobile phone and given a short familiarisation session. In one scenario, during morning rounds students would be directed to monitor the progress of an animal being treated. Their task would be to document case progress over time. They took pictures throughout the day, uploaded them to a blog, tagged them with caseID and key features, e.g. type of animal, the injury, condition. The students then used quiet moments to add details to the 'case' using blog postings. During the evening rounds, the students presented their cases in group discussion sessions with their tutor, using the images, blog posts and a projector. The group reviewed the diagnosis and the actions which were taken, and reviewed these in the light of revisiting the images and postings which acted as catalysts for evaluation of practice. Co-reflection was enhanced because of the availability of images which bring the medical case into the seminar room. It affected the students' tutorial conversation, providing ongoing formative contributions to the case in the form of postings. The discussion moved from abstract 'textbook theory' to what tutors called 'case presentation': how the particular condition presents itself in a particular case, how to analyse symptoms in real-world conditions and how to assess treatment. These are key skills which are often neglected due to the inability to have a concrete presence of the case in the seminar room as a focus for reflective and analytical discussion. The process of using images to capture cases also provided feedback to tutors on the students' learning. Tutors reported that observing students' pictures gave them a window on their thinking: what they noticed, where their attention was and where they assigned importance. This was the basis for modifying tutor input and the focus of the tutorial discussion.

DESIGN PATTERNS: SITUATED ABSTRACTIONS OF DESIGN NARRATIVES

The *Design patterns* paradigm (Alexander, Ishikawa & Silverstein, 1977) was developed as a form of design language within architecture. The core of a design pattern can be seen as a local functional statement: 'for problem P, under circumstances C, solution S has been known to work'. Such a structure reads like a direct generalisation of the design narrative form.

In order to include design patterns as elements of a scientific discourse, a clear path needs to be marked from narratives to patterns, and mechanisms established for validating them. Mor (2010) defined the following process:

1 A prominent design feature is identified in a design narrative, by linking it to a pedagogically effective outcome, or to the resolution of a critical problem.
2 The design feature is captured using a core template of *Problem*, *Context* and *Solution*. The source design narrative is noted.
3 Other narratives are searched for additional support.
4 The problem is expressed as a configuration of forces.
5 The initial context of the pattern is defined by the situational characteristics common to all supporting narratives.
6 The solution is articulated in the most specific detail that was still consistent with all supporting cases.

The identification and articulation of the initial set of patterns is typically followed by a phase of organising and refactoring the pattern language as a whole. The links between patterns are identified and noted, and new patterns are derived by structural manipulations, such as:

- *Specification*: when a pattern's empirical support is found to be weak, the pattern's scope is narrowed down to fit the evidence.
- *Decomposition*: where peer review indicates that patterns were too complex or too sensitive to contextual factors they are broken into several more robust components, each expressed as a separate pattern.
- *Extraction*: design features that recur in several patterns are expressed as a new pattern and noted as a component in the others.
- *Generalisation*: where the distinction between two patterns is unclear, they are merged and expressed as a pattern of a higher level of abstraction, and the source patterns noted as its extensions.

This process may be iterated until it produces a stable collection of linked patterns. Patterns which lack sufficient empirical support, or are poorly connected to the collection, should be removed from the collection but saved for future consideration. The guiding objective is to collate a coherent set of patterns, offering a solid base for a potential language of patterns. The patterns which are produced by this process should then be substantiated further by eliciting empirical and theoretical support from the relevant scientific and professional literature. Finally, visual aids such as metaphoric illustrations and structural diagrams are added to enhance the patterns' text. The same collection of design narratives could, theoretically, give rise to different sets of design patterns, reflecting the author's choice of interpretative framework and her focal domain of practice. The process of developing design patterns is accompanied and guided by constant monitoring of their quality along two dimensions: the scientific validity of the claims they encapsulate, and their ability to communicate these claims.

Every pattern language and collection defines a common template for all the patterns it includes. Such a template is useful for users of the collection, as it enables them to search and apply patterns as needed. At the same time, a carefully designed template safeguards rigour by prompting the pattern author to address all the important aspects of the patterns. An exemplar template can be found at: http://goo.gl/eyZQU.

As an example, The FEASST project report included 11 patterns derived from the narratives collected by the project. The Classroom Display pattern was derived from the CoMo narrative provided earlier:

CLASSROOM DISPLAY

http://patternlanguagenetwork.myxwiki.org/xwiki/bin/view/Patterns/Classroom-display

Summary

Share your work with a trusted audience.

Problem

Using learners' work as part of the instructional activity has several advantages; it:

- rewards participation;
- makes learning more meaningful, by relating it to learners' personal experiences;
- allows the teacher to align instruction with students' perspectives and current state of knowledge.

However, doing this poses some challenges:

- The teacher needs to have learners' works collated in a single, easy to access location, so that she can draw on them as needed.
- Learners might feel uncomfortable about presenting their work in a public space.
- There could be legal or other restrictions on sharing work.

Context

Most suited for small to medium size classes, blended learning, not one-off, where learning has an element of production/construction of visual artefacts. However, could be adapted and extended to a very wide range of settings.

Solution

Create a space within the learning environment where learners' works can be displayed side by side.

Works can be arranged thematically, chronologically, as an index or as a *Visual Narrative.*

The size and location of the display should allow learners and teacher to view a collection of learners' work simultaneously, and refer to them in the course of the learning activity.

The display should be visible for all learners, but may need to be concealed from the outer world. If not, it should at least function as a *Front Garden*[1].

DESIGN SCENARIOS: FRAMING REFUTABLE DESIGN CLAIMS

Design narratives represent design knowledge extracted from empirical evidence, capturing and interpreting the designers' experience. Design patterns attempt to organise this knowledge into complex modular structures. Design scenarios borrow the form of design narratives, adapting it from an account of documented past events to a description of imagined future ones. Scenarios function both as a scientific form and as a practical tool. From a scientific viewpoint, they offer a means for validating the design claims emerging from design narratives and encapsulated in design patterns, by formulating refutable predictions; if a narrative reports 'this worked', a pattern argues 'under such conditions this may work', a scenario claims 'if we do this, it will work'. From a practical stance, scenarios are a powerful tool in the hands of the designer. They allow her to articulate a thick description of a design challenge in a realistic context, and harness existing design knowledge and theoretical frameworks to propose a viable solution to this challenge. At the heart of a design scenario is a sequence of actions the protagonists may take to achieve their objectives, events they might encounter and their reactions to these, and finally—the ensuing results of this sequence. These actions, events and consequent results are afforded or driven by the qualities of new artefacts introduced into the context. Thus, they express a design claim: that introducing such artefacts into such a context may induce such results. However, this claim is stated in a thickly grounded form, submitting it to elaborate scrutiny.

Design scenarios retain the same basic components that constitute design narratives: context, challenge, theoretical framework, events and actions, results and reflections. However, these elements reflect a hypothesis about possible future states of the world. The context describes a current, existing situation, which is perturbed by the introduction of new material, social and intentional elements such as new technologies, new practices, or new objectives. Consequently, the challenge component might describe an existing conflict of forces, which is altered by the introduction of new contextual elements. Alternatively, it could consist of altogether new requirements arising from the reconfiguration of forces, such as the satisfaction of novel objectives. The protagonists in a design scenario do not need to refer to specific individuals in the real world, but they must describe persons who could, convincingly be present in the domain of practice being explored and be ascribed with the intentions and social relations included in the described context. Such constructs are often denoted Persona in HCI methodology—fictitious characters representing a typical person within the domain.

Ethnographic methods are used to construct an elaborate description of the context. This can include appropriate visual materials, such as photographs, videos and sketches. The contextual elements can be organised into a force map, as described earlier.

The proposed solution may be articulated as a storyboard: a series of sketches or diagrams depicting the protagonists' actions and their expected outcomes (Figure 17.3). In the case of technological innovation, a storyboard might include wireframe diagrams of the user interface. In case of innovation in pedagogical practice, it may include comic-style sketches of learners' and teachers' activities. Storyboards are very powerful in facilitating discussions with possible stakeholders.

The claim embodied in a design scenario can be judged theoretically, heuristically and empirically. Theoretical assessment would evaluate the statements in the scenario by comparing them to prior knowledge. For example, if the scenario includes an event to which a protagonist responds in a particular way, we can ask if this response is consistent with evidence of human behaviour in similar situations. Heuristic evaluation is a technique borrowed from usability research, where a group of experts is asked to assess a particular design using a given rubric (set of heuristics). It offers a low-fidelity rapid evaluation which often uncovers design flaws at an early stage. Finally, empirical evaluation consists of implementing the proposed design, introducing the new artefacts into the domain of practice, observing real participants' reactions to them and comparing their actions (and their results) to the ones in the scenario.

Whether they are used as a stage in an actual design and development process, or as a conceptual representation of possible innovations for the sake of discussion, scenarios are a powerful tool in making ideas explicit and grounding them in realistic contexts.

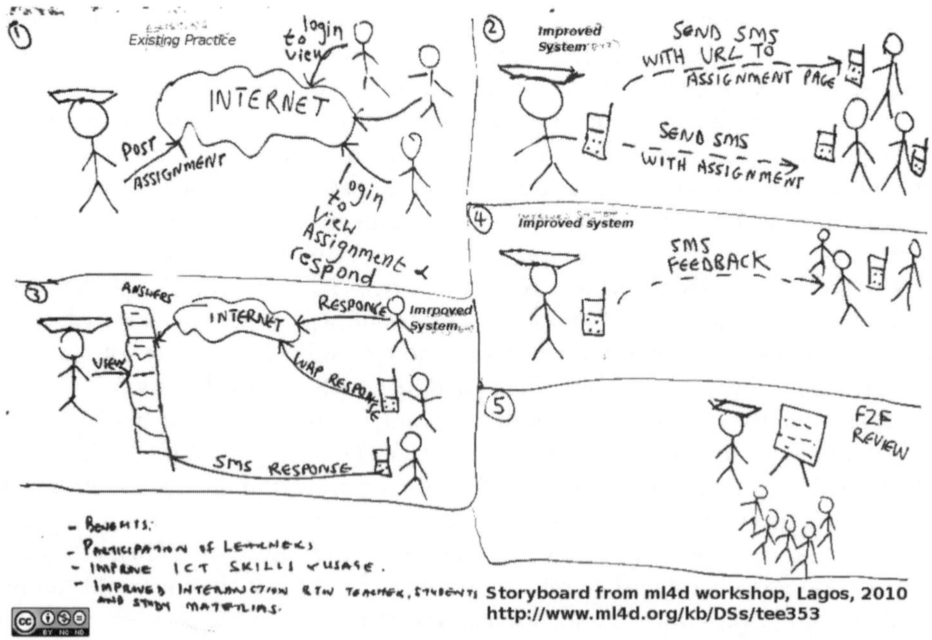

Figure 17.3 Example storyboard, from the ML4D project (http://www.ml4d.org/kb/DSs/tee353), describing a proposed innovation using mobile phones to enhance existing methods of managing assignments.

As an example, the FEASST project facilitated a workshop in which software developers reviewed the narratives and patterns collected from practitioners, and used them to develop scenarios of technological innovations. One of these scenarios is included in the project report:

Situation

First year undergraduate students starting a new subject in large classes (around 600) supported by small tutorial groups (6–12 students), taught on campus and with access to a VLE.

Task

A number of such courses require that students learn large new vocabularies quite quickly. Two contrasting examples would be biology where students are expected to master a large number of unfamiliar terms, and philosophy where students are expected to master the specific technical meanings of perhaps well-known words and phrases. Formative assessment has, potentially, an important role in the learning of these vocabularies.

Solution

Students would build up their own personal glossaries, individually typing in the words and their own definitions, illustrating use in context, and then come together to share these definitions. This is an application of the NARRATIVE SPACES pattern giving learners opportunities to express themselves in narrative form, supporting the use of the vocabularies in context, and then bringing them together into groups where again the discussion and comparison of the definitions practises the use of the language of the domain. In the case of biology the incorporation of images would also be important.

Using the pattern OBJECTS TO TALK WITH the vocabularies and definitions are made into objects to talk with through being externalised, resulting in the sharing of individual definitions in groups, with peer assessment, commentary on other definitions and voting for the best definitions.

The pattern CLASSROOM DISPLAY can be used as these meanings become more stabilised, enabling the sharing of personal understandings of vocabularies with a trusted audience.

The SHOWCASE LEARNING pattern becomes applicable as these definitions are refined, moving up from small groups to tutorial groups and finally to the whole class with a process of voting and selecting the best at each stage, enabling the public celebration of the students' work.

STRENGTHS AND CAVEATS

Design Patterns and Principles have been demonstrated as powerful mediators between theory and practice yet their abstract nature hinders widespread adoption by the practitioner community. Design Narratives have the potential of addressing this challenge by grounding design claims in concrete experiences, and Scenarios afford the formulation of refutable design claims. Design patterns, narratives and scenarios are derived from practical experience. As such, they are firmly grounded in reality, but often lack scientific rigour. It is important to ensure that the strong pragmatic intuitions are linked to hard evidence through appropriate theoretical frameworks.

Despite the prevalence of the narrative form in reports of design research (Bannan-Ritland, 2003) it raises several methodological and practical issues. In the words of Shavelson, Phillips & Towne (2003: 25), 'there is nothing in narrative form that guarantees veracity'. Practically, narrative accounts do not fit well into academic publication format (Reeves et al., 2005). One apparent source of methodological vagueness is the lack of upfront discussion of the narrative tools used by researchers. With a few notable exceptions (e.g. Barab et al., 2008) most studies intuitively use a narrative style of report without explicitly formulating it as a methodology. Even when the form is discussed, it lacks a rigorous definition: what is the core structure of a design narrative? How are its boundaries set? How are events selected and details filtered out? How should we judge if the narrative warrants the researchers' claims?

Another source of difficulty lies within the inherent nature of narrative. In a well-crafted narrative, the message of the story is left implicit (Mor & Noss, 2008). This feature may be epistemically powerful, as it provokes the reader to infer the message and construct her own logical structure to support it. However, it is incompatible with scientific discourse, which demands that the path from evidence to arguments to conclusions be exposed to peer scrutiny. The implication is that design narratives are incomplete as a scientific form, and need to be accompanied by a representation of the derived knowledge.

Finally, it is important to remember the interpretive quality of narrative. A narrative is not a neutral recount of events; it is the outcome of the narrator's immediate attempt at making sense of events, a conjecture regarding the semantics of occurrences. Arguably, this is common to all manner of organising evidence: the statistical analysis of a randomised experiment reflects the researcher's choice of parameters and variables. Yet in the case of statistical analysis, another researcher using the same choice of material could have produced the same result. A narrative is unique to its narrator. This subjectivity may be appropriate in design research, where the researcher is part of the phenomena, but nevertheless needs to be accounted for.

CONCLUSION

This chapter outlined a framework for constructing and sharing design knowledge using design narratives, patterns and scenarios. This framework harnesses the epistemic and expressive power of narrative form, and combines it with the modularity, abstraction and succinctness of design patterns. Scenarios, narratives and patterns have been used successfully, in various combinations, as a framework for design research in educational technology, a methodology for practitioner's collaborative reflection, and as a pedagogy for training educational practitioners. Readers interested in finding out more are invited to follow the links below.

- The Learning Design Grid lists a variety of representations, tools and methodologies, including patterns, narratives and scenarios, and links to several associated projects: http://www.ld-grid.org.

- The Learning Patterns project produced around 25 design narratives and 150 patterns, 50 of them at a beta or release level of maturity: http://lp.noe-kaleidoscope.org/.
- The pattern language network site lists over 100 design narratives, close to 30 design patterns and 13 scenarios: http://patternlanguagenetwork.myxwiki.org.
- The JISC funded FEASST project produced nine design narratives, ten patterns and two scenarios in the domain of formative e-assessment: http://feasst.wordpress.com/.
- Recently, the methodology has been used, with promising initial results, by the ML4D project in the domain of mobile learning for development: http://www.ml4d.org/.

NOTE

1. Front garden—a space that projects a clear group/personal ownership, and a sense of protection for the owner, even if it is publicly visible.

REFERENCES

Alexander, C., Ishikawa, S., & Silverstein, M. (1977). *A Pattern Language: Towns, Buildings, Construction.* New York: Oxford University Press.

Bannan-Ritland, B. (2003). The role of design in research: The integrative learning design framework. *Educational Researcher, 32*(1), 21.

Barab, S. A., Baek, E., Schatz, S., Scheckler, R., & Moore, J. (2008). Illuminating the braids of change in a web-supported community. In A. E. Kelly, R. A. Lesh, & J. Y. Baek, *Handbook of Design Research Methods in Education* (pp. 321–353). New York: Routledge.

Bell, P., Hoadley, C. M., & Linn, M. C. (2004). Design-based research in education. In M. C. Linn, E. A. Davis, & P. Bell, *Internet environments for science education* (pp. 73–85). Mahwah, NJ: Lawrence Erlbaum.

Derntl, M., & Motschnig-Pitrik, R. (2005). The role of structure, patterns, and people in blended learning. *The Internet and Higher Education, 8*(2), 111–130.

Goodyear, P. (2005). Educational design and networked learning: Patterns, pattern languages and design practice. *Australasian Journal of Educational Technology, 21*(1), 82–101.

Hoadley, C. P. (2002). Creating context: Design-based research in creating and understanding CSCL. In *Proceedings of Computer Support for Cooperative Learning (CSCL) 2002* (pp. 453–462), Boulder, CO: Lawrence Erlbaum.

Kali, Y. (2006). Collaborative knowledge building using the Design Principles Database. *International Journal of Computer Support for Collaborative Learning, 1*(2), 187–201.

Kali, Y. (2008). The Design Principles Database as means for promoting design-based research. In A. E. Kelly, R. A. Lesh, & J. Y. Baek (Eds.), *Handbook of Design Research Methods in Education: Innovations in Science, Technology, Engineering, and Mathematics Learning and Teaching.* Mahwah, NJ: Lawrence Erlbaum Associates.

Linn, M. C., & Hsi, S. (2000). *Computers, Teachers, Peers: Science Learning Partners.* Mahwah, NJ: Lawrence Erlbaum Associates.

Linn, M. C., Bell, P., & Davis, E. A. (2004). Specific design principles: Elaborating the scaffolded knowledge integration framework. In M. C. Linn, E. A. Davis, & P. Bell (Eds.), *Internet Environments for Science Education* (pp. 315–340). Mahwah, NJ: Lawrence Erlbaum Associates.

Merrill, M. David (2002). First principles of instruction. *Educational Technology Research and Development, 50*(3), 43–59.

Mor, Y. (2011). Design Narratives: An intuitive scientific form for capturing design knowledge in education. In *Learning in the Technological Era 6th Chais Conference* (pp. 57–63). Open University, Israel.

Mor, Y. (2010). A Design Approach to Research in Technology Enhanced Mathematics Education. PhD thesis, Institute of Education, University of London. http://www.yishaymor.org/phd.

Mor, Y., & Winters, N. (2007). Design approaches in technology enhanced learning. *Interactive Learning Environments, 15*(1), 61–75.

Mor, Y., & Noss, R. (2008). Programming as mathematical narrative. *International Journal of Continuing Engineering Education and Life-Long Learning (IJCEELL), 18*(2), 214–233.

Quintana, C., Reiser, B. J., Davis, E. A., Krajcik, J., Fretz, E., Duncan, R. G. et al. (2004). A scaffolding design framework for software to support science inquiry. *Journal of the Learning Sciences, 13*(3), 337–386.

Reeves, T. C., Herrington, J., & Oliver, R. (2005). Design research: A socially responsible approach to instructional technology research in higher education. *Journal of Computing in Higher Education, 16*(2), 96–115.

Retalis, S., Georgiakakis, P., & Dimitriadis, Y. (2006). Eliciting design patterns for e-learning systems. *Computer Science Education, 16*(2), 105–118.

Shavelson, R. J., Phillips, D. C., Towne, L., & Feuer, M. J. (2003). On the science of education design studies. *Educational Researcher, 32*(1), 25.

van den Akker, J. (1999). Principles and methods of development research. In J. v. d. Akker, N. Nieveen, R. M. Branch, K. L. Gustafson, & T. Plomp (Eds.), *Design Methodology and Developmental Research in Education and Training* (pp. 1–14). Dordrecht, the Netherlands: Kluwer.

18

GOING NATIVE

Autoethnography as a Design Tool

Margot Duncan

1 WHY GO NATIVE?—REASONS FOR USING AUTOETHNOGRAPHY

Autoethnography is a 21st-century research methodology that has evolved from much earlier ethnographic practices. In the early 1900s, British social scientists, fascinated by exotic cultures, would travel to distant lands to observe 'the natives'. They would collect artefacts and make observations which they recorded in journals to create stories, or ethnographies, of how other people lived. Over time, scientists became increasingly aware of how their presence in a foreign culture might influence the events that unfolded, potentially changing people's behaviour and altering the stories they were told. They realised that they were not separate from what they were studying. This new awareness about the influence of the researcher on what was being observed became one of the signatures of ethnography and eventually led some researchers to consider studying themselves—hence the term '*auto*ethnography'.

In autoethnography the premise is that you are the native in your own 'world' and your story is worth telling through your own eyes. In fact you might be the only one that can tell it. Inner knowing is valued and your influence on the environment of your interest is acknowledged. How you perceive your world, what you bring and how you work is the key to everything that happens. Therefore to know your world, you need to know yourself. This premise applies to any 'world', including that of educational technology.

While the logic of these statements is simple, the use of autoethnography in research has been slow to gain momentum. In a world where scientific paradigms dominate the construction of knowledge, there is a tendency to devalue the power of what we might call 'inner knowing'. Research proposals using autoethnography are received dubiously in many academic circles where scientific observations of a 'separate' external world are the preferred norm.

That being said, the realisation that investigating *the one who is looking* might be as valuable as investigating 'what' we are looking at, is not new. Buddhist scholars have explored the nature of 'looking' and its determining influence on reality for more than

2,000 years. 'With our thoughts we make the world' goes a famous Buddhist quotation, capturing the essence of the idea that objective reality is not as fixed as we might assume but is constantly being created through our mental predispositions (Chaskalson, 1997). The Dzogchen tradition (Wangyal & Klein, 2006) describes the true nature of our mind as not actually our thoughts, but 'the space in which those thoughts arise'. Taoists say it another way, that we have three minds—one in our head, one in our heart and one in our gut—emphasising the intelligent, wordless knowing of the whole body not just the head (Chia, 2008). These ancient understandings are the meaningful result of thousands of years of experiential research conducted by countless practitioners, documented in depth and still ongoing. The relevance of these understandings extends beyond the boundaries of philosophy or religion. Western science, which has spent most of its time looking at the external world and very little time looking at the nature or influence of thought, is only just starting to catch up with all that this might mean.

The few Western researchers that have explored the value of 'inner knowing' have made a controversial yet impressive impact on their disciplines. Michael Polyani, a Hungarian Professor of Chemistry, noted in the late 1950s that scientific observation is never entirely impartial. It is always influenced by the 'passions and commitments' of the observer. Furthermore, he considered that scientific discoveries benefited from this, appearing to come from breakthrough moments that tapped into a 'tacit' dimension (Polyani, 1967), which by nature was somewhat illogical and unscientific. In the 1980s Donald Schön influenced a generation of educators and organisational thinkers with his work on reflective practice (Schön, 1987). '*Knowing-in-action*' and '*the artist's conversation with materials*' became valid sources of understanding and informed a range of professional contexts. Similarly, Eliot Eisner (1991) noted that inner knowing and creativity, so highly valued in the arts, were greatly undervalued in other professions. He described what he called the 'enlightened eye' and advocated the idea of 'connoisseurship' as the way in which one could develop it. Connoisseurship involved becoming familiar with; then articulate about the elements, nuances, interactions, and interrelationships of a setting in order to form a deeper appreciation or 'enlightened' awareness. In other words, you develop a 'language' to describe and enhance the experience of your inner knowing, thereby giving the knowledge that 'arises from within' a new voice.

So, while we can say that the reasoning behind taking an autoethnographic approach in educational technology design is somewhat metaphysical (i.e. beyond that which is physical), it is in fact, entirely practical. There is great precedent for taking the approach seriously and exploring what it might contribute to educational design, research and learning contexts.

2 HOW TO GO NATIVE—AUTOETHNOGRAPHIC METHODS AND THEIR USE

Autoethnographers need to know: (1) how to define their study boundaries; (2) how to be a participant observer; (3) how to write reflectively; (4) how to collect artefacts; and (5) how to analyse what they have collected and written. This section looks at each of these in turn.

2.1 Study Boundaries

Autoethnographic studies must have clear boundaries—a specific 'environment of interest' clearly delimited in time and place. The time and place must align with the research question. In the study conducted for my doctoral thesis (Duncan, 2001), the logical boundary was the time and place connected to the particular series of projects I was working on. My research question was closely linked to these projects as I puzzled over how to design hypermedia in the early days of multimedia computing. For your study, other times and places might apply. The 'time' could include everything that happens in one week, everything that has happened in your life up to now or everything that happens during the time it takes to solve a particular problem. The 'place' of your study will involve your actual geographical location as well as the social and political context surrounding your work, the people you work with or serendipitously encounter, the technical and material resources you have access to, and the places you turn to for inspiration and guidance.

2.2 Participant Observation

Participant observation is the core method of all types of ethnography and the practice through which all data collection is organised. Since you are the main character in your autoethnographic study, organising participation is easy but how do you observe yourself and the inner workings of your creativity? While the use of audio, video or keystroke recording may be useful for some research questions, these never capture adequately the thought processes behind your activity. Reflective writing or journaling at specific intervals during the design process is by far the most common and purposeful approach. Many artists and designers already keep a design notebook or journal as part of their daily practice. However, in autoethnography more rigour is required in regards to how often you take notes and what those notes are about. A much more intense writing focus is applied during the specified timeframe than might be considered necessary for normal practice.

In my own autoethnographic work I use a written journal at regular, pre-determined intervals, choosing times when I would normally take a break such as after breakfast, at morning and afternoon teatime, and in the evening. The note taking sessions are brief, addressing different reflective questions each time. At the end of each week I include a longer writing session where I look back over the challenges and breakthroughs that occurred from a broader perspective. Great value lies in the connection between the participatory moments and the moments of reflection. The activity of reflective writing will help develop your 'inner language'. The realisations you gain will 'enlighten your eye' and develop your capacity for focused awareness in following participatory phases. In fact, it is the play between these two activities—participation and reflection—that highlights the relevance of autoethnography to educational technology design.

2.3 Reflective Writing

Journal writing can be a daunting task. Some people are afraid of looking into their 'thought stream' in case it is either empty or full of rubbish. These fears may be well founded. To avoid such dangers, it is helpful to use a journaling framework that triggers insightful reflections by posing questions related to your study purpose. Consider the potential of the following 12 categories of questions for designing a framework to suit your particular research focus. Choose the questions you think will most stimulate your daily or weekly journaling activities, adding new questions or categories as they arise. Your responses may be in point form or prose. Your journal could include mind maps and diagrams or sketches, photos and collages that symbolise your experience. Whatever gives a voice to your inner experience is worth including.

2.3.1 Potential Triggers for Reflective Writing by Category

- *Category #1—Inspiration*: This category of questions asks about what is inspiring you and provides a good way to get your writing started. Look at what you are most excited about, what motivates you, where the work is flowing well and how what you do connects to your highest values and commitments.
- *Category #2—Obstacles*: Often what will be foremost on your mind are the areas in which you feel stuck. Ask questions that help you identify where the major challenges are, where the distractions are coming from, what kind of 'being stuck' you are experiencing, and what types of tension or emotions are connected to these obstacles.
- *Category #3—Imagination and intuition*: Questions in this category tap into imagination and reverie to get intuitive or predictive answers and can be useful at times when you are beginning a new section of work, feel stuck or need to think outside the box. For example, ask 'If this situation was an animal, what type would it be and what would that animal be doing? What is my relationship to the animal and what is about to happen?' or try something like 'If a famous person relevant to this project was to visit, what would I ask them and how do I imagine they would reply?' Your answers and interpretations may reveal breakthroughs you would otherwise be unable to access.
- *Category #4—Transformation*: Questions in this category show the big moments of transformation in the design, in your thinking and in the environment and people around you. What were the key things that happened, the forks in the road, the defining encounters? What were the emotions and signals before and after these key transformative events? How have you been able to confirm or consolidate the transformation?
- *Category #5—Space*: This category asks questions about how often you connected with the *space in which thoughts arise* and how was that connection made? How did you get away from yourself? How did you clear the decks completely and refresh your thinking and how often did you do that? It is easy to overlook this question but that would be a mistake since your best performance will be related to how well you answer this.
- *Category #6—Emerging ideas*: Here we identify the ideas or issues that almost came forward from the tacit dimension, but then did not quite make it out into the open—those things you almost heard yourself say, the *half-thunk thoughts*, the answers on the tip of your tongue. The act of reflective writing can help these emerging ideas to form more clearly.
- *Category #7—Context*: Contextual questions ask about the main events, people or objects with which you interacted. Who did you talk to? What items came into the environment that made an impact on your design? What did you do or see outside of work that influenced you? Who did you influence? What serendipitous encounters did you have? What did you gain from these encounters?
- *Category #8—The collective consciousness*: Questions in this category are best asked when engaging in broader reflection about your work. They explore the view of the collective consciousness on an issue or challenge, your assumptions, the most commonly held views, the views that are on the leading edge and those that are on the dragging edge. Where is your thinking positioned? If there was a gap in the collective consciousness, then what would you see?

- *Category #9—Main themes*: This category helps you identify the main themes arising from your experience. What are the key words or phrases that describe your work and what you have been experiencing? Regularly asking this will reveal recurring patterns and show those areas worthy of further exploration.
- *Category #10—Essentials*: The environments in which we work are so full of sensory, mental and emotional stimulation it is easy to feel overwhelmed. This category of questions helps you to see through the plethora of potential information to identify what is essential. What are the most important things that have arisen out of everything you have been doing? What is most essential to your work? What is the area still needing the most attention? What are the priorities? What is the event or experience that connects most closely to your research question?
- *Category #11—New questions*: This category gets you to articulate more clearly the questions you have been asking yourself. When a question is worded exactly it becomes a very powerful tool in research, when left vague or unrefined it can waste time and effort. Take time to play with your question wording, extend or reduce the variety of questions you are asking, refocus and reconnect with your key question and you will better influence what comes into your awareness. Do this as often as possible.
- *Category #12—Freeform writing*: This category has no question. You are simply allowed to vent or write freely about anything that comes to your mind no matter whether it is fact or fiction, relevant or irrelevant (note: this is valuable but do not make it the only thing that appears in your journal as some people do).

Whether you use pen and paper, electronic notebooks or audio-visual equipment, it is important to time and date your entries. Give each entry a title after you have finished recording it, then log each title in an index to assist later analysis. Simply reading over the index creates a map of where you have been and where you might be going that is useful in itself. Make sure you practise your approach before formally starting your study to check how everything is working. The ways in which you go about observation and reflective writing will, of course, evolve as your experience deepens. Allow for that, but where you can, be clear in your planning at the beginning as this effort will help determine the quality of your end result.

2.4 Data Collection

In autoethnography, data collection begins with your journal entries but does not end there. Apart from your system of reflective writing and the filing of those notes, you will also be collecting corroborating evidence. This evidence will add an important dimension to your study, enabling a richer level of analysis and lifting your work from mere autobiographical musings to something substantial and verifiable in more traditional research terms. The data, or 'artefacts' you collect, will fall into two basic categories.

1. *Artefacts of the inner experience*—This is the evidence that documents the inner experience of design and the development of ideas related to your research question (other than your reflective journal). Artefacts in this category might include but are not limited to sketches; drafts of screen layouts; plots of interaction sequences; story boards; beta versions; loose notes; concept maps; and white board print-outs.

2 *Artefacts of the external environment*—This is the evidence that identifies and documents the external constraints and contextual factors related to your research question (other than your reflective journal). Examples here include items such as your original project proposal; records of user feedback; recordings of workplace visitors; photographs of how your workplace is set up; critical reviews of projects similar to yours; influential articles you might have read; and minutes of meetings.

2.5 Data Analysis

When your study reaches its final stage you will cease your participant observation and daily reflections and no longer collect data. Now you will look through each item you have collected with a fresh eye (all your reflective journal entries and artefacts). I recommend using a grounded theory approach to label and code them (Strauss & Corbin, 1990). Grounded theory is an iterative process that enables relationships between data items to emerge as you code, group and regroup elements of your observations; rethink their meanings and find new connections. Ultimately you will be looking for an answer to your original research or design question. For serious research studies, often what is being searched for is a theory that proposes or explains a new way of doing things. This task of theory creation is particularly suited to autoethnography whereas the testing of theories may be something you do later using a less personal approach.

For example, the following piece of data (a journal entry) captured an overheard conversation that the designer found interesting:

> *Journal entry 5.7* 'The elderly lady said her granddaughter showed her so many ways to do things on the computer that by the end she couldn't remember what to do! The granddaughter was so excited to show her but the elderly lady wished the young girl hadn't talked so fast and that she had only been shown one thing, then she might have been able to remember it.'

This entry could be labelled with the code 'Cognitive Overload'.

Each data item may be given more than one code. In the above journal entry the labels 'Elderly User' or 'Overenthusiastic Presenter' could also be applied. As your data coding continues you will find some codes reoccurring and these will coalesce into categories. For example, a screen snapshot on which you have scribbled the notes 'too many things going on, needs simplifying', might also be labelled 'cognitive overload'. Now the issue of cognitive overload is becoming a category. As you understand each category further you will be able to note their different properties and dimensions. From the preceding examples, we can see that the category 'cognitive overload' might include items that are operational (the elderly lady could not remember what to do) or visual (the screen view was too cluttered). You might also identify that the dimensions of cognitive overload include 'user experience' or 'presenter style'.

Theories start to emerge as you notice how categories and core categories are connected. For example, you might find a connection between the category 'cognitive overload' and another category called 'emotion'. What starts to occur to you as you look over your notes is *not* how cognitive overload causes a certain emotion, but how certain emotions, such as being overly enthusiastic about presenting, help create learning experiences where cognitive overload occurs. Noting this, you might decide to revisit your data to look for all other examples of how a certain type of emotion helped create a situation of cognitive overload, eventually developing a theory about, for example, 'the emotional causes of overloaded designs and how to mitigate them'. In the final phase of the analysis, your autoethnography will most likely be written up as a narrative based on the journey of recognising these deeper themes and their connections to your emerging theory.

3 WHERE TO GO NATIVE—CHOOSING APPROPRIATE SETTINGS AND CHALLENGES

Autoethnography is characterised by much experimentation and liberal interpretation about what counts as research and how to present findings. Anything from analytic reports (Anderson, 2006) to short stories (Gilbourne, 2010); personal memoirs (Sotirin, 2010); conversation, interview and diary studies (Balaam, 2011; Clark & Gruba, 2010; Wiebe & Guiney Yallop, 2010); narratives (Ellis, 2004; Trahar, 2009); artistic and photographic histories (Liamputtong & Rumbold, 2008; Holbrook, 2005; Luna Hernández, 2009; Suominen, 2003; Schneider, 2010); collaborative accounts (Zanker & Gard, 2008; Chang, Ngunjiri & Hernandez, 2012); personal documentaries (Costantini, 2012; Erhlich, 2003) and virtual interactive artworks (Morrison, Viller & Mitchell, 2010) may stake a claim for their research status under similar umbrellas. This provides a rich environment for researchers to explore new ways of knowing and sharing experience. To better understand how these opportunities for experimentation might apply in an educational technology setting, it can be helpful to see these different studies as happening along a continuum ranging from the very casual autoethnographic product at one end to the far more rigorous account, suitable for a doctoral research thesis, at the other. In the middle of the continuum you might find examples of autoethnography applied as an approach to workplace problem solving. The practitioner's purpose or question is always the rule by which you measure the 'goodness-of-fit' of the approach, be it experimental, casual or highly rigorous.

The *casual approach* may involve little more than the designer's notebook and an illustrated summary of their experience. In taking the time to develop a summary, the autoethnographic character of the activity will emerge as the designer develops categories of their ideas, prioritising some and eventually answering questions such as 'What do I like/not like as a designer (either in general or in relation to a particular project)?' 'What influences me?' Or something more challenging such as 'What are my strengths and weaknesses?' Since such an activity is not intended to be submitted as research, it need not bear the label autoethnography, although the designer would benefit from understanding the methods and techniques. Taking extra time with the question focus and exercising rigour with the definition of study boundaries, writing and data collection will do much to draw out the value of the designer's world, crystallising their learning.

The advantage of the casual approach is the freedom you have to do what you like, write what you like and stop when you want. You can present your work as an artist might present a painting, claiming that it is valid simply because it exists. You can decide the worth of the activity solely by what you got out of it and you need not even articulate that. If you show someone, you can count on not really being judged because no one knows on what grounds to critique you.

The disadvantage of the casual approach is that you might have a tendency to ramble or wander off topic, fail to gather momentum, become irregular in your writing and data collection, miss important opportunities for learning and, as a result, come to no conclusions or develop faulty ones. In the worst case scenario you will get lost in your own thoughts instead of clarifying their meaning and value. If you can manage some amount of personal rigour, a well-defined casual autoethnography can be an excellent personal learning tool and a great way to pilot your methodological approach before working on a research question that involves longer timelines and other stakeholders. Try a two-week autoethnography on a single focus question such as 'What I like/do not like about my own design work'. Buy a new journal, choose a set of sub-questions to use as a writing framework and book in a time with yourself twice a day to respond to these questions. Collect 'corroborating' data to add to your journal as you go along and, at the end of the fortnight, set aside a few one-hour sessions to see not only the obvious patterns but those hidden threads that are emerging, those seeds of new ideas that your autoethnographic attention has helped to germinate.

In a workplace setting, the application of autoethnographic techniques might involve more difficult or specific questions such as those discussed at the beginning of this chapter. They might address aspects of design related to a particular project, particular stakeholders, or environmental contexts. For example: 'What is the best way to incorporate existing learning applications within this project?' 'How can [insert the name of the latest technology] be applied to this project?' 'How does our design team work best together?' or 'How can my design help adult learners complete degree study while at work?' Any design question occurring in a day's activity can be addressed through autoethnographic methods. Whereas previously you may have left the question for the weekly team meeting, mapped out whiteboard solutions and run with the consensus opinion; now you will give this question 'research status' and address it through your personal practice.

You now value your own experience as a primary resource, intensify your focus and allow more time than normal to explore and develop your thinking and insight about the topic. You will triangulate different data sources and have a deadline requiring a final summary that will be presented to a specific target audience of your work team or project stakeholders. A higher level of rigour in note taking, data collection, data analysis and presentation will be required than in the 'casual approach'. As a result you will come up with revealing insights and valuable theories in answer to your questions that help solve real design problems, guide future work or sharply focus further enquiries. Your solutions are likely to be more original, more thorough and have greater relevance and longevity because of the deeper flow of attention you applied.

In the case of a *doctoral thesis*, you can expect a study that extends over a much longer time frame. As such your question will need to sustain interest and be considered academically significant. Any question we have asked so far could be a starting point. However, unlike the 'workplace' or 'casual' autoethnography, you will conduct an in-depth and ongoing literature review that will influence your inner language of design and help refine your question. In particular you will be analysing the literature for what your peers have *not* been writing about. Identifying this gap establishes how your research will make the 'significant' contribution to knowledge required of doctoral level research.

Here, the world of educational technology, characterised by rapid change, works to our advantage. Developers closely involved in creating innovations rarely have time to write about them, let alone complete doctoral level study. Consequently, there are few detailed maps showing which way to go. As designers, we frequently find ourselves in the role of pioneers, looking for new ways to help learners learn, not sure if the guidelines we followed yesterday still apply. We wonder if we are somehow blind to new thinking and search for ways to see things differently. In this environment there is clear justification for the use of autoethnography and a strong claim for the significance of your study.

The end product of your research may be a conservative, traditional, written thesis or include more creative outputs depending on your institution and supervisor (Doloriert & Sambrook, 2011). In either case, you will need to offer your reader guidelines on how to judge the worth of your study (Duncan, 2004). In new research methodologies just as in new media, the audience could feel lost when viewing your work, if no conventions are supplied. In more conservative environments, use your methodology chapter to clearly answer questions about your study's validity, utility and reliability—thus saving your examiner and peers the trouble of asking.

4 CONCLUSION

In our busy professional lives, it is rare to have the opportunity to stop and really look at what we have been doing. Undertaking an autoethnography provides that opportunity and offers structured methods for capturing the inner workings of the creative process and accelerating learning. With great scope for creativity in both the application of the methods and the end product, autoethnography is easily personalised to suit different work settings and research questions. In the world of educational technology design and use, there are many possibilities still to explore. If the researcher takes care to match the rigour of their research design with their question and context (i.e. goodness-of-fit), valuable understandings and insights can be assured. We must consider that, as both designers and learners, our primary piece of educational technology is our own mind and what we have been missing most are ways to look inside it.

REFERENCES

Anderson, L. (2006). Analytic Autoethnography. *Journal of Contemporary Ethnography, 35*(4), 373–394.

Balaam, M. (2011). An Autoethnographical Design: Using autoethnographic methods to understand and portray experience through design. 11 December 2011, from http://www.madelinebalaam.co.uk/assets/Uploads/submission-balaam.pdf.

Chang, H., Ngunjiri, F., & Hernandez, K. (2012). *Collaborative Ethnography (Developing Qualitative Inquiry).* Walnut Creek, CA: Left Coast Press.

Chaskalson, M. (1997). *Western Buddhism.* New York: Harper Collins

Chia, M. (2008). *The Healing Energy of Shared Consciousness: The Taoist approach to entering the universal mind.* Canada: Destiny Books.

Clark, C. & Gruba, P. (2010). The use of social networking sites for foreign language learning: An autoethnographic study of Livemocha. Proceedings ascilite, Sydney. Accessed 15 December 2011, from http://ascilite.org.au/conferences/sydney10/Ascilite%20conference%20proceedings%202010/Cclark-full.pdf.

Costantini, R. (2012). Social Documentary as a Pedagogic Tool: The experience of the Project Europa. *Conference Proceedings, International Conference 'The Future of Education'* 2nd Edition, 7–8 June 2012, Florence, Italy. *Accessed 19 June* 2012, *from* http://www.pixel-online.net/edu_future2012/common/download/Paper_pdf/636-MLE07-FP-Costantini-FOE2012.pdf.

Doloriert, C. & Sambrook, S. (2011). Accommodating an Autoethnographic PhD: The tale of the Thesis, the Vive Voce, and the Traditional Business School. *Journal of Contemporary Ethnography.* Accessed 15 December 2011, from http://org.sagepub.com/content/19/1/99.full.pdf+html.

Duncan, M. (2001). *Principles of hypermedia design: An autoethnographic case study.* Unpublished doctoral dissertation, Queensland University of Technology, Brisbane, Australia.

Duncan, M. *(2004).* Autoethnography: Critical appreciation of an emerging art. *International Journal of Qualitative Methods, 3(4), 1–14. Accessed 15 November* 2011, *from* http://www.ualberta.ca/~iiqm/backissues/3_4/pdf/duncan.pdf.

Ehrlich, M. (2003). Poetry on the margins: Ghetto Life 101, Remorse and the New Radio Documentary. *Journalism, 4*(4), 423–439.

Eisner, E. (1991). *The Enlightened Eye: Qualitative inquiry and the enhancement of educational practice.* New York: Macmillan.

Ellis, C. (2004). *The Ethnographic I: A methodological novel about autoethnography.* Walnut Creek, CA: AltaMira Press.

Holbrook, M. (2005). Customer value and autoethnography: Subjective personal introspection and the meanings of a photograph collection. *Journal of Business Research, 58*(1), 45–61.

Gilbourne, D. (2010). 'Edge of Darkness' and 'Just in Time': Two cautionary tales, two styles, one story. *Qualitative Inquiry, 16*(5), 325–331.

Liamputtong, P. & Rumbold, J. (2008). *Knowing Differently: Arts-based and collaborative research method.* New York: Nova Science Publishers.

Luna Hernández, J. R. (2009). Photo-ethnography by People Living in Poverty Near the Northern Border of Mexico. *Forum: Qualitative Social Research, 10*(2). Accessed 15 November 2011, from http://nbn-resolving.de/urn:nbn:de:0114-fqs0902353.

Morrison, A., Viller, S. & Mitchell, P. (2010). Ethnography considered useful: Situating criticality. In: OZCHI '10: Proceedings of the 22nd Annual Conference of the Australian Computer-Human Interaction Special Interest Group (pp. 184–187). Brisbane, Australia, 22–26 November 2010.

Polyani, M. (1967). *The Tacit Dimension.* London: Routledge Kegan Paul.

Schneider, A. (2010). Contested grounds: Fieldwork collaborations with artists in Corrientes, Argentina, *Performance, art et anthropologie.* Accessed 26 January 2012, from http://actesbranly.revues.org/43.

Schön, D. (1987). *Educating the Reflective Practitioner: Toward a new design for teaching and learning in the professions.* San Francisco, CA: Jossey-Bass.

Sotirin, P. (2010). Autoethnographic mother-writing: Advocating radical specificity. *Journal of Research Practice, 6*(1), Article M9. Accessed 1 June 2012, from http://jrp.icaap.org/index.php/jrp/article/view/220/189.

Strauss, A. & Corbin, J. (1990). *Basics of Qualitative Research: Grounded theory procedures and techniques.* London: Sage.

Suominen, A. (2003). *Writing with photographs, re-constructing self: An arts-based autoethnographic inquiry.* Doctoral Dissertation, Ohio State University. Accessed 11 December 2011, from http://etd.ohiolink.edu/view.cgi/Suominen,%20Anniina%20.pdf?acc_num=osu1061236352.

Trahar, S. (2009). Beyond the story itself: Narrative inquiry and autoethnography in intercultural research in higher education. *Forum: Qualitative Social Research, (10)*1. Accessed 24 November 2011, from http://www.qualitative-research.net/index.php/fqs/article/view/1218/2653.

Wangyal Rinpoche, T. & Klein, C. A. (2006). *Unbounded Wholeness, Dzogchen, Bön and the Logic of the Nonconceptual.* Oxford: Oxford University Press.

Wiebe, S. & Guiney Yallop, J. (2010). Ways of being in teaching: Conversing paths to meaning. *Canadian Society for the Study of Education, (33)*1, 177–198. Accessed 4 March 2011, from http://www.csse-scee.ca/CJE/Articles/FullText/CJE33-1/CJE33-1-WiebeYallop.pdf.

Zanker, C. & Gard, M. (2008). Fatness, fitness and the moral universe of sport and physical activity. *Sociology of Sport Journal, 25*(1), 48–65.

Part III
Implementation

INTRODUCTION

Barbara Grabowski and Niall Winters

May [we design and implement] . . . in interesting times.

Borrowing from a popular Chinese saying, we see this implementation section as presenting a purposefully eclectic series of implementation cases. Emerging and burgeoning advancements in technology, combined with continuing advancements in our understanding about learning contribute to making the process of design "interesting." While "interesting times" denotes challenges, innovative learning technologies provide not only challenges, but exciting and promising opportunities for improving learning. This section, therefore, is organized around four implementation challenges related to design in educational technology:

1. designing learning activities and support systems for complex thinking;
2. designing for collaborative interactions;
3. designing for learning with innovative technologies;
4. designing distant education with innovative technologies.

Each challenge should not be seen as a "stand-alone" as there is strong overlap between them. Exemplifying the diversity of TEL, each addresses, in a different manner, a variety of learning issues, levels of thinking, design strategies, contexts, content areas, learning environments and methods of evaluation. The authors conceptualized and put into practice their ideas, drawing together theoretical, methodological and critically practical issues. Contributions of the chapters are presented by their underlying contributions to addressing the four challenges.

The manner in which particular design decisions are implemented is crucial to the success of the design process and this section of the book presents the reader with specific examples of ways in which different techniques and strategies were actually operationalized and realized. Each chapter author begins with a particular implementation challenge and describes how it was met by including a discussion of its design history and theoretical grounding. The authors then connect the design history to particular justifiable design decisions that were implemented in specific ways unique to their context, content and learning environment constraints. This section of chapters also includes those implementation challenges at the programmatic level because of the implications technology can have on broader institutional policy.

1 IMPLEMENTATION CHALLENGES OF DESIGNING LEARNING ACTIVITIES AND SUPPORT SYSTEMS FOR COMPLEX THINKING

One of the most promising and challenging applications of technology-enhanced learning is to support and promote complex thinking. The first four chapters in this section describe support systems for: (1) learning and practicing creative problem solving at the college level (Lim, Lim, & Hong); (2) learning "complex, dynamic, risky, time-pressed information-laden" anesthesiology used by dental students (Choi, Hong, Park, & Lee); (3) learning how to engage in the complex process of critical and predictive writing of an action research proposal for graduate students (Sharma & Anderson); and (4) a twist on the theme, monitoring reading ability progress of elementary and special education students (Hooper, Miller, & Rose). In each case, some aspect of design-based research or iterative implementation was used to modify their designs.

Lim et al. describe support tools that integrate e-learning environments with the traditional classroom, specifically with Web 2.0 tools. They outline five theoretically based guidelines and demonstrate how they are applied for designing a creative problem-solving support system. Choi et al. present case-based learning scenarios that take advantage of electronic learning support systems, dynamic textbooks that provide relevant information keyed to need, decisions points, scaffolded summary notes, video representation of cases and expert reasoning, along with a data- based infrastructure. Six design decisions are detailed, theoretically justified and tested. Sharma and Anderson's case applies principles from scaffolding and vicarious learning theories in an online learning environment that includes design strategies called "Thought Tools," "Writer's Wisdom" and "Writer's Shelf."

Hooper et al.'s chapter presents technology support tools in a unique application, that is, a tool to assess and monitor student progress. Addressing the problem of grading and monitoring inefficiency of student essays, these authors describe four design cycles of experimenting with a web-based analytics support system that resulted in an affordable, efficient and scalable e-assessment system.

2 IMPLEMENTATION CHALLENGES OF DESIGNING FOR COLLABORATIVE INTERACTIONS

Two critical dimensions of learning include collaboration and interaction. Technology affordances enable the learning designer to include opportunities for both. However, simply using technology to enhance interaction does not mean it will be effective. Three chapters in this section deal specifically with the challenges of creating effective collaborative interactions. Maddrell and Morrison address crucial questions about when, why and how interactions should be included in the virtual space of distance education. They draw upon distance education literature, interaction theory and computer-supported cooperative literature to suggest five design strategies to promote workspace awareness as a means for making collaborative interaction efficient and effective.

Many questions have also been raised in regard to the use of social networking sites for collaborative learning in formal courses. Taking advantage of several key features in Facebook, Kurtz, Meishar-Tal and Pieterse applied connectivist theory to design interactions into a hybrid course for graduate students. Their implementation study investigated its effectiveness to promote interactive dialogue, sharing information and co-constructing knowledge.

Price and Marshall focus on innovation and innovative practice with tangible computing for learning, and provide an up-to-date overview of this research. Drawing on a number of key implementation pilot projects, they emphasize the importance of design, in particular detailing how tangibles can support collaborative learning activities and discussing how different forms of external representations influence interaction.

3 IMPLEMENTATION CHALLENGES OF DESIGNING FOR LEARNING WITH INNOVATIVE TECHNOLOGIES

When thinking about the implementation of learning technologies broadly across all sectors (and not just within the technology-enhanced learning community itself) one of the issues which is often overlooked is the design *process*. By this we mean design that addresses the needs of users directly in a "bottom-up" manner. This can be contrasted against the many implementation projects that seek to embed learning technologies in a "top-down" manner, which can result in wasted resources as take-up of the technology is low.

Winters addresses this point in his chapter by discussing the importance of a *participatory approach* to design and implementation of TEL interventions within the context of postgraduate medical education. He notes the need to focus not only on the design of the software but also on the design of the associated learning activities. The chapter stresses the importance of underpinning any TEL design (and indeed the design process itself) with an appropriate learning theory. Winters points to the key role of the researcher in supporting users to make an informed decision regarding this choice.

As is evident throughout this section, TEL researchers and practitioners use innovative technologies across the formal and informal learning sectors. We have already discussed the work of Price and Marshall on tangible computing. Heo, Jo, Lim, Lee and Suh work in the related area of ubiquitous technologies. Their chapter presents a unique model called CLUE (convergent learning in a ubiquitous environment) to suggest design strategies that converge formal with informal learning environments in which learners become "full participants in a social-cultural space." In the informal sector, one of the main areas of interest over the years has been detailed investigations of museum learning. Walker's chapter follows in this tradition. He discusses his PhD research, in which he focuses on how mobile devices can support meaning-making in museums. In particular he shows the importance of technology in supporting a core aspect of meaning-making, that of linkage—between artifacts and visitors, and between different interpretations and ideas.

4 IMPLEMENTATION CHALLENGES OF DESIGNING DISTANT EDUCATION WITH INNOVATIVE TECHNOLOGIES

Distance education, innovative practice and innovative technologies align in current practice not only at the lesson level, but at a programmatic level, as discussed in the last three chapters of this section. Arnone, Ellis and Cogburn discuss important theoretically driven design and implementation decisions that were made for a cyberlearning master's degree program for persons with disabilities (PWD) to become leaders in public policy. The design team faced many challenges specifically related to presentation methods and accessibility to content. Key to their design of distributed collaborative learning activities were Vygotsky's social constructivist and motivational theories.

From an even broader perspective, Romiszowski and Otamere focus on innovative advances of cloud computing and its potential for higher education distance education/ e-learning programs. They discuss its benefits and risks. Then, in two cases, one completed and one in the planning stage, they analyze and evaluate the implementation of a cloud-based e-learning system.

Finally, Ke and Zhu discuss how two innovative technologies, Tegrity lecture capture tool and Second Life virtual reality environment, were used to extend teaching presence in two unique cases. The effects of these two implementation cases were presented to argue for designing specifically for teaching presence to promote cognitive and social presence in a web-based learning environment.

5 CONCLUSION

As the chapters in this section testify, implementation is not a stand-alone concept. It is driven by a clear conceptualization from the outset of what needs to be achieved, a strong focus on learning theory and a necessary understanding of design practice. Pragmatically, the implementation stages of any TEL project or intervention help in gaining a better understanding of learners' needs, help to improve on the learning design through appropriate evaluation. Thus, we should be clear that implementation is not an end in-and-of itself but part of an overall process which seeks to make learning technologies relevant to learner needs within their own context.

19

A DEVELOPMENTAL STUDY FOR THE DESIGN OF THE CREATIVE PROBLEM SOLVING SUPPORT SYSTEM

Cheol Il Lim, Wan Chul Lim, and Miyoung Hong

1 INTRODUCTION

The design and development of learning support systems has been a prominent subject in educational computing recently. Jonassen, Howland, Marra, & Crismond (2008) suggested using a computer not just as a tutor but as a cognitive tool for critical and complex thinking processes, and many studies have been conducted to design learning environments in which computers work as supportive tools. Computers with network capabilities can play a key role in systematically guiding collaborative activities among learners. A structural approach for creativity such as Creative Problem Solving (CPS), for instance, can be successfully supported by an online system in which learners are guided and asked to join divergent and convergent activities collaboratively among team members. CPS as a model for guiding creative processes has long been the framework for teaching creativity (Treffinger, Isaksen, & Dorval, 2000, 2006). The model emphasizes a balance between divergent and convergent thinking in every step of the problem-solving process (Puccio, Firestien, Coyle, & Masucci, 2006). However, it has been used mostly in face-to-face classroom settings, and the possibility of using the model in an e-learning environment has not been well explored yet.

This case study delineates how an online support system can be designed and implemented for guiding learning activities by the CPS model. The main ideas of the study are twofold. One is that the design principles for the system could be developed and improved through *developmental research methodology* (Richey, 1997; Richey, Klein, & Nelson, 2004). The initial design principles were identified and elaborated through three specific steps in this study, and an online system was developed. Those principles for the system were improved by examining the learners' reactions which were collected in a real college course. This study specifies what steps and activities should be followed to implement design decisions successfully in developmental research. The other point is that the way to handle learner control for their learning activities is not just a matter of system design but an implementation strategy for advising the learners with appropriate information. This approach can be used practically before the design principles can be fully implemented to develop an online support system.

2 CREATIVE PROBLEM SOLVING AND ONLINE SUPPORT SYSTEM

The CPS model for creativity was originated from Osborn (1963) who suggested the idea of brainstorming, which emphasized the practice of divergent thinking to solve problems creatively. Osborn suggested the original CPS model which outlined his ideas on creative problem solving. The steps of Osborn's original model are: *Orientation, Preparation, Analysis, Hypothesis, Incubation, Synthesis and Verification* (Puccio, Murdock, & Mance, 2005). His model has been developed into more advanced ones in which orderly approaches to creativity are emphasized (Shneiderman, 2000, 2007). When a solution is suggested and explored, the creative experts evaluate its strengths and weaknesses, compare it to existing solutions and refine the promising solution to make it implementable. The structuralists emphasize orderly processes of problem solving such as CPS (Isaksen & Treffinger, 1985; Treffinger et al., 2000, 2006).

Treffinger and his colleagues (2000) added a meta-component (or management component) to their previous CPS model: "Planning Your Approach" which contains the two stages of *Appraising Tasks* and *Designing Process.* The prior step-by-step model has not theoretically allowed individuals or teams to customize their approach to applying CPS. However, for individuals or teams who want to use the CPS model flexibly, it is required to be able to engage in meta-cognition (Puccio et al., 2005). The meta-component serves as an operating system to guide the application of the three *process* components: *Understanding the Challenge; Generating Ideas; and Preparing for Action.* These process components are divided into six specific stages, during which creative and critical thinking activities are engaged in harmony. Figure 19.1 shows the latest CPS model which consists of six specific stages: *Constructing Opportunities; Exploring Data; Framing Problems; Generating Ideas; Developing Solutions;* and *Building Acceptance* (Treffinger et al., 2000).

In addition to the multiple steps of the CPS model, it emphasizes a balance between divergent and convergent thinking in every stage of the problem-solving process (Puccio et al., 2006). In the CPS process, some phases where the additional options are primarily needed may require great emphasis on divergent thinking, and other phases where analysis, evaluation and improvement are needed may call for an emphasis on convergent thinking. Successful use of the CPS involves knowing how to balance the use of both divergent and convergent thinking strategies (Isaksen, Dorval, & Treffinger, 1994). Therefore, it is necessary to strive for reasonable balance between divergent and convergent thinking. This dynamic balance is one of the most important factors that makes the CPS process so powerful and productive (Isaksen & Treffinger, 1985). An identified common feature of the CPS model is the use of various creative thinking tools to enhance divergent and convergent thinking skills (Higgins, 2006). Higgins (2006) classified various thinking tools into divergent and convergent ones. For instance, Brainstorming, Forced connection method, Morphological analysis, Osborn's checklist, Attribute listing, and SCAMPER are classified as the divergent thinking tools. The convergent thinking tools include Hits, Highlighting, Reverse brainstorming, Evaluation matrix, Paired comparison analysis, ALU (Advantage, Limitation, and Unique Qualities), and PMI (Plus, Minus, and Interesting). Externalized outputs by using such creative

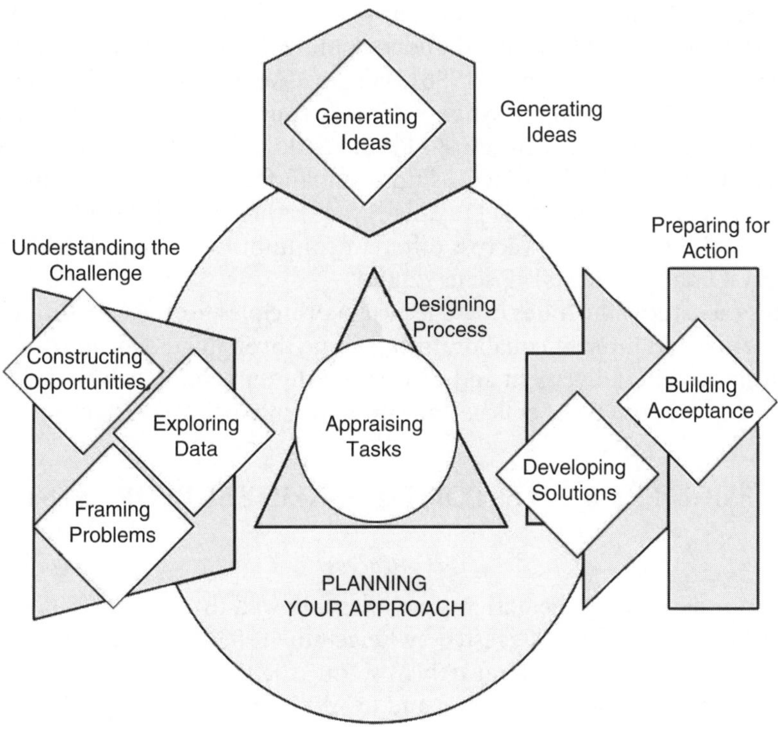

Figure 19.1 The CPS Version 6.1™ framework.

thinking tools may provide feedback for individual evaluation and facilitate the creation of common ground between collaborators.

As creativity has become one of the key competencies in this knowledge and information society, the use of the CPS model should be extended into the college education setting. The practical need of creativity in college education faced the challenge of integrating e-learning environments with the traditional classroom. Students could be well supported by the e-learning environment where they can interact online to solve a problem creatively as they follow the CPS steps and utilize divergent and convergent tools. The traditional approach to using the CPS model in the face-to-face classroom setting could not take advantage of technical artifacts in which people can collaborate and manage their activities effectively.

The e-learning environment design for the CPS model mainly comes from the question of how we can support the social aspect of creativity. Most human creativity is exhibited in a social context where interactions with other people and shared artifacts are important contributors. Social creativity comes alive in socio-technical environments in which individuals collaborate with shared technical artifacts (Mumford, 1987; Fischer, 2007). Creative actions cannot be completely planned actions; rather, they can only be situated actions, after reflecting upon the situational feedback from the environment, either technical or social. Therefore, creativity can be greatly enhanced by providing appropriate socio-technical environments (Mumford, 1987).

Individuals in the communities of creative problem solving are assumed to have unique experiences, varying interests and different perspectives about problems. They also use different cognitive structures in their work. Individuals' understanding of problems can be transformed into a shared understanding that supports collaborative learning and working. Csikszentmihalyi (1996) claimed, "An idea or a product that deserves the label 'creative' arises from the synergy of many sources and not only from the mind of a single person." However, Mumford's (1987) and Fischer's (2005) notion of sources for social creativity involved artifacts as non-human factors as well as human factors. Social creativity can be distributed (1) spatially (across physical distance), (2) temporally (across time), (3) conceptually (across different communities), and (4) technologically (between persons and artifacts) (Fischer, 2005).

Thus, this case study illustrates how the design principles for the CPS support system, in which learners can interact collaboratively online through guided steps and activities with the employment of divergent and convergent thinking tools, can be developed and implemented in the context of college education for enhancing creativity.

3 DESIGN PRINCIPLES FOR THE ONLINE SUPPORT SYSTEM

3.1 Process

The process for developing the design principles followed three steps for developing an instructional model that were suggested by Reigeluth (1983): (1) identifying the general principles from reviewing the literature; (2) setting the theoretical components for the system by categorizing those principles; and (3) developing specific guidelines for each principle. First, general principles were identified from the relevant studies on how to teach the CPS model and to help learners to engage with the CPS activities. The following studies were reviewed for developing design principles: studies on the balance between divergent and convergent thinking tools (Puccio et al., 2006), collaboration for social creativity (Shneiderman, 2007), and learner-centered problem solving environment for creativity (Kim, 2006). The suggested design principles were, next, categorized into a set of theoretical components. They can play an important function of providing a conceptual framework for developing the system. They explain the basic attributes of the newly designed system. The final step is to come up with specific guidelines for each general principle, which can guide the practical design and implementation of the system.

3.2 Principles and their Theoretical Ground

3.2.1 General Design Principles

First, general design principles for the online CPS Support System or CPS[3] were identified from respective studies. The design principles are as follows.

3.2.1.1 PROVIDE EFFECTIVE TOOLS SUPPORTING DIVERGENT AND CONVERGENT THINKING IN HARMONY

CPS is a model for solving problems creatively by using divergent and convergent thinking repeatedly. That is, in every stage within CPS, divergent and convergent thinking are used and a deliberate balance between the divergent and convergent phases is the critical factor to apply CPS effectively (Puccio et al., 2005). In accordance with Shneiderman (2007), creativity support tools would be needed to support not only individual aspects of creativity, but also social aspects of creativity. Tools supporting mass collaboration and social production such as citizen journalism (Blogger, Ohmynews), media sharing (Flickr, YouTube), wikis (Wikipedia), folksonomies (del.icio.us), and virtual worlds (Second Life) are other examples of support tools for social aspects of creativity (Shneiderman, 2007).

3.2.1.2 SUPPORT-STRUCTURED APPROACH

The school of structuralism embraces systematic approaches. There are some approaches around the traditional phases of preparation, incubation, illumination and verification (Shneiderman, 2007), but also often around more carefully defined methods such as the eight potential stages of CPS v6.1™ model (Isaksen, Dorval, & Treffinger, 2000).

However, it is difficult to provide precise guidance in a step-by-step manner. So rigid structured strategies were cast aside and replaced with semi-structured methods that include meta-cognitive or end user modifiability components, which have been shown to be beneficial (Isaksen et al., 2000; Fischer & Scharff, 2000). By using these methods, individual learners and their team can use a support system tailored to meet their needs.

3.2.1.3 MAKE LEARNERS WORK COLLABORATIVELY IN SOCIO-TECHNICAL ENVIRONMENTS

Socio-technical environments are necessary to collaboration and to bring social aspects of creativity alive (Mumford, 1987; Fischer, 2005, 2007). In these environments, learners can express themselves, articulate their own ideas and solutions, discuss their own perspectives, combine those perspectives, generate new understandings, and build up a single appropriate solution. In large and heterogeneous groups working together for long periods of time over complex design problems, the challenge is not to reduce heterogeneity and specialization but to support and manage them at both the technological and social level by finding out ways to build bridges between individuals and exploiting conceptual collisions and breakdowns to stimulate imagination and invention (Dede, 2008; Hewitt & Scardamalia, 1998; Clarke, Dede, & Dieterle, 2008; Csikszentmihalyi, 1996; Fischer & Konomi, 2007; Fischer, 2007; Shneiderman et al., 2005).

3.2.1.4 ENCOURAGE EVOLUTIONARY USING

Shneiderman (2007) emphasized the benefits of history-keeping in creative problem solving. He also stated, "Whether discoverers and innovators used structured or free-form thinking, the benefits of rich history-keeping are apparent." With regards to this perspective, learners have a set of alternatives they have tried in the process of problem solving. Learners can compare the alternatives throughout the whole processes and they can go back to previous ones to make modifications. Also, history-keeping on collaborative situations has still more benefits, such as sending interesting cases to colleagues for comments, continuing dialogues on those cases through the time line, and creating macro problem-solving processes that can be run repeatedly on new data.

3.2.1.5 MAKE LEARNERS DESIGN THEIR OWN CREATIVE THINKING TOOLS

Kim (2006) stressed the way to support learners in designing their creative thinking tools. He suggested a learner centered problem solving environment that can empower learners to engage in the problem-solving process rather than providing a problem solving environment restricted to the use of existing creative thinking tools. Learners can design their creative thinking tools in accordance with their extent of understanding. If creative thinking tools should effectively support creative problem solving, problem solvers should redesign creative thinking tools rather than simply use the assigned ones.

3.2.2 Theoretical Components for the CPS Support System

Three theoretical components for designing the system were extracted by categorizing the general design principles. The first theoretical component, systematic approach, is related to the structured process components of CPS, such as "Understanding the Challenge," "Generating Ideas," and "Preparing for Action." The second one is about the learners' collaborative activity, which should be supported in socio-technical environments. The last theoretical component is related to the learners' autonomy. The level of engagement that results from being able to pursue their own needs is one of the critical points of effective and creative problem solving.

3.2.3 Specific Guidelines

A set of specific guidelines was developed from the general design principles of the theoretical components. Table 19.1 summarizes the specific guidelines of the CPS support system.

3.2.3.1 SYSTEMATIC APPROACH

The CPS support system should provide the whole components and stages of the CPS process. Learners should be able to customize their CPS process based on their needs and the instructor must be able to control the learners' problem-solving process.

In addition, the CPS support system should provide thinking tools that support divergent and convergent thinking, data interoperability among the thinking tools, and user interfaces for viewing the results from various perspectives of learners to monitor the whole process of problem solving in progress. The CPS support system also has to support an on-going and dynamic balance of convergent and divergent thinking.

3.2.3.2 COLLABORATIVE ACTIVITY

The CPS support system should provide the feature of organizing the team flexibly, synthesizing individual learners' outputs into the team's, and the mutual evaluation of the learners' results. It should also be designed to select a team leader and set up the role, and to set up individual learners or the team as a fundamental unit of problem solving and the rules for sharing individual learners' outputs with the team.

In addition, with the CPS support system, learners can verify their fellow learners' results from using creative thinking tools, reflect on their processes of problem solving and share them. The team leader should be able to control the team's step-by-step process of problem solving.

3.2.3.3 LEARNERS' AUTONOMY

The CPS support system should be able to manage a variety of ways of viewing the results of problem solving and be able to select a thinking tool for each stage. In addition, with the CPS support system, the instructor could evaluate the result of each stage, and each team should be able to modify and redesign its own creative thinking tool.

4 IMPLEMENTATION AND DESIGN MODIFICATION

4.1 System Implementation

In the process of implementing the design principles, the support system was actually developed with the process below.

Table 19.1 Specific Guidelines for Designing the CPS Support System

Design Principles	Theoretical components	Specific Guidelines
Provide effective tools supporting divergent and convergent thinking in harmony	Systematic Approach	Provide data interoperability among the thinking tools. Provide thinking tools that could support divergent and convergent thinking. Support an on-going and dynamic balance of convergent and divergent thinking. Make it possible to set up the combination and sequence of the thinking tools. Provide user interfaces for the results with various perspectives of learners. Make it possible to monitor the whole process of problem solving in progress.
Support structured approach		Enable the instructor to register and manage the CPS model. Make it possible to use and modify the CPS model. Enable the instructor to control the problem-solving process. Provide of the whole components and stages of the CPS process.
Make learners work in socio-technical environments	Collaborative Activity	Make it possible to synthesize individual learners' outputs into the team's. Make it possible to organize the team flexibly. Enable learners to select team leader and set up the role. Enable team leader to control learners' step-by-step process of problem solving. Make it possible to set up individual learner or team as a fundamental unit of problem solving. Make it possible to set up the rules for sharing individual learner's output with team. Enable learners to verify their fellow learners' result of using creative thinking tools. Enable learners to reflect on their processes of problem solving and share them. Enable learners to evaluate each others' results. Provide each team with discussion board.
Encourage evolutionary using	Learners' Autonomy	Make it possible to view the results of problem solving in various ways. Enable instructor to evaluate the result of each stage and ask learners to 'redo' if necessary.
Make learners design their own creative thinking tools		Enable learners to select the thinking tool for each stage. Enable learners to use template of thinking tool designed by instructor. Enable each team to select and redesign its own creative thinking tool.

The first step was designing conceptual services on the basis of instructional goal and content, and then examining identifying design principles. The second was to design expected learners' usage flow, and then designing data for communication among learners and instructors and for interaction among thinking tools, CPS process, and the results of problem solving. In this step, the selection and adaptation of users' activities such as utilizing divergent and convergent thinking tools were made based upon the constraints

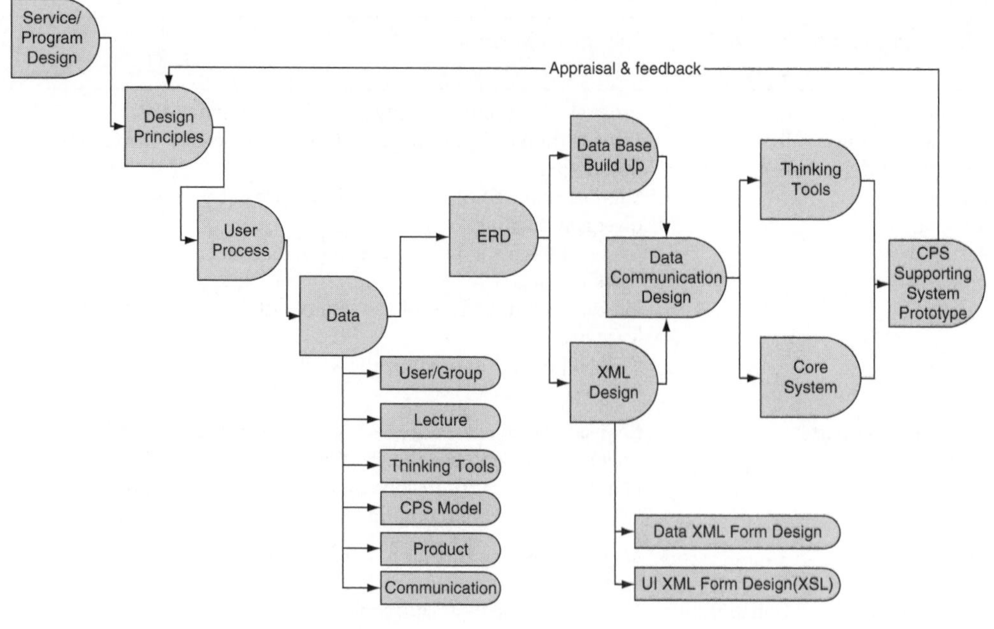

Figure 19.2 CPS³ prototype development process.

of resource and developing time. Six tools were selected and developed by the criteria of popularity for divergent and convergent thinking practices. The third step was designing an ERD (Entity Relationship Diagram) for developing a database, and XML form for data and the UI (User Interface). Finally, a prototype was developed, based on technological communication among data, and the thinking tools.

The actual system developed following the principles, and implemented in the practice, represented eight stages of the CPS v6.1™ process: *Appraising Task, Designing Process, Constructing Opportunities, Exploring Data, Framing Problems, Generating Ideas, Developing Solutions,* and *Building Acceptance.* The system also included six thinking tools: two divergent thinking tools (*Attribute Listing* and *Brain Storming*) and four convergent thinking tools (*HIT, PMI, ALU* and *Evaluation Matrix*).[1] Except for the first two stages, there were one divergent thinking tool and two convergent thinking tools in each stage.

Figure 19.4 shows a sample screenshot of the developed system. The thinking tools are originally set up by the instructor, but they could be modified and redesigned by each team. The result of using a thinking tool is displayed in the right of the menu. The instructor and learners can monitor the whole process of problem solving, results from using thinking tools and the various versions of the result with this system.

Figure 19.5 displays screenshots of one of the thinking tools, Evaluation Matrix, in use. Here, learners should list possible ideas on one axis of a grid and important criteria to be evaluated against on the other axis. This allows learners to compare and contrast several possibilities using similar criteria (Stead & Dorval, 2001). The instructor sets up the thinking tools for each stage, and then learners can select and redesign as they use them. The results are shown in various user interfaces such as individual user view or

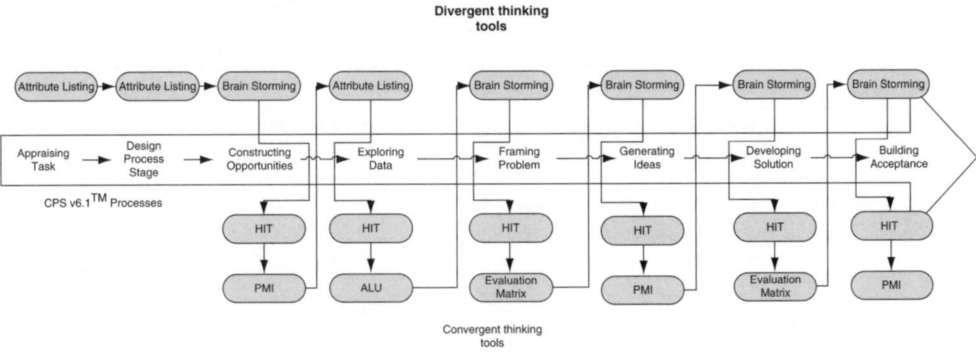

Figure 19.3 Sequence of thinking tools through CPS process.

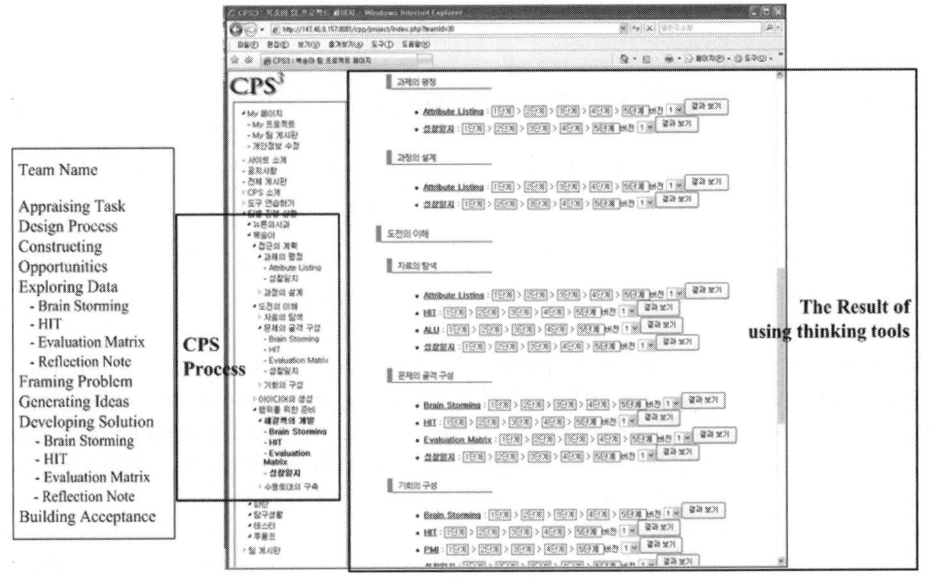

Figure 19.4 A sample screenshot of the CPS³.

team based view, etc. The left side of Figure 19.5 shows the example of using the Evaluation Matrix and the right side shows an individual user's view of the results.

4.2 Design Principles Improvement

The developed system was implemented in an undergraduate course, "Understanding Education," at Seoul National University in 2008. Thirty-three students participated in this study and they were engaged as four small groups (7–9 members) in solving an authentic educational problem of "differentiated instruction" creatively using the CPS³. Students' reactions about the system were collected through two channels: one from reflective journals that they reported in the system as they finished each stage of CPS; the other from intensive interviews with individual students. Twelve students, three

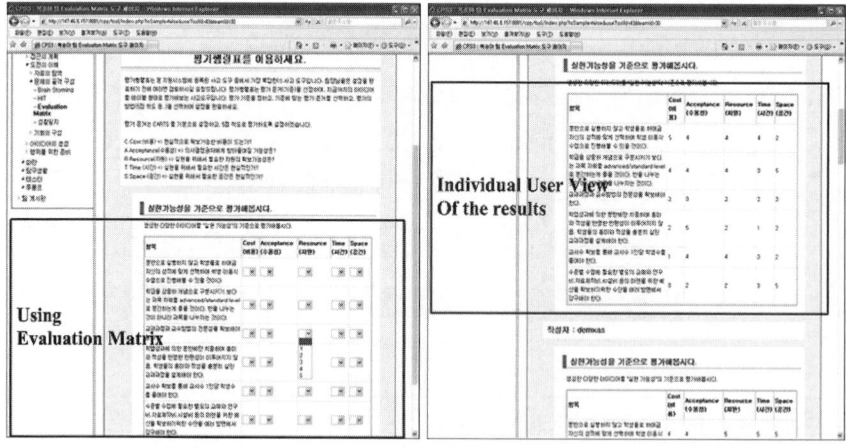

Figure 19.5 Using the Evaluation Matrix and individual user view.

from each team, were originally selected as interviewees based on their level of participation: four students with higher levels of participation, four students with lower levels of participation and four team leaders. However, the number of final interviewees was reduced to 10 because two students with lower levels of participation declined to be interviewed.

Learners' reactions were collected to improve the design principles and, eventually, the system. Table 19.2 represents their responses to the respective general design principles.

Although the learners responded positively to the design principles and the implemented system, they suggested the following three improvement areas, which should be examined in terms of learning system design and implementation in general. First, they wanted a more simple and flexible process rather than following all the stages of the CPS model. The issue of providing autonomy to learners should be more carefully examined in the design and implementation stages. The system was designed for the learners to complete all the stages from the beginning to the end, and it eventually did not work well. Although the whole process of any learning activity such as problem solving is designed and implemented in the system, the instructor and learners should negotiate whether they follow all the steps or not, and the system must support their decision.

Second, the learners asked for more choice of their own tools rather than the six tools the current system provided. This demonstrated the unavoidable gap between designers' analysis and decision and users' preferences, which are impossible to detect before the system is actually implemented. The theoretical solution to this problem can be suggested in two ways: One is to design more tools the learners would like to use, which might be difficult to put into practice within the limit of resources and time constraints, and the other one is to communicate with learners more specifically in the implementation stage: why the system has these types of tools and how they can use these tools more effectively. The latter solution is more practical within the limit of development constraints, and the designer should provide the instructor with guide-

Table 19.2 Learners' Reactions

Design Principles		Reactions
Support structured approach	Strength	• Ongoing development of discussion with a definite and structured process • Helpful for solving complex problems
	Weakness	• Uniform process for all teams restricted creative thinking • Too many stages
Provide effective tools supporting divergent and convergent thinking in harmony	Strength	• Approach complex problem efficiently with the thinking tool
	Weakness	• Need more diverse thinking tools • Need to enable each team able to select thinking tools
Make learners work in socio-technical environments	Strength	• Communicate efficiently as the result of team discussion for each stage being saved • Not only secure participation of all students, but also reflect diverse individual perspective • Put team members' ideas together and make it the final result of the team
	Weakness	• Hard to wait until all members participate and tutor's approval for the next stage
Encourage evolutionary using	Strength	• Observe the progress • Compare and refer to the previous version when the result is not satisfactory
	Weakness	• Inconvenient because it is focused on managing the version of the result only by the process, not by each specific thinking tool
Make learners design their own creative thinking tools	Strength	• Enabling each team able to design its own thinking tool motivates active participation • To efficiently access the complex problems within the framework of collaborative thinking tools designed by users themselves
	Weakness	• Hard to design team's own thinking tool in the early stage
Etc.		• Hard to figure out the whole context with only the short idea in the system • Unfamiliar with the system

lines, so they can explain the reason for the choice of limited tools to the learners more persuasively.

Third, the learners wanted to work more flexibly as a collaborative group. The current system was designed to require the instructor's approval at each stage, and proceed to the next stage only after all the members complete the stage. This brought unexpected results of delaying collaborative work if the instructor did not reply promptly or a member failed to do his/her duty. It was found that the group leader should have the autonomy to continue their process with the consensus of members to work more flexibly as a group while the instructor has the right to monitor their activities.

5 CONCLUSION

In educational computing, there has been a shift of emphasis from using the computer as a tutor to using it as a cognitive tool for complex thinking skills. This case study demonstrates how the online support system for creativity can be designed and implemented through developmental research methodology. The CPS model as a representative framework for teaching creativity was selected to be used in the college education context. Prior studies suggested that the model could be used more effectively with the online support system in which learners can work collaboratively following the stages and using tools for divergent and convergent thinking in the online environment.

This study extended the idea that the CPS model for teaching creativity could be supported by a web-based system, and conducted developmental research to develop the design principles. First, three specific steps for developing the design principles were taken, and they were: (1) identifying the general principles from reviewing the literature; (2) setting the theoretical components for the system by categorizing those principles; and (3) developing specific guidelines for each principle. Second, those design principles were implemented by following the prototype development process in which learners' usage flow and data communication flow among learners and instructors were considered. In this step, users' activities, such as utilizing divergent and convergent thinking tools, were selected and implemented within the constraints of resource and developing time. Finally, the online support system was actually used in a college course, and the learners' reactions were collected and analyzed to improve the design principles.

This case study intended to demonstrate the procedure to develop the design principles and implement them for teaching creativity. The structural approach to creativity such as CPS requires specific steps and activities to follow, and the designers tried to come up with the optimal solutions within the limits of constraints. However, the learners in practice did want more autonomy for their activities and more options for selecting tools. This brought us to think about how we can handle the traditional issue of learner control in the context of web-based support systems. Whether we provide the learners with full responsibility or not, it is not an easy decision to make which activities to follow or which tools to use. One lesson we learned from this study is to inform the learners systematically why a specific set of steps and activities are required before providing them with full autonomy and a well-equipped tool box. The issue is not just to design in full scale but how we can advise the learners with the best information for their learning activities.

NOTE

1. Attribute listing is used to create new values first by listing all possible aspects of a problem, and then considering the value of each attribute, and finally modifying the attributes in some way. Brain Storming is the most popular divergent thinking tool designed to generate a large number of ideas for the solution of a problem. HIT is used when there are various ideas and they should be examined, selected and narrowed by checking the most likely alternative. PMI is a valuable convergent tool and stands for "Plus/Minus/Interesting." By writing down all the positive results for "Plus," all the negative effects for "Minus" and the implications and possible outcomes for "Interesting," an alternative can be selected from a range of options. Evaluation Matrix tool is used for evaluating and prioritizing among choices based on your evaluation plan.

REFERENCES

Clarke, J., Dede, C., & Dieterle, E. (2008). Emerging technologies for collaborative, mediated, immersive learning. In J. Voogt & G. Knezek (Eds.), *The International Handbook of Technology in Primary and Secondary Education* (pp. 901–910). New York: Springer-Verlag.

Csikszentmihalyi, M. (1996). *Creativity: Flow and the psychology of discovery and invention.* New York: HarperCollins.

Dede, C. (2008). Theoretical perspectives influencing the use of information technology in teaching and learning. In J. Voogt & G. Knezek (Eds.), *The International Handbook of Technology in Primary and Secondary Education* (pp. 43–62). New York: Springer-Verlag.

Fischer, G. (2005). Challenges for future research activities and projects focused on "software tools and socio-technical environments to enhance creativity." *Creativity Support Tools*, NSF Workshop Report. pp. 74–75.

Fischer, G. (2007). Designing Socio-Technical Environments in Support of Meta-Design and Social Creativity. *Proceedings of the Conference on Computer Supported Collaborative Learning (CSCL '2007)*, Rutgers University, July, pp. 1–10.

Fischer, G., & Konomi, S. (2007). Innovative socio-technical environments in support of distributed intelligence and lifelong learning. *Journal of Computer Assisted Learning, 23*(4), 338–350.

Fischer, G., & Scharff, E. (2000). Meta-Design—Design for Designers. *3rd International Conference on Designing Interactive Systems (DIS 2000)*, New York, pp. 396–405.

Hewitt, J., & Scardamalia, M. (1998). Design principles for the support of distributed processes. *Educational Psychology Review, 10*(1), 75–96.

Higgins, J. M. (2006). *101 creative problem solving techniques: The handbook of new ideas for business.* Winter Park, FL: New Management Publishing Company Inc.

Isaksen, S. G., & Treffinger, D. J. (1985). *Creative Problem Solving: The basic course.* Buffalo, NY: Bearly Limited.

Isaksen, S. G., Dorval, K. B., & Treffinger, D. J. (1994). *Creative Approaches to Problem Solving.* Dubuque, IA: Kendall/Hunt.

Isaksen, S. G., Dorval, K. B., & Treffinger, D. J. (2000). *Creative Approaches to Problem Solving: A framework for change.* Dubuque, IA: Kendall/Hunt.

Jonassen, D., Howland, J., Marra, R. M., & Crismond, D. (2008). *Meaningful Learning with Technology.* Upper Saddle River, NJ: Pearson Education, Inc.

Kim, A. (2006). Empowerment learning: True learner-centered learning in online environment. In E. Pearson & P. Bohman (Eds.), *Proceedings of World Conference on Educational Multimedia, Hypermedia and Telecommunications 2006* (pp. 1109–1112). Chesapeake, VA: AACE.

Mumford, E. (1987). Sociotechnical systems design: Evolving theory and practice. In G. Bjerknes, P. Ehn, & M. Kyng (Eds.), *Computers and Democracy* (pp. 59–77). Aldershot, UK: Avebury.

Osborn, A. F. (1963). *Applied Imagination: Principles and procedures of creative problem-solving.* New York: Charles Scribner's Sons.

Puccio, G. J., Firestien, R. L., Coyle, C., & Masucci, C. (2006). A review of the effectiveness of Creative Problem Solving training: A focus on workplace issues. *Creativity and Innovation Management, 15*(1), 19–33.

Puccio, G. J., Murdock, M. C., & Mance, M. (2005). Current development in creative problem solving for organization: A focus on thinking skills and styles. *The Korea Journal of Thinking & Problem Solving, 15*(2), 43–76.

Reigeluth, C. M. (1983). Instructional design: What is it and why is it? In C. M. Reigeluth (Ed.), *Instructional Design Theories and Models: An overview of their current status.* Hillsdale, NJ: Lawrence Erlbaum.

Richey, R. C. (1997). Research on instructional development. *Educational Technology Research and Development, 45*(3), 91–100.

Richey, R. C., Klein, J. D., & Nelson, W. A. (2004). Development research: Studies of instructional design and development. In D. H. Jonassen (Ed.), *Handbook of Research for Educational Communications and Technology.* Mahwah, NJ: Lawrence Erlbaum Associates.

Shneiderman, B. (2000). Creating creativity: user interfaces for supporting innovation. *ACM Transactions on Computer-Human Interaction (TOCHI), 7*(1), 114–138.

Shneiderman, B. (2007). Creativity support tools: Accelerating discovery and innovation. *Communications of the ACM, 50*(12), 20–32.

Shneiderman, B., Fischer, G., Czerwinski, M., Resnick, M., & Myers, B. (2005). Introduction to Workshop Report. *Creativity Support Tools*, NSF Workshop Report, pp. 4–9.

Stead, S., & Dorval, K. B. (2001). The Power of the Evaluation Matrix. *CPSB's Communiqué*, Vol. 11, pp. 24–27.

Treffinger, D. J., Isaksen, S. G., & Dorval, K. B. (2000). *Creative Problem Solving: An introduction.* Waco, TX: Prufrock Press Inc.

Treffinger, D. J., Isaksen, S. G., & Dorval, K. B. (2006). *Creative Problem Solving: An introduction* (4th ed.). Waco, TX: Prufrock.

20

CASE-BASED LEARNING FOR ANESTHESIOLOGY

Enhancing Dynamic Decision-Making Skills through Cognitive Apprenticeship and Cognitive Flexibility

Ikseon Choi, Yi-Chun Hong, Hyojin Park, and Yunseok Lee

1. INTRODUCTION TO THE IMPLEMENTATION SITUATION THAT PROMPTED THE USE OF CASE-BASED LEARNING

College instructors often wrestle with contradictory educational goals, such as covering broader topics at a deeper level or enhancing higher order thinking with broader factual knowledge (Hung, Bailey, & Jonassen, 2003) in a very limited time. An introductory course in anesthesiology offered at dental schools in South Korea was not an exception. The goal of the *Introduction to Anesthesiology* course was to help dental students understand broad topics related to anesthesiology and gain deeper levels of understanding of an anesthesiologist's decision-making processes in a given timeframe of one semester credit hour. Consequently, the instructor had to focus on delivering massive amounts of factual knowledge through a given textbook. Unquestionably, the instructor rarely observed students engaging in reflective thinking or appreciating experts' decision-making processes. The decontextualized information received and memorized through this class had seemed to remain as "inert ideas" in students' minds, which is inactive knowledge constructed without critical thinking (Whitehead, 1927). This is a classic problem in education that most college instructors have experienced in their own practices.

Formulating an innovative educational solution to overcome this classic problem and to achieve the intended learning outcomes, we focused on both efficiency and effectiveness in learning, so students can learn the given broader topics meaningfully with richer contexts, and so they also can gain decision-making skills through authentic experiences. Therefore, we considered case-based learning (Allen, Otto, & Hoffman, 2000; Barnes, Christensen, & Hansen, 1994; Shulman, 1992) as the primary theoretical structure of the solution, while cognitive apprenticeship (Collins, Brown, & Holum, 1991; Collins, 2006) and cognitive flexibility (Spiro, Feltovich, Jacobson, & Coulson, 1992) were integrated into this basic structure as sub-solutions for further enhancing decision-making skills in particular. A critical review of the given class situation and a careful integration of three learning theories resulted in six design decisions that prescribed the architecture of the educational solution. These theoretically informed design decisions, in turn, had been actualized through the development of a video-based, case-based e-learning environment that was implemented into the anesthesiology course using an online and face-to-face blended approach.

2. INTRODUCTION TO THE LEARNING PROBLEM

2.1. The Nature of Learning Tasks: Dynamic Decision-Making in Anesthetization

Anesthetization is often characterized as complex, dynamic, risky, time-pressed, and containing highly information-loaded tasks (Gaba & Howard, 1995). For safe patient care during a surgery, anesthesiologists continuously monitor a patient, anesthesia equipment, and clinical procedures, and carry out necessary actions accordingly in the process of anesthetization (Gaba & Lee, 1990). Critical decisions are made in dynamically evolving surgical situations. Gaba and Howard suggested a pattern of the anesthesiologist's decision-making process: detecting cues from external devices or patient monitoring, identifying problems from the interpretation of cues, predicting future states based on reasoning, planning actions, implementing the actions, monitoring the effects of the actions, and evaluating the overall results of the decision-making process.

2.2. The Context of Learning and Challenges

The *Introduction to Anesthesiology* course is a one-semester credit hour course required for the third-year students at a dental school in South Korea. This course aims at helping students (1) construct scientific and clinical knowledge related to anesthesiology, including interactions between physiology and pharmacology, (2) understand a wide spectrum of anesthesiology and patient management in the operating room, and (3) make reasoned decisions for maintaining the appropriate anesthesia in expected and unexpected patient situations. It is a challenge for both the instructor and the students to achieve these goals in a large, traditional classroom setting.

This course was taught by a series of teacher-led lectures, and the learning outcomes evaluated by multiple-choice questions. This indicated that students would mainly engage in memorization of the decontextualized textbook information. An interview with a successful student who passed this course confirmed that he failed to remember the majority of what he had learned in the course after one year had passed.

3. LEARNING THEORIES/MODELS FOR DESIGN DECISIONS

3.1. Case-Based Learning

Having a long history in a variety of practices, case-based learning has been widely implemented with various formats and different names, such as case method and case-based instruction. In this chapter, case-based learning is defined as a set of learning and teaching models that uses real or realistic events holding multifaceted issues and complexity as part of learning resources, which engages students in individual and/or group inquiry on the given events with other relevant information, and which promotes students' reflections on their own learning and problem solving (Allen et al., 2000; Barnes et al., 1994; Shulman, 1992).

Recent empirical studies support that case-based learning improves students' knowledge acquisition (Abbott et al., 2010; Cendan, Silver, & Ben-David, 2011), reasoning skills (Nikendei et al., 2009), and problem-solving skills (Danielson et al., 2006). It is believed to be one of the most effective methods to bridge the gap between theory and practice (Barnes et al., 1994; Williams, 1992). Compared to other learning theories and models promoting experiential learning, such as problem-based learning and authentic learning, case-based learning has a wider spectrum of possible models and uses (Barrows, 1986) and has more flexibility to be adopted in a variety of learning environments that range between teacher-centered and learner-centered. This is a key reason to consider case-based learning for designing this educational solution, because the implementation site is based in a teacher-centered classroom culture, yet it requires a certain degree of experiential learning.

Our design decisions were influenced by two main characteristics shared by various types of case-based learning. First, real or realistic events involving multifaceted problems with richer contextual information are essential components of learning resources in case-based learning. A collection of meaningfully connected events, as a case, could be designed for several different functions of educational uses (Jonassen, 2011). For instance, a case with a complete set of events (e.g., legal cases or surgery cases) could be used as an example to enhance students' understanding of abstract concepts or to show a process of problem solving. In contrast, a case with incomplete events (e.g., business problems or ethical dilemmas) could be used as a problem situation to be solved by students. Furthermore, a series of cases with a certain theme could be utilized to promote case-based reasoning (Aamodt & Plaza, 1994) to solve new problems.

Second, case-based learning promotes students' active involvement in "systematic inquiry and rigorous reasoning about the substantive issues" (Christensen & Hansen, 1987, p. 4) that are raised in a case. Inquiry questions for guiding meaningful analysis and evaluation of the case and for promoting students' reflection on their experiences and learning are provided in an individual learning or group learning contexts (Ellet, 2007).

3.2. Cognitive Apprenticeship

Based on critical analysis of a traditional apprenticeship in which expertise is developed in the workplace, Collins, Brown, and Newman (1989) proposed cognitive apprenticeship as a model of instruction "that works to make thinking visible" (Collins et al., 1991, p. 6) and that applies the essential components of the traditional apprenticeship to the school system.

Cognitive apprenticeship recommends six methods to promote the development of expertise (Collins et al., 1991; Collins, 2006):

- *modeling*, allowing students to observe experts/teachers' performance;
- *coaching*, allowing students to perform a task with experts' observation and feedback;
- *scaffolding*, providing appropriate support to help students perform a task;
- *articulation*, allowing students to verbalize their knowledge and thinking;
- *reflection*, enabling students to compare their performance with others;
- *exploration*, allowing students to solve their own problems.

This model informed us about how to design inquiry activities and learning resources for the case analysis that developed students' thinking skills.

3.3. *Cognitive Flexibility*

Criticizing a reductive epistemic view, oversimplifying the complexity of real-world problems and believing the world is predictable and well-defined, cognitive flexibility theory (Spiro, Collins, & Ramchandran, 2006; Spiro, Feltovich, & Coulson, 1996) highlights the importance of, and the nature of, human knowledge being adaptable to understand multifaceted reality in diverse situations from multiple perspectives. This theory suggests learners should crisscross, compare, and contrast multiple cases through meaningful themes and different perspectives to enhance the flexibility of knowledge, so that the knowledge can be active and applicable in learning and solving problems in ill-defined domains (Spiro & Jehng, 1990; Spiro et al., 1992; Spiro et al., 2006).

The following four major components of designing a cognitive flexibility hypertext learning environment influenced our design decisions (Graddy, Lee, & Timmons, 2001; Spiro et al., 2006).

- *Crossroad case*: instead of being used for teaching one concept or one thing in particular, a major case should be rich and open so it provides the intersection of multiple themes, allowing multiple interpretations and the possibility of being used for multiple learning purposes.
- *Multiple conceptual themes*: top-level central concepts, ideas, or schema of the domain expressed by different experts. Multiple cases should be explored according to multiple themes to promote flexibility.
- *Many mini-cases*: the larger case can be broken down into small segments according to the themes. Utilizing many mini-cases according to a variety of themes can enhance flexibility.
- *Perspectives*: Contextual and semantic elements of cases or specific interpretations of cases are considered as perspectives which allow multiple representations of reality for important ideas and themes.

4. DESIGN DECISIONS INFORMED BY THE LEARNING THEORIES/MODELS

The theories/models identified in the previous sections informed our decisions on how to design case-based learning in a given implementation situation. Figure 20.1 presents how each of the theories and their characteristics are related to the decisions made for developing specific technology-embedded strategies. Figure 20.2 presents the interface of the case-based learning developed based on the design decisions.

4.1. *Design Decision 1: Provide Representative Cases Containing Educational Values, Multiple Challenges, and Rich Contexts*

To provide students with vicarious experiences, real or realistic events with rich situational information are essential learning resources. However, it is also important to consider whether a series of events, as a case, has educational values aligned with the course objectives. Taking into account the implementation context, we consider three aspects. First, cases should be linked to broader topics that the course aims to cover.

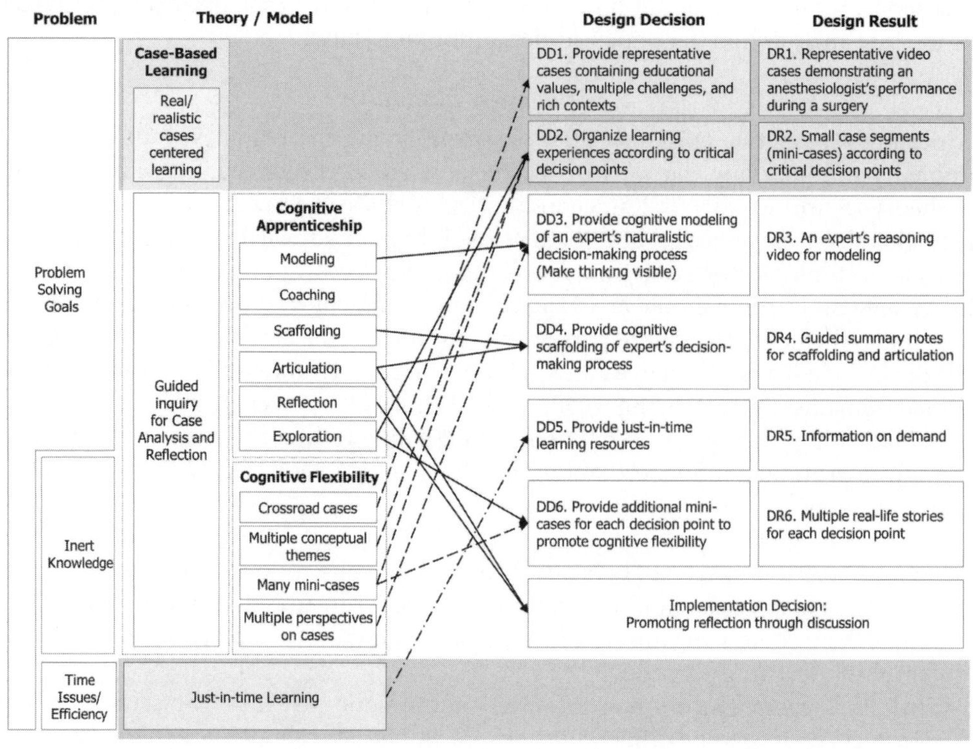

Figure 20.1 Relations among problems, learning theories/models, design decisions, and design results.

Different goals (conscious sedation or general anesthesia), types (nasal or mouth), and other important parameters of anesthesia (anesthesia drugs, operations, and others) are analyzed to characterize possible types of surgery cases that may provide a broader range of anesthetization procedures.

Second, cases should include important and multiple themes, authentic problems, and/or real-world challenges, so that the cases can be used for multiple themes and topics and can promote students' learning around important knowledge and skills that are worthwhile to learn. We searched over 2000 surgery cases for the characterized representative cases that hold multiple challenges in each single case. However, this effort failed. Thus, we decided to develop realistic case scenarios and embed valuable challenges into the stories.

Last, the case should provide rich, complex situational information so students have the opportunity to develop flexible and multiple representations of reality. Video technology was considered as an appropriate option among the currently available technologies (Spiro, Collins, & Ramchandran, 2007).

The consideration of these three aspects resulted in two realistic scenarios. The scenarios were two 10-minute-long representative video cases that provided a series of challenges and an expert's performance in the given context. So the students were able to vicariously experience authentic situations and the problem-solving processes that experts typically dealt with in their practices.

4.2. Design Decision 2: Organize Learning Experiences According to Critical Decision Points

Anesthesiologists are engaged in serious reasoning processes around critical decision points in order to understand problem situations and then to generate the appropriate courses of action based on existing medical knowledge. To teach experts' reasoning and decision-making skills along with the relevant basic medical knowledge related to anesthesiology, we believed that the critical decision points should be major problem units where the learner's attention is focused and where instructional efforts need to be made. Through a cognitive task analysis process (e.g., Flanagan, 1954; Klein, Calderwood, & Macgregor, 1989), we found that most critical decisions were made in the planning stage of anesthetization and during unexpected (or expected) incidents while surgery is performed. Based on the analysis, each representative video case was broken into segments less than two minutes long. Each segment was divided according to critical decision points. During a course of anesthesiologist's performance during a surgery case, 8–10 critical decision points were provided. Each decision point requires different kinds of knowledge, skills, and decisions. Thus, each decision point can be considered as an independent case. This design was aligned with the notion of themes (critical decision points) and mini-cases (small segments) recommended by cognitive flexibility and exploration by cognitive apprenticeship.

As shown in Figure 20.2, each segment is navigated through the decision-point navigation bar under the representative case screen. Students were advised to review decision

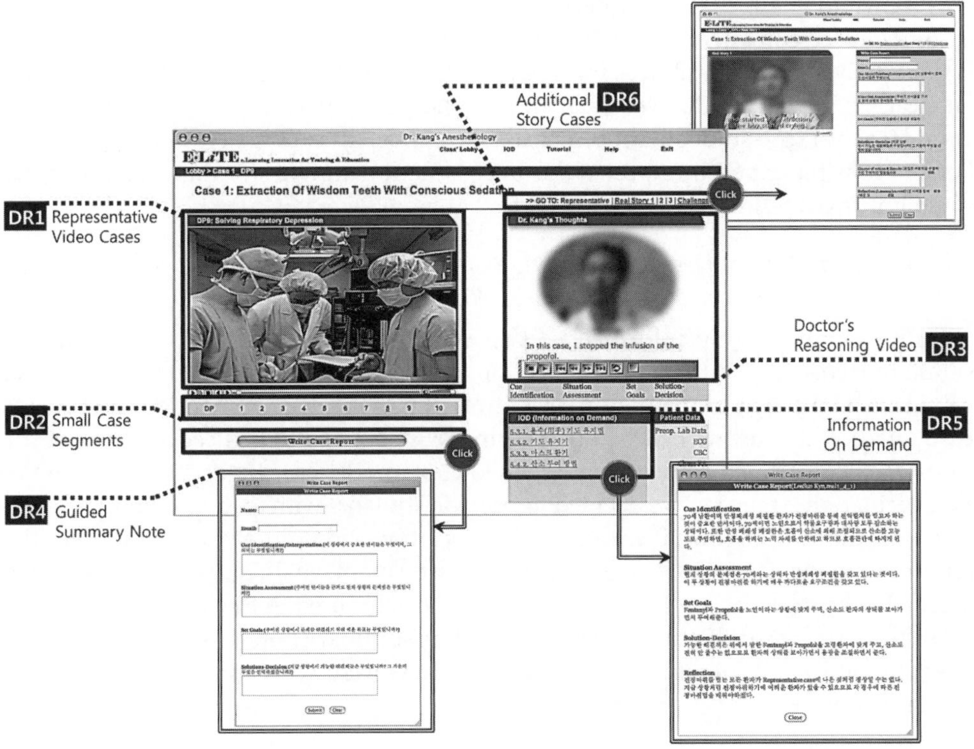

Figure 20.2 Design results.

points sequentially to understand how the case deployed. As they navigated each decision point, all other learning resources on the page were updated accordingly.

4.3. Design Decision 3: Provide Cognitive Modeling of an Expert's Naturalistic Decision-Making Process

Guided inquiry for the analysis of each small case problem would be the core learning activities in case-based learning. We believed that it was important to show students how experts made reasoned decisions when they faced a critical moment during the case analysis activities. Thus, we elicited an anesthesiologist's thinking process for each decision point by utilizing a critical incident method (Flanagan, 1954; Klein et al., 1989) and a stimulated recall method (Gass & Mackey, 2000). We also identified the following six common phases of thinking across the critical decision points: (1) identifying problem cues, (2) assessing situations, (3) setting goals, (4) generating solutions, (5) executing the solutions, and (6) evaluating the solutions. This frame of an expert's thinking process became a foundation of our remaining design decisions related to the guided case analysis activities, such as modeling and scaffolding an expert's thinking. We finally decided to provide students with the expert interview video on how the expert thought and made decisions at the critical moment, after they watched each segment of the representative video. We believed that listening to an expert's narrative explanations about his/her interpretations of a situation and his/her decision-making process would help learners model experts' reasoning. This design decision is based on the notions of cognitive modeling and "making thinking visible" from cognitive apprenticeship.

As shown in Figure 20.2, the interface was designed for students to watch an expert's reasoning video clip after reviewing each segment of the representative video. When the learners arrived at a critical decision point in the representative case video, they might not clearly understand what was going on and how an expert would deal with the situation. However, the students should be able to model an expert's reasoning process as they *saw* how the expert interpreted the given situation and how to make decisions that would improve the situation.

4.4. Design Decision 4: Provide Cognitive Scaffolding of Expert's Decision-Making Process

Cognitive apprenticeship informed us that multiple strategies—including modeling, scaffolding, coaching, articulation, reflection, and exploration—needed to be provided to students in a coherent manner in order to facilitate the development of the students' reasoning skills. Thus, we believed that further support would be needed after the students watched each expert's reasoning video clip (modeling). By applying scaffolding and articulation strategies, we decided to provide students with an opportunity to articulate what they would learn from an expert's reasoning video according to the identified frame of thinking, cue identification, situation assessment, goals, and decisions with justification. The students' summaries would then be submitted to the instructor.

As shown in Figure 20.2, a template of an online summary note was developed. In this note, the four phases of an expert's thought process were represented as the following four questions:

- What were the important cues in the given situation, and how would you interpret them (cue identification)?

- How would you define the problems in the given situation (situation assessment)?
- What goals would you set up to deal with the identified problems (set goals)?
- What were the possible solutions, and what solution(s) would you choose among them (solution/decision)?

A link for the "Writing a Case Report" was provided under the representative case video to open this summary note. Through the above guiding questions, the students were asked to articulate what they understood from listening to an expert's narrative about how to think about and react to the situation.

4.5. Design Decision 5: Provide Just-in-Time Learning Resources

If learning occurs at the moment of need, then the learning will be meaningful and efficient, improving human performance (Gery, 1991). However, this kind of learning rarely happens in education and performance settings. People often have either limited access to appropriate learning at the moment of need, or learning opportunities without any contextual needs. Just-in-time learning refers to learning systems or strategies providing appropriate learning resources to learners at the right moment of need (Gery, 1991). By applying database technology and cognitive task analysis methods, a variety of electronic performance support systems were introduced (Gery, 1991). The Ask System (Schank & Cleary, 1995), in which information was organized according to learners' questions, is a good example of the electronic learning system. More importantly, well-designed, just-in-time learning systems would allow learners to construct and index knowledge properly for later activation in appropriate situations (Aamodt & Plaza, 1994).

The idea of just-in-time learning helped us design a dynamic textbook that would provide a potential solution for the time limitation to cover broader topics. As the students would watch situation video clips, review expert's reasoning video clips, deploy their reasoning, and make decisions, they would want to know relevant facts, concepts, principles, and theories that were usually offered by their textbook. Thus, we decided to design a dynamic textbook that would provide only relevant pieces of information in order to understand the given problem situation and the expert's reasoning process. Through this solution, the students would be able to construct and index textbook knowledge within a meaningful context so they would activate and apply the knowledge at the moment of need.

To develop a dynamic textbook, what we called Information On Demand (IOD), we first divided the textbook information into small chunks and entered these chunks into a database. Each piece of information stored in the database was then indexed based on the relevance of each critical decision point. As shown in Figure 20.2, a set of information links was provided under the expert's reasoning video clips. As the students clicked on these links based on their needs while reviewing the problem situations and the expert's reasoning, the specific textbook information was provided through a small pop-up window. Therefore, they were able to access relevant information efficiently. IOD was also designed for the instructor to add to, delete from, and update information as they found further needs.

4.6. *Design Decision 6: Provide Additional Mini-Cases for Each Decision Point to Promote Cognitive Flexibility*

The cognitive flexibility theory informed us that experiencing a single case was not enough for learners to develop cognitive flexibility for solving similar problems. Instead it was recommended that different cases should be experienced under the same theme. Thus, we decided to provide two or three stories relevant to each critical decision point besides the main case video. Each story started with a similar decision-making problem raised at the decision point of the representative case. Then an expert's reasoning on cue identification, situation assessment, goal settings, and decisions followed. In addition, the story ended with the actual results of the decision and an expert's reflection on the decision and results. To facilitate the students' learning, we also provided a summary note with guided questions through which the students articulated what they learned. Also, we decided to add a test story that portrayed only the critical situation, so students were asked to make a decision to address the situation.

As shown in Figure 20.2, the additional story links were located above the expert's reasoning video box. The links trigger a small pop-up window to open where students can watch a mini-real-life story and can summarize their understanding in a given note template. Unlike the representative case, real-life story videos did not present the actual operation process. Although the problems might be more meaningful if an actual performance in the operation room was presented, we chose to use an expert's storytelling video for two reasons. First, using experts' storytelling videos could reduce the developmental cost. Second, we believed that the expert storytelling method might increase both efficiency and the transfer of learning. To be more specific, the students who watched a representative case (an actual operation video) would be able to gain a certain level of situational understanding, so these students would be able to visualize problem situations and build mental models of the problem situation from an expert's storytelling. Considering that most experts in the real world exchange their experiences and problems through storytelling (Orr, 1996), we believed that the students would become familiar with building their knowledge and understanding through storytelling.

5. IMPLEMENTATION CHALLENGES

Implementation should be aligned with our design and learning models/theories. Promoting reflective thinking in individual and group learning contexts is an important characteristic of case-based learning. While utilizing case-based learning, the instructor facilitated large group discussions. Some decision points were assigned as part of the students' homework, and the instructor led question and answer sessions for the assignment during classroom meetings. So through the implementation decision (see Figure 20.1), learning events attempted to promote reflection through group discussions.

We encountered three unexpected challenges during our implementation. First, students were focusing more on completing and submitting their assignments than they were on experiencing meaningful learning through recommended learning paths. For example, students were encouraged to watch a segment of the representative case, to review the expert's reasoning, to study a given set-up of content information, and finally to summarize and submit what they learned sequentially. However, after they completed a couple of decision points, they began to open the summary note first and tried to answer the guiding questions while searching for specific resources to help. This phenomenon is a well-known problem in designing artifacts; as Norman (1988) pointed out, there is a gap between a designer's conceptual model on how something should be used and a user's conceptual model on how it is actually used.

Second, we found a certain level of resistance against the adoption of the resources by other instructors. In our case-based learning, only one anesthesiologist's performance video and his reasoning processes were provided. Besides the anesthesiologist himself, other instructors in the same or other institutions hesitated to utilize the resources for their course. It might be related to a dominant paradigm based on the teacher-centered model that believes the instructor should be the center of the classroom and the source of knowledge. Thus, many instructors may not be comfortable with using another person's performance and his interpretation as primary learning resources. It is also possible that a single person's perspective might limit the students' flexibility of knowledge, as the cognitive flexibility theory recommends multiple perspectives for each case.

Last, we found that students were overwhelmed with the number of resources that they needed to study. Each decision point contains a problem video, an expert's reasoning video, two or three real-world stories, and a test story. In addition, they were supposed to summarize what they learned from each of these items. This might be a reason why students tried to complete the assignment instead of trying to learn from experiencing cases.

6. PRACTICAL CONSIDERATIONS AND RECOMMENDATIONS FOR PRACTICE

Based on our experience, we offer three recommendations for further design consideration. Most importantly, multiple perspectives by multiple experts and stakeholders should be included in these kinds of case-based learning resources. It would help students not only to develop cognitive flexibility but also to develop their ability to deal with real-world problems in which multiple, even conflicting, perspectives exist. It would also help to reduce unnecessary resistance toward the adoption of the learning modules by other instructors. Second, the designer should not assume that learners would use the tool in the way they planned. Appropriate affordance to guide users to maximize the given tools for learning should be considered. Last, relative learning loads, based on students' basic ability and prior knowledge, are an important factor that designers should consider in designing learning environments that guide students to achieve the intended learning outcomes.

REFERENCES

Aamodt, A., & Plaza, E. (1994). Case-based reasoning: Foundational issues, methodological variations, and systems approaches. *AI Communications, 7*(1), 39–52.

Abbott, A., Sullivan, M., Nyquist, J., Mylona, E., & Taylor, C. (2010). A "Medical student practice profile" as the foundation for a case-based curriculum revision. *Teaching and Learning in Medicine, 22*(4), 307–311.

Allen, B. S., Otto, R. G., & Hoffman, B. (2000). Case-based learning: Contexts and communities of practice. In S. Tobias & J. D. Fletcher (Eds.), *Training and Retraining: A handbook for business, industry, government, and the military* (pp. 443–471). New York: Macmillan/Gale Group.

Barnes, L. B., Christensen, C. R., & Hansen, A. J. (1994). *Teaching and the Case Method: Instructor's guide* (3rd ed.). Boston, MA: Harvard Business Publishing.

Barrows, H. S. (1986). A taxonomy of problem-based learning methods. *Medical Education, 20*(6), 481–486.

Cendan, J. C., Silver, M., & Ben-David, K. (2011). Changing the student clerkship from traditional lectures to small group case-based sessions benefits the student and the faculty. *Journal of Surgical Education, 68*(2), 117–120.

Christensen, C. R., & Hansen, A. J. (1987). *Teaching and the Case Method: Text, cases, and readings.* Boston, MA: Harvard Business School Publishing.

Collins, A. (2006). Cognitive apprenticeship. In R. K. Sawyer (Ed.), *Cambridge Handbook of the Learning Sciences* (pp. 47–60). Cambridge, UK: Cambridge University Press.

Collins, A., Brown, J. S., & Holum, A. (1991). Cognitive apprenticeship: Making thinking visible. *American Educator, 15*(3), 6–11, 38–46.

Collins, A., Brown, J. S., & Newman, S. E. (1989). Cognitive apprenticeship: Teaching the crafts of reading, writing, and mathematics. In L. B. Resnick (Ed.), *Knowing, Learning, and Instruction: Essays in honor of Robert Glaser* (pp. 453–494). Hillsdale, NJ: Lawrence Erlbaum Associates.

Danielson, J. A., Mills, E. M., Vermeer, P. J., Preast, V. A., Young, K. M., Christopher, M. M., George, J. W., et al. (2006). Characteristics of a cognitive tool that helps students learn diagnostic problem solving. *Educational Technology Research and Development, 55*(5), 499–520.

Ellet, W. (2007). *The Case Study Handbook: How to read, discuss, and write persuasively about cases.* Boston, MA: Harvard Business Press.

Flanagan, J. C. (1954). The critical incident technique. *Psychological Bulletin, 51*(4), 327–358.

Gaba, D. M., & Howard, S. K. (1995). Situation awareness in anesthesiology. *Human Factors, 37*(1), 20–31.

Gaba, D. M., & Lee, T. (1990). Measuring the workload of the anesthesiologist. *Anesthesia and Analgesia, 71*, 354–361.

Gass, S. M., & Mackey, A. (2000). *Stimulated Recall Methodology in Second Language Research.* Mahwah, NJ: Lawrence Erlbaum Associates.

Gery, G. J. (1991). *Electronic Performance Support Systems: How and why to remake the workplace through the strategic application of technology.* Tolland, MA: Gery Performance Press.

Graddy, D. B., Lee, J. T., & Timmons, D. (2001). Cognitive flexibility hypertext as a learning environment in economics: A pedagogical note. *Journal for Economics Educators, 3*(3). Retrieved from http://frank.mtsu.edu/~jee/PDF_Files/TEAcogpaper.pdf.

Hung, W., Bailey, J. H., & Jonassen, D. H. (2003). Exploring the tensions of problem-based learning: Insights from research. *New Directions for Teaching and Learning, 2003*(95), 13–23.

Jonassen, D. H. (2011). *Learning to Solve Problems: A handbook for designing problem-solving learning environments.* New York: Routledge.

Klein, G., Calderwood, R., & Macgregor, D. (1989). Critical decision method for eliciting knowledge. *IEEE Transactions on Systems, Man, and Cybernetics, 19*(3), 462–472.

Nikendei, C., Mennin, S., Weyrich, P., Kraus, B., Zipfel, S., Schrauth, M., & Ju, J. (2009). Effects of a supplementary final year curriculum on students' clinical reasoning skills as assessed by key-feature examination. *Teaching and Learning in Medicine, 31*(9), 438–442.

Norman, D. A. (1988). *The Psychology of Everyday Things.* New York: Basic Books.

Orr, J. E. (1996). *Talking About Machines: An ethnography of a modern job.* Ithaca, NY: ILR Press.

Schank, R. C., & Cleary, C. (1995). *Engines for Education.* Hillsdale, NJ: Lawrence Erlbaum Associates.

Shulman, J. H. (Ed.), (1992). *Case Methods in Teacher Education.* New York: Teachers College Press.

Spiro, R. J., & Jehng, J. C. (1990). Cognitive flexibility and hypertext: Theory and technology for the nonlinear and multidimensional traversal of complex subject matter. In D. Nix & R. J. Spiro (Eds.), *Cognition, Education, and Multimedia: Explorations in high technology* (pp. 163–205). Hillsdale, NJ: Lawrence Erlbaum.

Spiro, R. J., Collins, B. P., & Ramchandran, A. R. (2006). Modes of openness and flexibility in cognitive flexibility hypertext learning environments. In B. Khan (Ed.), *Flexible Learning in an Information Society* (pp. 18–25). Hershey, PA: Idea Group.

Spiro, R. J., Collins, B. P., & Ramchandran, A. (2007). Reflections on a post-Gutenberg epistemology for video use in ill-structured domains: Fostering complex learning and cognitive flexibility. In R. Goldman, R. D. Pea, B. Barron, & S. Derry (Eds.), *Video Research in the Learning Sciences.* Mahwah, NJ: Lawrence Erlbaum Associates.

Spiro, R. J., Feltovich, P. J., & Coulson, R. L. (1996). Two epistemic world-views: Prefigurative schemas and learning in complex domains. *Applied Cognitive Psychology, 10*, 52–61.

Spiro, R. J., Feltovich, P. J., Jacobson, M. J., & Coulson, R. L. (1992). Cognitive flexibility, constructivism, and hypertext: Random access instruction for advanced knowledge acquisition in ill-structured domains. In T. M. Duffy & D. H. Jonassen (Eds.), *Constructivism and the Technology of Instruction: A conversation* (pp. 57–75). Hillsdale, NJ: Lawrence Erlbaum Associates.

Whitehead, A. N. (1927). *The Aims of Education.* New York: The Free Press.

Williams, S. M. (1992). Putting case-based instruction into context: Examples from legal and medical education. *The Journal of Learning Sciences, 2*(4), 367–342.

21

SCAFFOLDING LEARNING IN A LEARNING MANAGEMENT SYSTEM

Learning to Write an Action Research Proposal

Priya Sharma & Alice E. Anderson

1. INTRODUCTION

Writing is a complex activity, dependent on various procedural, cognitive, and personal factors. Writing is an integral and prominent part of education, especially graduate education where masters and doctoral students produce culminating reports of research or practice in the form of papers, theses, or dissertations. Previous research has documented that even students at the doctoral level tend to encounter obstacles in writing well, especially within literature review and methodology sections of theses (e.g., Boote & Beile, 2005), and that their writing tends to exhibit flaws in analysis and reasoning. With the increasing number of online graduate programs and degrees, we can anticipate that online students might face similar problems with writing theses and papers. Indeed, this problem might be exacerbated, since writing supports that might be available on traditional campuses, such as writing centers, writing groups, etc., might not always be easily available in the online context.

Scaffolding has been documented as a successful strategy for advancing student learning in a variety of areas. Scaffolds can offer significant cognitive, metacognitive, and procedural support for developing skills and learning (Hannafin, Land, & Oliver, 1999). Various scaffolds have been successfully used to foster complex language skills, such as reading and writing, in both online and face-to-face settings (e.g., Palincsar & Brown, 1984; Lee & Tan, 2010; Li & Lim, 2008). Apart from procedural and cognitive support provided by scaffolds, affective models may also be useful in supporting the writing process (Bandura et al., 2003). One type of affective support is the provision of vicarious learning models, wherein novices can observe expert thinking and strategies. Specifically, vicarious learning models in the form of coping models might aid student writing by helping a learner to identify and avoid errors (Kitsantas, Zimmerman, & Cleary, 2000) as well as increasing learning, self-efficacy, and task persistence (Schunk & Hanson, 1985). Thus, well-designed cognitive scaffolds and vicarious learning models might also be able to support writing within online graduate classes.

2. THEORY-BASED DESIGN DECISIONS

2.1. *Writing as a Complex Problem*

Writing involves various cognitive processes, knowledge of content, and knowledge of the writing process to produce a final deliverable (Hayes, 1996; Saddler & Graham, 2007; Torrance & Galbraith, 2006). For many, it can be difficult to write about unfamiliar topics or in a new style. This was the double challenge faced by our graduate students enrolled in an upper-level course within an online master's degree program for education technology. In this course students are introduced simultaneously to two new content areas—use of technology to support complex learning and basics of action research methods. Concurrently, they are asked to formulate and articulate an action research proposal to investigate the application of technology to their professional context.

Despite the provision of multiple resources such as personally relevant project choices, content resources, practice with tools, and expert feedback on drafts, students' final design proposals were insufficiently grounded in theoretical and methodological justification. Two potential reasons for the low quality of the final product were identified as being low or late activity on the development of the proposals and sparse experience with argumentative writing strategies. To address these concerns, we used scaffolds to support cognitive writing processes, and vicarious learning models to provide affective support for student writing.

2.2. *Scaffolding Cognitive Aspects of Writing*

Scaffolding has successfully been used in a variety of educational settings to advance student learning. Typically, scaffolding is provided to help learners accomplish tasks that are just beyond what they are capable of accomplishing individually (Wood, Bruner, & Ross, 1976). Scaffolding can encompass conceptual, metacognitive, procedural, and strategic support (Hannafin et al., 1999). For example, procedural and strategic scaffolds support task sequence and decision-making while metacognitive and conceptual scaffolds support reflection and understanding of the content to be learned.

Conceptual scaffolds support students in focusing on important aspects of a task. Lai and Calandra (2007) found the use of conceptual scaffolds, such as question prompts, templates of the writing product, process displays, and modeling, to be useful to teachers in writing reflectively in an online environment. Specifically, the question prompts and modeling were perceived to be useful in supporting student writing by making specific links between the learner's own context and in considering more holistic perspectives. Similarly, Li and Lim (2008) also used conceptual prompts as fixed scaffolds within an online course to support historical reasoning, and supplemented the fixed scaffolds with questioning and modeling.

Procedural scaffolds are also useful in supporting writing. Yeh, Lo, and Huang's (2011) research indicates that scaffolding student writing in an online environment by providing a procedural guide was supportive and led to increased writing outcomes. In addition, Lee and Tan's (2010) research into the use of graphic organizers for managing and supporting metacognitive load for student writing suggests that metacognitive load affects the amount and relevance of ideas generated. Especially in online courses where students have to manage and coordinate across representations it is useful to provide visual organizers to scaffold metacognitive load (Lee & Tan, 2010). Their study suggests the utility of providing a planning space where students present their goals and their strategies for writing, and then explicitly supporting students in determining how the information they find aligns with their goals and strategies.

2.3. Vicarious Learning and Writing Process Models

In addition to support for cognitive aspects of writing, we also considered writing process models and principles of vicarious learning to address the affective aspects of the writing process. Depending on the model used, the term "writing process" describes one of several possible target phenomena. For example, some writing models address application of writing skills and describe how novice and expert writers progress towards producing better words, sentences, paragraphs, and papers (e.g., Bereiter & Scardamalia, 1983; Flower & Hayes, 1981; Hayes, 1996). Rather than fully describing the total phenomena of writing, they explain "the role of cognitive processes in students' writing *competence*" (Zimmerman & Risemberg, 1997, p. 75, emphasis in the original).

On the other hand, Zimmerman's social cognitive model attends to the activity of writing, describing *regulation efforts* to make writing happen. The key components of this model address behavioral, environmental, and personal strategies, which collectively are largely about ensuring that the activity of writing is, in fact, pursued. Thus, in addition to providing cognitive strategies, the writing process may also benefit from affective support (Bandura et al., 2003).

The hallmark of vicarious learning is observation, an activity we all employ throughout our lives. Models offer a type of vicarious learning and they are often substituted for live events. Models are seen as effective vehicles for providing information about concepts and processes that are not easily visible, and can be influential in novices' knowledge acquisition (Schunk & Zimmerman, 2007) and judgments of task self-efficacy (Bandura, 1997). Similarly, writing models have good potential to portray and influence the less visible efforts of composing a research proposal, such as composing and writing strong arguments and providing adequate justification for those arguments.

Models can be classed as mastery or coping. A mastery model is a near perfect or best case example performance. In learning to write academic research, research papers published in peer-reviewed journals can serve as examples of the target product, however they offer little in the way of performance insight. Schunk (2003) describes the utility of coping models in which the modeled performance is less than perfect but also demonstrates how progress is monitored and evaluated, and how improvements are planned. Observations of coping models enhance learners' confidence and subsequent task engagement more than observations of mastery models (Schunk & Hanson, 1985).

3. DESIGN OF COGNITIVE SCAFFOLDS AND VICARIOUS MODELS

As identified previously, our two main concerns within the course were low and late activity on the papers, as well as lack of knowledge of writing strategies. To address low activity on the paper, we established bi-weekly due dates for drafts of individual sections of the proposal, which eventually were submitted as part of the final proposal at the end of the semester. To address writing strategies, we decided to implement both cognitive and affective support for the writing process, using a combination of cognitive scaffolds as well as vicarious models in the form of coping models as the delivery mechanism.

3.1. *Cognitive Scaffolds for Goal Setting*

Planning is an important part of the writing process (Hayes & Nash, 1996).

To scaffold learner's goal setting, we revised the proposal outline by thoroughly explicating each section's content targets. In previous semesters, the syllabus contained instructions for the proposal that included an outline of first- and second-level headings, each labeled with a purpose statement. In the revised outline, each section contained numerous prompts and questions focusing on key concepts to be addressed, thus increasing the task's specificity. These questions could also be classified as reflective prompts about the writing, which were shown to be effective in other research on writing in online contexts (e.g., Lee & Tan, 2010; Li & Lim, 2008). The example in Figure 21.1 shows the detail included for one section of the expanded outline.

3.2. *Weekly Cognitive and Vicarious Writing Prompts*

Writers who maintain a regular writing schedule produce more writing and more ideas than writers who work in inconsistent spurts (Boice, 1985; Krashen, 2002). We anticipated that providing weekly prompts and bi-weekly deadlines would increase the frequency of text planning, generation, and revision cycles.

We structured each weekly prompt to have three types of support:

- *Thought Tools*, i.e., cognitive scaffolds—a restatement of the purpose of the section along with suggested steps for analyzing the writing task.
- *Writer's Wisdom*, i.e., affective support—a short opinion or saying based on other writers' experiences.
- *Writer's Shelf*, i.e., vicarious experience—extracts of previous proposal drafts with instructor feedback.

Each week, the three support types were arranged on a single web page (see Figure 21.2 for a sample web page) within the learning management system (LMS), and the presentation acted as a visual organizer (Lee & Tan, 2010) to focus attention on the three provided supports.

2. Area of focus: In this section, you need to expand and elaborate on the learning outcome that you are interested in supporting and exploring.

1. Identify your area of focus and identify the specific learning targets that you will examine. Identify the type of higher order thinking that is being addressed, and classify the targets within a taxonomy to identify their higher order nature.
2. Identify the problems that you have faced in the past- i.e., what problems do students encounter or exhibit in achieving the learning target? Provide any anecdotal descriptions or empirical results that illustrate evidence of the problem. Think back to the Knowing What Students Know chapter's description of cognition in the assessment triangle – what is the type of cognition that students need to engage in to achieve the target and what are they having trouble with?
3. Provide a description of other research or practice-based articles that have documented evidence of similar problem. Evaluate and synthesize the articles and identify how their description of the problem helps you extend your understanding of the problem and what kinds of challenges students might be facing.
4. Describe why addressing this problem is significant for you and why it is significant for teachers and learners in general.

Figure 21.1 Section of the scaffolded outline of a paper.

<table>
<tr><td>

Thought Tools

Section: Area of Focus.

This week your focus is on section 2 in your research proposal—i.e., area of focus. Look at your learning goals and try to identify how you could assess them. Think of assessment in terms of two things—first, what is the type of assessment outcome and second, how can you assess the process of demonstrating learning?

- What assessment outcome are you hoping for? Look at Nitko's chapter as a guide and try to identify what final format your assessment might take and why that is the most useful (consider practicality, validity, and reliability). Would you have students engage in solving problems or creating a portfolio or something else? What other examples of such assessment in your area can you find?
- How can you assess the process of learning? Look at the Knowing What Students Know chapter and identify the types of reasoning or learning processes you can evaluate while your students are engaged in learning or assessment activities. How could you observe processes of learning within your context and what kind of assessment or learning activity would allow you to explore this aspect? What literature in your area gives you more insight into this process?
- Based on the resources you find and the literature related to your area, try to frame an initial research question to investigate learning in your context. Remember, this is just a draft so we will get a chance to work on it during additional weeks.

</td><td>

Writer's wisdom

"Organizing is what you do before you do something, so that when you do it, it is not all mixed up."

~A. A. Milne, author, Creator of Winnie-the-Pooh

</td></tr>
<tr><td colspan="2">

Writer's Shelf

Sample Area of Focus: This is a decent example.
Another sample Area of Focus: This one is OK too but could use some subheadings to increase organization.

This sample needs work. It has some information out of place in the background section. Reordering and filling in missing learning objectives is required.

</td></tr>
</table>

Figure 21.2 Sample web page of weekly prompts.

The main area of the prompt page featured the cognitive scaffold. Titled "*Thought Tools*," the content represented an expert model for thinking through the writing problem. In classrooms, strategy instruction begins with an explanation of the steps to take, which is followed by the teacher performing a think-aloud while working through a problem (De La Paz, 2007). The restatement of the purpose focuses the reader on the task while the suggested cognitive steps represent the textual equivalent of the think-aloud. These detailed steps also offer the procedural scaffolding needed to complete the task.

The right-hand side bar, called "*Writer's Wisdom*," contained brief statements portraying attitudes or feelings about some portion of the writing process. Quotes were drawn from a variety of sources ranging from popular literature to successful authors.

The subjects of the quotes were selected to align with major cycles of the writing process such as planning, text generation, and revision. The quotes act as models of attitude, since attitude toward writing has been shown to affect writing achievement (Graham, Berninger, & Fan, 2007). Each week the quote was selected to coincide with the writing phase most likely to be prominent. For example, Figure 21.2 contains a quote about first drafts presented during week two. In contrast, at the end of the semester, when drafted sections need revision, we offered a quote from Harry F. Wolcott, a researcher and author of *Writing Up Qualitative Research.* "Careful editing is the antidote for the lack of giftedness among the huge corpus of us who recognize that we had better write but are not among the better writers."

The "*Writer's Shelf*" occupied the foot of the page and contained the final, but vital, leg in this triad of writing support. The course instructor had solicited student permission to use content submitted in previous semesters as examples for future students. This archive of proposals was searched for examples containing feedback that articulated areas for improvement. For each weekly prompt we sought both a strong and a weak example of the target section to extract and load to the LMS. Occasionally we were able to identify and offer a third, very weak example. We provided descriptive links to these extracts in the *Writer's Shelf.* Figure 21.3 shows a partial extract of an extract for section 3, the literature review.

Each writing sample served as coping model, i.e., a less than perfect, and sometimes very imperfect, example of learning efforts.

3. DESIGN RESULTS

We used a design-based research framework to evaluate and interpret the results, so as to inform subsequent revisions. We implemented the initial design in the summer semester of 2009, and implemented two revisions, in fall 2009 and summer 2010. Table 21.1 presents the sequence for implementation of different aspects of the design.

(Review of Literature)

Online Whiteboards

While I have struggled to find research that is on point with my proposed project, I have found some articles connected to the subject. When discussing the motivations of using an interactive whiteboard such as a SmartBoard or Promethian board, they found many benefits.

"Becta (2003) has summarised the main research findings and identified the following benefits for pupils:

- Increased motivation.
- Greater opportunity for pupils to participate and collaborate.
- Pupils are able to cope with more complex concepts as a result of clearer, more efficient and more dynamic presentations.
- Increased capacity to cater for different learning styles.
- Enables pupils to be more creative when making presentations to fellow pupils.
- Pupils do not have to use a keyboard to engage with the technology, increasing access to younger children and pupils with disabilities."

(Beauchamp & Parkinson, 2005)

In working with such technology in my own classroom, I have found a similar increased motivation, level of focus and participation, and level of creativity. It is something

Comment [PS1] : I understand some of the trouble you're having with framing the literature for your study – I think it would be good for you to separate in out into these distinct sections: 1. I think one of the cases you need to make is that whiteboards can easily give you access to thinking processes of students and how other folks have used Whiteboards (in terms of actual design and implementation) that you can employ in your design. 2. The second section is using technology and planning in general, which you have addressed. 3. The utility of think alouds for getting at thought processes and how you plan to use designs from other similar studies in your context.

Comment [PS2] : All direct quotations need a page number for citation. Also, check APA formatting for citing an author who is cited by another author.

Figure 21.3 Sample of *Writer's Shelf* content with instructor feedback.

Table 21.1 Design Implementation Sequence and Reasoning

Implementation	Supports implemented	Prior results that informed inclusion of support
Implementation 1: Summer 2009	• Sample proposals with intact feedback from instructor • Worksheets to support literature review and analysis	• Instructor was providing repetitive feedback on similar issues • Students' requests for sample work to inform their proposal development
Implementation 2: Fall 2009	• Detailed proposal descriptions • Weekly affective and cognitive writing support prompts • Drafts were solicited based on sequential proposal structure	• Proposals did not address all relevant aspects • Work on proposals seemed to come right at the end of the semester instead of a more continuous approach
Implementation 3: Summer 2010	• Detailed proposal descriptions • Weekly affective and cognitive writing support prompts • Reworked submission deadlines for documents to allow more time for revision and feedback	• Reduced the number of drafts and only requested sections on which most feedback was usually given • Discussion boards were set up to enhance discussion about proposal sections

All students in the three sections of the course agreed to provide access to their data for our evaluation (i.e., approximately 7–12 students per class). We collected the draft and final versions of the action research projects from three consecutive courses for analysis.

Our main focus was investigating the changes in quality of documents over these three iterations to identify whether the cognitive scaffolds and vicarious models supported student writing. We used a combination of anecdotal as well as numeric scores to interpret these results. Table 21.2 shows the data collected over iterations.

3.1. Overall Impact on Quality of Student Writing

Scores on the documents for implementation 2 and 3 are presented in Table 21.3. Score changes are not significant by any means. We noted that most students used the recommended outline provided as a cognitive scaffold in structuring their final paper. It also seemed that there was an attempt to follow the prompts presented within each section of the paper outline.

We then selected the artifacts from a few students in each of the classes to examine in more detail. Specifically, we were interested in examining the quality of students' reasoning within the literature review and methodology sections.

Thus, we selected a subset of student work focusing on those students whose scores dipped at the end as well as those whose scores indicated an increase. A total of ten student artifacts were analyzed in more detail to identify qualitative changes in their work. We used a rubric (adapted from Boote & Beile, 2005) to evaluate quality of the literature review and methodology sections evident in draft proposal documents as well as the final document. In addition, we looked at feedback that the instructor provided on different iterations to assess where improvement was needed in student work. Tables 21.4, 21.5, and 21.6 present the scores on selected student work.

In general, student scores did not vary significantly across the two artifacts that were most representative of the types of thinking being supported by the scaffolds and writing

Table 21.2 Data Collection Schedule

	Summer 2009 (10 weeks)	Fall 2009 (12 weeks)	Summer 2010 (10 weeks)
Weeks	**Activities to support proposal development**	**Activities to support proposal development**	**Activities to support proposal development**
1			
2			
3	Submit Draft 1 (Area of focus and assessment plan) for feedback		Submit Draft 1 (Sections 1 & 2) for feedback
4		Submit draft 1 (Sections 1 & 2)	Discussion forum: First iteration of research question and data collection
5	Submit Draft 2 (Instructional design and research question) for feedback		Submit Draft 2 (Section 3) for feedback Discussion forum: Literature review process
6			Submit Draft 3 (section 5 for feedback)
7		Submit draft 2 (sections 3 & 4)	
8	Submit Draft 3 (Theory base for activity design)		Final research proposal is due (based on revisions from previous feedback)
9			END OF COURSE
10	Final research proposal is due (based on revisions from previous feedback)	Submit draft 3 (sections 5 & 6)	
11	END OF COURSE		
12		Final research proposal is due (based on revisions from previous feedback)	

models. As might be expected, draft paper scores were generally lower than final paper scores since drafts were solicited to provide formative feedback on the focus and quality of writing. The most striking differences in performance over the artifacts are represented in our third implementation of the prompts, when two student scores dropped quite sharply for the final paper. We elaborate possible interpretations of this variation in the discussion section.

3.2. *Variation in Instructor Feedback over Iterations*

In an effort to further parse the quality of the papers, we decided to examine instructor feedback on the set of ten student artifacts to see where papers fell short of the expected level of quality. In all implementations, individual assignments were structured as pieces that eventually contributed to the final research paper, and feedback was intended to

Table 21.3 Scores over Iterations

Scores for summer 2009–15 students total

Student	Draft 1 (max score 20)	Draft 2 (max score 20)	Draft 3 (max score 20)	Final proposal (max score 100)
1	19	17	14	94
2	18	18	16	96
3	16	16	15	80
4	19	17	15	80
5	18	18	16	85
6	18	18	16	92
7	19	18	17	96
8	16	15	16	94
9	19	18	19	96
10	18	16	15	80
11	18	19	18	96
12	18	18	16	90
13	19	18	15	92
14	19	17	16	92
15	17	17	15	94
Class average	18.07	17.33	15.93	90.47

Scores for fall 2009–7 students total

Student	Draft 1 (max score 20)	Draft 2 (max score 20)	Draft 3 (max score 20)	Final proposal (max score 100)
1	20	20	20	90
2	20	20	20	94
3	0	20	0	88
4	20	0	0	0
5	20	20	20	95
6	20	20	20	90
7	20	0	0	0
Class average	17.14	14.29	11.43	65.29
Average without zero scores	20	20	20	91.4

Scores for Summer 2010

Student	Draft 1 (max score 30)	Draft 2 (max score 30)	Final proposal (max score 120)
1	27	27	110
2	22	25	90
3	27	27	112
4	0	28	108
5	28	24	108
6	27	29	90
7	27	27	115
8	25	28	114
9	26	28	112
10	25	25	95
11	26	25	100
12	29	29	117
13	26	25	105
14	25	25	105
15	26	26	95
16	0	0	0
17	26	26	115
Average scores	23.06	24.94	99.47
Average scores without zero grades	26.13	26.5	105.69

Table 21.4 Student Scores over Time for Implementation 1

Student	Score for draft (% of total)	Score for final paper (% of total)
L1Su9	17 (85%)	94 (94%)
L2Su9	15 (75%)	94 (94%)
H1Su9	18 (90%)	96 (96%)
H2Su9	19 (95%)	96 (96%)

Note: The L and H signify low and high scoring students although this is relative

Table 21.5 Student Scores over Time for Implementation 2

Student	Score for draft (% of total)	Score for final paper (% of total)
S1Fa9	20 (100%)	90 (90%)
S2Fa9	20 (100%)	90 (90%)

Table 21.6 Student Scores over Time for Implementation 3

Student	Score for draft (% of total)	Score for final paper (% of total)
L1Su10	25 (83%)	90 (75%)
L2Su10	25 (83%)	95 (79%)
H1Su10	27 (90%)	115 (96%)
H2Su10	26 (87%)	115 (96%)

Note: The L and H signify low and high scoring students although this is relative

provide formative guidance on progressing towards a good quality final product. In a sense, the feedback could be considered as a "soft" scaffold (Saye & Brush, 2002) aimed at supporting the static or "hard" cognitive scaffolds provided within the LMS. Usually, feedback contained editorial comments as well as suggestions for substantively addressing the focus and refinement of the argument within the paper.

Overall, the quality of the feedback was similar across high and low scoring students over the three iterations. In the first implementation, both low scoring students received comments related to (a) clearly identifying and justifying the instructional strategy they intended to use for their study (example comment: "what are you trying to improve with the use of the e-portfolios and where is the evidence to support the existence of the problem?"), (b) providing more empirical justification to support the utility of the strategy for their goals (example comment: "is there any research that talks about how to integrate prompts/activities that help students to better engage in the process of the e-portfolio?") and (c) making arguments in the paper more precise and focused (example comment: "there are a number of different things jostling for attention here—critical thinking, technology evaluation, reflection, constructivism, active learning, etc. I would try to focus my attention on a single outcome . . . to [support] the theoretical framework for design"). In these cases, instructor feedback seemed to focus both on procedural and conceptual issues with the writing, including the need to find additional resources and articulate arguments more clearly.

On the other hand, the two higher scoring students in the first implementation received comments that were primarily related to (a) making a clearer link between the presented literature and own context (e.g., "How is your project comparable to the [cited research]? How did they design their wiki and did you adopt any recommendations ensuing from their research?"), and (b) expanding on the justification for why cited strategies would work for own context (e.g., "I think you made a very good case for why the wiki will help you to document student thinking and discussion, I think there isn't as strong a case made for why you believe discussion is going to help students to make connections between ancient history and modern history"). Thus, it seemed that instructor feedback was primarily geared toward providing conceptual guidance on how to articulate and frame arguments more clearly.

In the second implementation, one set of artifacts (S1Fa9) received comments similar to those received by low scoring students in the previous implementation—i.e., suggestions to provide more empirical and theoretical support for the selected instructional strategy, to focus the argument, and to provide detail to match own context. In contrast, the second student (S2Fa9) received suggestions to more clearly articulate the link between cited research and own study, and to refine the description and support for the study more clearly based on the cited research.

For the third implementation, the two low scoring students received suggestions to (a) provide more detail for the literature being cited, (b) make stronger connections between cited literature and own context, and (c) refine the argument and structure of the paper. The two high scoring students received comments related to (a) relating research to own context and (b) providing more detail to support the use of design strategies in their own context.

In general, a weak trend related to instructor comments with regard to the high and low scoring students emerged. Low scoring students were usually provided both procedural and conceptual guidance on the paper to enhance both the scope and depth of the work. High scoring students, on the other hand, were provided conceptual feedback to refine the quality of their writing in making a clear link between their context and the cited research.

Overall, these results seemed to suggest that students tended to follow the cognitive scaffolds provided for goal setting since all documents contained the requisite sections and sub-sections. However, it seemed that the performance of low and high scoring students stayed consistent over the three implementations despite the scaffolds.

To explain this lack of change in quality over the three implementations and to better understand what might account for consistent differences between lower and higher scoring students, we decided to explore prompt use by students in the third iteration.

3.3. *Prompt Usage and Grades*

Students were reminded about the writing prompts every week, via course update emails from the instructor. In addition, every week's lesson pages showed the link to the prompts for that week. However, although prompts were made visible and emphasized to some extent, prompt use was voluntary. The LMS tracked access to prompts and we examined possible relationships between prompt use, grades, and scores on the writing confidence survey. First, we tabulated and summed the number of modules accessed by each student, and then compared prompt use to final proposal grades. As Figure 21.4 shows, prompt use only accounts for 1.3% of grade variance.

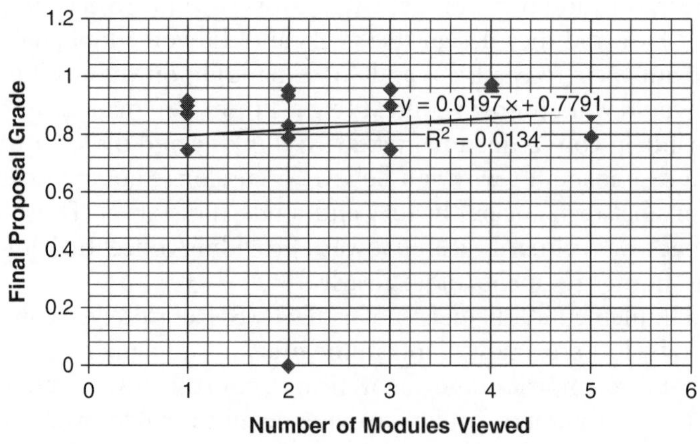

Figure 21.4 Prompt use and grade variance.

3.4. Writing Confidence and Grades

Confidence has been found to be a good predictor of success (Pajares, 2003). According to models of self-regulated learning, task requirements, achievement goals, and self-efficacy can influence planning decisions. Thus, for the third iteration of this course, we implemented a confidence survey that was delivered during the first week. Self-efficacy judgments are task specific (Bandura, 1997) and to obtain a good measure of self-efficacy, questions need to be sufficiently detailed and should cover all the tasks required for a successful execution. Therefore, we started with five questions from the Writing Self-Efficacy Survey (Pajares, 2007), choosing those that assess application of writing skills such as sentence, paragraph, and document structuring. In addition to these writing skill questions, we asked three questions on literature search and review, and six questions on the design of qualitative research.

Overall confidence accounts for 18.9% of the variance in proposal scores (Figure 21.5). Our reason for implementing the confidence survey was to influence planning. Because planning often includes locating and using helpful resources, we wanted to compare the confidence scores with prompt use and found that confidence accounts for 29% of the variance in prompt use (Figure 21.6). Indeed, this result provided a satisfying piece of empirical evidence that one of the design goals seemed to be met: those students who felt they needed additional help were able to access the supports, while those who felt no help was necessary were not burdened by having to use them.

4. DISCUSSION

Our goal in this series of iterations was to improve the quality of student research proposals, with a specific focus on improving the quality of writing for the final research proposal such that it was well grounded in empirical and theoretical literature, and provided adequate reasoning and analysis. Our investigations were situated within a real-life, messy context and the design-based research approach allowed us to make incremental changes to support our goals, as well as to examine our findings within the context of a specific implementation. Overall, we found that initial goal-setting scaffolds were largely

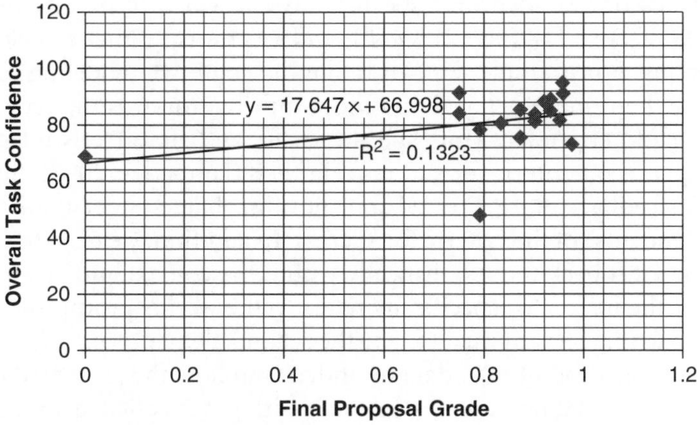

Figure 21.5 Writing confidence and grade variance.

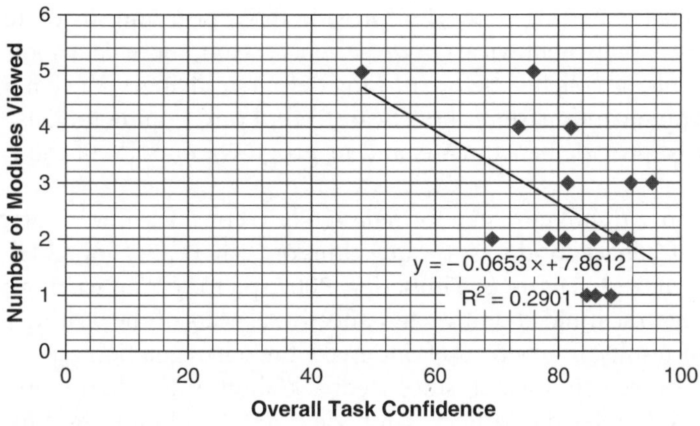

Figure 21.6 Writing confidence and prompt usage variance.

supportive of student writing in that the proposals contained the required sections and sub-sections. However, the weekly writing prompts did not significantly affect the quality of the proposals as measured by scores or grades. However, we did find a weak trend that suggested that low and high scoring students were given similar types of feedback over the three iterations. One explanation, provided by our examination of student use of the prompts, is that only students who needed the support tended to use it, while those students who felt more confident of their ability did not.

These findings pose interesting directions for subsequent design of similar interventions. Specifically, a question arises about how to support students with low and high confidence to create even more high-quality proposals. Although we made the weekly prompts more detailed in every successive iteration, student use of the prompts was not consistent. A strategy to engender more conscientious use of the weekly cognitive and vicarious learning prompts might be to link each week's prompt more clearly to the overall outline of the paper.

From our evaluation, we identified specific ways in which to modify the cognitive (*Thought Tools*), affective (*Writer's Wisdom*), and vicarious (*Writer's Shelf*) aspects of the weekly prompts. For example, we can refine the cognitive modeling aspect of the prompts to make them more detailed and more directed towards the types of writing outcomes we hope to engender. More specific goals can help direct student attention and provide emphasis on criteria for success (Hattie & Timperley, 2007). Specific goals also help to make feedback more directed and allow for shared understanding (between instructors and students) of the criteria for success. In addition, we need to consider the role of instructor's feedback more holistically within the context and ensure that feedback provided by the instructor specifically refers to the weekly prompts and cognitive scaffolds for articulating level of quality. For the second element, i.e., affective support, we would want to collect additional data to understand how the presented opinions or experiences affected (or did not affect) students' writing. We solicited student feedback in the last implementation but, unfortunately, none of the students chose to respond due to time constraints. In the last iteration we also integrated opportunities for students to discuss their proposal drafts on discussion boards within the LMS as another way of gaining affective support. In a subsequent iteration, we could consider posing weekly questions about the writing process to provide more peer and instructor support for writing. For the last element, vicarious experience, again, more data about the utility of the samples could be solicited before making definitive changes. We could also provide examples of coping and mastery models, instead of only coping models, from existing student work to provide benchmarks and in-progress examples of the type of writing that is needed.

In conclusion, a useful next step for redesign is to consider how to integrate prompts and instructor feedback to address the questions of "Where am I going? How am I going? and Where to next?" (Hattie & Timperley, 2007, p. 102). The writing prompts were selected mainly to scaffold cognitive and affective aspects of the writing process. However, from our results, it may be useful to make the self-regulation aspect of the writing process more prominent as well, since feedback about the task, the process, and self-regulation are interrelated (Hattie & Timperley, 2007) and important to achieve goals. Thus, successful writing outcomes can be fostered by closely linking task details, cognitive and affective support, instructor feedback, and design of the learning environment such that they all contribute to student understanding and self-regulation of the writing process.

REFERENCES

Bandura, A. (1997). *Self-efficacy: The exercise of control.* New York: W. H. Freeman and Company.

Bandura, A., Caprara, G. V., Barbaranelli, C., Gerbino, M., & Pastorelli, C. (2003). Role of affective self-regulatory efficacy in diverse spheres of psychosocial functioning. *Child Development, 74*(3), 769–782.

Bereiter, C., & Scardamalia, M. (1983). Levels of inquiry in writing research. In P. Rosenthal, S. Walmsley, & L. Tamor (Eds.), *Research in Writing: Principles and methods* (pp. 3–25). New York: Longman International.

Boice, R. (1985). The neglected third factor in writing: Productivity. *College Composition and Communication, 36*(4), 472–480.

Boote, D. N., & Beile, P. (2005). Scholars before researchers: On the centrality of the dissertation literature review in research preparation. *Educational Researcher, 34*(6), 3–15.

De La Paz, S. (2007). Managing cognitive demands for writing: Comparing the effects of instructional components in strategy instruction. *Reading & Writing Quarterly, 23*(3), 249–266.

Flower, L., & Hayes, J. R. (1981). A cognitive process theory of writing. *College Composition and Communication, 32*(4), 365–387.

Graham, S., Berninger, V., & Fan, W. H. (2007). The structural relationship between writing attitude and writing achievement in first and third grade students. *Contemporary Educational Psychology, 32*(3), 516–536.

Hannafin, M., Land, S., & Oliver, K. (1999). Open learning environments: Foundations, methods, and models. In C. Reigeluth (Ed.), *Instructional-Design Theories and Models: A new paradigm of instructional theory* (pp. 115–140). Mahwah, NJ: Lawrence Erlbaum Associates.

Harris, K. R., Graham, S., & Mason, L. H. (2006). Improving the writing, knowledge, and motivation of young struggling writers: The effects of self-regulated strategy development. *American Educational Research Journal, 43*, 295–340.

Hattie, J., & Timperley, H. (2007). The power of feedback. *Review of Educational Research, (77)*1, 81–112.

Hayes, J. R. (1996). A new framework for understanding cognition and affect in writing. In C. M. Levy & S. Ransdell (Eds.), *The Science of Writing: Theories, methods, individuals differences, and applications* (pp. 1–27). Mahwah, NJ: Lawrence Erlbaum Associates.

Hayes, J. R., & Nash, J. G. (1996). On the nature of planning in writing. In C. M. Levy & S. Ransdell (Eds.), *The Science of Writing: Theories, methods, individuals differences, and applications* (pp. 29–55). Mahwah, NJ: Lawrence Erlbaum Associates.

Kitsantas, A., Zimmerman, B. J., & Cleary, T. (2000). The role of observation and emulation in the development of athletic self-regulation. *Journal of Educational Psychology, 92*(4), 811–817.

Krashen, S. (2002). Optimal levels of writing management: A re-analysis of Boice (1983). *Education, 122*(3), 605.

Lai, G., & Calandra, B. (2007). Using online scaffolds to enhance preservice teachers' reflective journal writing: A qualitative analysis. *International Journal of Technology in Teaching and Learning, 3*(3), 66–81.

Lee, C. C., & Tan, S. C. (2010). Scaffolding writing using feedback in students' graphic organizers: Novice writers' relevance of ideas and cognitive loads. *Educational Media International, 47*(2), 135–152.

Li, D. D., & Lim, C. P. (2008). Scaffolding online historical inquiry tasks: A case study of two secondary school classrooms. *Computers and Education, 50*, 1394–1410.

Pajares, F. (2003). Self-efficacy beliefs, motivation, and achievement in writing: A review of the literature. *Reading and Writing Quarterly: Overcoming Learning Difficulties, 19*(2), 139–158.

Pajares, F. (2007). Empirical properties of a scale to assess writing self-efficacy in school contexts. *Measurement and Evaluation in Counseling and Development, 39*(4), 239–249.

Palincsar, A. S., & Brown, A. L. (1984). Reciprocal teaching of comprehension-fostering and comprehension-monitoring activities. *Cognition & Instruction, 1*(2), 117–175.

Saddler, B., & S. Graham (2007). The relationship between writing knowledge and writing performance among more and less skilled writers. *Reading & Writing Quarterly, 23*(3), 231–247.

Saye, J. W., & Brush, T. (2002). Scaffolding critical reasoning about history and social issues in multimedia-supported learning environments. *Educational Technology Research and Development, 50*(3), 77–96.

Schunk, D. H. (2003). Self-efficacy for reading and writing: Influence of modeling, goal setting, and self-evaluation. *Reading and Writing Quarterly: Overcoming Learning Difficulties, 19*(2), 159–172.

Schunk, D. H., & Hanson, A. R. (1985). Peer models: Influence on children's self-efficacy and achievement. *Journal of Educational Psychology, 77*(3), 313–322.

Schunk, D. H., & Zimmerman, B. J. (2007). Influencing children's self-efficacy and self-regulation of reading and writing through modeling. *Reading & Writing Quarterly, 23*(1), 7–25.

Torrance, M., & Galbraith, D. (2006). The processing demands of writing. In C. A. Macarthur, S. Graham, & J. Fitzgerald (Eds.), *Handbook of Writing Research* (pp. 67–80). New York: The Guilford Press.

Wood, D., Bruner, J. S., & Ross, G. (1976). The role of tutoring in problem solving. *Journal of Child Psychology & Psychiatry & Allied Disciplines, 17*(2), 89–100.

Yeh, S.-W., Lo, J.-J., & Huang, J.-J. (2011). Scaffolding collaborative technical writing with procedural facilitation and synchronous discussion. *Computer Supported Collaborative Learning*, 6, 397–419.

Zimmerman, B. J., & Risemberg, R. (1997). Becoming a self-regulated writer: A social cognitive perspective. *Contemporary Educational Psychology, 22*, 73–101.

22

CONSIDERING THE DESIGN OF AN ELECTRONIC PROGRESS-MONITORING SYSTEM

Simon Hooper, Charles Miller, and Susan Rose

1. INTRODUCTION

The relationship linking assessment and instruction is the cornerstone of student progress. This connection is likely to become increasingly important as technology makes it possible to use data to implement teaching practices that ensure individual student achievement (Hosp, 2010; Safer & Fleischman, 2005). This chapter describes the design of a web-based learning analytics system intended to improve children's literacy by tracking their academic performance over time and using the data to personalize instruction. We describe four design cycles that have occurred to date. Within each cycle we outline the theory behind the design, explain key design issues that influenced the design process, and examine data from implementation research. Throughout the design process we have faced complex challenges from which we have learned important lessons. We conclude by briefly describing our research agenda and reflecting on our experiences.

2. DESIGN CYCLE 1 (2005–2006)

The project began in 2005 with the goal of improving the efficiency of a laborious process faced by many teachers: Grading students' essays. The task we addressed differs from "traditional" essay grading. We were working with elementary school Special Education teachers who monitor their students' performance on frequent brief-writing tasks. The writing and grading processes are as follows: Students are provided with a story starter and given five minutes to write on paper; teachers grade an essay by marking each word-pair to reflect accuracy according to established criteria (e.g. spelling, semantics, grammar, punctuation, etc.); the total number of correct and incorrect marks are summed and entered manually into a grade book (Deno & Marston, n.d.). For example, grading the response "The big dog sat" involves judging the following word-pairs: The big; big dog; dog sat. Although teachers value the information gleaned from the grading process, the assessment is not used regularly because it is tedious and time consuming.

2.1. *Theoretical/Pedagogical/Technological Foundations*

Several possible benefits of a computer-based grading system were immediately apparent. It would allow for automatic data aggregation, thereby eliminating the need for counting and recording students' scores manually. Digital data storage would allow student performance charts to be generated dynamically and to facilitate comparison of individual with group growth patterns. Moreover, of great importance was the potential to change radically the grading experience for teachers. By carefully crafting interfaces, a system could highlight possible errors, change the mechanics of the grading process, and provide access to data visualizations that enhance decision-making. A well-designed scoring system could increase reliability, reduce grading time, improve teachers' ability to identify writing problems, and improve overall satisfaction with the assessment process.

2.2. *Design and Development Issues*

The software, which we named WordMark, includes separate interfaces for students and teachers. The teacher interface serves three functions: managing students (registering students' accounts), grading assessments, and viewing performance charts (see Figure 22.1). The main grading algorithm converts each word from the student's essay into a stand-alone object thereby enabling words to be formatted to highlight successive grading pairs (see Figure 22.2). Proficient users can grade an essay rapidly by using only four keys to score and navigate the document (i.e. up/down keys for correct/incorrect; left/right keys for previous/next). Visual feedback, in the form of grading symbols, indicates each grading decision. Total correct and incorrect scores, as well as total-word and character counts are aggregated, and recorded.

The student interface is quite simple. It establishes a space where the student can type short essays. The student is presented with a randomly selected prompt. Students are

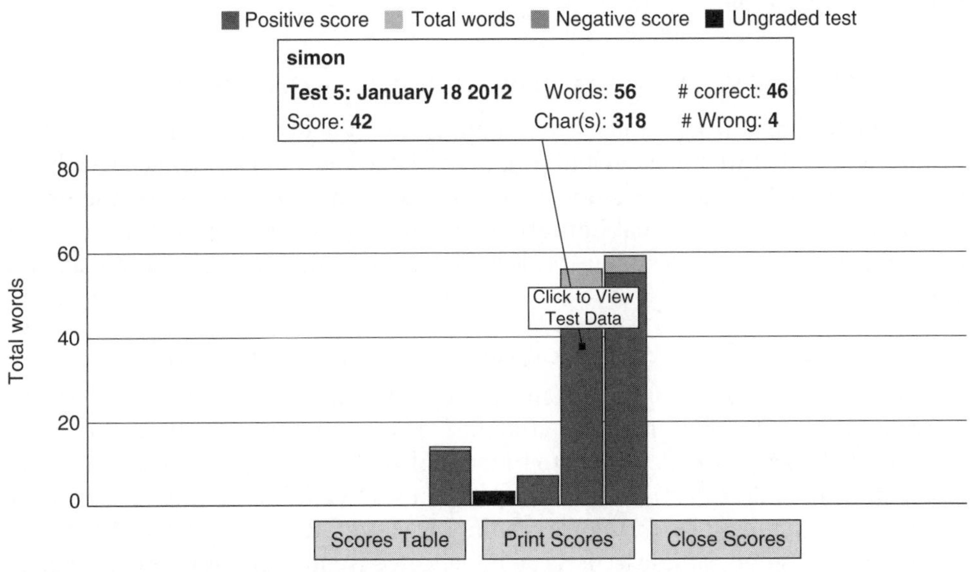

Figure 22.1 WordMark teacher grading interface.

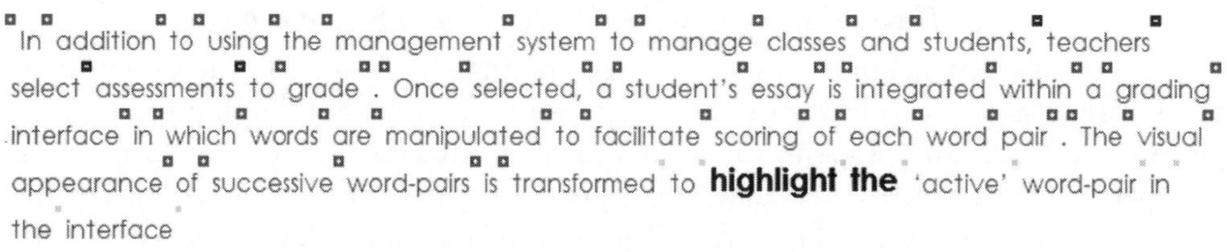

In addition to using the management system to manage classes and students, teachers select assessments to grade . Once selected, a student's essay is integrated within a grading interface in which words are manipulated to facilitate scoring of each word pair . The visual appearance of successive word-pairs is transformed to **highlight the** 'active' word-pair in the interface

Figure 22.2 WordMark performance chart.

given time to consider their topic and allocated five minutes to type a response. During the writing period students receive occasional system prompts indicating the remaining time. Data are stored automatically on the hard drive.

2.3. Implementation Research

Fifty teachers who had been using the software attended a workshop at which they requested various design changes. For example, they recommended distributing the software over the internet as distributing the software on CDs limited teachers' ability to compare student data, requires technical skills for installation, and limits the ability to update software automatically. One recommendation, that the interface should automatically transition the teacher to the next word-pair (instead of using the right-arrow key to navigate to the next word), reduced grading time by approximately 30% in timed tests. Teachers also asked for the ability to personalize story starters to connect students' story writing with in-class activities and for linguistics tools (e.g. spelling checker; grammar checker; morpheme counter; etc.) to cue writing errors. Although not all requests could be fulfilled as some of these features were not available in the development tools, we were able to extend programming functionality by creating "mashups" of diverse web technologies.

3. DESIGN CYCLE 2 (2006–2008—PROOF OF CONCEPT PHASE)

Implementation data from Design Cycle 1 stimulated the design of a more ambitious software system that we hoped would produce reliable and valid academic growth data that could be used to monitor students' literacy performance. We named the project Avenue DHH (i.e. Audio-Visual Educational Environments for Deaf or Hard of Hearing) evoking a previous assessment project for learning American Sign Language (i.e. Avenue ASL).

3.1. Theoretical/Pedagogical/Technological Foundations

The use of progress monitoring has increased exponentially over the past 20 years. Special Education teachers monitor students' progress by using Curriculum Based Measures (CBM) and use the results to individualize their instruction. CBM have several features that make them popular for school use: In addition to being sensitive to small changes in student performance (Espin, McMaster, Rose, & Wyman, 2012), they are easy to understand, simple to use, can be repeated frequently, and are cost effective and efficient.

Although widely used in schools, progress monitoring has been less successful with DHH children. Progress-monitoring tools and assessments used with DHH children are often unreliable, difficult to use, and time consuming, and thus do little to promote learning (Ewoldt, 1987; Luckner & Bowen, 2006; Paul, 2009; Traxler, 2000). Indeed, existing measures fail to provide teachers with formative data for making informed instructional decisions. Teachers often resort to anecdotal information, cumulative files, and check lists as documentation sources, resulting in assessment information that is frequently unused, misused, or misunderstood.

Other online CBM systems (i.e. EdCheckup, AIMS web, and DIBBELS) provide teachers with downloadable print assessments. Students complete the assessments on hard copy, and teachers manually score and enter data online. We determined that our software system should be internet-based to facilitate software distribution and data management. To guide our project, we generated several design considerations. Considerations are value statements that indicate the belief system. They are not rules to be applied in all cases, but rather guidelines that reflect the experiences, expertise, and philosophy of the design team.

- Scoring and data storage should be automated whenever possible.
- When assessments must be scored manually, interfaces should make the processes simple and efficient.
- Interfaces should create a positive emotional impact.
- The software should replicate and extend print-based interactivity.
- The software should support accepted teaching and learning pedagogy.

3.2. Design and Development Issues

We designed prototypes for three reading-comprehension assessment tools: Maze Test, Slash Test, and Real Time Reading (RTR).

3.2.1. Maze Test

Cloze tests, which have been used for decades to monitor literacy performance, are created by removing every seventh word from a text passage. Students complete the tests by writing into blank spaces the words they think were deleted. The Maze test is a modified Cloze procedure. A maze is a list of three words, the missing word and two distractors, that appear under the blank space; distractors are selected from different parts of speech from the correct word. For example, if the missing word were a verb, the distractors would be selected from one or more of the other categories (i.e. nouns, adjectives, prepositions, conjunctions, or determiners). The student uses a mouse to select a word from the maze to replace the blank space or vice versa (Deno & Marston, n.d.) (see Figure 22.3). Selecting appropriate distractors involves inspecting the codes to determine which parts of speech should not be used.

Maze tests are written at multiple reading levels and assigned according to each student's ability. We identified six performance levels reflecting average reading ability in grades 1–6. Students who master an academic level progress to the next, more complex, level. Thus, after initial placement students are expected to stay at a given level for an academic year. We developed a minimum of 13 different assessments for each grade level to minimize the possibility of repetition.

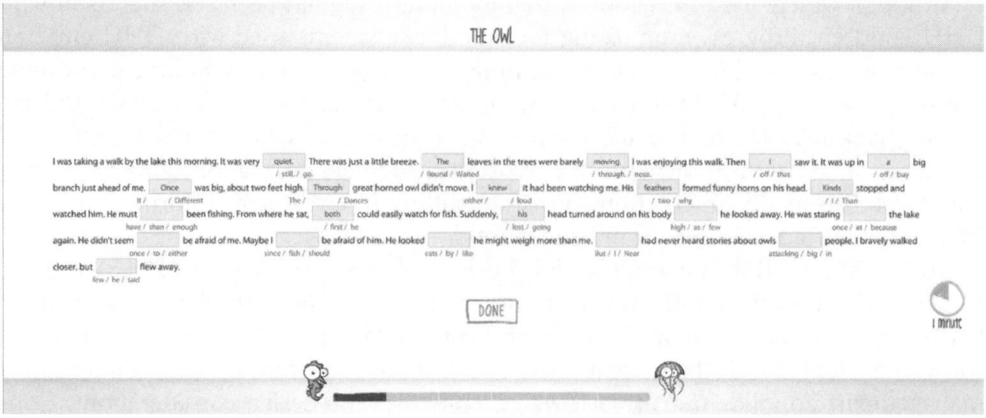

Figure 22.3 Maze test interface.

Design continued throughout the development process. We came to realize that each assessment could become a learning opportunity by using feedback to indicate response accuracy and, when wrong answers were selected, providing the student with knowledge of the correct response. We experimented with the look and feel of the mazes to maintain visual appeal, to address programming issues, and to create a positive user experience. For example, the blank spaces in the passages had to be styled to make them large enough to contain any word in the database, small enough to avoid visual imbalance, and yet remain visually appealing (see Figure 22.4). Moreover, we had not anticipated that extracted words might contain punctuation that could cue the correct answer. For example, when the missing word was the first word in a sentence, we had to ensure the correct answer did not appear in the maze in upper case. In general the process of selecting/deselecting words was carefully choreographed. For example, the opacity of each word was animated to its final state to maintain fluid interactions and smooth transitions.

3.2.2. Slash Test

Slash tests are text passages, displayed in upper case, in which the spaces between words are removed to create a continuous flow of characters. In print, students draw vertical lines where they believe word breaks should fall. On the computer, the student clicks between words to insert (or remove) word breaks between the characters. As with the Maze, Slash tests are written at multiple reading levels. We identified eight performance levels (covering reading levels from pre-K through 6th grades), and developed 40 different assessments for each level to minimize the possibility of repetition. Students begin at the lowest level and progress to subsequent levels when mastery within a level is achieved.

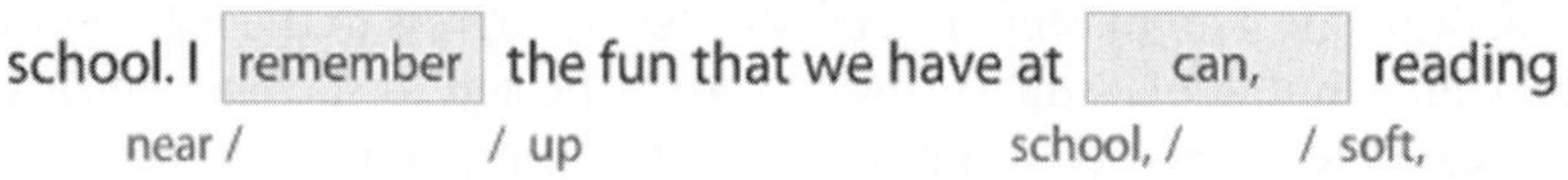

Figure 22.4 Detail of a maze used in the Maze test.

We considered deeply the experience of interacting with the text. When a word-break is identified, characters to the right of the word-break animate horizontally, and a vertical line appears between the words. Animation is used to emphasize the selection and to establish an aesthetically pleasing experience. Rolling the mouse over successive characters introduces a "temporary" vertical line—a visual cue suggesting how a word-break would appear if selected. By using different lengths, widths, and colors to draw vertical lines between characters, and carefully timing each animation we were able to increase usability by reducing inaccuracy and frustration, and to create a fundamentally different aesthetic experience from what is possible with paper and pencil.

3.2.3. Real Time Reading

RTR measures sign-language and oral-text fluency. The student is prompted to read a text passage within a set time period (i.e. 1 minute) then reads the text orally, in sign language, or in both. The student's performance is captured by a webcam and then stored online for teacher assessment. Separate interfaces are used for spoken and signed performances. Assessing oral reading involves tracking the number of words read correctly/incorrectly. Sign language is assessed using a rubric with descriptive qualitative measures for fluency, linguistics, accuracy, and expression.

Designing the RTR software was relatively straightforward as a version of the capture system had been developed for a previous project and the scoring interface was similar to that used in WordMark. However, the development processes for Slash and Maze were quite complex. In both cases, their functionality was to replicate that available in print versions. However, we wanted to use the interface design capabilities of the computer to establish a fundamentally different user experience.

Moreover, we knew we had to deliver potentially hundreds of versions of each assessment as we would be assessing students frequently within each grade and across six different grade levels, and we had to avoid delivering duplicate assessments. We began by developing static versions of each assessment but soon shifted to more dynamic approaches. Static design, which involves developing versions of each interface, is helpful for conceptualizing a tool's initial look and feel, or when only a few screens need to be developed, but is impractical when large numbers of assessments must be developed or when passage content might change. In contrast, dynamic design involves creating templates or shells that automate passage selection, content formatting and placement, grading, feedback, and data storage. Although complex initial programming is often required, dynamic design establishes considerable long-term flexibility. For example, interfaces can automatically scale to the end-users' hardware capabilities (i.e. large monitors, laptop screens, and mobile devices). Moreover, dynamic design makes it possible to use a content management system to store and update data. Throughout the development process design possibilities and issues emerged, each requiring a design solution, software prototyping, and feasibility assessment. Each feature added significant development time, but ultimately helped establish a strong sense of design quality.

Storing large quantities of end-user performance data and content for delivering dynamic versions of the assessment mandated the use of an online database. Using a database for storage created its own set of challenges requiring the implementation of important development techniques to maintain database security and prevent malicious hacking. One-way data encryption (also known as Cryptographic Hashing) was used to protect personally identifiable information and passwords. SQL-injection scripts were employed to prevent users from entering malicious string characters into forms. Without protection, hackers can compromise a server by entering commands that perform unintended operations such as revealing or deleting content.

3.3. Implementation Research DHH Teacher Workshop #2

We gathered design and usability data from design-team members and teachers attending a summer workshop. Entering Maze passages into the system was more complex than we had anticipated. Each Maze passage must be coded in the database by marking every seventh word to indicate its part of speech. We discovered that even minor coding errors caused the software to fail. In response, we developed a software tool, the Maze Content Creator (see Figure 22.5), that supports passage creation and classification, and assures error-free coded-data in the database.

The teachers recommended several additions and modifications to the system. They requested charts of student performance data. They recommended a more efficient student registration system, and they suggested doubling the number of reading levels for the Maze test to finely tune student progress at mid-year levels.

4. DESIGN CYCLE 3 (INITIAL FUNDING)

4.1. Theoretical/Pedagogical/Technological Foundations

Although teachers told us that the theoretical foundations behind each test were valid, we perceived that something was still missing in the software experience. We had replicated the paper-pencil versions of both Maze and Slash, and added auto-grading components that saved teachers time and provided performance feedback; however, interacting with the tests still felt "stale," similar to how teachers described other reading e-assessment environments. Some teachers commented that they wanted a "different" experience—something that extended traditional reading assessments.

At this point, an important shift occurred in our design; we introduced gaming features into the design. Our intent was to shift students' perceptions about the tasks from "testing" environments to "practice" or "gaming" environments. Well-designed game-like environments can create flow-states (Csikszentmihalyi, 1992) in which participants

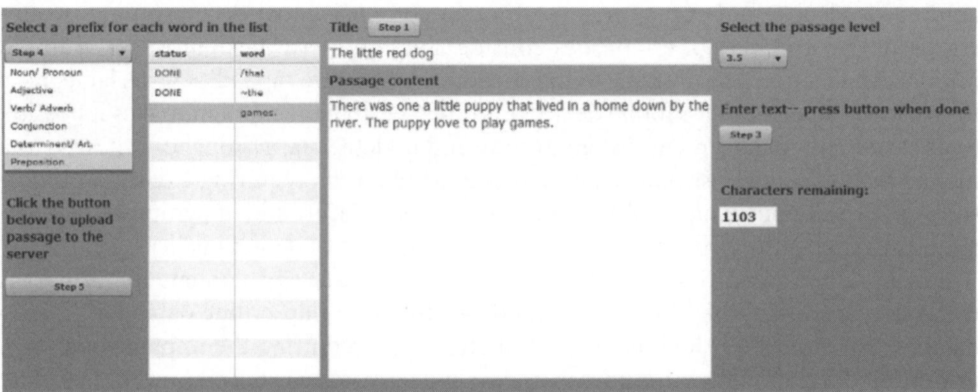

Figure 22.5 Maze Content Creator interface.

display states of deep concentration, enjoyment, and engagement (Johnson & Wiles, 2003).

4.2. *Design and Development Issues*

We received external funding to extend our design and conduct classroom feasibility analyses with DHH teachers and students. Our primary focus was on establishing system-wide software stability: Whereas our initial system was designed to work for use with a handful of users, the upgraded system would have to function effectively for hundreds, or perhaps thousands, of concurrent users. This shift required modifications to the database that controls all system information, security enhancements, and an upgraded server platform; these improvements allowed us to deploy Avenue DHH in multiple settings with ease from this point forward.

We also made additional design changes based on teacher feedback. In an attempt to focus student attention while completing the assessments, we added the functionality to make the browser invisible (in effect, removing extraneous browser buttons, bars, and text from the screen). We modified the Maze test layout to remove the need for scrolling as we believed that scrolling would decrease the usability. We added an automatic spell check to WordMark to help teachers identify misspelled words.

We added game-like features to the Maze and Slash tests to boost student engagement. We replaced numerical levels (e.g. a 3 or 4) with visually appealing imagery using smaller animal characters such as a fish or snail for lower difficulty levels, and larger animals such as an elephant or lion for higher difficulty levels. Within levels we added progressively complex success criteria (similar to an "energy graph" used in many console and online games) that varied the success criteria needed to progress between levels (see Figure 22.6).

Figure 22.6 Characters used to depict game levels.

4.3. *Implementation Research*

We continued gathering usability data throughout the period of the grant. At the end of year 1, we presented our designs to a focus group of 20 DHH educators during a one-day workshop. Three graduate students tested the design over a month-long period at the end of year 2. We invited 18 DHH educators to review the prototypes mid-year during year 3. Lastly, we pilot tested with university students during year 3.

It is not possible to anticipate how software systems will be used as they grow in complexity and are applied to specific settings, but pilot testing provided opportunities to explore real-world use of the system. Pilot testing allowed us to explore new design features (such as the addition of static and interactive charts to support progress monitoring), validate technical characteristics and security, and identify bugs that caused the software to fail when subjected to more stressful conditions than those typically experienced during development, but also to conclude that the software was fundamentally sound from usability and utility perspectives.

5. DESIGN CYCLE 4 (PHASE 2 FUNDING)

We recently received funding to expand the project for nationwide implementation. Although we are ready to conduct usability testing and implementation research, the system will continue to evolve. We will conduct a technological overhaul of the system, examine opportunities for data visualization for both teachers and students, and conduct a longitudinal study in which we examine the validity, reliability, and impact of the e-assessment system in K-8 classrooms.

5.1. *Theoretical/Pedagogical/Technological Foundations*

The theoretical and pedagogical foundations of our current design cycle focus primarily on the design of Information Visualization (InfoViz) components that will be integrated into the student and teacher interfaces. InfoViz in education is concerned primarily with how large datasets can support cognition. Although InfoViz can be used for lower-level learning outcomes such as knowledge acquisition (Keller, Gerjets, Scheiter, & Garsoffky, 2005), other common uses include visual data representation and manipulation to support decision- and sense-making. Visualizations create dynamic representations that can be manipulated, thereby allowing the viewer to ask "what if" questions leading to deeper insight of the topic along with the creation of rich and flexible mental models (Spence, 2007).

The support of decision-making goes beyond effective representation, to designing interfaces that allow users to engage with and transform the representations. Effectively designed interfaces allow information representations to be manipulated directly, thus allowing users to experience the immediate results (Chi, 2002). Designers must consider how such data transformation can allow users to sample, add constraints, scale, skew, or otherwise manipulate data (Spence, 2007). Transforming data creates new representations helping users to generate deeper insight.

In addition to developing and integrating these InfoViz components, we are also redesigning the entire system from the ground up using several new technologies. This system-wide transition of Avenue DHH forms the groundwork of our current design and development issues.

5.2. Design and Development Issues

The current versions of Avenue DHH were developed primarily using the Adobe Flash and Flex authoring environments, with the online environment running in a browser via the Flash Player. However, many teachers have reported problems installing the Flash Player on their computers, or that their technology staff do not allow webcams to be used in Flash-based environments (for security and privacy reasons). To bypass these issues, we will re-develop the software using device- and browser-agnostic technologies (i.e. a combination of HTML5, jQuery, and AJAX). The newly developed software will run on all platforms without the Flash plugin, aligning with common security protocols implemented in schools.

Moreover, with more than 25 million Apple iPads and 150 million iPhone and iPod Touch devices in use, educational institutions are using iOS platforms for face-to-face and online classrooms. We are currently developing custom Apps for the RTR tests. Students will be able to use camera-enabled iPads or iPod Touches to record and submit their reading assessments, which will then be accessible to their teachers either through a browser or the Avenue DHH App.

We will continue to design interactive InfoViz tools that help students to set and monitor goals, and teachers to support diagnosis and decision-making. Examples of two prototypes are described below.

5.2.1. Visualizing Task-Specific Performance

One design challenge explores the clear and concise communication of performance data to younger students, especially in relation to other students (while maintaining student privacy). Figure 22.7 illustrates a student's average test score compared to all students at the same level who have taken the same number of tests. The average scores of all relevant students in the system are represented by the dashed circle, with the larger circle representing the student's relationship to that average. In this example, the outer circle is larger than the dashed circle, indicating above-average progress through seven

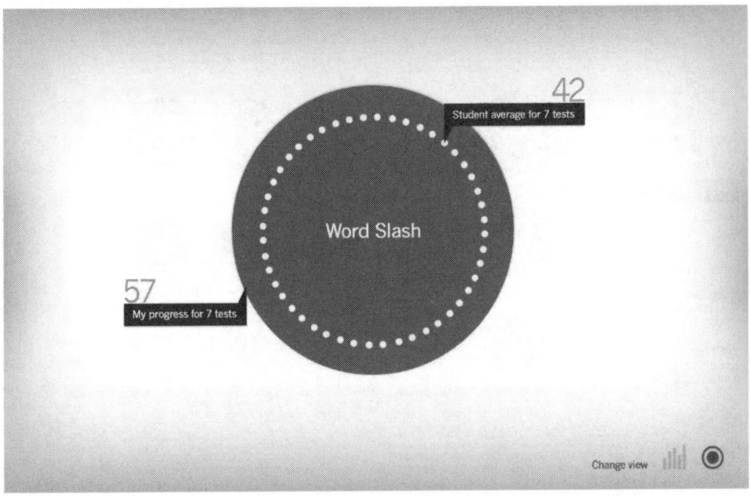

Figure 22.7 A representation of a student's task-specific performance compared to other students at the same level.

tests. The simplicity of the design allows students to quickly see their progress without being overwhelmed by unnecessary numerical data.

5.2.2. Visualizing Performance across Multiple Tasks for Multiple Students

We have examined how to present performance data to teachers for multiple students on multiple tasks. Figure 22.8 illustrates a potential solution to this challenge. Here, teachers can quickly compare students' performance on multiple tasks. Performances are represented by three categories that correspond to the color of the circles: successful performance (i.e. green), performance that requires intervention (i.e. red), and performance that is within 10% of average (i.e. blue)—shown in shades of grey in figure. The final category is particularly useful for teachers who aim to modify the future assessment difficulty to ensure a student is neither struggling nor insufficiently challenged.

5.3. Implementation Research

As we move forward our implementation research design will employ two distinct methodologies that will enable us: (a) to validate our measures; (b) to monitor the growth patterns of students in the academic areas of reading and written expression; (c) to analyze teachers' and parents' use of data generated by the software system; and d) to develop theories about the design and implementation of technological innovation. We will employ field-based research to determine the effectiveness of the system on the literacy performance of students who are DHH. In addition, we will continue to integrate Design Based Research with classical quantitative studies to modify and improve our design using data indicating the relative effectiveness, usability, and performances of the systems by teachers, students, and parents.

Specifically, our implementation research for Design Cycle 4 will involve: (1) validating the technical characteristics of all Avenue DHH e-assessment tasks and evaluation measures; (2) examining the impacts of the Avenue DHH e-assessment environment within authentic K-8 DHH settings; and (3) exploring longitudinal teacher, student, and parent use of the system.

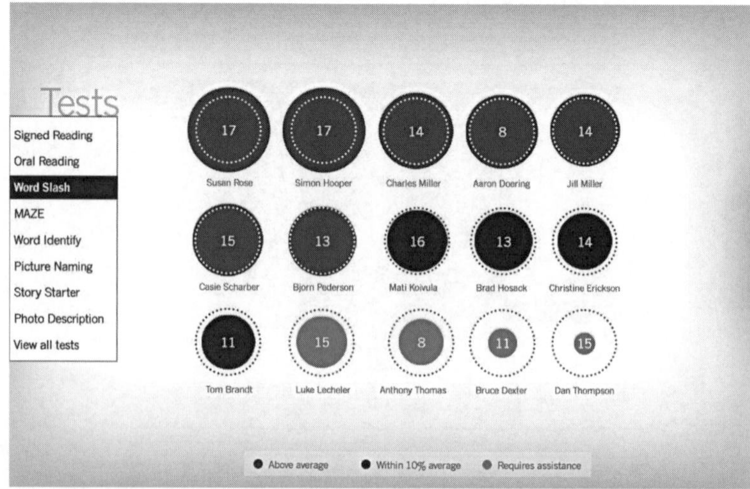

Figure 22.8 A visualization of students' task performance for teachers.

6. CONCLUSION

Ultimately, we believe that future design, integration, and evaluation of the Avenue DHH e-assessment environment will: (1) increase language, reading, and writing proficiency for DHH students in grades K-8; (2) achieve widespread integration of a flexible technology-based system that requires only minimal external maintenance and is scalable to diverse institutions; and (3) improve the nature of research and instructional decision-making by teachers in the DHH reading, writing, and language development community. Furthermore, we anticipate the theoretical, pedagogical, and technological evolution of the Avenue DHH environment will have significant implications for contemporary assessment methodologies in secondary DHH language development, as well as other K-12 world language development and assessment.

Finally, we believe it is important to describe our efforts in writing this chapter as many designers in the field have experienced similar design and development challenges (and opportunities), as well as analogous struggles in communicating their endeavors. The history of research in the field emphasizes empirical and interpretive findings from studies focused on the instructional outcomes of such online environments, and tends to overlook the narratives of the inherent design lifecycles. To enhance further collaborative design opportunities and inform the design processes of future online learning environments, we end with a call to arms for designers to share their design stories and document the vast array of design considerations that go into and evolve throughout each project. In turn, this may open the doors to a new format of publications (such as the *International Journal Of Designs For Learning*), conferences, and associations focused on illuminating the challenges and opportunities that arise when designing, developing, and integrating online and hybrid environments that focus on creating transformative learning and instructional experiences. In order to advance the quality of experiences in our designs, we must communicate and share the nuances and achievements of our work; otherwise, we are only sharing abridged conclusions without insightful context.

REFERENCES

Chi, E. H. (2002). *A Framework for Visualizing Information.* New York: Springer.

Csikszentmihalyi, M. (1992). *Flow: The Psychology of Happiness.* London: Random House.

Deno, S. L., & Marsten, D. (n.d.). Development of the Standard Reading Passages. Retrieved January 28, 2013, from http://www.edcheckup.com/Research/SRPDev.pdf.

Espin, C. A., McMaster, K. L., Rose, S., & Wyman, M. M. (eds.) (2012). *A Measure of Success: The Influence of Curriculum-Based Measurement on Education.* Minneapolis, MN: University of Minnesota Press.

Ewoldt, C. (1987). Reading tests and the deaf reader. *Perspectives for Teachers of the Hearing Impaired, 4,* 10–13.

Hosp, J. L. (2010). *Linking Assessment and Instruction: Teacher preparation and professional development.* Washington, DC: National Comprehensive Center for Teacher Quality.

Johnson, D., & Wiles, J. (2003). Effective affective user interface design in games. *Ergonomics, 46*(13/14), 1332–1345.

Keller, T., Gerjets, P., Scheiter, K., & Garsoffky, B. (2005). Information visualizations for knowledge acquisition: The impact of dimensionality and color coding. *Computers in Human Behavior, 22,* 43–65.

Luckner, J., & Bowen, S. (2006) Assessment practices of professionals serving students who are deaf or hard of hearing: An initial investigation. *American Annals of the Deaf, 151*(4), 410–417.

Paul, P. (2009). *Language and Deafness.* Sudbury, MA: Jones & Bartlett.

Safer, N., & Fleishman, S. (2005). Research matters: How student progress monitoring improves instruction. *Educational Leadership, 62*(5), 81.

Spence, R. (2007). *Information Visualization: Design for interaction* (2nd edition). Upper Saddle River, NJ: Prentice Hall.

Traxler, C. B. (2000). The Stanford Achievement Test 9th edition: National norming and performance standards for deaf and hard-of-hearing students. *Journal of Deaf Studies and Deaf Education, 5*(4), 337–348.

23

DESIGNING FOR AWARENESS

Purposeful Interactions in the Next Generation of Distance Education

Jennifer A. Maddrell and Gary R. Morrison

1. INTRODUCTION

In the fall 2010 semester, an estimated 6.1 million college students, approximately 30% of all enrolled students in degree-granting U.S. higher education institutions, were taking an online course (Allen & Seaman, 2011). This increase represents a 10% growth in online course enrollment from the previous year and far exceeds the less than 1% increase in overall U.S. higher education enrollment over the same period (Allen & Seaman, 2011). With prestigious universities, such as Harvard, Massachusetts Institute of Technology, and Stanford, recently announcing online courses targeting thousands of learners, some are forecasting a *campus tsunami* in which online education is a wave about to forever alter the landscape of higher education (Brooks, 2012; Mazoué, 2012).

Concurrent with the growth in online learning is the proliferation of computer-mediated communication (CMC) technologies to support virtual learning that offers students studying at a distance much of the same interpersonal communication and interaction of conventional face-to-face education (Keegan, 1996). CMC technologies are broadly categorized based on whether they support synchronous (real-time) or asynchronous (delayed-time) communication and interaction (Romiszowski & Mason, 2004). During the 2006–07 academic year, 65% of U.S. higher education institutions offered distance education courses and of those institutions 98% utilized asynchronous technologies, while 75% utilized synchronous Internet-based technology to facilitate at least some simultaneous online instruction for learners learning at a distance (Parsad & Lewis, 2008). Beyond the asynchronous communication and interaction features within an institution's learning management system, synchronous CMC tools in online conferencing systems typically offer text-chat, video and audio interfaces, web browsers, polling tools, application sharing, and whiteboards (Shi & Morrow, 2006). In addition, an ever evolving roster of Internet-based technologies are available to support virtual learning, including tools to support communication, publishing, resource searching and sharing, collaboration, and social networking (Grodecka, Wild, & Kielinger, 2009).

While the CMC technologies to support learners may be changing, research has for decades suggested no significant difference in learning outcomes based on the instructional delivery media, or based on whether the instruction is offered on-campus or via distance education (Bernard et al., 2004; Clark, 1983, 1994; Lockee, Burton, & Cross, 1999). Looking beyond the media to support communication and interaction, distance education theory and research have focused on the importance of cognitive engagement fostered through learner–content, learner–instructor, and learner–learner interactions (Anderson, 2003; Bernard et al., 2009; Moore, 1989).

Offering CMC technologies to support learner interaction with content, peers, and the instructor of the course is not sufficient to ensure quality interactions will occur (Bernard et al., 2009). Instead, as some argue, "the next generation of interactive distance education . . . should be better designed to facilitate interactions that are more targeted, intentional and engaging" (Abrami, Bernard, Bures, Borokhovski, & Tamim, 2011, p. 87), which begs several important questions for both researchers and practitioners. When students learn in a computer-mediated virtual space, what interactions should be supported (Ertmer, Sadaf, & Ertmer, 2011; Kanuka, 2011)? How should the instructional design support these purposeful interactions? Beyond merely replicating the face-to-face instructional experience, how can CMC technologies be utilized to maximize peer, content, and instructor interactions without causing unnecessary distractions to the learner? This chapter examines these questions through a review of distance education and computer-supported cooperative work (CSCW) literature to suggest design considerations to optimize learner interactions in virtual places.

2. INTERACTION THEORY AND RESEARCH

Interaction is a well-documented construct within distance and online education as well as education in general. A recent search of the Education Research Information Center (ERIC) database, with *interaction* as the subject field code, resulted in over 15,000 articles from 1966 to present. Various conceptions and operational definitions have been forwarded describing what interaction is and how instruction should incorporate interaction within a course (Bannan-Ritland, 2002). Noting that the range of definitions of interaction rendered the term useless as a descriptive construct, Moore (1989) appealed for clarity and consensus around three interaction types, including (a) learner–content, (b) learner–instructor, and (c) learner–learner. While learner–content interaction refers to the learner's interactions with the subject-matter content of the instruction, the other two types focus on learner–human level interactions.

A review of interaction in distance and online education literature suggests a focus in the past few decades on learner–human level interaction, such as patterns and amounts of communication, instructor activities and feedback, and other social exchanges or collaboration (Bannan-Ritland, 2002). The emphasis on human interaction in distance and online learning research has resulted in a multitude of recommended strategies to overcome the physical and time separation inherent in distance education, and to exploit the affordances of CMC technologies to facilitate improved interaction between the learner and others. In this section we will review the research on immediacy, learner–learner interactions, and effectiveness of the interactions.

2.1. Immediacy in Interactions

Immediacy is a construct studied extensively in distance education research, and refers to both verbal and nonverbal communication behaviors that influence perception of closeness to another (Mehrabian, 1968). A meta-analysis of instructor immediacy research suggests statistically significant positive correlations between instructor immediacy and both learner-perceived learning and affective outcome measures (r^2 = .24 to .25), but smaller positive correlations with objective measures of cognitive learning outcome (r^2 = .01 to .03) (Witt, Wheeless, & Allen, 2004). Similarly, the teaching presence construct, which focuses on how the instructor manages the discussion and helps build understanding, has been studied in distance education research to examine the influence of (a) instructional design and organization, (b) discourse facilitation, and (c) direct instruction (Anderson, Rourke, Garrison, & Archer, 2001). A statistically significant correlation (r^2 = .56) between the teaching presence construct and instructor immediacy has been reported (Baker, 2010). In addition, research findings suggested a statistically significant positive relationship between teaching presence and learner satisfaction (Abdous & Yen, 2010; Maddrell, 2011; Shin, 2003), as well as between teaching presence and student-perceived learning (Arbaugh, 2008; Maddrell, 2011; Shea, Li, & Pickett, 2006; Shea, Li, Swan, & Pickett, 2005; Shin, 2003; Swan & Shih, 2005). However, in a recent study, no significant relationship was found between teaching presence and objective measures of achievement (Maddrell, 2011).

2.2. Learner–Learner Interactions

Beyond learner interactions with the instructor, the learner–learner relationship has also been extensively studied. Numerous frameworks have been forwarded to describe how learner–learner interactions should occur, including cooperative and group-based mastery learning strategies (Johnson & Johnson, 1989; Slavin, 1987), classroom as community frameworks (Garrison, Anderson, & Archer, 2000; Rovai, 2002), and networked learning approaches (Cormier, 2008; Dron & Anderson, 2007; Siemens, 2005). Social presence theory builds upon the concept of social presence from the work of Short, Williams, and Christie (1976) and considers the degree to which learners feel connected while engaging in mediated communication (Swan & Shih, 2005). Theory and research have examined the effects of social presence on critical thinking and discourse within the mediated environment (Garrison et al., 2000). Some of this work is grounded in social-constructivist theories of learning and the CMC technologies are seen as tools to support learner–learner knowledge creation and negotiation of meaning (Paulus, 2007). Research on the relationship between social presence and perceived learning has shown mixed results with some studies finding a positive relationship (Arbaugh, 2008; Maddrell, 2011; Richardson & Swan, 2003; Swan & Shih, 2005) and others reporting no relationship (Akyol & Garrison, 2008; Shin, 2003). Similarly, some studies reported a positive correlation between social presence and measures of satisfaction (Akyol & Garrison, 2008; Arbaugh, 2008; Maddrell, 2011; Richardson & Swan, 2003; Swan & Shih, 2005), while others found either no relationship (So & Brush, 2008), or reported that social presence was not a predictor of satisfaction (Joo, Lim, & Kim, 2011). Findings are also mixed regarding the relationship between social presence and a learner's intent to persist with some indicating a correlation (Shin, 2003) and others reporting social presence was not a predictor of persistence (Joo et al., 2011). However, in a recent study, no significant relationship was found between social presence and objective measures of achievement (Maddrell, 2011).

2.3. *Effectiveness of Interactions*

While some researchers advocate a balanced approach in which learner–content, learner–learner, and learner–instructor interaction are all considered (Dunlap, Sobel, & Sands, 2007), others suggest deep and meaningful learning can be achieved as long as one of the three types of interaction is present at a high level (Anderson, 2003). A recent meta-analysis of distance education research offered support for the individual positive influence of all three interaction types on learning achievement, but the results revealed that the effects for learner–learner and learner–content interactions were both significantly larger than for learner–instructor interaction treatments, and that the effectiveness of learner–learner interaction was not different from learner–content interaction (Bernard et al., 2009). When interaction strength was considered, a significant positive relationship was suggested between effect size and (a) learner–content interaction strength, and (b) learner–content interaction in combination with either learner–learner or learner–instructor interaction. The findings from Bernard et al.'s (2009) meta-analysis suggest that strategies designed to encourage high levels of learner interaction with the content and with the instructor or other learners have a significant positive influence in learning achievement. However, it is important to note that results of the studies reviewed in the meta-analysis were heterogeneous based on a range of instructional strategies and interactions and that future research should focus on designs to support interaction to improve learning outcomes (Bernard et al., 2009).

3. INTERACTIONS IN VIRTUAL SPACES

The advent of teleconferencing and other types of synchronous technologies offered distance educators a new type of virtual classroom, which opened up interaction opportunities that more closely replicated the face-to-face classroom experience (Anderson & Garrison, 1995; Keegan, 1996; Simonson, Smaldino, Albright, & Zvacek, 2012). More recently, Internet-based social media, such as wikis and blogs, have allowed learners to create social ties outside the walled garden of the institution and have inspired instructors to look beyond replication of the face-to-face classroom experience to the facilitation of learner interactions in open networked environments (Buris & Levine, 2012; Cormier, Siemens, & Downes, 2011; Dron, 2007; Tu, Sujo-Montes, Yen, Chan, & Blocher, 2012; Wiley, 2007).

3.1. *Equivalency Theory*

However, regardless of the advances in CMC technologies to support interaction, the learning environments for local on-campus and distant students are fundamentally different due to the inherent physical (or time) separation of distance learners from others (Simonson, 1999). In distance education theory and research, the physical and time separation has been described as a *transactional distance* or a "psychological and communications space to be crossed, a space of potential misunderstanding between the inputs of instructor and those of learner" (Moore, 1993, p. 22). Yet, as *equivalency theory* suggests, the more equivalent the learning experiences of distance learners to local learners, the more equivalent the outcomes (Simonson, Schlosser, & Hanson, 1999).

With equivalency as a goal, what interactions should the virtual classroom support to both address learner separation and provide a learning experience of equal value for all students regardless of how the student joins the system? Theory and research on group awareness in both CSCW and computer-supported collaborative learning (CSCL) have also examined participant interactions in virtual spaces and may help answer this question.

3.2. *Fostering Group Awareness*

With a recognition that technology-enabled interactions lacked qualities of unmediated environments, theorists and researchers examining CSCW have focused on design solutions to achieve the same *awareness* qualities found in face-to-face interactions, while a primary goal of CSCL research continues to be an understanding of the relationships among group awareness, technology and design features, learning processes, and learning outcomes (Buder, 2011). While a multitude of conceptions and definitions of awareness exist (Schmidt, 2002), group awareness refers to the participants' knowledge of information and others' activities within the shared space (Gutwin & Greenberg, 1995). Whether in mediated or unmediated interpersonal communication, participants regularly monitor and manage the attention and commitment of others (Nardi, 2005). Thus, awareness is not a stable state, but rather a fluctuating perception that is created and fostered though participants' interactions (Gutwin & Greenberg, 2002). As such, awareness is sometimes described within a metaphor of a *shared mirror* in which all participants' presence and actions are reflected in the environment (Bodker & Christiansen, 2006).

In the context of cooperative work, physically separated individuals working together in shared virtual space lack knowledge of group members' activities and subtle cues to support interaction and to participate as part of the group, a design concept referred to as group awareness (Gutwin & Greenberg, 1995) that includes (a) physical environment awareness or basic information about the presence, identity, and location of other participants, (b) task environment awareness or information and artifacts associated with the task, as well as activities, action, intentions, and influence of others on the task at hand, and (c) social environment awareness or complex social conventions that provide subtle cues about those interacting in the group. Similarly, in cooperative learning, group awareness contemplates behavioral awareness related to learners' activities, cognitive awareness about the group members' knowledge, and social awareness about the group members' perceived functioning of the group (Bodemer & Dehler, 2011).

To foster awareness in a mediated space, participants must share activities to be discovered and noticed by others, process a diverse and constantly shifting flow of information about activities in the background, and possess the ability to effectively filter and select what they notice based on the information's relevancy to what they are doing (Heath, Svensson, Hindmarsh, Luff, & vom Lehn, 2002). However, in carrying out these interactions, a range of potential issues may result, including distraction from processing the information in the environment, difficulty in knowing what information is important for maintaining awareness, trouble communicating representations of an activity to others within the virtual space, and allowing participants to control what awareness information about themselves is shared (Gutwin & Greenberg, 1995).

4. RECOMMENDATIONS FOR PRACTICE

Research suggests the positive influence of learner–instructor, learner–learner, and learner–content interactions on learning achievement, as well as the importance of fostering group awareness as a means of optimizing interaction and communication in a collaborative learning environment. The latest synchronous and asynchronous technologies allow instructors and designers to overcome physical and time separation inherent in distance education and design virtual classrooms with equivalent learning experiences to face-to-face classrooms. Contemplating the central group awareness activities, Gutwin and Greenberg (2002) proposed a workspace awareness framework to aid in the design of awareness support in mediated spaces to reduce issues and effort and to increase efficiency among participants. The following considers this framework in the context of recommendations for creating, managing, and facilitating interactions in virtual classrooms.

4.1. Workspace Awareness in Collaboration

Workspace awareness is a type of group awareness that includes knowledge and information created and perceived by participants about a shared collaborative workspace (Gutwin & Greenberg, 2002). Recognizing that it is more difficult for participants in virtual spaces to maintain awareness than in face-to-face environments, Gutwin and Greenberg (2002) developed a descriptive framework of workspace awareness as an analysis tool to assist designers in determining what awareness support is needed. While each task and group situation has its own unique awareness requirements, Gutwin and Greenberg suggest that designers should contemplate a basic set of knowledge categories between a participant and the environment that comprise workspace awareness.

As shown in Table 23.1, these categories contemplate the *who*, *what*, *where*, *how*, and *when* related to interactions in the shared workspace. Based on these categories, specific elements of workspace awareness relate to knowledge about the present and/or past interactions, such as participant presence, identity, authorship, action, intention, artifacts, and location information. Table 23.1 presents these elements and the associated design questions related to each elements as identified by Gutwin and Greenberg (2002).

Table 23.1 Workplace Awareness

Awareness Knowledge Category	Workplace Awareness Elements	Awareness Design Questions
Who (present and past)	Presence Identity Authorship	Who is with me in the workspace? Who is (was) there? Who is doing (did) that?
What (present and past)	Action Intention Artifact	What activities are taking place? What is happening next? What objects are (were) worked on?
Where (present and past)	Location Gaze View Reach	Where are others located? Are they looking at the monitor or elsewhere? Can they see both the monitor and their desk? What objects are in their reach?
How (past)	Action history Artifact history	What steps were taken? What transformations were made to the artifact?
When (past)	Event history	When did that event happen?

Note. Adapted from Gutwin & Greenberg, 2002.

4.2. Designing for Workspace Awareness

With a goal of making collaborative interaction more efficient and effective, Gutwin and Greenberg (2002) suggested designers also contemplate five collaborative activities that are aided by greater workspace awareness. As outlined in Table 23.2, the following describes each of these five activities, suggests potential awareness issues, and proposes design considerations for virtual learning spaces.

4.2.1. Management of Coupling

During collaborative activities, participants move between individual and shared work, and *coupling* refers to the extent of work a participant is able to accomplish before they need to interact with others in order to continue (Gutwin & Greenberg, 2002). Participants realign from loose to tight coupling as they perceive the need to engage with others, and providing awareness information about what others are doing helps in the management of coupling. In a virtual learning space, learners and the instructor are physically separated and may never meet face-to-face, may not be familiar with peers (who), not know about potential collaborative opportunities (what), and have to overcome time delays (when) without the ability to meet in person (where). Potential design considerations to overcome these awareness issues may include facilitating formal learner–learner

Table 23.2 Designing for Workspace Awareness in Virtual Learning

Uses of Workspace Awareness	Awareness Issues in Virtual Learning	Potential Design Considerations
Management of coupling	Who: Unfamiliar peers What: Unknown collaborative opportunities When: Time separation (asynchronous) Where: Space separation	Facilitate formal learner–learner introductions Strive for transparency and reciprocity among participants Promote discussions of individual projects
Simplification of communication	When: Time-shifted asynchronous interaction What: Computer-mediated communication Where: Mediated environment	Manage communication and interaction expectations Incorporate backchannel communication Include audio and visual communication
Coordination of actions	Who: No informal peer connections What: Low level "sharing and comparing" Where: No small group workspace	Offer multiple communication options Encourage groups to set participant interaction expectations Provide group workspace options to support small group work
Anticipation	When: Unknown status and progress of others What: Out of sight/out of mind	Require updates on deliverables Incorporate group resource and deliverable repositories
Assistance	Who: No peer interaction What: Learner uncertainty Where: Unable to find support	Encourage informal learner–learner interactions Define and detail expectations Anticipate and address learner support needs

Note. Adapted from Gutwin & Greenberg, 2002.

introductions and offering spaces for learners to openly share and discuss individual projects by creating an open, off topic discussion area, which will increase transparency and promote reciprocity among participants.

4.2.2. Simplification of Verbal Communication

Collaboration research suggests that workplace awareness can simplify communication and improve the efficiency of participant interaction (Gutwin & Greenberg, 2002). Gutwin and Greenberg (2002) point to four important visual communicative actions that simplify communication, including (a) deictic reference, (b) demonstrations, (c) manifesting actions, and (d) visual evidence. Beyond verbal communication, collaborative discourse often includes referential communication (deictic reference), such as pointing or gesturing to an object. In addition, demonstrations inform others about the sequence of actions or how things operate. By manifesting these actions, verbal communication can be entirely replaced. However, these actions require visual evidence, including confirmation of understanding (or misunderstanding). Within virtual learning spaces, the time-shifted interaction (when), text-heavy CMC (what), and mediated environments (where) present potential awareness problems. Potential design considerations for the instructor to overcome these obstacles include managing communication and interaction expectations, incorporating synchronous backchannel communication among participants (i.e. text-chat occurring simultaneously with the live presentation), or augmenting text-based exchanges with either live or recorded audio and visual communication.

4.2.3. Coordination of Actions

Collaboration requires a coordination of participants' actions, including the planning of activity, the division of labor, and periodic reorganization of tasks and assignments (Gutwin & Greenberg, 2002). As such, workspace awareness focuses on the status of both the participants' activities and the task. However, in virtual learning spaces, there might be no existing peer connections (who), communication among peers might be primarily *sharing and comparing* versus critical discourse (what), and there might be no small group workspace available to learners. To address these awareness limitations in a virtual learning space, the instructional designer/instructor should contemplate multiple synchronous and asynchronous communication options (i.e. email, discussion boards, text-chat, or web conferencing), establish participant interaction expectations (both quantitative and qualitative parameters), and provide group workspace options.

4.2.4. Anticipation

Collaborative activity also includes predictions of others' actions that, in turn, influence the actions taken by others in response (Gutwin & Greenberg, 2002). Participants anticipate these actions based on learned patterns from observations that require current awareness knowledge about participants in the workspace. In virtual learning spaces, project commitments (what) tend to fall out of mind when participants are out of sight. In addition, the project status and progress of others (when) may be unknown. Requiring periodic updates and incorporating group resource and deliverable repositories that are open to all group members are potential design options to tackle these awareness issues.

4.2.5. Assistance

Collaboration also involves participants providing and receiving assistance, both requested and unsolicited when others perceive help is needed (Gutwin & Greenberg, 2002). Workspace awareness to support assistance includes knowledge of what others are doing, their goals, the stage of the task, and their status on the task. However, in virtual learning spaces, awareness may be impacted if there is little peer interaction (who), learners need help (what), but they cannot find support (where). Encouraging informal learner–learner interactions, defining and detailing expectations, and contemplating learner support needs will increase awareness and provide assistance to learners.

5. SUMMARY

Concurrent with the growth in online learning are advances in CMC technologies to support learner–content, learner–learner, and learner–instructor interaction in distance education. While the learning spaces for local on-campus and distant students are fundamentally different due to the physical separation of distance learners from others, theory and research suggest equivalent learning interactions and outcomes can be achieved. To that end, examinations of CSCW and CSCL have focused on design solutions to achieve the same group awareness qualities in technology-enabled interactions that are found in face-to-face interactions. Recognizing that it is more difficult for participants in virtual spaces to maintain awareness than in face-to-face environments, Gutwin and Greenberg (2002) developed a descriptive framework of workspace awareness as an analysis tool to assist designers in determining what awareness support is needed. Using this framework as a guide, this chapter examined collaborative activities that are aided by greater workspace awareness, as well as the categories of knowledge and information about the environment and participants that comprise workspace awareness. While each learning situation has its own unique awareness requirements, this chapter contemplated several potential awareness issues in virtual learning spaces, as well as possible design decisions to address these issues.

REFERENCES

Abdous, M., & Yen, C.-J. (2010). A predictive study of learner satisfaction and outcomes in face-to-face, satellite broadcast, and live video-streaming learning environments. *The Internet and Higher Education, 13*(4), 248–257.

Abrami, P. C., Bernard, R. M., Bures, E. M., Borokhovski, E., & Tamim, R. M. (2011). Interaction in distance education and online learning: Using evidence and theory to improve practice. *Journal of Computing in Higher Education, 23*(2/3), 82–103.

Akyol, Z., & Garrison, D. R. (2008). The development of a community of inquiry over time in an online course: Understanding the progression and integration of social, cognitive and teaching presence. *Journal of Asynchronous Learning Networks, 12*(3–4), 3–22.

Allen, I. E., & Seaman, J. (2011). *Going the Distance: Online Education in the United States, 2011.* (p. 44). Wellesley, MA: Babson Survey Research Group. Retrieved from sloanconsortium.org/publications/survey/going_distance_2011.

Anderson, T. (2003). Getting the mix right again: An updated and theoretical rationale for interaction. *The International Review of Research in Open and Distance Learning, 4*(2). Retrieved from http://www.irrodl.org/index.php/irrodl/article/view/149/230.

Anderson, T., & Garrison, D. R. (1995). Transactional issues in distance education: The impact of design in audioteleconferencing. *American Journal of Distance Education, 9*(2), 27–45.

Anderson, T., Rourke, L., Garrison, D. R., & Archer, W. (2001). Assessing teaching presence in a computer conferencing context. *Journal of Asynchronous Learning Networks, 5*(2), 1–17.

Arbaugh, J. B. (2008). Does the community of inquiry framework predict outcomes in online MBA courses? *The International Review of Research in Open and Distance Learning, 9*(2). Retrieved from http://www.irrodl.org/index.php/irrodl/article/view/490.

Baker, C. (2010). The impact of instructor immediacy and presence for online student affective learning, cognition and motivation. *The Journal of Educators Online, 7*(1), 1–30.

Bannan-Ritland, B. (2002). Computer-mediated communication, e-learning, and interactivity. *Quarterly Review of Distance Education, 3*(2), 161.

Bernard, R. M., Abrami, P. C., Borokhovski, E., Wade, C. A., Tamim, R. M., Surkes, M. A., & Bethel, E. C. (2009). A meta-analysis of three types of interaction treatments in distance education. *Review of Educational Research, 79*(3), 1243–1289.

Bernard, R. M., Abrami, P. C., Lou, Y., Borokhovski, E., Wade, A., Wozney, L., Wallet, P. A., et al. (2004). How does distance education compare with classroom instruction? A meta-analysis of the empirical literature. *Review of Educational Research, 74*(3), 379–439.

Bodemer, D., & Dehler, J. (2011). Group awareness in CSCL environments. *Computers in Human Behavior, 27*(3), 1043–1045.

Bodker, S., & Christiansen, E. (2006). Computer support for social awareness in flexible work. *Computer Supported Cooperative Work (CSCW), 15*(1), 1–28.

Brooks, D. (2012, May 3). The campus tsunami. *The New York Times.* Retrieved from http://www.nytimes.com/2012/05/04/opinion/brooks-the-campus-tsunami.html.

Buder, J. (2011). Group awareness tools for learning: Current and future directions. *Computers in Human Behavior, 27*(3), 1114–1117.

Buris, M., & Levine, A. (2012). Syllabus Summer 2012—ds106 docs. *Digital Storytelling Syllabus.* Course: Computer Science 106: Digital Storytelling, Summer 2012. Retrieved May 11, 2012, from http://ds106.us/docs/Syllabus_Summer_2012.

Clark, R. E. (1983). Reconsidering the research on media. *Review of Educational Research, 53*(4), 445–459.

Clark, R. E. (1994). Media will never influence learning. *Educational Technology Research and Development, 42*(2), 21–29.

Cormier, D. (2008). Rhizomatic education: Community as curriculum. *Innovate: Journal of Online Education, 4*(5), 6.

Cormier, D., Siemens, G., & Downes, S. (2011). change.mooc.ca. *change.mooc.ca.* Course. Retrieved May 11, 2012, from http://change.mooc.ca/index.html.

Dron, J. (2007). Designing the undesignable: Social software and control. *Journal of Educational Technology & Society, 10*(3), 60–71.

Dron, J., & Anderson, T. (2007). Collectives, networks and groups in social software for e-learning. In G. Richards (Ed.), *World Conference on E-learning in Corporate, Government, Healthcare, and Higher Education* (pp. 2460–2467). Quebec City, Canada: AACE.

Dunlap, J. C., Sobel, D., & Sands, D. I. (2007). Designing for deep and meaningful student-to-content interactions. *TechTrends: Linking Research & Practice to Improve Learning, 51*(4), 20–31.

Ertmer, P. A., Sadaf, A., & Ertmer, D. J. (2011). Student-content interactions in online courses: The role of question prompts in facilitating higher-level engagement with course content. *Journal of Computing in Higher Education, 23*(2–3), 157–186.

Garrison, D. R., Anderson, T., & Archer, W. (2000). Critical inquiry in a text-based environment: Computer conferencing in higher education. *The Internet and Higher Education, 2*(2–3), 87–105.

Grodecka, K., Wild, F., & Kielinger, B. (Eds.). (2009). *How to use social software in higher education.* Poland: iCamp. Retrieved from http://www.icamp.eu/wp-content/uploads/2009/01/icamp-handbook-web.pdf.

Gutwin, C., & Greenberg, S. (1995). Support for group awareness in real-time desktop conferences. *Proceedings of the Second New Zealand Computer Science Research Students' Conference.* University of Waikato, Hamilton, New Zealand.

Gutwin, C., & Greenberg, S. (2002). A descriptive framework of workspace awareness for real-time groupware. *Computer Supported Cooperative Work (CSCW), 11*(3), 411–446.

Heath, C., Svensson, M. S., Hindmarsh, J., Luff, P., & vom Lehn, D. (2002). Configuring awareness. *Computer Supported Cooperative Work (CSCW), 11*(3), 317–347.

Johnson, D. W., & Johnson, R. T. (1989). *Cooperation and Competition: Theory and research.* Edina, MN: Interaction Book Company.

Joo, Y. J., Lim, K. Y., & Kim, E. K. (2011). Online university students' satisfaction and persistence: Examining perceived level of presence, usefulness and ease of use as predictors in a structural model. *Computers & Education, 57*(2), 1654–1664.

Kanuka, H. (2011). Interaction and the online distance classroom: Do instructional methods affect the quality of interaction? *Journal of Computing in Higher Education, 23*(2–3), 143–156.
Keegan, D. (1996). *Foundations of Distance Education* (3rd ed.). London: Routledge.
Lockee, B. B., Burton, J. K., & Cross, L. H. (1999). No comparison: Distance education finds a new use for "no significant difference." *Educational Technology Research and Development, 47*(3), 33–42.
Maddrell, J. A. (2011). *Examining the community of inquiry framework and learning outcomes* (Doctoral dissertation). Norfolk, VA: Old Dominion University.
Mazoué, J. (2012). The deconstructed campus. *Journal of Computing in Higher Education, 24*(2), 74–95.
Mehrabian, A. (1968). Some referents and measures of nonverbal behavior. *Behavior Research Methods & Instrumentation, 1*(6), 203–207.
Moore, M. (1989). Three types of interaction. *American Journal of Distance Education, 3*(2), 1.
Moore, M. (1993). Theory of transactional distance. In D. Keegan (Ed.), *Theoretical Principles of Distance Education* (pp. 22–38). London: Routledge.
Nardi, B. (2005). Beyond bandwidth: Dimensions of connection in interpersonal communication. *Computer Supported Cooperative Work (CSCW), 14*(2), 91–130.
Parsad, B., & Lewis, L. (2008). *Distance Education at Degree-Granting Postsecondary Institutions: 2006–07* (No. NCES 2009044). National Center for Education Statistics, U.S. Department of Education. Retrieved from http://nces.ed.gov/pubsearch/pubsinfo.asp?pubid=2009044.
Paulus, T. M. (2007). CMC modes for learning tasks at a distance. *Journal of Computer-Mediated Communication, 12*(4), 1322–1345.
Richardson, J. C., & Swan, K. P. (2003). Examining social presence in online courses in relation to students' perceived learning and satisfaction. *Journal of Asynchronous Learning Networks, 7*(1), 68–88.
Romiszowski, A., & Mason, R. (2004). Computer-mediated communication. In D. Jonassen (Ed.), *Handbook of Research for Educational Communications and Technology* (Vol. 2, pp. 397–431). Mahwah, NJ: Lawrence Erlbaum Associates.
Rovai, A. P. (2002). Development of an instrument to measure classroom community. *The Internet and Higher Education, 5*(3), 197–211.
Schmidt, K. (2002). The problem with "awareness": Introductory remarks on "awareness in CSCW." *Computer Supported Cooperative Work (CSCW), 11*(3), 285–298.
Shea, P., Li, C., & Pickett, A. (2006). A study of teaching presence and student sense of learning community in fully online and web-enhanced college courses. *The Internet and Higher Education, 9*(3), 175–190.
Shea, P., Li, C., Swan, K. P., & Pickett, A. (2005). Developing learning community in online asynchronous college courses: The role of teaching presence. *Journal of Asynchronous Learning Networks, 9*, 59–82.
Shi, S., & Morrow, B. V. (2006). E-conferencing for instruction: What works? *Educause Quarterly, 29*(4), 42.
Shin, N. (2003). Transactional presence as a critical predictor of success in distance learning. *Distance Education, 24*(1), 69.
Short, J., Williams, E., & Christie, B. (1976). *The Social Psychology of Communications.* London: John Wiley.
Siemens, G. (2005). Connectivism: A learning theory for the digital age. *International Journal of Instructional Technology and Distance Learning, 2*(1), 3–10.
Simonson, M. (1999). Equivalency theory and distance education. *TechTrends, 43*(5), 5–8.
Simonson, M., Schlosser, C. A., & Hanson, D. (1999). Theory and distance education: A new discussion. *American Journal of Distance Education, 13*(1), 60–75.
Simonson, M., Smaldino, S., Albright, M., & Zvacek, S. (2012). *Teaching and Learning at a Distance: Foundations of distance education* (5th ed.). Boston, MA: Allyn & Bacon.
Slavin, R. E. (1987). Mastery learning reconsidered. *Review of Educational Research, 57*(2), 175.
So, H. J., & Brush, T. A. (2008). Student perceptions of collaborative learning, social presence and satisfaction in a blended learning environment: Relationships and critical factors. *Computers & Education, 51*(1), 318–336.
Swan, K. P., & Shih, L. (2005). On the nature and development of social presence in online course discussions. *Journal of Asynchronous Learning Networks, 9*(3), 115–136.
Tu, C. H., Sujo-Montes, L., Yen, C. J., Chan, J. Y., & Blocher, M. (2012). The integration of personal learning environments & open network learning environments. *TechTrends, 56*(3), 13–19.
Wiley, D. (2007). Intro Open Ed Syllabus. *INST 7150 Introduction to Open Education, Fall 2007.* Wiki. Retrieved May 11, 2012, from http://opencontent.org/wiki/index.php?title=Intro_Open_Ed_Syllabus.
Witt, P., Wheeless, L., & Allen, M. (2004). A meta-analytical review of the relationship between teacher immediacy and student learning. *Communication Monographs, 71*(2), 184–207.

24

LEARNING WITH *FACEBOOK GROUP*— INTERACTION IN ACTION

Gila Kurtz, Hagit Meishar-Tal, and Efrat Pieterse

1. INTRODUCTION

Though interaction is a critical component of the online learning process, it is a challenging task to promote an effective interaction that serves the collaborative educational process. Studies conducted on the use of course sites in higher education show that the use of these environments is usually limited to a one-way mediated communication from the professors to students by posting course materials and announcements (Coats, James, & Baldwin, 2005, Nachmias & Ram, 2009, Shemla & Nachmias, 2007). These studies suggest that course sites are usually used in an instructor-led lecture-based format and less in innovative ways, engaging students in collaborative activities and knowledge building through interpersonal interaction. The reasons for that phenomenon is partly related to the instructors' competencies and pedagogical background, and partly to the course site structure and the way it influences the learning dynamics occurring within its boundaries (Dillenbourg, Schneider, & Synteta, 2002).

The *Facebook group* has a unique structure and special characteristics that make it a potential candidate for holding innovative pedagogies and promoting productive online communication and interaction. In this case study we describe a pilot study to use a *Facebook group* as an interaction-based and content exchange course site.

2. BACKGROUND: SOCIAL NETWORKING AND LEARNING

Social networking sites, such as *Facebook*, are web 2.0 applications that are perceived to be the second generation of web development and design that facilitates communication and information sharing, interoperability and collaboration on the web (Web 2.0, 2012). Web 2.0 technologies place great emphasis on user-generated content, content sharing, and collaborative work, all of which can add significant value to deeper learning processes. Based on the unique characteristics of web 2.0 technologies, instructors and students can use these innovative technologies to interact, share and build a learning community (Harris & Rea, 2009).

A social network is a social structure made of nodes, generally individuals or organizations, which are connected by one or more specific types of interdependency (Social Networks, 2012). A social networking service, such as *Facebook*, is an online service, platform, or site that focuses on building and reflecting social networks or social relations among people, who, for example, share interests and/or activities. A social networking service consists of a representation of each user (often a profile), his/her social links, and a variety of additional services (Social Networking Service, 2012).

2.1. Learning with Facebook

Like any new web 2.0 environment, *Facebook* was not developed for learning and teaching purposes. Nevertheless, after a while, *Facebook* began to be used in the higher-education context. The first studies in using *Facebook* in higher education were conducted in order to examine the students' use of social networks in general (Pempek, Yermolayeva, & Calvert, 2009). More focused studies have examined the students' use of social networks for their studies. These studies found that social networks are one of the tools used by new students to adjust and meet other students before and during school (Madge, Meek, Wellens, & Hooley, 2009). A British study examined the content shared through *Facebook* by students in college. The research revealed that only 4% of the content posted by students contained material related directly to their studies. The content related to experiences outside of the university, the exchange of practical information about a course curriculum and for the sharing of academic information. *Facebook* was also used as a channel for expressing difficulties in learning so as to gain moral support from friends and for sharing humorous aspects related to the learning experience (Selwyn, 2009).

A recent study empirically examined cases in which *Facebook* and *Twitter* are being utilized for scholarly purposes by higher-education institutes in Israel. Research findings suggest that *Facebook* promotes knowledge sharing, thereby facilitating informal learning within community (Forkosh-Baruch & Hershkovitz, 2012).

In his chapter titled "Facebook or Faceblock: Cautionary tales exploring the rise of social networking within tertiary education," Peter Duffy (2011) summarizes the potential educational benefits of social networking technologies like *Facebook*:

> Firstly, they offer a set of affordances relating to the creation of online collaborative activities. Secondly, many students are already using these technologies for socialization and communication. Thirdly and lastly, many of the systems and tools are free to use and come without restrictions found in existing instructional management system (LMSs).
>
> (Duffy 2011, p. 289)

2.2. The Facebook Group *Interface*

At the heart of a *Facebook group* is the *wall*. Members of the group can share content, statuses (text messages), links to websites, pictures and videos on the wall. Each item uploaded to the wall can get responses, either by indicating *Like* or by writing a more detailed comment. The organization of the information on *Facebook* is dynamic, as new items appear at the top of the list and old items with new responses are also pushed to the top of the list. The wall is thus reorganized in such a way that the newest items and the newest comments are always at the top. The wall also allows the creation of documents. Another tool of the *Facebook group* is the *events* generator. Events are items that are time-dependent and allow the members of the group to *attend* or *not attend*.

The *profile pictures* of all members of the *Facebook group* appear on the group page. There is a special sign to indicate those currently on *Facebook*. Group members can use the one-to-one instant messaging system to chat with each other as well as group conferencing to chat with the entire group. The group also provides an internal search engine that supports information retrieval from the environment.

2.3. *The Uniqueness of a* Facebook Group *as a Learning Environment*

A main obstacle to the adoption of *Facebook* as a learning environment is related to the willingness of instructors to be "friends" of their students, thus exposing themselves to the students, and vice versa. The merging of the social with the educational environment is perceived as a violation of privacy in many cases (Abel, 2005; Mendez et al., 2009). Research conducted by Mazer, Murphy and Simonds (2007) examined the effect of the exposure of the personal lives of instructors to their students through *Facebook*. This study shows that in most cases the increased exposure of the instructor through *Facebook* helped the students to perceive the instructor as being more human and trustworthy. At the same time, the researchers emphasize that overexposure may be a sensitive matter. Many instructors are not interested in this exposure and prefer to keep their personal lives private from the students. Indeed, many students are not interested in this exposure either; they prefer a separation between learning space and social space. In light of these findings, it seems that *Facebook* is not a suitable environment for formal learning activities that require instructor–student interaction (Madge et al., 2009).

With the advent of groups on *Facebook* which do not require members of the group to be friends it became possible to create a study group in which students and

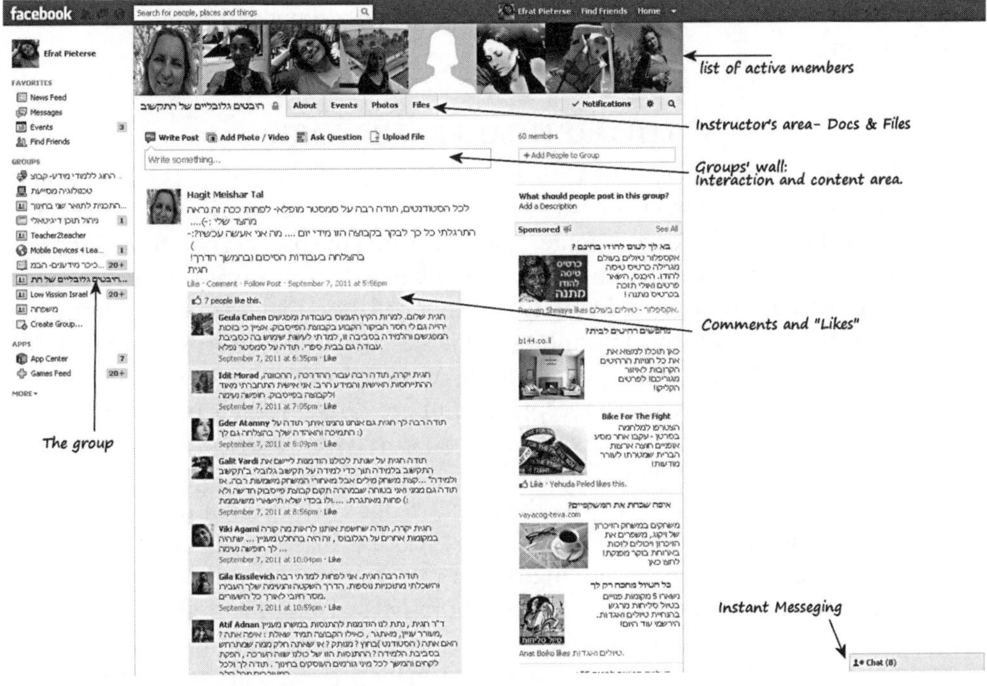

Figure 24.1 The *Facebook* group interface.

instructors participate without being friends. Under these conditions, the possibility of using a *Facebook group* as a teaching–learning space becomes more relevant.

A *Facebook group* can be created by any *Facebook* user. The creator of the group can invite other *Facebook* users to register for the group by forwarding a request to join it. The group administrator (creator) can choose to close the group or to leave it open. In the case of a closed learning group, the information published in the group does not appear on the user's wall as do all other activities on *Facebook*, but is published only among group members on the group wall.

Unlike other course sites that are controlled and managed by the institution, a *Facebook group* is a free platform. It does not require any maintenance and expenses. Participating in a *Facebook group* does not require handling another user account. The student can use the same username and password for learning purposes and for social purposes. Thus, the accessibility to the *Facebook group* is much higher. The students do not have to initiate a special entrance to the course site. Every time they are entering *Facebook* for other reasons they are exposed to the activity in the group.

Some other differences between a traditional course site and a *Facebook group* are related to the management and organization of content in the *Facebook group*. In the *Facebook group* all users, students and instructors, can create content and can delete content. News feeds are always at the top of the list, as are comments to old feeds that push old feeds to the top. The dynamic organization of the environment might make orientation and retrieval of content a bit difficult but, on the other hand, the dynamic organization generates intensive interaction and encourages active participation.

Another feature that contributes to students' participation in the *Facebook group* is the link between interactions and content. In the *Facebook group* each item published on the wall, whether it is content or an interaction, is automatically created with the option of commenting on it or adding "like" to it. This special design makes interaction inherent in the content.

3. THEORETICAL FRAMEWORK

Interaction and collaborative discourse are at the heart of the online learning experience (Harasim, 2012). Interaction is defined as a two-way communication process that involves two or more individuals (Berge, 2002). By using the process of interaction, data, information, and ideas are manipulated and enhanced, and transformed into newly acquired knowledge (Bolliger & Inan, 2012). In a collaborative learning environment, knowledge is shared or transmitted among learners as they work towards common learning goals; for example, a shared understanding of the subject at hand or a solution to a problem. Learners are not passive receptacles but are active in their process of knowledge acquisition as they participate in discussions, search for information, and exchange opinions with their peers. When learning by interacting, the learning process creates a bond between and among learners as their knowledge construction depends on each other's contribution to the discussion (Brindley, Walti, & Blaschke, 2009), thus, increasing motivation, mutual support, and high order thinking among the learners. Anderson (2003) argues that both interaction and collaborative learning methods can humanize the learning process through provision of effective interpersonal online exchange.

One of the new learning approaches that is based on the premise that people learn through interpersonal interaction is the Connectivist theory. Connectivism theorizes that learning is a process of building networks of information, contacts, and resources that can be applied to real problems (Siemens, 2007). According to Brindley et al. (2009), Siemens provides a framework that is very useful for understanding interaction and collaborative learning in an online environment. From his viewpoint, learning in the digital age is no longer dependent on individual knowledge acquisition, storage, and retrieval; rather, it relies on the connected learning that occurs through interaction with various sources of knowledge and participation in communities of common interest, social networks, and group tasks.

Siemens (2007) and Downes (2007) have written defining connectivist papers, arguing that learning is the process of building networks of information, contacts, and resources that are applied to real problems. Connectivist learning focuses on building and maintaining networked connections that are current and flexible enough to be applied to existing and emergent problems. Connectivism also assumes that information is plentiful and that the learner's role is not to memorize or even understand everything but to have the capacity to find and apply knowledge when and where it is needed (Anderson & Dron, 2011).

The main attributes of connectivism can be identified as follows:

1. Learning and knowledge rest in a diversity of opinions.
2. Learning is a process of connecting specialized nodes or information sources.
3. Learning may reside in non-human appliances.
4. Nurturing and maintaining connections is needed to facilitate continual learning.
5. The ability to see connections between fields, ideas, and concepts is a core skill.
6. Currency (accurate, up-to-date knowledge) is the intent of all connectivist learning activities.
7. Decision-making is a learning process. Choosing what to learn and the meaning of incoming information is seen through the lens of a shifting reality. While there might be a right answer now, it might be wrong tomorrow due to alterations in the information climate affecting the decision. (Siemens, 2005).

In the next section we describe an attempt to elaborate interaction and collaborative work methods in a graduate-level course setting, by using a *Facebook group* as its course site.

4. CASE STUDY

The course *International Aspects of ICT in Education* is a graduate course in the School of Education at the College for Academic Studies in Israel. The course is taught in a hybrid format by incorporating class meetings with online activities.

Fifty students registered for the course in the summer of 2011, all of them computer literate. Most students were in their late thirties or early forties, married, female and work full-time during the time they are in the program.

The *Facebook group* was opened at the beginning of the course. The students were required to register for it as part of the course requirements. The *Facebook group* was used to support the following pedagogical goals:

1. *The delivery of course content*: Course presentations were published in the group. Once the presentations were published, they were also accessible from the wall and everybody could comment on and download them.

2. *A shared space for collaborative course assignments*: The activity in the *Facebook group* consisted of five assignments, including searching, collecting information and sharing it with colleagues, peer assessment, online discussions and quantitative and reflective self-assessment. The tasks incorporated *Google Docs*. Students were asked to fill out forms prepared in *Google Docs*. After completing the forms, the database that was created as a joint task was published back on the *Facebook group* and analyzed by the students.
3. *Interacting and collaborating on course requirements*: The *Facebook group* was used for interaction by the instructor and the students with each other and other learning activities. The instructor also used the group to interact and collaborate with students on class projects, providing guidance and feedback on students' work. Students used the group space for information sharing, exchanging opinions with their peers and co-creating new knowledge not owned by one particular student.

5. STUDENTS' SELF-REFLECTIONS ON THE LEARNING EXPERIENCE WITH THE *FACEBOOK GROUP*

Toward the end of the course, students were asked to reflect on their activities in the *Facebook group* and to report on challenges tackled which had occurred during the learning process. A quantitative and qualitative content analysis of the 43 responses (86% response rate) was carried out. Recurring themes were identified by all three researchers independently and a list of the main themes was created based on an inter-rater agreement of 85%.

Analysis shows that the students experienced the interaction with their colleagues and with the instructor in the *Facebook group* as contributing to their learning as shown in the following paragraph:

> The messages and responses have been the most enjoyable part of the conversation in the group. The issues were raised not by the instructor but by the students who wished to respond and share. In some cases, a deep discussion developed and encouraged many class members to make interesting comments (like the discussion opened by XXX on whether to permit young children to go into Facebook). I really enjoyed taking part in these conversations. In my opinion, this is the real contribution of the Facebook environment for learning in this course.

Another student wrote: "We have been exposed to a variety of opinions and learning materials. An instant connection was created between everyone. I feel that the environment contributed to the consolidation of the group."

The *Facebook group* activities made the interaction with the instructor more accessible. A number of students mentioned the "just-in-time" support of the instructor as a meaningful experience: "The environment has allowed a direct link between the students and the instructor. She became an advisor; she gave us the tools and exposed us to information sources and learning tools, and gave us immediate feedback. This is meaningful learning for me."

It seems that the overall activity level of students was influenced by those experiences. Twenty-five percent of the students repeatedly emphasized that the online learning experience was intense, immediate, and fast. One of the students even defined the experience as "catchy": "There is something 'catchy' in the responses and therefore we see more comments."

An example of the experience of immediacy and intensity at all levels can be found here:

> We created an instant connection between us all. I feel that the environment contributed to the consolidation of the group, direct contact with the participants and of course, a place to "hear" all of them on any subject that came up. The ability to speak up immediately was very convenient and suited me very much. I used it in many cases. Rapid response of all the classmates gave a sense of a real "conversation" and made me continue responding and expressing agreement or disagreement, with the need to justify why.

Another finding is related to the contribution of the *Like* feature to the group dynamics. Students used *Like* to achieve an active presence whenever it was hard for them to express themselves, as shown in this citation: "I am not a big fan of Facebook and 'likes', but I didn't always have a chance to bring my own voice, so in some situations I just hit 'like'." The *Like* feature also served students who wanted to express themselves but did not want to repeat others, as expressed here: "I read my classmates posts and I responded by 'like'. I do not like to repeat what others have written so I did not respond verbally, unless I had something important to say."

The contribution of *Like* to the dynamic of the group is dual. From the perspective of the sender *Like* is a sign of presence and a gesture of support, and from the perspective of the receiver, it is a positive feedback as stated here: "My responses to the members of the group were by indicating 'like'. For me, it is a kind of response that shows support. I like (literally) when my friends 'like' my posts. I felt that what I wrote is significant to all."

6. CONCLUSIONS AND IMPLICATIONS

The implementation of the *Facebook group* and the self-reflections of the students on their experience indicate that the *Facebook* activities were perceived by students as a positive learning experience. The main advantage of the *Facebook group* is that it invites interpersonal interaction via response and involvement. This is the result of the unique structure of information organization on *Facebook*.

The case study described above demonstrates that design and operation of learning processes within a *Facebook group* can lead to a more engaging learning. The unique dynamic structure of the *Facebook group* can be leveraged to carry out learning processes that require collaboration among learners and between learners and the instructor.

The *Facebook group* is not just "another discussion group" but a unique environment that can serve as a viable alternative to traditional learning management systems that provides educators with an opportunity to further engage learners throughout the course, as well as to support development of learner skills and competencies needed for the "Knowledge Society." The *Facebook group* provides a shared space conducive to facilitating collaborative learning and knowledge building discourse.

The incorporation of a web 2.0 application such as a *Facebook group* into teaching helps elicit learner participation beyond the traditional class meetings and enables instructors to engage students in collaborative learning in a way that has been nearly impossible up to now. In fact, using social media can help students create new contexts for learning and communication for themselves. As Harris & Rea (2009) stated: "Students become part of the lesson!" (p. 141).

In light of the above, we need to acknowledge that the technology application itself is not solely responsible for the creation of learning discourse (Dillenbourg et al., 2002). The role of the instructor in designing the tasks, the immediate and detailed feedback of her responses during the learning process, the motivation of learners and the fact that the *Facebook* activity was part of the course requirements, all contributed to the positive aspects of the learning process. Future research that compares this application in other study groups' settings and with different models of teaching can broaden our understanding of the influence of the *Facebook group* as a teaching–learning environment.

REFERENCES

Abel, M. (2005). Find me on Facebook . . . as long as you are not a faculty member or administrator. *Resource for College Transitions, 3*(3), pp. 1–12.

Anderson, T. D. (2003). Getting the mix right again: An updated and theoretical rationale for interaction. *International Review of Research in Open and Distance Learning, 4*(2). Retrieved January 24, 2013 from http://www.irrodl.org/index.php/irrodl/article/view/149/230.

Anderson, T. D., & Dron, J. (2011). Three generations of distance education pedagogy. *The International Review of Research in Open and Distance Learning, 12*(3) Retrieved January 11, 2012 from http://www.irrodl.org/index.php/irrodl/article/view/890/1663.

Berge, Z. L. (2002). Active, interactive, and reflective elearning. *The Quarterly Review of Distance Education, 3*(2), 181–190.

Bolliger, D. U., & Inan, F. A. (2012). Development and validation of the Online Student Connectedness Survey (OSCS). *The International Review of Research in Open and Distance Learning, 13*(3). Retrieved June 29, 2012 from http://www.irrodl.org/index.php/irrodl/article/view/1171/2206.

Brindley, J. A., Walti, C., & Blaschke, L. M. (2009). Creating effective collaborative learning groups in an online environment. *The International Review of Research in Open and Distance Learning, 10*(3). Retrieved June 29, 2012 from http://www.irrodl.org/index.php/irrodl/article/view/675/1271.

Coats, H., James, R., & Baldwin, G. (2005). A critical examination of the effects of learning management systems on university teaching and learning. *Tertiary Education and Management, 11*(1), 19–36.

Dillenbourg, P., Schneider, D., & Synteta, P. (2002). Virtual learning environments. In A. Dimitracopoulou (Ed.), *Proceedings of the 3rd Hellenic conference on information and communication technologies in education* (pp. 3–18). Greece: Kastaniotis Editions.

Downes, S. (2007, June). *An introduction to connective knowledge.* Paper presented at the International Conference on Media, knowledge & education—exploring new spaces, relations and dynamics in digital media ecologies. Retrieved January 11, 2012 from http://www.downes.ca/post/33034.

Duffy, P. (2011). Facebook or faceblock: Cautionary tales exploring the rise of social networking within tertiary education. In Mark J. W. Lee & C. McLoughin (Eds.), *Web 2.0-Based E-Learning: Applying Social Informatics for Tertiary Teaching* (pp. 284–300). Hershey, PA: IGI Global.

Forkosh-Baruch, A., & Hershkovitz, A. (2012). A case study of Israeli higher-education institutes sharing scholarly information with the community via social networks. *Internet and Higher Education, 15*, 58–68.

Harasim, L. (2012). *Learning Theory and Online Technologies.* New York and London: Routledge.

Harris, A., & Rea, A. (2009). Web 2.0 and virtual world technologies: A growing impact on IS education. *Journal of Information Systems Education, 20*(2), 137–144. Retrieved from ABI/INFORM Global. (Document ID: 1755224731).

Madge, M., Meek, J., Wellens, J., & Hooley, T. (2009). Facebook, social integration and informal learning at university: "It is more for socialising and talking to friends about work than for actually doing work." *Learning, Media and Technology, 34*(2), 141–155.

Mazer, J. P., Murphy, R. E., & Simonds, C. J. (2009). The effects of instructor self-disclosure via Facebook on instructor credibility. *Learning, Media and Technology, 34*(2), 175–183.

Mendez, J. P., Curry, J., Mwavita, M., Kennedy, K., Weinland, K., & Bainbridge, K. (2009). To friend or not to friend: Academic interaction on Facebook. *International Journal of Instructional Technology & Distance Learning, 6*(9), 33–47.

Nachmias, R., & Ram, J. (2009). Research insights from a decade of campus-wide implementation of web-supported academic instruction at Tel Aviv University. *The International Review of Research in Open and Distance Learning, 10*(2). Retrieved June 29, 2012 from http://www.irrodl.org/index.php/irrodl/article/view/595/1214.

Pempek, T. A., Yermolayeva, Y. A., & Calvert, S. L. (2009). College students' social networking experiences on Facebook. *Journal of Applied Developmental Psychology, 30*, 227–238.

Selwyn, N. (2009). Faceworking: Exploring students' education-related use of Facebook. *Learning, Media and Technology, 34*(2), 157–174.

Shemla, A., & Nachmias, R. (2007). Current state of web supported courses at Tel Aviv University. *International Journal on E-Learning, 6*(2), 235–246.

Siemens, G. (2005). Connectivism: A learning theory for the Digital Age. *Elearn Space.* Retrieved January 15, 2012 from http://www.elearnspace.org/Articles/connectivism.htm.

Siemens, G. (2007). Connectivism: Creating a learning ecology in distributed environments. In T. Hug (Ed.), *Didactics of Microlearning: Concepts, discourses and examples.* Munster, Germany: Waxmann Verlag.

Social Networking Service (2012). http://en.wikipedia.org/wiki/Social_networking_service (accessed January 18, 2012).

Social Networks (2012). http://en.wikipedia.org/wiki/Social_network (accessed January 18, 2012).

Web 2.0 (2012). http://en.wikipedia.org/wiki/Web_2.0 (accessed January 18, 2012).

25

DESIGNING FOR LEARNING WITH TANGIBLE TECHNOLOGIES

Sara Price and Paul Marshall

1. INTRODUCTION

With the emergence of increasingly small, cheap and robust computing platforms and digital sensing technologies, the potential for embedding computing power into physical artefacts and linked to digital representations in flexible ways is increasing. A number of opportunities for tangible technologies to support learning in new ways have been made. Their very nature seems to foster hands-on learning, providing new explorative ways of interacting with information and engendering a more active approach to learning than traditional computing; digital augmentation offers opportunities to present information not normally available in the physical world e.g., through visualisation or sound (Rogers et al., 2005). In this chapter we adopt a broad definition of 'tangibles', following Shaer and Hornecker (2010): 'Interfaces that are concerned with providing tangible representations to digital information and controls, allowing users to quite literally grasp data with their hand and effect functionality by physical manipulations of these representations.' Examples of tangible systems designed to support learning include Resnick et al.'s (1998) pioneering digital manipulatives, Bakker, Antle and Van Den Hoven's (2012) Moving Sound Tangibles and Horn and Jacob's (2007) tangible programming blocks (see Figures 25.1a, 25.1b, and 25.1c). See Shaer and Hornecker (2010) for a detailed introduction to research on tangible interfaces.

The chapter begins by identifying key underlying theoretical and design-based drivers for engaging with tangibles in learning contexts, detailing the features of tangibles that underpin their perceived value for learning. Drawing across findings from the research field, the next section outlines emergent design themes, providing key illustrative research examples. The chapter then outlines a number of key research issues for tangible learning environments, and proposes key future research directions.

2. DESIGN DRIVERS FOR LEARNING

A number of inherent properties of tangible technologies make them appealing for supporting learning tasks. Their physical nature exploits our familiarity with the physical

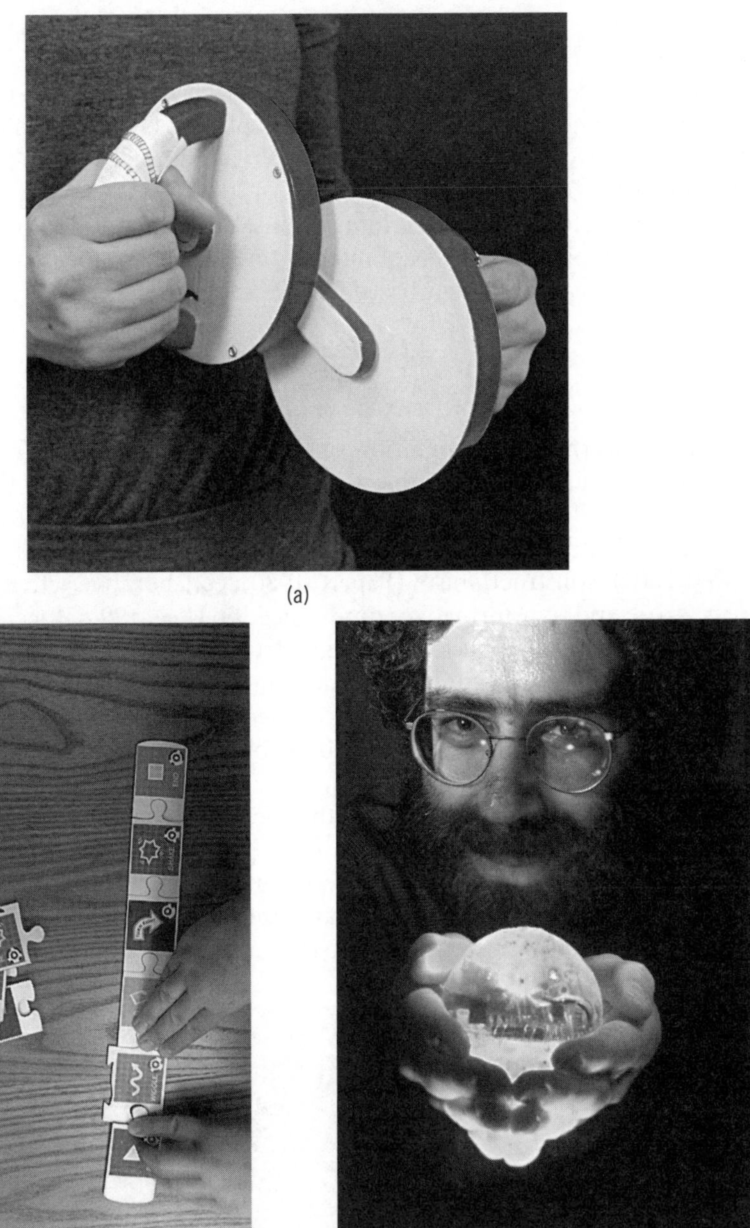

(a) (b) (c)

Figure 25.1 Examples of tangible systems designed to support learning.

world and enhances interaction in new ways that might foster more hands-on, physically engaging approaches to learning (Ishii, 2008). At the same time they offer new experiences through augmenting objects and action-on-objects with digital media (e.g. sound, narration, images, text or animation). Physical objects coupled with digital information in this way allow access to more or different information than is normally available in the immediate physical environment. For example, FlowBlocks links visual representation of electricity flow with physical blocks (Zuckerman, Grotzer & Leahy, 2006); Topobo (Raffle, Parkes & Ishii, 2004) offers a construction kit which can record and play back physical motion; or invisible scientific concepts can be dynamically linked to physical entities in the world, e.g. the LightTable (Price, Pontual Falcão, Sheridan & Roussos, 2009; see Figure 25.2).

The potential for flexibly combining physical artefacts and environments, sensor technologies and representations is of interest to designers in the context of learning from various theoretical and design-based perspectives.

2.1. Theoretical Perspectives

2.1.1. Developmental Psychology Approaches

Theories of learning and cognition offer a plausible rationale for designing tangible interaction to supporting learning (e.g. see also O'Malley & Stanton-Fraser, 2004). In particular, tangible interfaces are compatible with constructivist theoretical concepts that include hands-on engagement; experiential theories of learning (e.g. Bruner, 1973; Dewey, 2001); constructionism (Papert, 1980); collaborative activity (Pontual Falcão & Price, 2010); and transformative communication (Pea, 1994; Price, 2008).

Constructivist approaches (e.g. Piaget, Bruner) to learning advocate the active creation and construction of knowledge, and contrast with transmission models of learning. Piaget (1972) proposes that children's knowledge is initially focused on the manipulation of concrete materials, but through a process of internalisation they become able to think at higher levels of abstraction. Vygotsky (1978), on the other hand saw external action as a basis for children to 'internalise' the more abstract concepts they are learning (or practising) through physical interaction, e.g. planning. A key mediating process for this is independent exploration and discovery learning, where learners have the opportunity to test out and explore different ideas, and examine the consequences (e.g. Bruner 1973; Dewey 2001). Hands-on learning, where learners can explore through manipulation,

Figure 25.2 The LightTable.

building and creating, forms the foundation for constructionist approaches (Papert, 1980), which underpins much work on tangibles in the form of construction kits (e.g. Topobo, Raffle et al., 2004; Programmable beads, Resnick et al., 1998). These theoretical ideas correspond to the functional and interactional properties of tangibles, where physical interaction can be enhanced with digital representation. Yet, providing new technologies for learning that build on these ideas is complex: combined physical-digital environments increase the design parameters extensively.

2.1.2. Embodiment/Physicality

Recent work in embodied cognition has explored the idea that higher-level, supposedly abstract forms of cognition might be grounded in and built on top of the activity of sensori-motor systems (Barsalou & Wiemer-Hastings, 2005; Lakoff & Johnson, 1999). There is a wealth of evidence to suggest that physical actions are linked to cognition. For example, Glenberg and Kaschak (2002) report a phenomenon in language comprehension that they call the *action-sentence compatibility effect*: participants were asked to judge whether sentences were sensible or nonsense by either pushing or pulling a lever. If the sentence implied movement in one direction, this interfered with the participants' ability to move the lever in the opposite direction, suggesting the cognitive process interfered with action planning.

Theoretical work on embodied cognition has been adopted by some in the tangibles community who explore whether the physical manipulation of tangible artefacts might help to support learning, through engaging the same sensori-motor systems used in thinking about more abstract domains.

2.1.3. Motivation and Engagement

Physical objects have long been considered effective for fostering perceptual and sensory playful educational experiences (e.g. as used by Froebel in the schools he set up in 1837). Their similarity to toys makes them familiar to children, stimulating positive emotional associations, thus promoting engagement (Resnick et al., 1998). Their fun and 'motivating' qualities have inspired the development of various tangible systems, e.g. SystemBlocks and FlowBlocks, BitBall, and Thinking Tags. Fun and enjoyment are closely related to motivation, and are known to support learning and be effective in children's development (e.g. Clements, 1995; Ryan and Deci, 2000; Malone and Lepper, 1987).

2.1.4. Conceptual Frameworks

A number of conceptual frameworks around tangible technologies and their functionality have been developed (cf. Mazalek & Hoven, 2009). Early frameworks provide descriptive taxonomies, which specify configuration of different systems, but say little about the relative strengths and weaknesses of different designs in terms of interaction (e.g. Ullmer and Ishii, 2001; Koleva, Benford, Hui Ng & Rodden, 2003; Fishkin, 2004). More recent frameworks focus on human interaction and the relationship between design and interaction experience (Zuckerman, Saeed & Resnick, 2005; Hornecker and Buur, 2006). Other frameworks provide the basis for analysis, for example, Antle (2007), drawing on literature from cognitive psychology, identifies five properties of tangible systems for designers to consider, primarily concerning physical-digital mappings; or for empirical research approaches specifically for learning (Marshall, 2007; Price, 2008). Although many do not focus on learning per se, they are all important in informing design.

2.2. *Design-Based Approaches*

A number of projects have taken a design-based approach to develop tangible systems to support learning through prototyping and iteration. For example, Garzotto and Bordogna (2010) have carried out work with children with severe cognitive, linguistic and motor disabilities. They experimented with augmenting the existing low-tech paper materials that are already used by children in schools so as to link them with multimedia resources. In an iterative design-based approach they have highlighted a number of potential benefits of using tangible artefacts relating to emotional, cognitive and motor control, as well as benefits for non-disabled children involved in the design process.

A second design approach has been to explore the technical possibilities for supporting learning, an approach that can be described as 'technology inspired' (Rogers et al., 2002). For example, Ryokai Marti and Ishii (2005) describe the I/O brush, which uses a camera and sensors to enable children to 'pick up' colours and textures from the world and make paintings with them.

3. THEMES FOR DESIGN

A central theme that emerges from research on tangible learning environments is the possibility to promote exploratory interaction, to engender discovery learning. This is true for both non-collaborative and collaborative environments, and for single tangible systems, such as FlowBlocks or Topobo, as well as more complex systems such as the LightTable or 'of Pages and Paddles'. In this chapter we identify four key themes around explorative learning interaction through tangible interfaces and highlight the important associated design considerations. Each theme is illustrated with selected empirical examples, together with design issues that they raise.

3.1. *Representational Properties and Design*

Different forms of external representations have been shown to influence interaction and cognition (e.g. Kirsch, 2010) in a variety of ways. The representational properties of tangible interfaces are of particular interest given the diversity of representational media offered through these systems, ranging from the physical properties of the objects to the various properties of associated digital representations. The increased degrees of freedom, in terms of design choices, offer challenges to understanding the differential benefits and disadvantages of design combinations for learning.

3.1.1. *Representation Location*

Tangible technologies lend themselves to flexible linking of artefacts to representation. One design choice concerns the location of the digital representation relative to the physical object(s) (e.g. discrete—output is on a separate screen display; co-located—input and output are contiguous, the digital effect is directly adjacent to the artefact; embedded—within the object itself). Price et al.'s (2009) work explored the effect of different locations of visual representation related to interaction space. A comparative study investigated children's interaction with a tangible environment designed to enable students to explore light behaviour with objects. In one condition discrete representation was used, i.e. the location of digital visual representation was separate from the manipulation of object location, while in the other the digital representation was co-located with the physical objects. Findings suggest that the different location of representation (discrete, co-located or embedded) lends itself to representing concepts at different levels of detail. An embedded representation infers something going on inside the object, such as the light waves being absorbed, or transmitted; the co-located representations effectively show events that are closely coupled to the physical objects, but become problematic when illustrating, for example, refraction when the object itself is 'covering' the surface where the digital image is displayed. The discrete representation on the other hand enabled these details to be clearly displayed (Figure 25.3).

This is useful for developing design ideas particularly considering the different affordances of the representational opportunities—both physical and digital.

3.1.2. Physicality of Objects

The physical properties of tangibles are also important. The concrete nature of objects and physical interaction is thought to be beneficial for learning, being familiar to children, and offering a foundation from which to abstract symbolic relations from concrete instances of phenomena (O'Malley & Stanton-Fraser, 2004). However, some debate remains over the specific relationship between action and manipulation of representation, which is not yet well understood and is worthy of further investigation (Manches & Price, 2011). Antle, Droumeva and Ha's (2009) work explored differences in interaction between mouse-based and tangible-based interfaces using a jigsaw puzzle activity. Findings suggest that physicality through object (as opposed to mouse) manipulation encourages more epistemic actions, i.e. actions which change the world to ease task completion (e.g., rotating a Tetris shape to better understand what it looks like in different orientations), and supports more exploration. Such actions make difficult mental representation tasks explicit, and thus work as a form of cognitive support, whilst also fostering explorative forms of interaction. This would seem to suggest that the different manipulative properties of tangibles allow behaviours that are related to learning to be influenced by changing the 'cost' of carrying out particular kinds of interface actions (cf., O'Hara & Payne, 1998). However, more work is needed to understand the role of epistemic action for learning—is it the action of manipulation itself or the resultant representation that is important here? (Manches & Price, 2011).

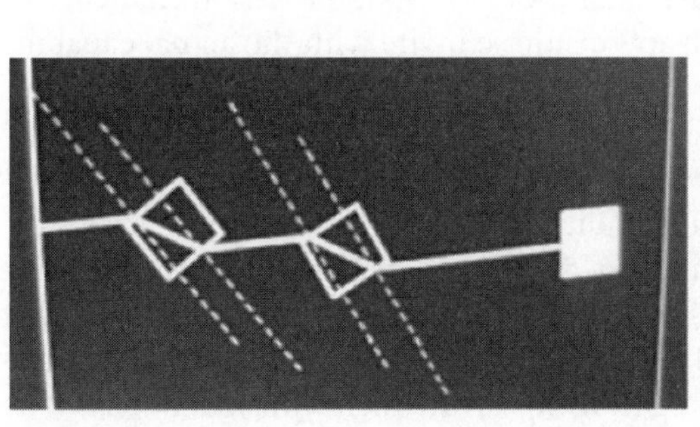

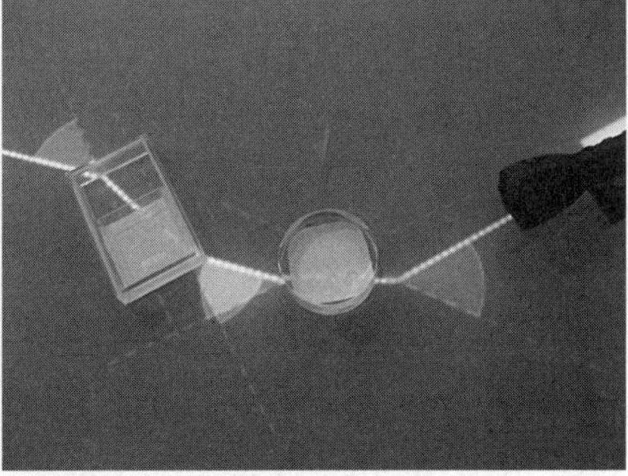

Figure 25.3 Discrete and co-located displays of refraction.

3.1.3. *Physical-Digital Mappings: Linking of Action and Effect*

The physical nature of tangibles inherently fosters physical action, e.g. manipulation. The linking of such actions and digital effect in terms of mapping between physical representation, physical action and digital representation—in other words physical-digital mappings—are critical in mediating interaction and an important design issue. Much work in this area draws on Lakoff and Johnson's seminal work on metaphor. Lakoff and Johnson (1999) suggest that communication and language show the extension of our experiences within our own body through the use of metaphor, which shapes our communication as well as the way that we think, act and perceive more abstract concepts. They describe image schemas and conceptual metaphor. Image schemas are recurring sensori-motor patterns that structure our experience—the basic ways through which we learn to interact with the world as children. For example, the CONTAINER schema is abstracted across our own experience of using containers of various kinds. We begin as children by placing objects in and out of containers, we learn that containers can hold items, and can be full or empty, and that containment is transitive: if a ring is in a box and someone is holding the box, then they are also holding the ring. Lakoff and Johnson suggest that these image schemas, which are abstracted from concrete experience, can through a process of metaphorical extension be used to enable expression of more abstract ideas. For example, Lakoff and Núñez (2000) suggest that Boolean Logic is an extension of the sensori-motor CONTAINER schema, with the same inferential structure of IN, OUT and transitivity, originally developed through experiences with real containers. This idea of embodied conceptual metaphors forms the basis of the design of many systems where mapping action to digital effects is central to interaction with the system (e.g. Price & Pontual Falcão, 2009; Antle, Corness, & Droumeva, 2009). For example, Bakker et al.'s (2012) Moving Sound (MoSo) Tangibles was a set of tangible artefacts that afforded different kinds of movement which mapped metaphorically onto the pitch, volume and tempo of sounds that children were able to manipulate to explore and learn about the abstract qualities of sound.

Price and Pontual Falcão (2009) analysed the effect of 'literal physical correspondence' design choices on learners' interpretations of light behaviour, i.e. objects acted as themselves: the torch represented a torch and the blocks behaved according to their 'real' physical properties (colour, opacity, shape and texture). Findings suggest that the designer's choice of correspondence does not necessarily result in learners inferring the same correspondence metaphor. Indeed, Hornecker and Dünser's (2009) study on tangible augmented reality showed how 'breakdown' in physical-digital mappings can detract from the learning experience. In particular they highlight the design challenge of matching 'the physical affordances and the actions these invite with the actual capabilities of the digital system and with users' understanding of interaction' (p. 106).

3.2. *Designing for Fun, Affect and Engagement*

Many studies highlight the fun and engaging quality of tangible technologies. For example, The Hunting of the Snark demonstrated successful use of tangibles for engendering playful learning: spontaneous exploration, which increased through experiencing unexpected events (Price & Rogers, 2003). With Topobo, a tangible assembly kit, children were reported to develop affective relationships with their constructions, while the simplicity of the interface was found to encourage playful expression through rapid experimentation (Raffle et al., 2004). While tangibles can be used to create novel, playful and pleasurable learning environments, which engage children in exploratory and reflective activities, other research suggests that children can become distracted by technology, through technical malfunctioning or breakdowns in physical-digital mappings (Hornecker & Dunser, 2009).

However, measuring fun and engagement is challenging, being dependent on the particular definition of 'engagement'. In emerging technology learning environments this challenge is heightened due to novelty and 'enchanting' factors (Read, MacFarlane & Casey, 2002), the potential for the Hawthorne effect (Draper, 2010) and the tendency for new artefacts to skew data on learning (Taylor, 2006). Measures of fun and engagement primarily focus on subjective measures (e.g. survey data using Likert scales (e.g. Ryan, 2006); rating scales (e.g. Read et al., 2002; 2006)); and/or objective measures (e.g. number of positive (smiles, laughter) and negative expressions (frowns, signs of boredom) (Read et al., 2002); amount of time spent on and off task (Africano et al., 2004; Inkpen et al., 1999) observation analysis (Xie, Antle & Motamedi, 2008)). More recent work has sought to establish detail on the properties of the environment that foster engagement to specify ways in which learners are 'engaged' in tangible environments, and to understand the implications for design (Price & Pontual Falcão, 2011). This analysis of 'engagement' in tangible environments that foster exploratory learning activity, determined three key foci of interaction: the learning concept, the tangential activity within which the learning concept is explored, and the technology itself. Findings suggest that each of these aspects leads to different forms of engagement, but the relationship between them can support the learning process: engaging with a tangential activity facilitated cognitive engagement with the learning domain concepts; while engaging with technology to understand the basics of the system's functioning fostered higher levels of conceptual abstraction. The design challenge that arises for developers is how to make effective links between the tangential activity, the functionality of the technology and the learning domain to create engaging environments that foster learning.

3.3. Designing for Collaboration

A third design consideration is how to design tangible learning environments that foster collaborative interaction. Collaboration can be important in promoting exploratory forms of interaction, and for fostering discovery learning. A broad range of studies has shown how tangibles and shared surfaces, often through forms of conflict, can promote collaborative engagement and interaction (Piper et al., 2006; Hornecker, 2008; Fleck et al., 2009; Pontual Falcão & Price, 2009, 2010; Olson, Leong & Horn, 2011).

Fernaeus and Tholander described how children working together to program their own simulations using tangible objects are able to use physical movement to signal a change in attention or to spatially index an interface object (2006), and how tangible artefacts can be used outside the interactive space to support social organisation (2005). In an informal comparison between children's interactions with physical paper prototypes and an interactive surface prototype, Marshall et al. (2009) show how children can use different mechanisms to mediate disputes over the control of interface objects, with subtle gestures, such as moving an object out of someone else's reach or closing fingers around it, being used when working with physical materials, whereas much more forceful and potentially disruptive actions such as pushing someone else out of the way or closing off an area of the space with both arms were used by the children using the interactive surface.

Similarly, Pontual Falcão and Price's studies (2010) of the LightTable showed how interference supported collaboration. Many instances where one child's actions 'interfered' with another's and provoked unexpected events in the dynamic display, were successful in provoking curiosity, drawing attention to relevant instances of the learning phenomena, engendering exploratory and inquiry activity, and promoting verbal negotiation and synchronisation of actions. Key design factors cited to influence interference include: having multiple resources enabling all participants to actively contribute to and engage in the activity; multiple simultaneous inputs enables each participant to physically engage in the activity at the same time, removing the need for sequential collaborative activity. Dynamic digital feedback shows immediate cause and effect through action, which renders 'surprise' or unexpected events to be visually explicit; a shared visual field means that they can readily see each others' actions.

These studies also illustrated how the design of the representation location influences collaborative interaction. Studies showed how a co-located design promoted a high level of awareness of others, and provided a common and unique focus of attention. Everyone's actions on the objects and the consequent digital effects were visible to all participants on the shared surface, which facilitated collective exploration and collaborative knowledge construction (Pontual Falcão and Price, 2010). In contrast, a discrete mode design where input and output were physically separate made the action–effect relationships less clear and awareness of others' actions problematic, and learners tended to work by themselves (Price et al., 2009).

3.4. Designing for Special Needs

A further development in empirical work on tangibles and learning is in the support of groups with special educational needs. Farr, Yuill and Raffle (2010a) described how a group of children on the autistic spectrum engaged in more social activities (i.e. more cooperative play, on-looking, and parallel play) when playing with Topobo, a tangible construction kit with kinetic memory, than when playing with conventional Lego. Similarly, Farr, Yuill, Harris and Hinske (2010b) showed how a configurable narrative play set, the Augmented Knights Castle, encouraged more collaborative play and less solitary play in a group of children on the autistic spectrum than a non-configurable version of the same set. Garzotto and Bordogna (2010) have experimented with augmenting existing low-tech paper materials used in schools with children with severe cognitive, linguistic, and motor disabilities so as to link them with multimedia resources. In a sustained design-based approach, they have highlighted a number of potential emotional, cognitive, and motor control learning benefits as well as benefits for non-disabled children involved in the design process. Hengeveld et al. (2009) examined how tangible interaction could support shy children in developing social skills and being accepted by their peers. They developed a tangible application for toddlers (ages 1–4) with multiple disabilities. They claimed multiple benefits that they attributed to tangibility, e.g. that the TUI is closer to a toddler's usual style of exploration, that the interface slowed down their interaction allowing more control over its timing, and that it provided more opportunities for facial, gestural and verbal expressions by the children. These statements were based on weekly 30-minute sessions with 15 children, for a period of six weeks. However, the methodology used (retrospective interviews with speech therapists and questionnaires after six weeks and no related observations and quantitative analysis) indicates that the conclusions should be treated with some caution.

4. THE EVALUATION CHALLENGE AND FUTURE RESEARCH

The design and development of tangible technologies specifically for learning, either for formal educational contexts or informal learning events, currently faces some ongoing challenges, particularly with respect to evaluating their learning value.

4.1. Evaluation Challenges

While increasing work has researched tangible technologies for learning, the need for more extensive evaluation remains: validation of whether the systems support learning process or outcomes is important, as well as better understanding of how and when learning is fostered. The field still faces some key challenges (e.g. see Price, 2007). The novelty of the environments inherently makes them motivating and fun for participants, a key finding across studies. The need for longitudinal studies is critical to factor out these findings and establish the sustainability and long-term effects of tangible systems for learning. Yet novelty is also seen as a core part of the appeal of tangibles, 'simply the novelty of seeing objects that would normally be regarded as inanimate, doing unexpected things, such as controlling the behaviour of a program or responding intelligently' (Xu, Read & Sheehan, 2008, p. 98).

A related key challenge is in establishing whether, how and when tangibles are effective in real-world settings—in the classroom, museums, or informal learning contexts. The novelty of such environments has meant that the majority of studies have been lab-based, or at least artificially contextualised in educational settings. This suggests the need for more 'natural-based' studies, where tangible systems are deployed in the context of their intended use, with the personnel involved in using them, e.g. teachers, curators, parents. Yet, there are differential costs and benefits to undertaking 'in the wild' studies or lab-based approaches to evaluation.

REFERENCES

Africano, D., Berg, S., Lindbergh, K., Lundholm, P., Nilbrink, F., & Persson, A. (2004) Designing tangible interfaces for children's collaboration. In: *Extended Abstracts of the Conference on Human Factors in Computing Systems CHI'04*, ACM Press, Vienna, Austria.

Antle, A. (2007) The CTI framework: informing the design of tangible systems for children. *Proceedings of the 1st International Conference on Tangible and Embedded Interaction*, ACM Press, 195–202.

Antle, A. N., Corness, G., & Droumeva, M. (2009) What the body knows: exploring the benefits of embodied metaphors in hybrid physical digital environments. *Interacting with Computers: Special Issue on Enactive Interfaces*, Elsevier, 66–75.

Antle, A. N., Droumeva, M., & Ha, D. (2009) Hands on what? Comparing children's mouse-based and tangible-based interaction. In *Proceedings of Interaction Design for Children (IDC'09)*, ACM Press, Italy, 80–89.

Bakker, S., Antle, A., & Van Den Hoven, E. (2012) Embodied metaphors in tangible interaction design. *Journal of Personal and Ubiquitous Computing, 16*(4), 433–449.

Barsalou, L. W., & Wiemer-Hastings, K. (2005) Situating abstract concepts. In D. Pecher and R. Zwaan (Eds.), *Grounding Cognition: The role of perception and action in memory, language, and thought* (pp. 129–163). New York: Cambridge University Press.

Bruner, J. (1973) *Going Beyond the Information Given*. New York: Norton.

Dewey, J. (2001) *Democracy and Education*. Pennsylvania State University.

Draper, S. W. (2010) The Hawthorne, Pygmalion, Placebo and other effects of expectation: some notes. Available at: http://www.psy.gla.ac.uk/~steve/hawth.html (accessed 22 January 2013).

Farr, W., Yuill, N., & Raffle, H. (2010a) Social benefits of a tangible user interface for children with autistic spectrum conditions. *Autism, 14*(3), 237–252.

Farr, W., Yuill, N., Harris, E., & Hinske, S. (2010b) In my own words: configuration of tangibles, object interaction and children with autism. *Proceedings of the 9th International Conference on Interaction Design and Children*, New York, USA, pp. 30–38.

Fernaeus, Y., & Tholander, J. (2005) 'Looking at the computer but doing it on land': children's interactions in a tangible programming space. In *HCI2005*, pp. 3–18.

Fernaeus, Y., & Tholander, J. (2006) Designing for programming as joint performances among groups of children. *Interacting with Computers, 18*(5), 1012–1031.

Fishkin, K. P. (2004) A taxonomy for and analysis of tangible interfaces. *Personal and Ubiquitous Computing, 8*(5), 347–358.

Fleck, R., Rogers, Y., Yuill, N., Marshall, P., Carr, A., Rick, J., & Bonnett, V. (2009) Actions speak loudly with words: unpacking collaboration around the table. *Proceedings of Interactive Tabletops and Surfaces*, ACM Press, 189–196.

Garzotto, F., & Bordogna, M. (2010) Paper-based multimedia interaction as learning tool for disabled children. *Proceedings of the 9th International Conference on Interaction Design and Children*, New York, USA, pp. 79–88.

Glenberg, A. M., & Kaschak, M. P. (2002) Grounding language in action. *Psychonomic Bulletin & Review, 9*(3), 558–565.

Hengeveld, B., Hummels, C., Overbeeke, K., Voort, R., van Balkom, H., & de Moor, J. (2009) Tangibles for toddlers learning language. *Proceedings of the 3rd International Conference on Tangible and Embedded Interaction*, New York, USA, pp. 161–168.

Horn, M. S., & Jacob, R. J. K. (2007) Tangible programming in the classroom with Tern. *Proceedings of CHI'07 ACM Human Factors in Computing Systems (CHI Trends Interactivity)*, New York, ACM Press.

Hornecker, E. (2008) 'I don't understand it either, but it is cool': visitor interactions with a multi-touch table in a museum. In *IEEE Tabletops*, ACM Press.

Hornecker, E., & Buur, J. (2006) Getting a grip on tangible interaction: a framework on physical space and social interaction. *Proceedings of CHI 2006*, Montreal, ACM Press, 437–446.

Hornecker, E., & Dünser, A. (2009) Of pages and paddles: children's expectations and mistaken interactions with physical-digital tools. *Interacting with Computers, 21*(1–2): 95–107.

Inkpen, K. M., Ho-Ching, W., Kuederle, O., Scott, S. D., & Shoemaker, G. B. (1999) This is fun! We're all best friends and we're all playing: supporting children's synchronous collaboration. *Proceedings of the Conference on Computer Support for Collaborative Learning* CSCL'99, Palo Alto, USA.

Ishii, H. (2008) Tangible bits: beyond pixels. *Proceedings of the 2nd International Conference on Tangible and Embedded Interaction*, New York, ACM Press.

Kirsch, D. (2010) Thinking with external representations. *AI & Society, 25*(4), 441–454.

Koleva, B., Benford, S., Hui Ng, K., & Rodden, T. (2003) A framework for tangible user interfaces. *Physical Interaction Workshop on Real World User Interfaces. Mobile HCI*, Udine, Italy.

Lakoff, G., & Núñez, R. E. (2000) *Where Mathematics Comes From*. New York: Basic Books.

Lakoff, G., & Johnson, M. (1999) *Philosophy in the Flesh: The embodied mind and its challenge to Western thought*. New York: Basic Books.

Malone, T. W., & Lepper, M. R. (1987) Making learning fun: a taxonomy of intrinsic motivations for learning. *Learning and Instruction, 3*: 223–253.

Manches, A., & Price, S. (2011) Designing learning representations around physical manipulation: hands and objects. *Proceedings of the 10th International Conference on Interaction Design and Children*, Ann Arbor, MI, ACM Press.

Marshall, P. (2007) Do tangible interfaces enhance learning? *Proceedings of 1st International Conference on Tangible and Embedded Interaction*, USA.

Marshall, P., Fleck, R., Harris, A., Rick, J., Hornecker, E., Rogers, Y., et al. (2009) Fighting for control: children's embodied interactions when using physical and digital representations. *Proceedings of ACM CHI 2009 Conference on Human Factors in Computing Systems*, pp. 2149–2152.

Mazalek, A., & Hoven, E. van den (2009) Framing tangible interaction frameworks. In 'Tangible Interaction for Design' a special issue of *AIEDAM, 23*, pp. 225–235.

O'Hara, K. P., & Payne, S. J. (1998) The effects of operator implementation cost on planfulness of problem solving and learning. *Cognitive Psychology, 35*, 34–70.

Olson, I. C., Leong, Z. A., & Horn, M. S. (2011) 'It's just a toolbar!' Using tangibles to help children manage conflict around a multi-touch tabletop. *Proceedings International Conference on Tangible, Embedded, and Embodied Interaction*, Funchal, Portugal. ACM Press, pp. 29–36.

O'Malley, C., & Stanton-Fraser, D. (2004) Literature review in learning with tangible technologies. *Nesta Futurelab Series*, Report 12.

Papert, S. (1980) *Mindstorms: Children, computers and powerful ideas.* New York: Basic Books.

Pea, R. D. (1994) Seeing what we build together: distributed multimedia learning environments for transformative communications. *Journal of the Learning Sciences, 3*(3), 285–299.

Piaget, J. (1972) *The Principles of Genetic Epistemology.* New York: Basic Books.

Piper, A. M., O'Brien, E., Morris, M. R., & Winograd, T. (2006) SIDES: a cooperative tabletop computer game for social skills development. *Computer Supported Cooperative Work*, ACM Press, pp. 1–10.

Pontual Falcão, T., & Price, S. (2009) What have you done! The role of 'interference' in tangible environments for supporting collaborative learning. *Proceedings of the 8th International Conference on Computer Supported Collaborative Learning*, CSCL'09, Rhodes, Greece, pp. 325–334.

Pontual Falcão, T., & Price, S. (2011) Interfering and resolving: how tabletop interaction facilitates co-construction of argumentative knowledge. *International Journal of Computer-Supported Collaborative Learning, 6*(4), 539–559.

Price, S. (2007) Ubiquitous computing: digital augmentation and learning. In N. Pachler (Ed.), *Mobile Learning: Towards a Research Agenda* (pp. 33–54). London: WLE Centre for Excellence, Institute of Education, University of London.

Price, S. (2008) A representation approach to conceptualizing tangible learning environments. *Second International Conference on Tangible and Embedded Interaction* (pp. 151–158). Bonn, Germany.

Price, S., & Pontual Falcão, T. (2009) Designing for physical-digital correspondence in tangible learning environments. *Proceedings of the 8th International Conference on Interaction Design and Children*, Como, Italy, pp. 194–197.

Price, S., & Pontual Falcão, T. (2011) Where the attention is: discovery learning in novel tangible environments. *Interacting with Computers, 23*(5), 499–512.

Price, S., Pontual Falcão, T., Sheridan, J. G., & Roussos, G. (2009) The effect of representation location on interaction in a tangible learning environment. *Proceedings of the Third International Conference on Tangible and Embedded Interaction*, Cambridge, UK, pp. 85–92.

Price, S., & Rogers, Y. (2003) Let's get physical: the learning benefits of interacting in digitally augmented physical spaces. In J. Underwood & J. Gardner (Eds.), *Computers & Education: Special issue: 21st Century Learning, 43*, 137–151.

Raffle, H. S., Parkes, A. J., & Ishii, H. (2004) Topobo: a constructive assembly system with kinetic memory. *Proceedings of the Conference on Human Factors in Computing Systems CHI'04*, ACM Press, Vienna, Austria.

Read, J. C., & MacFarlane, S. J. (2006) Using the Fun Toolkit and other survey methods to gather opinions in child computer interaction. *Interaction Design and Children, IDC2006*, ACM Press, Tampere.

Read, J. C., MacFarlane, S. J., & Casey, C. (2002) Endurability, engagement and expectations: measuring children's fun. *Proceedings of the 1st International Conference on Interaction Design and Children, IDC'02*, ACM Press, Eindhoven, the Netherlands.

Resnick, M., Maryin, F., Berg, R., Boovoy, R., Colella, V., Kramer, K., et al. (1998). Digital manipulatives: new toys to think with. *Proceedings of the SIGCHI Conference on Human Factors in Computing Systems, CHI'98*, Los Angeles, USA, pp. 281–287.

Rogers, Y., Scaife, M., Harris, E., Phelps, T., Price, S., Smith, H., et al. (2002) Things aren't what they seem to be: Innovation through technology inspiration. In B. Verplank, A. Sutcliffe, W. Mackay, J. Amowitz, & W. Gaver (Eds.), *Designing Interactive Systems* (pp. 373–379). ACM, London, 25–28 June.

Rogers, Y., Price, S., Randell, C., Stanton-Fraser, D., Weal, M., & Fitzpatrick, G. (2005) Ubi-learning integrates indoor and outdoor experiences. *Communications of the ACM, 8*(1), 55–59.

Ryan, R. M., & Deci, E. L. (2000) Self-determination theory and the facilitation of intrinsic motivation, social development, and well-being. *American Psychologist, 55*: 68–78.

Ryokai, K., Marti, S., & Ishii, H. (2005) Designing the world as your palette. *Proceedings of Conference on Human Factors in Computing Systems (CHI'05)*, ACM Press, pp. 1037–1049.

Shaer, O., & Hornecker, E. (2010) Tangible user interfaces: past, present and future directions. *Foundations and Trends in HCI, 3*(1–2), 1–138.

Taylor, J. (2006) Evaluating Mobile Learning: What are appropriate methods for evaluating learning in mobile environments? In M. Sharples (Ed.), *Big Issues in Mobile Learning: Report of a workshop by the Kaleidoscope Network of Excellence Mobile Learning Initiative*, University of Nottingham, pp. 24–26.

Ullmer, B., & Ishii, H. (2001) Emerging frameworks for tangible user interfaces. In Carroll, J. (Ed.), *Human Computer Interaction in the New Millennium* (pp. 579–601). New York: Addison-Wesley.

Vygotsky, L. S. (1978) *Mind in Society: The development of higher psychological processes.* (Edited by M. Cole, V. John-Steiner, S. Scribner & E. Souberman). Cambridge, MA: Harvard University Press.

Xie, L., Antle, A., & Motamedi, N. (2008) Are tangibles more fun? Comparing children's enjoyment and engagement using physical, graphical and tangible user interfaces. *Proceedings of the 2nd Conference on Tangible and Embedded Interaction, TEI'08*, ACM Press, Bonn, Germany.

Xu, D., Read, J., & Sheehan, R. (2008) In search of tangible magic. *Proceedings of 22nd British HCI Conference*, Liverpool, UK.

Zuckerman, O., Saeed, A., & Resnick, M. (2005) Extending tangible interfaces for education: digital Montessori-inspired manipulatives. *Proceedings of the SIGCHI Conference on Human Factors in Computing Systems, CHI'05*, pp. 859–868, Portland, USA.

Zuckerman, O., Grotzer, T., & Leahy, K. (2006) Flow blocks as a conceptual bridge between understanding the structure and behavior of a complex causal system. *Proceedings of the 7th International Conference on Learning Sciences*, Indiana, pp. 880–886.

26

AN INTRODUCTION TO TECHNOLOGY ENHANCED LEARNING DESIGN IN POSTGRADUATE MEDICAL EDUCATION

Niall Winters

1. INTRODUCTION

Postgraduate medical education in the UK has undergone significant change in recent years. Primarily, this is because of the European Working Time Directive (EWTD) which means that a trainee's working week is an average maximum of 48 hours, resulting in a time constraint on training which could result in a discontinuity of a trainee's experience due to increasingly distributed rotation rotas. As part of an overall approach to the continuous review and improvement of medical training in light of the EWTD, the role that new and emerging technologies can play has received renewed interest. Indeed, the 'application of learning technologies' has been identified as an emerging theme in the medical education literature (Harden, 2006). However, we argue that in order to make appropriate use of learning technologies in medical training, a more significant focus needs to be placed on learning design and design methodologies. By learning design, we mean the design of the software applications and their associated activities within a teaching context.

The nature of what is meant by a learning technology can differ between areas. In postgraduate medical education exemplar learning technologies include simulation, e-portfolios and social media, each with a different level of embeddedness within current teaching practice. We briefly discuss each of these here, along with their underlying motivation of use.

Medical simulation refers to the use of approaches and models in which trainees can practise and develop their skills without any risk to patients. Popular approaches include the use of role-play and realistic mannequins. A core underlying rationale for this is the understandable focus on patient safety: as noted by Okuda et al. (2009) '[a]s patients become increasingly concerned that students and residents are "practicing" on them, clinical medicine is becoming focused more on patient safety and quality than on bedside teaching and education'.

E-portfolios allow trainees to collect and critically reflect on data related to their professional practice. These data can be easily shared with their supervisor. E-portfolios are widely used by the Royal Colleges in the UK, and the motivation for doing so is stated by the Royal College of General Practitioners (RCGP) as follows:

> Its [the e-portfolio's] prime function is to be an educational tool that will record and facilitate the management of the journey of clinical and personal development through learning. It is the system used to record the evidence collected through the application of the WPBA [workplace based assessment] tools. It might be described as the 'glue' which holds the curriculum learning and assessment together.
>
> (RCGP, 2012)

The third technology that has received a lot of attention in recent years is social media. However, much of the research has focused on its use in the undergraduate curriculum and on generating statistics regarding how many doctors are using social media tools (e.g. Wu et al., 2011; McGowan, Vartabedian, Miller & Wasko, 2011) and what they need to know (McGee and Begg, 2008) in order to do so effectively. However, there has been very little research into the ways in which social media can be used as a *learning technology* to support postgraduate medical education.

An important rationale for the medical education community's focus on learning technology is the belief in its potential effectiveness. Post-implementation, it is usual to critique a learning technology with respect to its effectiveness, either for improving medical training or for improving patient outcomes. While there may be issues with this as an evaluation approach within the education community (based on their experience of similar evaluative criteria in support of technology enhanced learning (TEL) interventions, see for example http://www.nosignificantdifference.org/), the fact remains that this approach maintains its validity within the medical education community. Based on this, it is therefore appropriate to question the cyclic nature of this approach. This seems to follow a traditional—but nevertheless outdated—waterfall model of technology development and implementation. The key steps in this process are:

1. *Requirements gathering*: Determine the technical specifications that defines the purpose of the system.
2. *Design*: Develop the system to meet the requirements determined in step 1.
3. *Implementation*: Roll out the system for the user.
4. *Verification*: Test any issues *in-situ* and address them.
5. *Maintenance*: Keep the system running over time.

Evaluation can be viewed as fitting within the fourth step of this process, i.e. can we verify that the learning technology met its initial requirements? In the worst case, the outcome of such a 'top-down' model of design and implementation is that the learning technology is not fit-for-purpose, replicates existing solutions, or does not meet the needs of users within the context of existing cultures of work.

This chapter investigates a different approach to design and evaluation that takes place over the course of the development of any TEL tool. The approach is designed to better address the needs of supervisors and their trainees. Working in this way has the benefit of catching problems early, thus avoiding potentially costly learning technologies that do not seem to meet their stated aim.

2. A PARTICIPATORY APPROACH

A distinctly different approach to the 'top-down' design and implementation of a TEL tool is to use participatory design (Kensing & Blomberg, 1998). This approach emphasises the role of the users (and/or community) in the design and development of the tools they will use. Therefore, instead of simply having them 'feed into' the requirements analysis at the beginning of the project, they are seen as equal partners, involved in all stages of the design, development and implementation processes. Given this focus on the involvement and empowerment of people, it is no surprise that much work on the conceptualisation, refinement and implementation of participatory design has occurred within the development studies community (see Dearden & Rizvi, 2008 for a discussion of the links between those using participatory design in the technology and development communities, respectively). Drawing on this work, and noting that a key criterion is to empower people to be involved in solutions that address their own needs, Gow and Vascent (cited in Dearden and Rizvi, 2008) discuss the following advantages of participation:

- People organise best around problems that they themselves consider most important;
- Local people tend to make better economic decisions and judgements in the context of their own environment and circumstances;
- Voluntary provision of labour, time, money and materials to a project is necessary condition for breaking patterns of dependency and passivity; and
- Local control over the amount, quality and benefits of development action helps make the process self-sustaining.

Looking at this from the perspective of TEL in medical education, the clear way forward is for supervisors and trainees to be more involved in the design of their learning technologies. The claim being made is that if this were the case, they would be better organised and they could make more informed decisions about what the technology should do for them. This would result in more sustainable interventions that have the additional positive outcome of reducing the current dependency on unsuitable technologies.

While this is an idealised position, it nevertheless has merit based on the outcomes of sustainable participatory development projects analysed in the social studies of science literature—see, for example, the Bush Pump (de Laet and Mol, 2000). However, the process of engaging in a successful participatory design process is non-trivial. Heeks (1999) and Dearden and Rizvi (2008) both raise concerns and key questions that need to be addressed by researchers before delving into any participatory process. Here the questions raised by Heeks (1999) are contextualised to the area of TEL in postgraduate medical education:

- *What is the context?* The emphasis on context can be understood as gaining a good insight into the training approach both in terms of educational practices (by supervisors and trainees) and technical infrastructure. It should also be made clear that context is relevant not only for the *process* of participatory design but also for *developing* the learning software application. This is particularly true when designing new technology-based tools such as mobile phones. As discussed by

Kukulska-Hulme et al. (2009) 'mobile technologies can support diverse teaching and learning styles, and lend themselves particularly well to personalised, situated, authentic and informal learning. The common denominator is context: physical, technological, conceptual, social and temporal contexts for learning' (p. 22). This point is further supported by Roschelle (2003) who strongly promotes the identification of the 'simple things that technology does extremely and uniquely well' (i.e. their affordances), and thus being better able to 'understand the social practices by which those new affordances become powerful educational interventions'. This point is critical and cannot be overemphasised.

- *Who is initiating the participation?* A key point regarding the initiation of participation is that participants must want to be involved and have the skills and support to do so. Dearden and Rizvi (2008) note the need to concentrate on 'the skills and strategies required of practitioners', pointing out that 'participatory research has three key elements: power, people and praxis. In participatory processes, critical inquiry is informed by and responds to the experiences and needs of people involved.' Thus, the role of the researcher as a facilitator is critical to the success of the endeavour. The researcher must try their best to ensure that all of the key perspectives of participants are reflected in the participatory process and that any decisions taken are equitable.
- *Who is participation sought from, do they want to and can they take part?* Participation needs to involve all the key players, including trainees and they need to be adequately resourced to do so. For most, this means that time needs to be officially allocated to design activities. The role of the researcher is critical in ensuring that the participation process is structured to match participants' capabilities, particularly at the start of the process when the motivation, rationale and process of participatory design may be unfamiliar to them.

3. THE USE OF LEARNING THEORY IN POSTGRADUATE MEDICAL EDUCATION

A key choice to be made when designing any TEL intervention is the choice of underpinning learning theory. This choice will usually be informed by the researcher's perspective on how to best support trainees' learning practices. In medical education, the choice is made more complex by the fact that medical trainees are expected to be able to associate theory with practice directly. They need to understand, abstract and apply specialist theoretical knowledge in a practical and focused manner. Depending on their specialisation, they are required to work collaboratively and be expert communicators. Furthermore, during their training they need to become highly skilled reflective practitioners, so that they can continually improve their practice.

Despite this, medical education has traditionally focused on the development of the individual trainee and on their ability to work autonomously. According to Bleakley (2006) this means that there is a need to

> critically address the limitations of the current dominant learning theories informing medical education. An argument is made that such theories, which address how an individual learns, fail to explain how learning occurs in dynamic, complex and unstable systems such as fluid clinical teams.

The implication of this for designing a TEL intervention is that, unlike in most areas of learning technology research, the individualised structures contextualising medical training are very likely to have been in place for a long time. Thus, it is likely that the theories of learning in use will be those

> that focus upon an isolated individual rather than the sociocultural context for learning. The former include varieties of adult learning theory, experiential learning and reflective practice. In these approaches, the learner is viewed as an active agent, resonating with medicine's tradition of autonomy.
>
> (Bleakley, 2006)

This is not to say that the above approaches should not be used *where relevant* but instead to be explicit about the context in which the design of TEL interventions will take place. On the more positive side, there is a growing awareness of the potential benefits of socio-constructivist theories of learning (which, for example, surgical trainees are increasingly exposed to, given the nature of their team work). This is due to the self-reflectivity of the medical education community on the broad range of learning experiences trainees should be involved in. This means that, particularly within the context of a teaching hospital, training is not only about the development of trainees with respect to their competencies, skills and knowledge but it is also about how trainees work together within teams to collaboratively construct their knowledge:

> We need to know not only how established knowledge is constructed and reproduced, but how new knowledge is produced and held collaboratively in inherently unstable, complex systems. Socio-cultural learning theories are more powerful than those oriented to individual cognition when it comes to explaining how learning occurs in such systems.
>
> (Bleakley, 2006)

The challenge for TEL design is to be able to understand how a learning technology can be developed in order to support such knowledge construction in a complex setting. Research in this area is at an early stage and much remains to be done.

4. THE E-PORTFOLIO EXAMPLE

The position outlined up to this point has focused on the potential of bringing a participatory approach and an awareness of appropriate learning theories to TEL design in postgraduate medical training. At this stage, I want to contrast this somewhat idealised position—certainly to the extent that it has not been used at scale and has been restricted to small-scale pilot implementations—with a very practical example, the implementation and use of the e-portfolio in medical education. Specifically, the perspective of educational supervisors on the role the e-portfolio plays in supporting trainees and the challenges this raises for the ways in which technological solutions are implemented in practice will be discussed.

The e-portfolio was chosen because it is an example of a technology already embedded in practice and therefore helps to frame thinking—both positive and negative—regarding the design of future TEL interventions. Furthermore, the e-portfolio is a relatively mature technology in terms of its design and implementation and therefore has been subjected to critical analysis within the medical education literature. However, much of this work has focused on its 'effectiveness'. To take just one example, in a systematic review, Tochel et al. (2009) from NHS Education Scotland found 'good evidence that if well implemented, portfolios are effective and practical in a number of ways including increasing personal responsibility for learning and supporting professional development'. The interesting point here is the caveat 'if well implemented'. Our own research (Winters, Price, Oliver & Pelletier, 2012) has explored what implementation means on the ground for educational supervisors and their trainees. We found that, overall, educational supervisors and trainees supported the use of the e-portfolio in supervision but that it was viewed and used overwhelmingly as an *assessment tool* rather than a tool to support *developmental learning*. Essentially, rather than being used in a truly formative manner as was its intended design, in practice use was summative.

The way in which the e-portfolio frames and supports educational supervisory practice was also an issue. It was generally felt that the main downside of the e-portfolio was that it reduced aspects of supervision to a very procedural competency-based assessment: it became a tick box exercise, where there was not much freedom to go beyond the templates/forms. A typical comment from an educational supervisor was as follows:

> It is very competency-based and ticking boxes. There is one place where they can enter reflective practice but we don't really look into that when we do their annual reviews . . . because the Royal College, which sets all these standards, have given us the guidelines on, and it's basically a competency-based decision-aid making flowchart. (107)

The result of this was that a culture had developed around the e-portfolio that meant for some it was not viewed as a learning tool:

> Some educational supervisors also feel it is a tick box exercise. It will take a huge culture change to consider it as a learning tool. (106)

However, it was seen as valuable to educational supervisors as a way of looking back at a trainee's profile, helping them make sense of current problems, claims and so on. Educational supervisors felt that the e-portfolio represented the curriculum for trainees, so that supervisors could identify what trainees have not yet learnt as well as what they have experienced. They liked the fact that the e-portfolio allowed for the collation of, and access to, feedback on trainees in the one place:

> It is so much easier for people to get multi-source feedback when you are using an electronic system . . . it's so easy. (108)

However, there was clear recognition that practice varied widely:

> The e-portfolio is a tool. And it can be used badly or it can be used properly, and it can be used to its fullest intent, or not. (103)

> I think the ethos behind e-portfolios is excellent, encouraging reflective writing, storing your performance, allowing you to complete your ARCPs. [. . .] I think however

> the way people use it is different from the way it was designed to be used. Some people don't fully engage. They don't use the more touchy-feely aspects of e-portfolio such as the reflective areas, such as the skills log. (109)

What is interesting here, is that our findings support Bleakley's critique of the constrained nature of learning theories in postgraduate medical education. The e-portfolio is seen as supporting the individual trainee. There is no reference to its potential as a way of supporting more collaborative forms of learning and training.

Educational supervisors' perspective on how trainees view the e-portfolio: On the whole, educational supervisors felt that trainees viewed the e-portfolio negatively, seeing it as something they had to do rather than a tool to support their training and development:

> I think you are over-estimating the adult nature of their learning. They are very busy and they view the current NHS e-portfolio as something that they do to be monitored. (106)

> I think it is still quite mixed. Some people see it as a complete chore, and are very anti it and then we do have to use the stick approach I'm afraid. [. . .] They don't see it as being useful. (108)

In some cases, the e-portfolio is not treated as being an integral part of their training or clinical work and is instead something trainees fill in as a requirement:

> The systems trainees are given are not integrated into their work. (106)

This non-integration can lead to e-portfolios being filled in at the last minute, thus reflecting a crammed snapshot of practice, rather than a longitudinal view of how trainees are developing:

> [N]ow some of them are great, they keep it ticking over but then there are some, who, you know you can tell, you look at their e-portfolio and nothing and then there is concentrated activity before they have to do something. And even if you say you have to do X number of assessments within a 6- or an 8-month period. That still doesn't mean they have to spread them equally over that period. They can still choose to cram it all in at the last moment. (108)

These findings support our earlier assertion regarding the importance of context in the design of a TEL intervention. While the intentions regarding implementation of the e-portfolio were excellent, how this was instantiated in practice was very different. Such a position can only have been reached because the ways in which the e-portfolio should respond to supervisor and trainee needs were not fully explored at an early stage. Again, a more participatory approach to design and development could have ameliorated the chances of this occurring.

5. THE WAY AHEAD

TEL design is a significant challenge. Educational researchers have long promoted the benefits of appropriate design to encourage the learning. In particular, findings from the recent £12m Technology Enhanced Learning Research Programme (TLRP-TEL, 2012) in the UK stress that we need 'to design technology so that it addresses problems of learning and teaching', rather than relying 'on the crumbs of technologies designed for other purposes'. Approaching TEL design in this way will allow for an understanding of how technology-mediated learning happens. However, '[w]ithout that understanding, the evidence informed design of technology-enhanced learning systems is hampered, limiting our ability to provide rich and effective educational experiences' (ibid., p. 17).

In the context of postgraduate medical education, we have seen that participatory design methodologies and appropriate learning theories can support the developments of the kinds of learning interventions suggested by TEL researchers. However, the design challenge is complex. Understanding the context of the educational setting, its socio-cultural history and existing practices in order to inform the design of a TEL tool in a participatory manner is non-trivial. For one thing, it is time consuming but if done in an appropriate manner, the long-term benefits resulting from a learning technology designed to be embedded in practice are worth the effort and resources. The alternative of 'imposing' technical solutions in a 'top-down' manner is not recommended, as this has been shown to result in very limited take up and wasted resources.

Pragmatically, too, TEL tools in postgraduate medical settings have their own set of complexities. The needs of postgraduate medical trainees are very different, not just in terms of obvious things such as speciality and year but in determining how TEL tools can be tailored to both help trainees-in-difficulty and support excellence. Scaling up any learning technology that results from a participatory design approach is challenging and would require local training schemes. Finally, 'on-the-ground' issues such as technical barriers to implementation (including weak WiFi and mobile phone coverage in hospitals) and privacy concerns need to be addressed at the outset of the design process.

REFERENCES

Bleakley, A. (2006) Broadening conceptions of learning in medical education: the message from teamworking, *Medical Education*, 40: 150–157.

Dearden, A. & Rizvi, H. (2008) Participatory design and participatory development: a comparative review. In: *PDC'08: Experiences and Challenges, Participatory Design Conference*, Indiana University, Bloomington, IN, USA, October 1–4.

de Laet, M. & Mol, A. (2000) The Zimbabwe Bush Pump: mechanics of a fluid technology, *Social Studies of Science*, 30(2): 225–263.

Harden, R. (2006) Trends and the future of postgraduate medical education. *Emergency Medicine Journal*, 23: 798–802.

Heeks, R. (1999) The tyranny of participation in information systems: learning from development projects. Development Informatics Working Paper Series, Number 4, Institute for Development Policy and Management, University of Manchester.

Kensing, F. & Blomberg, J. (1998) Participatory design: issues and concerns. *Computer Supported Cooperative Work*, 7: 167–185.

Kukulska-Hulme, A., Sharples, M., Milrad, M., Arnedillo-Sánchez, I. & Vavoula, G. (2009) Innovation in mobile learning: a European perspective. *International Journal of Mobile and Blended Learning*, 1(1): 13–35.

McGee, J. & Begg, M. (2008) What medical educators need to know about 'Web 2.0'. *Medical Teacher*, 30: 164–169.

McGowan, B., Vartabedian, B., Miller, R. & Wasko, M. (2011) The 'meaningful use' of social media by physicians for learning. *Medicine 2.0 2011 Conference*. See: http://www.medicine20congress.com/ocs/index.php/med/med2011/paper/view/764. (For slides see: http://www.slideshare.net/cmeadvocate/medicine-2pt0-meaningful-use-of-so-me-by-physicians-final.)

Okuda, Y., Bryson, E. O., DeMaria, S. Jr, Jacobson, L., Quinones, J., Shen, B. & Levine, A. I. (2009) The utility of simulation in medical education: what is the evidence? *Mount Sinai Journal of Medicine*, 76(4): 330–343.

RCGP (2012) The trainee ePortfolio. Last accessed 23 July 2012, from http://www.rcgp-curriculum.org.uk/eportfolio.aspx.

Roschelle, J. (2003) Unlocking the learning value of wireless mobile devices. *Journal of Computer Assisted Learning*, 19(3): 260–272.

TLRP-TEL (2012) System upgrade: realising the vision for education (http://telit.org.uk/).

Tochel, C., Haig, A., Hesketh, A., Cadzow, A., Beggs, K., Colthart, I. & Peacock, H. (2009) The effectiveness of portfolios for post-graduate assessment and education: BEME Guide No. 12. *Medical Teacher*, 31: 299–318.

Winters, N., Price, N., Oliver, M. & Pelletier, C. (2012) A scoping exercise to explore the use of Web 2.0 and mobile technologies to support faculty development in postgraduate medical education across LP/LEP networks in London: Final Report, London Deanery (http://www.lkl.ac.uk/niall/Deanery/Web2andMobileEducationalSupervisionFINAL.pdf).

Wu, R., Rossos, P., Quan, S., Reeves, S., Lo, V., Wong, B., Cheung, M. & Morra, D. (2011) An evaluation of the use of smartphones to communicate between clinicians: a mixed-methods study, *Journal of Medical Internet Research*, 13(3): e59.

27

THE CONVERGENCE OF INFORMAL LEARNING AND FORMAL EDUCATION IN A UBIQUITOUS ENVIRONMENT

Heeok Heo, Il-Hyun Jo, Kyu Yon Lim, Hyeon Woo Lee and Soonshik Suh

1. INTRODUCTION

Technological advances such as mobile devices, context-aware computing and handheld personal organizers provide educators with opportunities and challenges to enhance teaching and learning, as Mark Weiser already proposed in the early 1990s. He envisioned the world of ubiquitous computing, where computers are available unobtrusively and invisibly to users throughout the physical environment (Weiser, 1993). When technologies become pervasive and connected with wireless networks, information will be accessible anytime anywhere, suggesting new paradigms of interaction inspired by computational capabilities (Abowd & Mynatt, 2000). Eventually, in the future, devices will be seamlessly integrated into the environment, enhancing our everyday activities including teaching and learning experiences. This trend of ubiquitous computing triggered this study in which the ultimate purpose is to promote meaningful learning from converging formal education and informal learning.

Individuals in real settings outside of schools can experience various objects in authentic contexts. Experience in real life provides individuals with natural and informal ways to learn new things as well as to use and transform existing knowledge and skills. However, not all of the experience in real settings may be transformed into meaningful learning, when people have little intention to learn, or when they are not aware of what they have experienced. Given that the experiences in informal settings can play a key role as the clues for enhancing systematic and efficient learning for formal learning, inadvertent yet rich experience from the real world should be further explored. That is why many educators have paid attention to developing ways to integrate experience in informal settings with formal education (Coffield, 2000; Resnick, 1987; Sefton-Green 2004; Clough, Jones, McAndrew, & Scanlon, 2008). Ubiquitous computing technologies can assist this integration by capturing individuals' feelings and thoughts in the real world and connecting to systematic school learning. This study tried to find a better way to capture natural experiences and integrate them with school learning with the help of technology. Following is a virtual scenario providing the overarching story of this study:

> Jane is an elementary school student, and her family is going to visit an amusement park on a sunny spring day. In the car headed toward the park, Jane is using her mobile device to search information about the amusement park and sending messages to her friends to boast about her trip. When she arrives at the main gate, Jane's device automatically runs the amusement park mobile application, giving her a welcome message. Hereafter, corresponding information is pushed to the device whenever Jane passes by the specific attractions and rides. Jane stands in a long line waiting for the pirate ship ride, and then the mobile application pushes information about the pirate ship ride, for example, a general history of the pirate ships, introduction to the ride, and scientific principles behind the ride. In addition, a message pops up so Jane becomes aware of the association between the science project carried out in her school and the pirate ship ride. Now Jane gets on the ride, and she makes a video of the pirate ship ride in order to share with her science project teammates. Jane becomes more interested in the science project, and her experience in the amusement park provides her with a critical clue to implement in her science project.

In this scenario, an elementary school student is experiencing a convergence between a school project and family activity, supported by ubiquitous computing technology. The researchers' aim in this study is to develop a model that illustrates a learning process in a ubiquitous computing environment. In other words, the suggested model entitled "convergent learning in a ubiquitous environment" (CLUE), will embrace formal education and informal learning in a seamless manner. Given that the ontological characteristics of ubiquitous computing are physically pervasive and phenomenologically embodied, learning experience in this environment will be different from the past. CLUE is a new, technology-enhanced approach that converges different forms of learning into a real setting. In this chapter, theoretical backgrounds, components of the CLUE model, design considerations and the implementation of the model will be described.

2. THEORETICAL BACKGROUND

2.1. The Integration of Informal Learning and Formal Education

Recently, much attention has been paid to informal learning, as formal education in schools has been facing challenges in coping with new societal and technological changes (Coffield, 2000; Resnick, 1987; Sefton-Green 2004). Informal learning happens voluntarily in minimally structured situations, without pre-set learning resources and predesignated teachers (Clough et al., 2008). That is, informal learning is likely to happen in a highly personalized manner based on learners' particular needs, interests, and past experiences. The claim that people learn through understanding and solving real-world problems in everyday lives shows that informal learning is the most natural way of learning. However, not all experiences in informal settings turn out to be meaningful, since it is spontaneous and unplanned (Greenhow & Robelia, 2009). On the other hand, formal education occurring mostly in school settings tends to be effective and efficient in providing learners with systematically organized and qualitatively decent information. Yet, there exist demerits of formal education: It is difficult to evoke learners' genuine interest due to the decontextualized learning contents, and it is also difficult to transfer knowledge obtained from school settings into real-life situations.

To overcome the limitations of informal learning and formal education, many educators discussed the interrelationships between these two different learning contexts (Coffield, 2000; Dewey, 1916/1980). More specifically, there have been some efforts to combine formal education and informal learning by employing student-oriented activities such as field trips. Most field trips, for example, have been conducted as a subsidiary strategy to enhance learning in formal settings (Kisiel, 2005; Phillips, Finkelstein, & Wever-Frerichs, 2007). To illustrate, it is necessary to provide learners with opportunities to contextualize their knowledge learned from the school curriculum into the real setting. On the other hand, learners' new experiences from informal settings can be limited to what they have already learned from classrooms. Various experiences in informal learning are important given that unexpected events in the informal settings arouse individuals' genuine senses and perception on real objects, and sometimes require their cognitive involvement beyond school learning.

This study supposes that the advancement of ubiquitous computing can open up a new way to integrate informal learning into formal education. When new technologies are pervasive in real life, teachers or instructional designers can engage learners by providing timely assistance in real settings. This relatively new approach can bring informal learning into a systemic learning environment by generating associations among bits and pieces of accidental learning experiences.

2.2. Situated Learning and Community of Practice

Scholars who are concerned with knowledge, recognition and learning in a ubiquitous society frequently discuss the approach of situated cognition and situated learning (Chen, Kao, Yu, & Sheu, 2004; Klopfer, Yoon, & Rivas, 2004). Often times, especially in formal education settings, skills and knowledge are operationalized differently from how real-world experts use them in real life (Choi & Hannafin, 1995). Thus, it is likely that learners who pass exams in formal settings may fail to transfer the same knowledge and skills into the real settings. From the standpoint of situated cognition, learners should be engaged with the context where knowledge is embedded in a natural way rather than in a decontextualized, simplified manner (Brown, Collins, & Duguid, 1989).

The situated view on learning does not only emphasize being physically present in a certain space and time, but has a stronger focus on working with others who are continually transforming themselves through their actions and relations in the world (Driscoll, 2005). According to Lave and Wenger (1991), learning can occur through situated activities that combine learners' personal activities in everyday lives with the socio-cultural settings in which learners belong. This socio-cultural situatedness is optimal when individuals participate in communities of practice where groups of people share a concern, a set of problems, or a passion about a topic, and deepen their knowledge and expertise in a specific area by continuous interactions (Lave & Wenger, 1991). That is, an individual can acquire knowledge and skills through the process of becoming a full participant in a socio-cultural practice.

Individuals may be involved in various communities; for instance, an elementary school student might be a member of a school, a family, and a play group. These communities affect the student's daily life and experience. An experience in the play group can be a trigger for school work and, at the same time, school learning can help the student become engaged deeply in an everyday game with friends from the play group. Every experience can be intertwined with each other in a tacit way. Ubiquitous technology can integrate these various activities from different communities in a meaningful way, and relate unintended experiences to the intended learning done in school.

Prior research results support the claim that learners' participation in authentic learning within the community of practice promoted knowledge acquisition, collaboration skill, and higher-order thinking skills in traditional or multimedia-based instruction settings (Herrington & Oliver, 1999; Lajoie, 2008; Utley, 2006). More recently, there exist efforts to investigate the application of ubiquitous technology to realize situated cognition, and the studies provided design suggestions from technological and pedagogical perspectives (Chu, Huang, & Tsai, 2010), although empirical studies are still rare (Zheng, 2010). These implications from prior research guided the researchers to design a model entitled Convergent Learning in a Ubiquitous Environment (CLUE).

3. DESIGN CONSIDERATIONS

3.1. CLUE Model

CLUE is a learning environment where learners experience situated-collaborative learning processes by being connected virtually with his or her community at any time at any place using ubiquitous computing technologies.

Based on the implications from the literature review, CLUE was designed according to the following assumptions. First, human experience occurs through continuous reconstructions and rigorous interactions between personal tendencies and the surrounding environment (Dewey, 1916/1980). Second, there are always some special moments when individuals feel the need for some assistance to figure out uncertain things in everyday life (Wretsch, 1998). At these times, they need to have various kinds of support for processing and using information, to ignite reflective thinking, and to connect them with others who may be concerned with them. Third, humans cannot understand every physical component and their hidden meanings and values in an external situation. Fourth, tools and resources are available for maintaining connections and valuable interactions among off-line and on-line communities. Fifth, teachers from formal settings can take on various roles to support learners in reconstructing meaningful experiences, through sensitive feelings, perceptive experience, logical thinking and collaborative activities in real settings, and then to continually open them toward subsequent experiences. In this environment, individuals can understand the intensive connectivity between abstract knowledge and real concrete situations, as well as obtain achievements beyond pre-set learning goals in formal settings.

The primary goal of CLUE is to build a learning environment in which learners can reconstruct and continually expand their own meaningful experiences through the processes of stimulating their feelings, perception and cognition in real informal settings, and to connect their experiences in formal school settings. The learning phases of CLUE are as follows (See Figure 27.1).

- *Provoking learning*: This is to make a possible connection between the unintentional sense and learners' cognition in real settings. It facilitates switching unexpected experiences into learnable and teachable moments. Since various feelings and actions in informal settings could be fragmented and scattered without any meaningful integration into genuine experiences, it is necessary to help learners

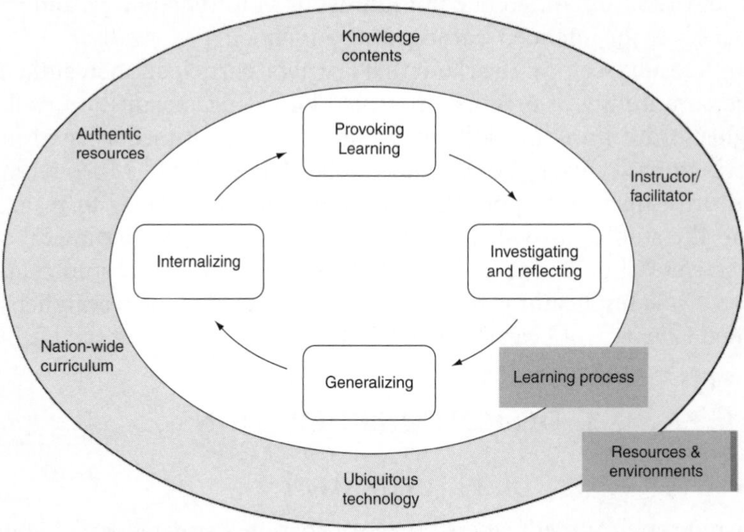

Figure 27.1 Conceptual framework of CLUE.

link those feelings and actions to generalized knowledge. This "provoking learning" may be triggered by a text message delivered by any technology, which involves a push from the instructor/designer or a pull from the user in CLUE.

- *Investigating and reflecting*: Once the unintentional experience and educational intention are successfully associated, individuals start to investigate various pieces of information and resources, and then reflect on them in action. This is very similar to a process of intellectualizing what at first is merely an emotional quality of the whole situation (Dewey, 1933, p. 109). Through this process, the personal experience can be articulated by language and becomes a socially consented meaning.
- *Generalizing*: Knowledge acquired from an authentic context needs to be transformed into a generalized form in order to be transferred into other settings and communicated to others. Classrooms, where the teacher facilitates learning and students meet their peers with similar intentions, are appropriate places for learners to bring in what they have learned and experienced from informal settings. At this point, learners can integrate unintentional everyday experiences into intentional learning goals and enhance collaboration with peers for achieving mutual learning goals.
- *Internalizing*: The process of generalization should lead to internalizing and personalizing for further learning attempts. As continuous and spontaneous learnability is a key attribute of the suggested model, the experience connecting informal and formal learning may be a clue for emerging conscious intention to new things and enhancing intrinsic interest to learn.

In order to successfully fulfill the whole process of integrating informal learning and formal education, the following components must be equipped in and outside of schools:

1. electronic knowledge contents accessible any time anywhere;
2. authentic objects provoking learners' emotion and curiosity in real settings;
3. flexible curriculum involving authentic experiences in informal settings;
4. teachers taking various roles for supporting learners; and
5. advanced technologies allowing seamless connections between informal learning and formal education.

3.2. Learning Context in CLUE Model

The learning context in CLUE is a physical and social context in which informal experience in real settings is integrated into structured experience in formal settings as a whole, and this integration enables the continuous reconstruction of experience. The following principles were considered in designing the learning context.

- Clarify how learners' experiences encountered in informal settings can be connected to their school learning.
- Prepare materials or devices to provoke learners' curiosity and cognitive thinking on real objects, and then embed these materials or devices into the informal setting.
- Maintain the connectivity among communities to which learners belong or among peers and colleagues with whom learners communicate regardless of location.
- Plan learning process and activities in class that integrate informal experiences.

3.3. Resources and Tools in CLUE Model

Resources and tools include e-Contents, learning tools, and communication tools. E-Contents, as a knowledge base, consist of relevant information, knowledge, and wisdom in web-based and/or mobile formats. For example, e-Contents can deliver opinions of experts, descriptions on specific objects, or a direction on how to use the provided advanced technology. Learning tools, on the other hand, are available for supportive learning activities such as concept mapping, visual thinking, note-taking and bookmarking during the process of learning. Lastly, interaction and communication among learners and teachers are enhanced by using electronic communication tools such as instant messaging, video chatting, blogging and discussion in both synchronous and asynchronous ways. These resources and tools are used for the following purposes:

- to accentuate the physical context of the place where the learner actually exists, and make connections with its related social context;
- to make visible some attributes of various objects in a certain physical place, stimulate different feelings and cognitions from what learners actually feel and think, and even connect learners to a virtual space;
- to allow learners to coexist temporarily and virtually, and merge different levels of experience as a whole entity.

4. IMPLEMENTATION: PRELIMINARY STUDY OF THE CLUE MODEL

4.1. Research Context

The preliminary study of CLUE was aimed at formative evaluation of the suggested model. For the preliminary study, an amusement park was chosen as the informal learning setting, and an elementary science class as the formal setting. Participants in this study used electronic devices, Ultra Mobile PCs equipped with a 7-inch LCD, a stylus pen, Windows XP operating system (tablet edition), a camera, and wireless LAN. Three fifth graders who fully participated in the entire process carried the portable PC with them at all times. Since participants were from a small town in Korea, they were relatively unfamiliar with using mobile devices for learning. The general academic achievement level of the participants was intermediate in terms of their grades achieved in the previous semesters.

The study followed the phases illustrated in Table 27.1.

A learning material as an e-Content delivered through the Ultra Mobile PC was developed to support students' experiences in the amusement park. The material included a road map, information of the attractions and learning contents that turn informal experiences into learnable and teachable moments. For example, the screen captures shown in Figure 27.2 explain how scientific knowledge indirectly relates to the pirate ship ride, which provokes learners' intention to learn. The information presented in Figure 27.3 encourages learners to record their feelings and thoughts to share with peers, which allows learners to generalize and reflect on their experience.

Learning tools such as note-taking, voice-recording, and making movies and photographs were available to support learning. Also, blogging, Skype meetings, and electronic bulletin boards were readily accessible for learners to promote communication among peers and between learners and teachers as well.

Table 27.1 Phases of Learning Experiences

Week		Formal setting	Informal setting
1	Activities	• Classroom instruction on 'energy' from the elementary school-level curriculum • Collaborative task: 'Create a story about energy'	NA
	Location	• Science classroom	NA
2	Activities	• Classroom instruction on 'energy' from the elementary school-level curriculum (cont.)	• Visit an amusement park. (Participants did not know from the start that there would be a learnable moment when they visited the park. That is, for participants, the purpose of visiting the amusement park was just to have fun.) • Guide scientific perspective through experiencing rides. • Facilitate learners to experience provoking, investigating and reflecting.
	Location	• Science classroom	• Amusement park (during weekend)
3	Activities	• Classroom instruction on 'energy' from the elementary school-level curriculum (cont.) • Student presentation on 'energy'	NA
	Location	• Science classroom	NA

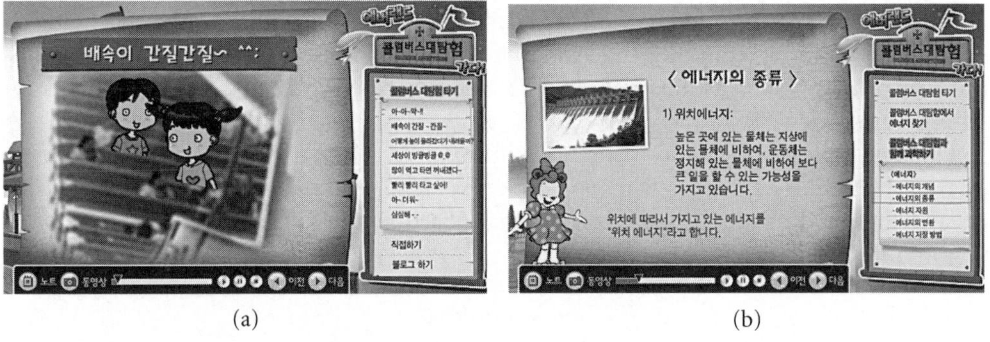

(a) (b)

Figure 27.2a and b Screen shots of the learning material: Provoking learning.

Figure 27.3 Screen shots of the learning material: Reflecting and generalizing.

4.2. Data Collection and Analysis

The main research question was to explore how learners would feel and act in given informal and formal settings. To answer the research question, this study employed qualitative methods to analyze the overall process and results of the implementation. First, audio-video recordings and unobtrusive observations were conducted by researchers throughout the whole process. Second, an unstructured interview was conducted to collect data about participants' perception on the informal learning experience. Three female students and a teacher who assisted them were interviewed. The students were fifth graders from a rural school and had never been to the specific amusement park before. They were selected from different science project groups by the teacher. The teacher explained the purpose of this trip in general to the participants, although he did not mention any explicit connection between the park visit and their science project. During the interviews, students were asked about their feelings and insights, focusing on situational contexts, technological availability, and lessons learned. Third, participants' learning products such as the final report, student-created contents, and personal storytelling were reviewed.

The data collected by various methods in this study were analyzed based on the four phases of CLUE. The interview responses were categorized independently by three coders and their coding results were combined. Subsequently, video recordings and observation notes were reviewed by the coders.

4.3. Findings

The findings from the qualitative study are as follows:

4.3.1. Provoking Learning

- *Consistency between physical space and learner's perceived context*: The e-Contents including general information about the amusement park and attractions stimulated students to be aware of the characteristics of the present physical space and the context in which learners were located.
- *Triggering a learnable moment*: This study assumed that students would wait approximately 30 minutes to ride a ride, which is a usual waiting time for a ride in the amusement park. Therefore, the researchers expected that if students were provided with content that provoked learning when they felt bored while waiting, they could switch their mind and cognition into learning mode in the amusement park. However, in the real setting of the study, the participants only waited 5 to 10 minutes for each ride, accordingly strategies for using the short waiting time more efficiently were required in order to trigger a learnable moment.
- *The value of everyday experience*: It was observed that the content including the value of everyday experience provided students with opportunities to make a connection between a ride in the amusement park and the classroom science project, which they valued as learning resources.

Student 2: Early on, I thought the Pirate ship ride was just an exciting, interesting thing . . . but it is more interesting to me now because I know that science is hidden in there.

4.3.2. Investigating and Reflecting

- *Converging entertaining context and learning context*: It was not easy to effectively converge students' cognition on "energy" and feelings about riding the pirate ship ride.

Student 3: I was a little bit frightened . . . I could not think about energy while I was on the ride . . . Anyway, there is some relationship between the pirate ship ride and energy. The ship swings up and down . . . kinetic energy . . . there might be a relationship.

In this case, the student felt fear while on the ride, so it was difficult for her to think about the topic of energy while riding the ship. This suggests personal feeling may take precedence over cognition, which is quite common in the real world.

4.3.3. *Generalizing*

- *Possibility for collaborative construction*: Participants had a struggle interacting with other students located in their hometown due to the limitation of wireless technology. However, they were finally connected with other students and discussed the science project, and they showed their intention to use the riding experience as an example for their project.

Student 2: After riding, I talked with my friends on Skype. At first, the video was slow and distorted . . . but audio was good. (skip) I talked with Hyun-a about the task. I will be able to use the ride as an example for kinetic energy later.

> *Observation note: The students seemed to be able to hear each other, so student 2 called her friends loudly and asked the same questions repeatedly. Later on, the technology worked fine.*

- *Using blogs for information sharing*: The blog was provided as a learning tool and assisted in creating and sharing information by research participants as well as other students from the learning community. In this study, there were two types of blogs; individual blog and learning community blog. Students participated more often in the learning community blog than their individual blogs to share information they collected. One of the communities used their blog for the final presentation of the science project.
- *Embracing various learning experiences*: The community, whose members visited the amusement park, reported about their experiences in the amusement park as well as live experiences of members from other real settings. In their presentation for the project, the use of slides, swings, and a jungle gym in a playground and the experience of other amusement parks were included. This means that the experiences from the amusement park inspired the students to connect the contents of the classroom science project with the real world and stimulated their curiosity for further experiences.
- *Personal responsibility for task completion*: After visiting the amusement park, the research participants showed a different attitude toward the science project from other students who did not visit the amusement park. The students who visited the amusement park were selected as presenters of their group and they worked very hard from a sense of responsibility which was caused by their perception that they were selected students for the amusement park visit.
- *Use of the pre-developed e-Contents*: The students did not actively use the e-Contents due to the technological limitations. Rather, asynchronous activities with peers, including reflections or thoughts through blogs, were more frequently observed.

4.3.4. *Internalizing*

- *Project presentation reflecting the amusement park experience*: In the final presentation, the learning communities whose members visited the amusement park appropriately linked the amusement park experience with the purpose of the project, even though it was not a requirement. The amusement park experience served as an important learning resource for understanding the "real experience related with energy."

- *Promoting changes in students' thinking*: Students who visited the amusement park indicated that their understandings of energy had been changed by completing this task. They also expressed that energy is very important and it is closely related with their everyday lives. However, students who did not visit the amusement park presented a general idea with little reflection on personal experience.
- *Providing clues for continuing development*: It was notable that various individual experiences were connected together under a mutual learning goal and then became collaboratively constructed collective knowledge. The product of collaborative construction would play a role as another starting point which continuously motivates learners in terms of constructing personal and collective knowledge.

5. CONCLUSIONS

At the very beginning, this study started with a question asking "what do individuals experience in ubiquitous environments?" and then made an attempt to theoretically build a ubiquitous learning environment in which informal learning and formal education converge together.

The results of this study are concluded as follows: First, participants were very impressed with the unexpected, informal learning experiences as well as new technologies. For them, the most interesting activity was to see and talk with their friends 200 kilometers away via computers while playing in the amusement park. Second, the preset e-Contents introducing some of the attractions in the amusement park were helpful in providing students with useful information and even provided them with scientific knowledge about the attractions. Even though a synchronous communication tool did not properly work at all times, most learning tools worked successfully and assisted the students. Third, there was some evidence that students encountered new challenges, connected new information to previous knowledge, and opened their thoughts toward a different world.

Results from this study suggest the following recommendations for further studies: First, implementations in different contexts must be carried out with recent technologies to revise the CLUE model and to enhance integration of informal experiences and formal learning. The theoretical assumption of the CLUE model was not fully implemented due to the technological limitations at that time. Recent development of information and communication technologies can better realize the gist of the suggested model.

Second, such external components as digital content, teacher education, resources in real context should be systematically organized to elaborate the CLUE model. For example, electronic devices are needed as physical objects to embed in the real world, so individuals can access the objects in both physical and virtual ways. Teachers also need to be aware of the importance of informal experiences in students' lives and the ways to combine them into the school curriculum.

REFERENCES

Abowd, G., & Mynatt, E. (2000). Charting past, present, and future research in ubiquitous computing. *ACM Transactions on Computer-Human Interaction, 7*(1), 3–28.

Brown, J. S., Collins, A. S., & Duguid, P. (1989). Situated cognition and the culture of learning. *Educational Researcher, 18*(1), 32–42.

Chen, Y., Kao, T., Yu, G., Sheu, J. (2004). *A mobile butter-fly watching learning system for supporting independent*

learning. Proceedings of the 2nd IEEE International Workshop on Wireless and Mobile Technologies in Education.
Choi, J., & Hannafin, M. J. (1995). Situated cognition and learning environments: Roles, structures, and implications for design. *Educational Technology Research & Development, 43*(2), 53–56.
Chu, H. C., Hwang, G. J., & Tsai, C. C. (2010). A knowledge engineering approach to developing mindtools for context-aware ubiquitous learning. *Computers & Education, 54*(1), 289–297.
Clough, G., Jones, A., McAndrew, P., & Scanlon, E. (2008). Informal learning with PDAs and smartphones. *Journal of Computer Assisted Learning, 24*(5), 359–371.
Coffield, F. (2000). *The Necessity of Informal Learning*. Bristol: The Policy Press.
Dewey, J. (1916/1980). Democracy and Education. In J. A. Boydston (ed.), *John Dewey: The Middle Works, vol. 9*. Carbondale, IL: Southern Illinois University Press.
Dewey, J. (1933). *How We Think*. Boston, MA: D. C. Heath and Company.
Driscoll, M. P. (2005). *Psychology of Learning for Instruction* (3rd ed.). Boston, MA: Allyn and Bacon.
Greenhow, C., & Robelia, B. (2009). Informal learning and identity formation in online social networks. *Learning, Media and Technology, 34*(2), 119–140.
Herrington, J., & Oliver, R. (1999). Using situated learning and multimedia to investigate higher-order thinking. *Journal of Educational Multimedia and Hypermedia, 8*(4), 401–421.
Kisiel, J. (2005). Understanding elementary teacher motivations for science fieldtrips. *Science Education, 89*(6), 936–955.
Klopfer, E., Yoon, S., & Rivas, L. (2004). Comparative analysis of palm and wearable computers for participatory simulations. *Journal of Computer Assisted Learning, 20*, 347–359.
Lajoie, S. P. (2008). Metacognition, self-regulation, and self-regulated learning: A rose by any other name? *Educational Psychology Review, 20*(4), 469–475.
Lave, J., & Wenger, E. (1991). *Situated Learning: Legitimate Peripheral Participation*. Cambridge: Cambridge University Press.
Phillips, M., Finkelstein, D., & Wever-Frerichs, S. (2007). School site to museum floor: How informal science institutions work with schools. *International Journal of Science Education, 29*(12), 1489–1507.
Resnick, L. (1987). Learning in school and out. *Educational Researcher, 16*, 13–20.
Sefton-Green, J. (2004). Literature review in informal learning with technology outside school. *A report for NESTA Futurelab (no. 7)*. Retrieved from http://www2.futurelab.org.uk/resources/documents/lit_reviews/Informal_Learning_Review.pdf.
Utley, B. L. (2006). Effects of situated learning on knowledge gain of instructional strategies by students in a graduate level course. *Teacher Education and Special Education, 29*(1), 69–82.
Weiser, M. (1993). Some computer science issues in ubiquitous computing. *Communications of the ACM, 36*(7), 75–84.
Wretsch, J. V. (1998). *Mind as Action*. London: Oxford University Press.
Zheng, R. (2010). Effects of situated learning on students' knowledge acquisition: An individual differences perspective. *Journal of Educational Computing Research, 43*(4), 467–487.

28

DESIGNING FOR MUSEUM LEARNING

Visitor-Constructed Trails Using Mobile Technologies

Kevin Walker

1. INTRODUCTION

Museums are broadly viewed as places of informal learning, and most people visit museums expecting to learn something (Moussouri, 2002; Ellenbogen, 2002; Falk and Dierking 2000; Falk, Moussouri and Coulson, 1998). My focus is not on measuring discrete 'learning outcomes', but on the processes by which visitors make meaning in relation to artefacts. According to Hooper-Greenhill (1999: 12), 'The process of meaning-making is the process of making sense of experience, of explaining or interpreting the world to ourselves and others. In museums, meaning is constructed from objects, and from the sites themselves'. What is crucial to museum meaning-making is linkage—between artefacts and visitors, and between different interpretations and ideas. Ham (1999) has shown that, in museums, the amount of information is not as important as the conceptual structure into which it is placed; such structures not only facilitate information integration but constitute most of what is remembered. This mirrors what many museum exhibitions generally do—present individual artefacts within a structure which links them together to form a larger narrative. And there is, according to McLellan (2006), substantial evidence of narrative as a meaning-making tool. Doering and Pekakirk (1996) believe that visitors to a museum arrive with their own 'entrance narratives'—a kind of internal storyline based on prior knowledge, which is then compared with the curatorial narrative(s) in a dialogic process. On the other hand, visitors with low subject knowledge willingly allow the museum to structure their visit to a certain extent (Smith and Tinio, 2008). Thus, there would seem to be scope for structuring visitors' personalised or collaborative knowledge construction.

Trails provide one way of linking individual artefacts in a narrative or thematic structure. This chapter investigates the concept of visitor-constructed trails across different topic areas, museums and visitor types. I focus on museums as informal places of learning which collect, display and interpret artefacts of some sort, for educational purposes, and not 'science centres' which utilise interactive exhibits to illustrate scientific concepts. Findings are analysed using a conceptual model grounded in museum learning and activity theory. The technologies of particular focus digital audio player/recorders.

2. TWO APPROACHES TO STUDYING MEANING-MAKING IN MUSEUMS

In the past two decades or so, the dominant approach to how people make meanings in, and from, museums has been Falk and Dierking's (2000, 1991) 'Contextual Model of Learning', which views meaning-making as both process and product, resulting from the integration, over time, of visitors' personal, physical and sociocultural contexts. The personal context encompasses an individual's prior knowledge, interests and beliefs, as well as motivations and expectations, choice and control. The physical context situates meaning-making 'in dialogue with the physical environment', according to Falk and Dierking (2008: 22). The sociocultural context includes visitor interactions within, and outside, their own social group.

According to Kaptelinin (2008: 6), the separation of context into three separate spheres permits a 'detailed understanding of the micro-dynamics of visitors' interactions in museums, which together are intended to depict the complexity of museum meaning-making'. But he contends that Falk and Dierking do not include a clear strategy for synthesising them into a whole (ibid.). Pierroux (2006) believes that viewing the personal, physical and sociocultural as separate contexts focuses too much on the assimilation of information by an individual visitor, treating context as an external, quantifiable variable. She also contends that the Contextual Model tends to freeze time at critical junctures, instead of looking at activity which has a history and which develops over time.

An alternative proposed by both Kaptelinin (2008) and Pierroux (2006) is based on activity theory. In activity theory (AT) as developed by Vygotsky (1978) and others, activities as a unit of analysis are seen in a rich social matrix of people, artefacts and other resources. Grounded in a social constructivist epistemology, AT foregrounds the social context of meaning-making without neglecting the role of the individual, regarding the boundary between individual and collective as overlapping. For example, in this view, competencies such as reading and writing begin as social functions and become internalised; conversely, they are externalised when a breakdown occurs, when knowledge is to be shared, or when activities are socially distributed.

In AT, activities are the 'minimal meaningful context' for analysing technology in use (Kuuti, 1991). AT subdivides activities into an 'object hierarchy' of activities, actions and operations (Leont'ev, 1978). Activities are seen to be driven by motives, which may be conscious or unconscious; actions are carried out to fulfil motives, and have conscious goals; and operations are subconscious, adjusting actions to situational changes. AT regards tools as mediating human actions and interactions in the world, differentiating physical from cognitive tools, and analysing an entire 'activity system'. While museums can be regarded as a physical context of meaning-making, the artefacts they collect and display have their own original contexts of creation and use, and are thus decontextualised and simultaneously re-contextualised in a new setting—usually the only physical setting in which visitors encounter such artefacts. Pierroux et al. (2007), therefore, discuss the 'double mediation' of tool-mediated meaning-making in museums, in which visitors' meaning-making can be mediated by museum artefacts as well as by technological and other tools. The authors propose that digital technologies can serve to bridge the 'activity contexts' of visitors with those of museum artefacts.

3. MUSEUMS' USE OF DIGITAL TECHNOLOGY

Technological tools can help to re-contextualise artefacts, for example in virtual re-creations of original contexts (Mintz, 1998: 25); in explorations of artefacts' design and use (Reynolds and Speight, 2008); by prompting visitors to look more closely at artefacts (ibid.); or by conveying scientific comparisons (Robinson, 1998: 50) or complex abstractions (Dierking and Falk, 1998: 60). While there is a tendency among curators to use computers to tell visitors more than they want to know about a topic, Mintz (1998: 32) contends that used well, technology can control the amount of information or expand visitors' options.

If, as Mintz (1998) claims, technology in museums gains legitimacy through its proximity to authentic artefacts, portable digital technologies could be considered more 'legitimate' through their use directly in the place of encounter between visitor and artefact. Small-screen presentations intended to mediate visitors' encounters with non-digital artefacts and environments can, however, add to the surfeit of information already in the museum environment, according to Fisher (2005).

4. LEARNING TRAILS

Peterson and Levene (2003) address the problem of navigating large amounts of data by drawing from Bush's (1945) concept of the 'Memex', a device to aid researchers in constructing and sharing trails through research data. In 'navigational learning' described by Peterson and Levene, a learner creates and edits a trail, and can then share it with others. Systematic recording and representation of a trail makes its use and sharing easier.

Initial implementations of an 'experience recorder' relied on automatic tracking of visitors' locations in a museum. However, the system generated huge amounts of quantitative data (Baker, Roussos and Levene, 2006), and reconstructing an accurate trail of a single visit required filtering out spurious data points and developing a complex algorithm (Papadogkonas, Roussos and Levene, 2006). In addition, the system relied heavily on quantitative location information, not qualitative data related to visitors' interpretations. While location-tracking technology can be very precise, without personal interpretation it can be meaningless, if for example a visitor is in front of a particular artefact but facing the other direction.

My intention in this research was thus to use qualitative data to focus on visitors' interpretations, with trails as a conceptual device for linking interpretations together, utilising off-the-shelf technologies such as many visitors already carry.

5. RESEARCH DESIGN

The following research questions were derived from a review of research on museums, technology and trails.

- (How) can trails be used to support meaning-making in museums?
- How do portable digital technologies mediate and support trail construction?

The most important data collection method used in this research was the recording of visitor monologues and dialogues using audio recording technology. The audio included semi-structured interviews, individual and group 'talk aloud' audio, and the products of trail construction in the form of audio trails. This diversity of recorded data affords a view into trail construction during the construction process, in reflection afterward, and in the final products constructed by the visitors.

5.1. Conceptual Model for Analysis of Trails: TrACE

To reconcile the Contextual Model of Falk and Dierking (2008) with AT, as described above, I devised a model specifically for design and analysis of trails, by situating the personal and social spheres of context as concentric rings around the visitor, and around an artefact encountered by the visitor; the artefact is additionally situated in a fixed physical context, which the visitor moves through. The encounter is mediated by tools and resources. A trail is conceptualised as a goal-driven process in which the visitor encounters a series of artefacts, the product of which is a re-contextualisation of artefacts from the physical to a virtual context, set within a thematic social context, with each artefact retaining its 'personal context'—its unique history and attributes. Trail construction is shown to take place within the broader physical context of the museum, while goal-setting and finalising of the finished trail can be completed either in or outside the museum. The model is shown in Figure 28.1.

Visitors' mediated encounters with artefacts were analysed individually and collectively using this model. Hereafter I refer to it as the TrACE model, for Trails of Activity Context Encounters. The iterative development of this model is detailed in Walker (2010).

6. TRAIL CONSTRUCTION BY ADULT VISITORS TO ART MUSEUMS

This study involved three London museums: Tate Modern, the British Museum, and the Victoria and Albert Museum (V&A). The sample included two adult individuals and one

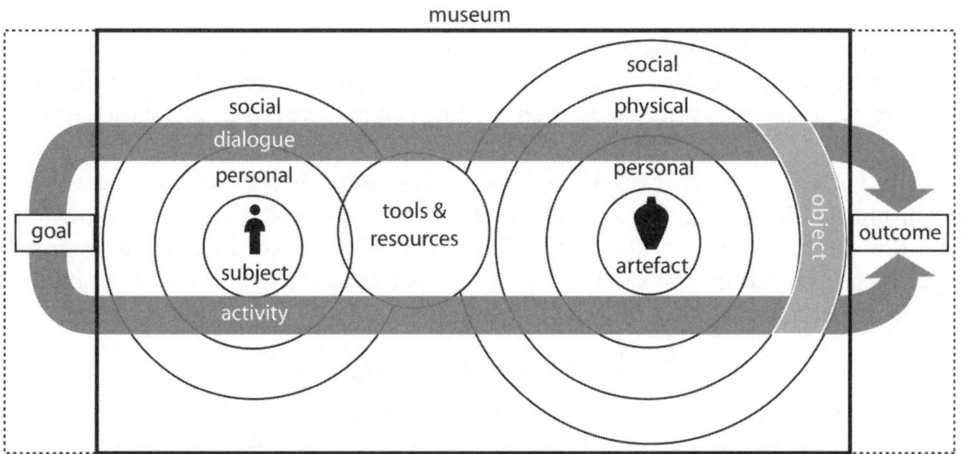

Figure 28.1 TrACE conceptual model.

pair, each of whom constructed trails using portable audio recorders. The sample was self-selected, being respondents to a call issued by me, via email, for participants, and they conformed to the average profile of adult casual museum visitors, who tend to have higher levels of education than the general population, and regularly attend cultural events and venues, though they may have little or no prior knowledge about a particular artist or exhibition.

I aimed to collect data for this study by means of 'experience recording' as described by Peterson and Levene (2003), but using readily available existing technology. A simple and seemingly effective solution was to record visitors' narration, or dialogue, as they navigated through a museum. I offered the option of using participants' own recording device, or an iPod recorder provided by me. Peterson and Levene envision an experience recorder as automatically tracking a visitor's location in the museum. However, I hypothesised that simple audio recording could eliminate the need for location-tracking technology if the visitor could simply speak the chosen location into the audio recording device. A precise location could be most easily pinpointed by reading an artefact label, or otherwise identifying an artefact of interest. Additionally, it could yield a valuable source of qualitative data, specifically visitors' own interpretations of artefacts and locations. The audio data from each trail were first transcribed by me, then analysed using the TrACE model. Names have been changed to protect anonymity.

6.1. Keith at the V&A

This trail was recorded in the China gallery of the V&A, which contains a mix of pre-historic, historical and contemporary artefacts. Keith is a social scientist living in London. An excerpt from one of his recordings follows.

> Recording 4 (Duration: 1:02)
>
> A big abstract painting, directly, or sort of right in the centre of the gallery, across from the, that sculpture . . . 'Dreaming'. Uh, it's watercolour and ink on paper, and it's by Chan Ky-yut [name spelled out]. It's from 2001, Canada. Um, it's big, it's about 12, 14 feet wide, by maybe 6 feet high. Uh, lots of different colours, looks quite contemporary. Um, very minimal and quite abstract.

From the transcript, Keith appeared to have selected individual artefacts based solely on aesthetic preference. He devoted most of the recordings to descriptions and locations of artefacts, reading text labels and even spelling out names. His trail is shown in Figure 28.2.

Keith visited a large portion of the gallery, choosing artefacts which appeared striking or unusual to him. He made little attempt to tie the artefacts together in the trail; in Recording 4, he referred to the artefact from the previous recording only as a means of describing his location. It is notable, however, that he restricted his trail to a single gallery, in contrast to the other trails collected in this study.

6.2. Tim at the British Museum

Tim is a computing lecturer living in New York City, and this trail was constructed during a visit to London to attend an academic conference. The following are excerpts from his trail.

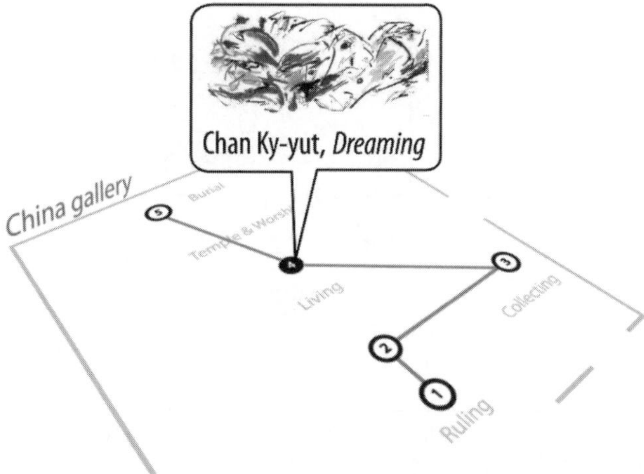

Figure 28.2 Representation of Keith's trail in the V&A's China gallery, with sections of the gallery labelled, and numbers representing each trail stop; one stop is highlighted with an image from the artist's web site.

> '. . . underscores how people everywhere deal with the tough realities of life, the challenges we all share with their many different responses.' Um, I kinda wanna go and see the Easter Island figure because after reading Collapse, I got really interested in Easter Island and how the um, they basically chopped down all the trees, and how that had everything to do with why the society died. And you know, he mentions in the book that you really just kinda wonder, What would make you chop down the last tree?
>
> [. . .]
>
> . . . sickness and dying. Just layers and layers and layers of pills. And, photos around the edge, of people from, you know various either illnesses, some x-rays, so-and-so taking his pills. I mean, the thing that strikes me about is, this really doesn't tell me anything about this whole line of pills in front of me. It just uses them as, sort of, wallpaper.
>
> [. . .]
>
> '. . . one man and one woman's life, and the various drugs they've taken over the course of a lifetime.' And um, that's a lot of drugs. It's actually pretty cool when you look at it that way.

Tim's trail is shown in Figure 28.3.

In contrast to Keith, Tim did not restrict his trail to a single gallery. Like Keith, Tim did not have a particular theme or goal in mind in navigating the museum. The first recording excerpted above was made at the entrance to the 'Living and Dying' gallery, where he read from a wall text introducing the gallery. He was then attracted by a large figure at the other end of the gallery, which reminded him of a book he read. Tim's next stop was a display of pills in the centre of the gallery, an art installation called Cradle to Grave. He expressed surprise at the lack of interpretation provided by the museum; in the subsequent recording, however, he had found a descriptive label.

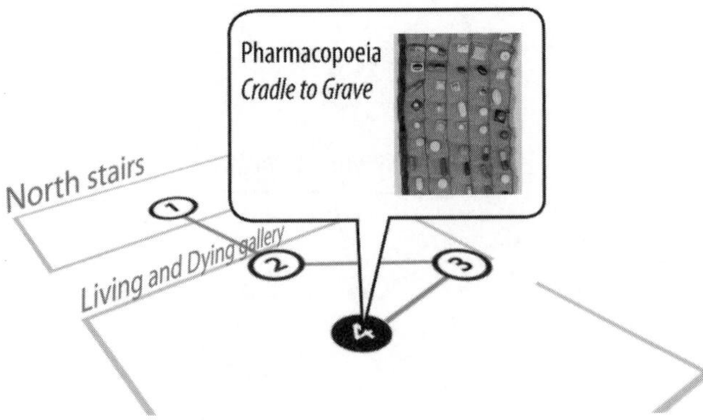

Figure 28.3 Representation of Tim's trail in the British Museum, with galleries labelled, and numbers representing each trail stop; one stop is highlighted using an image from the museum's web site.

6.3. Rachel and Adam at Tate Modern

Rachel is a London-based education researcher and former teacher. She created an audio trail with her partner, Adam, a musician, at Tate Modern, using her own digital audio recorder. The result was three digital files, with duration of 26:51, 21:27, and 2:27, respectively. The trail was recorded as a nearly continuous narration of the visit, Rachel carrying the recorder throughout, and the recording included her monologue as well as conversations between the pair.

Generally, the pair's references to particular artefacts were descriptive, the works identified by name in many cases, and most often these come with either a cursory reaction ('It's a nice painting of the sea though') or somewhat deeper interpretation ('He looks a bit worried, he has a furrowed brow'). A portion of the trail is shown in Figure 28.4.

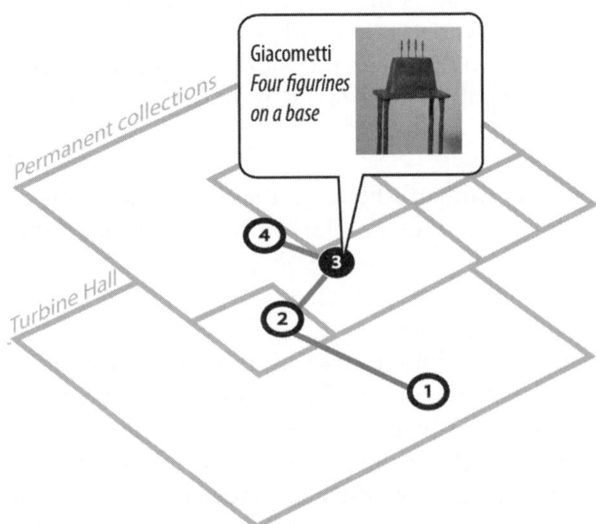

Figure 28.4 Portion of Rachel and Adam's reconstructed trail, shown stretching across two floors of Tate Modern, with one trail stop highlighted, using an image from the museum's web site.

6.4. Analysis of the Trail Data

The trails constructed in this study were intended to inform both research questions: to provide a baseline understanding of how adult visitors interpreted the trails concept (Question 1); and to investigate audio recording, as both a method of trail construction and a means of data collection (Question 2).

6.4.1. The Role of Contexts

The social context encompasses visitors' influences and interactions within their own social group, outside their social group, and in the broader cultural context. This is partly about how visitors communicate, for example by sharing facts, talking about their history or identity, using explanations and questions. This is found in the trails of Keith and Tim—specifically, sharing facts from text labels by reading them into the audio recorder. But for Rachel and Adam, closed-ended questions are much more frequent; for example, 'Is that a Jackson Pollock?' This illustrates a simple difference between a collaborative versus individual trail, between monologue and dialogue.

The personal context refers to personal and shared histories and experience. An example of a reference to the personal context is shown in Figure 28.5.

The physical context refers to the impact the physical environment has on visitors, how it accommodates the visitor group, and how they, in turn, use the space. For example, there were several instances in Rachel and Adam's trail in which crowds or queues (referred to in these environmental, not human, terms) changed the pair's planned navigation. Navigation, therefore, can be seen as the intersection of the physical context with visitor activity. Other visitors also mediated the pair's encounters with artefacts. An example of a reference to the physical context is shown in Figure 28.6.

6.4.2. Mediation

In museums, groups of two or more visitors typically engage in hushed conversations, and individual visitors tend not to engage other visitors in dialogue. The presence of

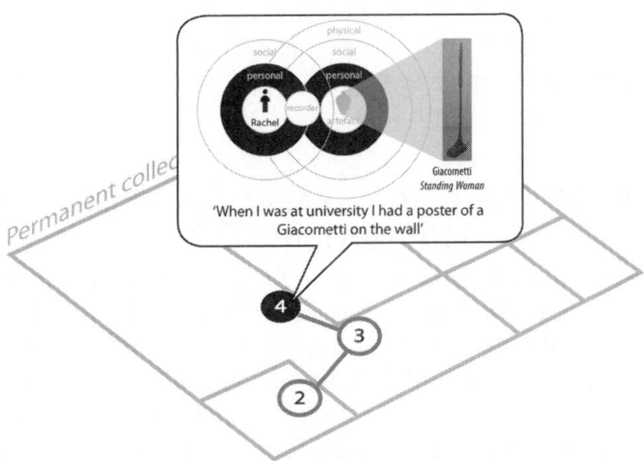

Figure 28.5 Excerpt from Tim's trail at the British Museum, with reference to his personal context highlighted in portion of the TrACE model.

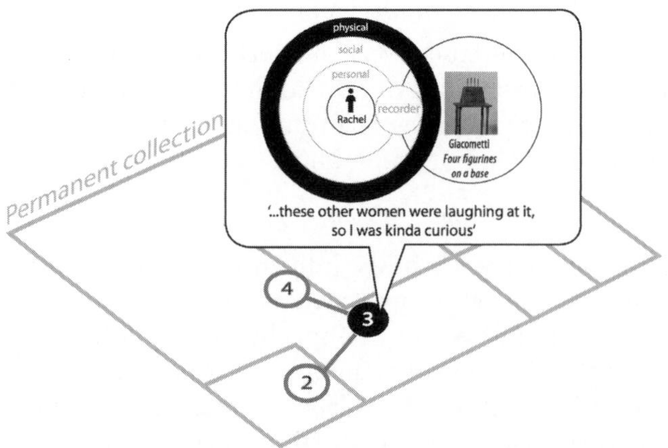

Figure 28.6 Excerpt from Rachel and Adam's trail at Tate Modern, with reference to the physical context highlighted in the TrACE model.

the recording tool—along with the trail construction activity linked to it—countered this social convention, prompting spoken monologues from Keith and Tim, and a running dialogue between Rachel and Adam (more so than would normally be expected). Therefore, the devices, even without special software, implicitly supported both internalisation (of the trails concept) and externalisation (of individual and shared interpretations), through the design of the activity, not of the technology itself.

There was a clear relation between the recorder and other tools—specifically, text-based interpretation which was transferred to the device via the visitors' narration, along with their interpretations. Subjects' interpretations were thus mediated by the museum-provided tools, as well as by the handheld device. But unlike portable digital technologies, museum-provided interpretive tools are, for practical purposes, inseparable from the physical context. Therefore, the construction of individual trail stops can involve a transference of information from one medium to another, or from the physical context to the visitor's personal context. When personal interpretations are added, this can be said to constitute personalisation of the trail; when such interpretations are negotiated in the form of dialogue (as in the case of Rachel and Adam), a trail can be characterised as both personalised and collaborative.

7. TRAIL CONSTRUCTION BY SECONDARY STUDENTS AT A HISTORY MUSEUM

This more focused study took place with a single group of three secondary students, at the Foundling Museum, a small history museum in London. It took place over five weekdays; this longer time scale meant that the students could become more familiar with the museum content and context than in an average visit of a few hours. The Foundling Museum chronicles the story of the Foundling Hospital, a purpose-built home for abandoned children which stood near the same site from 1739 to 1954. It contains original rooms and architectural features from the hospital, artworks donated by patrons such as the artist William Hogarth, and a gallery dedicated to the composer Georg Friedrich Handel (an early benefactor).

Three female students, all aged 16, took part in the study (hereafter identified as S1, S2, S3). Museum staff involved included two museum educators (E1 and E2 hereafter). In this study portable digital recorders were used, but in contrast to the previous study, the activity was much more structured and oriented towards museum artefacts and locations, the links between them, and the product or outcome of the trail. One of the recorders is shown in Figure 28.7.

The students used the audio recorders for rehearsing their narrative trail. Based on the research value of recordings of visitor conversations found in the previous studies, I also asked them to make long, continuous recordings while they navigated the museum, discussed and constructed the trail, for my own analysis. I also interviewed the students and museum staff before and after trail construction.

7.1. Description of the Data Collected

As the scope of trail construction was deliberately narrowed, the completed audio trail comprises only six recordings, averaging two minutes each. But the trail construction process was documented with approximately ten hours of audio recordings of discussions and rehearsals.

The students and educators generally took up my suggestion to use a small number of trail stops, one per room, each stop focusing on one or two artefacts. The students created characters derived from real historical figures they encountered in the museum, and set these characters in conversation within the audio trail. The following are excerpts from the completed trail:

Figure 28.7 SanDisk Sansa m240 MP3 Player, shown in the entry hall of the Foundling Museum.

Stop 1: Coram's Children gallery

S1: My name is Mrs Copperbottom and I am one important woman. I am the governess of the Foundling Hospital. . . . If you walk around the wall behind you, you will see what our hospital looked like. Don't you think it's a grand building?

Stop 4: Picture Gallery

S3: Taking my little baby to the Foundling Hospital brought a lot of different emotions to me. . . . I was asked to leave a token to my baby for easy access to reclaim her. I left a black and white beaded bracelet in the token box. It was the only thing my grandma gave to me before she passed away. . . . Seeing a picture of Thomas Coram, looking kinda nice with his big red coat, reassured me that my baby was in good hands.

Stop 6: Handel gallery

S1: My good friend Handel is an absolutely fabulous musician. He helped fund our hospital by making awesome concerts. He is an inspiration to a lot of our children. He was actually an orphan, and was in a similar situation to some of the foundlings at the hospital. He actually composed the Foundling Hospital's anthem. He is simply too great and will never be forgotten. Mrs Copperbottom, Governess of the Foundling Hospital.

The trail is depicted in Figure 28.8.

7.2. Analysis of the Data

7.2.1. Students' Personal and Social Contexts in Trail Construction

Each student assumed a historical character, with its own personal context, including attitudes, experience and motivations. The characters mediated the students' (and subsequently listeners') encounters with artefacts and their contexts. Because the students inhabited historical characters, they made very few references to their own personal lives

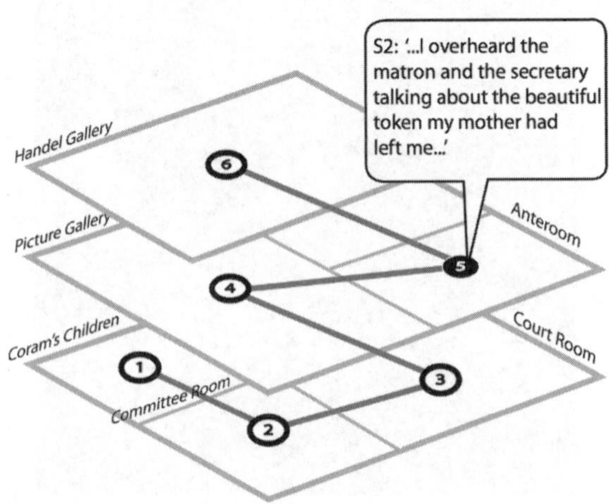

Figure 28.8 Students' complete trail through the Foundling Museum, with one stop highlighted and excerpted.

during the study. This trail consisted in large part of links between the social context of the students (as co-constructors of the trail) and the social contexts of artefacts (as illustrative of the history of the Foundling Hospital).

One of the students' early ideas was to create a page for the museum on MySpace, a social networking web site focused mainly on contemporary music. But they had difficulty imagining that it could attract young people with the music of Handel. By focusing solely on the trail and not creating a MySpace page, the students gave up trying to contemporise the museum, and instead immersed themselves in the historical context of their characters. It became an individual and shared effort to come to terms with the original social contexts of the artefacts, and to convey these in the contemporary medium of the audio trail.

This was done primarily through language. The students struggled with trying to portray historical speech and different social classes through speech, in order to lend authenticity to their dramatisations. However, as characters were negotiated and the story developed, the students 'got into character' (to use the theatrical term), adopting and adapting historical language for the trail. Here they repeated facts from museum labels, but placing them in the narrative form of a drama enabled them to embellish the factual history with fictional histories. Elsewhere, character monologues served to link individual artefacts to their broader social context.

7.2.2. Personal and Social Contexts of Artefacts

In this study, attributes of individual artefacts were referenced as a means to explore their broader historical significance. At the same time, the conventions of drama provided an effective means to 'personalise' the artefacts by attaching fictionalised stories to them—in effect, creating new personal contexts for them.

For example, in the Picture Gallery, the students were intrigued by the items that mothers were required to leave for their children as a means of identification. S3 selected one (a bracelet) and built a narrative around it, and this was then linked to a second artefact in the same room (a picture of Thomas Coram). S3 thus skillfully used narrative to create a shared social context for two artefacts which were not otherwise obviously linked, within the same trail stop and physical context, as shown in Figure 28.9.

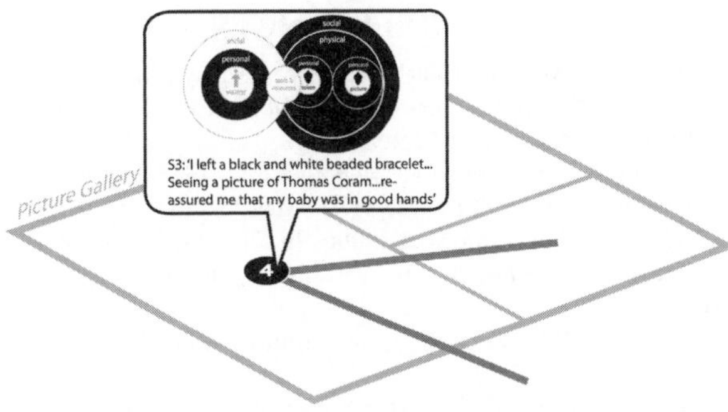

Figure 28.9 TrACE model highlighting two unrelated artefacts linked in shared physical and social contexts in Stop 4 of the trail.

7.2.3. Role of the Physical Context in Trail Construction

The students approached each room of the museum essentially as curators. More broadly, they considered how visitors would navigate the museum as a whole and, by extension, how linear the narrative should be.

After an initial tour with the educators, the students were given their own space—the education room—in which to work on their trail. However, they soon realised the value of being in the physical context of the galleries and, in the end, decided not only to revisit each room, but to work on and record each trail stop in the room for which it was intended. This enabled them to give precise directions in the recordings ('If you walk to your right . . .'), and to see the artefacts they referred to in the recordings.

7.2.4. The Role of Mediating Tools and Resources in Trail Construction

Even more so than in the first study, here the device was closely tied to the trail definition and product; specifically in this case it was not a trail of artefacts visited, but more clearly defined as a trail that would help other visitors in their encounters with artefacts.

The students had to come to terms with the technicalities of an audio trail, since they had never taken a museum audio tour before. The students also had to come to terms with linearity, and one student explained to another by referring to tracks in an MP3 player. In the end, the students balanced the nonlinearity afforded by the technology with the linearity of the storyline: characters recur in subsequent trail stops, their stories continue, and references are made to previous stops.

8. CONCLUSION

Trails were seen to support museum meaning-making among different visitor groups and in different museum types, by providing a curatorial scaffolding for visitors' re-contextualisation of artefacts, when they have a clear goal and product, and a limited scope, through the articulation of interpretations arising from navigation to artefacts—interpretations which are links between visitors' and artefacts' contexts, and are generally narrative in form. Technology can mediate the bridging of contexts by embodying the trails concept on the one hand, and by prompting articulation of personalised interpretations on the other. A key to visitor engagement thus may lie not in technology itself, but in the design of activities around it.

REFERENCES

Baker, R., Roussos G. and Levene, M. (2006) The Experience Re-player: Trail-based Reconstruction of Captured Experiences in Ubiquitous Computing Spaces. Workshop on Pervasive Image Capture and Sharing (PICS 2006) at UBICOMP 2006, Irvine, CA, 18 September.

Bush, V. (1945) As we may think. *Atlantic Monthly*, July 1945. http://www.theatlantic.com/magazine/archive/1969/12/as-we-may-think/3881/, accessed 27 May 2010.

Dierking, L. and Falk, J. (1998) Audience and accessibility. In Thomas, S. and Mintz, A. (Eds.) *The Virtual and the Real: Uses of multimedia in museums*, 57–70. Washington, DC: Technical Information Services, American Association of Museums.

Doering, Z. and Pekakirk, A. (1996) Questioning the entrance narrative. *Journal of Museum Education, 21*(3): 20–22.

Ellenbogen, K. (2002) Museums in family life: An ethnographic case study. In Leinhardt, G., Crowley, K. and Knutson, K. (Eds.) *Learning Conversations in Museums.* London: Erlbaum.

Falk, J. and Dierking, L. (1991) *The Museum Experience.* Walnut Creek, CA: Left Coast Press.

Falk, J. and Dierking, L. (2000) *Learning from Museums.* Walnut Creek, CA: AltaMira Press.

Falk, J. and Dierking, L. (2008) How visitors learn through media and interaction. In Tallon, L. and Walker, K. (Eds.) *Digital Technologies and the Museum Experience: Handheld Guides and Other Media.* Walnut Creek, CA: AltaMira Press.

Falk, J., Moussouri, T. and Coulson, D. (1998) The effect of visitors' agendas on museum learning. *Curator, 41*(2): 106–120.

Fisher, S. (2005) An evaluation of Learning on the Move and Science Navigator: Using PDAs in museum, heritage and science center settings. Nesta report.

Ham, S. H. (1999) Cognitive psychology and interpretation: Synthesis and application. In Hooper-Greenhill, E. (Ed.) *The Educational Role of the Museum* (2nd Ed.). New York: Routledge.

Hooper-Greenhill, E. (1999) *The Educational Role of the Museum* (2nd Ed.). New York: Routledge.

Kaptelinin, V. (2008) Meaning making in museums as bridging activity contexts: Toward a theoretical framework for interaction design. Working Paper WP-08.01. Department of Informatics, Umeaå University.

Kuuti, K. (1991) The concept of activity as a basic unit of analysis for CSCW research. In *Proceedings of the Second European Conference on CSCW.* Amsterdam, 249–264.

Leont'ev, A. N. (1978) *Activity: Consciousness and Personality.* Englewood Cliffs, NJ: Prentice Hall.

McLellan, H. (2006) Digital storytelling: Bridging old and new. *Educational Technology* Sept–Oct, 26–31.

Mintz, A. (1998) Media and museums: A museum perspective. In Thomas, S. and Mintz, A. (Eds.) *The Virtual and the Real: Media in the Museum,* 19–34. American Association of Museums.

Moussouri, T. (2002) A context for the development of learning outcomes in museums, libraries and archives. RCMG.

Papadogkonas, D., Roussos, G. and Levene, M. (2006) Discovery and ranking of significant trails. 2nd International Workshop on Exploiting Context Histories in Smart Environments (ECHISE 2006) at UBICOMP 2006, Irvine, CA, 17 September.

Peterson, D. and Levene, M. (2003) Trail records and navigational learning. *London Review of Education, 1*(3), 207–216.

Pierroux, P. (2006) *Meaning, Learning and Art in Museums.* Oslo: Unipub.

Pierroux, P., Bannon, L., Kaptelinin, V., Hall, T. and Walker, K. (2007) A Framework for Designing for Visitors' Augmented Activities in Museums. *Proceedings of ICHIM 07,* Toronto, 24–26 October.

Reynolds, R. and Speight, C. (2008) Trials and trails: Do HE design students need museum learning resources? *Art, Design and Communication in Higher Education, 7*(3): 185–193.

Robinson, M. H. (1998) Multimedia in living exhibits: Now and then. In Thomas, S. and Mintz, A. (Eds.) *The Virtual and the Real: Media in the Museum,* 37–55. American Association of Museums.

Smith, J. K. and Tinio, P. P. L. (2008) Audio augmentation of museum visits: Talking the walk. In Tallon, L. and Walker, K. (Eds.) *Digital Technologies and the Museum Experience: Handheld Guides and Other Media.* Walnut Creek, CA: AltaMira Press.

Vygotsky, L. S. (1978) *Mind in Society: The Development of Higher Psychological Processes.* Cambridge, MA: Harvard University Press. Published originally in Russian in 1930. http://www.marxists.org/archive/vygotsky/works/mind/.

Walker, K. (2010) Designing for meaning making in museums: Visitor-constructed trails using mobile digital technologies. PhD thesis, University of London.

29

A BLENDED INSTRUCTIONAL DESIGN APPROACH TO ACCESSIBLE CYBERLEARNING

Marilyn P. Arnone, Jennifer T. Ellis, and Derrick L. Cogburn

1. INTRODUCTION

Two major learning challenges for students with disabilities including impairments to vision, hearing, and mobility are accessibility of content and how it is presented. While strides have been made toward developing distributed learning communities that are more effective and efficient, most still do not have a high enough degree of accessibility to allow persons with disabilities to fully engage in the learning experience (Myhill, Cogburn, Samant, Addom, & Blanck, 2008). If students cannot easily access material or they encounter frustrations in doing so, chaos ensues and learning is compromised, if not rendered impossible. Not only is learning thwarted but motivation to learn is severely undermined.

These are learning issues facing all persons with disabilities (PWDs). In some parts of the world, this problem is magnified because of the sheer numbers of PWDs, especially in the Asia-Pacific Region with one of the highest levels of disability in the world (Officer & Posarac, 2011; ESCAP 2012). Many are marginalized in their own countries, and face significant barriers in terms of transportation, information and communication technologies, employment, and most importantly, education. Without education that acknowledges their unique learning needs *and* that prepares them to be leaders on disability issues in their region and the world, they have few opportunities for political participation in which their voices can be heard.

2. POLITICAL CLIMATE RIPE FOR CHANGE

Increasingly, there is a national, regional, and now global public policy framework emerging to address the needs of PWDs. Enforced on 3 May 2008, the United Nations Convention on the Rights of Persons with Disabilities (CRPD), with now over 140 signatories, the transition to a global, social-based approach to disability rights and policy is well under way. Also, keeping with the approach developed during the formulation of the CRPD—"Nothing About Us Without Us," it is especially important to increase the knowledge, skills and abilities of persons who themselves have disabilities. However, the development of national implementing legislation and monitoring the enforcement of these policies requires a specialized knowledge base that is severely lacking in the Asia-Pacific Region, and around the world. Advanced, post-graduate, academic training at the intersection of disability issues and public policy is required to address these growing global concerns. Moreover, such training would need to address the unique learning challenges and problems of PWDs who would enroll in the training. Finally, many persons who desire and could benefit from academic preparation in disability issues and public policy are already working, and need a flexible approach to completing an advanced degree.

Technological advances over the last decade have made distributed collaboration in knowledge work much more practical. Collaboratories, or "centers without walls" in the sciences and social sciences have made it possible to do extremely complex research work at a distance (Wulf, 1993; Berman & Brady, 2005). Virtual organizations of all types are appearing to support distributed work. The cyberinfrastructure to support these developments continues to be enriched by both commercially available "off the shelf" technologies, as well as a wide range of open source software tools. These developments led the US National Science Foundation to explore the potential of these cyberinfrastructure-based approaches to transform education and learning, in a program it calls "Cyberlearning" (NSF, 2008).

Against this backdrop, the Chairman and Executive Director of The Nippon Foundation of Tokyo, Mr Yohei Sasakawa and Mr Ohno, asked the question: "Is there some way to accelerate the needed human capacity development in disability policy through the use of information and communication technologies?" (Focus Group, Bangkok, August 2009). In response, the Center for Research on Collaboratories and Technology Enhanced Learning Communities (COTELCO, http://cotelco.net/), a joint social science research center between American University and Syracuse University, proposed to create the Institute on Disability and Public Policy (IDPP, http://aseanidpp.org/). The IDPP is the world's first virtual graduate institute focused on the intersection of disability and public policy (http://idpp-global.org/). While the IDPP also focuses on collaborative research, outreach, and continuing education, the centerpiece of the institute is its Masters of International Affairs in Comparative and International Disability Policy (CIDP). The CIDP is the first completely online degree offered by American University, and is accredited by the Middle States Commission on Higher Education (http://aseanidpp.org/admissions/). Of special concern to the CIDP was addressing the learning needs of the main audience for the new master's curriculum, PWDs.

3. THE LEARNING AUDIENCE: LEARNING PROBLEMS/CHALLENGES

Although the framework for the CIDP program had been carefully created, implementing this plan was challenging with respect to establishing a cyberinfrastructure to support the effective and efficient teaching and learning and curriculum for core courses, residency program and skills institutes. The primary audiences for the CIDP introduced new challenges that surfaced during the implementation, also. Early indicators showed the importance of an iterative process of instructional design and ongoing clarification of the learning needs and goals of students.

3.1. The Learning Audience

Ten students from Southeast Asia (Vietnam, Cambodia, Singapore, and the Philippines) were selected and supported by a fellowship provided by The Nippon Foundation as the initial cohort for the 39-credit CIDP master's program. Of these ten, four were blind or visually impaired; three were deaf or hard of hearing; and three were mobility impaired.

The CIDP was delivered by the IDPP through the School of International Service (SIS) at American University. Flexibility was a key value of the CIDP; candidates could participate in the master's program synchronously or asynchronously, and take as long as needed to finish the program. While the program could be completed entirely online within one year, there was a two-week face-to-face residency to prepare the students.

Faculty teaching in the CIDP were drawn from American University, but enabled by the distributed nature of the cyberlearning environment, they also came from around the world. Many faculty members were senior practitioners, embedded in the United Nations, regional organizations, and other disabled persons organizations (DPO). Finally, the IDPP was positioned within the Socio-Cultural Community of the Association of Southeast Asian Nations (ASEAN) led by civil society.

3.2. Diversity as Challenge and Opportunity

Multiculturalism when addressed in college courses often centers on gender, ethnicity, and race while frequently overlooking disability as contributing to a diverse campus. The students enrolled in the CIDP master's program at American University represented many aspects of diversity. Disability was one; gender was another. They also represented different cultures from the ASEAN region. Most importantly, these students represented great diversity in the knowledge and experience they brought to the program. Such a diverse group presented both an instructional challenge and an opportunity.

One single representation of knowledge or a limited teacher-centric mode of instruction would be inappropriate and inadequate to meet the learning needs of these future leaders in disability and public policy. Some have argued that electronically facilitated communication such as that provided in a cyberlearning environment may make cultural differences irrelevant (Jarvenpaa & Leidner, 1998). Cogburn and Levinson (2003) hold that such differences play a large role in the development of trust in cross-national collaborations using distributed communication, and that instructors must be keenly aware of such differences. Furthermore, students' understanding and embracing individual cultural differences among each other were viewed as strengths in the CIDP program where students have a future stake in policies that affect the *entire* region of Southeast Asia. A program that afforded a high level of social interaction to build trust and understanding would be required. To guide instructional design, we embraced a perspective that recognized the importance of both social interaction and sociocultural elements within a distributed collaborative cyberlearning environment.

3.3. Accessibility and its Impact on Learner Motivation

In addition to addressing cultural diversity, a crucial learning challenge for students with disabilities is accessibility in online learning posing major learning obstacles for PWDs (Myhill et al., 2008). Contributing to this learning problem is the undermining effect on student motivation, especially in terms of perceived competence and autonomy. Our instructional design required a strong emphasis on motivation as a critical element in learning.

4. A BLENDED APPROACH TO THEORY AND INSTRUCTIONAL DESIGN

The virtual nature of the institute and its target audience promised to be unlike any existing disability programs; it would require the development of a new approach to education. Therefore, a blended instructional design approach was utilized during the implementation phase in the development of the CIDP courses. This approach applied the strengths of the commonly recognized ADDIE and ASSURE models and blended them with the Universal Design for Learning (UDL), especially important in designing for PWD environments. Motivation theory and social constructivism informed the instructional design (see Figure 29.1).

The underpinnings and complementary methods of ADDIE (Reiser & Dempsey, 2012; Wang & Hsu, 2009) and ASSURE (Smaldino, Russell, Heinrich, & Molenda, 2005) strengthened the instruction (e.g. activities and assessments) and helped the team better understand the project's needs (learning goals) to develop effective assessments (evaluations). The U—utilize media and materials—of the ASSURE model highlighted the "5 Ps": Preview the Material, Prepare the Material, Prepare the Environment, Prepare the Learners, and Provide the Learning Experience, which are essential to the development of the cyberinfrastructure and require input from the key stakeholders who will use the cyberinfrastructure: students, faculty, staff, technical experts, etc.

Principles of UDL, that is, presenting information and content in different ways, differentiating the ways students can express what they know, and stimulating interest and motivation for learning, correlate importantly with student motivation (CAST, 2011) and brought these principles to the fore during design and development.

In addition, a blended and iterative instructional design approach, considered an eclectic postmodern approach to instructional design, recognizes the influence of four societal factors during the design:

1. Society is past the point where there are a limited number of authorities available to a classroom student.
2. No longer can there be an agreed-upon, single type of well-educated individual.

Figure 29.1 CIDP blended instructional design model.

> 3. The currently popular cognitive paradigm—constructivism—does not recognize or advocate a traditional, linear educational sequence.
> 4. No single, objective truth exists.
>
> (Brown & Green, 2011, pp. 13–14)

Thus, by integrating a constructivist approach, designers had to provide an instructional environment that allows the learners to have a forum for collaboration and discussion to construct knowledge (Fard, Tasir, & Ziden, 2010).

ADDIE, ASSURE, the principles of UDL, and the societal influences of a blended instructional design approach essentially ensure that a comprehensive and successful learning experience that focuses on addressing the needs of the end user is effectively created. As highlighted in Figure 29.1, the implementation phase was used as a bridge between the various models (Greer, 1996, in Reiser & Dempsey, 2012). The iterative and self-correcting nature of the instructional design process emerges as one of the greatest strengths (Reiser & Dempsey, 2012).

Therefore, the front-end analysis was extensive. A two-phased research project preceded the launch of the IDPP, with the first phase focusing on benchmarking data on disabilities indicators and statistics for the region, a modified Delphi-process to develop the curriculum based on data collected about the top-ranked programs in disability studies and public policy in the United States and around the world, and analysis of the tools to support the cyberinfrastructure for the institute. This procedure allowed for the incorporation of the assessments of a complex array of experts into the curriculum (Cogburn, Nelson, & Thomas, 2011). From this approach, we created and followed a guiding paradigm from constructivism and motivational theory.

4.1. A Guiding Paradigm

Vygotsky's social constructivist perspective was evident in the development of the master's program and the distributed collaborative learning environment. In this view, theoretical emphasis was placed on social and cultural processes and activities; it is through social negotiation that an individual constructs knowledge and moves toward higher mental processing (Woolfolk, 2007).

> Constructivist instructional design principles involve embedding learning in complex real world problems, providing a rich and flexible learning environment with goals and objectives set by the learner, emphasizing continuous assessment that is embedded in the instruction, facilitating multiple perspectives and social negotiation as integral parts of learning, and encouraging ownership in learning by actively engaging in the process of knowledge construction.
>
> (Chen, 2007, pp. 73–74)

An increasing number of instructors seem interested in adopting various constructivist approaches for the design and delivery of courses created for a cyberlearning environment.

> However, in a constructivist learning environment, to successfully promote active and meaningful learning, the instructor has to commit a significant amount of time and energy to develop complex, problem-based learning tasks; arrange an open and

> resource-rich learning environment; provide ample opportunities for social interactions; form and norm groups; offer cognitive scaffolds, continuously monitor and coach performance; and encourage collaboration and interaction to gain multiple perspectives.
>
> (Chen, 2007, p. 74)

Students engaged in constructivist learning also have to spend a substantial amount of time and effort on their learning experience and on managing logistical tasks, such as coordinating with other group members. Constructivist-based teaching and learning require more time and effort from both the instructor and the students than objectivist-based instructional approaches (Cavanaugh, 2005; Rajandran, 2003). These tenets from constructivism also influenced our design.

Students in the master's program came from different countries within the ASEAN region. They were expected to gain from the combined knowledge and practice of the group with the goal of students themselves creating meaningful knowledge that they could apply within the context of the cultures they would be serving after graduation. Their sharing backgrounds and experiences, social interactions, and cooperative and collaborative learning placed the emphasis of constructing knowledge on them as opposed to the instructor who acted as a guide on the side. The students and instructor together built the essential scaffolding for making meaning. This guiding paradigm is in concert with a distributed collaborative learning environment in which the learner is an active participant.

4.2. Motivation Theory

Self-Determination Theory (Deci & Ryan, 1985; Ryan & Deci, 2000) played a key role in guiding our instructional strategy decisions that impact student motivation. This theory holds that individuals have several basic and innate psychological needs that must be met for well-being and self-motivation: competence, autonomy, and relatedness. Studies across numerous domains including all levels of education (Chen, Jang, & Branch, 2008; Arnone, Reynolds, & Marshall, 2009; Black & Deci, 2000), across different cultural contexts (Lynch, La Guardia, & Ryan, 2009; Chirkov, 2009; Rudy, Sheldon, Awong, & Tan, 2007), and with PWDs (Perreault & Vallerand, 2007) provide empirical support for the principles underlying the theory. Considering these needs in designing both face-to-face and cyberlearning environments is essential to ensure persistent effort and a climate that allows all students to be curious and constructive.

When designing environments that serve PWDs, addressing perceived competence is of great importance. A video without closed-captioning, for example, will undermine a deaf or hearing-impaired student's confidence in learning the course material. Additionally, it impacts perceived autonomy support for learning as the technical infrastructure and instructor are, in essence, taking away personal control and limiting students' ability to self-regulate their learning. Such issues can contribute to higher attrition rates for PWDs who depend on technology affordances to succeed in online learning. Perceived autonomy was the most important predictor of students' intrinsic and extrinsic motivations in one study (Chen et al., 2008). Addressing accessibility beyond what is typically available at the present time in online learning management systems has been a large concern and implementation challenge for the technology team.

Our design strategies also considered ways in which to build a sense of community among students (social relatedness). Studies in online learning have demonstrated the importance of learners' affiliation to learning outcomes (Dennen, Darabi, & Smith, 2007) but this need is also culturally relevant. Describing the residency that brought together students from a number of countries in Southeast Asia, one facilitator noted, "Students seemed to make close friends very quickly. Now they had a face and a shared experience. They exchanged views. I noticed that these ties have been maintained in the virtual program. Students help each other out."

5. IMPLEMENTATION DESIGNS

In this section, we present several "implementation to reality" examples from the face-to-face residency component. Each situation was selected to exemplify how the design was influenced by a theory or model.

5.1. Residency in Bangkok, Thailand

With the two-week residency held in the summer in Bangkok, Thailand, it was the first time students met their cohort, some faculty, and staff. The first example relates to knowledge building of accessibility issues and public policy. The second focuses on a motivational design strategy.

5.1.1. Example #1

Since the residency was the first opportunity for students to meet and learn from each other, the instructional design focused on promoting active learning. Throughout the residency, students worked on a case study representing a problematic situation to redesign a café business that was not meeting guidelines for accessibility to PWDs.

This learning activity, initially scaffolded by the instructor and facilitators, remained student-centered and collaborative. Students tapped into their varied backgrounds including work, cultural, and disability experiences to share multiple perspectives in solving the problem contributing to scaffolding. The facilitators noted that students were motivated by sharing and building on each others' experience and knowledge.

For different aspects of the café problem, there was no obvious right solution. Problem-solving thus required a high degree of reflection by each student and as members of teams. One example involved making the bathroom accessible. It could be solved by building an entirely new bathroom or through some means of retrofitting such as adding rails, ramp, etc. Each student shared ideas and they used their individual strengths to contribute to the solution. One of the students was an architect and was able to use specialized software to lay out the design of the building; another student had organizational and research strengths and developed a policy matrix to evaluate the pros and cons of different options for the café. Perhaps, most importantly, each shared their view of potential solutions from the authentic experience of his or her specific disability, insuring that the ultimate solution was sensitive to a variety of needs of PWDs. Each solution was a viable one and represented an innovative approach to problem-solving.

5.1.2. Example #2

The second example relates to motivation, the social constructivist perspective, autonomy of SDT, relatedness and competence. In order to help build a sense of community (relatedness), the Bangkok residency included recreational trips for students to have leisurely communication with each other and establish bonds that could continue throughout the master's program's virtual components. Students indicated this as a satisfying aspect of the residency experience on their evaluations. Finally, the residency enabled instructors to embed learning in a rich authentic problem-solving environment in Bangkok. Students were amidst other students who had disabilities dissimilar to theirs and they had an opportunity to visit organizations that had an impact on disabilities and public policy.

5.1.3. Community Building

During the residency students did make knowledge gains in their understanding of public policy issues, assistive technologies, advocacy, and techniques for problem-solving, but we were particularly impressed by how important the residency was to building community and affiliation. Participants either agreed or, more often, strongly agreed with all three statements on the residency evaluation that related to the residency providing enough opportunities to work collaboratively with diverse teams, the policy exercise activities helping promote a sense of community, and creating a sense of being part of a group that would make a difference in the lives of PWDs in the ASEAN region.

6. IMPLEMENTATION CHALLENGES

There are many challenges faced in providing a higher education learning environment that supports the needs of PWDs beyond what has routinely been available to students. The most difficult challenge was technology and accessibility. Without solving these issues, the instructional design could not be properly implemented.

6.1. Technological and Accessibility Challenges

The organization of the IDPP and the delivery of the CIDP master's program would not be possible without the underlying technology infrastructure. While we had great success with the cyberinfrastructure we assembled from commercially available and open source software tools, we faced numerous implementation challenges. The "5 Ps" from the ASSURE model are evident in the examples that follow.

6.1.1. Asynchronous Technologies

The backbone of every distance learning program is its learning management system (LMS). The LMS defines how courses are organized, materials provided, assignments submitted, and discussions held. The team agonized over whether to use an open source LMS or the commercial system licensed by the university. Given our priority for accessibility, we leaned heavily towards one of the open source LMS options, i.e. Atutor, Desire to Learn, Moodle, and several other systems. Amongst these, Moodle and Atutor rated high on our list after extensive accessibility testing. However, in the final analysis, the benefits of using the enterprise-wide system, Blackboard Learn, outweighed the costs; at least for the first year, when other issues took priority.

6.1.2. Synchronous Technologies

Although the CIDP had an extremely flexible structure, and we wanted to ensure students could continue working while they pursued the master's degree if they liked, we felt it critical to include a synchronous component. Our first residency evaluation results confirmed that building community was important to our learners and using synchronous technologies added that element to the virtual program and supported our social constructivist approach to learning. However, this was a challenge.

Rather than explore more bandwidth-intensive and expensive options such as video conferencing or even high-end telepresence, following Cogburn and Kurup (2006), we focused on webconferencing solutions. The technical team evaluated a wide range of webconferencing tools. Based largely on their commitment to "No User Left Behind" which focuses not only on accessibility for low-bandwidth and cross-platform users, Blackboard Collaborate (formerly Elluminate Live!) was chosen. Blackboard Collaborate places a premium on accessibility for PWDs. The UDL principles influenced our decision, making the tool's technological features ideal for the *synchronous* cyberinfrastructure. However, it was also critical for the *asynchronous* strategy. Recorded sessions are compiled within 60 seconds after the conclusion of a session, and the link can be made instantly available to students through Blackboard Learn, our asynchronous platform, to be accessed at their convenience.

6.1.3. Accessibility and Usability

For each technology included in the cyberinfrastructure strategy, rigorous accessibility testing included both automated testing strategies, and actual user-testing with our three primary disability groups: (1) deaf or hard of hearing; (2) blind or visually impaired; and (3) mobility impaired. This testing carried over to testing content in the most accessible format. For example, we initially tested a survey design on a small group of non-participating PWDs using a matrix to present a number of items/statements. The matrix, while more efficient in terms of space and conciseness, worked fine for persons without disabilities but was problematic for PWDs. What worked best in the end with the user's software was to separate each statement individually. This rigorous accessibility testing was also considered to be extremely important because of its potential impact on student motivation in terms of perceived competence and autonomy.

6.1.4. Course Delivery and Innovations

By confronting these challenges, the team developed a number of innovations in course delivery. Some of the more important innovations include: (1) screen-reader accessibility. For students that are blind or visually impaired, screen reading software is critical to their ability to use and navigate electronic environments. The choice of Blackboard Collaborate ensured that students using these tools could successfully navigate the synchronous environment. (2) Closed-captioning. Blackboard Collaborate also has multiple channels of integrated closed-captioning. We contracted with a small California company that provides remote, real-time, closed-captioning for our webconferencing sessions all around the world. (3) American Sign Language (ASL) Interpretation. Not all students who are deaf or hard of hearing prefer closed-captioning as an accommodation. Sign language interpretation is the preferred method for many. However, one challenge related to sign language was trying to decide which version of sign language to use. Following the model set by the ASEAN Secretariat itself, ASL was chosen for the IDPP. ASL has very broad global acceptance and was implemented in an innovative way. After substantial testing and evaluation, a configuration that allowed real-time delivery of ASL interpretation over the webconferencing system was identified, representing a major breakthrough. Numerous members of our staff, sponsors, and colleagues at the National

Technical Institute for the Deaf (NTID) at the Rochester Institute of Technology (RIT) have confirmed its effectiveness. Providing different formats as part of the solution was in line with the UDL principle of multiple forms of representation of content.

7. CONSIDERATIONS AND RECOMMENDATIONS FOR PRACTICE

This case study highlighted success factors (and barriers to success) in customizing and applying several theories and instructional design models to distributed collaborative learning that supports PWDs. Further, this project and the research which will continue to flow from it will provide a synchronous and asynchronous pedagogical model that can inform efforts on other campuses around the world to be inclusive in the initial design and implementation, and to consider both the psychological and learning needs of all students including those with disabilities.

For each aspect of the design, development, implementation and evaluation of this project, a separate list of considerations could be presented. We will focus on several of the most valuable lessons learned to date. Undoubtedly, we will continue to learn new lessons as we strive to improve the program and experience for learners.

1. When designing a program in a cyberlearning environment consider using a blended instructional design approach to utilize the structure of a model such as the ADDIE model to design the curriculum and the ASSURE model to design the cyberinfrastructure and support faculty training. The social constructivist perspective guided the types of learning activities planned.
2. Using a modified Delphi technique in the analysis phase of an instructional design model is one effective means of establishing the goals and content for the curriculum.
3. Motivational design should include attention paid to a learner's perceived competence and the autonomy supportiveness provided by both the instructor and delivery system. This is especially important with regard to technology and PWDs. Without access and/or proper technology affordances, confidence in one's ability to successfully complete a course or program will be undermined, as will the ability to self-regulate learning, impacting perceived autonomy.
4. Consider adding face-to-face residencies as part of a virtual learning program. In our case, building community within the multicultural cohort gave students the opportunity to make ties, share customs, work on an authentic problem, and enjoy leisure activities together. The benefits of the residency appear to continue throughout the program.
5. Schedule sufficient time to test all components of the cyberlearning environment with members of the target audience.
6. Instructional design is an iterative process making it imperative to conduct ongoing formative evaluation to inform future decision-making.

8. CONCLUSION

The IDPP is working across numerous cultural orientations in ten countries of ASEAN with tremendous socio-economic considerations as well as religious, racial/

ethnic diversity, and approaches to disability issues. The cross-cultural and/or intercultural issues we faced in the IDPP are vast and emerged in a variety of ways, some subtle, some less so. From issues related to power distance, to high- and low-context communication styles, culture shaped the approach to building the IDPP. The IDPP project has opened many avenues for potential research in instructional design that supports learners with disabilities.

REFERENCES

Arnone, M. P., Reynolds, R., & Marshall, T. (2009). The effect of early adolescents' psychological needs satisfaction upon their perceived competence in information skills and intrinsic motivation for research. *School Libraries Worldwide*, 15(2), 115–134.

Berman, F., & Brady, H. (2005). Final Report: NSF SBE-CISE Workshop on Cyberinfrastructure and the Social Sciences. Retrieved September 14, 2010, from http://ucdata.berkeley.edu/pubs/CyberInfrastructure_FINAL.pdf.

Black, A. E., & Deci, E. L. (2000). The effects of instructors' autonomy support and students' autonomous motivation on learning organic chemistry: A self-determination perspective. *Science Education*, 84, 740–756.

Brown, A., & Green, T. (2011). *The Essentials of Instructional Design: Connecting fundamental principles with process and practice* (2nd ed.). Boston, MA: Pearson Education.

CAST (2011). Universal design for learning guidelines version 2.0. Wakefield, MA: Author.

Cavanaugh, J. (2005). Teaching online—A time comparison. *Online Journal of Distance Learning Administration*, 8(1), 1–9.

Chen, K. C., Jang, S. J., & Branch, R. M. (2008). Autonomy, affiliation, and ability: Relative salience of factors that influence online learner motivation learning outcomes. *Knowledge Management & E-Learning: An International Journal*, 2(1), 30.

Chen, S. J. (2007). Instructional design strategies for intensive online course: An objectivist-constructivist blend approach. *Journal of Interactive Online Learning*, 6(1), 72–86.

Chirkov, V. I. (2009). A cross-cultural analysis of autonomy in education: A self-determination theory perspective. *Theory and Research in Education*, 7(2), 253–262.

Cogburn, D. L., & Kurup, D. (2006). The World is our Campus: Web conferencing software lets colleagues, students and researchers from all over the globe collaborate. *Network Computing*, 17(7), 57–63.

Cogburn, D. L., & Levinson, N. S. (2003). U.S.–Africa virtual collaboration in globalization studied: Success factors for complex, cross-national learning teams. *International Studies Perspectives*, 4, 34–51.

Cogburn, D. L., Nelson, C., & Thomas, T. (2011). Participatory Mixed Methods Curriculum Design for the Institute on Disability and Public Policy. Paper presented at the *International Association for Media and Communication Research* (IAMCR) 2011, Istanbul, Turkey.

Deci, E. L., & Ryan, R. M. (1985). *Intrinsic Motivation and Self-determination in Human Behavior.* New York: Plenum.

Dennen, V. P., Darabi, A. A., & Smith, L. J. (2007). Instructor–learner interaction in online courses: The relative perceived importance of particular instructor actions on performance and satisfaction. *Distance Education*, 28(1), 65–79.

Economic and Social Commissions for Asia and the Pacific (ESCAP) (2012). *Disability at a Glance 2012: Strengthening the evidence base in Asia and the Pacific.* Bangkok: United Nations Publication. Retrieved October 5, 2012 from http://www.unescap.org/publications/detail.asp?id=1521.

Fard, H. E., Tasir, Z., & Ziden, A. A. (2010). Hybrid instructional design model based on constructivism for web. *World Applied Sciences Journal*, 11(1), 44–48.

Jarvenpaa, S. L., & Leidner, D. L. (1998). Communication and trust in global virtual teams. *Journal of Computer-Mediated Communication*, 3, 4.

Lynch, M., La Guardia, J., & Ryan, R. M. (2009). On being yourself in different cultures: Ideal and actual self-concept, autonomy support, and well-being in China, Russia, and the United States. *The Journal of Positive Psychology*, 4(4), 290–304.

Myhill, W. N., Cogburn, D. L., Samant, D., Addom, B., & Blanck, P. (2008). Developing accessible cyberinfrastructure-enabled knowledge communities in the national disability community: Theory, practice, and policy. *Assistive Technologies*, 20, 157–174.

National Science Foundation. (2008). Fostering learning in the networked world: The cyberlearning opportunity and challenge. *Report of the NSF Task Force on Cyberlearning*, 1–59.

Perreault, S., & Vallerand, R. J. (2007). A test of self-determination theory with wheelchair basketball players with and without disability. *Adapted Physical Activity Quarterly*, 24, 305–316.

Rajandran, V. (2003). A study investigating the impact of web-enhanced learning on student motivation. *CDTL Brief*, 6(9), 2005.

Reiser, R. A., & Dempsey, J. V. (Eds.) (2012). *Trends and Issues in Instructional Design and Technology* (3rd ed.). Saddle River, NJ: Pearson Education.

Rudy, D., Sheldon, K. M., Awong, T., & Tan, H. H. (2007). Autonomy, culture, and well-being: The benefits of inclusive autonomy. *Journal of Research in Personality*, 41, 983–1007.

Ryan, R. M., & Deci, E. L. (2000). Self-determination theory and the facilitation of intrinsic motivation, social development, and well-being, *The American Psychologist*, 55(1), 68–78.

Smaldino, S. E., Russell, J. D., Heinrich, R., & Molenda, M (2005). *Instructional Technology and Media for Learning* (5th ed.). Saddle River, NJ: Pearson Education Ltd.

Wang, S., & Hsu, H. (2009). Using the ADDIE Model to design second life activities for online learners. *Techtrends: Linking Research and Practice to Improve Learning*, 53(6), 76–82.

World Health Organization (WHO) (2011). *World Report on Disability*. Edited by A. Officer & A. Posarac. Retrieved January 17, 2011, from http://whqlibdoc.who.int/publications/2011/9789240685215_eng.pdf.

Woolfolk, A. (2007). Social cognitive and constructivist views of learning. In *Educational Psychology* (pp. 329–369). Canada: Pearson/Allyn & Bacon.

Wulf, W. (1993). The collaboratory opportunity. *Science*, 261, 854–855.

30

CLOUD-BASED ELEARNING FOR HIGHER EDUCATION

Realizing the Potential

Alexander Romiszowski and Elvis Otamere

1. WHAT IS CLOUD COMPUTING?

1.1. A Formal Definition of Cloud Computing

> Cloud computing is a model for the enabling of ubiquitous, convenient and on-demand network access to a shared pool of configurable computing resources (e.g., networks, servers, storage, applications, and other services) that can be rapidly provisioned and released with minimal management effort or service provider interaction. This cloud model promotes availability and is composed of five essential characteristics, three service models and four deployment models.
>
> (Mell & Grance, 2009)

This somewhat jargon-laden definition is from a document of the USA's National Institute of Standards and Technology (NIST), which also describes the characteristics of cloud-based computing. Many readers will already be familiar with the characteristics and claimed benefits of what is, arguably, the "IT buzzword of the decade" (CBS, 2009), but let us briefly review the five characteristics mentioned in the last sentence of the definition.

1.2. Five "Essential" Characteristics of Cloud Computing

The NIST document mentions five "essential characteristics" of cloud computing.

1. *On-demand self-service.* A consumer can "rent" computing capabilities, such as server time and network storage, as needed, automatically.
2. *Broad network access.* Capabilities are available and accessed through any Internet-enabled device (e.g. mobile phones, laptops, desktops, tablets and PDAs).
3. *Resource pooling.* The provider's computing resources are pooled to serve multiple consumers, with different resources dynamically assigned and reassigned according to consumer demand.

4. *Rapid elasticity.* Capabilities can be rapidly and "elastically" provided to quickly scale up or scale down the size and scale of services provided.
5. *Measured Service.* Resource usage can be measured, monitored, controlled, and reported, providing transparency for both provider and consumer of the service.

Given that the term *cloud computing* has come to be used so loosely, it might be useful to consider these five characteristics as a form of check-list by which one can verify that a given IT service really offers all the potential benefits. But what are these benefits?

2. WHY CLOUD COMPUTING? THE BENEFITS AND THE RISKS

2.1. Potential Benefits of "Leaping to the Cloud"

Investment in IT infrastructure and operational costs is much reduced. The first of the above characteristics may be of exceptional value to an institution which has yet to design its IT environment and invest almost "from scratch." Some case studies reported in the literature have claimed savings of 80% or more when an organization has opted for a cloud-based as opposed to an in-house solution. For an Open Distance Learning (ODL) institution embarking on a new IT-based venture, such as moving from a print-based to an online model of course delivery, the benefits may be immense (Kourik & Wang, 2012).

Operational costs are much reduced. By building vast "server farms" close to electrical generation facilities cloud computing providers save much of the 95% of energy normally lost in transmission lines. This lowers the computing energy consumption. Many large-scale cloud services providers are choosing to set up such "server farms" in locations where electricity supply is particularly cheap and reliable, for example in countries like Sweden and Finland, right next to major hydroelectric projects.

Processing times are much reduced. Cloud computing works by assigning resources. For example, many small computing jobs can be run on a single large computer and large tasks can be split up to run in parallel on several machines at the same time. This can speed up processing time enormously.

Investment in IT infrastructure for end-users is reduced. An important spin-off from the use of the Internet as the communication network between data and end-users is that access to the system is then by means of an Internet browser. Therefore, in principle, any Internet-enabled device can be used to access the data stored in the cloud. The benefit is that in many cases the end-users can access the system by means of devices that are already available to them for some other purpose. This can drastically reduce investment in additional hardware. This aspect of cloud computing has given birth to another trend: BYOD—Bring Your Own Device. In contexts where funds are in short supply, as is typically the case in education, BYOD might make an otherwise too expensive IT application affordable. Therefore, ever more often, BYOD is becoming a part of a school's technology-integration strategy (Cisco, 2012).

Providers assume all technical tasks of course delivery, management and maintenance. Another major benefit is that typically the cloud services provider assumes all, or most, of the technical tasks that the customer would have to undertake in the case of in-house IT services. This can result in significant savings on in-house staffing. Also, the efficiencies of large-scale server farms tend to lower staffing requirements and so reduce the net cost of technical support. Another related benefit of importance in the educational context is that educational institutions often do not possess the requisite numbers and quality of technical support staff, and if they do invest in the requisite levels of quantity and quality of staff required to manage the system during peak use, the staff are not used to full capacity most of the time—the result is either under-performance or over-expenditure (Nagel, 2009).

Providers charge a pro-rata fee, on a per-megabit or per-user basis. This benefit can make an otherwise unaffordable project viable, by making it very easy to progress from small- to large-scale use. For example, in the case of many online courses, it can be difficult to foresee the popularity of the course in advance of its launch. In the case of a totally in-house operation, the institution must make some estimate of the number of end-users and then invest in the creation of a system that will handle these numbers. If this estimate turns out to be incorrect (either too big or too small) the real costs incurred will be greater than would have been the case if estimates matched reality.

2.2. Possible Risks: Security of Data and Systems

How safe is it to entrust your organization's data to a third party so you are not sure where it is or how it is being protected? What if a service provider closes down—how will you recover the data? Is data in the cloud more at risk from hackers, viruses and spyware? These are typical concerns with a "leap to the cloud" (Syncplicity Inc., 2012). But here are some reasons why the concerns may be largely unfounded, especially in an educational-systems context.

We have all been using cloud-based services for ages, but just did not know it. In the first place, the basic concept of entrusting our data processing needs to "the cloud" is not at all that new. We all trustfully deposit much sensitive and confidential data online in databases managed by other organizations (e.g. banks). Oscar Wilde is reputed to have said: "Today I discovered that all my life I have been writing *prose*, but I never knew it." *Cloud computing* is similar—the name is new but the process it describes is not.

Who is more concerned about cloud services security than the providers? In the second place, the reputation and very business survival of cloud services providers depends on the provision of safe and secure services to their customers. The result should be even greater diligence concerning security. There is little evidence to suggest that data "in the cloud" is by definition any less secure than data stored in-house.

What do we have in an eLearning system that we really need to protect? Third, there is little in an eLearning system which is truly sensitive and secret. Indeed, so far as learning materials are concerned, the current trend is towards the provision of Open Educational Resources (OER)—free and open access to all.

We can make special arrangement to protect private and sensitive data. Fourth, any sensitive data, such as exam results and financial reports, need not be placed in the cloud. We might choose to outsource delivery and management of courses, but choose to keep any sensitive data in-house on a privately managed system, as before.

To what extent are our current in-house databases secure? Last, there is little to suggest that the in-house databases of a university, or indeed of many organizations in both the private and public sector, are all that secure. If outsourced to the "cloud," the data might then reside on a server-farm in, say, Ireland, Sweden or Finland, managed by highly skilled, dedicated, ethical and security-conscious professionals.

3. CASE EXAMPLE 1: ORGANIZATION X

In the literature there are few studies that describe, analyze or evaluate aspects of the implementation of cloud-based eLearning systems. This chapter, therefore, contributes by presenting two case examples, discussed from the project implementation perspective.

3.1. Organization X: The Context

The first case is an implementation of cloud-based eLearning involving:

- a USA-based multinational company which, although a manufacturing rather than educational entity, offers education and training programs to an adult audience comparable in size to a mid-size institution of higher learning;
- a small Cloud Services Provider (with some help from a bigger one);
- a project that was a spin-off from earlier R&D work at a university;
- some two years of accumulated practical experience since implementation.

At the request of the company that is the "star" of this case study, we refer to it as Organization X or just plain "X." To set the context, X:

- is a manufacturer/distributor of heating, ventilating and air conditioning systems;
- is a $12.5 billion company with over 40,000 employees serving customers in about 170 countries worldwide;
- trains many of its employees at some point in time;
- also trains the technical, maintenance, sales and other staff of its network of dealers and representatives;
- has factories in USA, Canada, Europe, Brazil, Mexico, China and India, so both the external and the internal trainees are distributed around the globe.

3.2. eLearning at Organization X

For some years now, Organization X has been using eLearning to train this large and distributed body of adult trainees. Three eLearning programs are now regularly used by about 6,000, soon to reach 7,000, trainees per year. The course topics are:

- Internal training of employees on diverse topics (5,000+ users/year)
- Maintenance technician training (1,000+ trainees, mostly external to "X");
- Refrigeration theory & practice (300+ internal and external engineers, etc.).

The HRD department of Organization X is located in a town where there is a university known for R&D on designing, developing and implementing technology-based training systems, so when "X" first started to use eLearning, it asked the local university for help. As a result, the courses were first developed for, and used on, the Blackboard LMS platform used by the university, with all the course materials and data stored on a university server. However, "X" was fully responsible for management, upgrading, updating and backup of course files, as well as all learning management aspects of the courses.

As the number of eLearning courses and number of students using them expanded, "X" faced some challenges. One challenge was to contain the overall costs by reducing up-front investment in producing and implementing new courses, and also the recurrent per-student operational and maintenance costs. The company was faced with increasing costs for the server space rented from the university to host its increasing portfolio of courses and data generated by the growing number of students. It was also faced with the prospect of increasing the number of technical staff devoted to maintaining the eLearning systems. At the same time, the local university entered into a downsizing mode, some staff reductions were in progress and the remaining IT support staff were no longer as able or willing as before to help the staff of Organization X to learn how to upload and maintain courses on the Blackboard platform or assist them if they had any problems with the server.

This apparent *problem* situation was seized as an *opportunity* by two university staff who had acted as consultants to Organization X, but were in the midst of university downsizing. They formed a small company and presented "X" with a proposal to move its eLearning operation to the cloud. "X" accepted. The process can be summarized as follows:

- "X" selected a "credible cloud services provider." This was the newly formed company of the two previously known and trusted consultants.
- The selected services provider performed a needs analysis—basically this involved an investigation of where and how "X" could benefit from moving its eLearning activities to the cloud (with emphasis on cost reduction and convenience).
- The provider, as a result of this analysis, recommended and organized a move of all the eLearning courses from Blackboard to the Moodle platform—this decision was largely driven by the no-cost OER nature of Moodle and the extensive and mostly free technical support that exists to help new users.
- The migration of existing courses from Blackboard to Moodle was performed by this small new company in a short period of time and at low cost.
- The small new company did not acquire any servers or other hardware, but instead outsourced the data storage to another "credible and reliable" (but much larger) server-farm-providing organization.

A breakdown of the services performed by the consulting company and the costs charged is worthy of analysis. The small provider performed these specific services:

- maintaining the data on servers it rented from another provider "in the cloud";
- uploading and maintaining all course materials and data, as directed by "X";
- looking after all security aspects (including daily backups of all files);
- providing online technical support to over 6,000 trainees, 24/7, worldwide.

For these services, the provider charged "X" an all-inclusive annual fee, which was $30,000 when "X" had in the region of 4,500 active trainees and was raised progressively to $40,000 as trainee numbers grew to 6,000. This annual fee represents the very reasonable-sounding cost of less than $7/student/year.

However, in order to evaluate the cost-benefit, we must also examine the cost savings:

- Infrastructure investment costs were minimally impacted, as the hardware platform previously used was rented (from the university)—however, there was an estimated one-time saving of about $10,000 associated with not buying and/or replacing equipment at the offices of "X" that would have been necessary for the projected additions of technical staff as use of eLearning grew.

- A significant saving was the elimination of LMS platform rental charges (Blackboard) previously paid to the university—$6,000/year.
- However, the greatest saving was obtained by a reduction of technical support staff employed by "X" to keep its eLearning courses running—$60,000/year.

It should be noted that these last savings were reductions in actual costs at the start of the changeover, before the later growth in the use of eLearning. Therefore, the substitution of previous internal staff costs ($60,000) by the cost of similar services offered by the small company formed by ex-university staff ($30,000) represented a 50% saving in operating costs. In addition, there was a further immediate annual saving of $6,000 in rental charges of space for hosting its courses on the university's Blackboard server. Thus, the overall savings in operational costs during the first year after changeover were about 60%. From that point onwards, the provider's fees increased in proportion to the number of actual users of the services. Since the changeover, the annual trainee numbers have increased by about a third and the service providing company has increased its annual fee by a third.

One final, less tangible but no less important, benefit obtained by Organization X as a result of the changes was that the management and other staff of the HRD department could concentrate on instructional improvement of the courses in terms of curriculum and/or learning materials, and on the effectiveness and efficiency of the "academic" trainee support services (guiding, tutoring, moderating and evaluating learning), without concern about the "technical" support services also required by the trainees, but now provided by the services company.

4. CASE EXAMPLE 2: NOUN

This second case study is not an account of an already implemented solution but, rather, a plan for the implementation of cloud-based eLearning at university level in the type of resources-starved organizational context that can be found in educational institutions all over the world, but most frequently and most obviously in some developing nations. Rather than referring to the "star" of this case study as "University Y" we name the institution, as the following case is based on a proposal by the authors of this chapter for implementing eLearning at the National Open University of Nigeria (NOUN).

4.1. NOUN: The Institutional Context

NOUN began full-scale operations in 2002. Since then, it has become Nigeria's leading provider of ODL at tertiary level and is the largest tertiary institution in Nigeria in terms of student numbers. As is the case with many ODL institutions, course delivery was originally in the form of printed modules, supported by facilitators working from a network of regional study centers. However, technology-based enhancements are being planned and implemented, starting with the examination system—*e-Exams*. Another innovation is the use of *e-TMAs*. Each unit of a module of learning materials includes a Tutor-Marked Assignment (TMA). The TMAs are being made available online as well as in printed form so that students can respond and receive facilitator support more quickly and effectively. This requires that students have regular access to the Internet, and so is a step towards fully online courses.

One of the major problems is the existing technology infrastructure. The headquarters in Lagos has a basic IT infrastructure, but this needs modernizing even as regards the administrative purposes for which IT is currently employed. It is in no way adequate for intensive and large-scale deployment of online courses. Funding restrictions are the main reason for this state of affairs. As early as 2002 a study was performed and a "blueprint" for an advanced technology infrastructure, capable of deploying online learning systems and solutions, was prepared. However, a decade has passed and little progress has been made to implement the proposals. In the meantime, the IT world has gone through not one but several "revolutions," so that the proposals of the 2002 blueprint are a long way from reflecting the "best" way to address IT infrastructure needs of the university and to exploit opportunities offered by recent technological innovations (including cloud computing).

Furthermore, there is the question of whether the university's students would be able to access eLearning materials. Currently, the student support system relies principally on the network of regional study centers. Students meet their facilitator individually or as participants in small group tutorial or facilitation sessions. Very few of these centers are equipped with computers for student use, and fewer still have Internet access. On the other hand, research indicates that in Nigeria the vast majority of adults have a mobile phone. By extension, most students already possess and use mobile phones as an integral part of their lifestyle, and a growing proportion of the Nigerian population who may be considered as candidates for higher education already own, or aspire to own, sophisticated "smartphones" capable of running many applications and offering access to the Internet.

4.2. Nigeria: The Wider Context

Some of the challenges NOUN is facing in the process of planned innovation in the use of ICT for teaching and learning are internal, such as the university's IT infrastructure which needs upgrading in order to maintain its study centers' functions and contact with students and with headquarters. But other challenges are external: deficiencies in the national infrastructure (e.g. affordable broadband Internet); unreliability of the power supply almost everywhere across a large country.

The unreliability of the power supply and the frequent drops and surges in voltage pose severe problems for any institution wishing to use sensitive electronic equipment and offer a constant and reliable technology-based service. NOUN, as a distance-learning university in the process of moving towards online course delivery, has to work with, or around, such external constraints in addition to improving its internal infrastructure.

A second, but no less important, consideration at national level is reliable access to the Internet. Broadband connectivity is available, at a price, in major cities, where the demand justifies investment in cable or satellite transmission. This is seldom the case, however, in less populated and rural areas. Also, as in the case of electrical power provision, and possibly due in part to the unreliability of this provision, most Internet Service Providers (ISPs) tend to provide unreliable services of fluctuating quality.

These conditions are well illustrated by the situation in NOUN. Despite the university's IT services providing all academic staff with connections to its servers and offering a centralized e-mail system, nearly everybody uses third-party systems such as yahoo, hotmail or gmail (which, incidentally, are cloud-based services). Even more relevant is the university's strategy to ensure Internet access for key academic and administrative staff: despite its own IT infrastructure NOUN issues all key staff members plug-in USB modems to access the Internet via the cellphone networks—currently the most widespread, most affordable and most reliable technology.

4.3. So, Why Move the University Towards an eLearning Model?

The original reasons for NOUN embarking on the use of online resources were to simplify, speed up and in general improve the end-of-course examinations process. Current developments have, for similar reasons, extended to online completion of TMAs included in each study module. But there is one important difference: whereas the e-exams occur at a predetermined time and place which all students attend and NOUN staff supervise and invigilate, the TMAs are completed "anytime, anywhere" in typical ODL fashion, which implies that all students should have access to the Internet throughout their course, preferably "any time, any place."

Thus, the transition to e-TMAs signals the need for flexible and affordable access to the Internet, which in turn opens the opportunity for more extensive use of online learning. An immediate possibility is the online study of the basic course materials that are already available in electronic format on the university's servers. Once students start to study course materials online, it makes sense to enrich the materials with video, animations, simulations and other ICT-based enhancements, thus moving further towards a full eLearning model. But given the infrastructure deficiencies, why move to eLearning?

One part of the answer is the amount of material available on the Web, the powerful tools available for repurposing it, and particularly the Open Educational Resources (OER) trend to share learning materials freely and allow for the integration of parts of different existing materials to create new derivative materials (as described in Creative Commons licensing agreements). This has transformed the nature of ODL course design and development. "Writing" has been replaced by "repurposing" or "mashing." So, one suggestion to course designers in general, and at NOUN in particular, is to *enrich both existing and new courses with repurposed online study materials.*

Second, the emphasis on "*course writing*" (as practiced in the case of NOUN and many other ODL institutions) has reinforced, rather than reduced, the emphasis on the simple communication of content from teacher to student. Course materials might be outstanding examples of content presentation, but often lack relevant learning exercises or are low on interactivity. Therefore, the second suggestion to course designers at NOUN is to *adopt a course design process which encourages not the authoring of all the content of a course, but rather the writing of course and lesson guides replete with questions, exercises and assignments, which allow students and facilitators to judge whether effective learning is taking place and, if not, to decide what to do about it.*

So, the reasons for moving an institution like NOUN towards an eLearning model are as much to do with the improvement of course design, development and evaluation as with course delivery or cost factors. The main reasons can be summarized as follows:

- to maintain closer and more interactive contact between students and faculty;
- to enrich course materials with multimedia/animations/simulations, etc.;
- to extend the market for courses to students in remote areas and other countries;
- to improve courses by focusing on the design of relevant learning activities;
- to improve efficiency and speed of course development—and lower its cost.

Given the situation at NOUN with respect to the current IT infrastructure and lack of funds for investment in its modernization and expansion, there seems to be no alternative, other than desisting from the pursuit of an eLearning policy, to seeking the cost-benefit advantages of a cloud-based solution.

5. CONCLUSION: A LEAP TO LOW-COST, HIGH-IMPACT, ELEARNING IN THE CLOUD

In the first case study discussed in this chapter, we saw how an organization already running a program of training by means of eLearning could implement it more cost-effectively by "leaping to the cloud." In the second case, we saw how, in addition to such cost-effectiveness benefits, a leap to the cloud can help to overcome many problems and deficiencies, both internal and external to the organization, which are hampering efforts to implement eLearning. From these cases, we can derive the following list of ten suggestions for the implementation of eLearning in an incremental and cost-controlled manner, enabled by recent developments in cloud computing.

1. Rather than investing in one's own infrastructure, rent state-of-the-art IT infrastructure and services, on a pay-per-student basis.
2. Delegate the supply and maintenance of this IT infrastructure, and the functions of data storage, processing, delivery and security to specialist organizations whose very survival depends on providing efficient and secure services.
3. Outsourcing these technical tasks to a cloud services provider, will allow the institution's academic staff to concentrate on their true professional tasks of instructional design and development, and learning facilitation and evaluation.
4. Initially, focus this design and development effort on the creation of interactive learning exercises to support the print-based courses that have already been written and are in use. This is an extension and enrichment of NOUN's current "TMA" model to include student–tutor and student–student interaction and collaboration during the whole of a module rather than just at the end.
5. Recognize that a network of physical spaces (study centers) where students can meet with tutors and with each other, although a valuable component of an ODL system, is by itself not sufficient to enable regular interactive and collaborative study. Therefore, implement interactive learning environments which integrate physical and virtual components in the most time- and cost-effective manner.
6. Design the presentation formats of online learning resources so they can be conveniently accessed and the learning activities performed on Internet-enabled devices that typical university students already own, or aspire to own.
7. Build on societal trends that are making mobile communication devices as essential an item of personal property as a wristwatch or a toothbrush, by promoting a BYOD policy and a culture of personal ownership.
8. In the design and development of new courses, and also the enrichment of existing ones, seek to adopt or adapt existing materials available on the Internet. Provide a digital-media-rich environment based on OER.
9. In addition to any pedagogical benefits, use of OER will reduce the cost of course provision for the institution and also reduce student expenditure on print

materials, thus generating an ROI (return on investment) for the students on the purchase of appropriate Internet-enabled mobile devices.

10. In this way, promote a "digital native" culture among the students. Rather than ignoring, or even opposing, the trends towards digital entertainment, video-gaming, or social networking, seek to capitalize on them through rationally planned use of edutainment, serious gaming and online communities of practice.

As implied by the Organization X case study, many of these hints for successful implementation are applicable to any eLearning project. However, the application of all of them might be more crucial to success and could also have more impact in contexts that share some of the characteristics, problems and risks illustrated by the NOUN case study.

The suggestions must, of course, be adapted to the characteristics of any specific case. For example, in the case of NOUN, we do not mean to suggest the abandonment of the already existing network of study centers where students meet with their facilitators or study together in collaborative groups. However, we do suggest that in order to implement eLearning, NOUN does not need to wait for the day when there are funds available to equip the study centers with computers and broadband access. One can start to implement full-scale eLearning, albeit initially on a small scale tailored to the available budget, well before that by "leaping to the cloud." In due course, when funding becomes available, the technology infrastructure of the study centers can be upgraded, but probably with newer cloud-based technologies which may enhance what can be achieved through personal mobile devices in ways that—from today's perspective—might not even be predictable.

Undoubtedly, just like other new technologies in the past, cloud computing will not be a panacea for every problem of eLearning implementation. However, it does offer a series of potential solutions and benefits that should be seriously considered during the design and implementation of eLearning systems—and it is a trend that is fast growing, not only in the extent of its adoption but, more importantly, in terms of the nature and variety of its potential applications and benefits. The prognosis for eLearning is cloudy.

REFERENCES

CBS (2009). *Cloud Computing Latest Buzzword or a Glimpse of the Future?* http://www.techrepublic.com/whitepapers/cloud-computing-latest-buzzword-or-a-glimpse-of-the-future/2314275.

Cisco (2012). University Embraces Bring-Your-Own-Device with Wireless Network. *eCampus News June 15th, 2012.* http://www.ecampusnews.com/white-papers/university-embraces-bring-your-own-device-with-wireless-network/

Kourik, J. L., & Wang, J. (2012). Cloud Computing's Software-as-a-Service (SaaS) Delivery Model Benefits Technical Courses in Higher Education. *International Journal of Social and Human Sciences, 6*, 581–585. http://www.waset.org/journals/ijshs/v6/v6-97.pdf

Mell, P., & Grance, T. (2009). *The NIST Definition of Cloud Computing.* National Institute of Standards and Technology, Information Technology Laboratory. http://www.nist.gov/itl/cloud/upload/cloud-def-v15.pdf

Nagel, D. (November, 2009). HP Launches Education Cloud Service with ClassLink. *THE Journal.* http://thejournal.com/articles/2009/11/17/hp-launches-education-cloud-service.aspx

Syncplicity Inc. (2012). *Securing Data in the Cloud: 10 Questions to Ask Your Cloud Provider.* http://blog.syncplicity.com/blog/2012/03/securing-data-in-the-cloud.html

31

ROLE OF WEB-BASED TECHNOLOGIES IN FRAMING TEACHING PRESENCE

Fengfeng Ke and Li Zhu

1. INTRODUCTION

Emerging web-based technologies have allowed for innovative learning and pedagogical practice. In this chapter, we examine the educational affordances of two web-based technologies, Tegrity lecture capture system and Second Life virtual reality environment, in providing instructors the ability to expand both cognitive and social dimensions of the teaching presence.

Whereas much has been written about non-traditional learning (Wedemeyer, 2009), much less has been discussed about benefits and strategies of non-traditional teaching with technology in an active, student-centered learning environment. According to the education literature, teaching is to "bring about" a specified sequence of intervening activities necessary to learners' intellectual development required for attainment of desired general educational goals (Hirst, 1971; Johnson, Rhodes, & Rumery, 1975, p. 280). Although researchers differ in defining the "intervening activities" or pedagogical tasks that compose teaching, they generally agree that teaching involves providing situations and materials that are necessary for learners' "coming to know" (or learning), exemplifying the desirable learning activities, and assessing the student's performance of these activities to advance learners or reinstate the activities (Gagné, 1985; Driscoll, 1994).

The pervasive impact of the web-based technologies, however, creates a unique environment for teaching or pedagogical tasks. Web-based lecture capture technologies, for example, can digitally record lectures for online delivery to students, and are challenging long-held teaching traditions, such as the role and style of lectures, the nature and delivery of learning content, and the way students interact with the instructor and content (Wingard, 2004; Jewels, de Pablos Heredero, & Campbell, 2004). They also blur the boundaries between face-to-face and online learning. The emergence of web-based virtual reality platforms is turning the text-intense, correspondence-type online education into an immersive, social-present teaching and learning experience by enabling the construction or embodiment of 3D identity presence (e.g., avatar) and highly personalized virtual interactions (Sköld, 2012).

Adopting the Community of Inquiry (CoI) framework (Garrison & Arbaugh, 2007; Garrison, Anderson, & Archer, 2000) and the relative cognitive and social cultural learning theories, this chapter examines the design, implementation, and potential effect of two web-technology-mediated learning environments in developing teaching presence in higher education, through web-enhanced direct instruction and virtual-reality-based learning-interaction facilitation.

2. THEORETICAL FRAMEWORK

Among theoretical frameworks unique to the online learning environment, CoI is the one that has been widely examined in the literature of different disciplines and has become increasingly used for conceptualizing the online teaching and learning process (Garrison & Arbaugh, 2007; Shea, 2007). Resonating with the work of Dewey and constructivist approaches to learning, the framework of CoI (Garrison et al., 2000) proposes that web-enhanced or web-based learning experiences should be embedded within an online learning community or CoI in which deep and meaningful learning results from the presence of three core elements: cognitive presence, social presence, and teaching presence.

Cognitive presence refers to the affordance of the environment in supporting the development of meaning-construction and sustained critical thinking among learners. It can be conceptualized as the extent to which learners interact with the learning content in a deep and meaningful manner via a cycle of exploration, integration, and application (Garrison & Cleveland-Innes, 2005). *Social presence* refers to the establishment of a supportive environment such that both learners and the instructor can project their identities into the class community, thereby presenting themselves to the other participants as "real and functional" people. Social presence should move beyond socio-emotional presence to cohesion that requires open and purposeful academic exchanges and finally, to achieving a feeling of camaraderie (Garrison & Arbaugh, 2007).

Of the three elements of the CoI framework, *teaching presence* has been mostly understudied but plays the central role in integrating the constituting elements (i.e., presences) to establish and sustain an online CoI (Shea & Bidjerano, 2009; Garrison, Cleveland-Innes, & Fung, 2010). Teaching presence begins before the course commences as the instructor designs and organizes the learning activities and materials, and continues during the course, as the instructor facilitates the learning and provides direct instruction when required.

Emerging research suggests that teaching presence influences social and cognitive presence (Ke, 2010; Garrison et al., 2010). Both social and content-related interactions among participants need to be clearly structured and focused to ensure effective online learning, hence are supported by teaching presence (Garrison et al., 2000). Teaching presence, in its essence, means the design, facilitation, and direction of cognitive and social presences or processes for the purpose of achieving meaningful learning outcomes (Garrison & Arbaugh, 2007). The structure, organization, and leadership associated with teaching presence (i.e., how the course content and participant interactions are structured and facilitated) create the environment where social and cognitive presence can be cultivated. Teaching presence can be operationalized through three components: (1) instructional design and organization, (2) facilitating discourse, and (3) direct instruction.

In spite of the central role of teaching presence, limited research examines the planning and design of teaching presence in web-enhanced learning environments to promote cognitive and social presence during the learning process. Therefore, this chapter examines and describes how emerging technologies can be adopted to construct teaching presence and then enhance the cognitive presence and social presence in learning, as depicted in Figure 31.1. The chapter encompasses two cases: (1) the deployment of web-based lecture capture technology to enhance the direct instruction, and hence cultivate and sustain meaningful interactions between students and lecturing materials (i.e., cognitive presence); and (2) the instruction design of a virtual-reality-based learning environment and organization of virtual-reality-based interactions to facilitate academic exchanges or discourses (i.e., social presence).

2.1. Web-Enhanced Instruction

In the past two centuries, there has been a dramatic increase in using web-based instruction in higher education to enhance traditional, on-campus courses. From the perspective of distributed cognition (Hutchins, 1995), the development of knowledge is attributed to the system of learners interacting dynamically with artifacts and external environment. As such, it is warranted to examine the interaction between instructors/learners and web-based technologies in order to determine how to best develop teaching presence in web-enhanced instruction.

In a multi-institution study, Wingard (2004) examined faculty's perceived changes with teaching activities when web enhancements were used in campus classes, via survey and semi-structured interviews. The study reported that web enhancements were initiated primarily for: (1) pragmatic purposes, such as convenient material distribution and easy student access, easy communication with students, and relevance of the technology to the course topic; or (2) pedagogical purposes, including organization of course materials, expanded web resources to illustrate content topics, and individualized instruction. The faculty in the study reported increased student-to-student and student-to-instructor interactions outside of classroom; they also reported decreased lecturing and minimized

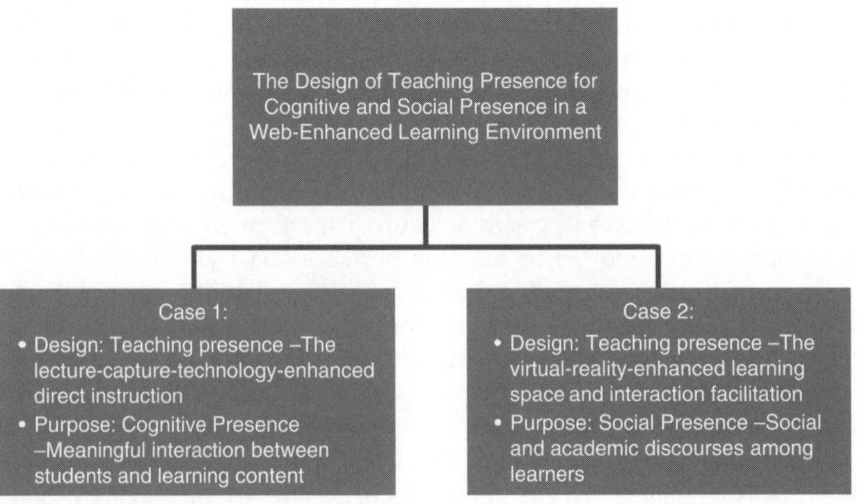

Figure 31.1 Emerging technologies that enhance presence.

note taking, increased student engagement in class, improved process continuity, more student-centered instruction, more readily available practice and feedback opportunities for students, and increased active learning along with the web enhancement usage in campus classes. Wingard's (2004) findings have demonstrated the promising nature of using web-enhanced instruction. But it should be noted that his study focused on instructors' perspectives without report of students' data.

2.2. Virtual-Reality-Based Learning Interaction and Facilitation

Sociocultural learning theories contend that learning only takes place when an individual has opportunities to express his/her identity within the social space of the learning group (Crichton & Kinsel, 2003; Nichani, 2000; Tu & McIsaac, 2002). Empirical research of online learning suggests that identity closely links to students' participation and collaboration within an online learning situation and hence influences the construction of knowledge (Crichton & Kinsel, 2003; Gunawardena & Zittle, 1997; Nichani, 2000; Palloff & Pratt, 1999; Tu & McIsaac, 2002). Interestingly, although identity is a key learning variable in prior educational research, limited work has been done to examine how identity is expressed within diverse online course contexts and whether identity presence relates to the learning and instruction processes. In a recent study, Ke (2010) found that online teaching presence comprises both academic and social presence of an instructor. Online learners, especially those of minority or non-traditional status, expressed a desire for "knowing" their instructors as a "social being".

Recently, Internet-based 3D virtual reality, such as Second Life (SL) developed by Linden Research Inc., has been adopted as an emerging learning platform to support a variety of education activities. Virtual reality (VR) or virtual world is a computer-generated 3D representation of real-life environments. A user can autonomously navigate around a VR (in the *form of virtual* representatives known as *avatars)* and interact with simulated objects, characters or other avatars in real time at the same pace one would experience events in the real world (Mitchell, Parsons, & Leonard, 2007). A recent literature review (Sköld, 2012) reported that VR has been used to support the educational activities of role-play, designing and building virtual presentations, and interacting with instructor-built scenarios. It was claimed that SL could offer a new and exciting perspective for learning facilitation via the development of an "embodied" identity presence. As yet, though, limited empirical research has explored whether and how the design and implementation of SL-like VRs can help instructors to facilitate learning along with identity construction.

3. CASE 1: WEB-BASED LECTURE CAPTURE TECHNOLOGY TO ENHANCE DIRECT INSTRUCTION

3.1. Introduction to the Learning Problem

There are constant and persistent needs from faculty and students in a four-year university to use various instructional technologies to help enhance the teaching and learning processes. Students often miss classes for a variety of reasons such as sickness, medical/dental appointments, family emergencies, etc., especially varsity student athletes who often miss classes due to intercollegiate sport competitions. Furthermore, students often need help with difficult course materials, with homework, or when they prepare for quizzes and tests. There is a need to capture instructor classroom lectures for on-demand student review. In addition, several university departments need to record training courses and make them available online for on-demand review in order to save manpower and resources to teach these training courses.

3.2. Design Decisions

A lecture capture system—Tegrity—was identified to help address these needs. The Tegrity system automatically captures audio and video portions of a course session including any information presented through a computer, a laptop/tablet, or a document camera. The resulting files are available for on-demand student review via the web or to download in various formats. Students can choose to review the entire session, review certain chapters of the session, or search for specific information. Furthermore, Tegrity can be easily integrated with Blackboard through a Blackboard building block to automatically post links to the recorded course sessions in corresponding Blackboard course sites.

3.3. Methodology

From the fall of 2008 to the fall of 2011, a total of 47 faculty members from various disciplines and departments used Tegrity in 156 courses/sections with over 6,000 students enrolled. A total of 3,729 recordings (2,869 hours) were produced. These recordings were viewed 8,609 times (3,507 hours). The recordings were downloaded as podcasts 309 times, downloaded as M4V files 392 times, downloaded as Tegrity sessions 424 times, and downloaded as MP3 files six times. The number of recordings has greatly increased over the past several academic years, so have the times viewed and the number of downloads.

Surveys were conducted at the end of each semester to evaluate faculty and student experiences with Tegrity. A total of 14 faculty members and 981 students took the survey. Of the 981 students who submitted the survey, 520 actually used Tegrity. The goal was to investigate whether this type of system can help enhance the teaching and learning processes.

3.4. Results

The majority of faculty and student participants suggested that the system helped enhance their teaching and learning processes. The results of the survey were grouped into two major themes: benefits of the system to faculty, and benefits of the system to students.

3.4.1. Benefits of the System to Faculty

When asked whether this system helped their teaching in any way, ten of the 14 faculty participants indicated that it did help, three indicated that teaching was largely unchanged, and the system neither helped nor hindered their teaching, and one indicated using the system slowed him down a bit.

Benefits of the system mentioned by faculty included, but were not limited to, the following: the system allowed faculty to review their own performance and improve their teaching, motivated faculty to be more prepared for classes, helped orient new instructors and helped ensure that multiple sections of the same course were covering equivalent material and moving at a similar pace, helped reach more students who missed classes for various reasons, saved instructors' time and effort when they had fewer extra instruction requests, and allowed faculty to teach at a distance if needed.

3.4.2. Benefits of the System to Students

When asked whether the recordings helped them learn the material, 463 out of the 520 students who used Tegrity indicated that it did help with their learning. They further explained the different ways the system helped enhance their learning.

Helped students who missed classes to catch up. Many student participants indicated that they used the system to review lectures because they missed classes. By watching the lectures at their convenience, it gave them a chance to keep up and stay connected to the class. For example, ST131 said, "The recordings were invaluable. For those times when class was missed or simply faded from memory, the recordings offered the chance to literally retake the class."

Helped students review/reinforce materials covered in class. Many student participants felt that watching the lectures helped them review materials covered in class. ST401 stated, "The mere fact that I was able to listen multiple times to a lecture previously attended helped with class. I was able to re-review the material, and digest some concepts that I had forgotten after class." Others felt it helped them reinforce difficult concepts covered in class that they did not fully understand the first time. ST860 said, "They did help me learn the material because I was able to still experience the lecture, and was able to re-listen to them if I didn't understand concepts. It was a classroom lecture without the teacher's presence."

Helped students with higher levels of learning. Some student participants stated it helped them with problem-solving skills. ST002 said, "Hearing my teacher explain it again helped me better understand how to work out problems and why the reactions occurred the way they did." ST742 also noted the recordings helped, "especially when I was having trouble solving a problem that we had skimmed through in class. I could go back and freeze the frame where the solution was worked out and follow along."

While explaining the benefits of the system, student participants noted several major advantages of the Tegrity system included, but were not limited to, the following: The course recordings were very accessible and very well organized, students were given maximum control over their learning, and the system accommodated different learning styles.

Accessibility of the course recordings. Student participants described various dimensions of the accessibility of the course recordings. They suggested the recordings were very accessible because they could be accessed anytime anywhere with an internet connection, and they were always there when the students needed them. Therefore, they could watch the lectures on demand at their own convenience. The recordings were usually available on the website soon after class ended so that students could start watching them. ST115 stated that "Tegrity is just like having personal access to a teacher at any time of day. This greatly helped me learn." Another student participant, ST917, said, "It was always available, like having a teacher in my computer if I needed it."

Organization and chunking of the recordings. Course recordings were grouped by course and were listed chronologically with the newest recording at the top. Each recording was automatically broken into different chapters based on the computer screen change. So students could easily find and locate specific information that they needed. ST259 noted, "The ability to access class anywhere in the lesson and the multi chapter set up with each lesson allowed me to find specific part of the lesson so I didn't have to go back over the whole lesson."

Learner control. Students were given maximum control over the recordings they were watching. They could choose which lecture and which chapter in that lecture to watch. They could play, pause, rewind, fast-forward, speed up and slow down, skip around, and replay a lecture. This allowed them to watch the lectures at their own pace. They could watch the lectures online or download them into different formats, and they could search for specific keywords. Many student participants indicated they liked the speed adjuster feature; it allowed them to watch the lecture in half the time. ST423 said, "I liked the speed adjuster. Sometimes I don't have enough time to listen to the whole lecture, so I speed it up and stop it where it doesn't make sense."

Accommodate different learning styles. Many student participants claimed they were visual learners. Therefore, watching the screen presentation along with the instructor's explanation helped them learn the material.

4. CASE 2: SECOND LIFE-BASED LEARNING INTERACTION AND FACILITATION

4.1. Introduction to the Learning Problem

The sampled course is a graduate-level, WebCT-based online course offered in a major Hispanic-serving research university. Adopting a constructivist and problem-based learning approach, the instructor of this course planned case-based group discussions around realistic situations as the major learning activity. Students performed this collaborative learning activity mainly via the text-based, asynchronous online discussion forum. The instructor facilitated learning through active responses toward students' online posts in the discussion forum.

However, the course evaluation results indicated that students, especially those with a high-context culture background (i.e., Hispanic and Navajo students), perceived the lack of social presence during online learning interaction. Students reported that the text-based asynchronous communication challenged the conventional way of "knowing and trusting" people. An exemplary comment was, "I don't feel like I have real openness with my classmates, which I would have if I was in a classroom sitting with them."

4.2. Design Decision

Second Life (SL) was adopted as an alternative platform to support case-based discussions that aimed to promote students' skills in negotiating with a client in an instructional design project. Students were randomly assigned into different learning groups. Within each group, two students acted as instructional designers with others acting as clients. Each group was randomly assigned with one of the two scenarios of negotiation that are described below:

1. The clients are going to convince instructional designers that their students, course content, and learning needs are unique, and, therefore, they need the designers to create a new learning management system for them. After the meeting begins, the designers will ask the client for their documents to understand their needs. The documents were provided via a PowerPoint slide displayed on a media stand in SL (see Figure 31.2).
2. The clients want to use every social software technology in the book: Twitter, web conferencing, YouTube, SMS. Designers, of course, have to negotiate with the client. Using every technology is going to be a bit overwhelming!

A heuristic guideline on negotiation was provided via the notecard feature in SL. The scenario-based role-playing lasted for an hour and was followed by a 20-minute reflective discussion.

4.3. Methodology

Forty-two students who were enrolled in the course participated in the study. Their SL-based communications and role-playing performance were observed and video recorded. The researchers conducted individual interviews with the instructor and six selected study participants. These participants were purposively sampled to represent the diverse ethnic, age, and educational backgrounds of the students. A questionnaire examining students' perceptions of their SL-based learning interaction experiences was also distributed to all student participants.

A content analysis was conducted with the observation notes and students' virtual interaction transcripts to generate a thick description of the interactions between the instructor and students. The researchers employed qualitative thematic analysis with the interviewing results to develop the narratives and systematically extract emergent themes on the nature of SL-based learning interaction and instructional facilitation. Descriptive statistics were run on the survey results to provide supplementary information on the profile of SL-based teaching and learning.

4.4. Results

The key themes associated with the SL-based interaction and facilitation emerged from the data. These themes, with supportive examples and citations, are presented and discussed below.

4.4.1. Uncertainty in Projecting Physical Learning Space into the Virtual Space

As observed, the SL-based virtual world had been designed to simulate the face-to-face learning environment. The color and style of the virtual building, the seating arrangement, and the media stand had all simulated the face-to-face learning setting in participants' real life. The instructor let students sit around the media stand in the conference room during discussion, "Follow me, we should get to the conference hall," "How about we sit and begin our role-playing activity?" Materials were presented via PowerPoint and a notecard, following a routine practiced at a face-to-face meeting. Some students did not question the necessity of sitting together, whereas the others were nonconforming in using the virtual space. Quzie, for example, left the meeting area on the virtual land (called *island* at SL) and walked toward the ocean, "By the way I'm going to go over and enjoy the water while we chat." She managed to continue text chat with her group-mates

Figure 31.2 SL-based learning interaction.

but her voice faded away when she was away from the meeting area. When interviewed, Quzie challenged the necessity of projecting the physical learning setting and interaction protocol into the virtual space:

> If we are truly going to embrace virtual realities then why do we make them look like the real thing? I found that if I wandered to the riverbank I lost contact with the group—how ridiculous! It is a virtual environment. Shouldn't group participation be controlled by log-ins not screen proximity? Do we have to choose an environment like the holograph room on Star Trek? To "teleport" to an amphitheater is completely senseless to me. I'd rather be sitting on a beach and hearing the surf in the background or sitting in the mist on top of a mountain if I'm going to be virtual.

Apparently, a virtual learning space in Quzie's mind should not be a mimic of her real-life classroom. The fantasy-like openness in the virtual world (e.g., "beach, surf, mist, and top of a mountain") was its uniqueness that was somewhat devastated when the instructor tried to project a traditional protocol of learning interaction and facilitation into this newfangled learning space.

4.4.2. Directions Required in the Virtual World

In spite of the instructor's effort in providing a variety of guidance materials, around 70% of the student participants reported that they needed more directions on the SL-based role-playing activity. As observed, it took an average of eight minutes for each group to start the activity. Such a tardy beginning was due to a poor *preparation for space orientation*, interruptions from *technical issues*, and the *distraction from the virtual-world fantasy*. There was not a virtual map on the university's SL island. "Where to go" was a frequent question popping up during the text chat. Students had difficulty transporting to the SL island where the activity occurred, or had been maneuvering around various buildings to find the designated meeting area. Besides, in spite of the provision of an orientation session, technical issues, such as the configuration of the voice-chat, the tweaking of the PowerPoint presentation on the media stand, and unstable internet speed, still interrupted students' participation in learning interactions. It was also found that participants could be distracted by the novel effect of the SL environment, as this instructional remark highlighted, "Susan, you look like you're having too much fun flying."

4.4.3. Chaos Management

The instructor appeared to be a chaos manager when facilitating SL-based learning interactions. She had to: (1) catch up messages in the text-chat window to follow through a discourse thread with each individual, (2) request technical support to deal with the technical details (e.g, "Can you give the instructions to everyone?"), (3) orient students around the virtual space (e.g, "Let me lead the way"), (4) monitor the virtual meeting (e.g., "Is everyone here? Who do I need to teleport?"), (5) facilitate the role-playing process (e.g., "Can you respond from the client's perspective?"), and (6) adapt the learning task to address the emergent technical issues (e.g., "Some students have issues with the media player. So we will go ahead without PPT"). As observed, the facilitation effort was spent more on the process management than interaction scaffolding.

4.4.4. Level of Engagement and Authenticity

More than 90% of the student participants agreed on the "engaging" and "interesting" nature of the SL-based learning environment. They had frequently reported the excitement of using body gestures and facial expressions during SL-based interactions, "It was interesting seeing the avatars' movements during the activity. It was interesting showing some agreement or disagreement faces, and boring ones."

On the other hand, student participants disagreed on the authenticity of SL-based role-playing. Because the university's SL island was designed as a public learning space, it was not attuned to the role-playing activity in an individual course. Correspondingly, students' interactions demonstrated a sense of disbelief during role-playing, "*I think* I am a client, *as* a client, I . . ." Recurrently, their interactions lacked elaborative arguments with real-life cases, as the following transcript demonstrated:

[18:58] OL:	What kind of disabilities? Do you know?
[18:59] Carolyn:	One possible student is visually impaired.
[19:00] OL:	That will make things very difficult. Audio teaching may be incorporated but not to full extent of the course.
[19:02] Carolyn:	Perhaps some accommodations can be made for her with a special monitor as well.
[19:02] OL:	You're talking a lot more cost. Are you willing to pay?
[19:03] Carolyn:	I believe we may be required to pay for "reasonable accommodations."
[19:04] OL:	Okay so far we have target audience of the general public, preferable Moodle and accommodating to visually impaired. Is that correct?
[19:05] Carolyn:	Yep.

When asked why their discourse was not elaborated as expected, the two participants responded with a short answer, "It was *surreal.*"

5. CONCLUSIONS AND IMPLICATIONS OF THE TWO CASES

In summary, the two cases indicate that emerging technologies can be adopted to construct the teaching presence and hence help promote the cognitive and social presence in a web-enhanced learning environment. Both the Tegrity lecture capture system and SL virtual reality have blurred the boundaries between face-to-face and online learning by providing an innovative way for learners to interact with the learning content and their instructor or peers in a web-enhanced learning environment.

A lecture capture system, as a web-based instructional technology, can be used as a supplemental tool to facilitate and expand instruction-oriented teaching presence from physical classroom to virtual online spaces. By expanding the time and space of teaching, it provides greater flexibility to accommodate various learning needs. Moreover, it helps to cultivate cognitive presence by: providing well-structured course content that is composed of instructor audio, video, and computer screen input; by providing maximum learner control that allows learners to decide when and where they need to review these recordings, how frequently, at what speed, which sections/chapters to review; and by accommodating different learning styles. The usage of the lecture capture system creates meaningful interactions between the students and course content, and hence involves students in deeper levels of learning.

The SL-based virtual learning space, on the other hand, has been used as an alternative learning platform to deliver facilitation-oriented teaching presence. The case study indicated that the SL-based learning environment affords both verbal and non-verbal communications and presents an engaging setting, thus promoting social presence in web-enhanced learning interaction and facilitation. However, transposing the traditional teaching customs to the virtual space has created uncertainty about the boundary and connection between the physical and virtual learning spaces. On one hand it makes virtual world and activity an extension of the regular course; on the other, it leads to students' sense of disbelief toward the virtual presence and activity, especially when the fantasy features of the virtual world are in conflict with the rigid, physical-environment-confined teaching and learning customs. In the case study, the instructor appears to face more challenges when managing learning facilitation in the SL-based virtual space.

Sköld (2012) has argued that every virtual or blended learning space should be a distinct learning environment, implying that the design of the learning space should be attuned to individual learning tasks, and vice versa. This argument is especially true in our second case. Even though students have developed a sense of engagement in the virtual world, the mismatch between a generic university island and the context-specific, scenario-based role-play activity leads to a low level of authenticity (or social presence), and hence fails to promote an immersive, meaningful performance of learning interactions. Therefore, designers and educators should seriously consider the affordance of the VR platform for each individual learning/teaching task, and if necessary, customize the design of the VR world for different tasks.

As the literature on web-based education emphasizes, instructors and learners need to develop the competence in using the multi-modal learning tools and the interface of the platform before they can comfortably and efficiently exploit the web-enhanced learning space to their advantage (Ke, 2010). Purposeful training should be designed to prepare instructors for using emerging technologies to construct teaching presence in a web-enhanced learning environment. Particularly, instructors and/or designers should explore and reflect on the necessity and strategies of developing technology-based teaching, cognitive, and social presence that are not available or affordable in a traditional classroom.

REFERENCES

Crichton, S., & Kinsel, E. (2003). Learning plans as support for the development of learner identity: A case study in rural western Canada. *Journal of Adult and Continuing Education, 8*(2), 213–226.

Driscoll, M. P. (1994). *Psychology of Learning for Instruction*. Boston, MA: Allyn and Bacon.

Gagné, R. M. (1985). *The Conditions of Learning and Theory of Instruction*. New York: Holt, Rinehart & Winston.

Garrison, D. R., Anderson, T., & Archer, W. (2000). Critical inquiry in a text-based environment: Computer conferencing in higher education. *The Internet and Higher Education, 2*(2–3), 87–105.

Garrison, D. R., & Arbaugh, J. B. (2007). Researching the community of inquiry framework: Review, issues, and future directions. *The Internet and Higher Education, 10*(3), 157–172.

Garrison, D. R., & Cleveland-Innes, M. (2005). Facilitating cognitive presence in online learning: Interaction is not enough. *The American Journal of Distance Education, 19*(3), 133–148.

Garrison, D. R., Cleveland-Innes, M., & Fung, T. (2010). Exploring causal relationships among teaching, cognitive, and social presence: Student perceptions of the community of inquiry framework. *The Internet and Higher Education, 13*(2), 31–36.

Gunawardena, C. N., & Zittle, J. F. (1997). Social presence as a predictor of satisfaction within a computer-mediated conferencing environment. *American Journal of Distance Education, 11*(3), 8–26.

Hirst, P. H. (1971). "What is Teaching?" *Journal of Curriculum Studies, 3*(1), 5–18.

Hutchins, E. (1995). *Cognition in the Wild*. Cambridge, MA: MIT Press.

Jewels, T. J., de Pablos Heredero, C., & Campbell, M. A. (2004). Does technology impact on teaching styles or do teaching styles impact on technology in the delivery of higher education? *Issues in Informing Science and Information Technology, 1*, 79–95.

Johnson, H. C., Rhodes, D. M., & Rumery, R. E. (1975). The assessment of teaching in higher education: A critical retrospect and a proposal. *Higher Education, 4*(3), 273–303.

Ke, F. (2010). Examining online teaching, cognitive, and social presence. *Computers & Education, 55*(2), 808–820.

Mitchell, P., Parsons, S., & Leonard, A. (2007). Using virtual environments for teaching social understanding to 6 adolescents with autistic spectrum disorders. *Journal of Autism and Developmental Disorders, 37*(3), 589–600.

Nichani, M. (2000). Differentiating between Communities of Practices (CoPs) and Quasi-Communities: Can CoPs exist online? *International Journal on E-Learning, 1*(3), 23–29.

Palloff, R. M., & Pratt, K. (1999). *Building Learning Communities in Cyberspace*. San Francisco: Jossey-Bass Publishers.

Shea, P. (2007). Towards a conceptual framework for learning in blended environments. In A. G. Picciano & C. D. Dziuban (Eds.), *Blended Learning: Research Perspectives* (pp. 19–35). Nedham, MA: Sloan-C.

Shea, P., & Bidjerano, T. (2009). Community of inquiry as a theoretical framework to foster epistemic engagement and cognitive presence in online education. *Computers & Education, 52*, 543–553.

Sköld, O. (2012). The effects of virtual space on learning: A literature review. *First Monday, 17*(1–2). Retrieved December 12, 2011 from http://firstmonday.org/htbin/cgiwrap/bin/ojs/index.php/fm/article/view/3496.

Tu, C. H., & McIsaac, M. (2002). The relationship of social presence and interaction in online classes. *American Journal of Distance Education, 16*(3), 131–150.

Wedemeyer, C. A. (2009). *Learning at the Back Door: Reflections on Non-traditional Learning in the Lifespan*. Madison: The University of Wisconsin Press.

Wingard, R. G. (2004). Classroom teaching changes in web-enhanced courses: A multi-institutional study. *Educause Quarterly, 1*, 26–35.

Part IV
Evaluation

INTRODUCTION

Sadhana Puntambekar

Technology-enhanced environments to support learning are becoming ubiquitous in both formal and informal educational contexts. Often, the use of technology presents many opportunities as well as challenges for evaluating what and how students learn. Further, the use of technology changes the interactions among the different agents and resources in the context; new routines, processes and curricula are often introduced to integrate technology in innovative ways. This warrants examining learning and interactions in the environment by using a variety of approaches. This section on evaluation, therefore, consists of a representation of methods that span a range of dimensions: qualitative and quantitative methodologies, understanding the context of learning and understanding individual learning gains, examining the processes of learning and the outcomes, to name a few. The data used range from the detailed log data and traces to an understanding of a product or artifact. The twelve chapters in this section bring these diverse perspectives together, to provide researchers with an array of methodologies for use in technology-supported environments. The twelve chapters fall into four main categories: understanding learning in all its complexity, artifacts and interactions, tools and methods, and cognitive and affective dimensions of learning.

Three chapters (Pellegrino, Sandoval, and Tabak) highlight the complexity of examining, measuring, and understanding learning in technology-supported environments. They discuss frameworks and the theoretical and practical dimensions of understanding learning. Of particular interest here are two ideas: (i) we need to pay attention to the context and take into account the learner's environment; and (ii) we need to design theoretically driven assessments that eventually inform practice.

In his chapter, Pellegrino provides an excellent introduction to assessment. The chapter presents assessment as a process of reasoning from evidence, which takes into account advances in cognitive theory and our understanding of how people learn. This provides us with the necessary basis to design our assessments. A key idea discussed in this chapter is to use what we learn from the assessments to improve teaching and learning.

Carrying forward the conversation on designing assessments and examining the complex nature of learning in technology-rich environments, as well as the connection between theory and practice, Sandoval presents an overview of Design-Based Research (DBR) methods. The central premise of DBR is to study an innovation in its natural context, through cycles of iterative design-enactment and redesign. DBR is now widely used to understand how technology-rich innovations can be designed and implemented, but there has been considerable discussion about what constitutes DBR. Sandoval presents the key ideas underlying DBR and, more importantly, gives practical suggestions on how design research is done, to orient readers interested in using the approach.

Tabak examines, in detail, a key aspect of design research, the role of the context in which we use technology. She discusses several dimensions of context such as, internal and external, affective, social, material, and cognitive resources that are available in a setting. She argues about the notion of context as a weave, or a web of interacting agents and resources, which needs to be understood in all of its complexity.

In the next three chapters (Halverson and Magnifico, Cress, and Manches), the authors discuss how student-created artifacts and interactions around them can be used as powerful data sources to understand learning.

Halverson and Magnifico discuss what they call bidirectional artifact analysis as a method for examining the process of digital production. The method uses a range of data types and qualitative methods to trace the development from an idea to an artifact, and from the product itself back to the idea. This bidirectional way of examining both the product and process provides insights into learning through artifacts, reflections, and critiques

In a similar vein, Cress discusses a framework for analyzing individual and group processes of learning. She puts forth the notion of the Co-Evolution Model of Individual Learning and Collaborative Knowledge Building, as a framework for examining the collaboration with social software. Specifically, she examines learning as the interplay between individual cognitive systems and the social system, represented in a shared artifact, such as a Wikipedia article.

Another chapter that uses emerging technologies is by Manches, who discusses the role of interactions with the technology (tool) for evaluation and design. Within the paradigm of embodied cognition, the chapter raises several interesting questions about how interactions with a physical device might provide insights into learning. Manches puts forward two key mechanisms, offloading cognition and providing conceptual metaphors, as the basis of understanding how we can understand the role of interactions in learning.

The next few chapters provide us with methods for analyzing and understanding learning in some detail. These methods focus on the data collected by a technology tool that can be analyzed to provide insights into the process of learning.

Leonard and Derry argue that video is a powerful data collection tool that can support multiple theoretical perspectives and practical considerations. Researchers can analyze a video from many perspectives to address different questions at different times. But using this technology also presents a range of new issues that researchers need to think about. Leonard and Derry discuss the issues of selection, analysis, technology, and ethics.

Reffay and Martínez-Monés present an overview of SNA (Social Network Analysis) as a method for analyzing collaborative interactions. They provide examples of the theoretical underpinnings and the methodological principles underlying SNA. Social networks allow us to understand interactions of the community as a whole, or relationships between individuals, providing a powerful method for visualizing collaborative interactions in technology-mediated learning situations.

The notion of visualizations to help understand interactions is also presented by Hmelo-Silver, Jordan, and Sinha. They discuss CORDTRA, Chronologically-oriented Representations of Discourse and Tool Mediated Activity (adapted from the CORDFU methodology developed to understand technology-mediated learning. This method addresses an important issue—that of temporality—by visualizing interactions and tool use, by chronologically representing discourse, gestures, and the use of a technology tool.

Discussing further the temporal dimension of learning, Reimann and Yacef present process mining, a type of data mining technique. They discuss process mining as a powerful method to understand the processes associated with learning, especially the temporal nature of the processes. This chapter discusses the underlying conceptual assumptions of the method, its advantages and disadvantages, and how to apply the method.

The last two chapters discuss methods to examine the cognitive and affective dimension of learning. Winne, discusses the use of log trace data to understand Self Regulated Learning (SRL). He proposes a class of software, Self Regulated Learning Engines (SRLE), that use log data and data mining in almost real time, together with self-assessments to provide feedback for learning. Rosé examines the motivational and socio-emotional states during social interactions that happen around a technology tool. This method helps eliminate some of the shortcomings of using questionnaires to assess motivational states, providing yet another way to understand factors that affect learning.

Together, the twelve chapters provide us with many techniques to understand learning. They discuss the role of novel technologies that offer us ways to document learning, and techniques through which this data could be analyzed.

32

MEASURING WHAT MATTERS

Technology and the Design of Assessments that Support Learning

James W. Pellegrino

1. INTRODUCTION

For more than a decade, assessment has constituted one of the most controversial issues in education with respect to matters of theory, design, implementation, and educational policy (see e.g., Pellegrino, Chudowsky, & Glaser, 2001). Many of the arguments surround what we assess, how we assess, and the ways in which information derived from assessments is used to shape educational practice. As argued in various sources (e.g., Pellegrino & Quellmalz, 2010), new technologies provide opportunities to shift our assessment systems from a primary focus on summative and accountability practices to one focused instead on formative uses in which assessment information becomes an integral part of the teaching and learning process. But it is not simply a matter of using technology to shift how we assess students, nor the uses to which we put the information. Most importantly, it is a matter of careful considerations of what can and should become the targets for assessment—the types of knowledge and skill that arise in a 21st-century digital world and that are essential for academic and personal success. It is the confluence of method, use, and content that offers the greatest chance for a dramatic shift in the productive integration of assessment into the processes of teaching and learning.

2. ASSESSMENT AS A PROCESS OF EVIDENTIARY REASONING

Educators assess students to learn about what they know and can do, but assessments do not offer a direct pipeline into a student's mind. Assessing educational outcomes is not as straightforward as measuring height or weight; the attributes to be measured are mental representations and processes that are not outwardly visible. Thus, an assessment is a tool designed to observe students' behavior and produce data that can be used to draw reasonable inferences about what students know. Deciding what to assess and how to do so is not as simple as it might appear.

The process of collecting evidence to support inferences about what students know represents a chain of reasoning from evidence about student learning that characterizes all assessments, from classroom quizzes and standardized achievement tests, to computerized tutoring programs, to the conversation a student has with her teacher as they work through a math problem or discuss the meaning of a text. People reason from evidence every day about any number of decisions, small and large. The first question in the assessment reasoning process is "evidence about what?" *Data* become *evidence* in an analytic problem only when one has established their relevance to a conjecture being considered. Data do not provide their own meaning; their value as evidence can arise only through some interpretational framework. What a person perceives visually, for example, depends not only on the data she receives as photons of light striking her retinas, but also on what she thinks she might see. In the present context, educational assessments provide data such as written essays, marks on answer sheets, presentations of projects, or students' explanations of their problem solutions. These data become evidence only with respect to conjectures about how students acquire knowledge and skill.

In the NRC report *Knowing What Students Know: The science and design of educational assessment* (Pellegrino et al., 2001) the process of reasoning from evidence was portrayed as a triad of three interconnected elements: the *assessment triangle.* The vertices of the assessment triangle (see Figure 32.1) represent the three key elements underlying any assessment: a model of student *cognition* and learning in the domain of the assessment; a set of assumptions and principles about the kinds of *observations* that will provide evidence of students' competencies; and an *interpretation* process for making sense of the evidence in light of the assessment purpose and student understanding. These three elements may be explicit or implicit, but an assessment cannot be designed and implemented, or evaluated, without consideration of each. The three are represented as vertices of a triangle because each is connected to and dependent on the other two. A major tenet of the *Knowing What Students Know* report is that for an assessment to be effective and valid, the three elements must be in synchrony. The assessment triangle provides a useful framework for analyzing the underpinnings of current assessments to determine how well they accomplish the goals we have in mind, as well as for designing future assessments and establishing validity.

The *cognition* corner of the triangle refers to theory, data, and a set of assumptions about how students represent knowledge and develop competence in a subject matter domain (e.g., fractions; Newton's laws; thermodynamics). In any particular assessment application, a theory of learning in the domain is needed to identify the set of knowledge and skills that is important to measure for the intended context of use, whether that be

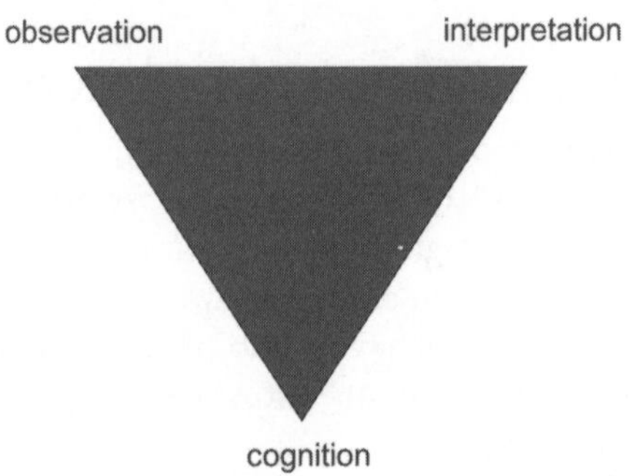

Figure 32.1 The *Assessment Triangle*

to characterize the competencies students have acquired at some point in time to make a summative judgment, or to make formative judgments to guide subsequent instruction so as to maximize learning. A central premise is that the cognitive theory should represent the most scientifically credible understanding of typical ways in which learners represent knowledge and develop expertise in a domain.

Every assessment is also based on a set of assumptions and principles about the kinds of tasks or situations that will prompt students to say, do, or create something that demonstrates important knowledge and skills. The tasks to which students are asked to respond on an assessment are not arbitrary. They must be carefully designed to provide evidence that is linked to the cognitive model of learning and to support the kinds of inferences and decisions that will be made on the basis of the assessment results. The *observation* vertex of the assessment triangle represents a description or set of specifications for assessment tasks that will elicit illuminating responses from students. In assessment, one has the opportunity to structure some small corner of the world to make observations. The assessment designer can use this capability to maximize the value of the data collected, as seen through the lens of the underlying assumptions about how students learn in the domain.

Every assessment is also based on certain assumptions and models for interpreting the evidence collected from observations. The *interpretation* vertex of the triangle encompasses all the methods and tools used to reason from fallible observations. It expresses how the observations derived from a set of assessment tasks constitute evidence about the knowledge and skills being assessed. In the context of large-scale assessment, the interpretation method is usually a statistical model, which is a characterization or summarization of patterns one would expect to see in the data given varying levels of student competency. In the context of classroom assessment, the interpretation is often made less formally by the teacher, and is usually based on an intuitive or qualitative model rather than a formal statistical one. Even informally teachers make coordinated judgments about what aspects of students' understanding and learning are relevant, how a student has performed one or more tasks, and what the performances mean about the student's knowledge and understanding.

A crucial point is that each of the three elements of the assessment triangle not only must make sense on its own, but also must connect to each of the other two elements in a meaningful way to lead to an effective assessment and sound inferences. Thus to have an effective assessment, all three vertices of the triangle must work together in synchrony. Central to this entire process, however, are theories and data on how students learn and what students know as they develop competence for important aspects of the curriculum.

3. ASSESSMENT DEVELOPMENT: EVIDENCE-CENTERED DESIGN

While it is especially useful to conceptualize assessment as a process of reasoning from evidence, the design of an actual assessment is a challenging endeavor that needs to be guided by theory and research about cognition as well as practical prescriptions regarding the processes that lead to a productive and potentially valid assessment for a particular context of use. As in any design activity, scientific knowledge provides direction and constrains the set of possibilities, but it does not prescribe the exact nature of the design, nor does it preclude ingenuity to achieve a final product. Design is always a complex process that, while guided by theory and research, involves optimization under a series of multiple constraints, some of which are outside the realm of science. In the case of educational assessment, the design is influenced in important ways by variables such as its purpose (e.g., to assist learning, measure individual attainment, or evaluate a program), the context in which it will be used (classroom or large-scale), and practical constraints (e.g., resources and time).

The tendency in assessment design is to work from a somewhat "loose" description of what it is that students are supposed to know and be able to do (e.g., standards or a curriculum framework) to the development of tasks or problems for them to answer. Given the complexities of the assessment design process, it is unlikely that such a loose process can lead to generation of a quality assessment without a great deal of artistry, luck, and trial and error. As a consequence, many assessments are insufficient on a number of dimensions including representation of the cognitive constructs and content to be covered, and uncertainty about the scope of the inferences that can be drawn from task performance.

Recognizing that assessment is an evidentiary reasoning process, it has proven useful to be more systematic in framing the process of assessment design as an evidence-centered design process (e.g., Mislevy & Haertel, 2007; Mislevy & Riconscente, 2006). Figure 32.2 suffices to capture three essential components of the overall process. As shown in the figure, the process starts by defining as precisely as possible the claims that one wants to be able to make about student knowledge and the ways in which students are supposed to know and understand some particular aspect of a content domain. Examples might include aspects of algebraic thinking, ratio and proportion, force and motion, heat and temperature, etc. The most critical aspect of defining the claims one wants to make for purposes of assessment is to be as precise as possible about the elements that matter and express these in the form of verbs of cognition that are much more precise and less vague than verbs such as *know* and *understand* which are high-level cognitive superordinates. Example verbs might include compare, describe, analyze, compute, elaborate, explain, predict, justify, etc. Guiding this process of specifying the claims is theory and research on the nature of domain-specific knowing and learning.

While the claims one wishes to make or verify are about the student, they are linked to the forms of evidence that would provide support for those claims—the warrants

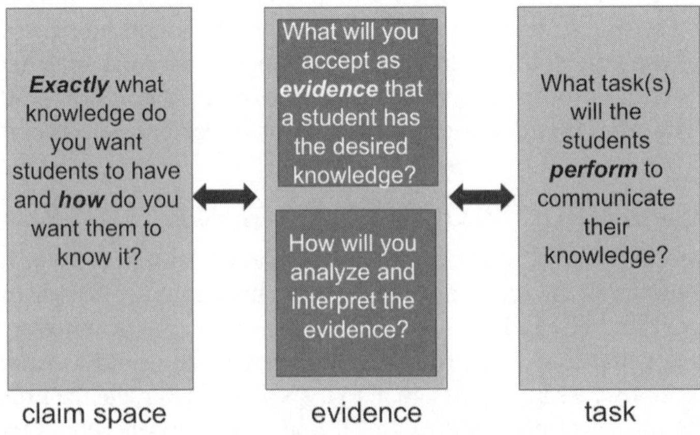

Figure 32.2 Simplified representation of three critical components of the evidence-centered design process and their reciprocal relationships.

in support of each claim. The evidence statements associated with given sets of claims capture the features of work products or performances that would give substance to the claims. This includes which features need to be present and how they are weighted in any evidentiary scheme—i.e., what matters most and what matters least or not at all. For example, if the evidence in support of a claim about a student's knowledge of the laws of motion is that the student can analyze a physical situation in terms of the forces acting on all the bodies, then the evidence might be drawing a free body diagram with all the forces labeled including their magnitudes and directions.

The precision that comes from elaborating the claims and evidence statements associated with a domain of knowledge and skill pays off when one turns to the design of tasks or situations that can provide the requisite evidence. In essence, tasks are not designed or selected until it is clear what forms of evidence are needed to support the range of claims associated with a given assessment situation. The tasks need to provide all the necessary evidence and they should allow students to "show what they know" in a way that is as unambiguous as possible with respect to what the task performance implies about student knowledge and skill—i.e., the inferences about student cognition that are permissible and sustainable from a given set of assessment tasks or items.

4. TECHNOLOGY AND THE DESIGN OF *ASSESSMENTS FOR LEARNING*

Across the disciplines, technologies have expanded the phenomena that can be investigated, the nature of argumentation, and the use of evidence. Technologies allow representations of domains, systems, models, and data, and their manipulation in ways that previously were not possible. Dynamic models of ecosystems or molecular structures help scientists visualize and communicate complex interactions. Models of population density permit investigations of economic and social issues. This move from static to dynamic models has changed the nature of inquiry among professionals as well as the way that academic disciplines can be taught. Correspondingly, a new generation of assessments is well on its way to transforming what, how, when, where, and why assessment occurs and its linkages to teaching and learning.

Although early uses of technology in assessment focused on relatively straightforward logistical efficiencies and cost reductions in large-scale testing programs (see e.g., Bennett, 2008; Pellegrino & Quellmalz, 2010), a new generation of innovative assessments is pushing the frontiers of measuring complex forms of learning. The computer's ability to capture student inputs permits collecting evidence of processes such as problem-solving sequences and strategy use as reflected by information selected, numbers of attempts, approximation to solutions, and time allocation. Such data can be combined with statistical and measurement algorithms to extract patterns associated with varying levels of expertise (e.g., Vendlinski & Stevens, 2002). Research in the learning sciences is simultaneously informing the design of innovative, dynamic, interactive assessment tasks and powerful scoring, reporting, and real-time feedback mechanisms. When coupled with technology, such knowledge has propelled various advances in adaptive testing including knowledge and skills diagnosis, the provision of immediate feedback to teachers and students accompanied by scaffolding for improvement, as well as the potential for accommodations for special populations. Technology also supports movement towards the design of more balanced sets of coherent, nested assessments that operate across levels of educational systems.

A distinction has been made between assessments *of* the outcomes of learning, typically used for grading and accountability purposes (summative assessment), and assessments *for* learning, used to diagnose and modify the conditions of learning and instruction (formative assessment) (Stiggins, 2005). The formative use of assessment has been repeatedly shown to significantly benefit student achievement (Black & Wiliam, 1998; Wiliam, 2007). Technologies are well suited to supporting many of the data collection, complex analysis, and individualized feedback and scaffolding features needed for the formative use of assessment (Brown, Hinze, & Pellegrino, 2008). Two illustrative projects, one drawn from science and the other from mathematics, rely on detailed analyses of subject matter domains and student thinking to provide in-depth assessment and feedback during instruction.

The DIAGNOSER project is based on the facets framework for mapping aspects of student knowledge (Minstrell & Stimpton, 1996) combined with principles of guided inquiry (see Minstrell & Kraus, 2005). It has set out to do the difficult work of breaking down physics concepts into requisite knowledge sets and misconceptions (facets). The facet framework is based on the understanding that students have preconceptions about scientific concepts that are not necessarily unique. For example, students may think that magnets only exert a force when they touch an object, or that "cold" can flow out of something that feels cold. For each of a number of physics concepts appropriate for middle-school to high-school level courses, a series of multi-response items have been created that are designed to have every facet represented at least once in a response choice. An example of an item available online in the DIAGNOSER system is provided in Figure 32.3. Occasionally, students are asked to provide their reasoning for a response by choosing an option, encouraging consistent scientific reasoning. Each topic contains two question-sets, and prescriptive learning activities are supposed to be used in between question-sets. Other resources are provided as support materials.

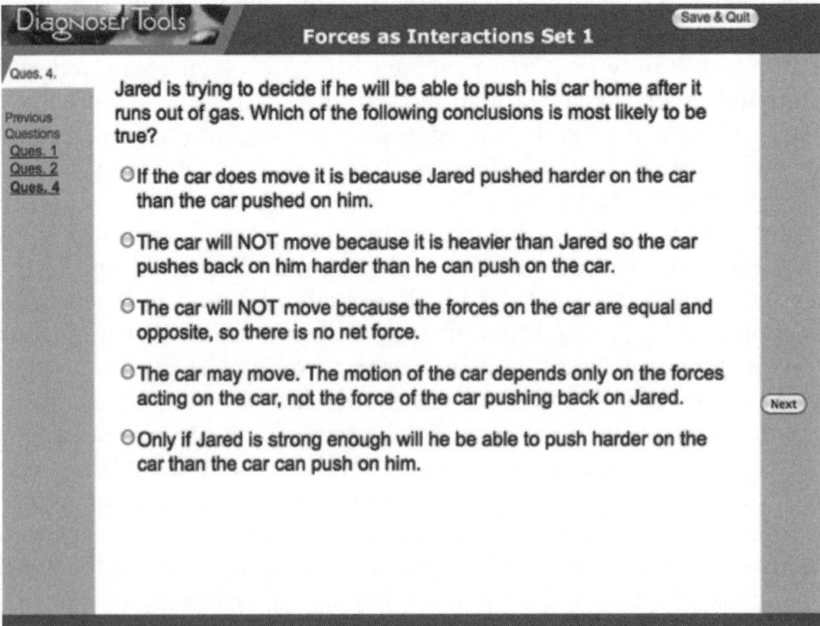

Figure 32.3 Example of a DIAGNOSER physics assessment item.

Based on a student's response to an item such as that shown in Figure 32.3, as well as others in a set related to this topic area, a diagnosis is done of the student's level of understanding. Through the Web-based system, students respond and receive immediate and cumulative constructive feedback. Teachers receive the results immediately and can refer to a series of prescriptive activities that are tailored to address each facet. It would be difficult to replicate the feedback system without the Web-based design, which provides opportunities for self-regulated learning on the part of the student as well as targeted interventions on the part of the teacher. Providing two question-sets along with supplemental material allows for intervention and re-assessment to work toward advancing student understanding.

Another example is the ASSISTment system which is a pseudo-tutor for middle-school level mathematics. Originally based on items from the Massachusetts state standardized test, researchers have developed a feedback system for each item through discussions with teachers. The system uses scaffolding questions, optional hints, and *buggy messages* (specific feedback given after student errors) for each item. Students must eventually reach the correct answer and scaffolds/hints are limited so as not to give away the answer (Feng, Heffernan, & Koedinger, 2009). Teachers receive feedback on student and class progress both on general summative measures (e.g., time to completion, percent correct) and on more specific knowledge components. Students are also provided item-level analyses to identify specific issues with problems (Feng & Heffernan, 2005). Evaluation of the efficacy of ASSISTments has shown that performance is predictive of performance on randomly selected standardized test questions in paper-and-pencil format and finer-grained models predict standardized-test performance better than typical scores (Feng et al., 2009) indicating that providing this analysis to teachers should be useful in interpreting students' skills. Over 60% of students self-report that the ASSISTments help them with the standardized tests, and there is some evidence that scaffolds help students transfer knowledge better than hints, especially on difficult problems.

In addition to assessment of student knowledge and skills in highly structured problems with one right answer, technology can also support the design of complex, interactive tasks that extend the range of knowledge, skills, and cognitive processes that can be assessed (Quellmalz & Haertel, 2004). For example, simulations can assess and promote understanding of complex systems by superimposing multiple representations and permitting manipulation of structures and patterns that otherwise might not be visible or even conceivable. Simulation-based assessments can probe basic foundational knowledge such as the functions of organisms in an ecosystem, but, more importantly, can probe students' knowledge of how components of a system interact along with abilities to investigate the impacts of multiple variables changing at the same time (Quellmalz, Timms, & Buckley, 2009). Moreover, because simulations use multiple modalities and representations, students with diverse learning styles and language backgrounds may have better opportunities to demonstrate their knowledge than are possible in text-laden print tests.

In an ongoing program of research and development, WestEd's SimScientists projects are studying the suitability of simulation-based science assessments as summative assessments with the technical quality required for components of an accountability system (Quellmalz et al., 2008; http://simscientists.org). SimScientists projects are also studying use of simulations for curriculum-embedded formative uses of assessment. Figures 32.4 and 32.5 present screen shots of tasks in a SimScientists summative, benchmark

Figure 32.4 Screenshot of SimScientists ecosystems benchmark assessment showing a food web diagram interactively produced by a student after observing the behaviors of organisms in the simulated Australian grasslands environment.

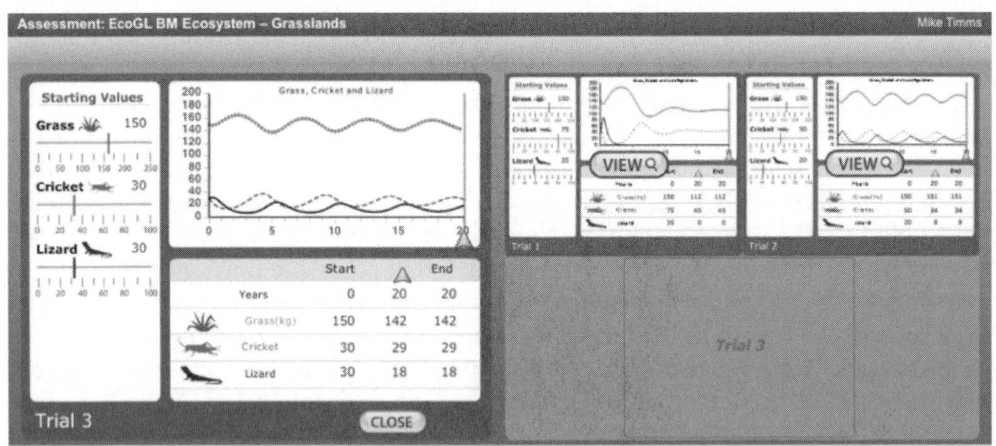

Figure 32.5 Screenshot of SimScientists ecosystems benchmark assessment showing a student's investigations with the interactive population model.

assessment designed to provide evidence of middle-school students' understanding of ecosystems and inquiry practices after completion of a regular curriculum unit on ecosystems.

Students are presented with the overarching problem of preparing a report to describe the ecology of an Australian grasslands for an interpretive center. They investigate the roles and relationships of the animals, birds, insects, and grass by observing animations of the interactions of the organisms. Students draw a food web representing interactions among the organisms in the novel ecosystem. The assessment then presents sets of simulation-based tasks and items that focus on students' understanding of the emergent behaviors of the dynamic ecosystem by conducting investigations with the simulation to predict, observe, and explain what happens to population levels when numbers of particular organisms are varied. In a culminating task, students present their findings about the grasslands ecosystem. In a companion set of curriculum-embedded, formative assessments situated in a different ecosystem, a mountain lake, the technological infrastructure identifies types of errors and follows up with feedback and graduated coaching.

5. CONCLUSIONS, IMPLICATIONS, AND FUTURE DIRECTIONS

It is an exciting time in the field of assessment for several reasons. First, individuals have realized that there are multiple roles for assessment to play in the educational process and that one of the most valuable roles is the formative function of assisting student learning. Second, cognitive research and theory have provided us with rich models and representations of how students understand many of the key principles in the curriculum, how students develop knowledge structures, and how to analyze and understand simple and complex aspects of student performance. Third, technology makes possible more flexible, tailored presentations to students of a much wider and richer array of tasks and environments where students can learn and where they can show us what they know and how they know it. Thus, there is an interesting and powerful confluence among theory, research, technology and practice, especially as regards the integration of curriculum, instruction, and assessment.

In numerous areas of the curriculum, information technologies are changing what is taught, when and how it is taught, and what students are expected to be able to do to demonstrate their knowledge and skill. These changes, in turn, are stimulating people to rethink what is assessed, how that information is obtained, and how it is fed back into the educational process in a productive and timely way. This situation creates opportunities to center curriculum, instruction, and assessment around cognitive principles. With technology, assessment can become richer, more timely, and more seamlessly interwoven with multiple aspects of curriculum and instruction. The most useful kinds of assessment for enhancing student learning emphasize knowledge integration and extended reasoning, support a process of individualized instruction, allow for student interaction, collect rich diagnostic data, and provide timely feedback. The demands and complexity of these types of assessment can be quite substantial, but technology makes them feasible. In diagnostic assessments of individuals' learning, for example, significant amounts of information must be collected, interpreted, and reported. No educator, whether a classroom teacher or other user of assessment data, could realistically be expected to handle the information flow, analysis demands, and decision-making burdens involved without technological support. Thus, technology removes some of the constraints that previously made high-quality formative assessment of complex performances difficult or impractical for a classroom teacher. Examples described earlier illustrate how technology can help infuse ongoing formative assessment into the learning process.

Technological advances will allow for the attainment of many of the goals that educators, researchers, policymakers, teachers, and parents have envisioned for assessment as a viable source of information for educational improvement (U.S. Department of Education, 2010). When powerful technology-based systems are implemented in classrooms, rich sources of information about intellectually significant student learning will be continuously available across wide segments of the curriculum and for individual learners over extended periods of time. This is exactly the kind of information we now lack, making it difficult to use assessment to truly support learning. The major issue is not whether this type of innovative assessment design, data collection, and information analysis is feasible in the future. Rather, the issue is how the world of education anticipates and embraces this possibility, and how it will explore the resulting options for effectively using assessment information to meet the multiple purposes served by current assessments and, most important, to enhance student learning.

REFERENCES

Bennett, R. E. (2008). *Technology for large-scale assessment.* ETS Report No. RM-08-10. Princeton, NJ: Educational Testing Service.

Black, P., & Wiliam, D. (1998). *Inside the Black Box: Raising Standards through Classroom Assessment.* London, UK: King's College.

Brown, J., Hinze, S., & Pellegrino, J. W. (2008). Technology and formative assessment. In T. Good (Ed.), *21st Century Education. Vol 2. Technology* (pp. 245–255). Thousand Oaks, CA: Sage.

Feng, M., & Heffernan, N. T. (2005). Informing teachers live about student learning: Reporting in the ASSISTment system. *Technology, Instruction, Cognition and Learning, 3*, 1–14.

Feng, M., Heffernan, N. T., & Koedinger, K. R. (2009). Addressing the assessment challenge in an online system that tutors as it assesses. *User Modeling and User-Adapted Interaction: The Journal of Personalization Research (UMUAI), 19*(3), 243–266.

Minstrell, M., & Krause, P. (2005). Guided inquiry in the classroom. In J. Bransford & S. Donovan (Eds.), *How Students Learn History, Mathematics, and Science in the Classroom.* Washington, DC: National Academy Press.

Minstrell, J., & Stimpton, V. (1996). A classroom environment for learning: Guiding students' reconstruction of understanding and reasoning. In L. Schauble & R. Glaser (Eds.), *Innovations in Learning: New Environments for Education* (pp. 175–202). Mahwah, NJ: Erlbaum.

Mislevy, R., & Haertel, G. D. (2007). Implications of evidence-centered designs for educational testing. *Educational Measurement: Issues and Practices, 25*(4), 6–20.

Mislevy, R. J., & Riconscente, M. M. (2006). Evidence-centered assessment design: Layers, concepts, and terminology. In S. Downing & T. Haladyna (Eds.), *Handbook of Test Development* (pp. 61–90). Mahwah, NJ: Erlbaum.

Pellegrino, J. W., & Quellmalz, E. S. (2010). Perspectives on the integration of technology and assessment. *Journal of Research on Technology and Education, 43*(2), 119–134.

Pellegrino, J., Chudowsky, N., & Glaser, R., (Eds.) (2001). *Knowing What Students Know: The Science and Design of Educational Assessment.* Washington, DC: National Academy Press.

Quellmalz, E. S., Timms, M., & Buckley, B. (2009). *Using Science Simulations to Support Powerful Formative Assessments of Complex Science Learning.* Paper presented at the annual meeting of the American Educational Research Association. San Diego, CA.

Quellmalz, E. S., & Haertel, G. (2004). *Technology supports for state science assessment systems.* Paper commissioned by the National Research Council Committee on Test Design for K-12 Science Achievement.

Quellmalz, E. S., DeBarger, A. H., Haertel, G., Schank, P., Buckley, B., Gobert, J., Horwitz, P., & Ayala, C. (2008). Exploring the role of technology-based simulations in science assessment: The Calipers Project. In

J. Coffrey, R. Douglas, and C. Stearns (Eds.), *Science Assessment: Research and Practical Approaches* (pp. 191–202). WDC: National Science Teachers Association.

Stiggins, R. (2005). From formative assessment to assessment for learning: A path to success in standards-based schools. *Phi Delta Kappan, 87*(3), 324–328.

U.S. Department of Education (2010). *National Educational Technology Plan.* Washington, DC: U.S. Department of Education.

Vendlinski, T., & Stevens, R. (2002). Assessing student problem-solving skills with complex computer-based tasks. *Journal of Technology, Learning, and Assessment, 1*(3). Available from http://ejournals.bc.edu/ojs/index.php/jtla/article/viewFile/1669/1511.

Wiliam, D. (2007). Keeping learning on track. In F. K. Lester Jr (Ed.), *Second Handbook of Mathematics Teaching and Learning* (pp. 1051–1098). Greenwich, CT: Information Age Publishing.

33

EDUCATIONAL DESIGN RESEARCH IN THE 21ST CENTURY

William A. Sandoval

INTRODUCTION

Since the term "design experiments" was coined two decades ago (Collins, 1992), what is now more commonly known as educational design research has moved out of the nascent learning sciences community and into the mainstream of educational research (Levin & O'Donnell, 1999; NRC, 2002; Schoenfeld, 2006). The strengths and weaknesses of the approach have been described and dissected over the last decade, reflecting a tension between advocates for educational design research and observers who worry about the rigor and epistemic standing of the alleged methodology (for example, in Barab, 2004; Kelly, 2003). Historically, educational design research is closely tied to the development of educational technologies, but is currently conducted across a wide range of learning settings, with and without technology. As an approach to studying learning and education, it seems here to stay. Still, two decades in, there remains not inconsiderable confusion over what "it" really is, and, perhaps more importantly, how to do "it." The aim of this chapter is to provide an overview of the writing about design research to outline the core features of the approach and discuss core methodological issues to doing design research.

The question most often asked of educational research by policymakers and the public seems to be, "What works?" The educational design researcher asks a different question, "What works, for whom, under what conditions?"[1] In fact, from the perspective of design research, "what works?" is exactly the wrong question to ask because it ignores all those aspects of difference between people and places that are likely to affect how any particular educational innovation plays out. Educational design research is centrally concerned with context. This concern carries with it a variety of methodological implications and challenges that, to date, scholars and practitioners of design research have only partially managed to address. Educational design research can trace its roots in a variety of intellectual traditions of psychology dating back to the early twentieth century, including the emergence of sociocultural perspectives on learning and development (a good history is Confrey, 2006), and Cronbach's (1975) reflections on aptitude-treatment interactions.

This variety is reflected in the theoretical breadth visible in educational design research as it has been practiced over the last two decades, and the concomitant methodological variety (Bell, 2004). Consequently, descriptions of design research have leaned much more towards epistemic and social commitments rather than descriptions of methods.

WHAT EDUCATIONAL DESIGN RESEARCH IS

There has been an explosion of writing about design research in the last decade. Special issues of well-regarded and influential journals have been devoted to its characterization (Barab, 2004; Kelly, 2003; Sandoval & Bell, 2004). It appears in the American Educational Research Association's major methods handbook (Schoenfeld, 2006), and even featured in two chapters in a recent handbook on the learning sciences (Barab, 2006; Confrey, 2006). Various formulations and facets of design research figured prominently in a recent handbook on science and mathematics education research design (Kelly & Lesh, 2000). More recently, it has been examined and described in edited volumes (Dai, 2011; Van den Akker, Gravemeijer, McKenney, & Nieveen, 2006) and even has its own handbook (Kelly, Lesh, & Baek, 2008).

Core Features of Design Research

Examination of this volume of writing on design research reveals a range of characterizations of the nature and purposes of design research and ways to carry it out. Bell offers a succinct yet inclusive definition of design research as, "those enterprises that involve intentional design coupled to empirical research and theorizing about what takes place in the authentic contexts where the designed objects come to be used" (Bell, 2004, p. 245). Looking across the writing on design research, such enterprises can be characterized as research that holds a set of epistemic and social commitments. Namely, design research:

- pursues joint goals of improving practice and refining theory;
- occurs through iterated cycles of design, enactment, and analysis;
- employs methods that link processes of enactment to outcomes;
- involves sustained engagement with stakeholders;
- strives to produce usable knowledge.

It is critical to understand what design in design research means. Design research refers to a mode of research and development on educational innovations. The *research* in "design research" refers to the systematic study of designed learning environments. Thus, the *design* in "design research" can refer, and has, to just about any facet of a designed environment that researchers feel requires systematic study. This can include instructional strategies, broader pedagogical frameworks, or computational and other tools designed to support some kind of learning. Many, if not most, design research examples include all of these elements.

HOW EDUCATIONAL DESIGN RESEARCH IS DONE

Given the variety of work described as design research, it would be misleading to argue that there is a single way to do design research correctly, or even a finite set of ways to do it. In light of the theoretical variety evident in design research and the different strengths apparent in such variety, it may not even be desirable to articulate a single approach to the conduct of design research (Bell, 2004). There is a common idea of the general approach that can be summarized. More crucially, design research frames and addresses a set of methodological issues that demarcate it from other approaches to educational research.

The General Cycle of Design Research

Design research is often described as research that iterates through a cycle of design, enactment, analysis, and revision (Bielaczyc & Collins, 2007; Cobb, Confrey, diSessa, Lehrer, & Schauble, 2003; Design-Based Research Collective, 2003). Of course, designs are developed to solve particular kinds of problems, so design research really starts with problem analysis (Edelson, 2002). A good problem analysis has what Bereiter (2002) observes is a visionary quality focused on innovation that goes well beyond notions of program improvement or increasing efficiency—an ethos of potential and possibility.

A problem analysis leads to an initial design of some environment. Crucially, design research sees design as theoretical, as a means of embodying theoretical conjectures about learning in the chosen problem context and how such learning can be supported (Cobb et al., 2003; Confrey & Lachance, 2000; Sandoval, 2004). Since Edelson's (2002) initial effort to describe a process of design research, several efforts to characterize the design process have appeared. Some of these are idiosyncratic, in the sense they offer a particular example as a model (Barab, 2006), others describe heuristics that guide the design process (Confrey, 2006; Edelson, 2002; Gravemeijer & Cobb, 2006), while others present structural models of the process (Middleton, Gorard, Taylor, & Bannan-Ritland, 2008; Sandoval, 2004, in press). For developers of educational technologies, it is particularly crucial to recognize that social elements of learning environments also require design (Bielaczyc, 2006).

Initial designs are then enacted in some sample of setting for which they have been designed. Design research is characteristically open to revision on the go, during enactment, as both a means to improve learners' experiences as needed and to pursue hypotheses about learning or its support that arise in the moment (Gravemeijer & Cobb, 2006). Obviously, any such revisions must be carefully documented as they are made. Following an enactment, retrospective analyses (Cobb, 2001) focus on generating or testing hypotheses about how a designed environment functioned to produce its outcomes (intended and unintended). Insight from the analysis of unintended outcomes has been cited as an advantage of design research (Brown, 1992; diSessa & Cobb, 2004). Retrospective analyses are used to revise designs and the cycle continues. Of course several issues arise in this process.

Methodological Issues in Design Research

Educational design research shares the challenges of any empirical research, but both the role of design in the approach and the contextualization assumption raise issues unique to design research. Defining and accounting for contextual variations and their influences on the conclusions that can be drawn from design research have been the focus of much writing about design research (Barab, Hay, & Yamagata-Lynch, 2001; Brown, 1994; Cobb et al., 2003; Collins, 1999; Collins, Joseph, & Bielaczyc, 2004; Hoadley, 2002; Steffe & Thompson, 2000; Tabak, 2004). The discussion here addresses this overarching concern in terms of some concrete issues of method.

Site Selection

Sampling is an issue in any research design, and how samples are chosen has a serious influence on the validity of consequent claims. Traditional concerns of representativeness or equivalence (Raudenbush, 2005) can be a factor in design research, but the acute issue of sampling for design research is selecting sites for research where the problem one is trying to solve exists, or the opportunities one is trying to exploit can be realized. It is usually crucial to choose sites that are open to innovation and have the interest and capacity to collaborate at the level required by the research team. Site selection, in the early stages of design research is, therefore, more about selecting collaborators than sites. The collaborative nature of design research highlights that site selection affects not just issues of sampling, but influences the designed environment directly because of the inevitably blurry intermingling of the external design and the existing, ongoing designed and emergent features of the setting into which designs are imported (Tabak, 2004).

Instrumentation and Outcome Measurement

The core aim of educational design research to link targeted outcomes to the functional processes created through designs raises, perhaps, the central methodological challenge of design research. The variability in approaches to design research, and the wide spread in researchers applying the label to their own work has led to a concern that design research lacks an argumentative grammar to describe how such links can be warranted (Kelly, 2004). The theoretical variety among approaches to design research probably makes a singular description of such a grammar unlikely (Bell, 2004). This section and the next decompose the linkage of outcomes to processes to separately examine issues of outcome measurement and process observation.

Design research, especially technology-oriented work, often aims to transform both how and what students learn (Roschelle, Pea, Hoadley, Gordin, & Means, 2000). This creates the challenge of designing instruments that can measure the outcomes of interest. Schwartz, Chang, and Martin (2008) argued that design researchers can profit from more attention to issues of instrumentation and measurement. The design of good measures, they argue, is crucial for generating evidence appropriate to the innovations of design research, for the simple reason that more widely available measures are tuned to current practice rather than possibility. Schwartz and colleagues describe a process of "assessment experiments" they use to tune measures to innovations.

Characterizing Relevant Processes

Assuming a design research team has access to good outcome measures, the enterprise requires methods to characterize the processes at work in a learning environment that are causally responsible for those outcomes. It would be impossible and even absurd to attempt to completely specify how the relevant functional processes in a designed learning environment might be observed. Bell (2004) indicates some of the range of possibility in his discussion of differing theoretical approaches to educational design research, and particular methodological approaches are explicated in a recent handbook on design research (Kelly et al., 2008).

The use of video records of interaction seems almost a central feature of design research, given its central place in Brown's (1992) seminal discussion and its subsequent ubiquity in the learning sciences community. Clearly, video records of the enactments of specific versions of a learning environment design can support detailed analyses of the function of the design in use, analyses that are crucial to progress in any design research effort. There are several features of video recordings that lead design researchers to prefer them as data sources for capturing and analyzing relevant processes of design function. Instructive resources on techniques for capturing and analyzing video are available and interested readers would be well served by two recent discussions of video analysis (Derry et al., 2010; Erickson, 2006). Two points warrant emphasis here, especially for newcomers to educational design research. First, recording video is itself an act of theorizing that involves choices about who and what to record, for how long, on what schedule, and so on (Hall, 2000). Such choices inescapably entail decisions, usually tacit, about what *not* to record. Second, once recorded, video can be analyzed in a number of ways. Erickson (2006) describes three approaches to video analysis that vary markedly according to differences in theoretical orientation. Design researchers must think carefully about their guiding theoretical orientations and the specific hypotheses they have, or do not have, at any particular point in a design research cycle.

A final note about process observations: critics of design research worry that designers are biased toward showing their intervention works (Shavelson, Phillips, Towne, & Feuer, 2003). On the contrary, design research demands attention to negative results or the aim of sustainable innovation cannot be reached (Bereiter, 2002). Design is iterative by nature because early designs rarely solve their target problem fully, and the impetus of design is improvement. This naturally tunes design researchers to shortcomings in designs and focuses analytic attention on their causes and possible solution (Sandoval, 2004). This is how educational design research advances theoretical insight, by driving analyses of processes of design enactments that refine the conjectures embodied in designs.

Working across Levels of Analysis

Design research takes place in authentic settings where learning occurs; that is, pretty much everywhere. Obviously, each of these settings is comprised of individuals who participate in it, and their very participation is itself embedded within social, institutional, cultural, and historical contexts. It is now taken for granted that all of these layers influence how any educational intervention might function (Collins, 1999). Understanding how a design functions in a particular setting, and how that function could vary across settings, requires attention to how the researchers' level of analysis interacts with adjacent levels of analysis.

Collins (1999; Collins et al., 2004) has articulated several levels at which particular designs could be analyzed, moving from the individual cognitive level through to the institutional level (e.g., the school), and lists a range of variables design researchers might attempt to measure at each level. It is not at all clear that any single design research effort within a particular research cycle could attend to all of these levels at once. Collins et al. (2004) suggest that multi-disciplinary teams with expertise distributed across all of these levels could do the job, but it may not be feasible, especially in the early stages of a design research effort, to engage such teams. Bell (2004) points out that the theoretical breadth observed across the landscape of design research includes a wide variety of aims and it is quite possible that different aims would appropriately lead researchers to focus on one level of the educational system over others.

Coordinating across levels of analysis requires methods tuned to each. Collins et al. (2004) make very specific suggestions of the kinds of data and analyses best suited to characterizing different levels, and these could be particularly useful for newcomers to educational design research, although it might well be that these or any specific set of prescriptions would be contested from other theoretical perspectives. A methodological issue that can be easily forgotten is that these different planes of analysis operate at different time scales (Lemke, 2000), and research methods must be tuned to these differences. For instance, community level norms are relatively stable and usually tacit, so brief records of interpersonal interaction may not surface them. Rather, observing the function of norms within a community and their influence on interpersonal interactions requires longer scales of observation (e.g., Cobb, Stephan, McClain, & Gravemeijer, 2001).

Trajectory

A final methodological challenge of design research that has not been treated much in the literature is the issue of trajectory. There are examples of design research trajectories, of course, but little discussion of how cycles progress, how later cycles might vary from earlier ones. The few design researchers who have addressed trajectory suggest a progression from small to broad scale, with an orientation on practical design improvement (Bannan-Ritland, 2003; Edelson, 2002; Middleton et al., 2008). These descriptions tend not to address how shifts in scale actually change the research effort, either in terms of the object of design work as projects increase their scale or the attendant research focus. Fishman, Marx, Blumenfeld, and Krajcik (2004) provide a well-articulated example of how the movement of technology-supported curricula from small to large scale changed the nature of both the design and research efforts. Clearly, any move to scale is not simply an issue of a project getting bigger, but entails a shift in the objects of design and the focus of research.

It is not obvious that a trajectory of increasing scale is the only, or most important, trajectory for design research. There are examples of design research projects that seem more focused on digging deeper into the learning phenomena of interest, rather than getting bigger, such as the example of Lehrer and Schauble's work on children's reasoning about data (Lehrer & Schauble, 2000, 2004; Lehrer, Schauble, & Lucas, 2008).

These and other examples of design research efforts that have traveled longer trajectories are certainly available, but the educational design research community has yet to write in a generalized way about the potential trajectories of design research, how some trajectories might privilege practical innovation over theoretical development and vice versa, or even how these conjoint goals can really be pursued. A crucial issue is figuring out how to specify design principles and domain theories in practically usable terms and avoid articulating principles at a vacuous level of abstraction (Bielaczyc & Collins, 2007).

CONCLUSIONS

The summary of design research offered here is intended mainly to orient newcomers to design research to the commitments inherent in the approach and convey the variety of ways the expanding design research community has pursued them, as well as to characterize methodological issues that seem, to me, to be inevitable to doing design research. This chapter is a complement to the chapter by Reimann in the Foundations section of this volume. It does not seem possible to be entirely comprehensive about design research today, but the structure laid out here should be enough to point readers to relevant scholarship. As the possibilities for educational technologies in the 21st century become more ubiquitous, mobile, and personal, no doubt design research will migrate into many more kinds of settings to investigate many more contexts of learning.

NOTE

1. I owe this succinct formulation of the question to Louis Gomez (personal communication, October 2011).

REFERENCES

Bannan-Ritland, B. (2003). The role of design in research: The integrative learning design framework. *Educational Researcher, 32*(1), 21–24.

Barab, S. A. (2004). Design-based research: Clarifying the terms [Special Issue]. *Journal of the Learning Sciences, 13*(1).

Barab, S. A. (2006). Design-based research: A methodological toolkit for the learning sciences. In R. K. Sawyer (Ed.), *The Cambridge handbook of the learning sciences* (pp. 153–172). New York: Cambridge University Press.

Barab, S. A., Hay, K. E., & Yamagata-Lynch, L. C. (2001). Constructing networks of action-relevant episodes: An in situ research methodology. *Journal of the Learning Sciences, 10*(1&2), 63–112.

Bell, P. (2004). On the theoretical breadth of design-based research in education. *Educational Psychologist, 39*(4), 243–253.

Bereiter, C. (2002). Design research for sustained innovation. *Cognitive Studies, Bulletin of the Japanese Cognitive Science Society, 9*(3), 321–327.

Bielaczyc, K. (2006). Designing social infrastructure: Critical issues in creating learning environments with technology. *Journal of the Learning Sciences, 15*(3), 301–329.

Bielaczyc, K., & Collins, A. (2007). Design research: Foundational perspectives, critical tensions, and arenas for action. In J. C. Campione, K. E. Metz, & A. S. Palincsar (Eds.), *Children's learning in and out of school: Essays in honor of Ann Brown* (pp. 89–111). Hillsdale, NJ: Lawrence Erlbaum Associates.

Brown, A. L. (1992). Design experiments: Theoretical and methodological challenges in creating complex interventions in classroom settings. *Journal of the Learning Sciences, 2*(2), 141–178.

Brown, A. L. (1994). The advancement of learning. *Educational Researcher, 23*(8), 4–12.

Cobb, P. (2001). Supporting the improvement of learning and teaching in social and institutional context. In S. M. Carver & D. Klahr (Eds.), *Cognition and instruction: 25 years of progress* (pp. 455–478). Mahwah, NJ: Lawrence Erlbaum.

Cobb, P., Confrey, J., diSessa, A., Lehrer, R., & Schauble, L. (2003). Design experiments in educational research. *Educational Researcher, 32*(1), 9–13.

Cobb, P., Stephan, M., McClain, K., & Gravemeijer, K. (2001). Participating in classroom mathematical practices. *Journal of the Learning Sciences, 10*(1&2), 113–163.

Collins, A. (1992). Toward a design science of education. In E. Scanlon & T. O'Shea (Eds.), *New directions in educational technology* (pp. 15–22). New York, Berlin: Springer-Verlag.

Collins, A. (1999). The changing infrastructure of education research. In E. C. Lagemann & L. S. Shulman (Eds.), *Issues in education research: problems and possibilities* (pp. 289–298). San Francisco, CA: Jossey-Bass.

Collins, A., Joseph, D., & Bielaczyc, K. (2004). Design research: Theoretical and methodological issues. *Journal of the Learning Sciences, 13*(1), 15–42.

Confrey, J. (2006). The evolution of design studies as methodology. In R. K. Sawyer (Ed.), *The Cambridge handbook of the learning sciences* (pp. 135–151). New York: Cambridge University Press.

Confrey, J., & Lachance, A. (2000). Transformative teaching experiments through conjecture-driven research design. In A. E. Kelly & R. A. Lesh (Eds.), *Handbook of research design in mathematics and science education* (pp. 231–265). Mahwah, NJ: Lawrence Erlbaum Assoc.

Cronbach, L. J. (1975). Beyond the two disciplines of scientific psychology. *American Psychologist, 30*(2), 116–127.

Dai, D. (Ed.). (2011). *Design research on learning and thinking in educational settings.* London: Routledge.

Derry, S. J., Pea, R. D., Barron, B., Engle, R. A., Erickson, F., Goldman, R., et al. (2010). Conducting video research in the learning sciences: Guidance on selection, analysis, technology, and ethics. *Journal of the Learning Sciences, 19*(1), 3–53.

Design-Based Research Collective. (2003). Design-based research: An emerging paradigm for educational inquiry. *Educational Researcher, 32*(1), 5–8.

diSessa, A. A., & Cobb, P. (2004). Ontological innovation and the role of theory in design experiments. *Journal of the Learning Sciences, 13*(1), 77–103.

Edelson, D. C. (2002). Design research: What we learn when we engage in design. *Journal of the Learning Sciences, 11*(1), 105–121.

Erickson, F. (2006). Definition and analysis of data from videotape: Some research procedures and their rationales. In J. Green, G. Camilli, & P. B. Elmore (Eds.), *Handbook of complementary methods in education research* (pp. 177–205). Washington, DC: AERA.

Fishman, B. J., Marx, R. W., Blumenfeld, P. C., & Krajcik, J. S. (2004). Creating a framework for research on systemic technology innovations. *Journal of the Learning Sciences, 13*(1), 43–76.

Gravemeijer, K., & Cobb, P. (2006). Design research from a learning design perspective. In J. Van den Akker, K. Gravemeijer, S. McKenney, & N. Nieveen (Eds.), *Educational design research* (pp. 17–51). London: Routledge.

Hall, R. (2000). Video recording as theory. In R. A. Lesh & A. E. Kelly (Eds.), *Handbook of research design in mathematics and science education* (pp. 647–664). Mahwah, NJ: Lawrence Erlbaum.

Hoadley, C. (2002). Creating context: Design-based research in creating and understanding CSCL. In G. Stahl (Ed.), *Proceedings of the international conference of computer support for collaborative learning (CSCL) 2002* (pp. 453–462). Hillsdale, NJ: Erlbaum.

Kelly, A. E. (2003). Theme issue: The role of design in educational research. *Educational Researcher, 32*(1), 3–4.

Kelly, A. E. (2004). Design research in education: Yes, but is it methodological? *Journal of the Learning Sciences, 13*(1), 115–128.

Kelly, A. E., & Lesh, R. A. (Eds.). (2000). *Handbook of research design in mathematics and science education.* Mahwah, NJ: Lawrence Erlbaum Associates.

Kelly, A. E., Lesh, R. A., & Baek, J. Y. (Eds.). (2008). *Handbook of design research methods in education: innovations in science, technology, engineering, and mathematics learning and teaching.* New York: Routledge.

Lehrer, R., & Schauble, L. (2000). Developing model-based reasoning in mathematics and science. *Journal of Applied Developmental Psychology, 21*(1), 39–48.

Lehrer, R., & Schauble, L. (2004). Modeling natural variation through distribution. *American Educational Research Journal, 41*(3), 635–679.

Lehrer, R., Schauble, L., & Lucas, D. (2008). Supporting development of the epistemology of inquiry. *Cognitive Development, 23*(4), 512–529.

Lemke, J. L. (2000). Across the scales of time: Artifacts, activities, and meanings in ecosocial systems. *Mind, Culture, and Activity, 7*(4), 273–290.

Levin, J. R., & O'Donnell, A. M. (1999). What to do about educational research's credibility gaps? *Issues in Education, 5*(2), 177–229.

Middleton, J., Gorard, S., Taylor, C., & Bannan-Ritland, B. (2008). The "compleat" design experiment: from soup to nuts. In A. E. Kelly, R. A. Lesh, & J. Y. Baek (Eds.), *Handbook of design research methods in education.* New York: Routledge.

NRC. (2002). *Scientific research in education.* Washington, DC: National Academy Press.

Raudenbush, S. W. (2005). Learning from attempts to improve schooling: The contribution of methodological diversity. *Educational Researcher, 34,* 25–31.

Roschelle, J., Pea, R. D., Hoadley, C., Gordin, D. N., & Means, B. M. (2000). Changing how and what children learn in school with computer-based technologies. *The Future of Children, 10*(2), 76–101.

Sandoval, W. A. (2004). Developing learning theory by refining conjectures embodied in educational designs. *Educational Psychologist, 39*(4), 213–223.

Sandoval, W. A. (in press). Conjecture mapping: An approach to systematic educational design research. *Journal of the Learning Sciences.*

Sandoval, W. A., & Bell, P. (2004). Design-based research methods for studying learning in context: Introduction. *Educational Psychologist, 39*(4), 199–201.

Schoenfeld, A. H. (2006). Design experiments. In J. Green, G. Camilli, & P. B. Elmore (Eds.), *Handbook of complementary methods in education research* (pp. 193–206). Washington, DC: AERA.

Schwartz, D. L., Chang, J., & Martin, T. (2008). Instrumentation and innovation in design experiments: Taking the turn towards efficiency. In A. E. Kelly, R. A. Lesh, & J. Y. Baek (Eds.), *Handbook of design research methods in education.* New York: Routledge.

Shavelson, R. J., Phillips, D. C., Towne, L., & Feuer, M. J. (2003). On the science of educational design studies. *Educational Researcher, 32*(1), 25–28.

Steffe, L. P., & Thompson, P. W. (2000). Teaching experiment methodology: Underlying principles and essential elements. In A. E. Kelly & R. A. Lesh (Eds.), *Handbook of research design in mathematics and science education* (pp. 267–306). Mahwah, NJ: Lawrence Erlbaum Assoc.

Tabak, I. (2004). Reconstructing context: Negotiating the tension between exogenous and endogenous educational design. *Educational Psychologist, 39*(4), 225–233.

Van den Akker, J., Gravemeijer, K., McKenney, S., & Nieveen, N. (Eds.). (2006). *Educational design research.* London: Routledge.

34

LIGHTS, CAMERA, LEARN

When the Set is as Important as the Actors

Iris Tabak

1. INTRODUCTION

> All of our acts, even the simplest, which are so familiar to us in everyday life, become strained when we appear behind the footlights before a public of a thousand people.
>
> (Constantin Stanislavski; Appears in Wilson & Goldfarb, 1996, p. 44)

In discussing the training of aspiring actors, Stanislavski makes explicit a simple, intuitive, idea that the setting or circumstances influence how we act. Conversely, the expectation that people are characterized by traits and abilities, and that they employ them with regularity and consistent outcomes across time and space, seems just as intuitive. Despite its surface intuitive appeal, empirical support for the consistency of performance across contexts is not as strong. In fact, context-dependent variation in performance has been documented by behavioral, cognitive, social and sociocultural psychologists. It is therefore ironic that the expectation of consistent performance has traditionally guided educational research and practice.

Underplaying the role of context in performance has negative consequences for both learners and educators. It can obscure competent performance that comes into play in some, but not all settings, leading to false assumptions of deficit. It can curtail the range of supports provided for learners, which can impede their learning. Similarly, it can lead to an impoverished view of which elements in a setting supported learning and were part of the performance. This, in turn, leads to an incomplete characterization of what constitutes the educational intervention, which undermines dissemination, adoption and change.

There is a growing interest in, and attention to, the role of context in learning and in the design of technologies for learning. But, there are many unanswered questions concerning appropriate theoretical and application frameworks. In this chapter, I present a conceptualization of context as weave, which is increasingly adopted in educational research. I also present a brief overview of empirical research that demonstrates the role of context in learning and in variations in performance. The conceptualization of context as weave and these empirical findings are used to discuss implications for research and design of learning technologies.

2. CONCEPTUALIZATIONS OF *CONTEXT*

There are two predominant ways of conceptualizing context. One conceptualization views context as that which surrounds an object or objects of focus. This way of thinking of context sets up a hierarchy between the foregrounded object of focus and the background or contextual elements. It also connotes an expectation of stability within the object. Conceiving of context in this way has typified much educational research and practice.

This view has been called into question. The argument against this way of conceiving of context is that there are important phenomena that lie outside its purview. For example, it does not readily lead us to consider how the "object" might influence the "background." Similarly, this foreground background notion of context does not lend itself well to examining additional mediating interactions such as those that might occur between elements within "that which surrounds" the object.

An alternative conceptualization tied to the linguistic roots of the word "context" refers to texture, weave (Goodwin & Duranti, 1992) or connection (Burke, 2002). This conceptualization highlights the notion of interaction among many interconnected relatively symmetric elements. Conceiving of context as a weave invites us to consider how all the resources available in a particular time or space, people, objects, language or affect might play a role in the activities and performances we observe. This allows for a richer (albeit "messier" and harder to study) explanation.

The weave approach to context is becoming the preferred approach, especially among scholars who subscribe to sociocultural theoretical perspectives[1] (Burke, 2002; Cole, 1996; Nardi, 1996). In considering implications for educational research, practice and design, it is important to consider the different knowledge goals to which we aspire. Attending to context, conceived as weave, might be more difficult for some knowledge goals than for others.

3. CONTEXT AND KNOWLEDGE GOALS IN RESEARCH AND DESIGN OF LEARNING TECHNOLOGIES

Educational researchers who design learning technologies adopt two broad categories of knowledge goals: analysis and explanation, and prediction and design. Analysis and explanation goals describe a situation and attempt to answer questions of: "what is," "how something happened," "why," "when," and "where," while prediction and design goals also describe "what *will* be," and "how to do something" (Gregor, 2006). Design refers both to the creation of artifacts and technology and to the articulation of design principles.

These goals are often adopted in an iterative fashion. Analysis and explanation are mainly used to identify educational problems, and to develop conceptual blueprints for technological and other pedagogical designs that can address these issues. Design is used to conceive of and apply these interventions. Analysis and explanation come into play again in trying to empirically understand the ways in which the infusion of technological tools and additional practices and supports have advanced our understanding of these issues and offered pathways to solutions.

3.1. *How Design Goals are Informed by Empirical Studies on Variation in Performance across Contexts*

3.1.1. *Contextualizing as a Practice to Promote Transfer*

As early as the 1920s, experimental psychologists have shown that consistency or variation in the background stimuli can affect recall in memorization tasks (e.g. learning a list of paired words). This was formalized by Tulving and Thomson (1973) as the encoding specificity, which roughly states that when we encode information about a certain "stimulus" we also encode additional contextual information (visual, auditory or olfactory) of that which surrounds the stimulus. This additional information is used in retrieval. Similar contextual cues are favorable for effective retrieval, and dissimilar cues hamper retrieval.

Most people have encountered similar phenomena in their daily lives. For example, you realize, while standing in the kitchen that you want to fetch your glasses from your bedroom. You go to your bedroom, but have no idea why you came there. You have to go back to the kitchen in order to remember, because the features of the kitchen have been encoded with the "fetch your glasses" stimulus, and thus aid in the retrieval of this information.

Semantic context (or priming) also affects encoding and retrieval (Polyn, Norman, & Kahana, 2009). For example, different features are recalled depending on the meaning of the words that precede the stimulus; if "cat" is preceded by "lions," its feline qualities are more likely to be recalled, but if "cat" is preceded by "dogs," its domesticated animal qualities are more likely to be recalled. Recent findings suggest that qualities of the participants, such as cultural background, also explain variations in performance between people and across contexts (Zhou, Gotch, Zhou, & Liu, 2008).

Variations in memory and performance also stem from social and affective cueing. A dramatic finding in these studies was the identification of stereotype threat that revealed that people could perform better or worse on subject-matter tests depending on whether they perceived that a negative stereotype of their social group was confirmed. Research in this area continues to make finer distinctions concerning the circumstances that heighten or dampen these effects (Marx & Stapel, 2006).

These findings concerning encoding specificity, contextual cues and priming imply that learning should occur in settings that are similar to their future application context. Future retrieval will be more likely, because of the similarity in cues at time of encoding and retrieval. These ideas were elaborated to include the importance of having the learning environment resemble the practice environment so that the underlying rationale, social and cultural values that are true for the practice environment are available to learners as part of the learning experience (Bransford, Brown, & Cocking, 2000; Collins, Brown, & Newman, 1989).

A central technological example of this approach is the development of the Jasper Woodbury series (Cognition and Technology Group, 1990). It was designed to help learners develop skills by considering a real-world scenario in which planning and computation are needed (such as a pilot that needs to get to a location within time and resource constraints). Thus, the learning context was similar to later application contexts, because people often need to use computation to utilize time and financial resources in their lives. This distinguishes the Jasper series from prevailing decontextualized materials, such as worksheets that only include symbol-based computations, which share little perceptual and experiential features with out of school activities.

3.1.2. Distributed Scaffolding: Rich Support for Robust Learning

Examining how people perform activities in real-world settings, reveals how performance arises from peoples' interactions with each other and with tools (Wertsch, 1998). A person who finds it difficult to compute fractions, might be able to make use of inventive representation from happenstance materials to transform the problem from abstract symbol manipulation to concrete cutting and assembly and derive an appropriate solution (Brown, Collins, & Duguid, 1989; Nardi, 1996). Resources that support performance can be affective, material, physical or cognitive/computational. For example, a task may be more readily accomplished in the presence of a friend than in the presence of other collaborators (McDermott, 1993).

These findings highlight the importance of conceiving of context as a web of interacting agents and resources, because it helps to keep us from denigrating the role that situation-specific resources play in performance. The implication for the design of learning technologies is that providing a rich set of resources can enhance performance and support learning. If these resources are also similar to those available in contexts outside of the classroom, then this quality performance will be more likely to continue outside of the learning setting.

In the field of design of learning technologies, this approach has taken the guise of *distributed scaffolding* (Puntambekar & Kolodner, 2005). In this approach, multiple means of support, within and outside of technological tools, are included in the design. Different resources are matched to different aspects of performance and to different learning needs and integrated into the broader learning environment.

For example, technological tools that are used in teaching science through design may include diary prompts that encourage learners to reflect on the features and considerations of their design. These supports are combined with pin-up sessions, which build on shared presentation and critique of design rationales, to provide a social and material resource for composing scientific justifications (Puntambekar & Kolodner, 2005). Similarly, interface queries of a database that reflect the conceptual questions of scientists can help novices perform sophisticated comparisons that are aligned with expert practice (Tabak & Reiser, 2008). Working side-by-side with a teacher who voices her rationale for making inquiry actions can provide better support for learning to coordinate intermediate inquiry steps (Tabak & Baumgartner, 2004).

Such supports complement each other, but none can function well alone (Tabak, 2004b). In this way, distributed scaffolding departs from a reductive view of learning that asserts that learning can be achieved through, or attributed to, a single support.

3.2. How Analysis and Explanation Goals are Informed by Empirical Studies on Variation in Performance across Contexts

3.2.1. The Need to Bracket Investment in the Designed Learning Technology in the Study of Enactments

A context as weave approach also recognizes the ways in which individuals can shape, alter, affect and create contexts. For example, learners can use resistance strategies such as humor to divert the classroom script from an academic to a social script, thus changing the setting from "a place where one learns facts" to "a place where one socializes and has fun" (Gutierrez, Rymes, & Larson, 1995). Similarly, a child in conversation with her parents can invoke a technical term, unfamiliar to her parents, such as Euler's formula, in order to change her status from a subordinate that is being quizzed to a more knowledgeable other in an intellectual exchange (Wertsch & Rupert, 1993). In addition, as people move "in and out" of a particular setting, traversing multiple contexts and sources of affiliation, they "import" and "export" knowledge, resources, values and experiences, so that they are continually changed-by and changing their environment.

In design research (Design Based Research Collective, 2003), attending to context as weave requires designers to distance themselves from their design, and view the enactment as an organic whole. This perspective is key prior to design in understanding existing resources and practices that can inform the design. During and after enactment, it is important in order to evaluate, understand and explain performance without giving special regard to the design. Researchers need to be open to seeing how participants import ideas into the setting, and how they define their own ways of interacting with and interpreting the innovations. This can be very difficult, because of the researchers' inherent investment in the designed artifacts, and consequent preconceived notions concerning which aspects of the context may contribute to learning and in what ways (Tabak, 2004a). Despite the difficulty, in order to fully attend to the multiple facets of the situation, it is imperative that designers bracket their expectations.

3.2.2. The Need to Reconceptualize Assessment Practices in Light of Studies of Variation in Performance across Contexts

The findings reviewed above, also suggest that it is problematic to judge ability in isolation of the context in which it is exhibited. This idea has been further explored through research that has examined the ways in which youth interact and perform across different configurations of people, space, time and allocation of resources. It highlights how performance, by the same individuals on the same or very similar tasks, can vary across contexts.

These studies challenge assumptions about the construal and stability of competence. For example, McDermott questions a deeply rooted notion of the trait-like approach to learning disabilities by showing how the learning disability may be more or less salient in different settings (McDermott, 1993). Other studies have recast deficit attributions. One study revealed how the norms that governed interaction in different activity structures made participation prohibitive or possible for a group of Native American children (Philips, 1972). Thus, rather than view the children as lacking a capacity for academic engagement, Philips showed that the context provides different opportunities for engagement, and consequently, exposes different levels of performance. Similarly, "gangsta" (affiliated with gangs) adolescents were regarded, in school settings, with deficit, due, in part, to their indifference to adopting conventional writing styles. In contrast, outside of school, they readily engaged with and internalized specialized and complicated gang writing styles (Moje, 2000b). So, they displayed, across contexts, different orientations toward, and capacities to engage in, practices that draw on similar abilities.

Performance also varies as a function of task or problem framing. African American youths were asked to solve problems that were presented as either typical school mathematics problems or as relating to basketball (Suad Nasir, 2000). Although the problems targeted the same abstract principles, and could be solved using the same means, the youths approached the two problems very differently. In the basketball scenario they used inventive strategies and were more successful, but, in the school scenario, they tried to apply recalled algorithms in ways that were often flawed.

Additional aspects of context such as temporality and physical configurations within spaces also influence performance. In the mathematics and basketball study just described, problem order affected performance. Students who received the basketball scenario first performed better on both tasks (Suad Nasir, Hand, & Taylor, 2008). In another study, young children who were initially regarded as not inclined to read incidental print and signage, turned out to do so when the print appeared at their eye level (Orellana & Hernandez, 1999).

This collection of studies challenges the notion of fixed traits and abilities that carry over with regularity across settings. If research and design of learning technologies is to align well with these characterizations it has to attribute performance to available resources and not just to an individual performer. In the area of assessment, which is gaining momentum in the design of learning technologies (e.g., Linn, Lee, Tinker, Husic, & Chiu, 2006; Thadani, Stevens, & Tao, 2009), this might require departing from deeply rooted and long-held beliefs.

Most of the work in this area has focused on contextualization. That is, creating problem contexts that reflect features of real-world applications and track students' step-by-step work (e.g., Thadani et al., 2009), but not on exploring how different resources contribute to performance in different settings. Despite some recent calls to attend to context as weave in assessment (Gee, 2010), there has been more progress achieved in instructional aspects of learning technologies.

This is not surprising. We might be comfortable describing the role that collaborators play in achieving certain levels of performance, but are we willing to base graduation requirements on a collaborative effort between parents, peers and youths? This is essentially what would be required to truly adopt an attending to context as weave stance. The performances that "count" for assessment would have to come from a variety of occasions and situations and not just "on the test." In addition, we would need to be open to having these performances mediated by various resources and tools. Assessment through e-portfolio (e.g., Connolly, 2010) that documents performance across settings is in line with some of these ideas, but it seems that we still expect high-stakes assessment to be based on individual intramental performance. Fully attending to context as weave might require that we abandon many formal assessments, and rely heavily on the display of competence in real-world activities. The barriers to such a model are socio-political as well as theoretical and logistical, because, in a competitive society with limited resources, assessment serves as a gate-keeper as much as it serves as an index of mastery.

4. THEORETICAL AND METHODOLOGICAL CHALLENGES IN CONCEPTUALIZING CONTEXT AS WEAVE IN RESEARCH AND DESIGN OF LEARNING TECHNOLOGIES

There is much support and motivation for attending to context as weave in research and design of learning technologies. Yet, despite its ideational allure, this conceptualization lacks some analytic advantages available in the traditional foreground/background model. In fact, it entails an inherent tension between theoretical fidelity and methodological feasibility. It is practically impossible to study a site or event without having a particular focus. Even the studies reviewed above, which were quite true to the context as weave model, had a particular analytic focus: Adam the boy with the learning disability, the group of Native American children, the group of basketball players, or the group of "gangsta" adolescents. The weave metaphor does not offer a formal "slot" for this analytical focal point, and it is difficult to compose an account that does not privilege these focal points. A singling out which is arbitrary outside of the research goal.

A grounding assumption that underlies the weave approach is that none of the elements in a situation have an a priori higher significance. The intent is to develop a veridical account of the situation that obviates the notion of focus by treating all elements with symmetry. Rogoff (2003, pp. 50–62) draws on a photography analogy to mitigate this tension. In the photography analogy, "all" the elements of a situation are present and "symmetric," but only some can be captured by the lens. This is governed by where the researcher aims and centers the camera. At different stages of the research the camera may zoom in on different aspects or levels of analysis. This analogy offers a way to consider the possible simultaneity of focus and symmetry, but does not resolve the problematic rhetorical privileging of the object of research.

Another artificial constraint imposed by the research stance is the need to delimit the boundaries of the particular context that is studied. The need to attend to the texture of the situation implies that even a small "space" entails considerable complexity. It is likely that much of what determines what will be captured in the researchers' lens will be practical, logistical, and even unintentional rather than a product of theoretical deliberation and choice. Recently, researchers have begun to involve participants in defining the scope of a context. This mitigates the artificial asymmetry introduced by the research, and reflects the subjective nature of what is a context. For example, participants articulate how they frame and circumscribe their neighborhood (Brooks-Gunn, Duncan, & Aber, 2000) or community (Moje, 2000a).

A recent and comprehensive example of an attending to context approach in learning technologies is the ecology of resources model (Luckin, 2010). One way in which this example stands out is in attending to the resources that are brought in from other spaces, and in following participants to other spaces of affiliation and action. A methodological practice that has received limited attention and even less so in relation to learning technologies. The ecology of resources model negotiates some of the difficulties that go along with adopting the context as weave stance by using an individual learner and his or her subjective perspective and traversal of daily activity as the pivot around which analysis evolves. This is accomplished through the use of mobile and ubiquitous computing.

This makes the approach susceptible to privileging focal aspects, but it provides a means for attending to a greater than typical range of configurations of resources in time and space. It also offers a theoretical "slot" for analyzing and describing these resources as part of explanations of performance and development by extending the notion of the Zone of Proximal Development to also include the concept of Zone of Available Assistance.

5. CONCLUSION

A rich corpus of evidence from a variety of theoretical traditions shows that the level of skill and proficiency that one exhibits under one set of circumstances might not be the same as in another set of circumstances. This suggests that a more veridical account of human performance should include a depiction of these circumstances. Thus, we need to think of context not as a secondary backdrop to the intramental functioning of individuals, but as a collection of interacting resources arranged in different configurations across time and space.

If we design learning environments and learning technologies based entirely on the analysis of specific content and skill, without consideration to other times and spaces in which similar abilities can come into play, we deprive our students of important resources for learning. Similarly, if we do not attempt to gain a purview into the ways in which learners perform in and out of school through different configurations of resources, we will end up with an impoverished representation of learner development. This is a deficit that will be more costly to some learners than others.

NOTE

1. I use this term as a shorthand to refer to a number of frameworks such as situated action, or cultural historical activity theory and others, which share some essential theoretical commitments and perspectives, but are also theoretically and methodologically distinct.

REFERENCES

Bransford, J., Brown, A., & Cocking, R. R. (Eds.). (2000). *How People Learn: Brain, Mind, Experience and Schools.* Washington, DC: National Academy Press.

Brooks-Gunn, J., Duncan, G. J., & Aber, J. L. (2000). *Neighborhood Poverty: Context and Consequences for Children.* New York: Russell Sage Foundation.

Brown, J. S., Collins, A., & Duguid, P. (1989). Situated cognition and the culture of learning. *Educational Researcher, 18,* 32–42.

Burke, P. (2002). Context in context. *Common Knowledge, 8*(1), 152–167.

Cognition and Technology Group. (1990). The Jasper series as an example of anchored instruction: Theory, program description, and assessment data. *Educational Psychologist, 27,* 291–315.

Cole, M. (1996). *Cultural Psychology: A Once and Future Discipline.* Cambridge, MA: Harvard University Press.

Collins, A., Brown, J. S., & Newman, S. E. (1989). Cognitive apprenticeship: Teaching the crafts of reading, writing, and mathematics. In L. B. Resnick (Ed.), *Knowing, Learning, and Instruction: Essays in Honor of Robert Glaser* (pp. 453–494). Hillsdale, NJ: Erlbaum.

Connolly, S. (2010). *Developing authentic achievement for disengaged young people using an electronic portfolio system.* Paper presented at the 35th International Association for Educational Assessment (IAEA) Annual Conference: Assessment for a Creative World, Brisbane, Queensland.

Design Based Research Collective. (2003). Design-based research: An emerging paradigm for educational inquiry. *Educational Researcher, 32*(1), 5–9.

Gee, J. P. (2010). Human action and social groups as the natural home of assessment: Thoughts on 21st century learning and assessment. In V. J. Shute & B. J. Becker (Eds.), *Innovative Assessment for the 21st Century: Supporting Educational Needs* (pp. 13–40). New York: Springer.

Goodwin, C., & Duranti, A. (1992). Rethinking context: An introduction. In A. Duranti & C. Goodwin (Eds.), *Rethinking Context: Language as an Interactive Phenomenon* (pp. 1–42). Cambridge, UK: Cambridge University Press.

Gregor, S. (2006). The nature of theory in information systems. *MIS Quarterly, 30*(3), 611–642.

Gutierrez, K. D., Rymes, B., & Larson, J. (1995). Script, counterscript, and underlife in the classroom: James Brown v. Board of Education. *Harvard Educational Review, 95*(3), 445–471.

Linn, M. C., Lee, H. S., Tinker, R., Husic, F., & Chiu, J. L. (2006). Teaching and assessing knowledge integration in science. *Science, 313*(5790), 1049–1050.

Luckin, R. (2010). *Re-designing Learning Contexts: Technology Rich, Learner Centred Ecologies.* London and New York: Routledge.

Marx, D. M., & Stapel, D. A. (2006). Distinguishing steretotype threat from priming effects: On the role of the social self and threat-based concerns. *Journal of Personality and Social Psychology, 91*(2), 243–254.

McDermott, R. (1993). The acquisition of a child by a learning disability. In S. Chaiklin & J. Lave (Eds.), *Understanding Practice* (pp. 269–306). Cambridge: Cambridge University Press.

Moje, E. B. (2000a). Circles of kinship, friendship, position and power: Examining the community in community-based literacy research. *Journal of Literacy Research, 32*(1), 77–112.

Moje, E. B. (2000b). "To be part of the story." The literacy practices of Gangsta adolescents. *Teachers College Record, 102*(3), 651–690.

Nardi, B. A. (1996). Studying context: A comparison of activity theory, situated action models and distributed cognition. In B. A. Nardi (Ed.), *Context and Consciousness. Activity Theory and Human-computer Interaction* (pp. 69–102). Cambridge, MA: MIT Press.

Orellana, M. F., & Hernandez, A. (1999). Talking the walk: Children reading urban environmental print. *The Reading Teacher, 52,* 612–619.

Philips, S. (1972). Participant structures and communicative competence. In C. Cazden (Ed.), *Functions of Language in the Classroom* (pp. 370–394). New York: Teachers College Press.

Polyn, S. M., Norman, K. A., & Kahana, M. J. (2009). A context maintenance and retrieval model of organizational processes in free recall. *Psychological Review, 116*(1), 129–156.

Puntambekar, S., & Kolodner, J. L. (2005). Distributed scaffolding: Helping students learn science from design. *Journal of Research in Science Teaching, 42*(2), 185–217.

Rogoff, B. (2003). *The Cultural Nature of Human Development.* New York: Oxford University Press.

Suad Nasir, N. i. (2000). "Points ain't everything": Emergent goals and average and percent understandings in the play of basketball among African American students. *Anthropology and Education Quarterly, 31*(3), 283–305.

Suad Nasir, N. i., Hand, V., & Taylor, E. V. (2008). Culture and mathematics in school: Boundaries between "cultural" and "domain" knowledge in the mathematics classroom and beyond. *Review of Research in Education, 32*(1), 187–240.

Tabak, I. (2004a). Reconstructing context: Negotiating the tension between exogenous and endogenous educational design. *Educational Psychologist, 39*(4), 225–233.

Tabak, I. (2004b). Synergy: A complement to emerging patterns of distributed scaffolding. *Journal of the Learning Sciences, 13*(3), 305–335.

Tabak, I., & Baumgartner, E. (2004). The teacher as partner: Exploring participant structures, symmetry and identity work in scaffolding. *Cognition and Instruction, 22*(4), 393–429.

Tabak, I., & Reiser, B. (2008). Software-realized inquiry support for cultivating a disciplinary stance. *Pragmatics & Cognition, 16*(2), 307–355.

Thadani, V., Stevens, R. H., & Tao, A. (2009). Measuring complex features of science instruction: Developing tools to investigate the link between teaching and learning. *Journal of the Learning Sciences, 18*(2), 285–322.

Tulving, E., & Thomson, D. M. (1973). Encoding specificity and retrieval processes in episodic memory. *Psychological Review, 80,* 352–373.

Wertsch, J. V. (1998). *Mind as Action.* New York: Oxford University Press.

Wertsch, J. V., & Rupert, L. J. (1993). The authority of cultural tools in a sociocultural approach to mediated action. *Cognition and Instruction, 11*(3 & 4), 227–239.

Wilson, E., & Goldfarb, A. (1996). *Theater: The Lively Art* (2 ed.). New York: McGraw-Hill.

Zhou, J., Gotch, C., Zhou, Y., & Liu, Z. (2008). Perceiving an object in its context—is the context cultural or perceptual? *Journal of Vision, 8*(12), 1–5.

35

BIDIRECTIONAL ARTIFACT ANALYSIS

A Method for Analyzing Digitally Mediated Creative Processes

Erica Halverson and Alecia Magnifico

In this chapter, we describe *bidirectional artifact analysis*, an analytic method for understanding creative, digital production processes through ethnographic observations of participants in situ, the artifacts they create, and interviews with participants as they describe their activities over time. Marrying narrative analysis (Halverson, 2008; Labov, 1997), discourse analysis (Wood & Kroger, 2000), and artifact analysis, this framework echoes and extends Enyedy's (2005) description of bidirectional analysis: "go[ing] 'backwards' in time in an attempt to trace the origins of this intervention and 'forwards' in time to examine what subsequent impact it had on the way other students reasoned" (p. 437). While typical descriptive analyses move forward, we, like Enyedy, have found that moving bidirectionally—from final product backward and from initial idea forward—helps us to better understand participants' learning, as well as the role of social and collaborative audiences in that learning.

For researchers seeking to understand and design environments that honor and encourage the development of new literacies through technology, the current focus on production-oriented definitions of literacy requires a complementary shift in methodology and analysis. Learning in digitally mediated environments often focuses on project creation, and learners often save and reflect on many incomplete versions as they work toward a final artifact. To understand these processes, we extend methodological tools such as case study (e.g. Stake, 1995), ethnographic observation (e.g. Geertz, 1973), thematic coding (e.g. Boyatzis, 1998), grounded theory analysis (e.g. Strauss & Corbin, 1998), and discourse analysis (e.g. Wood & Kroger, 2000) to focus on process and, specifically, the relationship between the creation of artifacts over time and learners' discussions of these emergent artifacts.

The development of this method responds to recent research on new media and new literacies, which has begun to re-focus the meaning of "literacy" and "multi-literacies" (Cope & Kalantzis, 2009; Jenkins, Purushotma, Clinton, Weigel, & Robison 2007; Moje, Overby, Tysvaer, & Morris, 2008; New London Group, 1996). Beyond the comprehension and production of texts, "being literate" in a particular context or content area has come to describe fluency in specific "constellations" (Steinkuehler, 2007) of practices, modes, spaces, and ways of knowing. These new understandings of what it means to become literate and to be literate have particular purchase in digital environments where social interactions are often shaped by the production and critique of artifacts for a responsive audience (Magnifico, 2010). In order to understand and, ultimately, design learning environments that support these complex practices, we must develop methods that specifically help researchers to describe the processes of digital production and how they lead to the creation of successful literacy artifacts. These new methods require analytical lenses that take complex creative works themselves—from online video to school essay to multimedia collage—as units of analysis and trace these works through the often-complex process of creation and revision.

For learning sciences researchers studying learning progressions, bidirectional analysis may also provide a robust system for analyzing students' increasingly sophisticated reasoning within various content domains (Duncan & Hmelo-Silver, 2009). Learning progressions provide a foundation for aligning assessment, curriculum, and external standards, but their design provides little information for how researchers ought to analyze their utility or success. Bidirectional analysis can give researchers an analytic approach to studying the development of learning progressions in situ and create the capacity to examine how progressions develop in the context of the learning environment over time.

THEORETICAL PERSPECTIVES

In order to produce creative work—or to teach creative processes to others—producers must consider not only the quality of their original ideas (i.e. whether an idea is "good"), but also how these concepts will be translated to consumers (i.e. how others will engage with the idea). In our attempts to trace the learning of creative processes, we have found it useful to pay explicit attention to several factors: (1) the representations that artists use to build their ideas and describe them to others, (2) the role that audiences play in the creative process, and (3) the metrics of quality used to evaluate creative products. These factors are relevant to creative processes regardless of technological mediation, but have come to the forefront as increasing numbers of learners use digital technologies to create and share their work in a more public sphere.

The Role of Representation in Creative Processes

Di Sessa (2004) argues that representation design is a fundamentally creative endeavor, "a venue in which creative and artistic skills are at a higher than normal premium" (p. 300). Like any representational domain, "getting smart" in the context of producing art "means coming to know the potential of the materials in relation to the aims of a project or problem" (Eisner, 2002, p. 72). The capacity to build the right representation in the right situation is a marker of creative expertise (Hayes, 1989), and thus, creative production means learning how to construct and evaluate these representations. While producers might use many media to draft a poem, video, or piece of visual art, and these multiple representations may transform over time and drafts, understanding how these artifacts contribute to the final "text"—the final draft of the creative production—is necessary to understanding the relationship between process and product. Bidirectional artifact analysis traces how artifacts are produced and edited over time in response to critiques from audience members and "key moments" (Halverson & Gibbons, 2010) in the production process.

The Role of Audience

Placing the construction of artifacts at the center of technologically mediated learning processes draws attention to the role that audiences play in production. While audience is often seen as what happens at the end of a learning process, cognitive and sociocultural perspectives on technologically mediated environments have noted the crucial role that audiences play throughout the production process. Members of an interactive audience can talk back and become collaborators, and their feedback is often immediate. Online producers can read their audience's preferences in comments and post additional drafts if they choose. Workshop participants in the same physical space can work together to help producers clarify artifacts. Focusing on the role of audience throughout the production process has become increasingly important because this kind of analysis can provide additional theoretical insight into creative practices (Magnifico, 2010).

What Makes a Quality Creative Product?

Audience members also matter in the production because they serve as judges of the success of a creative product. Narrative theorists describe two key features of "good" products: reportability—that which makes an artifact unique—and credibility—that which allows an audience to understand and relate to it. This "reportability paradox" (Labov, 1997) introduces a key tension across creative production processes. Using a creative medium to tell a certain story or express a specific meaning demands engagement with *both* genre typicality and uniqueness. Beyond letting learners "be creative," good mentors must help novice artists to understand and wrestle with these concepts in their work. Narrative methods help us capture the evolving relationship between an artifact's reportability and credibility, as well as young artists' attempts to work with this tension.

BIDIRECTIONAL ARTIFACT ANALYSIS

To these three central constructs—representation, audience, and the reportability paradox—we add an understanding of time, and how young producers use the artifacts they produce to move backwards and forwards through their creative work. This understanding stands in contrast to most education, and most education research, which moves forward in time. Teachers and education researchers create curricular interventions, they teach those curricula to learners, and they observe the effects on learners' learning. Learning continually builds up from prior knowledge and, therefore, researchers teach and analyze in this direction, too. Prior's (2004) multi-textual "tracing" methodology, developed in higher education settings, deepens this notion of learning over time and captures multiple and contextual threads of students' writing and learning. He analyzes assignments and "initiating texts," classroom discourse, drafts of writings, teacher and peer feedback, and students' reflections to trace how particular texts, arguments, or intellectual ideas are written into being, often as hybridizations of student interest and teacher guidance. Similar multi-layered evolutions might be traced over time for any student in a school or creative production environment.

Enyedy (2005) turns this forward-development timeline metaphor on its head in a study of elementary students working progressively to "inven[t] representations and iteratively refin[e] solutions to problems" (p. 428). Enyedy analyzes these social and mathematical activities in a bidirectional way. Instead of examining students' successive representations, his analysis reaches both backward and forward, examining how each new representation is built as a revision of prior ideas. By turning the analytical lens, this study shows *how* students' reflections on past representations become a base of shared prior knowledge that is used in whole-class inquiry.

In our work, we extend Prior's notion of tracing development and Enyedy's conception of bidirectional discovery to creative production endeavors. Learning in creative production settings often runs closely to the writers' workshop or the design crit models of instruction that are common across literacy and arts education. Young writers and artists present drafts to an audience of mentors and peers, assess their current successes and difficulties, and receive revision suggestions. While we focus on creative production in this chapter, the cross-content implications for this approach to analysis are clear: When we analyze drafts as representations that grow and change as a result of individual cognitions, mentor responses, and social reflections, it becomes possible to build models for developmental learning progressions (e.g. Duschl, Schweingruber, & Shouse, 2007) that account for collaboration in many subject areas.

A Summary of the Process

Briefly, bidirectional artifact analysis involves the following steps:

- *Identify* a learner-created digital artifact (i.e. start with the final product).
- *Document* relevant data around the artifact. Trace each step in the process of the artifact's creation, identify all draft artifacts that relate to this production process, and create a timeline of all exogenous research data related to this particular artifact's production. Not all process work might be evident in the final product; rather, the form and presentation of the artifact could change over the course of drafts and critiques.
- *Construct* narrative threads across the data types that trace the core ideas and tools present in the final product back through their development. The narrative threads could include artifact analysis (demonstrating the evolution of text and/or image over time), multimodal analysis (demonstrating changes in tool use over time), and discourse analysis (using critiques, conversations with mentors, interviews, journals, and the like to triangulate individuals' interpretations of what their creative work means over time). In this step, examine the data timeline in both a "backwards" and "forwards" direction: Look for how later drafts and conversations reference and reflect earlier ideas, and how early drafts and conversations provide starting points for later representations.

These brief bullet points will be contextualized in an example that highlights how we trace one learner's trajectory from his initial ideas to his final multimedia installation. In this example, we show how examining drafts and reflections alongside of each other enriches our understanding of his creative process, and, more broadly, his learning.

FRANK AS BORDER CROSSER

This example demonstrates how bidirectional artifact analysis allows researchers to "see" how students engage with their compositions and audiences, as well as their growing mastery of appropriate representational tools. We demonstrate how the method works and how it helps us to understand young people's emerging access to, and use of, the new literacy practices that researchers describe as crucial for 21st-century success. This example is drawn from Halverson's case studies of four United States youth media arts organizations; this larger project shows how young people learn to make art about their own stories and how this process contributes to identity development and literacy learning (Halverson, 2010, 2012; Halverson & Gibbons, 2010). Data collection traced students' digital art from initial program applications to final public presentations, and included ethnographic observations, artifact collection, semi-structured interviews, and post-mortem reflections.

Frank's piece (Figure 35.1) is an autobiographical graphic design piece created through Street Level Youth Media's 2007 program, "Represent!: Exploring your identity through history and culture." This piece includes three elements: (1) a photoshopped image of himself in front of two flags; (2) a black and white line drawing of a person split down the middle; (3) below the images, a series of names/nicknames printed on individual placards. The meaning and genesis of these elements can be traced by examining Frank's journal, interviews, and final piece. Frank's artist statement describes his work as: "a graphic design piece dealing with him being a Mexican American, crossing borders each day going to different places with his art work and gathering all of his names." Each of the elements is analogous to the components described in the statement; they are all connected with this vision for his art and how it represents his identity.

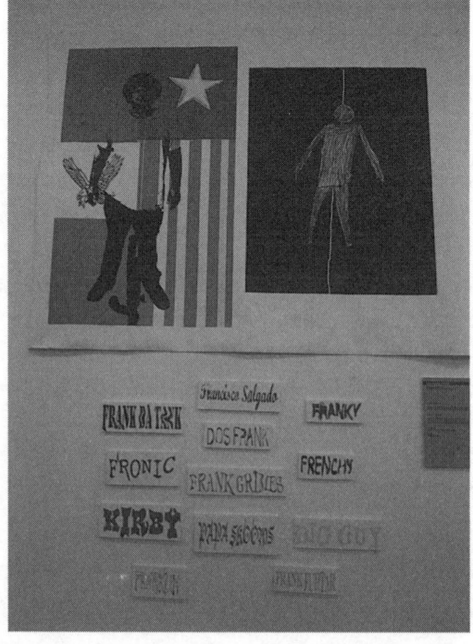

Figure 35.1 Frank's final piece: Represent!

Self-portrait

Frank uses a visual self-portrait as one way to represent himself through his art. Frank first considers a visual representation of himself in one of his journal entries. The entry contains a line sketch of Frank with the words, "Find images that represent me??" printed underneath. In an interview, Frank describes his struggle with the representational process:

> I was kind of straying from what this actually was [gesturing to his final piece]. I wanted to do different things about me. And [my mentor] told me, "Well, why don't you just put yourself, why don't you just take a picture of yourself? A picture of yourself basically represents who you are."
>
> (Interview, 09/15/08)

Frank and his mentor set out to create an image of himself (rather than the "finding" an image suggested in the journal) by taking digital photographs. The image of Frank and the two flags is one of these photos, and his description of the photograph alternates between collaborative and independent—"*we* took about 100 pictures and *I* had to choose the right one . . . *we* did a few inside and *we* did a few outside. And *I* chose this one." Frank notes that it represents something, but not enough on its own. He says, "I was kind of looking at it, and it's like, 'alright, what else am I?'" Frank incorporates his mentor's suggestion of a photograph, but points out that he is more than this picture, that an image does not equal an identity.

Frank da Tank

The first time participants shared their project ideas, Frank used his journal to craft a speech about what his piece would be about (see Table 35.1).

While Frank does not explain the meaning of "Frank Da Tank," this description remains at the center of his representation. The next substantive entry in Frank's journal is a two-page entry with a series of images and texts that becomes the outline for his final piece (Figure 35.2). The first component is an image of a list: "List of names friends and family use to refe[r] to me like 'frank the tank' and 'papa skoons'." "Frank Da Tank" has become a concept, and nicknaming as identity emerges as a method for self-representation. He builds a representation of a concept—the list of names that people call him—in his journal. Frank lists his nicknames and attributes (most) of them to a person or people. While there is no reflection on the meaning of this list, it is clear from the earlier

Table 35.1 Initial Text for Frank's Final Exhibit Piece

Original version	Analytic version
(1) Well I am Frank Da Tank. (2) i like screen printing (3) it shows what i am who i am and what i am about (4) makeing dighens and puting it on my clothe (5) gives me owner ship of my clothe (6) there is no . . . (7) Printing whats in his head out here	1. Well I am Frank Da Tank. 2. I like screen printing. 3. It shows what I am, who I am, and what I am about: 4. Making designs and putting it on my clothes. 5. [It] gives me ownership of my clothes 6. There is no . . . 7. Printing what's in his head out here

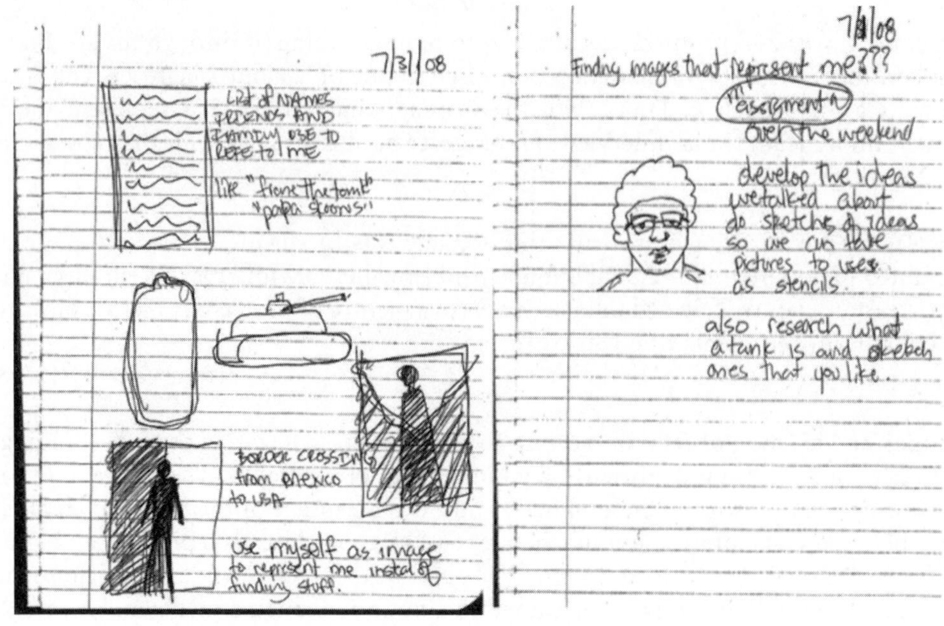

Figure 35.2 Frank's journal entries outlining core components of his piece

representation that he is trying to populate the image of "what people call him" in an identity display. Others' naming becomes Frank's identity representation.

This list becomes a series of printed placards across the bottom third of his final piece (see Figure 35.1). Their attributions are gone, so the audience might interpret that these are names for the artist, but not who made them or why. The through-line for this aspect of Frank's piece began with his assertion that he is "Frank da Tank." Next, he abstracts naming to a list, abandoning specifics for the idea of naming (see Figure 35.2). A real list of his names and social relationships follows. In the end, he chooses several names, each of which stands in for a social relationship and a narrative. Taken together the names represent how Frank sees himself through the eyes of others.

Border Crossing

The largest image in Frank's final piece is a screen print, a color image of him and two simplified flags, American and Mexican (see Figure 35.1). The initial idea for the dual flags appears in his journal as a drawing of a black figure standing in front of a box that is half white and half grey. This image is accompanied by the text, "border crossing from Mexico to USA" (see Figure 35.2). Frank attributes this idea to his father. In a post-mortem interview, he describes struggling to represent himself in his final piece of art. His father asked him, "Why don't you do something about you being Mexican American?" Not only did Frank embrace the idea, he felt motivated by this contribution: "That's like, part of the reason I did this. Because of my dad. He helped me too" (09/15/08).

Frank's journal entries end with the list of nicknames, but interviews with Frank reveal how he got from border crossing to the two flags present in the piece. He describes beginning by, "tak[ing] a regular flag from here and a regular Mexican flag and put[ting] them in the background," behind his photo. The simplified, adapted flags emerged from his artist-mentor's suggestion—"[he] gave me the concept of make your own flag"—and an image from an album cover. He compares that flag to his own: "I had saw a flag that Trent Reznor did . . . It's basically black. It's all red. It's like blood dripping down from the flag. I wanted to do that, but it kind of, it strayed from who I am" (09/15/08).

In describing the flag from a *Nine Inch Nails* album, Frank identifies what he likes about a self-made flag. The reason that he does not import this image, however, was that, "it strayed from who I am." He recognized the need to keep his representation of himself at the forefront of his art. So he chose an aesthetic that appealed to him and created a Mexican-American border-crossing version of this image.

The black and white image to the right replicates the sketch from Frank's journal. He describes this image as, "basically the same thing, have to dealing with borders. Only it's . . . it's the same thing as this only it's stripped down of everything." He sees the two images conveying similar meaning: Frank as border crosser. However, where the large image refers specifically to Frank's Mexican-American identity, this "stripped down" version is different: "It can mean anything. I'm basically walking into anywhere. With the same concept of walking into different borders or different places" (Interview, 09/15/08). The final image included both border crossing representations, the full color image of Frank in front of two flags, and this initial sketch. But Frank transforms the initial sketch to represent himself as a border crosser more generally. He now understands and represents himself as someone who can "go anywhere," a broader scope than his dad's original idea.

The above analysis traces each of the three key components of Frank's piece from initial conception to final piece. However, this division is more analytic than temporal; Frank did not conceptualize each of these elements independently. Bidirectional analysis allows us to understand Frank's artistic process and the evolving relationship between his concept (identity) and his representational choices (graphic design). Frank struggles initially, but through conversations, interviews, whole- and small-group instruction, and journal entries, he determines that he wants to create a visual representation of himself that portrays his identity as a Mexican American, a border crosser more generally, and a friend and family member with many roles and names. He marries his narrative perspective to the affordances of the tools, which results in his final piece and an artist statement that explains this relationship to an audience.

ADVANTAGES

Bidirectional artifact analysis directly juxtaposes two kinds of data: learners' work and what learners say about their work. While many methodologies analyze these two data streams separately, we believe that we can learn more by examining them together. By employing this methodology, instructors and researchers can produce fine-grained maps of the learning inherent in creative processes. The analysis is rooted to the context of learning, and thus, this methodology is particularly useful for examining innovative, non-traditional learning environments and contexts.

In environments where researchers are interested in the role of technological tools in the making of creative products (e.g. Clark & Sheridan, 2010; Halverson, 2012), bidirectional artifact analysis shows how learners use tools for creating, reflecting, editing, and drafting over time. Formulating a timeline of artifacts, learners' conversations about those artifacts, and feedback on those artifacts allows researchers to specifically analyze how learners used earlier representations to plan and produce later drafts—and how planning was mediated by the tools used. While it is often tempting to center an analysis on learners' interactions with digital tools, bidirectional artifact analysis documents how tool use becomes part of a learning process.

DISADVANTAGES AND CHALLENGES

Bidirectional artifact analysis allows mentors and researchers to remain close to learners as they draft representations. We see this feature of the method as a strength, but this analysis should be accompanied by descriptive observations to avoid eliding the broader environment. Detailed analyses of artifacts, critiques, and conversations are useful for uncovering micro-contextual patterns and specific details of the learning process, but at this tight focus it is easy to lose a full sense of the context. That is, bidirectional analysis is an effective tool for focused case studies—for example, zooming in on focal learners—but ineffective for creating general pictures of events in a large learning space. In addition, bidirectional artifact analysis is most useful when learning is process oriented and learners frequently reflect on their work, document their thinking, or receive feedback on interim drafts. This process can occur in many ways: for example, a learning environment might create small-group critiques, solicit online peer feedback, and mandate key moments for presentation of in-process work (Halverson & Gibbons, 2010). Without these elements of reflection on drafts or processes, too much inference is necessary to effectively trace and understand the links between various phases of a process or draft representations of a work.

The necessity of interpretation and inference represents, perhaps, the greatest challenge of this work. Bidirectional artifact analysis is a method for understanding qualitative, learner-focused, product-based, and, often, multimodal data over time. While the steps we describe here provide a starting place for this work, engaging in this method demands a commitment to detailed interpretive work: careful organization, reading and re-reading, drawing connections through code tables, and pattern collation. A similar commitment is necessary for most fine-grained qualitative analyses, particularly those that engage many data sources, but it can be challenging for time- or resource-limited projects.

CONCLUDING THOUGHTS

Frank designs and refines his autobiographical screen print by creating drafts in several media, consulting with his mentor and family, and journaling about his evolving thoughts. Taken together, these data sources demonstrate his representational decisions and his understanding of the role of digital media tools in representing self. Bidirectional analysis—with its focus on both draft artifacts and young artists' interactions around those artifacts—shows us how internal and external representations shift through creative processes, how mentors can provide feedback to encourage these shifts, and how young artists use this feedback to refine their creative works and their knowledge of representational materials (Eisner, 2002).

No single analytic tool provides enough information to gain an understanding of how production processes and artifacts lead to literacy learning in complex environments.

These complex tasks and questions require broader methods that help researchers to parse macro-level and micro-level data and to use data drawn from observation, conversational discourse, and artifacts in careful combination. Bidirectional artifact analysis offers a way forward by articulating an analysis framework that combines methodologies for conducting inquiry with complex qualitative datasets.

REFERENCES

Boyatzis, R. E. (1998). *Transforming qualitative information: Thematic analysis and code development.* Thousand Oaks, CA: Sage Publications.

Clark, K., & Sheridan, K. (2010). Game design through mentoring and collaboration. *Journal of Educational Multimedia and Hypermedia, 19*(2), 125–145.

Cope, B., & Kalantzis, M. (2009). Multiliteracies: New literacies, new learning. *Pedagogies: An International Journal, 4*, 164–195.

di Sessa, A. A. (2004). Metarepresentation: Native competence and targets for instruction. *Cognition and Instruction, 22*(3), 293–331.

Duncan, R. G., & Hmelo-Silver, C. (2009). Learning progressions: Aligning curriculum, instruction, and assessment. *Journal of Research in Science Teaching, 46*(6), 606–609.

Duschl, R. A., Schweingruber, H. A., & Shouse, A. W. (Eds.). (2007). *Taking science to school: Learning and teaching science in grades k-8.* Washington, DC: National Academies Press.

Eisner, E. (2002). *The arts and the creation of mind.* New Haven, CT: Yale University Press.

Enyedy, N. (2005). Inventing mapping: Creating cultural forms to solve collective problems. *Cognition and Instruction, 23*(4), 427–466.

Geertz, C. (1973). *The interpretation of cultures.* New York: Basic Books.

Halverson, E. R. (2012). Digital art-making as a representational process. *Journal of the Learning Sciences, 21*(2), 121–162.

Halverson, E. R. (2010). Film as identity exploration: A multimodal analysis of youth-produced films. *Teachers College Record, 112*(9), 2352–2378.

Halverson, E. R. (2008). From one woman to everyman: The reportability paradox in publicly performed narratives. *Narrative Inquiry, 18*(1), 29–52.

Halverson, E. R., & Gibbons, D. (2010). "Key moments" as pedagogical windows into the digital video production process. *Journal of Computing in Teacher Education, 26*(2), 69–74.

Hayes, J. R. (1989). Cognitive processes in creativity. In J. A. Glover, R. R. Ronning, & C. R. Reynolds (Eds.), *Handbook of creativity.* New York: Plenum.

Jenkins, H., Purushotma, R., Clinton, K., Weigel, M., & Robison, A. (2007). Confronting the challenges of participatory culture: Media education for the 21st century. Building the field of digital media and learning. Retrieved from http://www.newmedialiteracies.org/articles/.

Labov, W. (1997). Some further steps in narrative analysis. *Journal of Narrative and Life History, 7*(1–4), 395–415.

Magnifico, A. (2010). Writing for whom? Cognition, motivation, and a writer's audience. *Educational Psychologist, 45*(3), 167–184.

Moje, E. B., Overby, M., Tysvaer, N., & Morris, K. (2008). The complex world of adolescent literacy: Myths, motivations, and mysteries. *Harvard Educational Review, 78*(1), 107–154.

New London Group. (1996). A pedagogy of multiliteracies: Designing social futures. *Harvard Educational Review, 66*(1), 60–92.

Prior, P. (2004). Tracing processes: How texts come into being. In C. Bazerman & P. Prior (Eds.), *What writing does and how it does it: An introduction to analyzing texts and textual practices* (pp. 167–200). Mahwah, NJ: Lawrence Erlbaum Associates.

Stake, R. (1995). *The art of case study research.* Thousand Oaks, CA: Sage Publications.

Steinkuehler, C. (2007). Massively multiplayer online gaming as a constellation of literacy practices. *E-learning and Digital Media, 4*(3), 297–318.

Strauss, A. L., & Corbin, J. (1998). *Basics of qualitative research: Grounded theory procedures and techniques* (2nd edition). Newbury Park, CA: Sage Publications.

Wood, L. A., & Kroger, R. O. (2000). *Doing discourse analysis: Methods for studying action in talk and text.* Thousand Oaks, CA: Sage Publications.

36

MASS COLLABORATION AND LEARNING

Ulrike Cress

1. A THEORETICAL FRAMEWORK FOR LEARNING PROCESSES IN MASS COLLABORATION

New technologies and services, so-called Web 2.0 tools, such as wikis, weblogs, podcasts, folksonomies, file sharing and virtual online worlds, are changing their users' handling of data, information and knowledge. The new Web technology not only gives users access to a vast amount of data, information and knowledge, it also breaks with the distinction between consumers and producers of knowledge. Web 2.0 gives people the opportunity to contribute information, which then might be a small but nevertheless relevant piece in the collective development of knowledge. When people contribute information others might rely on it, link it to other contributions or even modify it. In an interactive process, the collective can make use of anybody's contribution and shape it in such a way that it fits the needs of the community. Through such collaborative processes the community can enhance its knowledge base and build new knowledge. But it is not only the community that learns, it is also the individual that benefits and whose knowledge is expanded. In mass collaboration with Web 2.0 tools these individual and collective processes of learning and knowledge building are greatly intertwined.

Of course, in large groups and in mass communication the group processes are not as obvious as in small groups, where the members know each other personally, where they coordinate themselves explicitly, take over roles and divide their work among themselves. Instead, in mass collaboration the people may remain anonymous, and they do not really work together, but more in parallel. They sometimes do not even have a common goal. In a forum, for example, a participant might just be interested in getting an answer to his specific question; he might not perceive himself as working with others on a common goal. But also, in this situation, people's contributions could lead to emergent processes, people might provide answers, and others might rely on these answers. So a dynamic process can be triggered where contributions are provided. But in these mass scenarios knowledge cannot be considered just an individual factor, as it is emergent in a way that it develops from the communication and activities among different users. In this way knowledge can be considered a community factor.

A shared artifact, where people have access to the contributions of others, where they can locate their own contributions and where they can eventually even revise others' contributions, can act as catalyst for such emergent processes. Scardamalia and Bereiter, for example, described these emergent processes in their framework of collaborative knowledge building and developed the "Knowledge Forum" as a tool to support school classes in their knowledge-building activities (Scardamalia & Bereiter, 1996, 2006). Knowledge Forum is a platform where pupils generate their own theories about a given topic, describe it and share it with others by writing contributions into a shared artifact. There it can be discussed with others who provide further support for these ideas, discuss or even find them false. Through this collaborative process good ideas will survive, while bad ones will fail over time. Through this kind of communication the group as a whole then gains deeper insights into the domain of interest and it develops its own shared understanding. Scardamalia and Bereiter used the Knowledge Forum mainly for school classes. In principle, a similar process can be observed with social software tools, which also provide a shared artifact and give people not only access to it, but also the possibility to link their own contributions to others' contributions. Such tools are frequently used in informal settings where communities exchange and build knowledge (Bruckman, 2006; Kolbitsch & Maurer, 2006; Leuf & Cunningham, 2001; Makice, 2006).

The Co-Evolution Model of Individual Learning and Collaborative Knowledge Building (Cress & Kimmerle, 2008; Kimmerle, Cress & Held, 2010; Kimmerle, Moskaliuk, Cress & Thiel, 2011), that is shown in Figure 36.1, provides a general framework for these mass processes. The model takes into account that the users need not necessarily form a group with common interests or common goals. Instead, they can just work in parallel and make use of the shared artifact. This means that each user is confronted with the artifact that results from these activities. The group working on this artifact

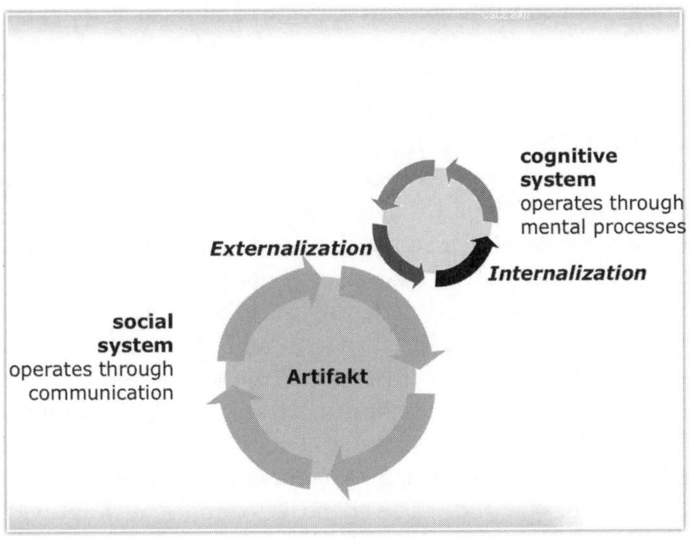

Figure 36.1 Co-Evolution Model of Individual Learning and Collaborative Knowledge Building (Cress & Kimmerle, 2008).

represents a self-organizational system. So the model proposes a systemic and cognitive view: A user as well as the community that communicates through a shared artifact are self-referential systems and auto-poietic systems, in the way they have been described by Luhman (1984), von Foerster (2003), von Bertalanffy (1968), or Maturana and Varela (1987).

The user represents a cognitive system, which processes information in its specific way: It does this by perceiving, reasoning, problem solving and all the mental processes that are included in the information processing approach. The system is closed, as it can only operate within these cognitive processes. Its environment can stimulate it, but it is up to the system itself how it perceives and processes these external stimuli. So the system builds knowledge about its environment. But all of its knowledge still represents a subjective construction of the environment. Different users, of course, represent different cognitive systems. They all might have different goals, different knowledge, and different mental representations of their environments. They could have expertise in different areas, and different views on the same topic.

The second part of the model is the community as it is represented in the artifact. This community is a *social system*. Its operation mode completely differs from that of cognitive systems, as its operation mode is communication. Each social system is defined by a specific code that it applies in its communication (Luhmann, 1984). This code is constructed by all the implicit and explicit norms and rules of the system. For example, the Wikipedia as a prominent Web 2.0 knowledge system operates on self-assigned pillars, which shape the activity of the users. This code prescribes that each article must provide a neutral point of view, and a reference must be given for all information. For example, Wikipedia operates by deleting articles that do not fit these criteria. Further, it adds references, changes text passages and interlinks the article with articles about similar topics. Other social systems that are established through Web 2.0 tools also have their specific ways of operations. With Twitter, for example, people have to put their messages into very short texts, they can refer to other tweets, or they can follow tweets of specific people or to specific topics. In forums, the code and operation mode tend to be more implicit, describing which kind of contributions are expected and socially accepted.

Tools that make the users' contributions tangible and independently available from their creators are most suited for mass collaboration. Most of these provide a shared artifact where the communicative acts crystallize and where the community knowledge is presented. With some tools the contributions remain linked to their owners and are identifiable as such, with other tools they fuse into one homogeneous product where which member provided which part is hardly traceable.

The Co-Evolution Model also assumes that a social system is operatively closed. It only exists through communication and can only operate on information that has been communicated and now exists independently from the person who communicated it. Similarly to the cognitive system, a social system can be stimulated by its environment. But in order to be able to operate on any stimulus of the environment, it has to transfer it into some kind of message. Insofar as these messages show a development in their content and/or in the depth of elaboration, the system can be considered as learning.

As already mentioned, both systems, the cognitive system as well as the social system, have their own modes of operation. The cognitive operates intra-individually through mental processes, the social interpersonally through communication processes. Both systems are autopoietic, self-referential and closed, as they can only operate on their own operations. This means that two systems cannot simply merge. But they can stimulate each other and induce a dynamic development. The Co-Evolution Model states that (individual) learning and (collaborative) knowledge building result from the interaction of cognitive and social systems as they deal with knowledge. These interactions can be described as externalization and internalization. In order to interact with the social system individuals have to *externalize* their own knowledge (which can, of course, be considered as an internationalization from the view of the social system). But in order to become part of the social system this has to be done in a way that conforms to the norms of the social system. In Wikipedia, for example, a text passage has to fulfill the Wikipedia guidelines and norms to be acceptable; in Twitter it has to fulfill the code of Twitter. The social system then will process the externalized knowledge further. Other individuals will refer to these contributions, and—if the artifact permits this—they will delete, change or revise it. In a wiki, for example, a paragraph provided by a user can be linked and interwoven with other paragraphs, and further paragraphs will, in turn, rely on this new text in the future. The model states that through these processes new knowledge can emerge which transforms the system into a dynamic knowledge-building system.

But such dynamic development does not only take place in the social system, it also happens in the cognitive system. By being forced to externalize one's own knowledge in order to bring it into the artifact, a user may learn through the externalization process, which itself leads to a deeper understanding (Flower & Hayes, 1980; Webb, 1982). But a user also learns through processing the information already in the artifact. By this internalization a cognitive system learns and develops its own individual knowledge structure. The Co-Evolution Model states that through these processes of internalization and externalization the cognitive and the social systems co-evolve. This co-evolution is triggered by incongruities between both systems (Moskaliuk, Kimmerle & Cress, 2009, 2012). Perceived incongruity between one's own knowledge and the information in the artifact leads to a cognitive conflict. According to Piaget's Equilibration Theory (1977) an individual resolves this conflict by assimilation or accommodation. Thus he can either integrate new information into his own cognitive structure without changing his own structure (internal assimilation), or he can change his own structure to accommodate the new information (internal accommodation). But whereas Piaget localizes these two processes in the individual and describes them as internal processes in the cognitive system, the Co-Evolution Model states that in mass collaboration analogous processes take place in the social system and its artifact. Through processes of externalization people can simply add information into the artifact, without changing its structure (external assimilation), or they can integrate information by changing the external structure (external accommodation).

So in mass collaboration four processes of learning can be distinguished: An individual can learn by internal assimilation or accommodation, and the social system can build new knowledge by external accommodation or external assimilation. All these four processes need to be taken into account while we investigate how to measure learning in mass collaboration (see Table 36.1).

2. MEASURES FOR MASS COLLABORATION AND LEARNING

Mass collaboration takes place "in the wild," that is, when people use Web 2.0 tools out of random interest, for example in wikis, blogs, Twitter or tagging systems. But these

Table 36.1 Four Forms of Learning in Mass Collaboration with a Shared Artifact

	Processes in the cognitive system: Individual learning	**Processes in the social system: Collaborative knowledge building**
Adding new concepts	Internal assimilation	External assimilation
Conceptual change	Internal accommodation	External accommodation

tools can also be used in an instructional context, such as when a teacher uses a wiki for supporting the collaboration of her students (Richardson, 2006). If we evaluate learning and test if learning processes have taken place in mass collaboration, we should consider both levels of learning that are part of Table 36.1: The individual as well as the collective level. This means that we have to deal with different units of analysis (Strijbos & Fischer, 2007): On the lowest level it is the single contribution that can be considered as the basic element of communication. Then it is the user who learns, though in the end it might be the community as a whole that builds new knowledge (Cress & Hesse, in press). Some data that are collected for evaluation purposes may be nested in these levels (for example, contributions may be nested within users), whereas some other data might just describe the mass collaboration as a whole.

On the lowest level, *activity data* can serve as first indicators for an effective collaboration. Of course the activity data are not indicators for learning, but they can give a first overview of how the activities are distributed among the learners. These data may result from logfiles but in principle could also be collected by questionnaires from the users. The data show how many people read the contributions of others, and how many provided any content. They also show if people related their contributions to the others' contributions. This level of contribution can also provide the opportunity to qualitatively analyze the trajectory of relevant contribution: Which contributions are taken up by others? How are they modified? Examples for such analyses that try to overcome a purely qualitative approach and try to provide also qualitative analysis are provided by Suthers and Medina (2011), or Halatchliyski et al. (2010, 2012). Both work with datasets from small groups. Considering all contributions and finding patterns in large groups becomes very complex and therefore is seldom done.

On the *individual level* each user can be described by his activity. How many contributions from others has a person read, how much content has he or she produced? Are there interindividual differences in the way people receive and produce these contents? Activities of the users often provide necessary but insufficient pre-conditions for learning. So, whenever it is possible one should also measure how much learning has occurred. For assessing such *internal processes of learning* it would be optimal if knowledge tests could be administered that each learner has to complete after a collaborative activity. With regard to the Co-Evolution Model, such a test could measure the knowledge of facts as well as conceptual knowledge. Factual knowledge can be considered the result of internal assimilation processes, conceptual the result of internal accommodation processes (Moskaliuk et al., 2009; Held, Kimmerle & Cress, 2012).

On the *community level* aggregated activity data across the users describes the liveliness of a community and its ability to bind its members and stimulate relevant activities. In regarding these data, the average activity of the users might be as important as the variation between them. In order to measure *external processes of knowledge building* one must observe the dynamic of the artifact. How does the artifact develop quantitatively and qualitatively? Quantitative development could be a sign of external assimilation, qualitative development a sign of external accommodation. For wikis, for example, the History Flow Diagram (Viegas, Wattenberg & Dave, 2004) provides an overview of the dynamic development of an article. It shows which sections are deleted, added or modified by the different authors. A history flow diagram can also provide a first impression of where sections are just added (external assimilation) and where the structure of the whole text is changed (external accommodation). A more complex method of observing the development of an artifact is a social network analysis (SNA). This kind of analysis can take into account links and references within the artifact. It can provide a visual representation for the development of the artifact and provide measures for density or clusters of contributions (Kimmerle, Moskaliuk, Harrer & Cress, 2010). Insofar as the SNA takes into account not only the artifact but also the authors, it deals with the bi-partite artifact-author network. Such an SNA can, for example, provide measures of centrality of users or contributions within the network, or even the dynamics of their centrality. For example, it could show that an article or an author who was not central at the beginning, became more and more central over time.

The quantitative analysis of the artifact often might not suffice to measure creative knowledge and its resulting collective knowledge building. Expert ratings could be necessary to detect levels of knowledge building. Moskaliuk, Kimmerle and Cress (2009), for example, measured external accommodation with expert ratings. Changes in a wiki article counted for external accommodation if a user brought in a new idea, linked or weighted two different arguments, or formulated conclusions. Based on those expert ratings, Moskaliuk et al. (2011) developed a tool that automatically measures "knowledge maturing" in a collaboratively written text. The authors used machine-learning algorithms for detecting external accommodation.

3. EXAMPLES FOR EVALUATING MASS COLLABORATION

When studying mass collaboration, a researcher often will not be lucky enough to have access to all the measures described in Table 36.1. In most cases she might have access to the artifact and its logfiles, but not to the users themselves. So she will have data about the users' activities and the dynamic development of the artifact created by the users, but not data about their individual learning. Direct access to the users is needed to measure their learning. In the following section we provide an example of an evaluation of the learning and knowledge-building processes in Wikipedia where we sought access to the users. We chose the German Wikipedia article about the nuclear power plant Fukushima-Daiichi and studied its development during the first nine days after the devastating tsunami (see also Oeberst, Halatchlyiski & Cress, subm). We expected that during that time a lot of knowledge building should have taken place, because many things happened around the power plant that had to be integrated into a Wikipedia article about it.

We first present activity measures and discuss the indicators for individual learning or collaborative knowledge building as they result from the Co-Evolution Model.

Activity Measures: The Wikimedia Toolserver with MySQL databases provides access to all activity data. With this tool we could analyze all contributions concerning their authorship, the data of activity, and the content that was changed. These data show that more than 60 different authors contributed to the article; in sum they revised the text about 200 times. About half of them contributed just once, others made a lot of edits on single days, and some authors were active over a period of several days. There are instances of intense work by some authors on certain days, but no single person dominated the process.

Collective knowledge building: An overview about the development of the article provides the History Flow Diagram shown in Figure 36.2. It shows the development of the article during the first 100 revisions of the article. The different shades of grey indicate different authors. The *x*-axis is a time axis, in its middle March 11 is marked, which is the date when the tsunami occurred.

We can see that before March 11, the article had been a product of just a few people. After March 11, more authors contributed, and some of the sections were revised continuously. Just from this diagram it is obvious that processes of different depth took place. In some phases information was just added, in some the structure was also changed. A qualitative analysis could show these processes of external assimilation and external accommodation in detail. It revealed that a typical kind of external accommodation was that an author changed a reference in order to furnish a better reference, while a typical example for external accommodation was that one author revised and changed the interpretation of an ongoing event. With regard to the growing amount of text and growing number of relevant concepts mentioned in the text, we can conclude that collaborative knowledge building took place. Experts who gave a high-quality rating to the resulting text strengthen this conclusion.

Individual learning: In order to test whether individual learning also took place, we had to contact the authors. In Wikipedia an author can be contacted if he or she provides personal information on the contact page. But—and this is typical for Wikipedia—only very few authors provided this information. In order to reach more authors we placed

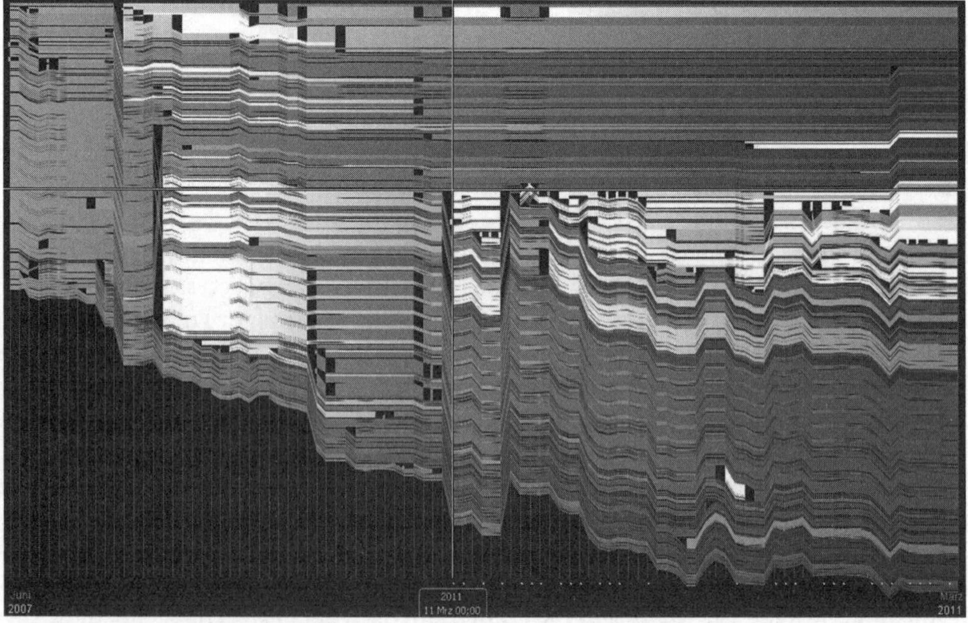

Figure 36.2 Temporal development of a Wikipedia article. The *x*-axis describes the time, the *y*-axis the different sections of the article. The different shades of grey indicate different authors.

a message into the talk site where we explained our study and provided a link to a questionnaire. About half of the active contributors participated in the survey. Because of the different levels of expertise of the authors and because of the high variation in their educational background, we could not apply any objective knowledge test. So we decided to use some rating scales where an author had to self-assess his own learning.

4. CONCLUSION

This example shows that mass collaboration often does not provide optimal opportunities for measuring all the processes that are relevant for learning. This is especially the case for cognitive systems, where learning is difficult to observe. But the artifact can indeed be analyzed with a holistic approach as well as in detail. This enables us to trace and analyze in depth the collective knowledge building. In particular, we can see how the rules of the social system shape individual behavior. In Wikipedia we can observe that its explicit norm—to present information from a neutral point of view and to provide references for all relevant information—leads to fruitful processes of external assimilation and external accommodation. The rules and norms of other communities might be quite different and the co-construction of knowledge may consider other criteria of knowledge validation (see, for example, rules and norms in minority communities; Kimmerle et al., in press). Also, other tools, such as forums, tweets or blogs, might not have such a strong affordance to completely integrate an individual's contributions into those of others. In such cases, the emergent processes might be detected when people take up others arguments and refer to each other's contributions. So with these social software tools the collaborative product is not a linear text, but a network of references. But, in general, the model described here can be applied for all settings where masses of users collaborate via a shared artifact. It is just the way the social system operates and communicates that is different.

REFERENCES

Bruckman, A. (2006). Learning in online communities. In R. K. Sawyer (Ed.), *The Cambridge Handbook of the Learning Sciences* (pp. 461–472). New York: Cambridge University Press.

Cress, U., & Hesse, F.W. (in press). Quantitative methods for studying small groups. In C. E. Hmelo-Silver, A. O'Donnell, C. A. Chinn, C. Chan (Eds.), *The International Handbook of Collaborative Learning*, Taylor & Francis.

Cress, U., & Kimmerle, J. (2008). A systemic and cognitive view on collaborative knowledge building with wikis. *International Journal of Computer-Supported Collaborative Learning, 3*, 105–122.

Flower, L., & Hayes, J. R. (1980). The cognition of discovery: Defining a rhetorical problem. *College Composition and Communication, 31*, 21–32.

Halatchliyski, I., Oeberst, A., Bientzle, M., Bokhorst, F., & van Aalst, J. (2012). Unraveling idea development in discourse trajectories. In J. van Aalst, K. Thompson, M. J. Jacobson, & P. Reimann (Eds.), *The Future of Learning: Proceedings of the 10th International Conference of the Learning Sciences* (Vol. II, pp. 162–166). Sydney, Australia: International Society of the Learning Sciences.

Halatchliyski, I., Moskaliuk, J., Kimmerle, J., & Cress, U. (2010). Who integrates the networks of knowledge in Wikipedia? *Proceedings of the 6th International Symposium on Wikis and Open Collaboration.* New York: ACM Press.

Held, C., Kimmerle, J., & Cress, U. (2012). Learning by foraging: The impact of individual knowledge and social tags on web navigation processes. *Computers in Human Behavior, 28*, 34–40.

Kimmerle, J., Cress, U., & Held, C. (2010). The interplay between individual and collective knowledge: Technologies for organisational learning and knowledge building. *Knowledge Management in Research & Practice, 8*, 33–44.

Kimmerle, J., Moskaliuk, J., Cress, U., & Thiel, A. (2011). A systems theoretical approach to online knowledge building. *AI & Society: Journal of Knowledge, Culture and Communication, 26*, 49–60.

Kimmerle, J., Moskaliuk, J., Harrer, A., & Cress, U. (2010). Visualizing co-evolution of individual and collective knowledge. *Information, Communication and Society, 13*(8), 1099–1121.

Kimmerle, J., Thiel, A., Gerbing, K.-K., Bientzle, M., Halatchliyski, I., & Cress, U. (in press). Knowledge construction in an outsider community: Extending the communities of practice concept. *Computers in Human Behavior.*

Kolbitsch, J., & Maurer, H. (2006). The transformation of the web: How emerging communities shape the information we consume. *Journal of Universal Computer Science, 12*(2), 187–213.

Leuf, B., & Cunningham, W. (2001). *The Wiki Way. Quick Collaboration on the Web.* Boston, MA: Addison-Wesley.

Luhmann, N. (1984). *Soziale Systeme. Grundriß einer allgemeinen Theorie.* Frankfurt am Main: Suhrkamp.

Makice, K. (2006). PoliticWiki: Exploring communal politics. *Proceedings of WikiSym'06,* International Symposium on Wikis 2006, pp. 105–118.

Maturana, H. R, & Varela, F. J. (1987). *The Tree of Knowledge: The Biological Roots of Human Understanding.* Boston, MA: New Science Library/Shambhala Publications.

Moskaliuk, J., Kimmerle, J., & Cress, U. (2009). Wiki-supported learning and knowledge building: Effects of incongruity between knowledge and information. *Journal of Computer Assisted Learning, 25*, 549–561.

Moskaliuk, J., Kimmerle, J., & Cress, U. (2012). Collaborative knowledge building with wikis: The impact of redundancy and polarity. *Computers and Education, 58*, 1049–1057.

Moskaliuk, J., Rath, A., Devaurs, D., Weber, N., Lindstaedt, S., Kimmerle, J., & Cress, U. (2011). Automatic detection of accommodation steps as an indicator of knowledge maturing. *Interacting with Computers, 23*(3), 247–255.

Oeberst, A., Halatchlyiski, J., & Cress, U. (subm). Knowledge: What is it? How is it gathered? Who creates it? Who possesses it? Answers from individual, social, and systemic perspectives: A review and a case study.

Piaget, J. (1977). *The Development of Thought: Equilibration of Cognitive Structures.* NewYork: The Viking Press.

Richardson, W. (2006). *Blogs, wikis, procasts, and other powerful web tools for classrooms.* Thousand Oaks, CA: Corwin.

Scardamalia, M., & Bereiter, C. (1996). Student communities for the advancement of knowledge. *Communications of the ACM, 39*, 36–37.

Scardamalia, M., & Bereiter, C. (2006). Knowledge building: Theory, pedagogy, and technology. In R. K. Sawyer (Ed.), *The Cambridge Handbook of the Learning Sciences*, pp. 97–118. NewYork: Cambridge University Press.

Strijbos, J.-W., & Fischer, F. (2007). Methodological challenges in collaborative learning research. *Learning and Instruction, 17*, 389–393.

Suthers, D. D., & Medina, R. (2011). Tracing interaction in distributed collaborative learning. In S. Puntambekar, G. Erkens & C. E. Hmelo-Silver (Eds.), *Analyzing Interactions in CSCL: Methods, Approaches and Issues* (pp. 341–366). New York: Springer Science+Business Media, LLC.

Viegas, F. B.,Wattenberg, M., & Dave, K. (2004). Studying cooperation and conflict between authors with history flow visualizations. *Proceedings of SIGCHI,* Vienna, Austria, April 24–29, pp. 575–582.

von Bertalanffy, L. (1968). *General System Theory: Foundations, Development, Applications.* New York: George Braziller.

von Foerster, H. (2003). *Understanding Understanding: Essays on Cybernetics and Cognition.* New York: Springer.

Webb, N. M. (1982). Student interaction and learning in small groups. *Review of Educational Research, 5*(3), 421–445.

37

EMERGING TECHNOLOGIES FOR YOUNG CHILDREN

Evaluating the Learning Benefits of New Forms of Interaction

Andrew Manches

1. INTRODUCTION

The most typical form of interaction with learning technologies is through a mouse and keyboard. These devices not only constrain interaction, but can challenge younger children's dexterity. Emerging technologies present novel ways to interact with digital materials. Touch screen computers, gesture recognition devices, and tangibles (digitally augmented physical objects) exemplify technologies that offer alternative, more accessible and, arguably, more engaging, forms of interaction. Yet, focusing on 'accessibility' or 'engagement' reflects a limited vision of their potential to support learning. The last couple of decades have furthered our understanding of the role of interaction in thinking and learning. By changing the way that children interact with materials, we need to consider how new devices may change the way children think and learn. This is particularly important in children's early years, given the significance attributed to their physical interaction with the world.

1.1. The Aim of the Chapter

This chapter considers what we know about the role of children's actions in their learning, and the implications for emerging technologies. Two key learning mechanisms are identified, which structure four questions to guide evaluation of emerging technologies for young children. An illustrative example is then provided using a recent design to support early numeracy.

2. THEORETICAL BACKGROUND

Understanding how children's interaction influences learning depends on our theories about the nature of cognition. Traditional perspectives, influenced greatly by pioneers such as Piaget, highlight how materials can help children articulate their thinking, whilst framing developmental progress as gradual independence from these materials. This 'concrete to abstract' perspective of development has significantly influenced instructional theories, such as Bruner (1966) who described children's knowledge as progression through enactive to iconic, and ultimately symbolic, forms of representation. More recently, however, proponents of Embodied Cognition have criticised this 'concrete to abstract' framing of development.

2.1. Embodied Cognition

Various claims can be identified under the umbrella term of Embodied Cognition. Wilson (2002) distinguishes six, of which the first five describe the dynamic relationship between cognition and our immediate environment: how the environment guides and supports our 'online' thinking. Claims from this perspective draw largely upon research in the field of External Cognition that considers thinking in terms of an interplay between internal and external representations. This theoretical perspective has provided a popular framework for examining the effect of different forms of digital interface and information (Scaife & Rogers, 1996).

According to Wilson, the sixth claim is more controversial, reflecting its more significant implication for the nature of cognition. The claim is that cognition is grounded in mechanisms that evolved for interaction with the environment, even when we are not actually immersed in that environment. In other words, our 'off-line' thinking cannot be considered 'abstract' but, rather, inseparable from prior sensory and motor experiences. If this is the case, children's early interaction with materials may provide the foundations to groundbreaking concepts (see Lakoff & Núñez, 2000).

Embodiment theories, therefore, have important implications for our understanding of cognition, and the role that physical actions play in cognitive development. Nevertheless, we are still not clear what the implications are for new forms of interaction with digital technology; we cannot simply assume that providing more physical forms of interaction will improve learning. The next section, therefore, draws upon Embodied Cognition as a conceptual framework to critically examine the learning mechanisms of physical interaction.

3. LEARNING MECHANISMS OF PHYSICAL INTERACTION

McNeil and Jarvin (2007) identify three main learning benefits of physically manipulating materials: providing an additional channel for conveying information, activating real-world knowledge, and improving memory through physical action. Yet, a common criticism is such mechanisms tend to lack the detail to evaluate the importance of physicality. Indeed, much research discussing the benefits of action, or manipulating materials, has been carried out on computers controlled by a mouse, suggesting that physicality itself is not important.

There is, therefore, a lack of clarity over the unique learning benefits, if any, of manipulating materials physically as opposed to through other forms of interaction. In fact, studies comparing physical and virtual learning materials have tended not to find any differences in learning outcome (e.g. Triona & Klahr, 2003).

More recently, Manches and O'Malley (2011) attempted to disentangle the possible unique mechanisms of physically manipulating materials in their work evaluating tangible technologies. Their paper draws significantly on External and Embodied Cognition literature, notably Mix's (2009) review of concrete materials. Manches and O'Malley present arguments for the benefits of physical manipulation under two headings: '*Offloading Cognition*'– where physical interaction might help children by freeing up valuable cognitive resources during problem solving, and '*Conceptual Metaphors*'— where perceptual information or actions with objects have a structural correspondence with more symbolic concepts.

3.1. *Actions to Offload Cognition*

Research in External Cognition literature demonstrates how individuals can manipulate information to help 'offload' cognitive work in tasks. Individuals do not simply manipulate information to carry out moves they have planned but can manipulate information to inform their plans; for example, rotating pieces in the on-screen game of Tetris to help identify what moves are possible (Kirsh & Maglio, 1994).

Martin and Schwartz (2005) have extended arguments to consider learning. According to their Theory of Physically Distributed Learning, individuals can learn by manipulating (physically distributing) the environment and (re)-interpreting the resulting changes. They demonstrated their theory by showing how children developed fraction concepts by manipulating physical tiles in presented problems.

3.1.1. Form of Actions

The Theory of Physically Distributed Learning emphasises the outcome, rather than the form, of interaction. Indeed, Martin has adopted the theory to consider virtual materials manipulated on a computer (Martin, 2007). Manches and O'Malley, however, argue that the way that children manipulate materials can significantly affect what ideas they develop.

In a series of studies looking at the role of physical interaction in children's numerical development, the authors demonstrate a wide range of actions children carry out with physical blocks in a mathematics problem (Manches, O'Malley, & Benford, 2010). These include actions such as halving or swapping over groups, stacking objects, or moving pieces near or away to help remember when to use them. Importantly, children's actions related to different problem-solving strategies, with children often constraining their own actions to focus their approach. This is significant because the authors showed how using a mouse to solve the same problem constrained children's actions (and strategies) and consequently reduced opportunities for children to constrain their own actions. A central question is how the opportunity to explore and constrain strategies using physical materials might have supported learning.

According to Schwartz, Bransford and Sears (2005), it is possible to consider learning in terms of a trade-off between efficiency and innovation. Efficiency refers to the way learners can practise, improve and become adept at particular strategies. In contrast, innovation refers to how learners are able to adapt to novel problems: identify what strategies are relevant in different contexts. Innovation is consequently related to transfer ability. It is suggested that innovation is fostered by opportunities for exploration and for selecting the most efficient strategies from a variety.

A key benefit of physically manipulating materials, therefore, may lie in the way children can adapt materials easily through a range of actions, interpreting the result of their actions, and then using this information to select particular strategies or approaches.

3.2. *Actions as Conceptual Metaphors*

Actions with materials can represent certain concepts. These actions can be more or less explicit, or intentional. For example, a child might intentionally move their hands around in circles to explain planetary motion, or raise their hand to articulate rising musical pitch: as a form of analogical reasoning. In contrast, the relationship between actions and concepts might be more implicit, echoing the Embodied Cognition claim that concepts may be grounded upon particular motor experiences. For example, Lakoff and Núñez (2000) suggest that children's developing numerical concepts, such as how numbers can be added and broken down, are grounded in prior physical experiences with manipulating physical objects. Increasing evidence for this claim has come from gesture research. Gesture research has demonstrated how individuals use specific gestures to support their thinking when explaining concepts. Indeed, children often express their thinking through gestures before they can do so verbally (Goldin-Meadow, 1999). Significantly, gestures often reflect prior actions with materials. This has been shown for discussing a range of concepts such as counting (Alibali & DiRusso, 1999) or the conservation of liquid (Ping & Goldin-Meadow, 2008).

Interaction with physical materials may therefore develop motor schemas with which to ground later concepts in learning. However, research shows how gestures may relate to interaction with other materials. Cook and Tanenhaus (2009), for example, showed how adults' gestures reflected previous actions manipulating on-screen objects using a mouse, although these were less expansive than gestures used by adults who had manipulated a physical version of these materials.

Therefore, whilst young children might develop motor schemata from interaction with different materials, physical interaction may provide more frequent, pronounced, and 'body-based' actions on which to ground developing concepts.

4. EVALUATING FORMS OF INTERACTION FOR YOUNG CHILDREN'S LEARNING

Research into the role of physical manipulation in learning is ongoing, and it remains difficult to draw firm conclusions about the impact of different forms of interaction with digital materials. Nevertheless, this section uses the two key mechanisms previously discussed: *offloading cognition* and *conceptual metaphors*, to consider the potential of emerging technologies.

4.1. Actions to Offload Cognition

4.1.1. Facilitating Interaction

Currently, the dominant form of interaction with digital technology is through the mouse and keyboard, where children's actions are indirect and constrained to single input. Although children as young as five can use the basic functions of the mouse (Donker & Reitsma, 2007), the demands on fine-motor control skills will be challenging for younger children. On a simple level, therefore, we can evaluate how different forms of interaction now allow younger children to access digital materials.

Usability studies can inform us about how easily children manipulate materials using difference devices. Actions such as swiping and tapping visual objects directly will be easier than the less direct actions with a mouse. Nevertheless, further work is needed to assess possible barriers to interaction such as the lack of tactile information, small screen size, and the difficulties of knowing the exact point that the finger makes contact, particularly when children's fingertips obscure their view (Figure 37.1).

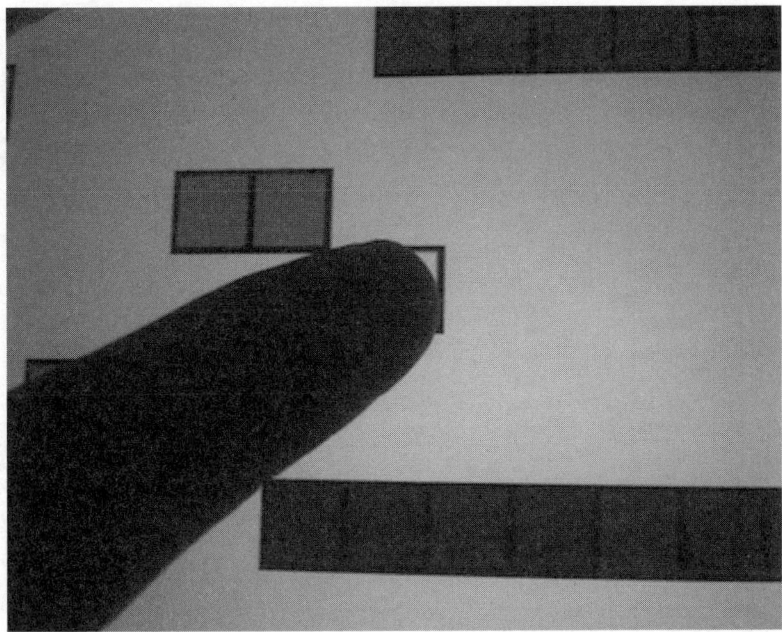

Figure 37.1 Fingers obscuring vision on screen.

Whilst accelerometers in devices such as Tablets or mobile phones provide novel ways to manipulate information on-screen (e.g. tilting device), this form of interaction does not offer the variety of actions possible with more tangible technologies. By integrating technology into physical materials, it is possible for children to interact through simple, intuitive actions such as tagging, grabbing, stacking, grouping, sliding, lifting and swapping over single or multiple objects. Indeed, various tangible designs have taken advantage of young children's aptitude with physical actions. Electronic Blocks (Wyeth, 2008; Figure 37.2), for example, allow young children to explore ideas about electronics by investigating the outcome of combining blocks marked with different symbols. With such designs, however, we always need to consider both how the technology responds to different actions and how the physical design may hinder certain actions, such as retracing moves.

4.1.2. Constraining Interaction

There might be times when we wish to constrain children's actions with materials to support learning. Reducing the ways children can manipulate information may help focus their attention on certain ideas: promoting efficiency rather than innovative learning. For example, although employing a variety of engaging digital effects, many learning apps for children follow a basic multiple-choice format. This relatively constrained form of interaction might help children to practise certain knowledge (e.g. addition facts).

There could also be cognitive benefits from hindering children's interaction. Research (with adults) has shown how increasing the demands of interaction can encourage greater planning in problem solving (O'Hara & Payne, 1998). Similarly, by hindering interaction through devices such as the mouse, it might be possible to encourage children to think more before acting. However, not only might this be frustrating, but it

Figure 37.2 Electronic Blocks (from Wyeth, 2008).

assumes children have sufficient understanding of the problem to plan their moves. This may be less likely for young children exploring relatively novel ideas.

4.1.3. Summary

Evaluating how the form of interaction helps children's offload thinking, therefore, requires us to consider our learning objectives and how we want children to explore different ideas. Emerging devices may support learning by providing children, particularly younger children, with simple and intuitive ways to explore a range of ideas, constraining their own actions as they learn. Yet, we need to consider when actions permitted in a virtual world (e.g. restarting) may be beneficial and if it is helpful to constrain actions to focus on particular strategies or ideas.

Questions for evaluation:

- What actions can children carry out to explore different possibilities in the learning domain?
- How easily are children able to carry out actions to explore different possibilities?

4.2. Actions as Conceptual Metaphors

4.2.1. Implication for Technology

The argument that concepts can be grounded upon perceptual experiences such as physical actions has important implications for technologies that can detect and respond to these actions. This presents the challenge of first identifying the relationship between certain concepts and actions, and then designing ways that technology can take advantage of this relationship to support learning.

Abrahamson and colleagues provide a good example of work addressing this challenge. Having identified how children are able to demonstrate their implicit understanding of proportionality through gestures before they can do so verbally, they examined how gesture recognition devices (Nintendo Wii remotes: Figure 37.3a) can help children make this knowledge more explicit (Abrahamson, Trninic, Gutiérrez, Huth, & Lee, 2011). Other work has investigated more body-based interaction. Fischer, Moeller, Bientzle, Cress and Nuerk (2010), for example, have investigated using a dance mat to respond to children's movement along a line to develop their concepts of numerical magnitude.

It is important to consider how designs respond to children's actions. In Abrahamson's design, the vertical movement of both hands is linked to onscreen representations. By graduating these on-screen representations to more symbolic notation (numerals), the design aims to scaffold children's formal concepts of proportionality. Other designs might seek to draw children's attention to particular actions through simpler perceptual feedback. For example, Price et al. (Figure 37.3b) link the acceleration of a container to colour changes in embedded lights. Both designs require us to think about the role played by others.

4.2.2. Summary

By considering how actions relate to learning concepts, we can evaluate how designs seeks to leverage this learning mechanism. Sometimes the relationship is not clear. For example, with several learning applications designed for Tablets, it is claimed that interaction builds upon embodied mechanisms because children solve problems by tilting the device or sliding their fingers across the screen. But the mapping between these actions and the learning concepts (e.g. increasing number magnitude) is often not clear. Also with some tangible designs, we have to consider whether actions are building upon conceptual metaphors or are simply making it easier to manipulate materials (i.e. offloading cognition).

Questions for evaluation:

- How do actions with materials relate to the learning concepts?
- To what extent do designs use digital technology to link actions with materials to more symbolic representations?

5. SCOPE

Whether a design will support learning will depend on a range of factors including the children's initial understanding, the task, or how the technology is used with others. In this regard, focusing on the potential value of the form of interaction is quite limited. Yet, it is argued here that the form of interaction does play an important role in how children can explore ideas and build upon previous experiences; and that emerging devices thereby offer new possibilities for learning. This section, therefore, looks briefly toward how factors such as activity, age or domain, influence the learning mechanisms discussed. In doing so, it is intended to highlight where this approach could be particularly effective.

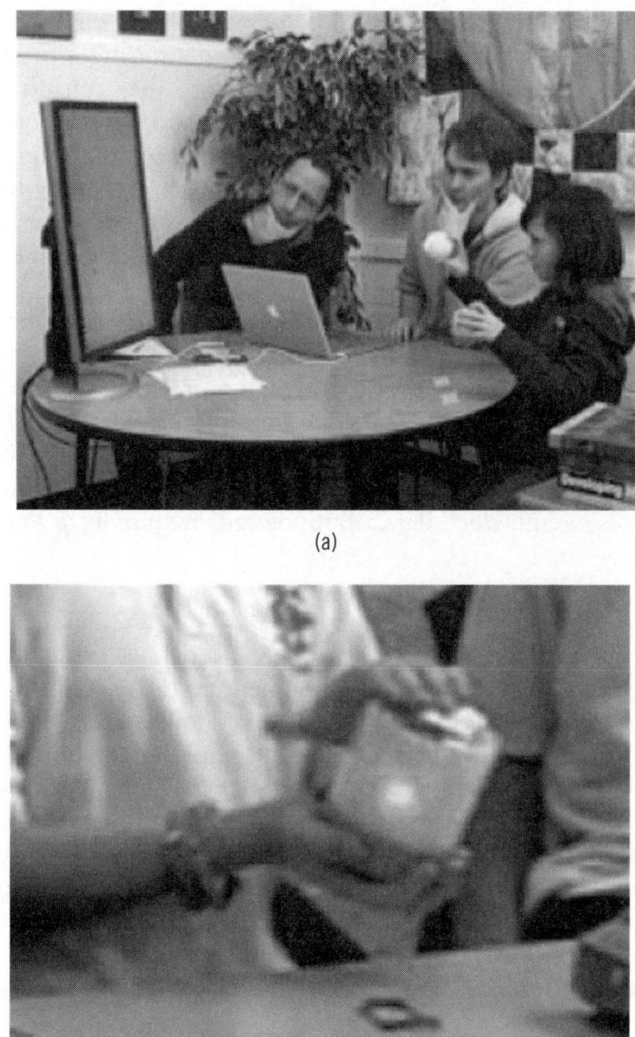

(a)

(b)

Figure 37.3 (a) Exploring proportionality through gesture recognition devices (from Abrahamson et al., 2011); (b) Exploring motion concepts through tangible technology (© Price, Roussos, Pontual Falcao, & Airzantis (http://www.lkl.ac.uk/research/tangibles/))

5.1. Individual/Collaborative

This chapter has focused on individual rather than more social interaction around emerging technologies. By providing multiple points of interaction, emerging technologies offer new possibilities for children to work together, thereby attracting both commercial and research interest (e.g. Dillenbourg & Evans, 2011).

Collaboration can indeed provide children with opportunities to reflect upon each other's actions and articulate thinking about how their actions are linked to digital information. It is important, however, to question how the technology encourages children to share their ideas, or even whether it is beneficial for multiple children to be interacting simultaneously (see Marshall et al., 2009).

5.2. Age

Research into emerging technologies demonstrates how new ways to manipulate information can benefit learners across ages. However, this chapter emphasises the benefits for young children for several main reasons: dexterity; greater emphasis on exploration and creativity (innovative thinking); and the importance of building on physical knowledge and experiences from before school.

5.3. Domains

Arguments in this chapter focus on manipulating information spatially. Consequently, we can reflect on which domains this may be particularly relevant for. In mathematics, spatial arrangement (i.e. groupings) of objects can represent a wide range of concepts, particularly in early mathematics. Yet, as spatial location can illustrate how information is related, it is possible to consider how facilitating manipulation of symbols, from letter tiles to electronic icons, can foster exploration of a wide range of ideas.

The movement of objects is also conceptually important in various domains, again particularly so in mathematics, but also in physics where force and motion concepts can be represented through actions. In both domains children's and adults' use of gestures can illustrate the possible link between action and concept. However, actions can also provide metaphors for ideas in other domains. For example, Antle, Droumeva and Corness (2008) have examined how certain gestures relate to musical concepts such as pitch.

6. CASE STUDY: DIGICUBES

6.1. Design Background

Digicubes are a digital representation of number that emerged from research into children's interaction and thinking in early mathematics. The research approach, which is not uncommon, was to examine young children's (4–7 years) interaction with physical materials in order to inform the design of digital materials.

The research examined children's use of physical materials to explore the different ways a single-digit number (e.g. 7) could be broken down into pairs (e.g. 2 & 5). The research highlighted the wide range of actions children carried out in problem solving and, importantly, the way children chose to manipulate single or multiple objects at a time (e.g. swapping over groups of plastic blocks to identify commutative solutions such as 2 + 5 after 5 + 2) (Figure 37.4).

Another finding was how children often created valid groupings without verbally identifying the numerical solution. This finding informed the design of Digicubes which change colour according to quantity attached in order to highlight numerical changes (Figure 37.5a, 37.5b). The materials have been further developed to perceptually highlight the decade structure of numbers 11–19 (Figure 37.5c).

Digicubes were initially designed on a computer using a mouse. Cubes could only be manipulated one at a time using typical drag and drop. We translated the design to a Tablet (iPad) to facilitate interaction for younger children and allow for multi-point interaction (although currently still single input). Whilst it would be possible to translate Digicubes to different devices such as gesture recognition or tangibles, it is important to evaluate what additional benefit these devices would offer. The following section adopts

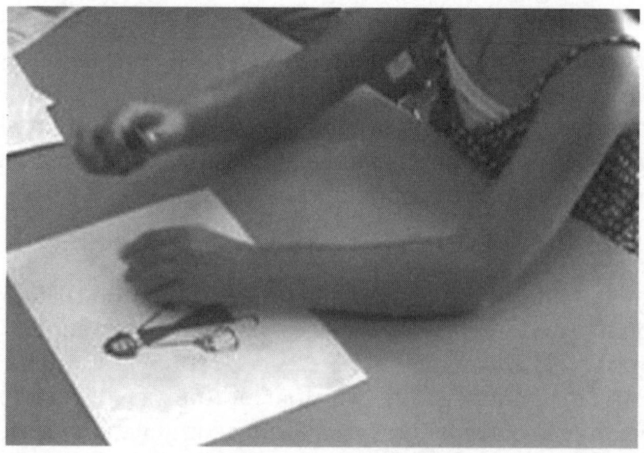

Figure 37.4 Child swapping over groups of objects in a mathematics task (Manches, O'Malley, & Benford, 2009).

the questions put forward previously to reflect upon the current form of interaction (Tablet) and how the design might be further developed to build upon physical learning mechanisms.

6.2. Actions to Offload Cognition

What actions can children carry out to explore different possibilities in the learning domain?

Children are able to move single or multiple objects, although there is an option to constrain actions so only one object can be moved at a time as previous research showed how this could encourage children to identify consecutive solutions (e.g. 7 & 2 following 8 & 1)—promoting efficiency. Current work is examining the extent to which children can constrain their own actions toward this more efficient strategy over time.

The tablet design does limit a range of actions observed with physical materials. Children move multiple objects by sliding rows; they cannot grasp collections. They cannot stack objects. Again, whilst it is not clear what ideas children may develop from such actions, children often experimented with these actions, ceasing when they realised they were less effective. The virtual design does, however, allow changes not possible by physical blocks, such as clearing the screen or saving configurations.

How easily are children able to carry out actions to explore different possibilities?

We found that children tend to push at the edge of a block as they might with a physical block. As there is no tactile feedback and children's fingers obscured the point of contact, there were many times that children would fail to move a block as they started pushing from outside the block area (see Figure 37.6). Another issue resulted from children placing their resting hand on the screen. We are investigating how we might address these issues; however, it does illustrate the challenges of translating from physical to virtual designs.

We plan to examine if multi-touch will support interaction by helping distinguish moving objects (sliding using one finger) from separating a group (pulling apart using two fingers). However, we predict challenges in helping children place two fingers accu-

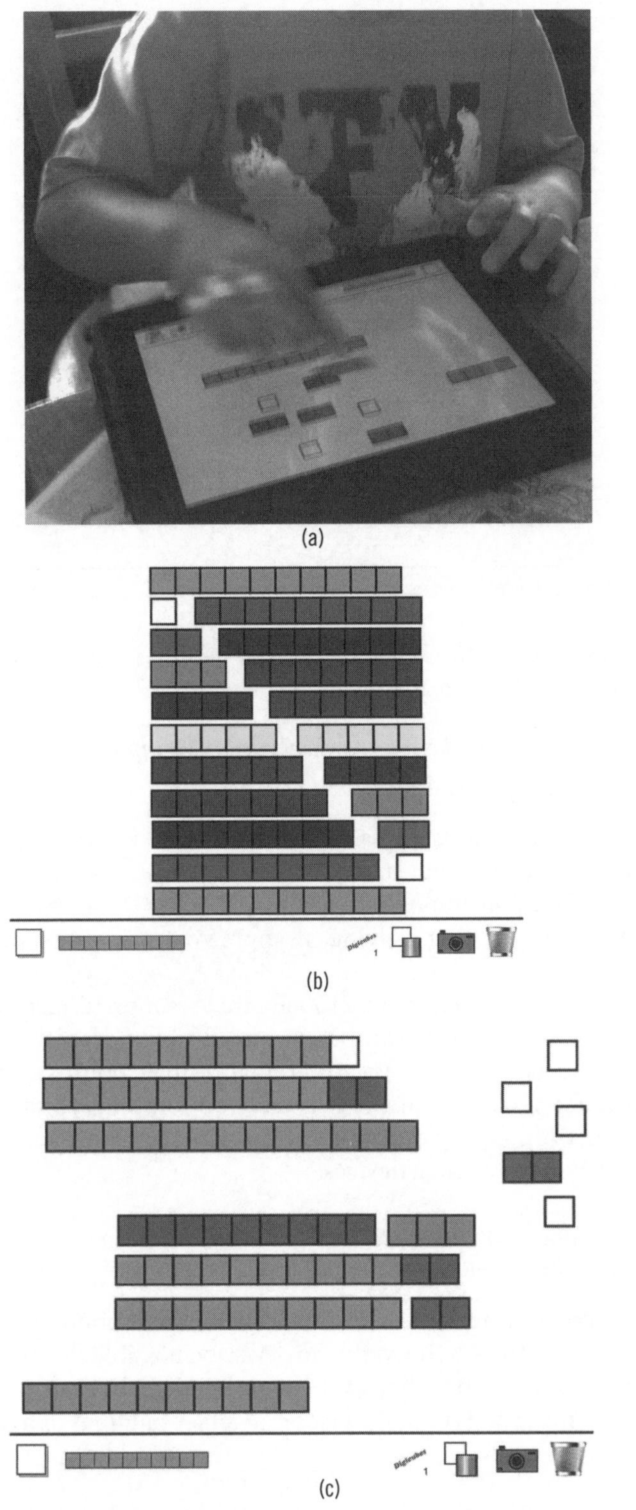

Figure 37.5 Digicubes: (a) and (b) exploring number through colour; (c) decade structure .

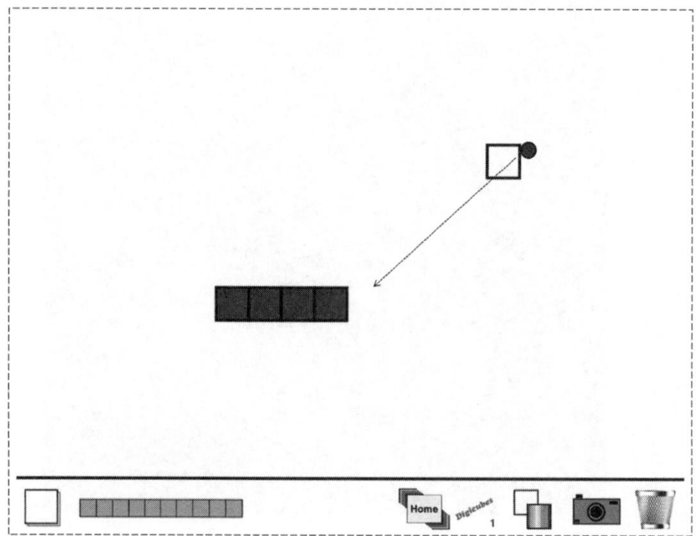

Figure 37.6 Pushing from outside of a square.

rately on the blocks with no tactile feedback. And we also noted that children often used their second hand to hold or steady the device.

6.3. *Actions as Conceptual Metaphors*

How do actions with the materials represent aspects of the learning concepts?

It has been shown how adults explaining fraction concepts use gestures relating to partitioning physical objects (Edwards, 2009). Therefore, evaluating how actions with Digicubes could build upon embodied learning processes would require investigation of how certain actions (e.g. adding, halving, swapping over amounts) correspond to early number concepts.

The current form of interaction on a touch screen is more direct than with a mouse, and sliding objects with a finger can be compared to children sliding single physical objects across a table. However, interaction remains single point and confined to a relatively small flat surface. A larger surface (e.g. tabletop computer) and multi-touch would make actions more pronounced but would still lack the more expansive actions detected by gesture recognition or tangible devices.

To what extent do designs use digital technology to link actions with materials to more symbolic forms of expressions?

Digicubes change colour when attached: digital effects correspond to the discrete result of actions rather than the process. It would, however, be possible to envisage an alternative design that did focus on actions. For example, using digital effects (e.g. sounds) to link actions such as moving groups of objects closer together (adding) or apart (subtraction).

6.4. *Conclusions*

This section illustrates how focusing on actions is informing the ongoing development of digital materials for young children. Initial work has identified limitations of the current design. Whilst some of these can be addressed (e.g. moving multiple objects), others require consideration of other devices (swapping objects). The goal, as described in this chapter, is to provide children with opportunities to explore with ease, constraining their own actions as they examine particular ideas, and to generate actions with materials that serve as metaphors for developing concepts.

REFERENCES

Abrahamson, D., Trninic, D., Gutiérrez, J. F., Huth, J., & Lee, R. G. (2011). Hooks and shifts: A dialectical study of mediated discovery. *Technology, Knowledge and Learning*, 1–31.

Alibali, M. W., & DiRusso, A. A. (1999). The function of gesture in learning to count: More than keeping track. *Cognitive Development, 14*(1), 37–56.

Antle, A. N., Droumeva, M., & Corness, G. (2008). Playing with The Sound Maker: Do embodied metaphors help children learn? In *Proceedings of the 7th International Conference on Interaction Design and Children.*

Bruner, J. (1966). *Toward a Theory of Instruction.* Cambridge, MA: Harvard University Press.

Cook, S. W., & Tanenhaus, M. K. (2009). Embodied communication: Speakers' gestures affect listeners' actions. *Cognition, 113*(1), 98–104.

Dillenbourg, P., & Evans, M. (2011). Interactive tabletops in education. *International Journal of Computer-Supported Collaborative Learning*, 1–24.

Donker, A., & Reitsma, P. (2007). Young children's ability to use a computer mouse. *Computers & Education, 48*(4), 602–617.

Edwards, L. D. (2009). Gestures and conceptual integration in mathematical talk. *Educational Studies in Mathematics, 70*(2), 127–141.

Fischer, U., Moeller, K., Bientzle, M., Cress, U., & Nuerk, H. (2010). Sensori-motor spatial training of number magnitude representation. *Psychonomic Bulletin & Review, 18*, 177–183.

Goldin-Meadow, S. (1999). The role of gesture in communication and thinking. *Trends in Cognitive Sciences, 3*(11), 419–429.

Kirsh, D., & Maglio, P. (1994). On distinguishing epistemic from pragmatic action. *Cognitive Science, 18*(4), 513–549.

Lakoff, G., & Núñez, R. (2000). *Where Mathematics Comes From: How the Embodied Mind brings Mathematics into Being.* New York: Basic Books.

Manches, A., & O'Malley, C. (2011). Tangibles for learning: A representational analysis of physical manipulation. *Personal and Ubiquitous Computing, 16*(4), 405–419.

Manches, A., O'Malley, C., & Benford, S. (2009). Physical manipulation: evaluating the potential for tangible designs. *Proceedings of the 3rd International Conference on Tangible and Embedded Interaction.* Cambridge, UK: ACM.

Manches, A., O'Malley, C., & Benford, S. (2010). The role of physical representations in solving number problems: A comparison of young children's use of physical and virtual materials. *Computers & Education, 54*(3), 622–640.

Marshall, P., Fleck, R., Harris, A., Rick, J., Hornecker, E., Rogers, Y., et al. (2009). Fighting for control: Children's embodied interactions when using physical and digital representations. In *Proceedings of CHI 2009*, Boston, pp. 2149–2152.

Martin, T. (2007). Physically distributed learning with virtual manipulatives for elementary mathematics. In D. Robinson & G. Schraw (Eds.), *Recent Innovations in Educational Technology that Facilitate Student Learning.* Charlotte, NC: Information Age Publishing.

Martin, T., & Schwartz, D. (2005). Physically distributed learning: Adapting and reinterpreting physical environments in the development of fraction concepts. *Cognitive Science, 29*, 587–625.

McNeil, N. M., & Jarvin, L. (2007). When theories don't add up: Disentangling the manipulatives debate. *Theory into Practice, 46*(4), 309–316.

Mix, K. S. (2009). Spatial tools for mathematical thought. In K. S. Mix, L. B. Smith & M. Gasser (Eds.), *The Spatial Foundations of Cognition and Language* (pp. 40–66). New York: Oxford Scholarship Online Monographs.

O'Hara, K. P., & Payne, S. J. (1998). The effects of operator implementation cost on planfulness of problem solving and learning. *Cognitive Psychology, 35*(1), 34–70.

Ping, R. M., & Goldin-Meadow, S. (2008). Hands in the air: Using ungrounded iconic gestures to teach children conservation of quantity. *Developmental Psychology, 44*(5), 1277.

Scaife, M., & Rogers, Y. (1996). External cognition: How do graphical representations work? *International Journal of Human-Computer Studies, 45*(2), 185–213.

Schwartz, D., Bransford, J. D., & Sears, D. (2005). Efficiency and innovation in transfer. In J. Mestre (Ed.), *Transfer of Learning from a Modern Multidisciplinary Perspective* (pp. 1–51). Greenwich, CT: Information Age Publishing.

Triona, L. M., & Klahr, D. (2003). Point and click or grab and heft: Comparing the influence of physical and virtual instructional materials on elementary school students' ability to design experiments. *Cognition and Instruction, 21*(2), 149–173.

Wilson, M. (2002). Six views of embodied cognition. *Psychonomic Bulletin & Review, 9*(4), 625–636.

Wyeth, P. (2008). How young children learn to program with sensor, action, and logic blocks. *Journal of the Learning Sciences, 17*(4), 517–550.

38

INSIGHT INTO TEACHING AND LEARNING

The Complex Face of Video Research

Mary J. Leonard and Sharon J. Derry

1. INTRODUCTION

Video is becoming an indispensable tool in education research, capturing detail and complexity in teaching and learning situations that other data collection approaches cannot. Yet with these advantages come new considerations for each step of the research process. Here we describe how video has helped researchers document and study complex technology-rich learning environments, and summarize experts' thinking about how video research is best conducted and reported.

Part of video's power as a data source is that it supports multidisciplinary research on teaching and learning. A video corpus can be selected from, analyzed, and re-analyzed by multiple researchers using different analytic approaches and theoretical frameworks. That said, underlying our discussion is an assumption that the actions people take and the ideas they communicate are expressions of cognition. Video captures settings, actions and talk, which are then analyzed in accordance with one or more methodological and theoretical positions, to advance and/or test hypotheses about cognition. Our discussion applies to video used to capture any situation where cognition is happening, whether in formal or informal "designed" educational environments, in the laboratory, or in natural experiential settings. We focus on video as a primary data source for studying learning and teaching in complex environments that incorporate learning technologies, broadly defined as anything human-made that supports or enhances learning.

Conducting video research in complex settings requires attending to intersecting issues of selection, analysis, technology, and ethics. We present an example to illustrate these issues in practice, then separately examine each issue. Detailed treatments of these issues are available in previous publications (Derry, 2007; Derry et al., 2010; Goldman, Pea, Barron & Derry, 2007).

2. EXAMPLE: VIDEO RESEARCH IN A SCIENCE CLASSROOM

Video was the primary data source in our study of knowledge building in a science classroom where students worked in small groups to design and build miniature balloon-powered cars (Leonard & Derry, 2011). Because the miniature cars were "vehicles" for learning science concepts, we consider them here as learning technologies. The study employed activity theory and discourse analysis to examine how the design task afforded and constrained students' learning of science and engineering concepts and skills.

This was a secondary data analysis. The original purpose for videotaping the classroom was to create a video case of an innovative middle-school curriculum for use in pre-service teacher education. Decisions about what to capture were guided by this purpose. While these decisions constrained the research questions that could later be asked and the types of analyses that could be conducted, the video corpus remained a rich resource for yielding insights into teaching and learning.

Video collection was contracted to a local video company, although a researcher was present for several days to guide collection. Two cameras were used: Camera A was stationary, capturing in-classroom actions and focusing on the teacher when she was present; Camera B roved, focusing on students and groups wherever they worked. The first audio track continuously recorded the teacher's clip-on microphone; a boom microphone followed Camera B and fed the second track.

As researchers we approached the resultant video corpus both deductively and inductively, identifying and analyzing relevant data in a combination of theory-driven and emergent processes that led to progressive refinement of our research questions. We began by viewing the video corpus in time order from the beginning to become deeply familiar with the corpus and the activity itself. We viewed the video with a focus on students' explanations for balloon-car motion, engaging first in open coding to identify where students expressed their ideas, then in focused coding to identify the types of explanations they gave. We derived focused codes from the theoretical framework and orienting research questions, but revised and supplemented them through iterative analysis. We transcribed the entirety of one group's independent work and the whole-class sessions throughout multiple viewings of the video, refining the transcript each time to draw out nuances of action and speech.

Transana (Transana, 2006) video transcription and analysis software allowed us to transcribe from video and to synchronize the transcript with the video. It further enabled us to build multiple collections of video clips, including video coordinated from both cameras, to segment and organize the corpus in multiple ways (e.g., by activity versus by individual groups). Following analysis, we included video clips and stills in research presentations and reports. Our analysis showed how students and the teacher struggled to use science to understand balloon-powered car motion and suggested improvements for curriculum and teacher professional development.

3. SELECTION

As in our example, selection occurs at every step of video research: planning the project, shooting the original footage, selecting clips for analysis, developing final products for presentation, and dealing with issues related to archiving and curatorship. During video recording, selection is shaped by practical and technical concerns. Practically, while one can never capture everything, supplementing video with other data—such as observer notes, screen capture, or student work products—allows robust analysis and triangulation. Technically, there are multiple issues to consider, including: Choice and numbers of cameras and microphones, placement of recording equipment, when to start and stop recording, shooting wide-angle or close-up, and panning and zooming decisions (Derry (2007) and Derry et al. (2010), provide advice on these issues).

Selection during analysis involves choosing events from a larger video corpus. Events are segments of activity comprising multiple parts and timescales (Zacks & Tversky, 2001) and thus can be defined at multiple levels. To provide another example, the Video Mosaic online repository (http://videomosaic.org) contains selections from the Robert B. Davis Institute for Learning (RBDIL) video archive containing more than 3,500 hours of recordings collected during studies of children's mathematical thinking (Maher, 2005, 2008). The selections enable study of the development of children's mathematical thinking in specific strands of mathematics activity, such as combinatorics and fractions. Using Video Mosaic, researchers or educators can, for example, select and examine events in which children work in small groups to solve combinatorics problems using unifix cubes. These selected events could be parsed further into sub-events that could be sampled for study: presentation of an argument by one student, the response of another, negotiation of meaning, etc. Sub-events can be selected from and examined at a still smaller scale, as in the study of gestures. Alternatively, selected small group problem-solving sessions could be analyzed as aspects of a longer-term macro-event representing longitudinal development of students' understanding of fundamental concepts such as exponential reasoning.

Decisions about how and what to select are driven by researchers' perspectives and goals. For example, if the researcher is concerned with relative frequency of events, a statistically defensible event sample might be required. In contrast, when the objective is telling an insightful story, or creating a narrative, researchers select interesting and illustrative clips. What one selects is also shaped by the reasoning approach—inductive, deductive, or both. Emerging themes drive selection in inductive approaches. In deductive approaches, data are selected that inform one's hypotheses and questions. As with our science classroom study, these approaches can be used in combination when researchers set out to investigate hypotheses but remain open to what presents itself in the situation under study. Our example also illustrates how selection decisions made for a particular purpose or from a particular analytical or theoretical framework might constrain what analyses are later possible with the resultant dataset.

4. ANALYSIS

Minimally edited video becomes data when the researcher strategically selects video segments from a corpus and uses them for a specific analytic purpose (Goldman & McDermott, 2007). The specifics of how to go about analysis are dependent on one's theoretical commitments, research questions, the audience for the analysis, and practical constraints of time, money and personnel. Here we address several approaches and recommendations for analyzing video that were illustrated in our science classroom study and are generally applicable.

Experienced researchers start analyses with orienting questions but expect to discover unanticipated phenomena that can be theoretically fruitful (Engle, Conant, & Greeno, 2007). Approaching analysis with theoretically motivated questions helps manage the complexity of video data, preventing the researcher from becoming lost in the details. At the same time one is working with guiding questions, it is important to be open to discovering new phenomena. In the example video study described above, we started with a theoretical framework that indicated what to look for in a design-based science classroom, but discovered the enacted curriculum required students to engage in scientific practices not anticipated by the researchers (or the teacher).

The process of analyzing video is iterative and researchers should expect to engage in multiple cycles of analysis. Regardless of approach, one generally views a video corpus in its entirety then selects events to consider in greater depth. Analysis involves moving between the process of video selection, one's evolving interpretations and hypotheses, and intermediate representations.

Intermediate representations summarize the contents of video records, assisting researchers in identifying segments for analysis and in detecting patterns. Like many video researchers, we employed a variety of representations to outline events and to identify key events and participants. These include *time-indexed field notes* made during video collection, *content logs* created while viewing collected video, and macrolevel coding of video in the form of *flow charts* (Ash, 2007) or *workflow visualizations* (Hackbarth, Derry, Eagan, & Gressick, 2010). Some researchers develop descriptive, *narrative summaries*, lengthy descriptions of action and dialogue captured in the video (e.g., Powell, Francisco, & Maher, 2003). Researchers may summarize aspects of video records using *still frames* or *diagrams* that characterize actions of interest (e.g., Angelillo, Rogoff, & Chavajay, 2007). Most researchers eventually produce *transcripts* that represent events (see Derry (2007) for common transcription choices). Transcripts are iteratively revised over the course of analysis, until they provide a reliable record of what researchers deem most relevant for answering their research questions (e.g., Engle et al., 2007).

Video records can be analyzed and reported using quantitative, qualitative, or mixed methodologies. Video technology greatly enhances the researcher's capacity to quantify qualitative data (for quantification methods, see Bakeman & Gottman, 1997; Chi, 1997; Erickson, 1986). The practice of disciplined observation, a core feature of scientific methodology, relied on pre-established coding schemes that could be applied reliably by multiple observers in situ. Video now allows coding schemes to be developed after data collection, often collaboratively among researchers, over multiple viewings or over multiple research projects (e.g., Ash, 2007; Powell et al., 2003). In other approaches, researchers might instead focus on developing rich examples of phenomena, for example, providing "play-by-play" descriptions of a sequence of selected events (e.g., Koschmann, Glenn, & Conlee, 1999; Ochs & Taylor, 1996). Video analysis is a complex, iterative, social process that benefits from technological support.

5. TECHNOLOGY

Technologies are being developed to support a workflow which, as in our science classroom example, proceeds somewhat as follows (Pea & Hoffert, 2007). As video is collected, a researcher labels and organizes recordings. The researcher may then chunk video records into segments, marking segments of interest, transcribing at different levels of detail, and developing and applying analytic categories that interpret events, all in a recursive manner until achieving a desired level of understanding. The work then moves to presenting and sharing analysis, either formatively, as researchers collaboratively develop and comment on a video analysis, or summatively, when an account of the analysis is published and commented on by others.

Current technologies support certain phases of this workflow process but no one tool supports its entirety (see Pea & Hay, 2003). Video researchers must investigate available tools and create a toolkit that is accessible and supported in their research environment. An appropriate toolkit will match the researchers' analytic practices and goals; fit their budgets; and, ideally, involve them in a supportive community of users. In our example study, the video analysis tool Transana met these needs. Derry et al. (2010) identify other current or historically important tools of video research, but others exist and new tools continue to be developed.

Digital video and easy access to online environments have created possibilities for sharing video data, so that "each part of the research process can now be a community activity" (Goldman, 2007, p. 6). This provides opportunities for broader participation in sense-making.

Video records may be included when an analysis is *reported*, via an accompanying CD-ROM/DVD, by linking to video on a website, or in an online journal. Including video opens up new levels of transparency in research, allowing readers to evaluate arguments based on the data. In a classic example, Goodwin (2000, 2003) created and disseminated multimedia versions of publications on CD-ROMs to interested colleagues. Records from research video can be included in online reports open to commentary by others (e.g., Goldman-Segall, 1998) or in teacher professional development materials (e.g., Hammer & van Zee, 2006). Few education journals have yet to include video records with publications, but one that does, and includes peer-reviewed articles, is *Education Next.*

Video records may be shared along with analyses by multiple researchers. A special issue of *Discourse Processes* (Koschmann, 1999) published independent analyses of one video by several leading researchers with differing theoretical perspectives and distributed a CD-ROM including the video record with the printed journal (see Clarke (2001) for an edited book example). In other examples of multiple analysis studies, the video was not disseminated but was represented by transcripts, exhibits, and images within the publication (e.g., Kamen et al., 1997; Koschmann, 2011).

Collected video can be openly shared in *repositories* and *collaboratories.* Often hosted in online databases, these open up video records to analysis (or reanalysis) by multiple, non-collaborating individuals or research groups, as well as for use in education settings. For example, the recent addition of the VMC Analytic component to the online Video Mosaic collaboratory (Video Mosaic Collaborative (VMC), 2012; VMC at UW-Madison, 2012) enables researchers and students from multiple fields to contribute and share analyses of videos hosted there.

While such projects evoke visions for the future of collaborative research with video data, they also raise important issues, such as funding and managing collaboratories, balancing capacity limitations and issues of quality control with the ideals of free access to data and of open sharing and reporting, and addressing ethical issues concerning research using human subjects.

6. ETHICS

Our video study required finding appropriate ways to accommodate both research needs and participant privacy and confidentiality. Like most researchers we presented our proposal to our institution's review board (IRB); because we partnered with researchers from another institution to collect the video, we additionally submitted our proposal to their IRB. The IRBs interpreted regulations and assessed the suitability of our planned human subject involvement and protection. Research using video, an inherently non-anonymous medium, raises unique concerns for privacy and confidentiality.

Requirements designed to protect participants can create challenges in using video for research. Anonymity cannot be guaranteed unless participants are technically filtered or masked in videos, expensive processes that compromise the video records for some research purposes. Confidentiality, however, can be protected by restricting access to video and any identifying information such as individuals' and school names. Honoring individual participants' wishes to not be recorded might require real-time editing, such as moving the camera before they come into view or seating them outside of camera range. These solutions are not always practical (students may be mobile) or desirable (special seating arrangements may marginalize students) and could limit the video's utility for research.

Sharing video records raises additional concerns but two forces are reshaping the conversation: (a) video is becoming ubiquitous in life and social acceptance of its use for many purposes is increasing, and (b) research communities and funding organizations are emphasizing the need for broad sharing of data sources. Yet challenges remain. One is deciding what parts of a video corpus should be shared and for what purposes. Another is the question of how shared video will be used and by whom; as records travel further from the source the possibilities expand unpredictability. It is, therefore, a matter of ethical concern that adequate documentation about the video, including information about the research participants, be included so that new users are adequately informed and can appropriately select, use, and interpret the records. Sharing such information, however, might not be perceived as adequately protecting privacy and confidentiality of participants.

Several models exist that may accommodate both research and human subjects requirements. For example, a *two-stage model* uses two protocols: (1) a collection protocol that uses an informed consent form (ICF) and covers data collection, its archiving and immediate use; and (2) a use protocol dependent on the collection protocol that covers access, publication and, possibly, destruction of video in subsequent analyses. Both protocols are reviewed by the IRB of the institution that owns and maintains the data corpus and often by the institution of the researcher requesting access. ICFs themselves can range from highly permissive (requesting unrestricted use of the video with no guarantees it will be used only for research purposes) to highly restrictive (promising access limited to the research staff only, full anonymity by masking of faces and voices when presented or shared, etc.). Video sharing is best supported by creating the least restrictive ICF possible that adequately protects participants but also encourages broad and appropriate uses of video. Researchers must become knowledgeable about ethics and regulations and might need to educate IRBs about risks and safeguards in video research.

7. VIDEO IN EDUCATIONAL COMPUTING RESEARCH

Video as a data collection tool supports myriad purposes, questions, and approaches to research in educational computing environments. For example, Lantz-Andersson (2009) collected video in the classroom to study how secondary students using an interactive Web-based multimedia mathematics program framed computer-supported collaborative learning situations. Mullins, Rummel and Spada (2011) videotaped students in the laboratory to study effects of individual versus collaborative learning with computer-supported instruction in secondary mathematics. Video was the primary data source in Greiffenhagen's (2012) study of how teachers interacted with students who were collaboratively using educational computing technologies in a secondary English classroom. Tanner and Jones (2007) collected video of classroom lessons to serve as a stimulus for elementary and middle-school students' reflections on their learning using an interactive whiteboard during the lessons. Rowe and Jacobs (2002) collected video as means to establish *intra*rater reliability of in-situ evaluations of middle-school students' posture at computer workstations. The full range of video's application in educational computing research has yet to be realized.

8. ADVANTAGES AND CHALLENGES

In video research, advantages are one side of the coin; challenges are the other. Video is an excellent source for analysis because it captures more complexity than even a team of ethnographers can keep up with in the field (Ruhleder & Jordan, 1997). But while the detail in video records allows analytical flexibility and depth, it can make that analysis overwhelming. As previously emphasized, video records facilitate multiple viewings that bring to light new aspects of discourse (Gee, 1999). Yet issues related to human subjects' privacy may prohibit broad sharing of video data. Also, the richness and volume of video records makes turning them into useful data enormously time consuming. The increased complexity of video records creates the need for new forms of representation that can handle the complexity captured (e.g., ways to represent and visualize the flow of ideas among collaborating students). Because video research is inherently complex, it is highly vulnerable to criticisms of subjective bias in selection and interpretation. However, these can be countered by accounts that describe rigorous attention to the logic of one's inquiry; by being systematic in the collecting, documenting, archiving, and selecting of video records; and by fully articulating the processes used to create explanations and generate claims.

REFERENCES

Angelillo, C., Rogoff, B., & Chavajay, P. (2007). Examining shared endeavors by abstracting video coding schemes with fidelity to cases. In R. Goldman, R. Pea, B. Barron, & S. J. Derry (Eds.), *Video research in the learning sciences* (pp. 189–206). Mahwah, NJ: Erlbaum.

Ash, D. (2007). Using video data to capture discontinuous science meaning making in non-school settings. In R. Goldman, R. Pea, B. Barron, & S. J. Derry (Eds.), *Video research in the learning sciences* (pp. 207–226). Mahwah, NJ: Erlbaum.

Bakeman, R., & Gottman, J. M. (1997). *Observing interaction: An introduction to sequential analysis.* Cambridge, England: Cambridge University Press.

Chi, M. T. H. (1997). Quantifying qualitative analyses of verbal data: A practical guide. *Journal of the Learning Sciences, 6,* 271–315.

Clarke, D. J. (Ed.). (2001). *Perspectives on practice and meaning in mathematics and science classrooms.* Dordrecht, Netherlands: Kluwer Academic Press.

Derry, S. J. (Ed.). (2007). *Guidelines for conducting video research in education: Recommendations from an expert panel.* Chicago: Data Research and Development Center. Retrieved from http://drdc.uchicago.edu/what/video-research.html.

Derry, S. J., Pea, R. D., Barron, B., Engle, R. A., Erickson, F., Goldman, et al. (2010). Conducting video research in the learning sciences: Guidance on selection, analysis, technology, and ethics. *The Journal of the Learning Sciences, 19*, 3–53.

Engle, R. A., Conant, F. R., & Greeno, J. G. (2007). Progressive refinement of hypotheses in video-supported research. In R. Goldman, R. Pea, B. Barron, & S. J. Derry (Eds.), *Video research in the learning sciences* (pp. 239–254). Mahwah, NJ: Erlbaum.

Erickson, F. (1986). Qualitative methods in research on teaching. In M. C. Wittrock (Ed.), *Handbook of research on teaching* (3rd ed., pp. 119–161). New York: Macmillan.

Gee, J. P. (1999). *An introduction to discourse analysis: Theory and method.* New York: Routledge.

Goldman, R. (2007). ORION™, an online digital video data analysis tool: Changing our perspectives as an interpretive community. In R. Goldman, R. Pea, B. Barron, & S. J. Derry (Eds.), *Video research in the learning sciences* (pp. 507–520). Mahwah, NJ: Erlbaum.

Goldman, R., Pea, R., Barron, B., & Derry, S. J. (Eds.). (2007). *Video research in the learning sciences.* Mahwah, NJ: Erlbaum.

Goldman, S., & McDermott, R. (2007). Staying the course with video analysis. In R. Goldman, R. Pea, B. Barron, & S. J. Derry (Eds.), *Video research in the learning sciences* (pp. 101–113). Mahwah, NJ: Erlbaum.

Goldman-Segall, R. (1998). *Points of viewing children's thinking: A digital ethnographer's journey.* Mahwah, NJ: Erlbaum.

Goodwin, C. (2000). Action and embodiment within situated human interaction. *Journal of Pragmatics, 32*, 1489–1522.

Goodwin, C. (2003). Pointing as situated practice. In S. Kita (Ed.), *Pointing: Where language, culture, and cognition meet* (pp. 217–242). Mahwah, NJ: Erlbaum.

Greiffenhagen, C. (2012). Making rounds: The routine work of the teacher during collaborative learning with computers. *Computer-Supported Collaborative Learning, 7*, 11–42.

Hackbarth, A., Derry, S. J., Eagan, B., & Gressick, J. (2010). Adapting workflow technology to design-based research: Development of a method for organizing the "messiness" of research in technology-rich online learning environments. In K. Gomez, L. Lyons, & J. Radinsky (Eds.), *Learning in the Disciplines: Proceedings of the 9th International Conference of the Learning Sciences (ICLS 2010)—Volume 1, Full Papers* (pp. 667–674). Chicago IL: International Society of the Learning Sciences.

Hammer, D., & van Zee, E. (2006). *Seeing the science in children's thinking.* Portsmouth, NH: Heinemann.

Kamen, M., Roth, W.-M., Flick, L. B., Shapiro, B., Barden, L., Kean, E., et al. (1997). A multiple perspective analysis of the role of language in inquiry science learning: To build a tower. *Electronic Journal of Science Education, 2* [Online]. Retrieved from http://unr.edu/homepage/jcannon/ejse/kamen_etal.html.

Koschmann, T. (1999). The edge of many circles: Making meaning of meaning making. *Discourse Processes, 27*, 103–117.

Koschmann, T. (Ed.). (2011). *Theories of learning and studies of instructional practices.* New York: Springer.

Koschmann, T., Glenn, P., & Conlee, M. (1999). Theory presentation and assessment in a problem-based learning group. *Discourse Processes, 27*, 119–133.

Lantz-Andersson, A. (2009). The power of natural frameworks: Technology and the question of agency in CSCL settings. *International Journal of Computer-Supported Collaborative Learning, 4*, 93–107.

Leonard, M., & Derry, S. (2011). *"What's the science behind it?" The interaction of engineering and science goals, knowledge, and practices in a design-based science activity* (WCER Working Paper No. 2011-7). Retrieved from http://www.wcer.wisc.edu/publications/workingPapers/papers.php.

Maher, C. (2005). How students structure their investigations and learn mathematics: Insights from a long-term study. *Journal of Mathematical Behavior, 24*, 1–14.

Maher, C. (2008). Video recordings as pedagogical tools in mathematics teacher education. In D. Tirosh & T. Wood (Eds.), *Tools and processes in mathematics teacher education* (pp. 65–83). Rotterdam, the Netherlands: Sense Publishers.

Mullins, D., Rummel, N., & Spada, H. (2011). Are two heads always better than one? Differential effects of collaboration on students' computer-supported learning in mathematics. *Computer-Supported Collaborative Learning, 6*, 420–443.

Ochs, E., & Taylor, C. (1996). The "father knows best" dynamic in family dinner narratives. In K. Hall (Ed.), *Gender articulated: Language and the socially constructed self* (pp. 97–121). New York: Routledge.

Pea, R. D., & Hay, K. (2003, March). *Report to the National Science Foundation: CILT workshop on digital video inquiry in learning and education, November 25–26, 2002* (based on NSF #0124012). Stanford, CA: Stanford Center for Innovations in Learning. Retrieved from http://www.stanford.edu/~roypea/RoyPDF%20folder/A112_Pea_Hay_CILT_DVI_2003.pdf.

Pea, R., & Hoffert, E. (2007). Video workflow in the learning sciences: Prospects of emerging technologies for augmenting work practices. In R. Goldman, R. Pea, B. Barron, & S. J. Derry (Eds.), *Video research in the learning sciences* (pp. 427–460). Mahwah, NJ: Erlbaum.

Powell, A. B., Francisco, J. M., & Maher, C. A. (2003). An analytical model for studying the development of learners' mathematical ideas and reasoning using videotape data. *Journal of Mathematical Behavior, 22,* 405–435.

Rowe, G., & Jacobs, K. (2002). Efficacy of body mechanics education on posture while computing in middle school children. *Work, 18,* 295–303.

Ruhleder, K., & Jordan, B. (1997, June). *Capturing complex, distributed activities: Video-based interaction analysis as a component of workplace ethnography.* In A. S. Lee, J. Liebenau, & J. I. DeGross (Eds.), *Information Systems and Qualitative Research* (pp. 246–275). London: Chapman & Hall.

Tanner, H., & Jones, S. (2007). Using video-stimulated reflective dialog to learn from children about their learning with or without ICT. *Technology, Pedagogy and Education, 16,* 321–335.

Transana 2.10 [Computer software]. (2006). Madison, WI: The Board of Regents of the University of Wisconsin System. Retrieved from http://www.transana.org.

Video Mosaic Collaborative at University of Wisconsin–Madison. (2012). Retrieved from http://vmc.wceruw.org.

Video Mosaic Collaborative. (2012). Retrieved from http://videomosaic.org.

Zacks, R., & Tversky, D. (2001). Event structure in perception and conception. *Psychological Bulletin, 127,* 3–21.

39

BASIC CONCEPTS AND TECHNIQUES IN SOCIAL NETWORK ANALYSIS

Christophe Reffay and Alejandra Martínez-Monés

1. INTRODUCTION

Evaluation has to be aligned with the goals pursued in each particular design, and is influenced by the theoretical principles on which these designs are based. Situated learning, which considers learning as a complex interplay between the individual and the collective (Lave & Wenger, 1991), leads to questions related to how learners interact with their context, in the classroom or in any community where learning can take place. As pointed out by Sfard (1998), issues related to the evolution of participation in those classes or communities become relevant questions to evaluate learning.

Another scenario where these issues are the appropriate questions to ask is when teachers try to orchestrate their classes using ICT resources and collaboration. Besides the inherent complexity of managing these scenarios (Prieto et al., 2011), teachers also need to know if the activity has developed as expected. Monitoring has to be provided at a coarse granularity (Dillenbourg et al., 2011), or otherwise teachers would be unable to integrate it into their practice. Issues such as whether the students have participated as expected or some of them have assumed a more (or less) prominent role, or whether subgroups of more inter-related students have emerged from the activity, are relevant to the teachers even if the information on which these indicators are based is not complete.

If the presence of computers makes the ecosystem described above more complex, it is also an opportunity to answer these demands: Computers can, at least potentially, store the actions performed by the users and run automatic parts of analysis methods to better understand the activity (Harrer, Martínez-Monés, & Dimitracopoulou, 2009). Beyond the basic statistics revealing the number of (low-level) actions of each actor that can be built on the technical log files, it has been shown useful to compute higher-level indicators. These indicators do not consider only actions in an actor-centered manner but, rather, the interaction between each pair of actors or even at various group levels.

A field that has been shown to be especially well suited to study these issues is Social Network Analysis (SNA) (Wasserman & Faust, 1994; Scott, 2000). It focuses on the study of the relationships among members in a community or a group. Since the first works at the end of the 1990s (Nurmela, Lehtinen, & Palonen, 1999; Wortham, 1999), SNA has been increasingly employed in the fields of technology enhanced learning (TEL) and computer-supported collaborative learning (CSCL).

The rest of this chapter describes the basic concepts and processes of SNA and the implications of its application to the study of learning in TEL. The following section introduces the theoretical and practical approaches from which SNA has been found to be appropriate. Then, section 3 discusses the basic concepts of the approach, illustrated with examples. Section 4 includes a short review of the current trends of research on the application of SNA to TEL. The chapter finishes with a discussion on the issues presented and open research lines.

2. THEORETICAL UNDERPINNINGS

Social Network Analysis, also named *structural analysis*, takes its roots from sociometry, group dynamics, graph theory and their intersection with structural and functional anthropology (Scott, 2000). Instead of taking an individualistic approach, as in traditional social and behavioral sciences, SNA assumes the pre-eminence of the relationships between individuals as a starting point, and defines structural variables, referred to the properties of links between actors. As pointed out by Scott (2000) and Wasserman and Faust (1994), the novelty in this vision is not so much the study of relationships but the denial of certain traditional assumptions in the social sciences that assume the statistical independence of the individuals, even when the interactions among them are the main focus of study.

Within the learning sciences, SNA is especially well suited to study issues highlighted by the situated theories and the participatory metaphor of learning (Sfard, 1998). These approaches stress the mutual dependence between the individual and the social, so that one cannot be understood without the other. This perspective states the need to study the situations at different levels: individual, group and the community. Learning is conceptualized as the development of new forms of participation in communities of practice. From this perspective, some of the relevant questions to ask are: Who are the most active actors? What is the structure of participation in a concrete community? Is there a progression in the level of implication of the different actors in the community? Traditional research methods, be they quantitative or qualitative, are not adequate to answer these questions. On the one hand, the size of large groups and the nature of the interactions in CSCL make it difficult to capture them by traditional ethnographic data sources. On the other hand, quantitative methods do not address the structural aspects of interaction, as they are focused on the individual properties and assume the independence between actors. On the contrary, SNA is based on the fact that individuals are interdependent, and provides techniques and indexes to analyze this interdependence.

Evaluating learning in TEL poses many practical problems, especially when social interaction among students is at stake. Recently, the need to provide teachers with means to orchestrate their classes, giving them support to integrate the large amount of tools and activities normally involved in a CSCL setting, has been stressed (Dillenbourg et al., 2011). In this sense, when conducting a collaborative learning scenario teachers are not normally interested in gaining insight into the cognitive processes that the experience might provoke in the learners, but in getting an overall impression of the enacted practices, and whether they match or not with what they had previously designed. SNA, with the help of automatic data logging has the potential to provide help in this direction. For this reason, a focus on participative aspects is also a practical approach to support teachers in their CSCL situation orchestration.

Section 4 will provide further details of the current research trends and open issues in the application of SNA to the fields of TEL and CSCL. Before that, the next section describes the main concepts and procedures used when applying SNA to evaluate interactions.

3. BASIC CONCEPTS AND TECHNIQUES IN SNA

The current section focuses on the conceptualization of the network and presents some important indices and techniques to enable social network analyses.

3.1. Social Networks: An Analytic Representation of Relationships

Basically, a social network is a set of actors and a set of relationships among them. An actor is a discrete social entity (such as individuals, corporations or collectives). A relationship is a specific kind of interaction between actors (Scott, 2000). The researchers, according to their goals determine this relationship. Relationships such as: (1) "A collaborates with B," (2) "A talked to B," or (3) "A used document X," are examples that can be modeled to study interaction in TEL. We already can observe that each of these examples does not convey the same type of information: the first relationship is symmetrical; the second is oriented from A to B; and example 3 connects entities of different types (i.e. actors and documents).

One of the reasons why SNA has received so much attention in recent decades is the fact that a social network (or sociogram) can be modeled as a graph, i.e. a set of nodes connected by ties. Depending on the direction, value and number of sets of actors participating in the relationships, different kinds of graphs can be represented (Scott, 2000): directed graphs (or digraphs) where ties are oriented (see Table 39.1: graphs #1 & #3) vs. undirected ones (graphs #2, #4 & #5), valued graphs (#3 & #4) vs. unvalued ones (graphs #1, #2 & #5). 1-mode networks are employed when nodes are all of the same type, such as, for example, *students* (Table 39.1: graphs #1 to #4), and 2-mode networks when two sets of distinct nodes (i.e., *students* and *documents*, see graph #5) participate in the relationship. These three independent dimensions (with two values each) offer eight potential combinations from directed valued 1-mode network to undirected unvalued 2-mode network.

Table 39.1 gives examples of the mentioned types of 1-mode networks. Graph #1 could represent actors (if connected) sharing documents. On graph #3, (connected) actors share a defined number of documents. These graphs (#1 and #3) are alternative ways to represent the 2-mode network graph #5 that could define links between actors (A, . . ., G) and documents (X, Y, Z). If graph #4 defines the flow and intensity of messages between actors, graph #2 only represents the existence of a link, and the direction of the flow. These examples also illustrate how graphs can be derived by transformation from previous ones, such as graph #2 from graph #4. Such transformation offers a wider choice of analyses (that apply only to simple graphs) at the cost of information loss.

Representing a sociogram by a graph enables researchers to exploit the knowledge on graph theory to visualize and manipulate data. A graph can be represented as a matrix

Table 39.1 Examples of different types of social networks, according to the direction and value of the links (graphs #1 to #4), and to the number of sets of nodes represented in the network: 1-mode (graphs #1 to #4) and 2-mode (graph #5) networks.

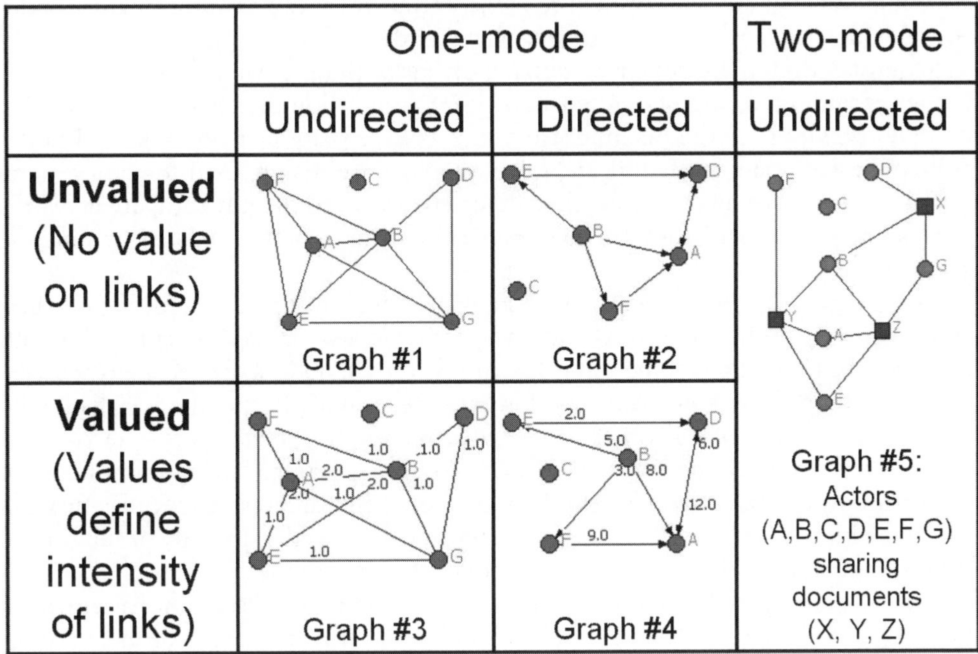

M (called adjacency matrix, see Table 39.2). For 1-mode networks, *M* is a square matrix with *n* rows and columns where *n* is the number of actors. The existence of a link between actors *i* and *j* is represented by a non-zero value (1 for unvalued graphs, any value *v* for valued graphs) in the element M_{ij}. Undirected graphs can be represented either by symmetric matrices or triangular ones. The 2-mode network can have a rectangular matrix where rows represent a first type of nodes (e.g. actors in graph #5), and columns, the other type (e.g. documents in graph #5).

Matrices are formal ways to represent sociograms, but it is sometimes (e.g. sparse matrices) more convenient to represent them by a list of (typed) nodes and a list of (valued) ties. Many tools[1] accept both of these representations as possible entries and may use a variety of graph description languages (e.g. GraphML, VNA, DL, etc.).

Table 39.2 Examples of the adjacency matrices that model the networks #2, #3 and #5 represented in Table 39.1.

↗	A	B	C	D	E	F
A	0	0	0	1	0	0
B	1	0	0	0	1	1
C	0	0	0	0	0	0
D	1	0	0	0	0	0
E	0	0	0	1	0	0
F	1	0	0	0	0	0

Adjacency matrix of graph #2

	A	B	C	D	E	F	G
A							
B	2						
C	0	0					
D	0	1	0				
E	2	2	0	0			
F	1	1	0	0	1		
G	1	1	0	1	1	0	

Adjacency matrix of graph #3

	X	Y	Z
A	0	1	1
B	1	1	1
C	0	0	0
D	1	0	0
E	0	1	1
F	0	1	0
G	1	0	1

Adjacency matrix of graph #5

3.2 Basic Indices and Techniques

The analysis of a social network can be done at different levels, focusing on the network as a whole (density of links and cohesion of the community), on the relationships between individuals (proximity, betweenness centrality, cohesion) or on singular nodes (central nodes, bridges, local bridges, peripheral nodes).

The most common indices characterizing the network (as a whole) are: *order*, or the number of nodes; *size*, number of edges; *density*, proportion of actual ties vs. possible ones; and *diameter*, or the maximum distance between any pair of connected nodes (if disconnected, diameter is infinite). These indices are mainly used to get a general impression of the overall characteristics of the network, or to roughly compare networks to one another. However, the structure of a network can be better analyzed by studying its subsets.

In simple graphs (not valued), we distinguish subsets of nodes depending on their connectivity with other nodes. As such, we find *components* (i.e. we can find a path between any pair of nodes of the subset), *k-cores* (i.e. each node is connected to at least k other nodes of the subset) and *cliques* or *k-cliques* (i.e. a set of k nodes where each of them is connected with the $(k - 1)$ other ones). Subsequently, a *k-clique* is a $(k - 1)$-*core* of k nodes. According to Granovetter (1973), cliques are subgroups having more frequent and intense interaction (strong ties). People connecting different cliques (with weak ties) have a higher "social capital": they are connected to a wider diversity of subgroups. This gives them more choice for a new job or house, for example.

Besides the group and subgroup levels, a major issue in SNA is the measurement of centrality at an individual level. Actors' centrality can provide an idea of their prominence and brokerage. The most common centrality indices, defined by Freeman (1979) are: degree, betweenness and closeness. *Degree* indicates the activity of an actor in the network (i.e. the number of neighbors); *betweenness* refers to the influence of actors in controlling the relationships of others (i.e. their brokerage); and *closeness*, represents the facility of an actor to reach the rest of the members of the network, which gives an idea of his or her independence to establish new relationships.

For illustration purposes, we will use a graph produced by Moreno (1934) where the 32 nodes are pupils (diamonds are boys, circles are girls) and oriented ties represent the two friends a pupil would choose as neighbors. By defining the size of each node according to *indegree* (Figure 39.1a), or to *directed betweenness* (Figure 39.1b), we can illustrate either the popularity (i.e. node #19) or the importance of nodes that connect all pupils, and here, particularly, boys with girls subgroups (nodes #10 and #22).

It is interesting to see that popular pupils emphasized on Figure 39.1a, (like #19 or #23) are not necessarily the best intermediaries (like #22 and #10 on Figure 39.1b). The importance of bridges between boys and girls (in this example) can also be explained by the theory of *structural holes* (Burt, 1992). Node #10 is important for his connection with node #22 because none of his other contacts (even indirect ones) can connect to any of the 18 girls. This bridge (from #10 to #22) can be used by all 14 boys to reach nine of the 18 girls. The other bridge connecting girls to boys (#29 to #11) only enables six girls (#22, #24, #26, #31, #30, #29) to reach six boys (#11, #3, #7, #5, #4, #10). It is interesting to observe that, except #29, five of these girls need both bridges, going through the boys (#3, #7, #5) to reach six other girls (#22, #23, #19, #20, #17, #27). Conversely, node #11 is the only boy who enforces other boys to go through some girls (#22, #30, #29) to reach him.

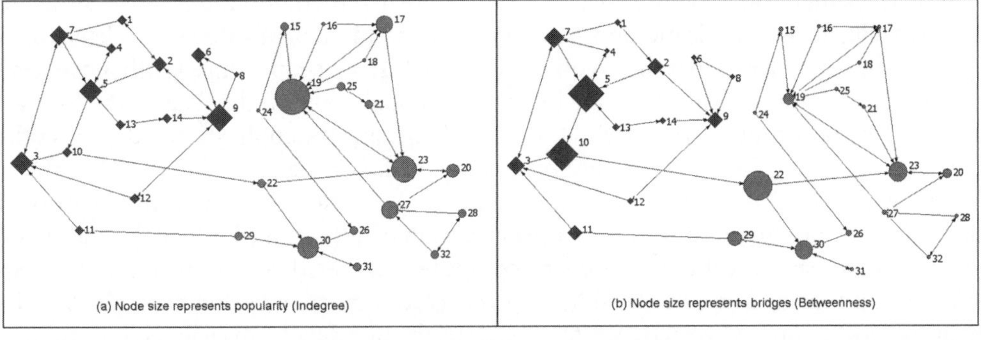
(a) Node size represents popularity (Indegree)

(b) Node size represents bridges (Betweenness)

Figure 39.1 Two representations of Moreno's graphs (1934), that use node size to visualize actors' (a) popularity and (b) betweenness.

Once the basic concepts and procedures of SNA have been described, the following section presents concrete examples of how these concepts and procedures are being used for the evaluation of learning in TEL scenarios.

4. SNA IN TEL: AN OVERVIEW OF EXPERIENCES

SNA is becoming a prominent approach in the evaluation of learning in TEL scenarios that have some form of collaboration within medium- or large-size groups. Several approaches to the use of SNA in these contexts can be identified.

Some researchers employ SNA methods to test hypothesis about the characteristics of the social structures emerging from CSCL scenarios and the positions of the actors in them. For example Cho, Stefanone and Gay (2002) use centrality degree, and Bonacich power (Bonacich, 1987) to detect the most prominent actors in a network. Aviv, Erlich and Ravid (2003) compare two CSCL communities by identifying the emerging *cliques*, to study their social capital. Reffay and Chanier (2003) combine *cliques* identification and *hierarchical clustering* in valued graphs to measure cohesion. The common characteristic of all these works is their use of SNA as a tool to gain insight into the characteristics of collaboration in a particular CSCL setting.

Other researchers take a pragmatic approach, focusing on methodological aspects. These focus on how SNA can be combined with other methods to help researchers and practitioners in the evaluation of CSCL practices. For example, Martínez-Monés, Dimitriadis, Gómez-Sánchez, Rubia and de la Fuente (2003) propose a mixed evaluation method that defines how to use SNA in combination with quantitative and qualitative methods for the evaluation of participatory aspects of learning in CSCL settings. A tool, named SAMSA, which will be discussed later in this section, supports this mixed method. Building on this idea, Daradoumis, Martínez-Monés and Xhafa (2006) propose a layered framework to support evaluation of different dimensions of collaboration at a distance, including SNA for the social level. In these cases, a research question that remains open is how to combine the different levels of analysis, as envisioned by the workshops on multivocality in the analysis of collaborative learning at ICLS 2010 and CSCL 2011 conferences (Suthers et al., 2011), where several works combining SNA with other research approaches were presented.

Finally, as mentioned before, SNA is based on formal methods and it is well suited to being applied to automatic methods and tools. The standard SNA software packages have the great inconvenience that they require a certain degree of experience for their use, and that preliminary work must be done by the researcher to set up the data in the formats accepted by those tools. To cope with these problems, specific applications adapted to the particular needs of TEL scenarios are being proposed. For example, SAMSA (Martínez-Monés et al., 2003) was developed with the main motivation of integrating the distinct data sources that can be employed in the evaluation of TEL scenarios, which range from ethnographic data to different forms of computer-mediated communication. SAMSA takes its input using a standardized XML protocol, described in Harrer et al. (2009). The data sources are pre-processed by filters that take the raw data from each data source and transform them into the XML protocol. Furthermore, SAMSA provides an interface to select and to configure the network to study, selecting dates, actors, and the relationship types among them. From the interactions file and from these configuration parameters, the matrix that represents the net is built, providing the results to the researcher.

Other examples of tools that exploit the potential of automatic analysis have been proposed. For example, CoNaVi (Harrer et al., 2007) visualizes the dynamics of the networks. The combination of SNA with automatic or semi-automatic tools adapted to CSCL has also raised the possibility to use it for new goals, such as supporting teachers' and students' self-regulation (Bratitsis & Dimitracopoulou, 2009).

All these works show the interest that SNA has raised during the last decade in the TEL arena. Current research is focusing on limitations of the initial proposals, such as the difficulties to convey the dynamic evolution of the networks, or the too limited semantics of the relationships being represented. For example, Harrer, Zeini and Ziebarth (2010) propose a 3-D network visualization technique that represents time on the *z*-axis, which allows capturing the evolution of the activity of the actors. Several works are relying on automatic or semi-automatic content analysis to add richer semantics to the relationships represented in the networks (Li, Liao, Wang, & Huang, 2007; Harrer et al., 2007). Sha, Teplovs and van Aalst (2010) describe an approach based on latent semantic analysis to add semantics to an already existing tool named KSV (Knowledge Space Visualizer) that allows conveying knowledge building structures based on Knowledge Forum{R} notes.

5. DISCUSSION

In this chapter we have introduced the main concepts related to the application of SNA to the evaluation of learning in TEL scenarios. We have described the main benefits of the approach, which are related to its alignment with the theoretical principles of situated learning and the fact that SNA-based indicators can provide information of interest to teachers. Being based on formal models (graph), easy to represent and manipulate computationally, this approach is particularly well suited for online collaborative learning, either for automatic feedback to actors involved in the setting, or for post-hoc analysis by researchers.

But SNA has also limitations that point to open research issues. We have already mentioned some of these and how researchers are dealing with them, such as the proposals to display the evolution of the networks in intuitive manners, or the works that are adding semantics to the relationships, in order to enable richer automatic analysis of knowledge building processes. Besides these, some aspects remain open, and we mention them here as pointers to future research.

The first issue to consider is the transferability of findings from sociology to computer-mediated communication (CMC)-based studies. The meaning and nature of the relationships in traditional studies is different from the ones typical in CMC-based studies. This calls for specific research on how standard SNA indices should be adapted to the specific characteristics of TEL and how these indices may be validated in a perspective of sociology of learning using CMC, following the line opened by the work of Reyes and Tchounikine (2005) that proposes new models for measuring group cohesion and actors' status, adapted to the specificities of interaction through forum-like tools.

In most empirical settings, the log data used for the analysis may need complementary sources. While some research has focused on the integration of different sources of data as the input of the analysis (Martínez-Monés et al., 2003), other approaches such as exploring multiplexity of networks can provide new insights into this problem.

As mentioned previously, SNA is potentially well suited to serve teachers to monitor the evolution of collaboration in their classes. However, interpretation is hard for novices (and especially for teachers, monitoring their group on the fly). There is still room for the development of simplified representations that would enhance the strongest evidences of a given sociogram especially for teachers and students (vs. researchers) in the context of a live setting monitoring (vs. a post-hoc analysis). The link between automatic smart display of social networks and their interpretation by novices also needs deeper studies.

In conclusion, after more than ten years of research using SNA in TEL and CSCL we can state that the field has great potential for future research. The complexity of learning, the development pace of new communication and collaborative tools, make learning settings a challenging ground in which to use, adapt and develop SNA techniques.

NOTE

1. List of SNA software provided by INSNA: http://www.insna.org/software/index.html.

REFERENCES

Aviv, R., Erlich, Z., & Ravid, G. (2003). Cohesion and roles: Network analysis of CSCL communities. In V. Devedzic, J. Spector, D. Sampson and Kinshuk (Eds.), *Advanced Learning Technologies: Technology Enhanced Learning* (pp. 145–149). Los Alamitos, CA: IEEE Computer Society.

Bonacich, P. (1987). Power and centrality: A family of measures. *The American Journal of Sociology*, 92(5), 1170–1182.

Bratitsis, T., & Dimitracopoulou, A. (2009). Studying the effect of interaction analysis indicators on students' selfregulation during asynchronous discussion learning activities. In C. O'Malley, D. Suthers, P. Reimann, & A. Dimitracopoulou (Eds.), *Computer Supported Collaborative Learning Practices—CSCL2009 Conference Proceedings* (pp. 601–605). ISLS.

Burt, R. (1992). *Structural Holes. The Social Structure of Competition.* Cambridge: Harvard University Press.

Cho, H., Stefanone, M., & Gay, G. (2002). Social information sharing in a CSCL community. In G. Stahl (Ed.), *Computer Support for Collaborative Learning: Foundations for a CSCL Community* (pp. 43–50). Hillsdale, NJ: Lawrence Erlbaum Associates.

Daradoumis, A., Martínez-Monés, A., & Xhafa, F. (2006). A layered framework for evaluating on-line collaborative learning interactions. *International Journal of Human-Computer Studies*, 64(7), 622–635.

Dillenbourg, P., Zufferey, G., Alavi, H., Jermann, P., Do-Lenh, S., Bonnard, et al. (2011). Classroom orchestration: The third circle of usability. In H. Spada, G. Stahl, N. Miyake, & N. Law (Eds.), *Proceedings of the Conference on Computer Supported Collaborative Learning, Vol I: Long papers* (pp. 510–517). ISLS.

Freeman, L. C. (1979). Centrality in social networks conceptual clarification. *Social Networks*, 1(3), 215–239.
Granovetter, M. S. (1973). The strength of weak ties. *American Journal of Sociology*, 78, 1360–1380.
Harrer, A., Malzahn, N., Zeini, S., & Hoppe, U. (2007). Combining social network analysis with semantic relations to support the evolution of a scientific community. In C. Chinn, G. Erkens, & S. Puntambekar (Eds.), *Proceedings of the 7th Computer Supported Collaborative Learning Conference* (pp. 267–276). ISLS.
Harrer, A., Martínez-Monés, A., & Dimitracopoulou, A. (2009). Users' data. Collaborative and Social Analysis. In N. Balacheff, S. Ludvigsen, T. Jong, A. Lazonder, & S. Barnes (Eds.), *Technology-Enhanced Learning* (pp. 175–193). Netherlands: Springer.
Harrer, A., Zeini, S., & Ziebarth, S. (2010). Visualisation of the dynamics for longitudinal analysis of computer-mediated social networks-concept and exemplary cases. *From Sociology to Computing in Social Networks*, 1, 119–134.
Lave, J., & Wenger, E. (1991). *Situated Learning. Legitimate Peripheral Participation.* Cambridge: University of Cambridge Press.
Li, Y., Liao, J., Wang, J., & Huang, R. (2007). CSCL interaction analysis for assessing knowledge building outcomes: Method and tool. In C. Chinn, G. Erkens, & S. Puntambekar (Eds.), *Proceedings of the 7th Computer Supported Collaborative Learning Conference* (pp. 428–437). ISLS.
Martínez-Monés, A., Dimitriadis, Y., Gómez-Sánchez, E., Rubia, B., & de la Fuente, P. (2003). Combining qualitative and social network analysis for the study of classroom social interactions. *Computers and Education*, 41(4), 353–368.
Moreno, J. L. (1934). *Who Shall Survive? Foundations of Sociometry, Group Psychotherapy and Sociodrama.* Beacon, NY: Beacon House.
Nurmela, K., Lehtinen, E., & Palonen, T. (1999). Evaluating CSCL log files by Social Network Analysis. In C. Hoadley, M. Christopher, & J. Roschelle (Eds.), *Computer Supported Collaborative Learning Conference (CSCL '99)* (pp. 434–444). ISLS.
Prieto, L., Villagra-Sobrino, S., Dimitriadis, Y., Schank, P., Penuel, W., & Haydel DeBarger, A. (2011). Mind the gaps: Using patterns to change everyday classroom practice towards contingent CSCL teaching. In H. Spada, G. Stahl, N. Miyake, & N. Law (Eds.), *Proceedings of the Conference on Computer Supported Collaborative Learning, Vol I: Long papers* (pp. 518–525). ISLS.
Reffay, C., & Chanier, T. (2003). How social network analysis can help to measure cohesion in collaborative distance-learning. In B. Wasson, S. Ludvigsen, & U. Hoppe (Eds.), *Designing for Change in Networked Learning Environments: Proceedings of the International Conference on Computer Support for Collaborative Learning 2003* (pp. 343–352). Dordrecht, Netherlands: Kluwer Academic Publishers.
Reyes, P., & Tchounikine, P. (2005). Mining learning groups' activities in forum-type tools. In T. Koschmann, D. Suthers, & T.-W. Chan (Eds.), *CSCL 2005. The Next 10 years! Proceedings of the International Conference on Computer Supported Collaborative Learning (CSCL 2005)* (pp. 509–513). ISLS.
Scott, J. (2000). *Social Network Analysis: A Handbook*, (2nd ed.). London: Sage.
Sfard, A. (1998). On two metaphors for learning and the dangers of choosing just one. *Educational Researcher*, 27, 4–13.
Sha, L., Teplovs, C., & van Aalst, J. (2010). A visualization of group cognition: Semantic network analysis of a CSCL community. In K. Gomez, L. Lyons, & J. Radinsky (Eds.), *Learning in the Disciplines: Proceedings of the 9th International Conference of the Learning Sciences (ICLS 2010)—Volume 1, Full Papers* (pp. 929–936). ISLS.
Suthers, D., Lund, K., Rosé, C., Dyke, G., Law, N., & Teplovs, C. (2011). Towards productive multivocality in the analysis of collaborative learning. In H. Spada, G. Stahl, N. Miyake, & N. Law (Eds.), *Proceedings of the Conference on Computer Supported Collaborative Learning, Vol III* (pp. 1015–1022). ISLS.
Wassermann S., & Faust, K. (1994). *Social Network Analysis: Methods and Applications.* New York: Cambridge University Press.
Wortham, D. (1999). Nodal and matrix analyses of communication patterns in small groups. In C. Hoadley, M. Christopher, & J. Roschelle (Eds.), *Computer Supported Collaborative Learning Conference (CSCL '99)* (pp. 681–686). ISLS.

40

SEEING TO UNDERSTAND

Using Visualizations to Understand Learning in Technology-Rich Learning Environments

Cindy E. Hmelo-Silver, Rebecca Jordan, and Suparna Sinha

Sociocultural and social constructivist theories of learning argue that learning is inherently social and is often situated in complex technologically mediated learning environments (Cole, 1999; Palincsar, 1998; Pea, 1993). In such environments, learning is fostered through technology related tools but also through the joint discussion of conceptions and meaning-making. Because learning results from this participation, understanding and designing technology to support the development of ideas requires analyzing data simultaneously across various sources through time. More specifically, studying learning in these environments requires understanding of how learning unfolds in context, how knowledge and strategies are constructed, and how the learning process is mediated by technological tools and resulting artifacts.

As we noted earlier, trying to understand complex learning often requires that we integrate information across different sources of data and use multidimensional coding schemes (Dyke, 2009; Dyke, Lund, & Girardot, 2009; Hmelo-Silver, Chernobilsky, & Jordan, 2008; Hmelo-Silver, Liu, & Jordan, 2009; Suthers, Dwyer, Medina, & Vatrapu, 2009). We propose that one way of integrating across these different sources of data and coding schemes is through the use of visualizations. Visualizations take advantage of peoples' innate perceptual capabilities (Dyke, 2009). Visualizations also allow one to view and search a large amount of information in a single glance (Larkin & Simon, 1987). They can support perceptual inference and pattern recognition (Dyke, 2009). When computer tools are used to create these visualizations, they can be used to manipulate the representations created, allowing an analyst to examine different parts of interactions, zooming in and zooming out as needed (Dyke et al., 2012; Hmelo-Silver, Liu, & Jordan, 2009). A key concern in our analyses is to understand how processes unfold chronologically (Reimann, 2007).

Our goal in this chapter is to show how visualization can enhance analysis of collaborative learning in technology-rich learning environments. We first demonstrate this as we look at collaborative engagement with different tools over time. We then demonstrate how we have used Chronologically-oriented Representations of Discourse and

Tool-related Activity (adapted from the CORDFU methodology developed by Luckin (2003) to understand technology mediated learning.

OTHER APPROACHES

To contextualize our approach to using visualization, we first describe other approaches to visualization of technology-rich learning environments. For example, directed graphs have been used to map the semantic space of instructional discourse as students coordinated conceptual and procedural knowledge (Strom, Kemeny, Lehrer, & Forman, 2001). Elsewhere, Martinez, Dimitriadis, Rubis, Gomez, and de la Fuente (2003) analyzed data using quantitative measures, social network analysis, and qualitative data. Even though the sociogram allowed visualization of interaction patterns, it was not easily integrated with other sources of data.

Another approach involves constructing diagrams to show how ideas are taken up in a collaborative learning group and coordinated across media (Suthers et al., 2009). In addition to this uptake analysis, inquiry threads can enable an understanding how ideas emerge over time (Zhang, Scardamalia, Lamon, Messina, & Reeve, 2007). This approach shows how the content of threads in an online database is engaged over time. Stahl (in press) has used vertical representations to show how asynchronous chats unfold over time, using a combination of arrows and colors to show different aspects of the interaction and how ideas are taken up by different speakers. None of these approaches necessarily integrates across multiple forms of data but they serve to support understanding how learning occurs over time.

One approach that seems particularly promising is Tatiana, because it is specifically designed to support computer-supported collaborative learning (CSCL) analysis and integrate across different data sources (Dyke et al., 2009). Tatiana is representative of a need for researchers to use analysis methods that allow for synchronizing, visualizing, and analyzing their data. One method, in particular, involves the creation of CORDTRA diagrams.

CORDTRA REPRESENTATIONS

CORDTRA diagrams contain a timeline where multiple processes are plotted on this timeline in parallel. This allows a researcher to juxtapose a variety of codes to understand an activity system through a sociocultural lens—for example, these might be discourse, gestural, or tool-related codes as shown in Figure 40.1. At first, we used this technique to examine face-to-face collaboration in a problem-based learning (PBL) tutorial to understand how learning was mediated through constructing a flow chart to help medical students to understand a patient's problem (Hmelo-Silver, 2003). In this work, a multidimensional coding scheme was used to code discourse at a fine grain of analysis to capture different features of the discourse. These discourse features were initially used to compile frequency counts and, later, used as part of the CORDTRA diagram, along with information on drawing activity and gestures, to get a sense of how the PBL tutorial unfolded and what role an external representation played in mediating this collaborative learning.

CORDTRA diagrams contain a single timeline that allows researchers to put a variety of codes side by side to help understand and, ultimately, design complex learning

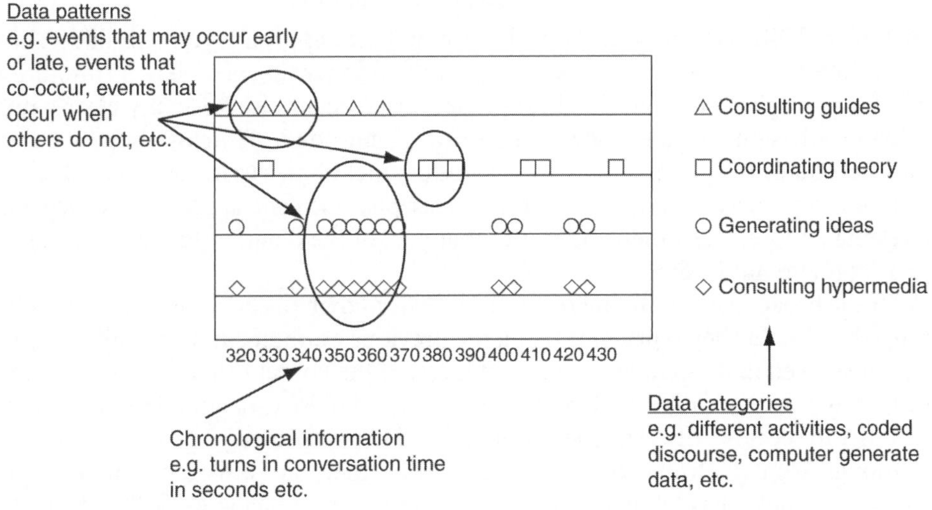

Figure 40.1 Explanation of CORDTRA.

environments—for example, these might be discourse, gestural, or tool-related codes. The specifics of the codes or computer logs chosen will depend on the research questions being asked. The CORDTRA diagrams are created as scatterplots in an off-the-shelf spreadsheet program. This technique was also used to examine an online CSCL environment for preservice teachers as it juxtaposed log data and discourse codes (Hmelo-Silver et al., 2008; Hmelo-Silver, Nagarajan, & Chernobilsky, 2009). These CORDTRA diagrams were helpful in understanding the differences in strategies used by more- and less-effective groups (Hmelo-Silver et al., 2008). They demonstrated how students' strategies changed over time as they became more familiar with both the tools and the PBL activity structure.

The CORDTRA technique is appropriate when there are either multiple data streams or multiple dimensions of an analysis that unfold over time. This is often the case when trying to understand learning in natural group contexts. We have used this technique for both children and adult learners, for learning that is entirely online and learning that is face to face (and in this setting with and without technology). It is a broadly applicable technique. The initial foray into using CORDTRA involved exporting the codes from qualitative data analysis software, which serendipitously had a limit of 26 codes that could be exported into Excel (Hmelo-Silver, 2003). This analysis of a PBL tutorial focused on an episode in which medical students were drawing an informal concept map as they were constructing explanations of a patient's problem. This was a face-to-face tutorial group and the CORDTRA diagram included discourse codes, gestures, and drawing activity. This meant that researchers needed to carefully consider the codes displayed in relation to research questions. In a subsequent attempt at using CORDTRA, we coded directly in Excel resulting in 80+ coding categories. We found the diagram generated from these codes to be nearly uninterpretable (Hmelo-Silver et al., 2008). Codes used in this analysis included computer log data, discourse content, and computer logs. Based on our experience with this diagram, we advise using far fewer coding categories.

Reading CORDTRA Diagrams

To "read" a CORDTRA diagram, we advise a multistep approach (Hmelo-Silver, Liu, & Jordan, 2009). First, we find it best to step back and take a broad view. Without looking at the graph legend, hold the diagram at a distance and look for any clear patterns or obvious divisions. In the analysis of a drawing episode in Hmelo-Silver (2003), this broad view made it clear that there were three distinct phases to the activity, which provided hints for where to look back at the transcripts. The central phase was particularly interesting and we could then zoom into that part of the diagram to see what was happening at that point in time.

After the broad inspection, the researcher needs to then orient to how the symbols are arranged and what they represent. Using the previous example, in the middle phase, the diagram showed that as students changed levels of the content that they were drawing, they were generating causal explanations near each of these time junctions, allowing the researcher to see how different codes were related to each other.

Although we have found this approach useful, there are also some disadvantages. Most importantly, it is labor intensive to create these manually as well as to recreate them at the different time scales. Second, it is important to be careful to try not to cram too much information into any one visualization or the patterns may become obscured. Tools such as Tatiana might eventually be helpful in dealing with these disadvantages.

In the remainder of this chapter we show two examples of how we have used CORDTRA to understand different aspects of learning in a technology-rich learning environment. In the first example, we study how content and strategies can be examined simultaneously in discourse. In the second example, we use visualization to study collaborative engagement using multiple dimensions.

CASE 1: CORDTRA FOR STUDYING CONTENT AND STRATEGY USE

This case is drawn from students working together around a computer simulation in the context of the RepTools software suite (Hmelo-Silver, Liu, & Jordan, 2009). This example focuses on looking at the relationship between different kinds of discourse moves and the content that the students discuss as they work with a computer tool. The RepTools suite includes computer-based representational tools for inquiry into complex biological systems. The design of our instructional intervention was informed by structure-behavior-function (SBF) theory, which originated in artificial intelligence research (Goel et al., 1996). Structures refer to components of a system, in this case an aquarium (e.g., fish, plants, filter, water). Behaviors refer to how the structures of a system achieve their output. These are the interactions or mechanisms that yield a product, reaction, or outcome (e.g., bacteria remove waste by converting ammonia into harmless chemicals). Finally, functions refer to the role or output of an element of the system (e.g., lights provide energy). SBF theory suggests that by considering structures, behaviors, and functions, one can reason effectively about complex systems and, indeed, in the domain of instruction, experts reason in ways consistent with SBF theory (Hmelo-Silver, Marathe, & Liu, 2007). The RepTools toolkit includes a function-oriented hypermedia and two NetLogo computer simulation models (Wilensky & Reisman, 2006). We used two NetLogo simulations—the fish spawn model and the nitrification process model—to provide models of aquaria at different scales. The fish spawn model at a macrolevel, simulated population density because of fish spawning within an aquarium. The purpose of the model was to help children learn about relationships among different factors in an aquarium ecosystem, such as the initial gender ratio, amount of food, filtration, water quality, and reproduction. The nitrification simulation presented a microlevel model of how chemicals reach a balance in an aquarium. In both simulations, students could adjust the values of variables such as fish, plants, and food and observe the results of the adjustment. Counters and graphs provided alternative representations for students to examine the results of their investigation. Students could observe the simulations, generate hypotheses, test them by running the simulation, and modify their ideas based on the results.

The data for this case study were drawn from a larger study by Liu (2008). The participants in the larger study were 145 middle school students who participated in a unit that was two and a half weeks long. Students showed significant gains in understanding (Liu, Hmelo-Silver, & Marathe, 2007). Three sets of codes were applied to investigate students' collaborative learning through different lenses: collaborative discourse, epistemic practices, and the content related to the student's learning goals (i.e., regarding the content: the structures, behaviors, and functions (SBF) in the system; Hmelo-Silver, Liu, & Jordan, 2009). To show the affordances of the CORDTRA diagrams, we contrast them here with a histogram of frequencies in a comparative case analysis. As determined by pre-post test gains, Group 8 was a high-achieving group and group 14 was a lower achieving group. Figure 40.2 shows the frequency distributions for the three dimensions of the coding scheme for the two groups.

From these frequency snapshots, we can see that the more successful group is engaged in asking explanations questions and warranting claims with greater frequency than the lower achieving group. But the lower achieving group is spending considerable time designing experiments and discussing behaviors. These latter epistemic and content-related codes suggest that there is some sophisticated reasoning going on. We get an alternative perspective from studying the CORDTRA diagrams and using those as an index into some hotspots in the transcripts that are worthy of further examination.

With respect to SBF content, we also noted differences between groups. When inspecting the SBF frequencies, shown in Figure 40.2, the high-achieving group appears to talk more about function than the low-achieving group, which was more likely to talk about structure and behavior. Although the students in both groups were talking about behavior and function as they explored the simulations, which are associated with deep understanding and not often seen in learners of this age (Hmelo-Silver et al., 2007), the low-achieving group talked more about behaviors than the high-achieving group, a result that we found puzzling. By looking at isolated frequencies in terms of behaviors and functions it was difficult to understand how the collaborative processes, epistemic practices, and discussion of content were related both within a particular coding scheme and across coding schemes.

CORDTRA Analyses

Overview

To understand how students' discourse unfolded, we delve more deeply into the CORDTRA diagrams in Figures 40.3 and 40.4. In particular, these diagrams focus on one of the more difficult pieces of the task—student discourse as they tried to make sense of the nitrification process while working with the microlevel NetLogo simulation. The horizontal axis in the CORDTRA diagram represents turn number, which is a rough

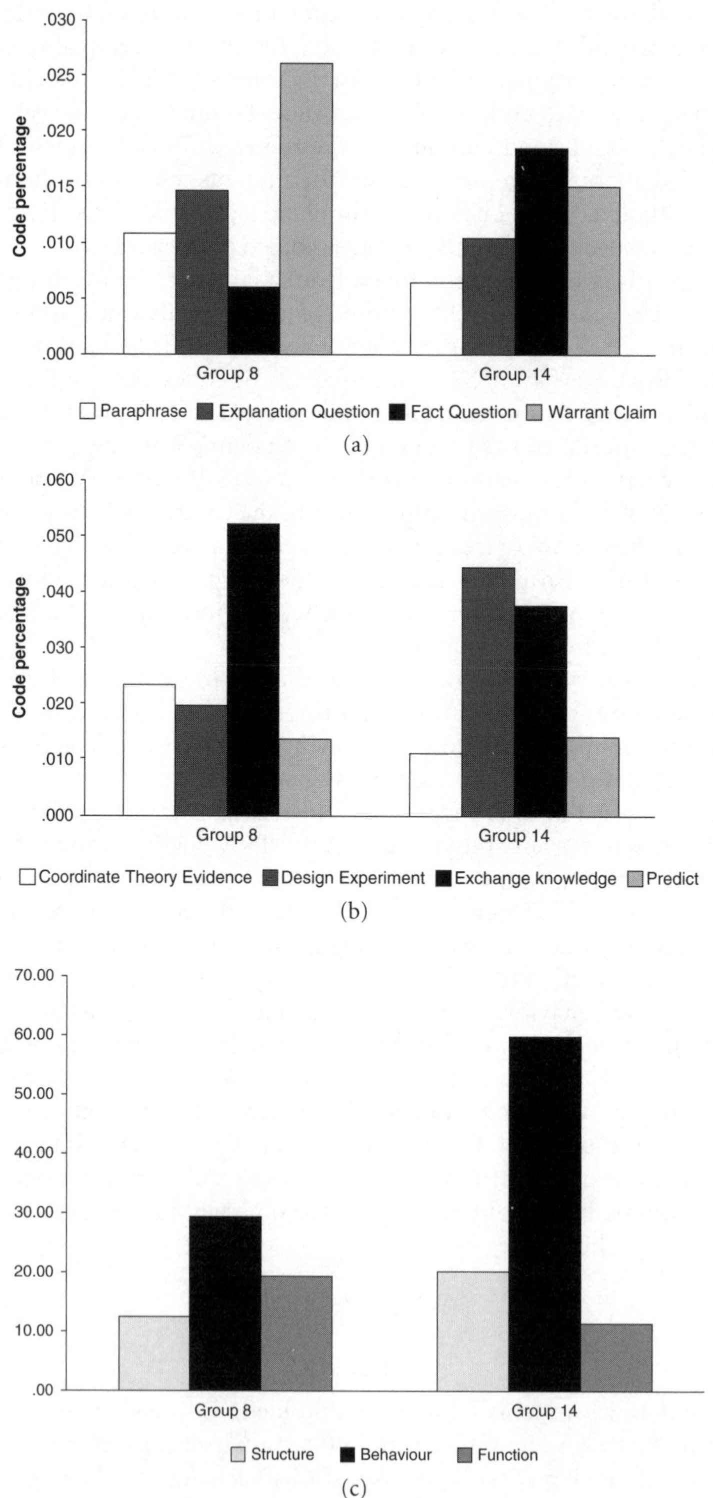

Figure 40.2 Percentage frequencies of (a) collaboration; (b) epistemic practices; and (c) SBF.

approximation of time. The vertical axis represents the different coding categories indicated by the legend on the right.

We started our analysis using the CORDTRA diagrams with a broad overview of the full diagrams held at a distance. This big picture view began by just looking at the overall patterns without attending to the legend for any specifics. The first obvious difference was in the overall amount of talk, with the high-achieving group (Figure 40.3) having more conversational turns than the low-achieving group (Figure 40.4). A glance at the high-achieving group suggested that they had 3–4 distinct phases of activity: an initial portion dominated by sharing knowledge and warranting claims, a middle portion that involved a great deal of observation, and then (starting around turn 400) open ended questioning and knowledge exchange, and ended with continued work with the simulation and focus on function. The low-achieving group looked quite different, and their phases were almost the opposite of the high-achieving groups. These students jumped right into exploring the simulation and describing their observations, then in a second phase, near turn 50, engaged in knowledge exchange and theory generation, and then by around turn 225, a third phase began that focused on working with the simulation and talking about behaviors.

Our initial inspection suggested some places to go back to the transcript for analysis. In addition, this big picture made clear how some codes from the collaboration and epistemic practices categories were overlapping. It is not surprising that the "observe" and "describe observations" categories are almost completely overlapping. There was also some overlap between "warranting claims" and "coordinating theory and evidence," though this was more apparent in the high-achieving group.

The process described here shows how CORDTRA diagrams provide information at a glance that is helpful at guiding further analysis. Next, we describe how further analysis was conducted and how we drew conclusions based on these diagrams.

High-Achieving Group

Inspection of the CORDTRA diagram for group 8 (the high-achieving group shown in Figure 40.3) showed that there was both an ongoing discussion of structures, behaviors, and functions and "describing observations." At about turn 270, there was increased engagement in epistemic practices of "designing experiments," "coordinating theory and evidence," and "checking knowledge validity." This change in the coded discourse suggested that we needed to go back to the transcript.

We did not expect the students to move between SBF levels so early in the discussion. In the early part of the discussion, the students talked in terms of observations about colored dots (which represent different chemicals in the simulation) and patches (which represent two types of bacteria) during the first half of the discussion; in the second half, the students talked more about what those patches represent. Further, Figure 40.2b demonstrates that the group conversation shifted across SBF levels and initially shifted largely between structures and behaviors, as they were trying to understand what was happening in the simulation. Inspection of Figure 40.3 also shows that associated with this shift, the students often engaged in "exchanging knowledge," "warranting claims," and in the middle part of the discourse, with "designing experiments." This observation suggested the need to zoom into that initial part of the discourse both by looking at a section of the CORDTRA diagram and the actual transcript. The following example shows the group trying to figure out the relations between the movement of the dots and the patches based on observations of the simulation:

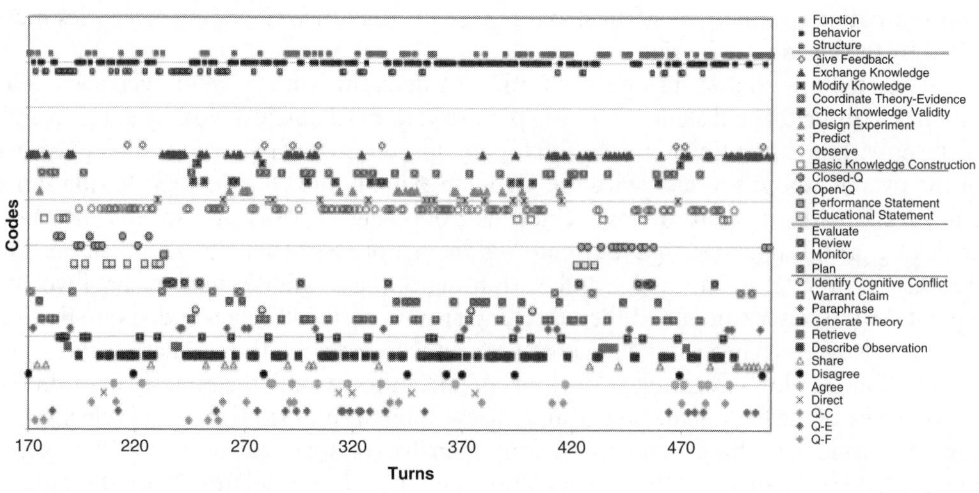

Figure 40.3 CORDTRA for high achieving group.

203 Ada — So the white goes to the blue, but it doesn't matter. And the blue goes to the purple, and the red goes to anything . . .
207 Ada — The white one is going in the blue and nothing happens.
208 Siddarth — The red one . . .
209 Siddarth — So the white one goes into blue and nothing happens, right?
217 Ada — And then the yellow one, just . . .
219 Siddarth — The . . . red one goes into the purple and becomes white.
220 Siddarth — And then the white one goes into the blue one, and then becomes yellow.

In this segment, Ada and Siddarth were exchanging information about their observations as they discussed the structures and functions in the simulation. First Ada observed that red dots went into the blue patches and became white dots (turns 203 and 207, coded as behavior and observation). Then Siddarth noticed that white dots became yellow once they got into patches (turns 219 and 220). The discussion of the structures and behaviors of the dots and patches later became the supporting evidence for their meaning-making of the representations of the bacteria in the model (i.e., the blue and the purple patches). An enlarged CORDTRA section allowed the analyst to see what the major processes and content were in this early excerpt. We report further detailed analyses in Hmelo-Silver, Liu, and Jordan (2009) as they engaged in further construction of a coherent explanation as they attempted to integrate nitrification and photosynthesis processes in a coherent explanation. We reached these conclusions through our interpretation of the CORDTRA diagrams and the pieces of transcript that the diagram suggested would be fruitful for further analysis.

Low-Achieving Group

The CORDTRA diagram for the low-achieving group is shown in Figure 40.4. In contrast to the high-achieving group, we observed that this group began their discussion at the structural and behavioral level. They engaged in some discussion of function in the middle, but then ended with continued discussion of experimental designs, which were not driven by explicit goals and were not associated with shifting between SBF levels. This resulted in a discussion of behaviors that created a description rather than an explanation. Although there was an increase in explanation questions over time, these students were still asked many fact-oriented questions about what they directly observed. Similar to the high-achieving group, the times when this group shifted between SBF levels was associated with knowledge exchange. Again, we include an excerpt from near the end of the group's work with the nitrification simulation.

256 Jean Look how high it is going because there is . . .
257 Judy But either way it went high
258 Jean Yea it speeds up even more with less amount of plants, but why? The whole cycle speeds up
259 Judy Because it didn't have anything to stop them . . .
260 Jean Yea you can have a group of plants it'd stop the fertilization, you'd like block them
261 Judy Exactly. Look the ammonia . . .
262 Judy Quicker
263 Robby Yea the ammonia went high really quick
264 Judy What wait look the plants eat . . . no the plants eat the nitrite but how come the nitrite isn't going up if the plants still eat it?
265 Jean Yea, I thought the nitrite would go up
266 Judy Nitrite is down . . . it hardy went down
267 Jean Yeah, it's practically the same, which makes no sense
268 Robby All the acids are going up rapidly
269 Judy Our predictions were wrong for decrease.

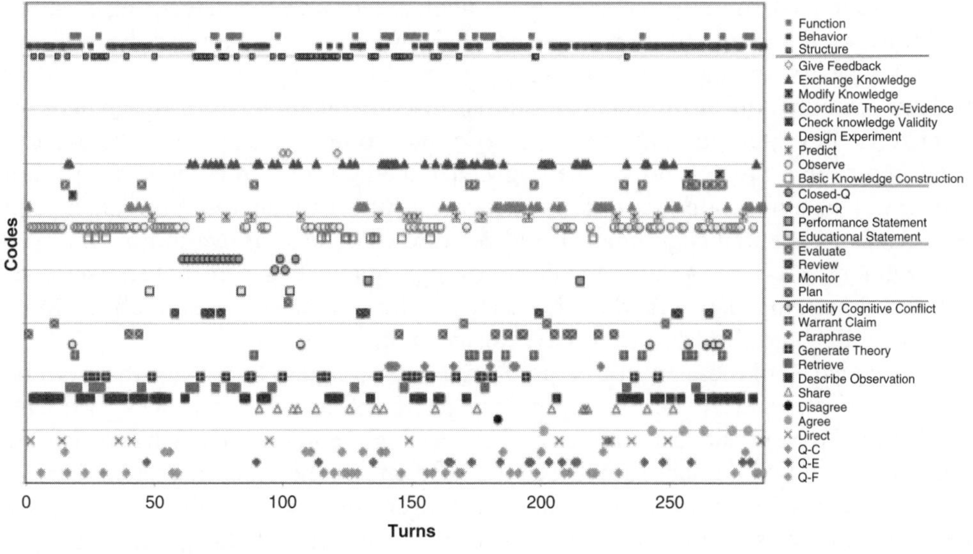

Figure 40.4 CORDTRA for low-achieving group.

In line 256 Jean began by describing the observed behavior in the simulation. They noticed associations between different behaviors of water quality indicators in the next several lines as they tried to coordinate theory and evidence and make predictions. The functional question asked in line 264 had the potential to lead to construction of an explanation but the functional topic got lost in the group discussion as the groups went on to other predictions and describing behaviors through to the end of their discussion of this simulation. Although the discourse included many instances of warranting claims and identifying cognitive conflicts, a large portion of the discourse stayed at the behavioral level. The group focused on manipulating the simulations and observing relationships but not getting to the functional aspects that would let them construct an explanation. This CORDTRA analysis, as opposed to the inspection of the histograms, enabled us to generate an explanation for why the low-achieving group had more discussion on behaviors but failed to reach a productive conversation.

Without comparing the different aspects of the discourse, including the SBF content, the discourse, and the epistemic practice features, it is unlikely that we would see the whole picture regarding the quality of the collaboration and how that was mediated by the technology. The CORDTRA diagram helped us see relations between SBF topics and the discourse and epistemic features. This method affords a comprehensive understanding of students' discourse by looking into the interrelated aspects of students' engagement in collaboration, epistemic practices, and talking about different levels of science content (e.g., SBF).

CASE 2: STUDYING COLLABORATIVE ENGAGEMENT

In a brief second example, we again used a multidimensional coding scheme, this time as a window into how learners collaboratively engaged with different technologies (Sinha, Adams, Rogat, & Hmelo-Silver, 2012; Sinha, Adams, Rogat, & Hmelo-Silver, 2012). We coded video data of students working with simulations and the Environmental Modeling Toolkit (EMT; Vattam et al., 2011). We defined high-quality task engagement (TE) as attempts to plan, monitor the plan's enactment, and move beyond focusing on superficial features. Planning was more than superficial when it moved toward the task solution and problem solving. Behavioral engagement (BE) referred to the extent to which students remained off or on task. Conceptual-to-consequential (CC) engagement was characterized by attempts at connections to domain content and practices that were on a continuum that range from simple knowledge telling (low), to content connections (moderate), to connections to prior knowledge, everyday experiences or the larger problem (i.e., consequential engagement). Videos were segmented at five-minute intervals. Each segment was coded as low-, medium-, or high-quality engagement (on a scale of 0 to 3, with 0 marking instances when the teacher addressed the entire class, 1 being low, 2 medium and 3 high) for BE, TE, and CC engagement.

As we coded all of these on a three-point scale, we wanted to know how these dimensions co-varied (i.e., were they measuring qualitatively different aspects of engagement), whether they were sensitive to differences between high- and low-achieving groups, and whether they showed variability between the different technologies that we were enacting. Moreover, we were curious as to how that engagement was sustained (or not) over the course of a class period. Overall means mask the fact that this group was highly engaged at a CC level at times during the simulation and occasionally during EMT use, as shown in Figures 40.5 and 40.6.

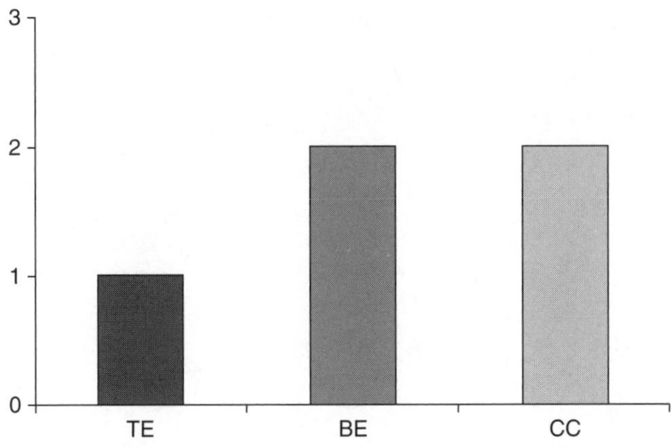

Figure 40.5 Group 1's engagement with simulation.

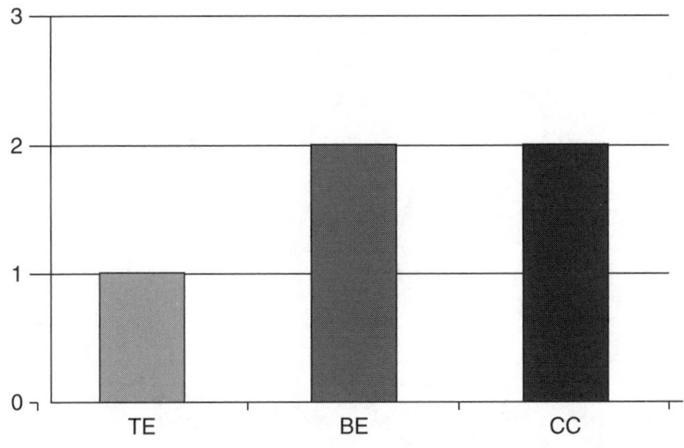

Figure 40.6 Group 1's engagement with EMT.

Graphing engagement patterns was beneficial at multiple levels of data analysis. At a quick glance the visual representations allowed us to identify types of engagement that were evoked as a result of interaction with the tools. For instance, engagement with EMT was predominantly behavioral in nature. Similarly the simulations prompted moderate conceptual engagement and low TE. A deeper analysis of the graphs allowed us to zero in on specific segments of class time when collaboration resulted in high levels of engagement (see Figures 40.7 and 40.8).

Analysis of the group's engagement patterns while working with the simulation indicated an overall high level of CC engagement. We observed several instances where the group made connections to uncovering the problem of fish dying. However we were equally interested in looking at the group's engagement with the task. Based on our coding we observed numerous instances in the class period when the group manipulated variables within the simulation to test their hypotheses. We noted that most often such activities were preceded by a group discussion where the group proposed hypotheses

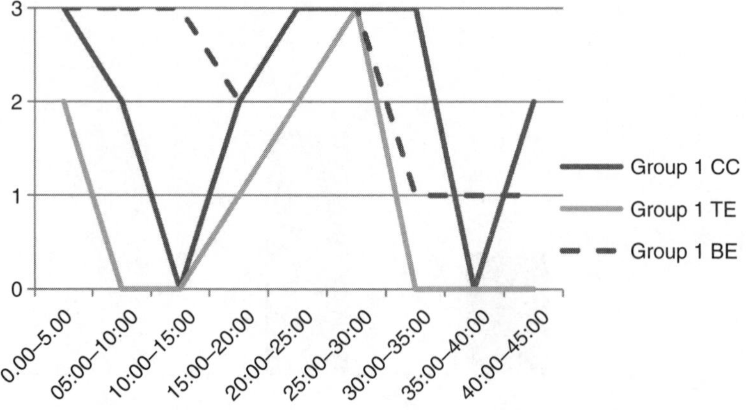

Figure 40.7 Group 1's engagement with simulation over a class period.

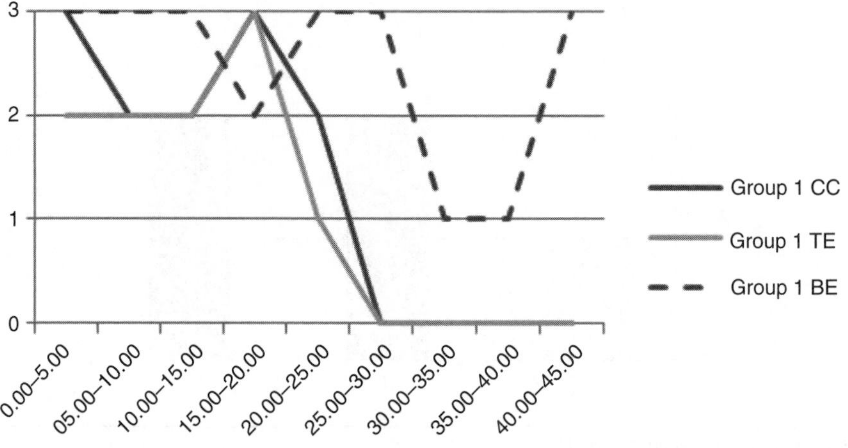

Figure 40.8 Group 1's engagement with EMT over a class period.

that would help uncover the cause of sudden death of fish. For instance, they kept one variable constant while modifying the others to determine its relevance to the problem. This indicated to us that the group's TE was important for them to clarify conceptual connections between variables present in the simulation. Importantly it advanced their CC engagement by moving them closer to understanding the science behind the problem. The graph also indicated the tool had the students behaviorally engaged throughout the class period. We argue that this might be so because the tool affords dynamic feedback. That is, as the students can instantly observe the output of their hypotheses they are not given the opportunity to engage in off-topic discussions.

The students used EMT software to create models of their evolving understanding of the problem. We observed that collaboration at the beginning of the activity led the students to consider adding key components such as sunlight and algae to their model. However, as the discussion did not result in connections to the larger problem, we saw that this had a bearing on their TE as well. The groups appeared to focus on superficial aspects of the model such as spelling of components and its final shape. As a result we felt that the group predominantly displayed moderate TE initially. We observed a similar pattern towards the middle of class when CC engagement once again appeared to influence TE. This was important as it indicated that collaboration led them to share their thinking. As a result students discussed the relative importance of numerous components prior to adding or deleting them from their model. Interestingly we observed the groups' BE decrease from high to moderate while working on model creation. We attribute it to the fact that once the group had discussed the components to be added or deleted within their model, the student in front of the laptop was engaged in carrying out the edits. Other group members would engage in off-topic discussions during such intervals.

This visualization led us to conclude that even though both tools offer opportunities for engagement, there are differences in the time course and intensity. We can also see how the chronology of different kinds of engagement is related to the tools. For example, in the simulation, TE and CC engagement follow similar time courses but it is clear from looking at both figures, that students may demonstrate BE in the absence of CC engagement. The histograms showed only the totals (and indeed in the simulation show the same frequency for BE and CC). Further work is needed to examine these relationships but this analysis suggests that the way that tools support engaged participation varies and that they offer different affordances for mediating learning (Hickey & Zuicker, 2005). We suspect we would gain further insights if this were analyzed along with log data so that we might look closely at the relation between engagement and use of the technological tools.

CONCLUSIONS

To paraphrase what Larkin & Simon (1987) noted so many years ago, a diagram can be worth more than 10,000 words. Technology-rich learning environments are part of a complex learning ecology when used in formal and informal settings, making them challenging to study. Visualizations can support analysis of complex learning environments by making relationships among different variables salient as in the two examples presented here. Moreover, visualizations support seeing the temporal relationships in technology-rich learning environments. It allows analysis that is consistent with a sociocultural view of the learning that considers the social and material dimensions of learning as important mediators.

The downside of these tools is that the visualizations are often challenging to create manually, and analysts need to be oriented to the complexity of the diagrammatic representations that may be used. General purpose tools such as Tatiana (Dyke et al., 2009) offer promise in this regard.

Visualizations can be a particularly valuable addition to mixed methods research (Puntambekar, in press; Puntambekar, Stylianou, & Goldstein, 2007). They can be useful for understanding individual learning in technology-rich learning environments as well as the increasing complexity of small-group and whole-class interactions with technology. Even more importantly, they can help track the sequential relations between tools, discourse, and other indicators of engagement to help researchers see between the lines.

ACKNOWLEDGMENTS

We gratefully acknowledge the support of the National Science Foundation and Institute for Education Sciences for their support. Opinions, findings, and conclusions or recommendations expressed in this material are those of the authors and do not necessarily reflect the views of IES. We thank Gregory Dyke for sharing his dissertation with us and providing additional insight on the role of visualizations in analyzing collaborative learning.

REFERENCES

Cole, M. (1999). Cultural psychology: Some general principles and a concrete example. In Y. Engström, R. Miettinen, & R. Punamaki (Eds.), *Perspectives on Activity Theory* (pp. 19–38). New York: Cambridge University Press.

Dyke, G. (2009). *A model for managing and capitalising on the analyses of traces of activity in collaborative interaction.* Doctoral Dissertation, École des Mines de Saint-Etienne, Lyon, France.

Dyke, G., Kumar, R., Ai, H., Rosé, C. P. (2012). Challenging assumptions: using sliding window visualizations to reveal time-based irregularities in CSCL processes. *The Future of Learning: Proceedings of the 10th International Conference of the Learning Sciences (ICLS 2012) Volume 1* (pp. 363–370). Sydney, Australia: ISLS.

Dyke, G., Lund, K., & Girardot, J. (2009). Tatiana: An environment to support the CSCL analysis process. In C. O'Malley, D. Suthers, P. Reimann, & A. Dimitracopoulou (Eds.), *Computer Supported Collaborative Learning Practices: CSCL2009* (pp. 58–67). Rhodes, Greece: International Society for the Learning Sciences.

Goel, A. K., Gomez de Silva Garza, A., Grué, N., Murdock, J. W., Recker, M. M., & Govinderaj, T. (1996). Towards designing learning environments I: Exploring how devices work. In C. Fraisson, G. Gauthier, & A. Lesgold (Eds.), *Intelligent Tutoring Systems: Lecture notes in computer science* (pp. 493–501). New York: Springer.

Hickey, D. T., & Zuicker, S. J. (2005). Engaged participation: A sociocultural model of motivation with implications for educational assessment. *Educational Assessment, 10*, 277–305.

Hmelo-Silver, C. E. (2003). Analyzing collaborative knowledge construction: Multiple methods for integrated understanding. *Computers and Education, 41*, 397–420.

Hmelo-Silver, C. E., Chernobilsky, E., & Jordan, R. (2008). Understanding collaborative learning processes in new learning environments. *Instructional Science, 36*, 409–430.

Hmelo-Silver, C. E., Liu, L., & Jordan, R. (2009). Visual representation of a multidimensional coding scheme for understanding technology-mediated learning about complex natural systems. *Research and Practice in Technology Enhanced Learning Environments, 4*, 253–280.

Hmelo-Silver, C. E., Marathe, S., & Liu, L. (2007). Fish swim, rocks sit, and lungs breathe: Expert-novice understanding of complex systems. *Journal of the Learning Sciences, 16*, 307–331.

Hmelo-Silver, C. E., Nagarajan, A., & Chernobilsky, E. (2009). Two sides of the coin: Multiple perspectives on collaborative knowledge construction in online problem-based learning. In K. Kumpulainen, C. E. Hmelo-Silver, & M. César (Eds.), *Investigating Classroom Interaction: Methodologies in action* (pp. 73–98). Rotterdam: Sense Publishers.

Larkin, J. H., & Simon, H. A. (1987). Why a diagram is (sometimes) worth ten thousand words. *Cognitive Science, 11*, 65–99.

Liu, L. (2008). *Trajectories of collaborative scientific conceptual change: Middle school students learning about ecosystems in a CSCL environment.* (PhD Dissertation), New Brunswick.

Liu, L., Hmelo-Silver, C. E., & Marathe, S. (2007). *Reptools: Representational tools to supporting learning about complex systems.* Paper presented at the NARST 2007 [CD ROM], New Orleans LA.

Luckin, R. (2003). Between the lines: Documenting the multiple dimensions of computer-supported collaborations. *Computers & Education, 41*, 379–396.

Martinez, A., Dimitriadis, Y., Rubia, B., Gomez, E., & de la Fuente, P. (2003). Combining qualitative evaluation and social network analysis for the study of classroom social interactions. *Computers and Education, 41*, 353–368.

Palincsar, A. S. (1998). Social constructivist perspectives on teaching and learning. *Annual Review of Psychology, 45*, 345–375.

Pea, R. D. (1993). Practices of distributed intelligence and designs for education. In G. Salomon & D. Perkins (Eds.), *Distributed Cognitions: Psychological and educational considerations* (pp. 47–87). New York: Cambridge University Press.

Puntambekar, S. (in press). Mixed methods for analyzing collaborative learning. In C. E. Hmelo-Silver, C. Chinn,

C. K. K. Chan, & A. M. O'Donnell (Eds.), *International Handbook of Collaborative Learning.* New York: Taylor & Francis.

Puntambekar, S., Stylianou, A., & Goldstein, J. (2007). Comparing classroom enactments of an inquiry curriculum: Lessons learned from two teachers. *Journal of the Learning Sciences, 16,* 81–130.

Reimann, P. (2007). Time is precious: Why process analysis is essential for CSCL (and can also help to bridge between experimental and descriptive methods). In C. A. Chinn, G. Erkens, & S. Puntambekar (Eds.), *Proceedings of CSCL 2007: Mice, minds, and society* (Vol. 8, pp. 605–614). New Brunswick, NJ: International Society of the Learning Sciences.

Sinha, S., Adams, K., Rogat, T., & Hmelo-Silver, C. (2012). *The Role of Technologies in Facilitating Collaborative Engagement.* Paper presented at the 2012 Subway Summit, New York.

Sinha, S., Adams, K., Rogat, T. K., & Hmelo-Silver, C. (2012). *The role of technologies in facilitating collaborative engagement. The Future of Learning: Proceedings of the 10th International Conference of the Learning Sciences (ICLS 2012) Volume 2* (pp. 489–490). Sydney, Australia: ISLS.

Stahl, G. (in press). Interaction analysis of a biology chat. In D. Suthers, C. P. Rosé, & K. Lund (Eds.), *Productive multivocality.* Cambridge, MA: MIT Press.

Strom, D., Kemeny, V., Lehrer, R., & Forman, E. (2001). Visualizing the emergent structure of children's mathematical argument. *Cognitive Science, 25,* 733–774.

Suthers, D. D., Dwyer, N., Medina, R., & Vatrapu, R. (2009). Exposing interactional processes in online learning. In K. Kumpulainen, C. E. Hmelo-Silver, & M. César (Eds.), *Investigating Classroom Interaction: Methodologies in action* (pp. 121–144). Rotterdam: Sense Publishers.

Vattam, S., Goel, A. K., Rugaber, S., Hmelo-Silver, C. E., Jordan, R., Gray, S., et al. (2011). Understanding complex natural systems by articulating structure-behavior-function models. *Educational Technology & Society, 14,* 66–81.

Wilensky, U., & Reisman, K. (2006). Thinking like a wolf, sheep, or firefly: Learning biology through constructing and testing computational theories—an embodied modeling approach. *Cognition and Instruction,* 171–210.

Zhang, J., Scardamalia, M., Lamon, M., Messina, R., & Reeve, R. (2007). Socio-cognitive dynamics of knowledge building in the work of 9 and 10 year olds. *Educational Technology Research and Development, 55,* 117–145.

41

USING PROCESS MINING FOR UNDERSTANDING LEARNING

Peter Reimann & Kalina Yacef

1. INTRODUCTION

Modern educational technology has made it easy to record how learners interact with an application (a hypertext, a problem-solving program, a computer simulation) and with each other. And since log files recorded on individual devices or on specific web applications can continuously be uploaded to web-based servers (e.g., data warehouses, see Koedinger et al., 2010), it becomes even easier to analyze data from many sites. It is not astonishing that the field of educational data mining is burgeoning (Yacef & Baker, 2009). With it comes an increasing awareness that since many of the data that become available from log files contain temporal information, new opportunities arise to study learning from a longitudinal, process-oriented perspective; both individual learning (Azevedo, Moos, Johnson, & Chauncey, 2010) as well as collaborative learning (Reimann, 2009).

In this chapter, we introduce a group of computational methods that go by the name of process mining (PM) (Trčka, Pechenizkiy, & van der Aalst 2010), sometimes also called workflow mining (van der Aalst, Weijters, & Maruster, 2004). Methods under these labels take information from event logs as input (i.e., time-stamped or fully ordered sequences) and produce process models that describe the information in the event logs in a comprehensive manner. These models can be subjected to conformance checks on new data, and/or be extended by analyzing new data. Models can also be formulated by the researcher in a non-inductive manner, and checked against observed sequences.

The situation that is typical for educational PM is this: In a learning environment, interactions with tools and/or collaboration processes are enacted, supported by a software system such as a chat tool or an argument editor or a more general Learning Management System such as Moodle. The system records the interactions and transactions to some extent in an event log. The event log is used for process model mining. PM can serve a number of purposes, such as:

- *Discovery*—No a-priori model exists. Based on an event log a model is constructed.
- *Conformance*—An a-priori model exists. Event logs are used to determine the extent to which the enacted interaction/collaboration corresponds to the model.
- *Extension*—An a-priori model exists. The goal is not to test but to extend the model, for instance with performance data (e.g., durations of activities). Extended models can then be used, for example, to optimize the process (van der Aalst & Günther, 2007).

We argue that this kind of temporal data analysis has a number of advantages. For one, process modeling languages are designed to accommodate concurrency, or parallelism. This is particularly interesting when the learning under study is taking place in groups and teams, and in classrooms, where division of labor and partial parallelism are afforded. Another advantage is that process models come with a multi-level representational notation: the model of a process can look quite different from the event sequence itself. This makes it easier to communicate models, for example, in the design process.

But for us the most important property is that process modeling imposes—and presupposes—a holistic view of a "process": as something with a beginning, and end, intermediate steps, constraints on how the process can unfold, and perhaps roles for those participating in the activity. Hence, they are particularly well suited to analyze temporal aspects of processes that occur in the context of a designed educational setting, such as a multi-step inquiry activity or a collaboration script. Thus, process models are particularly appropriate, so we argue, in situations where notions of (individual) habits, (collaborative) routines, and (collective) practices seem appropriate to characterize resources the actors in the situation can draw upon.

A frequently employed strategy is to use an external criterion for success, such as course grades, and then to look for patterns that are predictive of performance on the criterion. For instance, one can identify two sets of groups, the "successful" and the "less successful" students, and look for process models that are characteristic for the successful groups. This way, we would find activity patterns that are indicative of successful learning, but not necessarily, themselves, learning processes in the strong sense. While this strategy is obviously practical, it has the usual disadvantages of purely inductive approaches. We will come back to this.

2. METHODOLOGICAL AND CONCEPTUAL ROOTS

Process modeling has roots in Business IT and theoretical computer science rather than research computing, but has a number of characteristics that make it interesting as a process analysis method for learning research. A process model, in the meaning intended here, is a formal model, a parsimonious description of all possible activity sequences that are compatible with a model. A defining characteristic of process modeling is that log file data are seen as being generated by a process (in general, this can be multiple processes, but to keep the explanation concise we will speak of one process only) and that this underlying process can be modeled as a discrete event system. More precisely, the log file is interpreted as a sequence of activities that result from (typically) multiple enactments of a process; these enactments form the process instances. Since the events in the log file correspond to a more or less small number of activity classes, they can be described with a limited vocabulary.

The class of processes models we want to concentrate on here pertain to the large class of discrete event systems (Cassandras, 1993). Finite-state machines are one type of modeling language that can be used to describe and analyze discrete, deterministic, sequential events systems (Gill, 1962). A more powerful one is the language and theory of Petri Nets (Reisig, 1985), which present the advantage of modeling concurrency in addition to logic sequencing. Petri Nets can be mathematically described as bipartite directed graphs with a finite set of places P, a finite set of transitions T, both represented as nodes (round and rectangular, respectively), two sets of directed arcs, from places to transitions and from transitions to places, respectively, and an initial markup of the nodes with tokens (usually representing resources). The Petri net shown in Figure 41.1, for instance, expresses a process starting with transition A and ending after transition D, with two transitions B and C in between that can be executed in parallel, or in any order. The black circle in the initial node represents a token, which enables the transition A to be fired. A transition can only be fired if all the predecessor nodes have at least one token. So, for example, here transition D cannot be fired until both B and C have been fired. This model could, for example, represent a script for a collaborative writing scenario where the final version of a paper (D) cannot be submitted before two peer reviews (B, C) have been solicited.

Process Model representations that take the form of Petri Nets and similar formalisms have several interesting features. For instance, since they have formal semantics, they can be used to determine computationally if a specific activity sequence is commensurate with a model or not; like a grammar, a model can "parse" an activity sequence. For the same reason, they can be used to simulate potential (non-observed) model behavior computationally, and to compare different models with respect to certain formal parameters.

In the context of analyzing data from a collaborative learning environment, such representation could, for instance, be used to check which groups were following a specific process, and which not. For such a question, the deterministic nature of Petri nets might not be a problem. However, the smallest deviation from the behavior sequences captured by the model, e.g. due to a slip, would result in rejecting the model as an account for that event sequence. Hence, to account for human behavior probabilistic modeling formalisms are, by and large, more appropriate. One of these are Markov Models (Rabiner, 1989), which model the probabilistic process over a set of transitions, with the probability of any transition depending on the conditional probabilities of the

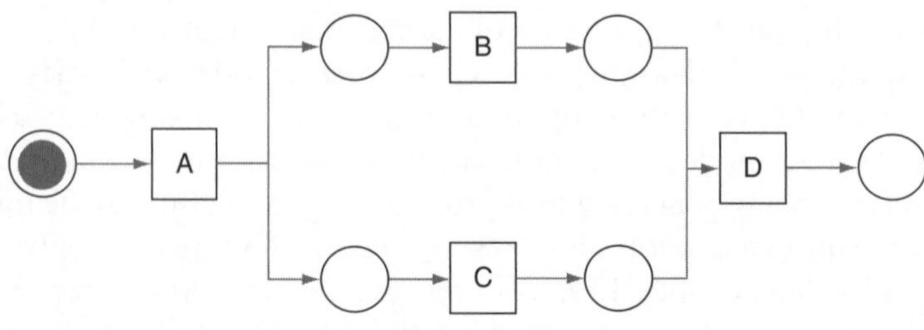

Figure 41.1 Example of a Petri Net description of a process.

transitions prior to that. Formal approaches to process modeling usually afford a graphical notation (such as the one in Figure 41.1) that can be exploited for learning purposes: the graphical representations can be made an object for comparison and reflection for the group members, i.e. serve as a mirroring or feedback device (Southavilay, Yacef, & Calvo, 2010).

3. HOW TO CONDUCT PROCESS MINING

PM refers to the identification of model based on the analysis of an existing data set. The three main steps are preprocessing, mining, and model testing. We illustrate these steps using the ProM process mining framework and a data set from a collaborative writing setting. ProM is a very comprehensive shell for accessing a large library of PM algorithms, developed at Eindhoven University.[1]

3.1. Step 1: Preprocessing

As is the case for most research, "data" are rarely "given," but need to be constructed. In the case of PM, the main data type to be constructed is the event. This is, in general, not a trivial step at all (Abell, 2004). In our example data set (Reimann, Calvo, Yacef, & Southavilay, 2010), we were interested in analyzing collaborative writing events, based on log files from Google Docs. These log files track the text changes to documents, which in our case were written by pairs of two students. The preprocessing involved, amongst other things, constructing a sequence of collaborative actions on the text based on a log file of individual writing and editing activities. The analysis proceeded in multiple steps, applying text analysis methods (Villalon & Calvo, 2009) and heuristic methods, and involved moving from identifying individual actions on Google documents to expressing these as collaborative writing steps expressed in the taxonomy suggested by Lowry (Lowry, Curtis, & Lowry, 2004).

3.2. Step 2: Identifying a Process Model from Data

After preprocessing, the resulting event log consisted of 8,233 events. There were five different types of events corresponding to five types of writing activities: Brainstorming, Outlining, Drafting, Revising, and Editing. The Dotted Chart Analysis utility of ProM [12] was used to analyze students' writing activities descriptively. The dotted chart shows the spread of events over time by plotting a dot for each event in the log. Figure 41.2 illustrates the output of the Dotted Chart Analysis of students writing their PSD documents. In the figure, points represent writing activities.

While dotted charts and similar formats that organize temporal data along a time axis are easy to interpret and can allow for visual identification of patterns, they become harder to interpret as the number of cases and/or the number of events increases. This simple visual representation does not afford a compact expression of process patterns. Discrete event models, such as Petri nets and finite-state machines, provide a more compact, yet more abstract representation. However, such deterministic models are not suited to fit human process data, at least not from learning environments where there are elements of choice. In these circumstances, heuristic methods or stochastic methods need to be applied.

In this study, we employed the the HeuristicMiner (Weijters, van der Aalst, & de Medeiros, 2006), also available in ProM, which uses a frequency based metric to express

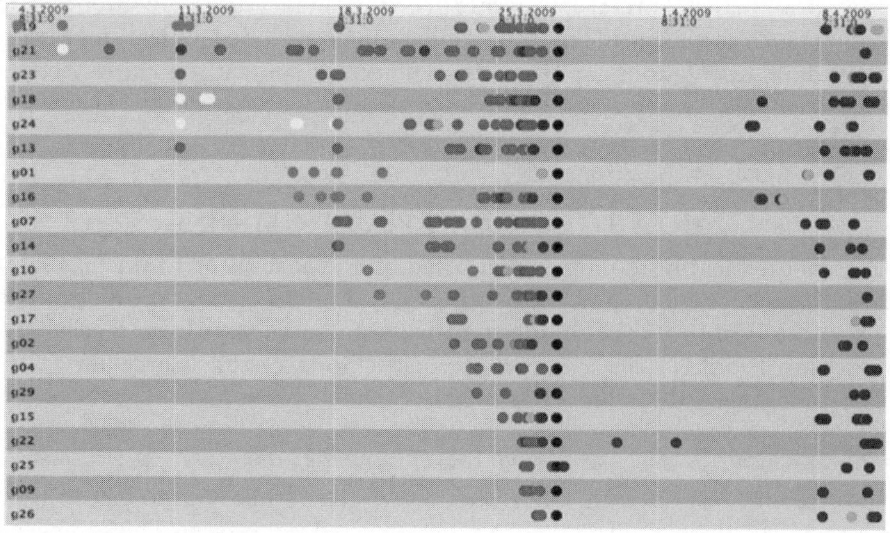

Figure 41.2 Dotted chart of 21 groups of students writing collaboratively (from ProM tool).

the degree of certainty of a dependency relation between two events A and B based on an event log. The result of applying this algorithm takes the form of a dependency graph depicted in Figure 41.3. The arcs on the right side of the boxes that point back at their own box indicate loops, meaning that statements of this type often occurred multiple times in a row. The numbers along the arcs show the dependency of the relationship between two events. The second number indicates the number of times this order of events occurred. The numbers in the boxes denote the event frequency.

Note that in this representation, as was the case with Petri nets and Markov Models, time is no longer directly represented. Furthermore, the model aggregates individual event sequences into a comprehensive display, one that is representing multiple instances of the process. While in this example display the model for writing all (21) documents is shown, one can also compute models for subgroups, such as for documents produced by successful and less successful students, and compare these.

3.3. *Step 3: Testing a Model*

In cases where PM is employed in the context of theory development, the researcher will not be content with finding a model that fits the data used for identifying the model, but will like to establish that the model is valid in other settings as well. One way to generalize the initial model beyond the data points that went into its identification is conformance checking, applicable when the model is deterministic, for instance, a Petri Net model. For this purpose, the ProM framework includes the Conformance Checker that allows calculation of the fit between a model (in form or a Petri Net) and an event sequence (Trčka et al., 2010). The comparison between the proportion of sequences matched by the model with those not matched yields a conformance measure.

In case of heuristic or probabilistic models, conformance checking as described above is not possible. In these cases, statistical methods will need to be employed to answer questions such as “How can it be established that a sequence pattern is above chance?”

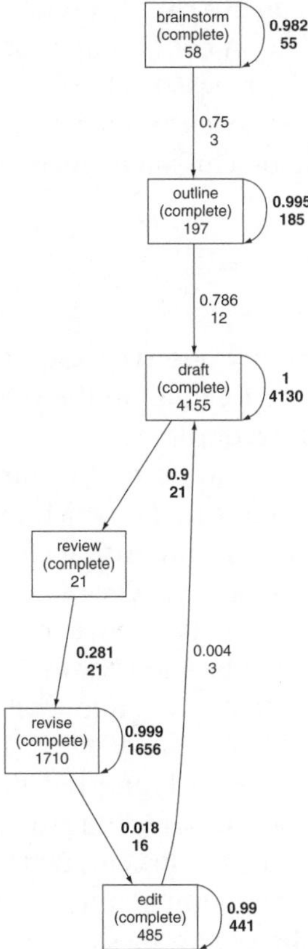

Figure 41.3 The collaborative writing process model (combining all process instances) in form of a transition diagram as mined from log data.

and "How can it be established, when we are interested in comparisons between individuals or groups, that the frequencies in patterns between these entities are statistically significant?"

The answer to the first question is also interesting because it leads to a statistical method to identify patterns in sequence data, as well as methods to test the significance of patterns identified by other (non-statistical) methods, such as described above. At the core of these methods (see Bakeman & Gottman (1997) for an excellent introduction) stands the notion of transitional probability, a kind of conditional probability where the target and the given events occur at different times. For instance, if the data are represented as event sequences, then one can describe the probability that the target event, T, occurs immediately after event G (i.e., at lag 1) as $p(T + 1|G0)$, occurring after an intervening event (lag 2) as $p(T + 2|G0)$, etc. In case the data come with time stamps, the transitional probabilities are written as $p(Tt + 1|Gt)$, $p(Tt + 2|Gt)$, etc.

To identify if particular chains are significantly more likely than others, one can employ goodness-of-fit testing, such as chi-square for the simplest case. For this, it is necessary to estimate transitional probabilities for some model, and compare them with the observed probabilities. For instance, if we had sequences based on a coding scheme that distinguishes five event types ($K = 5$), and we were interested in event sequences of length 2 (lag 1, L = 2), then one can observe theoretically $K^L = 5^2 = 25$ different types of sequences (for the case where adjacent codes cannot be identical). We might argue that the probability of any one kind of them is .05 (1/20). For any specific observed sequence (N = 127 two-event sequences, say), we can then determine the expected frequency as N × P: 127 × .05 = 6.35. The Pearson chi-square formula

$$X^2 = \Sigma \frac{(obs - exp)^2}{exp}$$

gives us then a way to decide for any observed lag 1 frequency if it deviates from the model (chance here, essentially) by looking up the value for the theoretical chi-square contribution (with one degree of freedom).

In lag-sequential analysis, this method can, in principle, be applied to sequences of increasing length (lag 2, 3, . . .) to test if and which longer sequences are significantly frequent. We say "in principle" as with increasing length of sequences, the number of possible sequences increases exponentially, hence expected frequencies become so small that huge data sets are required to evaluate their significance with confidence. As a general heuristic, the total sample should be 4 to 5 times KL+1 when consecutive codes may repeat, and 4–5 times K(K−1)L when they cannot, with K the number of codes, and L the sequence length (Bakeman & Gottman, 1997, p. 125). Note that sample required increases exponentially with increases in K and L. Nevertheless, for small K and L the method is practical; see, for instance, Kapur (2011) for an application to CSCL data, also illustrating the software package MEPA (Erkens, 2002), which has been developed for performing lag-sequential analysis on human interaction data.

Space does not allow us to elaborate on these methods further. We want to end this section by pointing out that in research settings where the sequence analysis is part of a larger design, such as comparing between experimental groups the effectiveness of certain pedagogical-technical interventions, scores such as Yule's Q can be used in analysis of individual or group differences. Bakeman and Gottman (1997) advise against the use of z-scores for this purpose, and recommend measures of effect size, such as Yule's Q instead.

4. DISCUSSION

4.1. When is the Method Appropriate?

In the terminology suggested in Reimann (2009), PM is appropriate when event sequences can be meaningfully conceptualized as being generated by a process (or a number of processes) with internal structure. This means that processes are seen as being more than chains of atomistic events (the "sequence view" of process). At the same time, process models are conceptually appropriate if reflection and interpretation on the process itself either does not take place in the settings studied, and/or is not relevant for the research questions raised. That is, the process is causally effective without having to undergo transformative interpretations by the agents involved. The process is a (useful) resource for the agents; it provides a kind of routine, practice, or habit as a guideline for action. The process has "structure," for instance in the form of roles it provides for division of labor; the process reflects adaptations to constraints and encapsulates former planning and experience. The process itself, however, is not reflected upon and/or changed, at least not in a manner that changes the course of action. If it was, then this kind of meta-development/learning could not be modeled with process modeling methods as introduced here. Good examples for educational situations where these constraints may apply are learning strategies for individual learning, and collaboration scripts for group learning.

Those process model formalisms that have a flat, event-based ontology cannot be used to link observables directly to "hidden" states, or latent constructs, such as knowledge, skill, attitude, motivation, belief, dispositions. To capture this, modeling languages need to be employed that distinguish between observed events and latent constructs, such as hidden Markov models (Rabiner, 1989).

One could apply event-ontology PM methods to sequences of "real learning" events, provided the event sequence captures what is considered learning directly, e.g., based on measurements of learning, such as gleaned from tests or from interpretation. However, such data are not contained in the typical "activity" log files. Similarly, for the case of collaborative learning, what we typically find in log files are group activities on the "operational" level (groups getting tasks done, achieving certain goals states, working with constraints), not learning processes. Learning on the group level taking the form of changes in these operational processes over time, such as "optimizing" a process, can be analyzed by process modeling: For instance, by exploring if groups/teams change from model A to model B over time.[2]

In terms of place within a larger research process, PM is in our view more appropriate in situations where the researcher already has a conception of the process she is studying. If the objective is to find out if there are temporal regularities in a data set at all, and when it is not clear how long these sequences will be, then methods for sequence mining (for instance, with lag-sequential approaches as described, or with methods for sequence pattern mining such as sequential pattern mining (Srikant & Agrawal, 1996; Perera, Kay, Koprinska, Yacef, & Zaiane, 2008) are more appropriate. As said before, PM is best used when one is looking for processes that function as resources for the agent(s) involved.

PM, like other forms of data mining, cannot replace theory building. While it is tempting to turn observations on "what worked" in some settings into predictions of what will happen in the future—and perhaps into prescriptions of what should be done in the future—for comparable situations, both types of inferences are difficult to justify based on an event ontology. To move to deeper explanations, one needs to move from statements of regularities to causal connections (House, 1991).

4.2. Advantages, Disadvantages and Challenges

We have mentioned some of the advantages of PM before: An important value lies in the type of description provided; the graphical/formal nature does direct attention to the whole, not only the parts. The textual and graphical format of the model descriptions can be stored, distributed, and extended. The representations are compact, and can be compared with each other. They can be tested against new data largely automatically. For deterministic models, such as Petri Nets, it can be decided with certainty if a model can account for an observed sequence or not. For pedagogical purposes, the visualizations that come with process models can be used as information for teachers and/or as feedback for students. And while this has not been much considered so far in the educational literature, in situations where concurrency and parallelism become the object of study (e.g., Hamilton & Jago, 2010), modeling languages that can express this become important.

A potential disadvantage of PM methods is the need for large amounts of data (pertaining to the same process or processes), certainly if one wants to establish the quality of a model by statistical means. Another disadvantage is that the methods are, as of yet, not well understood in terms of the applicability to educational research questions and data. In many cases, such as for instance for the heuristic mining algorithm described above, there are a great many parameters one can tune in the course of the mining process, and it is less than clear what the conceptual implications of these tunings are, with resulting risks of over-fitting models to data. Also, given current practices, PM methods, as other data mining methods, are not part of the canonical method education for educational researchers and learning researchers, with corresponding challenges for managing effort and establishing methodological quality.

Nevertheless, we see numerous potential applications for this method in the future. An immediate challenge is to articulate the relation between PM and more established educational research methods, and to raise in general the awareness for temporal issues in educational research.

NOTES

1. http://www.processmining.org
2. Note that this is not contradicting what we said before, that process modeling itself cannot model changes to models; in this case, it is the researcher who creates the changes between models. However, work on meta-modeling architectures (Karagiannis & Kühn, 2002) demonstrates how one can make changes to model on level L an activity that can be modeled on level L+1. But to our knowledge for PM no such meta-architectures exist at this point in time.

REFERENCES

Abell, P. (2004). Narrative explanations: An alternative to variable-centered explanation? *Annual Review of Sociology, 30,* 287–310.

Azevedo, R., Moos, D. C., Johnson, A. M., & Chauncey, A. D. (2010). Measuring cognitive and metacognitive regulatory proceses during hypermedia learning: Issues and challenges. *Educational Psychologist, 45*(4), 210–223.

Bakeman, R., & Gottman, J. M. (1997). *Observing Interaction: An introduction to sequential analysis* (2nd ed.). Cambridge: Cambridge University Press.

Cassandras, C. G. (1993). *Discrete Event Systems.* Homewood, IL: Richard D. Irwin, Inc.

Erkens, G. (2002). MEPA (Multiple Episode Protocol Analysis).

Gill, A. (1962). *Introduction to the Theory of Finite-state Machines.* New York, London: McGraw-Hill.

Hamilton, E., & Jago, M. (2010). Toward a theory of personalized learning communities. In M. J. Jacobson & P. Reimann (Eds.), *Designs for Learning Environments of the Future* (pp. 263–282). New York: Springer.

House, E. R. (1991). Realism in research. *Educational Researcher, 20*(6), 2–9.

Kapur, M. (2011). Temporality matters: Advancing a method for analyzing problem-solving processes in a computer-supported collaborative environment. *International Journal of Computer-supported Collaborative Learning, 6*(1), 39–56.

Karagiannis, D., & Kühn, H. (2002). *Metamodelling Platforms.* In (Ed.), 3rd International Conference EC-Web 2002—Dexa 2002, Aix-en-Provence.

Koedinger, K. R., Baker, R. S. J. D., Cunningham, K., Skogsholm, A., Leber, B., & Stamper, J. (2010). A data repository for the EDM community: The PSLC DataShop. In C. Robero, S. Ventura, M. Pechenizkiy, & R. Baker (Eds.), *Handbook of Educational Data Mining* (pp. 43–56). Boca Raton, FL: Chapman & Hall/CRC.

Lowry, P. B., Curtis, A., & Lowry, M. R. (2004). Building a taxonomy and nomenclature of collaborative writing to improve interdisciplinary research and practice. *Journal of Business Communication, 41*(1), 66–99.

Perera, D., Kay, J., Koprinska, I., Yacef, K., & Zaiane, O. (2008). Clustering and sequential pattern mining of online collaborative learning data. *IEEE Transactions on Knowledge and Data Engineering, 21*(6), 759–772.

Rabiner, L. R. (1989). A tutorial on hidden Markov models and selected applications in speech recognition. *Proceedings of the IEEE, 77*(2), 257–286.

Reimann, P. (2009). Time is precious: Variable- and event-centred approaches to process analysis in CSCL research. *International Journal of Computer-supported Collaborative Learning, 4*, 239–257.

Reimann, P., Calvo, R. A., Yacef, K., & Southavilay, V. (2010). Comprehensive computational support for collaborative learning from writing. In S. L. Wong (Ed.), *Proceedings of the 18th International Conference on Computers in Education.* Putrajaya, Malaysia: Asia-Pacific Society for Computers in Education.

Reisig, W. (1985). *Petri Nets. An introduction.* Berlin: Springer.

Southavilay, V., Yacef, K., & Calvo, R. A. (2010). *Process mining to support students' collaborative writing.* Paper presented at the Third International Conference on Educational Data Mining (EDM2010).

Srikant, R., & Agrawal, R. (1996). Mining quantitative association rules in large relational tables. *ACM SIGMOD Record, 25*(2), 1–12.

Trčka, N., Pechenizkiy, M., & van der Aalst, W. M. P. (2010). Process mining from educational data. In C. Robero, S. Ventura, M. Pechenizkiy, & R. Baker (Eds.), *Handbook of Educational Data Mining* (pp. 123–142). Boca Raton, FL: Chapman & Hall/CRC.

van der Aalst, W. M. P., & Günther, C. W. (2007). Finding structure in unstructured processes: The case of process mining. In T. Basten, G. Juhas, & S. Shukla (Eds.), *Proceedings of the 7th International Conference on Applications of Concurrency to System Design (ACSD 2007; Bratislava, Slovak Republic)* (pp. 3–12). Los Alamitos, CA: IEEE Computer Society Press.

van der Aalst, W. M. P., Weijters, A. J. M. M., & Maruster, L. (2004). Workflow mining: Discovering process models from event logs. *IEEE Transactions on Knowledge and Data Engineering, 16*(9), 1128–1142.

Villalon, J., & Calvo, R. A. (2009). *Single document semantic spaces.* Paper presented at the The Australian Data Mining Conference.

Weijters, A. J. M. M., van der Aalst, W. M. P., & de Medeiros, A. K. A. (2006). *Process mining with the heuristics miner-algorithm. BETA Working Paper Series WP 166.* Eindhoven, the Netherlands: Eindhoven University of Technology.

Yacef, K., & Baker, S. J. D. (2009). The state of educational data mining in 2009: A review and future vision. *JEDM—Journal of Educational Data Mining, 1*(1), 3–17.

42

SELF-REGULATED LEARNING ENGINES

Software Technologies for Researching and Promoting Self-Regulated Learning

Philip H. Winne

Learners are agents with "ability to control their actions and, through them, events in the external world" (Haggard & Tsakiris, 2009, p. 242). As agents, learners engage in goal-directed self-regulated learning (SRL), testing and adapting (regulating) tactics and strategies to improve their effectiveness. This has profound implications for designing research on learning and for engineering artifacts to promote learning (Winne, 2010, 2011; Winne & Hadwin, in press).

AGENTS SET GOALS

Goals contrast to a learner's current situation. Goals can refer to:

- a process the learner intends to engage ("I'll memorize key terms");
- knowledge or skill the learner aspires to develop ("I should understand hyperbolas"); and
- time allocated to a process ("I'll study economics for 45 minutes").

Goals constrain learning with varying degrees of clarity, explicitness and force by identifying content learners target for study and methods used to study. Content and methods determine what learners achieve. Choosing different goals can change levels as well as kinds of achievement.

Goals are typically assigned. As agents, however, learners exercise options about goals that others set. A learner's goal may match assigned goals; or, it may complement, decouple from or contravene assigned goals. For example, learners might be assigned: "Check your understanding of parabolas." This goal is imprecise. Learners who elect to pursue it determine what constitutes understanding and how they will check it. Their standards for sufficient understanding and methods for evaluating understanding can vary widely. Even precisely stated goals afford opting out or altering parameters. In short: agents *always* set their own goals; sometimes, these match assigned goals.

PHASES OF SRL

SRL can be modeled in four phases (Winne, 2011; Winne & Hadwin, 1998). In phase 1, learners survey context to identify factors they perceive could affect the course of learning and achievements. In phase 2, learners set goals. This positions them to retrieve or design plans for reaching goals. Plans can involve a single, simple tactic, for example, identify sentences containing bold terms and rehearse them until they can be recalled verbatim. Or, plans can be multiply branching strategies that are sensitive to unfolding conditions while conforming to general principles, for example, "maximize benefits relative to costs." In phase 3, learners enact plans by operating on information. Operations generate products that self-regulating learners might choose to monitor and, based on results of monitoring, they might adjust tactics or strategies if they forecast a benefit. In phase 4, learners might make large-scale revisions to features of any preceding phase, including phase 4, regarding whether and how to deliberately reflect on learning overall.

Three features of this model are key. First, SRL is not necessarily serial across phases. Learners can switch to any phase while engaged in any phase. This allows for recursion whereby products are inputs to the same operations that generated them. Second, as tactics and strategies are practiced, learners' opportunities to observe them degrade due to increasing automaticity (McKoon & Ratcliff, 1992). Third, SRL depends on information from two primary sources. One source is what a learner can recall about knowledge of the topic being studied, themselves, and tactics and strategies for learning; plus what the learner perceives and understands about the environment. The second influence on SRL is feedback about tactics, strategies, and products these operations generate. Feedback may be spawned internally when, for example, learners estimate the results of choosing one tactic over another. Or, external feedback can originate in the environment (Butler & Winne, 1995; Winne, 2011).

SELF-REGULATING LEARNERS ARE RESEARCHERS

Allowing for various phrasings, research has three main functions:

- identifying and describing features that define phenomena and other features that can be disregarded;
- developing accurate correlations and predictions about what happens given a particular disturbance or intervention in a particular context; and
- influencing or controlling outcomes by manipulating factors independently of how those factors would manifest naturally.

A learner's SRL is like a learning scientist's research program. In phase 1 of SRL, learners identify factors they judge can affect learning. They ignore other factors they predict will not matter. While learners' models are perhaps not as "sophisticated" as educational researchers' models, learners develop models about factors they believe affect their learning.

In phase 2, self-regulating learners choose goals to pursue—describing, predicting, and identifying causes—and choose tactics and strategies (treatments) they plan to achieve those outcomes. This parallels a researcher's hypothesis about how a treatment (the learner's plan) might promote particular effects (the learner's goals) in a particular context (setting). In phase 3, self-regulating learners do research as they learn. They gather data for testing their hypotheses about "what works" and, over time, strive to improve the validity and precision of their model of learning. Across studying episodes—akin to researchers' replications and variations across a series of studies—learners develop theories about why learning unfolds as it does and which outcomes they can achieve in contexts where they control some conditions but not others. In phase 4, self-regulating learners interpret accumulating results. They update their theory about learning across contexts and modify frameworks for testing the validity of their upgraded theory.

Challenges to Researching SRL

In a program of SRL-as-research, learners face the same challenges as researchers who investigate "what matters" and "what works" in learning science. These challenges are:

- How complete and valid is the model of learning? Which factors are focal, which can be controlled and which can be ignored? How should a factor's influence on learning be weighted?
- How can data be gathered about factors that affect learning?
- Are data reliable? Are data adequate for examining the model?
- How should data be analyzed?
- What do results of data analyses mean?
- How can interpretations of results be justified? Are interpretations valid?
- How generalizable are findings?

Regarding the challenge of having a model to direct research, learners' models of learning are partial, brittle and need improvement (Winne & Jamieson-Noel, 2003). Two reasons may explain this. First, learners are rarely taught how to research their learning. Second, learners receive little to no support to mitigate difficulties—described later—that hinder a progressive program of SRL-as-research.

Compared to researchers, learners are inadequately prepared to research their learning. Their grasp of the scientific method is tenuous. They have few resources to support focused and sustained research into learning. For example, learners cannot search databases such as PsycINFO to supplement incomplete and unrepresentative samples of personal experience or correct fallible memories about learning. Learners rarely profit from their peers' research into learning. Whereas learners are frequently evaluated on what they have learned, they have practically no instruments for gathering or analyzing data about how they learn. In short, compared to "professional" learning scientists, learners are practically bereft of resources needed to discover how to productively self-regulate learning.

EXTENDING RESEARCH ON LEARNING WITH SELF-REGULATING LEARNERS

Software technologies can help learners meet challenges in systematically researching learning. These same technologies can appreciably expand and accelerate learning science. Next, I sketch how software can facilitate learners' and learning scientists' research programs. Some of these technologies exist now; others are on the horizon.

Gathering Data to Trace Learning and SRL

Theories describe cognitive operations—for example, rehearsing, monitoring—that learners apply to information to create, extend or revise knowledge (and attitudes, motivational orientations, etc.; Winne, 2011). To research a theory, learning scientists establish a setting in which participants study; then, manipulate one or a few factors—for example, presence or absence of instructions to highlight. After learners study, they take an achievement test. The logic is that learners use different operations (or more of an operation) due to manipulated variables—the instructions, in this example. If operations matter, achievement will change when learners experience a treatment.

Most experiments suffer an important deficit because operations are inferred rather than documented by data. These studies are black box experiments (Winne & Nesbit, 2010). Software can strengthen these inferences by gathering data that provide clearer and stronger signals about whether a learner applies operations and the information those operations targeted.

Suppose a learner is instructed (or agentically chooses) to highlight "important" information while studying a text. Software can log data about: (a) the time when a highlight was enacted and (b) the words highlighted. Each logged trace of highlighting offers strong evidence that the learner (a) metacognitively monitored information in the text for importance and, on finding text judged to meet that standard, the learner (b) exercised metacognitive control to highlight. Trace data speak to treatment fidelity (and learner activity) by describing *every* highlighting event rather than memories about them (as in a questionnaire) or a sample of them (as in a think aloud protocol).

Better traces minimally intrude on the learner's work. Whenever the learner judges it is appropriate to highlight and is motivated to do it, text is highlighted. Tracing metacognitive monitoring this way, however, does not reveal something a researcher might like to know which, presumably, the learner knows. Did the learner metacognitively monitor text using an "importance" standard to discriminate what should be highlighted?

Designing a tool that generates traces revealing learners' standards for metacognitive monitoring is straightforward—provide a tool that labels highlights. These are tags. Examples might be "review this" or "key idea." Tags identify why text is highlighted, and different tags differentiate standards for highlighting plus metacognitive control.

An inference about the learner's planning is afforded by tags. What purpose could tags serve? If the learner tags information with "review this," it is likely the learner plans to review that information. More elaborate technology might record gaze durations for tagged text. Adding this dimension to trace data indicates degrees of reviewing.

If the tool allows learners to create tags, these constructions trace active SRL. Creating a new tag indicates a learner metacognitively monitored (a) features of the learning task and tools available in relation to (b) goals, and (c) judged currently available tags as inadequate or inefficient for achieving goals. Creating a new tag traces an instance in phase 4 of Winne and Hadwin's SRL model—the learner is regulating a strategy for learning.

Benefits of Trace Data

Trace data depict how learners operate on information, the information operated on and temporal features of operations (onset, duration). Trace data open the black box between the bookends of pretests and posttests in experiments (Winne & Nesbit, 2010). In contrast to think aloud data, trace data directly manifest products of cognition rather than a learner's commentary about those events that is difficult to verify for completeness and veracity.

Trace data avoid challenges of interpreting self-report data (Winne, Zhou, & Egan, 2011). Self-report items require learners to (a) generalize over unspecified contexts

("When you study . . ."), (b) mentally compute typicality with vague metrics such as "true of me" or (c) estimate frequency of use in ambiguous terms such as "sometimes" and "often." Self-report data can be accurate only if the learner fully and correctly recalls the population of relevant experiences referred to by a questionnaire item, then computes a valid summary of those recollections. Also, because only one response is allowed, self-reports require the researcher to assume every instance of metacognitive monitoring has one consistent expression in metacognitive control. Traces document behavioral variability across contexts and time.

Interpreting Trace Data

Does Tracing Affect SRL?

This issue parallels methodological concerns about pretest sensitization. Two points merit consideration. First, every measurement is an intervention (Winne, 2010). Thus, effects that measurement-generating interventions might have when learners experience them should be investigated. Access to a tool, for example, a tagging tool, might suggest a new action that a learner might never have invented otherwise. This same concern arises if self-report survey items describe contexts, studying operations or motivational constructs that learners might never have considered otherwise. This issue does not arise in data generated by think aloud protocols if instructions do not introduce new topics or cues in the learning environment that could become subjects of learners' reports.

Second, a benefit of trace data created when learners use tools is that learners choose whether data are generated. In contrast, directions and common social norms might push learners to provide self-reports regardless of whether they have grounds for responding or would prefer not to respond. It is rare (and generates problematic missing data) if a survey offers a response option, "Does not apply" or "Don't know." In think aloud protocols, researchers commonly remind learners to think aloud. This acknowledges a concern about missing data but prompts learners to generate data that might not be generated without prompting.

Are Trace Data Reliable?

"The question of 'reliability' . . . resolves into a question of generalization" (Cronbach, Gleser, Nanda, & Rajaratnam, 1972, p. 15). Thus, reliability entails questions about learners' characteristics, contexts within which traces emerge, and other facets. Two key issues merit consideration.

First, over what facets are generalizations sought? The software environment in which a learner uses a tool can be completely characterized in terms of features and functionality. Content the learner studies also can be automatically characterized in many ways that are difficult or expensive to do outside software environments. For example, every web page the learner visits can be stored for analysis of content-related features (e.g., whether a disciplinary term introduced previously appears in a page currently in view), linguistic features (e.g., readability), and design attributes (e.g., headings, emphasis using font styles). Software learning environments significantly increase opportunities to investigate facets that may affect generalizations based on trace data.

Second, generalizations based on trace data representing SRL might differ fundamentally from, for example, self-reports. Psychometrically, reliability concerns the degree to which responses do not vary when the factor(s) theorized to underlie a response does not vary. But SRL is about changing cognitive operations, for example, taking notes in a structured way vs. copying and pasting text; or changing the environment, for example, splitting a window into two panels so a page's overview can be scanned for guidance while analyzing a particular paragraph in the second panel. Thus, what is dependable about SRL is that learners judge learning might be more productive if they adapt method(s) for learning. The nature of the change might not matter so much as that a change occurs.

In sum, because traces of SRL-in-action originate with learners' choices, the question "Does a tool undermine reliability of data?" morphs into questions about "Under what conditions is a learner a reliable tool user?" and "Under what conditions does a learner *not* use tools as before?" Trace data provide raw material for answering these questions about generalization.

Other issues bearing on the validity of interpretations of trace data are beyond the scope of this chapter (see Winne, 2010; Winne et al., 2011).

DESIGN SPECIFICATIONS FOR SELF-REGULATED LEARNING ENGINES

Engines are machines that move a payload forward or, more abstractly, tools that advance a purpose. Can software technologies be engines helping learners improve SRL? Yes. Can these technologies accelerate learning science? Yes. This section sets out generic specifications for self-regulated learning engines (SRLE).

Logging

Because learners and researchers alike use fallible methods to gather samples of data, data for researching learning and SRL can be randomly or systematically missed. Systematic exclusions might reflect deliberate bias. For example, learners who believe they are "visual learners" might selectively avoid websites without spatial information displays, for example, graphs or flowcharts; but their choice neither benefits nor harms memory or understanding (Krätzig & Arbuthnott, 2006; Mayer & Massa, 2003). Bias can occur due to conditions beyond a learner's control, for example, some attributes of context may be beyond perception or never attended to if a task overloads cognition.

Researchers might not foresee value in gathering particular data about factors that actually predict or influence learners' online studying. For example, some web pages provide headings for sections of information but researchers might not think to record this subtle "treatment" that affects learning (Surber & Schroeder, 2007).

Software can store a copy of every website learners visit. Websites visited can be distinguished from websites studied by an operational definition of studying. For example, studying might be operationally defined to occur only if the learner tags or annotates information. This affords opportunity to investigate post hoc some naturally varying factors that might affect studying as operationally defined even if learners and researchers are a priori unaware of those variables.

Software can record every instance of learners' observable operations on information during studying. For example, suppose learners are offered a web form to describe goals. Fields in the form might include: title, benefit if achieved, percent completed, resources needed, and quality of work. The number, temporal record of re-access, and qualities of goals set can then be identified. Moreover, learners can be reminded of goals, perhaps sparking SRL.

In sum, one design specification for SRLEs is that they should log many features of learning. How might this be realized?

Operations and Information

Distinguishing operations learners apply to information from information on which learners operate is helpful. I hypothesized five primitive cognitive operations in learning and SRL: searching, monitoring, assembling, rehearsing, and translating (the "SMART" operations; Winne, 2001). Each operation receives information as input and outputs information. For example, translating receives information in one format, perhaps a mathematical expression. Translating outputs essentially that same information in another format, perhaps a sentence describing what the expression represents or a graph.

Where possible, tools that trace learning in SRLEs should set a stage for researchers to discern which operation(s) learners apply to information and what information is operated on. For example, an SRLE could log that a learner highlights a symbolic expression such as $y = ax^2 + bx + c$. This signals the learner was monitoring for specific information and which information the learner judged met those standards. If the learner annotates that selection, for example, "general formula for a parabola," the trace reveals the learner assembled the formula with a particular attribute ("general") in translated form (words).

Some operations and information operated on will not be traced. In the preceding example, the logged data do not unambiguously reveal (a) standards the learner used to metacognitively monitor the content being studied, (b) why the learner judged the equation worthy of an annotation, and (c) why a translation was enacted. One remedy for these gaps could be to provide a tagging tool, as previously described.

On-the-Spot Tagging

Studying tools such as tags creates opportunities to trace standards learners use in metacognitive monitoring or plans to reach goals. Another example is a note form where learners title the note (monitoring fit to a category), elaborate content presented in websites (assembling), and tick checkboxes that trace reasons for creating the note, for example, "test item?" or "valid?" (monitoring content).

Time Stamps

Learning unfolds in sequences and patterns (strategies) over time. The log generated by an SRLE should time stamp traces to allow analyzing duration as well as repetitions or adaptations of patterns. Methods of social network analysis can support this work (Winne & Hadwin, in press; see Wasserman & Faust, 1994).

Semantic Tools for Self-Testing

Self-regulating learners need formative feedback about gains in knowledge. To correct a common bias of overconfidence, learners can be encouraged to actually retrieve or use information versus estimating their knowledge (e.g., Miller & Geraci, 2011). Leading edge work in natural language processing could generate probes based on information viewed compared to information selected for study, helping learners sharpen their judgments (Winne, Popowich, & Nesbit, 2012).

Given the present state of natural language processing, machine-generated probes have moderate probability to be off target. When this happens, self-regulating learners can be invited to correct probes, a generalization of self-explaining (Fonseca & Chi, 2010) that cognitively engages learners in productively rehearsing and assembling information. A further advantage of correcting infelicitous probes is that, as learners search for and operate on information, additional traces are generated about how and what is studied. These trace data plus learners' corrected versions of probes are raw material for machine learning systems to bootstrap better probes tailored to individual learners.

Mediated SRL

Beyond solo studying and collaborative learning (see Chapter 36 in this volume), learners can benefit from mediated SRL. As many learners use an SRLE's tools to study online, each learner's trace data is streamed to a server where pooled data are mined for profiles of studying that correlate strongly with learning gains. From that time forward, when another learner's studying profile parallels a productive profile, the system issues two kinds of just-in-time feedback to mediate SRL. Process feedback describes how a learner is currently studying, expressed in terms of traces, compared to the more effective profile. Formative feedback describes information that can be beneficially reviewed or inspected. Groundwork for this kind of system is suggested by studies of externally regulated learning (Azevedo, Moos, Greene, Winters, & Cromley, 2008).

As learners experiment with learning based on the SRLE's recommendations, additional data are generated for cross-validating profiles and refining them. Mediating SRL in this way induces constantly adaptive learner-centered design experiments consistent with learners' agency. A massively distributed SRLE thus promotes rapid and continuous evolution of evidence-based learning tactics and strategies that are swiftly trialed in fully authentic settings. As participating learners express agency, they very likely originate customized methods for learning and invent new methods. Because the SRLE traces these "mutations" in response to process and formative feedback, this accelerates the evolution of more successful and varied and tailored learning strategies.

NSTUDY: A PROTOTYPE SRLE

A software environment called nStudy is a prototype SRLE (Beaudoin & Winne, 2009; Winne & Hadwin, in press). As learners study information online, nStudy gathers and sends to our server fine-grained, time-stamped data tracing their activities. nStudy's highlighting and tagging were introduced previously.

nStudy offers learners other tools that generate trace data. For example, when learners bookmark a website, this traces a metacognitive judgment that the site contains information judged useful for a task and the learner intends to revisit it. A title the learner assigns the bookmark may reveal standards used to metacognitively monitor content or a category to which the website's information is assembled.

In nStudy, learners can select text in a web page—a "quote"—and link quotes to notes or other nStudy "objects." Quotes are automatically copied to a quote field in notes. Clicking a quote returns the learner to its source, tracing that the learner (a) judged recall about the website was incomplete or inaccurate and (b) predicted the quote or surrounding information would repair this gap. Learners (and researchers) can structure notes' contents by creating web forms. A form has a title (e.g., argument, hypothesis) and might include: labeled text fields (e.g., claim, evidence, warrant), checkboxes (e.g., interesting; proven), radio buttons, sliders, dates, drop-down lists, and other features. Choosing a particular note form reveals standards a learner used to metacognitively monitor information in the note's source. If a learner builds a new note form or adapts a form, this signals SRL of the same sort as described earlier about creating new tags. Because note forms are more elaborate than a tag's title, this trace reveals additional information about the learner's schema for annotating content yet to be studied.

Learners can create other containers for information in nStudy: documents (e.g., essays or lab reports), text chats with peers, terms in a glossary, and concept maps. Every information object's title plus other of its metadata can be viewed in nStudy's Library table. The Library allows learners to: organize objects in a tree of titled folders, sort items by metadata columns of the Library table (e.g., date modified, author), filter the table by various features (e.g., notes only, a particular tag) and search for content. Operating on the Library table generates trace data indicating standards for search and instances of metacognitive control. Learners (and researchers) can query logs of trace data to generate focused process feedback about studying activities and formative feedback about content studied.

CONCLUSION

Learners are agents who self-regulate learning according to their goals. SRL is an inherent and useful source of variance to examine in learning science. Logging traces of SRL helps to penetrate the black box of how learners study and learn. Software tools designed to generate trace data lay a foundation for providing process and formative feedback, and mediating SRL to help learners gain knowledge and improve learning skills.

Rather than striving to erase natural variance that SRL generates by random assignment and experimental controls, modern software technologies can be designed to profit from learners' exercise of agency in natural learning environments by logging traces. Provided feedback about potentially more productive forms of studying, learners can seamlessly collaborate in advancing learning science as they pursue their goals. SRLEs offer the double promise of helping learners bootstrap achievements simultaneously with accelerating learning science.

REFERENCES

Azevedo, R., Moos, D. C., Greene, J. A., Winters, F. I., & Cromley, J. G. (2008). Why is externally-regulated learning more effective than self-regulated learning with hypermedia? *Educational Technology Research & Development, 56*(1), 45–72.

Beaudoin, L. P., & Winne, P. H. (2009, June). *nStudy: An internet tool to support learning, collaboration and researching learning strategies.* Canadian e-Learning Conference, Vancouver. http://learningkit.sfu.ca/lucb/celc-2009-nStudy.pdf.

Butler, D. L., & Winne, P. H. (1995). Feedback and self-regulated learning: A theoretical synthesis. *Review of Educational Research, 65*, 245–281.

Cronbach, L. J., Gleser, G. C., Nanda, H., & Rajaratnam, N. (1972). *The Dependability of Behavioral Measurements: Theory of generalizability for scores and profiles.* New York: John Wiley & Sons.

Fonseca, B., & Chi, M. T. H. (2010). Instruction based on self-explanation. In R. E. Mayer & P. A. Alexander (Eds.), *The Handbook of Research on Learning and Instruction* (pp. 296–321). New York: Routledge.

Haggard, P., & Tsakiris, M. (2009). The experience of agency: Feelings, judgments and responsibility. *Current Directions in Psychological Science, 18*, 242–246.

Krätzig, G., & Arbuthnott, K. (2006). Perceptual learning style and learning proficiency: A test of the hypothesis. *Journal of Educational Psychology, 98*, 238–246.

Mayer, R., & Massa, L. (2003). Three facets of visual and verbal learners: Cognitive ability, cognitive style, and learning preference. *Journal of Educational Psychology, 95,* 833–841.

McKoon, G., & Ratcliff, R. (1992). Inference during reading. *Psychological Review, 99,* 440–466.

Miller, T. M., & Geraci, L. (2011). Unskilled but aware: Reinterpreting overconfidence in low-performing students. *Journal of Experimental Psychology: Learning, Memory, and Cognition, 37,* 502–506.

Surber, J. R., & Schroeder, M. (2007). Effect of prior domain knowledge and headings on processing of informative text. *Contemporary Educational Psychology, 32,* 485–498.

Wasserman, S., & Faust, K. (1994). *Social Network Analysis: Methods and applications.* New York: Cambridge University Press.

Winne, P. H. (2001). Self-regulated learning viewed from models of information processing. In B. J. Zimmerman & D. H. Schunk (Eds.), *Self-Regulated Learning and Academic Achievement: Theoretical perspectives* (pp. 153–190). Mahwah, NJ: Lawrence Erlbaum.

Winne, P. H. (2010). Improving measurements of self-regulated learning. *Educational Psychologist, 45,* 267–276.

Winne, P. H. (2011). A cognitive and metacognitive analysis of self-regulated learning. In B. J. Zimmerman & D. H. Schunk (Eds.), *Handbook of Self-Regulation of Learning and Performance* (pp. 15–32). New York: Routledge.

Winne, P. H., & Hadwin, A. F. (1998). Studying as self-regulated learning. In D. J. Hacker, J. Dunlosky, & A. C. Graesser (Eds.), *Metacognition in Educational Theory and Practice* (pp. 277–304). Mahwah, NJ: Lawrence Erlbaum Associates.

Winne, P. H., & Hadwin, A. F. (in press). nStudy: Tracing and supporting self-regulated learning in the Internet. In R. Azevedo & V. Aleven (Eds.), *International Handbook of Metacognition and Learning Technologies.* New York: Springer.

Winne, P. H., & Jamieson-Noel, D. L. (2003). Self-regulating studying by objectives for learning: Students' reports compared to a model. *Contemporary Educational Psychology, 28,* 259–276.

Winne, P. H., & Nesbit, J. C. (2010). The psychology of school performance. *Annual Review of Psychology, 61,* 653–678.

Winne, P. H., Popowich, F., & Nesbit, J. C. (2012). *Architecture for Automatically Generating Self-Tests of Knowledge.* Burnaby, BC: Simon Fraser University.

Winne, P. H., Zhou, M., & Egan, R. (2011). Assessing self-regulated learning skills. In G. Schraw & D. H. Robinson (Eds.), *Assessment of Higher-Order Thinking Skills* (pp. 89–118). Charlotte, NC: Information Age Publishing.

43

ASSESSING SOCIO-EMOTIONAL LEARNING AROUND EDUCATIONAL TECHNOLOGIES

Carolyn Penstein Rosé

1. INTRODUCTION

Past research has shown relationships between student dispositions and motivational states and productive interaction with learning technologies. Much of this work has treated learning as an individual activity, without explicit consideration of how the social context influences student motivational states or how the social context reflects the ways in which these states wax and wane over time. An important limitation of this paradigm is that it does not consider the ways in which the presence of the technology within the social context affects social interactions within that context, despite the fact that such effects are undoubtedly present for better or for worse. The danger is that iterative development methodologies that are blind to these effects may produce technologies that are optimized for effective individual use but with unknown, and possibly negative, effects on the social environment in which the learning takes place. In this chapter, we propose a technical infrastructure and evaluation methodology in which instructional technology is situated in an intelligent environment where social interactions are monitored using machine learning technology, and those analyses prompt the environment to mediate the interaction between students and the technology with the goal of maintaining a positive effect on those social interactions. This infrastructure has been used effectively within the field of computer supported collaborative learning. Here we propose its broader use in connection with interactive learning interventions more generally.

The vision is for a microgenetic methodology in which the social context is sampled on a moment-by-moment basis. In microgenetic studies of learning, the learning process is analyzed so that changes in this process over time can be considered as part of the analysis, and naive assumptions about the ways in which behaviors are distributed over time can be challenged. Such process analyses have demonstrated that distributions of social behaviors are far from uniform over time (Wang, Rose, & Chang, 2011). Also, as more evidence is amassed that motivation waxes and wanes in a statelike manner, it has become suboptimal to measure these constructs just at pre-test and post-test time.

Connections between conversational behaviors and motivational states are just beginning to be investigated (Howley, Mayfield, & Rosé, 2011; Howley, Mayfield, & Rosé, 2013). In this chapter, we offer a path towards monitoring motivational and socio-emotional states that can be applied in lightly structured environments. Specifically, when students engage together with technology, their social interaction around and within the technology has the potential to provide another channel of information about motivational and socio-emotional states. If we can assess motivational states and related socio-emotional processes through analysis of social interaction in and around educational technologies such as tutoring systems, games, and simulation environments, we can get the benefits of microgenetic paradigms of research without the distraction of repeated use of questionnaires during learning interventions.

2. THEORETICAL UNDERPINNINGS

In the computer supported collaborative learning community there has been extensive work developing coding schemes for representing collaborative processes. These coding schemes have been motivated by theories and models from cognitive psychology and social psychology situated within the learning sciences more broadly. These frameworks are applications of constructs from the learning sciences to language interactions such that they represent the ways in which learning processes are viewed through language. They are composed of categories of conversational behaviors that represent steps within the processes they operationalize. Thus, a process analysis consists of a segmentation of an interaction into basic units, each of which is assigned one or more categories of behavior.

In our earlier work (Howley et al., 2013) we have contrasted this general approach with the idea of linguistic analysis of collaboration. Linguistic analyses of collaboration target language processes rather than learning processes. For example, that might include rhetorical strategies that are employed as a means for participation in language interactions within a learning context. In recent years we have explored how frameworks from sociolinguistics can be simplified and made more precise in order to be implemented in computational models, which has resulted in the multi-dimensional Souflé framework (Howley et al., 2013).

Souflé has three primary dimensions, one of which is cognitively focused, which we refer to as Transactivity, and the other two of which are more socially orientated, which we refer to as Authoritativeness (Martin & Rose, 2003) and Heteroglossia (Martin & White, 2005). While the cognitive dimension of that analysis scheme, which codes contributions according to whether they explicitly display reasoning, and whether that reasoning represents a new direction in reasoning within the conversation or builds on previously displayed reasoning (Sionti, Ai, Rosé, & Resnick, 2011; Gweon, Jain, McDonogh, Raj, & Rosé, 2012), other dimensions of that scheme are drawn from the broad subfield of linguistics referred to as Systemic Functional Linguistics. We have had particular success with computational models of the Negotiation coding scheme (Martin & Rose, 2003), from which we derive our Authoritativeness dimension, which encodes linguistic actions that can be employed to position a person as more or less authoritative within an interaction (Mayfield & Rosé, 2011; Mayfield, Garbus, Adamson, & Rosé, 2011). We attribute our success in these computational efforts to the natural fit between the language and the language behaviors these frameworks operationalize.

The question we address in this chapter is how motivational states and socio-emotional processes are displayed through language behaviors. Some progress towards this end has already been made. For example, Howley et al. (2011) demonstrated that self-efficacy is correlated with the occurrence of patterns of codes from the Negotiation framework. We will begin by explaining how basic language processes already reflect basic social and psychological processes that are related to the constructs we want to predict. We will then discuss the connection between these basic language processes and the three dimensions of the Souflé framework.

What we aim to convey in this chapter is an explanation for why a linguistic analysis of discussions is the right angle for formalizing how motivational states and socio-emotional processes can be detected within language interactions. We begin with one of the most fundamental concepts within the social sciences, the concept of power (Guinote & Vescio, 2010). Models of motivational states have a natural connection with the concept of power. Consider, for example, a model of social problem solving from social cognitive theory (Flavell & Ross, 1981). In that model, an agent seeks to achieve a goal. A plan is generated through means ends analysis. For each step in the plan, two motivational constructs are important to consider. First, how capable does the agent feel to accomplish that step insofar as that accomplishment depends upon his actions. That concept is self-efficacy. And second, to what extent might external threats prevent that action from being accomplished. That concept is locus of control. Power subsumes both of these concepts. A powerful individual is both capable and in control of his own destiny. Thus, if power is displayed through language processes, then linguistic analyses should be predictive of these important motivational constructs.

At the foundation, basic concepts of power and social distance from social psychology explain social processes operating within interactions. Roles within interactions are negotiated through manipulations of perceived social distance. Intimacy, or low horizontal social distance, is associated with equality of power within an interaction. Intimacy is achieved through in-group identification. Equality of power is also associated with low social distance on a vertical dimension. Authority is achieved through distancing on this dimension.

Social processes are reflected through patterns of language use at multiple levels, from pronunciation, to lexical choice, to rhetorical strategies. These patterns act as signals that are used as tools and resources to manipulate horizontal and vertical social distance in ways that manipulate perception of relative power within interactions. At the top layer of our model is the technology for monitoring social processes through language. If we can understand the connection between basic processes of power and social distance and patterns of language use, we can build computational models that fit interaction data more effectively. Beyond that, those models should be capable of leveraging patterns in language data that then become evidence of the manifestation of these social processes, as we have begun to see in our recent work (Howley et al., 2011).

The area of linguistic style accommodation describes how shifts in language behavior within interactions reflect relative power between conversational participants (Giles & Coupland, 1991). Specifically we refer to the finding that conversational partners may shift their speaking style within an interaction, either becoming more similar in order to decrease perceived social distance, or less similar to one another in order to increase perceived social distance. Stylistic shifts can occur at a variety of levels of speech or language representation. It has long been established that while some speech style shifts are subconscious, speakers may also choose to adapt their way of speaking in order to achieve social effects within an interaction (Sanders, 1987). One of the main motives for accommodation is to manipulate perceived social distance. If the amount of shift is asymmetric between speakers, it is typical for the speaker perceived as lower on the vertical dimension to shift towards the speaker perceived as higher on the vertical dimension. In that way, the lower status speaker shifts to close the gap in vertical social distance.

Insights related to language accommodation have important implications for the computational work related to the Souflé framework. For example, one dimension of that framework is Transactivity, which is the property of explanations that make reasoning visible and connect that displayed reasoning to previously articulated reasoning. The idea of Transactivity comes from a Piagetian theory of learning where this conversational behavior is said to reflect a balance of perceived power within an interaction. In terms of our discussion of language accommodation and social distance, we would then expect that linguistic accommodation would predict the occurrence of Transactivity, and we have found this (Gweon et al., 2012). What we have also found is that in a variety of efforts to automatically identify transactive conversational contributions in various forms of conversational data, those in which we have included a feature that represents language similarity have been the most successful (Rosé et al., 2008; Ai, Sionti, Wang, & Rosé, 2010). This confirms that consideration of basic language processes and how they relate to categories of behavior informs the design of effective representations for making a coding scheme learnable.

On the other two dimensions, we have not explicitly tested the connection between language accommodation and language representation directly, but we can make some cautious speculations. First, we consider the Heteroglossia construct. In this construct, openness to alternative perspectives is shown by attributing ideas to external sources of authority. This avoids presenting an idea as though it is the only way of thinking about something. In our prior work, we have found that the presence of heteroglossic contributions either from a computer agent (Kumar, Beuth, & Rosé, 2011) or other human conversational partners (Howley et al., in press) is associated with increases in articulation of reasoning or idea contributions. Frequently, heteroglossic contributions include making reference to other perspectives explicitly. Thus, we expect a similar pattern to what we found with Transactivity where language similarity would make positive predictions about the occurrence of heteroglossic contributions. Where deference is displayed towards others, we expect to see an influence on framing of contributions in line with what that audience would consider acceptable. This also predicts a linguistic convergence.

A final dimension is the Negotiation coding scheme, which is related to the idea of authoritativeness. This coding scheme is more related to vertical social distance than horizontal social distance. In our computational model of Negotiation, it has been important to encode constraints related to the qualitative motivation for the coding scheme that comes from Systemic Functional Linguistics. Specifically, the constraints enforce the idea that conversation is organized around flows of knowledge and action, where more authoritative parties more frequently act as the source and the less authoritative parties more frequently act as the sink. The formal constraints that are derived from this qualitative notion formalize the asymmetry between the two speaker roles. That in itself is one way in which the formulation of the construct reflects basic ideas of vertical social distance. In the case of big differences in authoritativeness, we expect role differentiation within the conversation, and thus, overall, we expect speakers to remain linguistically distinct. In this coding scheme, similarity has been found to be useful for linking core moves that belong on the same thread. Thus, lexical content reflects the flow of knowledge or action from the source to the sink. If there is a big difference in authoritativeness between speakers, we expect that there might be an asymmetrical linguistic shift such that the low authority party would shift to become more like the high authority party.

3. CHALLENGES

Since the recent turn of the century, we have already seen success at using machine learning in analysis of group discussions, especially in the field of computer supported collaborative learning. This technology holds the potential to speed up the research and make it feasible to analyze vastly larger amounts of data, and impressive demonstrations of this potential have been published (Dönmez, Rosé, Stegmann, Weinberger, & Fischer, 2005; Mu, Stegmann, Mayfield, Rosé, & Fischer, 2011). Many successful proofs of concept related to analysis of conversation for learning and how it enables automatic interventions that support facilitators, teachers, or students in their groups have also been published in recent years (Dönmez et al., 2005; Rosé et al., 2008; Ai, Kumar, Nguyen, Nagasunder, & Rosé, 2010; Mu et al., 2011), and tool sets for facilitating this work have been made available as well (Rosé et al., 2008; Mayfield & Rosé, in press).

However, despite the published demonstrations of success, the finding of many unpublished voices has been that the result did not measure up to the expectation. One issue is the amount of time it takes to annotate enough data to train a high performing model. The large effort required means that unless a researcher is working with a very large amount of data, the upfront investment in building a machine learning model does not pay off. The upfront effort might only yield a desirable return on investment if a researcher either plans to analyze data from a whole series of studies with the same coding scheme, so that the same model can be reused, or if the model will be used in a real-time analysis setting, in which case hand annotation is not even an option. Another issue is level of performance success. Faith in the power of machine learning has led researchers to expect that machine learning models will achieve a level of accuracy that they would trust for the analysis of their data. However, even among language technologies researchers working with very large annotated datasets, state-of-the-art performance has frequently been lower than levels required by quantitative research methodologies. Another issue is generalization. The finding has often been that models trained on one set of data do not perform as well on subsequent sets of data where the researcher would like to apply the same coding scheme.

Frequently the problem has been that too little attention has been given to the problem of representing data appropriately or consideration about how the structure or type of model makes about the way in which the target of the classification is displayed through the language. When it comes to applications of machine learning to language, the data must first be represented in terms of a list of attribute-value pairs referred to collectively as a vector space representation. In order for the model to generalize well, these features and the modeling technique must be selected carefully.

In this chapter we have written specifically about linguistic style accommodation and how that reflects social processes. Let us now consider the issue of model generality in light of this analysis problem specifically. Prior research has attempted to quantify accommodation computationally by measuring similarity of speech and lexical features either over full conversations or by comparing the similarity in the first half and the second half of the conversation. When analyses of stylistic shifts target specific linguistic features, then measuring the extent of the stylistic accommodation is simple since a speaker's style can be represented on a one- or two-dimensional space, and movement can then be measured precisely within this space using simple linear functions. However, the rich sociolinguistic literature on linguistic style accommodation highlights a much greater variety of speech style characteristics that may be associated with social status within an interaction and may thus be beneficial to monitor for stylistic shifts. Unfortunately, within any given context, the linguistic features that have these status associations are only a small subset of the linguistic features that are being used in some way. Furthermore, which features carry this social interpretation are specific to a context. Thus, separating the socially meaningful variation from variation in linguistic features occurring for other reasons can be like searching for a needle in a haystack.

In some of our recent work, we have sought to overcome this challenge by measuring accommodation using Dynamic Bayesian Networks (DBNs) that leverage an important insight from sociolinguistics. The insight behind our unsupervised modeling approach is that we can leverage the social reasons behind the accommodation in a way that better captures the inherent structure within the speech. Specifically, we can leverage this consistency of style shift to identify socially meaningful variation without specifying ahead of time which particular stylistic elements we are focusing on (Jain et al., 2012).

4. IMPLICATIONS FOR DESIGN AND USE OF LEARNING TECHNOLOGIES

This chapter presents a vision for instructional technology embedded in an intelligent environment capable of monitoring social interactions in and around the instructional interventions so that they can be administered in a way that is sensitive to that social context. The realization of such a vision would potentially have impact both on the effectiveness of the instructional technology itself in social contexts but also offers the capability to study the social aspects of learning in new ways.

At the heart of such a vision is the capability to monitor the social interaction using machine learning technology. Above we suggested that models that are capable of making predictions about motivational and socio-emotional states from interaction data can be seen as expansions of current models that make predictions about motivational states from key-click behavior. Similar to work using physiological sensing to make such predictions, this technology holds the potential to enable context-sensitive support to be administered even within less structured instructional activities than those featured in state-of-the-art key-click assessment work. Furthermore, it might be considered less invasive than many of these approaches since it does not require that students remain seated in one location or wear sensors on their skin. The sensors could be located instead on the instructional technology itself. For example, modern computers almost always have a microphone embedded in them. Cellphones can also be used as speech input devices for distributed collaboration. Eventually, the distinction between technology for supporting face-to-face collaboration and distributed collaboration might begin to blur.

By itself, however, this sensing technology would have little value. It must be embedded within an architecture that enables it to be used effectively. The Basilica architecture (Kumar & Rosé, 2011) is such an architecture. In the Basilica architecture, all interactions between students and instructional interventions are mediated by a channel that monitors all social interactions in the vicinity. The behaviors of the instructional interventions can then be managed in a way that takes the social context into account. A series of successful classroom studies demonstrate that this architecture can be used effectively as a test bed for evaluating the design of dynamic forms of collaborative learning support (Kumar, Rosé, Wang, Joshi, & Robinson, 2007; Kumar, Ai, Beuth, & Rosé, 2010; Ai, Sionti, Wang, & Rosé, 2010; Kumar et al., 2011; Howley et al., 2011). In this work, support was administered by means of conversational agents. But the architecture itself is agnostic to the form of the interactive instructional intervention. Logging from the architecture allows post hoc analyses of the conversational behaviors that occurred during the instructional activity to be analyzed from multiple perspectives. Thus, it is possible to assess the extent to which interventions are more or less successful at eliciting a density of particular desired behaviors from students summatively, or to analyze the way in which distributions of behaviors shifted over time or locally around specific interventions.

The Basilica architecture is a reconfigurable collection of component modules. Each component implements a behavior that could be conceptualized metaphorically as a combination of perception (by means of filters), thought (by memory/storage units) and action (by means of interactive interventions). Within this framework, support for collaborative learning comes in two forms, which could be thought of as microscripting and macroscripting, respectively. The macroscripting interventions are meant to provide the high level structuring of the instructional activity, for example, introducing the task, and introducing each phase of the activity at the appropriate time. The microscripting interventions are more reactive. In response to student behaviors and collaborative states that are detected during the activity, interventions are initiated to respond directly to these behaviors and states, locally within the context in which they are detected. Specifically, paired actor and filter components might be implementations of directed lines of reasoning, each designed to teach one concept, or separate conversational behaviors used to manage group interactions. Filters may annotate turns with applicable interaction categories, accumulates them, for example, to identify inactive participants, and then generates events that regulate the coordinators, which are responsible for triggering behaviors.

Ideally, the assessment technology envisioned in this chapter would be useful in connection with the full spectrum of instructional technologies and informal learning environments that are in use. However, social interaction is not always an integral part of the learning that students do in these environments. Insights about motivational and socio-emotional states may still be able to be gleaned. For example, we have observed that students respond to negative affective behaviors from classmates by positioning themselves as less authoritative and become correspondingly less engaged in problem solving in response to impasses (Howley et al., in press). The assessment technology we are proposing in this chapter would potentially enable monitoring for such events in the learning environment around educational technologies even when social interaction is not an integral part of the learning activity.

5. ACKNOWLEDGMENTS

This work was funded in part by National Science Foundation Grant SBE 0836012.

REFERENCES

Ai, H., Kumar, R., Nguyen, D., Nagasunder, A., & Rosé, C. P. (2010). Exploring the effectiveness of social capabilities and goal alignment in computer supported collaborative learning. *Proceedings of Intelligent Tutoring Systems*, LNCS.

Ai, H., Sionti, M., Wang, Y. C., & Rosé, C. P. (2010). Finding transactive contributions in whole group classroom discussions. *Proceedings of the International Conference of the Learning Sciences*, International Society of the Learning Sciences.

Dönmez, P., Rosé, C. P., Stegmann, K., Weinberger, A., & Fischer, F. (2005). Supporting CSCL with automatic corpus analysis technology. *Proceedings of Computer Supported Collaborative Learning*, International Society of the Learning Sciences.

Flavell, J., & Ross, L. (1981). *Social Cognitive Development: Frontiers and Possible Future*. Cambridge University Press.

Giles, H., & Coupland, N. (1991). *Language: Contexts and Consequences*. Thomson Brooks/Cole Publishing Co.

Guinote, A., & Vescio, T. (2010). *The Social Psychology of Power*. The Guilford Press.

Gweon, G., Jain, M., McDonogh, J., Raj, B., & Rosé, C. P. (2012). Predicting idea co-construction in speech data using insights from sociolinguistics. *Proceedings of the International Conference of the Learning Sciences*, International Society of the Learning Sciences.

Howley, I., Mayfield, E., & Rosé, C. P. (2011). Missing something? Authority in collaborative learning. *Proceedings of Computer Supported Collaborative Learning*, International Society of the Learning Sciences.

Howley, I., Mayfield, E., & Rosé, C. P. (2013). Linguistic analysis methods for studying small groups. In Cindy Hmelo-Silver, Angela O'Donnell, Carol Chan, & Clark Chin (Eds.), *International Handbook of Collaborative Learning*. Taylor & Francis, Inc.

Howley, I., Kumar, R., Mayfield, E., Dyke, G., & Rosé, C. P. (in press). Gaining insights from sociolinguistic style analysis for redesign of conversational agent based support for collaborative learning. In D. Suthers, K. Lund, C. P. Rosé, C. Teplovs, & N. Law (Eds.), *Productive Multivocality in the Analysis of Group Interactions*. Springer.

Jain, M., McDonogh, J., Gweon, G., Raj, B., & Rosé, C. P. (2012). An unsupervised dynamic Bayesian network approach to measuring speech style accommodation. *Proceedings of the European Association for Computational Linguistics* (pp. 787–797), Avignon, France, April 23–27, Association for Computational Linguistics.

Kumar, R., & Rosé, C. P. (2011). Architecture for building conversational agents that support collaborative learning. *IEEE Transactions on Learning 4*(1), pp. 21–34.

Kumar, R., Rosé, C. P., Wang, Y. C., Joshi, M., & Robinson, A. (2007). Tutorial dialogue as adaptive collaborative learning support. *Proceedings of Artificial Intelligence in Education*, IOS Press.

Kumar, R., Ai, H., Beuth, J., & Rosé, C. P. (2010). Socially-capable conversational tutors can be effective in collaborative learning situations. *Proceedings of Intelligent Tutoring Systems*, LNCS.

Kumar, R., Beuth, J., & Rosé, C. P. (2011). Conversational strategies that support idea generation productivity in groups. *Proceedings of Computer Supported Collaborative Learning*, International Society of the Learning Sciences.

Martin, J. R., & Rose, D. (2003). *Working with Discourse: Meaning Beyond the Clause*. Continuum.

Martin, J. R., & White, P. R. (2005). *The Language of Evaluation: Appraisal in English*. Palgrave.

Mayfield, E., Garbus, M., Adamson, D., & Rosé, C. P. (2011). Data driven interaction patterns: Authority and information sharing in dialogue. *Proceedings of the AAAI Symposium on Building Representations of Common Ground with Intelligent Agents*, American Association for Artificial Intelligence.

Mayfield, E., & Rosé, C. P. (2011). Recognizing authority in dialogue with an integer linear programming constrained model. *Proceedings of the 49th Annual Meeting of the Association for Computational Linguistics: Human Language Technologies*, Association for Computational Linguistics.

Mayfield, E. & Rosé, C. P. (in press). LightSIDE: Open source machine learning for text accessible to non-experts. Invited chapter in the *Handbook of Automated Essay Grading*. Routledge Academic Press.

Mu, J., Stegmann, K., Mayfield, E., Rosé, C. P., & Fischer, F. (2011). ACODEA: A framework for the development of classification schemes for automatic classification of online discussions. *Proceedings of Computer Supported Collaborative Learning*, International Society of the Learning Sciences.

Rosé, C. P., Wang, Y. C., Cui, Y., Arguello, J., Stegmann, K., Weinberger, A., & Fischer, F. (2008). Analyzing collaborative learning processes automatically: Exploiting the advances of computational linguistics in

computer-supported collaborative learning. *International Journal of Computer Supported Collaborative Learning, 3*(3), pp. 237–271.
Sanders, R. (1987). *Cognitive Foundations of Calculated Speech.* State University of New York Press.
Sionti, M., Ai, H., Rosé, C. P., & Resnick, L. (2011). A framework for analyzing development of argumentation through classroom discussions. In Niels Pinkwart & Bruce McClaren (Eds.), *Educational Technologies for Teaching Argumentation Skills,* Bentham Science.
Wang, H. C., Rose, C. P., & Chang, C. Y. (2011). Agent-based dynamic support for learning from collaborative brainstorming in scientific inquiry. *International Journal of Computer Supported Collaborative Learning, 6*(3), pp. 371–396.

INDEX